CALL
Environments

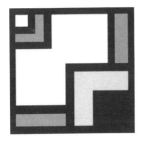

Research, Practice, and Critical Issues

Second Edition

Edited by Joy Egbert and
Elizabeth Hanson-Smith

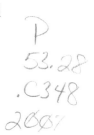
 T E S O L Teachers of English to Speakers of Other Languages, Inc.

Typeset in ITC Novarese and Vag Rounded
by Capitol Communication Systems, Inc., Crofton, Maryland USA
Printed by United Graphics, Inc., Mattoon, Illinois USA
Indexed by Pueblo Indexing and Publishing Services, Pueblo West, Colorado USA

Teachers of English to Speakers of Other Languages, Inc.
700 South Washington Street, Suite 200
Alexandria, Virginia 22314 USA
Tel 703-836-0774 • Fax 703-836-6447 • E-mail tesol@tesol.org •
http://www.tesol.org/

Publishing Manager: Carol Edwards
Copy Editor: Sarah J. Duffy
Additional Reader: Ellen Garshick
Cover Design: Tomiko Chapman

ISBN 9781931185431
Library of Congress Control Number 2007930167

Dedication

We dedicate this work to Jack Thompson, Arthur C. Hanson, and Jamie and David Jessup—inspirations all.

Table of Contents

Part III. Authentic Task

Part IV. Exposure and Production

Part V: Time and Feedback

References

Appendixes

Contributors

Index

Acknowledgments

This book is the result of a great deal of hard work by many dedicated people. We thank all of the contributors for their outstanding effort in making this text a seminal work in the field.

We are also grateful to Marilyn Kupetz, TESOL's former managing editor, who provided encouragement to proceed with both editions of this text; to Carol Edwards, who continues TESOL's tradition of publishing excellence; and to Sarah Duffy, for unflagging efforts in getting the editing right.

We also thank all of the software publishers and Web site developers who gave us permission to use images from their products in this volume.

Finally, and most important, we would like to thank our families and friends for their support of this 2-year project. Many thanks to Jack Thompson, Elizabeth's husband, whose patience and endurance sustained her work, and to the vibrant online community Webheads in Action, whose spirit of comradeship, experimentation, humor, and inventiveness led the way in creating new cutting-edge CALL adventures. Thanks are due to Cary Anderson, Levi McNeil, and Leslie Huff for helping Joy keep life in perspective during this long haul. Also, thanks to Keun Huh, who provided support in the early stages of this project.

Chapter 1 🔲

Introduction: Foundations for Teaching and Learning

Joy Egbert, Elizabeth Hanson-Smith,
and Chin-chi Chao

Focus

Wiki, weblog (blog), RSS, social software, chat room, m-computing, pop mailer, phishing, Web 2.0, *virus*—educational technologies involve a lot of scary-sounding jargon. In fact, technology presents a whole new language, but the language of technology, although important, is not the most crucial information that educators need in order to use technology effectively in their language classrooms. More important is an understanding of good pedagogy and the relationships among teaching, learning, and technology.

In 1990, Levy pointed out the need for a theory of computer-assisted language learning (CALL) that would provide educators with a framework for teaching and learning with technology. He noted that "our language teaching philosophy, method, or approach needs to be broadened to encompass new technologies, and the inter-relationship between language teaching and computing needs to be carefully explored" (p. 5). Supporting the need for a theory of CALL was the increase in the number of computers available to language educators and learners and the desire of educators to apply theories of second language acquisition (SLA) to the computer-using classroom. Hypothetically, a theory of CALL could assist teachers in making decisions about ways to prepare language learners for the high-technology future that they face; in describing the kinds of theoretically sound, vital changes in curricula that can and should be made; and in assessing the types of technology needed to assist in the effective and efficient learning and teaching of additional languages. At that time, the thought was that a theory of CALL could help educators evaluate how and which students learn with different kinds of technology, identify factors that must be addressed in the application of the technology, and serve as a guide for research on language learning.

If *technology* is replaced with *textbook* in the preceding paragraph, the hypothetical theory of CALL sounds not much different from an integrated theory of language acquisition; in fact, it is the same. In the years since

Levy's proposal, CALL educators have understood that a theory of CALL is a theory of language acquisition; the fact that the technology changes does not mean that the principles of language development do. Therefore, rather than making the use of technology in language classrooms focal, we now talk about how additional languages are learned and how this learning might be supported by technology.

This chapter introduces the concepts and ideas that ground the chapters in this book by first discussing how languages are learned and then describing goals for and of language learners. Next, the chapter posits conditions for optimal language learning environments and suggests how technology might support the development of such environments. The chapter ends with a discussion of how educators might investigate their own technology-supported language learning environments.

Background

Language Learning Theory and the Learning Environment

The number of theories of language acquisition and knowledge of the processes underlying these theories increase slowly but surely. Researchers and teachers generally accept that language acquisition is the result of an interplay between some kind of cognitive mechanism and environmental factors. They also acknowledge that not all language learners learn in the same way, at the same rate, or for the same purposes. Spolsky's (1989) still-viable general theory of conditions for language acquisition encompasses these variables in the form of the equation in Figure 1-1. According to this theory, *abilities* include physiological, biological, intellectual, and cognitive skills. *Opportunity* implies the learning environment, or time multiplied by exposure to the language. In the classroom, how or when a learner acquires language depends on the optimal strength of each of these variables for each learner.

Figure 1-1. Spolsky's (1989) Theory of Conditions for Language Acquisition

The learner's:

	Kp	Knowledge in the present
	A	Abilities
	M	Motivation/affect
+	O	Opportunity
	Kf	Knowledge and skills in the future

Although it is not yet known for certain whether nature (cognition) or nurture (the classroom environment) is more important in the acquisition of additional languages, researchers have shown that the learning environment (*opportunity*, the term used by Spolsky, 1989) is a critical component. In addition to being a valid predictor of learning outcomes (see, e.g., Fraser, 1986), the classroom environment can mediate between the learner and macroenvironmental variables such as socioeconomic status, family circumstances, and language status. Most important, the classroom language learning environment is also the component of language acquisition that teachers, researchers, learners, and technology use can directly influence.

Creating optimal language learning environments is the essential business of the language teacher. Understanding this, educators and their language learners can observe circumstances under which learners acquire language and make adjustments to the classroom environment, thereby playing an instrumental role in students' learning. Because computers are becoming an increasingly significant element in the teaching and learning environment, a clear theory of language learning that takes into account the significance of that environment in turn has critical implications for CALL. In other words, educators do not need a discrete theory of CALL to understand the role of technology in the classroom; a clear theory of SLA and its implications for the learning environment serves this goal.

In each part of this book, language learning theory and research and their implications are discussed before technology is addressed because of our understanding that technology use is *support for* the central objective: meeting language learners' needs and goals. Some books about technology use in classrooms focus on one learning theory or philosophy as a guide for technology use; throughout this book, however, the authors call upon a variety of philosophical stances and literatures, just as effective teachers do. More important than a single theoretical viewpoint is a focus on basic principles of language learning and essential learning goals in creating effective classroom language learning environments.

Establishing Goals for Language Learning Classrooms

Language learning classroom goals can be established in a number of ways, but effective learning environments emphasize the needs of both the learner and other stakeholders. Goals for language learners at all levels have moved beyond a mere understanding of language. For example, national and state legislation throughout the world—such as the U.S. national ESL standards (TESOL, 2006), technology standards (ISTE NETS Project, 2000–2005c), the Council of Europe's (2001) *Common European Framework of Reference for Languages*, and various content-area standards—determines in large part what kindergarten through adult students are expected to learn and be able to do. Most of these standards for language, technology, and content areas have in common seven *21st-century goals* for all learners:

1. knowledge acquisition
2. productivity
3. creativity
4. communication
5. research
6. problem solving
7. critical thinking

Closely tied to these learning goals are *new literacies*, or new ways of being knowledgeable. Recent attention has been drawn to the idea that, along with traditional text literacy and numeracy, *visual, information, technological, and media literacies* are crucial to help learners succeed outside of classrooms. In addition, standardized tests, student interviews, and nontraditional assessments can uncover areas where language development is most needed and explore the needs of students for engagement and relevance in their learning.

These learning goals, widely supported in the literature as essential to helping learners become fully realized human beings, are addressed in many ways throughout this book. Central is the idea that language is learned through and in pursuit of these goals, and that language learning environments must provide opportunities for language learners to reach these goals.

Conditions for Optimal Language Learning Environments

In the first edition of this book, we proposed a model of eight conditions comprising a variety of classroom environmental variables that may affect learners' acquisition. Research since that time has further supported this model; therefore, these variables still form the theoretical framework for this volume's discussion of CALL.

In the SLA, ESL, and learning theory literatures, research repeatedly points to eight conditions (see Figure 1-2) that, when present in the language learning environment in some form and in some amount, seem to support optimal classroom language learning. Although other factors may come into play, and different names are often applied, these eight are the most widely researched and supported in the literature and make up a general model of optimal environmental conditions. Below is a brief overview of these conditions, each of which is described in more detail in later chapters. This model forms the book's theoretical framework, one that you as a teacher can use to guide your deployment of technology in the language classroom.

Figure 1-2. Conditions for Optimal Language Learning Environments

1. Learners have opportunities to interact and negotiate meaning.
2. Learners interact in the target language with an authentic audience.
3. Learners are involved in authentic tasks.
4. Learners are exposed to and encouraged to produce varied and creative language.
5. Learners have enough time and feedback.
6. Learners are guided to attend mindfully to the learning process.
7. Learners work in an atmosphere with an ideal stress/anxiety level.
8. Learner autonomy is supported.

Condition 1: *Learners have opportunities to interact and negotiate meaning*

Many researchers have noted that learning is essentially the result of inter-action between learners and others (see, e.g., Ahmad, Corbett, Rogers, & Sussex, 1985; Kelman, 1990; Levin & Boruta, 1983; Vygotsky, 1978). If learn-ing is a social process, then interaction with other people is necessary. This concept, addressed in Part I, is not new to second language instruction, as many researchers have called attention to the importance of the negotiation of meaning and modification of interaction in second language development (Long, 1985; Long & Porter, 1985; Pica, Holliday, Lewis, & Morgenthaler, 1989; Porter, 1986).

Condition 2: *Learners interact in the target language with an authentic audience*

Researchers (see, e.g., Ernst, 1994; Pica, 1987; Pica, Young, & Doughty, 1987; Webb, 1982, 1985) have found that language learners must be involved not only in social interaction but in *purposeful* interaction, which includes a real audience that is actively involved with the learners. The implication, then, is that involving learners in authentic social interaction in the target language with a knowledgeable source (e.g., the teacher, another learner, a family doctor, another person who can negotiate in the target language) facilitates language acquisition. The question of audience is taken up in Part II.

Condition 3: *Learners are involved in authentic tasks*

Many researchers (e.g., Chun, 1994; Kelm, 1992; Meagher, 1995) have reported that learners tend to be inspired by having not only a real audience but also an authentic goal for their work, and in this context the language used tends to be candid and heartfelt. Authentic tasks are those having the same types of cognitive challenges as complicated real-world tasks do. The cognitive demands, that is, the thinking required, should be consistent with the cognitive demands in the environment for which the learner is being prepared. In the context of language learning, this means, for example, that language teachers want students not simply to learn *about* English or French but rather to be engaged in the use of English or French in ways that native speakers normally are. It is important to design tasks so that students can use their current proficiency level to function in authentic communications. Even less proficient students should have the ability to handle the task well and gain confidence from it. As Vygotsky (1978) believed and research has shown, learners grow into an activity that has meaning for them in its own right and at the same time grow out of the need for external support in the activity. The notion of task is addressed in Part III.

Condition 4: Learners are exposed to and encouraged to produce varied and creative language

Spolsky (1989) claims that

> whatever the language learner brings to the task, whether innate ability, a language acquisition device, attitudes, previous knowledge, and experience of languages and language learning, the outcome of language learning depends in large measure on the amount and kind of exposure to the target language. (p. 166)

An authentic task alone, therefore, may not be sufficient for language acquisition; the phrase *varied and creative language* implies that learners are involved in a diversity of tasks with a variety of sources of language input (Krashen & Terrell, 1983). In addition, Swain (1985) and others have confirmed the need for output as a means to language development. The use of varied and creative language also means that learners tap both receptive and productive language skills and that the tasks take into account the multiple learning styles and preferences among learners. Research on and examples of exposure and production are discussed in Part IV.

Condition 5: Learners have enough time and feedback

Learners need adequate time and feedback, both of which facilitate the formulation of ideas. Within the classroom, individual differences in ability, motivation, and other factors determine how much time each learner requires to complete a task successfully. This fact implies that some flexibility must be built into the timeline for the task. In this way, all learners have the opportunity to reflect on and communicate their ideas.

In addition, explicit, appropriate, individualized feedback is critical in helping learners reach the goals of a task. *Explicit* feedback addresses the learner's task-related questions; an example is help with the ordering of subtasks, with a relevant grammar point, or with general task instructions. *Appropriate* signifies as much assistance as the learner needs but neither less nor more. Learners also vary in the amount and kind of task feedback that they require. This condition does not indicate, however, that teachers must act as private tutors; it suggests that tasks, the grouping of learners, and learners' opportunities to receive help should be planned carefully. Part V addresses this topic, looking particularly at assessment in the classroom as a means to both feedback and learning.

Condition 6: *Learners are guided to attend mindfully to the learning process*

An authentic task and audience, exposure to and opportunities to produce language, and sufficient time and feedback do not imply that learners will take these opportunities or make the best of them. During the learning process, learners must be *mindful* (Salomon, 1990); that is, they must be motivated to take the opportunities presented to them and to be cognitively engaged as they perform them. A certain degree of metacognitive guidance (instructions and examples about how to learn), whether from peers, teachers, or others, may facilitate learning and promote cognitive engagement (Vygotsky, 1978; Zellermayer, Salomon, Globerson, & Givon, 1991). Research has repeatedly shown that the conscious or deliberate use of learning strategies is related to language achievement and proficiency (Oxford, 1994). By consciously understanding and applying metacognitive strategies, learners are prompted to be aware of their language use and learning and thus become more efficient in both. Learning styles and strategies and related issues are discussed in Part VI.

Condition 7: *Learners work in an atmosphere with an ideal stress/anxiety level*

Before becoming mindfully engaged and willing to communicate their ideas, learners must experience an optimal level of anxiety in the language learning environment; any feelings of worry or apprehension must be facilitative rather than debilitative (H. D. Brown, 1994; Krashen & Terrell, 1983; Lozanov, 1978). Educators can assist in the development of an environment with an optimal stress level by creating a learner-centered classroom, which implies that learners have some control over their learning (see, e.g., Bereiter & Scardamalia, 1987; Kremers, 1990; G. Robinson, 1991). A learner-centered environment also suggests that the teacher's expectations are reasonable and that goals are attainable. Peyton (1990b) suggests that giving more control to the learner removes the confounds of teacher, learner, school personalities, styles, and goals. These issues and their applications in the language classroom are discussed in Part VII.

Condition 8: *Learner autonomy is supported*

Thein (1994) describes a learner-centered classroom as one that develops learners' confidence and skills to learn autonomously and to design and coordinate tasks in a variety of contexts. In a learner-centered classroom, learners are given ownership of the process of developing solutions to their learning tasks and may, in fact, with the teacher's guidance or mentorship, devise their own learning agenda. This does not mean that learners have complete autonomy in the classroom; the instructor should determine boundaries so that learners can develop meaningful problems or tasks in that domain. Savery and Duffy (1995) believe that a teacher's role is to challenge learners' thinking, not to dictate or attempt to regulate their thinking for them. In this context, the learner decides on learning goals, but the modeling, mediation, and scaffolding provided by the instructor are indispensable. Consultation with and feedback from the instructor are crucial, as students require varying degrees of control. Issues of autonomy and their relationship to the CALL environment are discussed in Part VIII.

These eight conditions affect and overlap each other; thus, so do the chapters in this volume. The literature does not suggest the nature or impact of interplay among the conditions or their necessary or relative optimal strengths. What is known, however, is that the eight conditions act and interact in different ways in different classrooms depending on variables such as student population, content area, and learning context. Therefore, teachers must attempt to tailor these conditions in ways that are best for the learners in their specific classrooms. Classroom-situated research, or action research, discussed below, is one way to determine if and how the conditions are being met.

Using Electronic Technologies in Optimal Learning Environments

The focus of this volume is electronic technology because technology-enhanced environments can readily support optimal learning conditions. Electronic technologies include, in general, hardware, software, and the connections among them. Although the emphasis has until recently been on computers and the Internet, technologies such as iPods, handheld personal digital assistants, and cell phones are increasingly being used to create effective learning environments for language learners. Further, the current generation of *digital natives* (Prensky, 2001) that teachers encounter in their classes increasingly expects technology to be a part of the learning experience. As technology access improves around the world, teachers owe it to their students to explore the tools and resources it provides.

In supporting learning goals and conditions for optimal learning environments, technology can be used to change and improve how learning occurs in classrooms. Children and adults learn at home and in the world in very different ways than they do in classrooms. A huge disconnect exists when learners are asked to memorize and listen in class but outside of class learn naturally by exploring, inquiring, experimenting, and working together with teammates or peers. Technology can make it possible for language students to learn in more natural ways by offering resources, support, and feedback that teachers alone may not be able to provide. Of course, teachers must use technology in ways that support the goals of language learning and the creation of optimal language learning environments. The goal is to make the technology itself invisible while exploring the interactions, content, and processes of the learning that occurs with, through, and around technology.

Exploring the CALL Environment Through Research

Throughout this text, particularly in the *Explorations* sections, we propose questions that should be asked about CALL; however, even if all these questions are answered to our satisfaction, there will still be much to learn. The brief discussion below presents general guidelines for developing inquiries in the area of CALL. The purpose of classroom research is to find out what works for you as a teacher and to add to the growing body of knowledge concerning the CALL environment. The framework provided below for the exploration and presentation of research on CALL should have the very practical effect of leading you to uncover ways to meet the eight conditions for learning in your own setting.

Purcell (1996) notes that research generally has six levels—observation, recording, investigation, use of a model, experimentation, and enlightenment. He adds that the conduct of research involves six steps of analysis, synthesis, and evaluation:

1. Describe a question significant enough to merit research.

2. Review in the relevant literature the knowledge to date about the research question.

3. State a tentative answer to the research question, or declare the further knowledge required to answer the question.

4. Determine how to test the research question or gather the required information, and state it as an *if-then* sentence.

5. Test the hypothesis or gather the data carefully.

6. Refine the tentative answer to the research question, or present the clarification derived from the data; generalize the result of the particular research performed, and suggest ways to further study the research question.

These generic steps do not speak to specific research methods or measurement tools; researchers should use whatever is appropriate to the study. (See the article on Research [2006] for many more specifics and definitions of various types of research.) Even though conducting research following these guidelines seems simple enough, CALL environments require further considerations as noted by many of the authors in this volume. However, the most critical step in conducting research is formulating a research question of significance, Purcell's Step 1.

Step 1: *Ask the right questions*

In the years since the first edition of CALL *Environments*, research in CALL has exploded. Refereed journals focusing on language (as well as general) learning with computers abound and are readily accessible online (see, e.g., *Language Learning & Technology*, *Innovate*, *Reading Electronically*). Some of these, for example, TESL-EJ and *Teaching English With Technology*, focus particularly on foreign language teaching. Likewise, many new books on teaching with computers have appeared in the past few years, such as CALL *Essentials* (Egbert, 2005), *Learning Languages Through Technology* (Hanson-Smith & Rilling, 2006), *Laptops and Literacy* (Warschauer, 2006), and far too many others to list in this short introduction. However, research in computers and language learning can never tell teachers exactly how to use computers in a particular class. Just as there seems to be no one right way to teach or learn language (see Stevick, 1976, for numerous examples underscoring why this is so), there is no one best way to use computers for language learning. Researchers and educators looking for the CALL research study that can answer specific questions about the best way to teach must look also to the large body of research in SLA and language learning; in fact, much of the outstanding research cited in this volume comes from these and other academic fields or areas of study, as has the framework of environmental conditions that serves as the structure for this book. As we suggest above, perhaps the best way, if there is one, to teach in a CALL classroom is to create an optimal language learning environment for each learner.

One difficulty in researching CALL environments has been controlling all the variables. Even early on, Salomon (1990) and Ehrmann (1995) clearly saw that computers (or the introduction of any new factor) can radically change many parts of the environment. New skills are needed to perform the task, motivation to do the task may increase, and the task itself may be defined in new and different ways. Because technology introduces many new variables and myriad other, even more subtle changes, the comparison of a CALL environment with a non-CALL environment is misleading and can rarely describe accurately the effectiveness of computers for language learning in terms of simple linguistic measures, standardized tests, or discrete environmental variables (Salomon, 1990). Good research questions should focus on whether the *system* of teacher, student, and technology is working for the learners (see Egbert, 1993, for an example of a systemic approach to CALL research).

The *Explorations* sections at the end of each chapter in this volume demonstrate what we consider some of the right questions to ask about the

CALL environment. Questions that focus on conditions in language learning environments go far toward educating teachers about the effectiveness of technology in language learning. For example, the questions that Pica (1994, p. 52) asks of language learning research are just as critical in the computer-assisted classroom:

- How effective is group work as an aid to second language learning? What kinds of groups work best?

- Should students drill and practice new structures? If so, what kind of feedback should be given?

- What can be done to encourage participation among students who seldom ask questions or initiate interaction? Are these students more apt to interact when online? Under what conditions?

- To what extent does the correction of errors assist second language learning? How can errors best be corrected?

In addition, as Ehrmann (1995) notes, some technologies support some teaching methods better than others do, leading to the question:

- Which technologies are best for supporting the best methods of teaching and learning? For which type of student?

Studies of CALL environments must consider other important factors in SLA research. Ehrmann (1995) points out that one teacher using technology can influence a student's learning but that the cumulative effects of many teachers supporting good learning across the curriculum are far more significant. Therefore, what is needed are questions that address the study of CALL within and across courses and programs. Along the same lines, Chapelle (1995) notes that the many layers of the language learning environment can affect what happens in the classroom. Questions that investigate the political and social milieus in which CALL takes place are no less important than those that investigate CALL activities within one classroom. One may ask, for example, *What are some of the assumptions that come with technology? What are the goals of technology use in my school?*

Step 2: Review the literature

In CALL research, Purcell's (1996) Step 2 may involve more careful selection and analysis of research literature than is the case with typical SLA research. Much that has been written about using computers in language education has been descriptive rather than analytical: Technology-using teachers explain their program and curriculum and the way they have integrated CALL. Although these anecdotes are useful, they do not constitute rigorous research and should be used as guidelines for practice and as a starting point for scientific inquiry rather than as support for specific theories. A large body of research regarding educational technology does exist (see the journals and books mentioned earlier); this might be one place to start in conducting a research review for answers to theoretical CALL questions.

Another pitfall to watch out for in the literature (and in any SLA research) is the *Hawthorne effect*: Any group that is being studied while doing a new or different activity usually performs better. As noted earlier, this is only one way that the language learning environment changes upon the introduction of technology.

Step 3: State a hypothesis

Your search of the literature, beginning perhaps with some of the articles cited in the chapters in this volume that are pertinent to your inquiry, should give you a fairly comprehensive overview of what has already been accomplished in CALL research. Your study might lead you to replicate prior research, making appropriate corrections in procedures, or you may wish to strike out in a new direction. A tentative research question reflects only what you hope to find.

Step 4: Determine how to test the research question

Purcell's (1996) Step 4 is fraught with hazards. One truism of quantitative research in the past was the attempt to reduce or eliminate all variables except the one to be researched. However, testing pedagogical theory and application is one of the most difficult undertakings in the social sciences, because so many variables are at work at the same time. A quantitative focus cannot deal adequately with this "anarchic" environment. Happily for both researchers and classroom educators, many paradigm shifts have taken place since the days when only quantitative methodologies constituted "real" research. Structured qualitative studies, complementary analytic and systemic views, action research, and many other designs have successfully shed new light on what occurs in language classrooms (see D. Johnson, 1991, for an overview). Rather than forcing the design to fit into expected or traditional paradigms, you as a classroom CALL researcher should consider a design that takes into consideration what your questions are really asking.

Step 5: Gather data

Purcell's (1996) Step 5 cautions researchers to gather data accurately in order to test the hypothesis carefully. As we pointed out earlier, the CALL environment does not compartmentalize neatly into either *quantitative* or *qualitative* research and should be viewed through a lens that either combines these two paradigms or considers the classroom as the interacting system that it is.

The computer itself allows the generation of considerable data for many kinds of analyses. For instance, the usefulness of saving students' e-mail files to study as examples of interaction strategies is demonstrated in chapter 11. You might also have students save separately all drafts of a word-processed essay and later use them for an analysis of composing and editing strategies. Blogs and wikis are organized so that you may easily view successive drafts of a composition. Many software programs, for example, Live Action English Interactive (2006), also assist in data collection because a built-in record keeper notes the parts of the software that were accessed, the time spent on a task, and the results of tests or exercises. Collecting the same information about students working in a traditional classroom or studying the same material at home would be very difficult. At the University of Puerto Rico, Cayey's self-access lab, the coordinator created a similar but far simpler record keeper with HyperStudio (2005): Before logging out, students write up a record of their work with any questions they have after each session in the lab. A brief video clip on the first card explains how to use the software. Similarly, in an Internet-enabled lab, log-out could trigger a link to *SurveyMonkey* (Survey Monkey.com, 1999–2006) for a brief questionnaire.

The computer combined with video and audio recording also presents interesting opportunities to collect data about students' behavior with technology. Pujol (1995/1996) provides an excellent model for CALL research in which learners were video- and audiotaped as they used software. For more on interviewing and recording students' aural production, see chapter 27. Although video and audio recording may be used successfully in a traditional classroom for data collection, professionally developed software can allow sound files to be kept as records and later reviewed by the teacher, researcher, and student with regard to such variables as pronunciation and accent. Podcasts offer simple ways to maintain and access students' recordings online (for examples of student work, see Yeh, n.d.). A record of all keystrokes as students work at a terminal would allow close observation of how they use a tutorial, compose and revise an essay, or conduct an Internet search. Excellent models for quantitative research in CALL are to be found in *Language Learning & Technology*, a free, wholly online, refereed journal.

Many research models can be used to collect data for the study of a CALL environment, among them a discourse model with a hierarchical analysis of the interaction (Chapelle, 1990), a systemic model of the language learning environment like the one proposed in this book (see, e.g., Egbert, 1993; Egbert & Petrie, 2005), and a set of indicators like those proposed by B. F. Jones, Valdez, Nowakowski, and Rasmussen (1995) and by others. Regardless of the model, technology clearly does not dictate methods or questions; however, the model chosen must be appropriate to the setting and the technology under study. Questions of media are not of prime importance—questions about what is being taught and what is being learned must be the focus.

Step 6: *Refine your answer*

In both CALL and non-CALL research, Purcell's (1996) final step is sometimes treated with the perfunctory phrase "more research is needed in this area." A considerably more useful approach is to determine exactly where your research design may have gone astray or how data unaccounted for by your initial hypothesis might be incorporated into a different design or analytical framework. A number of the studies cited throughout this volume (e.g., in chapter 8) follow the latter approach and thus present useful starting points for your own research project. Action research, in which teachers carefully try out specific approaches and techniques with their students, making notes of successes and setbacks, is particularly suited to successive refinements as the teacher explores lesson plans and classroom strategies.

Conclusion

The eight learning conditions presented here can help meet goals in the language classroom by means of many general strategies, including using group work, providing concrete opportunities to interact in English, focusing on survival skills and functions or on content-based tasks, using problem solving, and recycling lesson content in various ways while providing open-ended opportunities for meaningful language use. In addition, you can provide adequate time for tasks, adequate feedback, appropriate prompting and other assistance, and adequate information or research resources while giving learners opportunities to choose goals and participate consciously in the learning process. The environmental conditions, however, do not dictate specific methods, techniques, content, or tools. Language educators are now using technology effectively to support these learning conditions in a wide variety of settings.

Chapters 2–27 explore in more depth the research that provides the empirical basis for each of the optimal language learning conditions. Each part of this book contains a chapter detailing research and describing the present state of theoretical knowledge about classroom language learning, especially as it relates to CALL (*Theory and Research*). Subsequent chapters discuss current teaching practices that apply the theory to computer-enhanced instruction, including activities, software, and hardware that support an optimal learning environment (*Classroom Practice*). Also included are chapters on matters related to the environment in which technology is used (*Critical Issues*). As requested by readers of the first edition of CALL *Environments*, each chapter now closes with suggestions for projects and questions for reflection that will help you understand more about CALL practices and conduct research with your own students in a computer-enhanced learning environment (*Explorations*). The text concludes with a reprise of "20 Minutes Into the Future" (Meskill, chapter 28) from our first edition, flanked by a new chapter, "The Future Is Now" (Price, chapter 29), which explores the new inventions and tools that will form the groundwork for CALL in the next several years. The appendixes provide names and uniform resource locators (URLs) for key World Wide Web sites and software, contact information for professional development, and other resources to help you explore the CALL environment with students. A new feature in this second edition, requested by our readers, is an index of terms used throughout the book.

Explorations

1. This chapter began with some computer jargon: *wiki, blog,* RSS, *social software, chat room, m-computing, pop mailer, phishing,* Web 2.0, *virus.* Begin a technology vocabulary journal by finding out what each of these terms means and how they might apply to your students'— or potential students'—learning situation. Keep a record of new terms and their uses throughout your reading of this text.

2. Examine the lab and/or other computer opportunities available to students in your school or a neighboring community. What types of access are available, and what limitations might be imposed on students (e.g., cost, limited time, lack of knowledgeable staff)? What remedies for these limitations might be found?

3. If you are currently working with a group of students or a tutee, follow the six steps outlined in this chapter to develop a research question and an appropriate means to explore it. Begin a preliminary exploration of the Internet and a range of journals in the profession for information about topics related to your question, and try to formulate a working hypothesis. Discuss your question and hypothesis with others in your class or in your work community, and revise as needed.

4. You may wish to begin classroom-situated action research either by observing a class or by collecting artifacts from your students. Be sure to obtain your students' informed consent before undertaking research with them.

5. As you sift through and organize the data you collect, be sure to refine your hypothesis and discuss your research with others in your working community. Decide what kinds of action you might take based on your hypothesis, your paper and Internet research, and the data you have explored. If you are in a teacher education class, your instructor may want you to submit oral and/or written reports based on your findings.

PART I

Interaction

Chapter 2 ⊞

Theory and Research: Interaction via Computers

Datta Kaur Khalsa, Diane Maloney-Krichmar,
and Joy Kreeft Peyton

Focus

It was interesting to get to know other children from different countries, it was very exciting. (Student in the MovingVoices project [iEarn, 2004, ¶ 3])

This chapter examines the use of emerging computer and Internet-based technologies to supplement traditional oral and print-based language and literacy teaching and learning with new forms of text-based and multimedia interaction. It provides an overview of theoretical concepts that support the use of interactive technologies, discusses the benefits and challenges of computer-mediated interactions, and suggests implications for instruction. The chapter describes the dynamic forces that shape online interaction and examines the uses and outcomes of these opportunities. It discusses the ways in which the effective use of computers and the Internet can provide highly motivating, multidisciplinary, problem-solving techniques and tools to prepare students more effectively for their future roles in a diverse world.

Background

Language learning in educational programs is shaped by the teacher's goals and methods and the students' motivations and activities. In the 1980s, the goals of language learning shifted from a focus on vocabulary and grammar knowledge to include authentic, meaningful communication and integrative, creative construction of language skills (Rodgers, 2001; Sullivan, 2000). These interactive language learning methods collectively became known as *communicative language teaching* (CLT; Rodgers, 2001). CLT emphasized the importance of genuine communication, student-centered teaching, and the learning of language forms in communicative contexts (Beale, 2002). This sociolinguistic approach provided opportunities for natural communication and often required that the teacher take a less dominant role in instruction and that learners negotiate meaning with each other (Larsen-Freeman, 1986). The communicative goals of CLT necessitated responsiveness to learners' needs and interests; interactive, authentic language use; risk taking and choice making; self-discovery in the process of learning; and integration of speaking, listening, reading, and writing (Beale, 2002; Finocchiaro & Brumfit, 1983). CLT has become one of many language teaching and learning approaches that H. D. Brown (1994) calls "enlightened eclecticism" (p. 74).

The use of computers and the Internet in language learning not only supports the development of students' language skills but also fosters students' interests and motivation (Cononelos & Oliva, 1993; Fujiike, 2004; Warschauer, 1996a). Although the primary goal of CALL activity is to increase and enhance the participation of language learners in linguistic interactions (Chapelle, 1997), technology also creates new social and electronic spaces that support collaboration and social interaction (Bruce, Peyton, & Batson, 1993; Fujiike, 2004; Jeon-Ellis, Debski, & Wigglesworth, 2005). In addition, technology can support the development of language and cultural knowledge in all of the areas covered by the standards for foreign language learning—communication, communities, cultures, and connections (American Council on the Teaching of Foreign Languages, 1983).

Learning through interaction, social constructivism, and identity theory are theoretical positions that build on communicative language development and co-construction of knowledge. These theories clarify why and how people observe, imitate, and learn in social, interactive contexts (Bandura, 1971, 1986; Rotter, 1982; Vygotsky, 1978; see also Khalsa, 2005b, for discussion of how these theories apply to online language learning). Social learning theory, also known as social cognitive theory (Bandura, 1971, 1986), explains how thoughts, feelings, and behavior are affected by the actual or implied presence of others. The social and cultural context of the individuals and how they perceive and interpret information from others is the basis of this theory. Likewise, identity theories, which describe the influence of sociocultural constructs and the relationship of culture, identity, and community in a collaborative culture, can also add to an understanding of virtual learning possibilities for language learners (Fearon, 1999; E. Hall, 1990; Hofstede, 2001; Hoppe, 2004; Voronov & Singer, 2002; Wenger, n.d.; Zhang & Storck, 2001). Each theory contributes to an understanding of coexistence in complex social learning systems and development of self-identity in a global community. Cognitive skills, attitudes, and behavior have an impact on the environment, and the environment has an impact on these personal factors (Huitt, 2002, 2004). Because of the current access to and popularity of the Internet, language learners can participate in genuine contexts to discuss and share ideas as they work and plan together.

Discussion and Examples

Development of and involvement in online interaction apply emergent uses of technology in language learning. They incorporate social learning theory and social constructivism into language learning environments and provide opportunities for students to share and experience diverse ideas, values, cultures, and language skills (Bandura, 2001). Merging social and language learning with technology can also strengthen skills that students need to be successful in society (National Institute for Literacy, n.d.). These skills include the following:

- ability to access information
- voice (ability to express ideas and opinions)
- independent action (ability to solve problems and make decisions)
- ability to participate in lifelong learning

Socially based computing tools, such as instant messaging, discussion threads, weblogs (blogs), and wikis to develop collaborative tasks and projects, provide a "holistic learning approach aimed at employing modern technology to trigger students' ability to act with words and create social realities in and out of the classroom, and thus to facilitate learning" (Jeon-Ellis et al., 2005, p. 121). As Holum and Gahala (2001) note, electronic tools available in Internet-based environments have moved language and literacy teaching and learning from its oral and print-based traditions to new forms of text-based and multimedia interaction. These technologies are changing how people learn to read, write, listen, and communicate. Teacher exploration of the basic characteristics of the interactive tools in online environments facilitates understanding of computer-mediated communication and provides opportunities to engage students in interactive and authentic learning experiences.

Online communication technologies are divided into two basic types: (a) those that make possible simultaneous or synchronous interaction, such as instant messaging, text and voice chat rooms, and videoconferencing; and (b) those that occur through delayed (asynchronous) communication, such as e-mail, discussion boards, blogs, podcasting, and webcasting. Synchronous interaction tends to be characterized by more informal written exchanges that more closely resemble speaking, whereas asynchronous communication modalities give the creators (or speakers in the case of multimedia technologies) the chance to review and edit their work (Preece, 2000; Preece, Maloney-Krichmar, & Abras, 2003).

Benefits of Computer-Mediated Interaction

Educators who have embraced the use of online communication technologies describe a number of benefits, including connectivity and fulfillment of social needs. For example, Khalsa (2005b) cites a New York City public school educator with 11 years of experience who spoke of the "amazing possibility ... to all of us. ... [to] participat[e] in an ongoing forum with people of very diverse cultural backgrounds from all over the world" (p. 145). Another New York teacher noted, "It encouraged my students to learn and inquire about cultural sameness and customs that our children were not aware of. The interest level of the children was amazing" (p. 147). A new educator in Delaware was surprised at the results of using computer-mediated communication in her teaching. She wrote, "The collaboration and the smiles I see on my students' faces when they receive a response from a fellow student sometimes 1000's of miles away [is very encouraging]" (p. 167).

Benefits include the following:

- *authenticity*—Learners gain access to an unlimited source of authentic language as they engage in interaction with native and nonnative speakers of the contact language (Bolter, 1990; Herring, 1996; Lemke, 1998). This provides a sociocultural environment that is realistic, natural, and meaningful and that reinforces and motivates learners (LeLoup & Ponterio, 2003). It also provides opportunities for target language practice that more closely match real-world needs (Jeon-Ellis et al., 2005; Jepson, 2005).

- *voice*—As learners engage in a variety of online communication activities and interact with a wide range of persons (peers and teachers), they are empowered to find and use their own voice (Kramsch, A'Ness, & Lam, 2000).

- *equal learning opportunities*—The online environment tends to promote more equitable sharing of ideas than the face-to-face classroom, which is delimited by space and time (Kramsch et al., 2000; Kremers, 1993; LeLoup & Ponterio, 2003; Odasz, n.d.). Face-to-face classrooms can be dominated by a few outstanding students, which tends to discourage participation of students with less language ability.

- *individual attention*—The online environment provides unique opportunities for individual relationships (student-teacher and student-student) and private conversations that may not be easily negotiated in face-to-face classes (Kramsch et al., 2000; LeLoup & Ponterio, 2003; Odasz, n.d.).

- *freedom of expression*—Research has shown that people often feel freer to express their feelings online than in person (Walther & Boyd, 2002). Students may feel more comfortable asking questions and expressing ideas to their teachers and other students in online environments (Jiang & Ramsay, 2005).

- *convenience and accessibility*—Students can work at their own speed, engage in a variety of learning activities, and have access to class participants and materials at all times (Kramsch et al., 2000; Odasz, n.d.). Researchers have long reported that many students like being able to access curriculum content, complete course work, and interact with other students and the teacher at any time from any place, and they especially like the immediacy of the feedback they receive (Bruffee, 1993; Dede, 1996; Harasim, Hiltz, Teles, & Turoff, 1995; Haythornthwaite & Kazmer, 2002; Renniger & Shumar, 2002).

- *engagement*—A greater depth of engagement in the curriculum content is promoted by a variety of textual and multimedia instructional modalities that address an array of learning styles (Kramsch et al., 2000; LeLoup & Ponterio, 2003; Odasz, n.d.). Multimedia and collaborative project-based learning activities can be tailored to the interests, learning styles, and motivations of specific groups (L. Lee, 2004; Shneiderman, 2002b). For example, a teacher in Tasmania, working with a group of reluctant readers, arranged for them to have an outdoor skateboard lesson. Following the lesson, the group documented what was involved with their own texts, digital photos, and multimedia slide presentations. This assignment provided a variety of learning activities that promote literacy skills while giving the students with lower skill levels a chance to contribute to the project (Connor, n.d.).

- *collaboration*—The online environment promotes collaborative learning and community building (Jeon-Ellis et al., 2005; L. Lee, 2004; Shneiderman, 2002b). In the process of acquiring language skills, networked students can collaborate to discuss real-life topics. In these discussions, they help each other learn how to explain and defend their thoughts and ideas, which can foster a sense of community and sharing (Jeon-Ellis et al., 2005; Jepson, 2005; Jiang & Ramsay, 2005; L. Lee, 2004).

- *technological literacy*—Uses of technology promote students' mastery of valuable computer and information literacy skills, which enhance self-efficacy and can also bring recognition from peers and teachers (Jeon-Ellis et al., 2005; Khalsa, 2005b). Van Dijk (2005) states that individuals learn more from practical applications of computer/information technology than from formal computer education. Mastery of computer and information literacy skills within a collaborative project-based learning environment can help students become more marketable as the need for technologically competent workers increases worldwide (Haythornthwaite & Kazmer, 2002; Katz & Rice, 2002).

Challenges of Computer-Mediated Interaction

As shown in the previous discussion, the online environment provides opportunities for mastery of curriculum content, development of the social relationships that promote language use and support learning, and acquisition of computer and information literacy skills. However, major challenges are inherent in the use of online technology and computer-mediated communication for language learning. Challenges include access to technology and the requisite computer and information literacy skills, absence online of social cues (oral and facial cues and body language) that help establish meaning and intent, and the need to develop trust and realistic expectations.

Access to technology and skills

The *digital divide* refers to complex and dynamic factors that determine who has access to which computer-mediated technology. Even the term *access* is complex, because there are several different types of access. *Physical access* to the hardware; software; and services of computers, computer networks, and other digital technologies is the most fundamental type of access. For privileged populations in developed nations, physical access to computer technology typically occurs at work, at school, and at home. In contrast, for disadvantaged and marginalized groups and developing nations, public places such as libraries; community centers; churches; the homes of neighbors, relatives, and friends; and commercial sites, such as Internet cafés, usually serve as points of access. The most important factor in determining physical access to computer technology is income, but access also strongly correlates with education, employment status, and occupation (Katz & Rice, 2002; Van Dijk, 2005; Warschauer, 2003).

A second type of access is becoming increasingly important. *Conditional access* refers to the applications, programs, and contents of specific software and data carriers (CDs and DVDs) that are available through purchase or membership only. In developed nations, companies are using marketing strategies that lower the costs of physical access to computer technology but increase the costs of conditional access. That is, while the price of computer hardware is falling, the cost of software programs and access to some Internet resources (e.g., research databases, electronic libraries, online journals) is increasing (Van Dijk, 2005). New initiatives to build computers that cost US$100 (OLPC, n.d.) will only address problems related to physical access; lack of conditional access will continue to plague minority and disadvantaged populations worldwide as access to software and Internet resources is restricted through high fees (Van Dijk, 2005).

While physical and conditional access present formidable challenges to educators working with disadvantaged and marginalized populations and those living in developing nations, the inequalities of *skills access* are an even larger challenge. Mastery of the following skills allows individuals to benefit from the use of modern computer and information technologies (Van Dijk, 2005, p. 75):

- *Operational skills* are required to read, write, view, listen to, create, and operate computers and computer programs.

- *Informational skills* are required to search, select, and process information from various text, statistical, visual, and multimedia sources and computer and network files.

- *Strategic skills* are required to improve one's position in life through effective utilization of information and resources accessed through computer and information technologies.

Researchers engaged in examining the digital divide note that people with high levels of traditional literacy, the ability to read and write, also tend to have high levels of operational, informational, and strategic skills and the ability to access and use information to obtain desired results (Katz & Rice, 2002; Van Dijk, 2005; Warschauer, 2003). In addition, social and cultural factors influence who masters the skills needed to use technology (Van Dijk, 2005). Educators must be sensitive to these issues when developing new and innovative programs using computer-mediated technologies to foster language acquisition and literacy.

Absence of social cues

How well a particular type of media conveys a sense of the participants being physically present was coined *social presence* by Short, Williams, and Christie (1976). Social presence affects how people sense emotion, intimacy, and immediacy (R. E. Rice, 1993). Reduced social presence is a characteristic of many types of computer-mediated communication: E-mail, discussion boards, blogs, and electronic journals are all types of text-based communication that do not convey nonverbal cues such as gestures and other body language, facial expression, appearance, and social context. Low bandwidth reduces nonverbal cues because in text-only modalities, both message and social information are carried by the same verbal/linguistic symbols (R. E. Rice, 1987, 1993).

The consequences of this absence of information vary depending on the communication task. Those working in text-only environments need to be aware of these limitations and be sure that they are sensitive to problems that can arise. People use nonverbal cues to enhance understanding (e.g., a quizzical look can send the message that the speaker has not been understood), and reduced social cues may result in behavior that would not occur in face-to-face interactions. For example, individuals may reveal more personal information online than appropriate (i.e., *hyperpersonalization*), and people may become frustrated and misunderstand the intentions of others, leading to hostile or aggressive communications (Lea, O'Shea, Fung, & Spears, 1992; Spears, Lea, & Lee, 1990; Walther, 1996; Walther & Boyd, 2002). Khalsa (2007) indicates that humor also must be treated carefully in online environments because it can be easily misunderstood without the usual array of nonverbal cues that help make it clear. In summary, Olson and Olson (2000) argue that differences in local context, time zones, culture, and language persist in spite of the use of communication technologies that reduce distances between people.

Need to develop trust and realistic expectations

It is important to develop strategies to foster trust in the online environment. Clear and sensible guidelines for interaction help students understand what the norms of behavior are in what may be a new environment for them (Khalsa, 2005a, 2005b, 2007). In addition, establishing the purpose of online activities and the roles that students and teachers will play is an important step in facilitating meaningful online interaction and managing expectations (Preece, 2000). For example, students tend to expect immediate feedback in an interactive environment that is available 24/7, and they may feel hurt if the teacher or other students do not respond quickly enough. However, if teachers inform the group that they will post responses or grade assignments within a specific time frame, they can strengthen the communication process and foster greater trust between themselves and their students. With proper guidelines for communication, teachers and students can capitalize on the advantages that electronic interaction offers.

Implications for Instruction

The availability of electronic media for interaction opens new doors to educators, giving them new options for instruction. At the same time, teachers need to carefully select and plan how they will use these media. The computer tools and activities selected depend on the learners, the learning goals, the teacher's technology skills, and the students' access to technology (Khalsa, 2005b). *First-generation* technology includes tools such as instant messaging, videoconferencing, e-mail, discussion forums, and learning management systems such as Blackboard (2005; Godwin-Jones, 2003). Some students have reported feeling comfortable writing e-mail to other nonnative English speakers, with the *anytime* convenience of writing and reflection (Jeon-Ellis et al., 2005; Volle, 2005). Other studies have found that the practice of language learning in synchronous chat rooms produced not only improved attitudes toward language learning but also more language, not to mention more complex language, than learning in face-to-face contexts (Payne & Ross, 2005; Warschauer, 1996a). Chat rooms have even been used for synchronous online debates (Fujiike, 2004). Computer classroom management systems provide a safe area for practicing language skills and sharing documents or interesting resources.

Second-generation technology, based on extensible markup language (XML), includes applications such as blogs, wikis, and really simple syndication (RSS) feeds (Godwin-Jones, 2003; RSS is a format for syndicating news and the content of newslike sites, including major news sites, news-oriented community sites, and personal blogs). These applications allow language learners to use audio, video, or text blogs as personal reflective journals, where they have additional opportunities to express themselves effectively and appropriately, while interacting with others who read and leave comments on their reflections. Wikis provide an authentic Web-based "shared repository of knowledge, with the knowledge base growing over time" (Godwin-Jones, 2003, p. 15). Some believe that these new and powerful collaborative tools are so important that their arrival signals a second generation of Web use (referred to as *Web* 2.0) that moves beyond information delivery and allows reflection on and interaction with that information and with others (Godwin-Jones, 2003).

Technology for language learning may include project-oriented computer-assisted language learning (ProCALL). Projects can include brainstorming topics while evaluating Web sites, compiling key words for Internet searches, conducting peer reviews, and presenting projects on Web sites for other groups (Jeon-Ellis et al., 2005). Global projects extend communication to native speakers and language learners around the world (Khalsa, 2005b; see also Kennedy, 2006, for a description of the GLOBE project). These efforts combine two or more technology tools such as discussion threads, instant messaging, and videoconferencing to help students compare local and global data and cultural experiences and to create learning products that can help others. An example is a collaborative project entitled *MovingVoices* (iEARN, n.d.), which engages a community in making digital videos while enhancing language learning, social studies, and community development as participants interact and collaborate online.

Conclusion

Computer and information technologies are creating opportunities for writing and learning that were never before possible, and teachers are central to the process of enabling students to interact and learn in this fast-paced technological era. Teachers must recognize that individuals have unique social and educational needs that require social connectivity, transparent application of technology, authentic learning, and opportunities to cultivate meaningful change in their world. At the same time, teachers must be aware of the dynamic forces that shape online interaction and continually examine the uses and outcomes of these opportunities. The language learning needs of today's students are complemented by effective use of computers and the Internet, which can provide highly motivating, multidisciplinary problem-solving techniques and the tools to prepare students more effectively for their future roles in a diverse world.

Explorations

1. As noted in chapter 11, and elsewhere in this volume, communicative language teaching emphasizes genuine communication, student-centered teaching, and the learning of language forms in communicative contexts. Computer-mediated interaction provides a number of opportunities for this type of learning. Which of the opportunities described in this chapter best fit the goals of your course and the needs of your students? Why?

2. Design a project for students that involves online interaction (through e-mail, discussion boards, blogs, etc.) or the use of online tools such as wikis and RSS feeds. Describe the student population involved, the knowledge and skills to be developed, the activities to be engaged in, and the expected outcomes.

3. Social interaction via electronic media is a popular form of social learning for youth. Research the most popular socially oriented Web sites for youth (e.g., *MySpace* [MySpace.com, 2003–2006], *Facebook*, 2007). Pick three of these Web sites and introduce them to your students. Formulate discussion questions and activities that will stimulate their examination of and involvement with these sites.

4. Why are some students reluctant to participate in interaction with their peers? What can teachers do to encourage the participation of students who do not commonly interact in class? How can technology assist in supporting such interaction? (You may find other chapters in this volume of help in exploring this question.) Do certain students learn better with less interaction? Why might this be the case? Discuss with your class or group some ways that you might study these questions in the research literature and in action research in the language classroom.

5. Formulate a research question related to interaction and technology, and conduct a literature search in the ERIC database to address the question. The following steps should be of help.

Performing a Boolean Search with the ERIC Database

1. Plan the search strategy by describing the question and deciding on the concepts that a record must contain to be relevant to the search. A concept can be a topic, an author's name, a key word or descriptor, a document type, a range of years, and so forth. Your concepts for this search might be *interaction, technology, research reports, 2000–2006*.

2. Determine possible synonyms or alternative words for each concept and group the synonyms together—for example, *interaction/communication/computer-mediated; technology/technology education/technological literacy*.

3. Connect to the ERIC Web site: http://www.eric.ed.gov/. Go to the >THESAURUS tab to identify additional ERIC synonyms, descriptors, and terms that might be used for your concepts. Link to >THESAURUS HELP to find out more.

4. Now click on the >ERIC SEARCH tab to try out a Basic Search. From the pull-down menu, select >DESCRIPTORS (FROM THESAURUS) and enter the terms you have found using the command OR between the synonyms—e.g., *interaction* OR *communication* OR *computer-mediated*. Click on the >SEARCH button to execute this step.

5. On the next screen that appears (there may be thousands of items resulting—don't worry, you will narrow the choices step by step), click on >SEARCH WITHIN RESULTS. This screen will allow you to enter your second concept and its synonyms. On the left-hand side of the screen, look for the directions: "Use the fields below to narrow your original search results."

6. Using the Boolean operator OR, add the synonyms chosen for your second concept in the box labeled *Keywords* (e.g., *technology* OR *technology education* OR *technological literacy*). Limit your search further by selecting various options (e.g., full text availability, range of dates, publication types).

7. Complete the search by clicking on the >SEARCH button.

8. You will be able to read the ERIC entries resulting from the search in the right-hand column of the subsequent page. Continue narrowing the search as needed, by adding and deleting concepts within your results (e.g., possibly eliminate *technology*).

In terms of Boolean logic, the sequence you have just followed uses the commands (also known as operators) OR and AND as follows:

interaction OR *communication* OR *computer-mediated*

AND

technology OR *technology education* OR *technological literacy*

AND

research reports

AND

publication dates=2000–2006

Chapter 3 ▧

Classroom Practice:
Problem-Based Language Learning

Joy Egbert and Leslie Huff

Focus

A major foreign manufacturer wants to build a new plant near an impoverished rural community in your region. The area is known for its natural beauty. Supporters of the plant claim that the jobs it will bring to the local people will make a big difference in their lifestyles and that the taxes and fees the plant pays will improve their health and education opportunities. Opponents claim that pollution from the plant will spoil the surroundings and cause more health problems and that the low-paying jobs will not raise the standard of living in the area. Supporters and opponents have scheduled separate meetings for the same night later this week.

You are concerned and want to get all the facts. Which meeting will you attend? Why? Use the Internet, interviews of local experts, newspaper articles and editorials, and any other resources you can find to solve both your own problem and the problem that this community faces.

This scenario depicts a problem-solving situation that occurs regularly around the world. People everywhere are concerned about jobs, health, and opportunity. However, without good reasoning and problem-solving and inquiry skills, many learners who may find themselves in similar situations will not be able to make effective decisions and change their lives for the better. Language learners need the language, thinking skills, reasoning strategies, and tools to address such real-world problems. Gordon (1998) notes,

> whether it's a relatively simple matter of deciding what to eat for breakfast or a more complex one such as figuring out how to reduce pollution in one's community, in life we make decisions and do things that have concrete results. (p. 391)

This chapter describes the problem-solving process and problem-based language learning (PBLL) and suggests how technology can be used to learn about and support this instructional approach.

Background

Problem solving is a process in which learners apply critical and creative thinking skills to a problem. The product of this process is a decision. Learners typically face two types of problems. The first type is *close-ended* problems to which there is a "correct" solution. Most students readily use a set process to find the solution to close-ended problems. The other type is *open-ended* or ill-structured problems. These problems, like the one in this chapter's Focus section, may have more than one solution and no "correct" answer. Open-ended problems require students to apply a variety of strategies and knowledge to making a decision. They also require a great amount of language and interaction to come to a logical solution.

With the current focus on 21st-century skills, research is being conducted in every area to look at the problem-solving process and determine how to produce more efficient and effective problem solvers. To date, research has determined that

1. problem-solving can depend on the context, the participants, and the stakeholders

2. students retain better after problem solving

3. the use of technology in problem-based learning (PBL) increases learning gains (Stites, 1998)

The problem-solving literature points out that both knowledge of the problem content and problem-solving skills are necessary for making effective decisions (Abdullah, 1998), and language is central to both learning and using those skills and knowledge. However, individual differences among students may impact their success. For example, students from some cultures will not be familiar with this kind of learning, and others may not have the language to work with it. According to the literature, the bias of limited or different experience can make it hard to understand all sides of a problem. Teachers must consider these challenges in teaching and supporting student problem solving.

To be successful in a PBLL environment, students need to have skills that enable them to reach the goals of the lesson. Some of these skills include the ability to synthesize information, work cooperatively (Larsson, 2001; M. Peterson, n.d.), compare and contrast data, prioritize, and use language to accomplish these goals. These skills can be difficult to teach because practice is a key factor in the ability to use them. However, certain strategies can be used to teach these essential skills and help students develop them effectively.

Direct instruction is one way to introduce skills, language, and the importance of using problem-solving skills effectively. Direct instruction consists of explicit instruction and demonstration, which increase the students' awareness of the skills so that they become the focus of thought. Didactic questioning is a valuable method of determining and assessing why and how certain skills can be used to achieve goals in the PBLL environment.

Indirect instruction provides a means through which students can practice and develop their problem-solving skills; students' skills progress as they use them to complete different tasks. Concept mapping is one way to increase students' abilities to synthesize materials. For example, after students have found individual sources for researching the impact of manufacturing plants on the environment, they can come together in a small group to synthesize their findings in a concept map. Comparing and contrasting, prioritizing, and working cooperatively are all skills that can be developed though small-group reflective discussions. For example, small groups can read a short scenario similar to that used in the Focus section of this chapter and then come to a consensus on the problems they found in the text and decide which are the most important. *Think-pair-share* (Ledlow, 2001) is another useful way of consciously thinking about strategies and how they can be applied to solving problems. In think-pair-share activities, students have think time to reflect on their own ideas, followed by collaboration with a partner and then sharing with the larger team or the whole class.

Self-directed learning is another important aspect of learning that must be developed in order for problem-based language instruction to be success-ful. Students must lessen their need for structured study and learn how to recognize their language learning needs and how to satisfy them effectively (Ngeow & Kong, 2001; Samford University, 2006). Developing effective groups to accomplish tasks can be one strategy for increasing student independence in learning. *Effective* in this case means that students can make "optimal use of their time and resources while working in groups. Functioning effectively in groups involves knowing how to organize the work, distribute responsibility, break up complex tasks, and provide useful feedback on work that is done" (Ngeow & Kong, 2001, n.p.). By allowing students to scaffold each other and rely less on teacher support, students have more power in the learning process and more opportunities to learn both language and problem-solving skills.

The benefits of PBLL make it worth facing the challenges. Using problems as a basis for language and content learning at all levels means that students can become more engaged in their learning, which can lead to gains in lan-guage learning and increased abilities for solving social problems (Elias & Tobias, 1996). As important, in learning language through problems, students better understand concepts, learn and practice skills that are necessary in their lives, and become independent and self-directed learners and thinkers outside of classrooms. In addition, students can develop better language skills by working on problems that require a high level of social interaction (Dooly, 2005). These social interactions in the language classroom can lead to some of the optimal conditions for learning expressed in chapter 1 of this volume.

Throughout the literature, the following steps in problem solving are often presented:

1. Define the problem: Think about what problem needs to be solved.

2. Identify options: Think about the things you can do about the problem.

3. Identify the best solution: Look at all the options from Step 2 and decide which one(s) would work best.

4. Plan how to achieve the best solution: Once you have picked your option(s), you need to plan how you will carry it out.

5. Evaluate results: Once you have carried out your plan, you need to decide if it worked the way you wanted it to and how much was accomplished. (Ohio Literacy Resource Center, 2006)

Teachers can demonstrate, model, and teach problem-solving strategies directly or incorporate them implicitly into tasks. The most important aspect of this instruction is the process, including, in part, examining cultural, emotional, intellectual, and other differences that impact the process.

Examples and Discussion

As discussed in chapter 1, the focus of technology use should be the learning opportunities that it presents. A variety of tools can support aspects of the problem-solving process: computer-aided design software, advanced expert systems that try to reproduce expert thinking processes, semantic mapping software such as Inspiration (2006), and so on. Even a word processor, a database, and spreadsheet software can help students organize and present data to be used in decision making. Throughout this process, learners work with a variety of language forms, skills, and content that are authentic to the task. Whichever tool is used, teachers must design instruction carefully to make sure that it contains an appropriate focus on both language and thinking skills. This section describes some useful tools for PBLL and then presents sample student activities.

Sample PBLL Tools

- *WebQuests*—A WebQuest (Dodge, n.d.-b) is a specifically formatted Web-based activity. Although few WebQuests are currently available for language learners—particularly at lower proficiency levels—there are advantages to creating and using WebQuests as problem-solving and language learning tools at all levels. For example, the WebQuest format includes preselected Web resources that can be differentiated by student level, collaboration and social interaction are required, and students have a variety of choices in ways to present their language-based solutions.

- *ThinkQuests*—Along the same lines as WebQuests, students can solve problems with their teams by building a ThinkQuest (Oracle Education Foundation, n.d.-a) or participating in a Web Inquiry Project (Molebash, n.d.).

- *TourMaker*—Tramline has developed field-trip generator software called TourMaker (n.d.), which is inexpensive and helps the user create interesting excursions. The problem-solving/creativity/critical thinking exercises require language that is part of many curricula. Ready-made Virtual Field Trips are linked from the Tramline site.

- *Your Sky* (*Walker, n.d.*) *and* Water on the Web (WOW, 2004)—These sites allow learners to explore problems presented by natural phenomena with minimal science equipment. When working with raw data, students have to draw their own conclusions based on evidence. Students develop important problem-solving skills while using authentic, content-based language.

- *Filamentality*—Through fill-in-the-blank activities, students choose a topic, conduct Internet searches, compile a list of links, and create online learning activities. The *Filamentality* Web site (AT&T Knowledge Ventures, 2007b) provides support "along the way through Mentality Tips. In the end, you'll create a web-based activity you can share with others even if you don't know anything about HTML or serving web pages" (¶ 1). The Mentality Tips are instructional guides to common technology activities, such as copying and pasting, searching for Web sites, and so on. *Filamentality* is free and easy to use, so any teacher (or student) with an Internet connection can build or solve a problem using this site. The focus on a variety of language modes is a central part of activities with *Filamentality*.

- *simulation software and* Web *sites*—A number of interesting simulations are discussed in several chapters of this volume (e.g., chapters 13 and 26). Simulations often present problems such as a mystery to be solved, a city or country to run (which may involve political, economic, and social decisions), or decisions to be made about where to go and how to achieve a goal or complete a quest. Chapter 26 describes several simulations constructed purposely for language learners. (See the *e*-GAME Web site [University of Essex, 1999–2001] for content-based business simulations; and Fasli & Michalakopoulos, 2006, for the pedagogical foundation.)

Content Sites for PBLL

- The Discovery Channel (Discovery Communications, 2006) and Discovery Education (2006a) Web sites present globally oriented problems, some of which focus on language.

- The NASA (n.d.) *SciFiles* present problems, video cases, quizzes, and tools for problem solving.

- *Nature for Teachers* (Public Broadcasting Service, n.d.) provides lesson plans for K–12 students and guides for teachers that involve animals and habitats and use thinking tools such as graphic organizers and Web searches.

- *Superthinkers* (Verizon New Media Services, 1996–2006) is an effective problem-solving site that can be used or adapted in many ways. In addition to various other resources, the site hosts the imaginary and thought-provoking Peetnik Mysteries.

- *Come Visit Wisconsin!* (Hayden, 2006; based on a similar WebQuest by Patricia Link about New Jersey) offers a lesson in which students research information in various categories to compile a brochure to advertise a vacation destination. This idea could be adapted to the students' local community.

- Innovative Designs for Education's (IDE, 2005) *Great Sites for Educators* provides numerous links to authentic learning units, including a PBL link of the month.

Teacher Tools

Instructional strategies, tips, and materials for teaching and supporting student problem solving can be found all over the Web and in a number of technology texts (see, e.g., Egbert, 2005; Hanson-Smith & Rilling, 2006; and chapters in this volume). Abdullah (1998) provides a sample step-by-step process for language teachers to follow in using PBL. Other resources include the following:

- Simple situations for adults to practice PBLL can be found at the Ohio Literacy Resource Center's (2006) *Problem-Solving* site.

- An excellent site with articles, activities, and explanations of PBL in the content areas of math and sciences is the *Problem-Based Learning Network* @ IMSA (Illinois Mathematics and Science Academy, 1993–2006).

- Research summaries can be found on the *Project-Based Learning Research* page of the George Lucas Educational Foundation (2006) Web site.

Other tools, both online and off, that support problem solving are mentioned in chapters 7 and 14, and elsewhere in this volume.

Technology-Enhanced PBLL Activities

Teachers can use tools like those mentioned previously to present learners with problems, or they can develop their own open-ended PBLL activities such as those presented in the following examples. Throughout, a focus must be kept on both the language and the process of problem solving. (For more on combining task-based and language learning, see chapter 13.)

Example 1: Cliffhanger

The teacher (or student) chooses a stopping point in a text where one of the story characters must reach a decision. Students discuss the choices that the character has and potential consequences for each. Students choose the most likely decision for the character (and can compare it to the best decision, if the two are not the same). They base their choice on an understanding of the story line and the character. Students create a story line and use a video camera to make a short video that presents their solution to what the character should and will do. Students evaluate both the proposed solution and the real one as they continue to read the text.

Example 2: World's worst problem solver

The teacher explains to students that they will have a competition to see who can propose the worst solution to a problem. The teacher proposes a problem that relates to current curricular goals and/or content. Students use preselected Web sites to research possible solutions and create Microsoft PowerPoint (2007) presentations to explain their solution. Students must reach an ineffective and inefficient but possible solution, and they must describe why their solution is the worst.

Example 3: Librarian

Students pretend to be a committee of librarians deciding which books to order for the school library. They have access to any book in the world but can choose only 10 books due to funding. (The teacher may choose to give students a preset amount to spend.) Their goals are to entice other learners to read, to meet the school's curricular goals, and to get the best deal for their money. During the process, students frame the problem, research and review books online, consider relevant factors such as what the other students might like to read and which curricular goals are most important, choose their books, and present their suggestions to the school in an electronic format.

Example 4: A *new flag*

The U.S. legislature has decided that the American flag no longer represents the country well. They are asking for well-supported suggestions for a new flag. The teacher asks students to work on this problem; the class will send one suggestion from the class to be voted on by the legislature. Student teams define the problem (e.g., Is it that the flag does not represent the country or that the legislature needs to be convinced that it does?). They research facts about the current flag and the United States on the Web and in texts. They prepare electronic presentations for class members, and the class evaluates each presentation based on known facts. Finally, students use an electronic voting system to choose the class's best solution.

Example 5: *Budgeting for food*

A certain country is in desperate need of money for food for the coming year or many of its people will starve. All together, the country requires US$7 billion. The governments of two countries that want to help are asking for public input on their budget choices. Because of projected budget problems, the political leaders in these two countries are deciding which programs could be cut, and to what extent, in order to help pay for the food. Because it is an election year, these leaders are interested in hearing where the public thinks the money could come from. After listening to this scenario, students at two different school sites must decide what the question is (e.g., How should they deal with the budget? Is this an election-year ploy? How much does the needy country actually require? What are some other potential problems?). Students perform a cost-benefit analysis using financial data, supplied in a spreadsheet, about the needy country and the (imaginary) helper countries (i.e., the two schools). They propose and weigh different solutions and type up a proposed budget for their helper country. Each helper country collaborates with the "public" (students) from the other country to determine which portion of the food money each will contribute.

Example 6: *Treeless*

The owners of the local mall have decided that the trees along the street in front of the mall are obscuring the view of passers-by and costing them business. They hire a tree service to cut down every other tree, providing a much better view of the mall from the street. Many residents of this "Tree Town USA" are upset and angry about the trees being cut down and decide to file a legal action against the mall owners. Students, acting as mall owners, Tree Town officials, town residents, and a mediation team, perform their various roles by counting and researching trees and tree growth, investigating all sides of the issue, and working with others to come to a decision about what should happen next. Students organize their data in a spreadsheet, use decision software to discuss, and use word-processing software to type up their reflections on the process and its outcomes.

These PBLL activities can all be adapted for a variety of student language levels and content, and different electronic or paper tools and processes can be used to meet the goals of each. As stated previously, the focus must be on the content to be learned, the thinking and reasoning skills to be practiced and acquired, and the language needed to succeed in the tasks. Technology helps create an optimal learning environment in which students can readily collaborate, find an authentic audience for their resulting decisions, and reflect on what they have learned.

Conclusion

The world is becoming "smaller" each day, and language students require new skills to mediate and navigate its impact on their lives. Helping students develop problem-solving skills, and supporting their understanding and use of technology, is an integral part of the language learning process.

Explorations

1. How did you learn to solve problems? What skills work best for you in problem-solving situations? How do your skills continue to develop now?

2. How can the strategies and activities that you are already using or are familiar with be adapted to cultivate students' problem-solving strategies? How can technology use support students' problem solving?

3. What are some of the difficulties of or obstacles to developing a technology-enhanced PBLL curriculum in your school or country? How can these difficulties and obstacles be effectively addressed?

4. Develop a problem scenario similar to those in this chapter on one of the following topics that is relevant to your language students: the environment, rural education, globalization, travel, or charity. Write a short introduction explaining the situation and contextualizing the problem. Provide appropriate Web-based resources to help students learn about the issues, for example, in the form of a WebQuest.

5. Visit some of the Web sites that feature problem-based instruction. How can information from these sites be incorporated in your language classroom? Share your discoveries with classmates or your working group.

Chapter 4 ⊞

Critical Issues: Places and Spaces

Elizabeth Hanson-Smith

Focus

Walk into many new computer labs in the 21st century, and you are apt to see a design that is based on the 18th-century school room: rows of computers with seats facing the board at the front of the room. It may be a whiteboard, not a chalkboard, but pupils are to focus on the sage on the stage at the head of the class. The space formerly taken up by books and paper is now held by the computer monitor, whether embedded in the desk or sitting on the table. To see what students are doing, the teacher must walk back along the rows of desks and stand behind them. What's wrong with this picture?

Take a look now at a corridor in my campus's Student Union: Just off the pizza parlor, all abuzz with foosball and incessant TV, small tables line the walls, each with an electric outlet. Some students have their laptops open and snack on an apple or sip an espresso while tapping the keys. Others sit in pairs or small groups, chatting and sharing their screens as they work. The entire building, like most others on the campus, is wireless-capable, so students may access their professors' Web pages for assignments and announcements, complete exercises with online software, e-mail their groups as they work on collaborative projects, and chat live through their headsets—anywhere on campus, anytime. One might ask: How does a student get anything done in all this chaos?

The issues of when, where, and how instruction is delivered—the places and spaces of learning—are not one-size-fits-all, however. Each of the two spaces described above may provide an optimal language learning setting for a particular student at a particular point in engagement with the target language. This chapter discusses how different types of computer and Internet access work to achieve a wide variety of instructional goals across different educational settings. Along with many other writers in the field of technology, Foshee (1997) reminds us that "any technical design or equipment strategy is only as good as it is relevant to the instructional goals, needs and pedagogies of the end user" (p. 3).

Background

The Instructional Lab

In the early days of CALL, I wrote a short monograph, *How to Set Up a Computer Lab* (Hanson-Smith, 1991), in which I suggested that an optimal lab environment would have computers placed around the periphery so that teachers could easily see the monitors. The central space had moveable tables to form groups away from the computers, and a whiteboard and master computer/projection system (in those days, a large TV screen) for display were placed at one end of the room beside an overhead projector for whole-group work (see Figure 4-1). I had the pleasure of using such a lab, which was state of the art at that time, once a week, for 50 minutes of my composition classes. I deployed a combination of activities and seating configurations:

- whole-group moments away from the computers to set the task and instruct, for example, to help students brainstorm and organize an essay outline or to demonstrate with a computer or overhead projection how to use a piece of software

- small groups of two to three students at each workstation for grammar games or writing, where they might use both paper and pencil and software

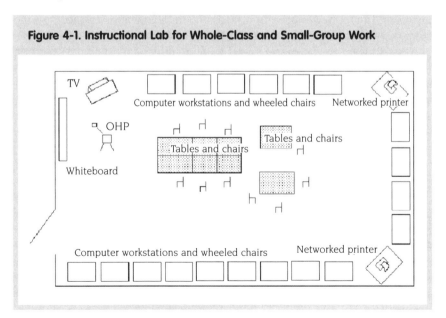

Figure 4-1. Instructional Lab for Whole-Class and Small-Group Work

- individual tasks at the workstations, followed by assembly into groups at the tables, for example, to read each other's drafts of very short writing assignments or sentences

Evaluations at the end of the semester indicated that lab times were my students' favorite activity and, they felt, the most directly relevant to improving their compositions. Other tasks, such as grammar exercises or playing Scrabble to build vocabulary, were assigned as homework and completed outside of class on the mainframe, where scores and time-on-task records were kept. Essays were word-processed in one of the many computer labs found around campus, including those in the Learning Skills Center and English Department buildings. (Almost no student had a personal computer in those days, and we didn't yet have the Internet or e-mail.)

I also used this type of lab environment on a daily basis with middle school and high school students new to computers. To introduce these newcomers to lab procedures initially, we walked around the room from station to station as I demonstrated how to turn on the machine, insert the disks we were going to use, and connect with a password to the Internet. When two or three students felt confident enough, they sat down together at a station and began work. The last few groups saw the demonstration about five times—once might have been enough, but they were the most cautious of the group of 30. Later the same procedure was used to introduce the use of a scanner or access to a particular piece of software or Web site. At a high school where I consulted, space was very limited, so workstations were arranged in two concentric squares with barely enough room to squeeze between them. However, the teachers could still see all monitors by standing in the center of the room. The room was used by classes and for afterschool free access—the most popular afterschool program in the school.

Fast-forward to the present, and many multiuse instructional labs in a variety of configurations reflect spaces conducive to the optimal conditions for learning languages. Stevens (2000), whose lab had seating in large rectangular groups (see Figure 4-2), mentions such refinements as

- an instructor's computer to one side of the classroom controlled by a remote from anywhere in the room
- an instructor's computer that switches easily to TV reception, which is then projected on a screen
- multimedia enhancements, such as earphones and microphones
- custom-designed workstations with fully recessible monitors so that paper tasks may be performed (see Figure 4-2)
- an adjustable-height teacher's station so that the instructor may sit or stand while using the computer or lecturing

Other recent lab variants include U shapes, pods with four computers back to back in a star shape, or high-mobility laptops and rolling desks for a variety

Figure 4-2. Teacher's Workstation and Recessed Monitors in Student Desks

Note: Photo: Vance Stephens. Reprinted with permission.

of configurations (see, e.g., C. Taylor, 2005). These variations represent both best technologies and preferred instructional styles: Some activities, such as testing, reading an electronic text, or doing individualized grammar exercises, demand single-person workstations; collaborations on projects may require that several wheeled chairs be pulled together. To hold students' attention, work often must start away from the monitors at a central table or in a side room. In a technology center for adults that I observed in Sacramento, California, in the United States, for example, teachers worked through role-plays and exercises from *Classic Classroom Activities: The Oxford Picture Dictionary Program* (Weiss, Adelson-Goldstein, & Shapiro, 1999) with the whole class. In the next hour, they walked students next door to the lab (similar to that in Figure 4-1), where students sat down at a central table to receive instructions, including a sheet of paper containing computer directions and passwords. They then moved to the computers at the periphery to work on electronic games and quizzes in The Oxford Picture Dictionary Interactive software (Shapiro, Adelson-Goldstein, Hanson-Smith, & Fella, 1999).

If you have only a traditionally arranged lab, it may nonetheless be put to a variety of uses, depending on your pedagogical strategies. For a controlled communicative activity, M. Chan (2003) suggests having students perform speaking tasks in pairs or groups spread apart from each other in the lab so that learners must rely only on listening to communicate or perform collaborative tasks, such as a jigsaw reading/listening activity or peer-to-peer testing of minimal pairs. This strategy works equally well in an audio lab or with voice chat or voice mail in an Internet-enabled computer lab (which need not be otherwise networked) or in a wholly online course. Similarly, text chats can operate in a traditional instructional lab online or from separate locations at a distance over the Internet for prewriting, brainstorming, or revising and editing groups. Wireless technology has redefined the concept of *networking*, which may now include an entire building or campus, the whole city—or the world. In a local CALL lab, a network's chief purpose, whether wired or wireless, may be primarily to protect younger students from online intruders. Secondarily, it can serve to keep students from wandering about the Internet when they should be doing classwork.

Although the instructional computer lab on some campuses may retain its traditional look—straight rows facing an instructor at the head of the class—its purpose is gradually being transformed. Rather than simply distributing content, in best practices the lab has become a place for communicative, constructivist language learning, where students interact in groups, each learner assigned a specific role and held accountable for results as they engage in authentic tasks (e.g., researching, creating, and presenting a project), communicate with partners around the globe, and reflect on their own learning in online journals and electronic portfolios. Instead of delivering content, students are creating it, as many of the chapters in this volume demonstrate.

Wireless Library and Internet Cafe

A truism of lab design in the 1990s was selecting the software first, then determining the hardware needed to run it (see Sachs, 1996, quoted in Sivert & Egbert, 1999). In the decade at the beginning of the 21st century, in which cross-platform capabilities are generally achieved, technicians are more concerned with what kind of Internet access will be provided: wired or wireless (see J. Schwartz, 2003). Wired facilities are the fastest, but wireless ones appear to be winning out because of their convenience. As Strauss (2003) points out, the laptop + wireless combination is like an ATM: You can take out the money when you need it, not just when the bank is open (p. 1). Many campuses today have wireless access in dorms, libraries, and most public spaces (see Figure 4-3). Off campus, one may connect with the Internet in local coffee shops, airports, hotels, public libraries, senior centers, and so forth, whether in Ulaanbaatar or San Francisco. Wireless connections are increasingly popular in developing nations because they can leapfrog the lack of infrastructure. In areas without electricity, laptops may be powered by rechargeable solar batteries or hand cranks (see MIT Media Laboratory, n.d.).

Because so much content and instructional material is online, the burgeoning wireless expansion in Africa, South America, and India (where only 2% of rural areas have access to fixed-line or cellular phones; Jain, 2005) holds the promise of connecting ever more people in new and potentially educational ways. Mobile technology, relying on satellite relay, makes the World Wide Web portable, not just to laptop computers, but to an array of new types of video cell phones, iPods, and personal digital assistants (PDAs). The lines are fast blurring between radio, TV, telephone, and print media (see numerous articles on convergence, e.g., Trumbull, 2005; for more on new technologies, see chapter 29 in this volume). As with other developments in technology described throughout this book, total access and compatibility will eventually impact education everywhere. As a small example, a commercial company now offers audio iPod-based test-taking tips and strategies in preparation for a major U.S. college entry examination, the Scholastic Aptitude Test (SAT).

Figure 4-3. The Lounge at California State University, Sacramento's Computer Resources Building

The Test of English as a Foreign Language (TOEFL) is already offered online. Dodd (2003) describes how Voice over Internet Protocol (VoIP) can spare colleges the expense of costly telephone equipment for distance learning. Free or low-cost Web-based VoIP services, such as Skype (2006), are already widely used for personal telephone calls and are being applied to webcasts and other classroom uses, such as virtual office hours. Whereas in 1994, only 3% of K–12 classrooms in the United States had Internet access, by 2003, 93% of classrooms had access (U.S. Department of Education, 2004, Figure 1). And many North American students have personal computers at home, as well as iPods, Blackberries, and cell phones in their pockets. Countries in Europe and parts of Asia have similar rates of access. While each successive generation of youngsters increasingly depends on technology for their daily social and school needs, the debate continues: Are computers good for education?

Access to computers and the Internet continues to expand from communal locations that might range from a single, locally owned, Internet-enabled cell phone shared for a fee, to widely available community and personal sites. An individual anywhere in the world, sitting in an Internet cafe, at a library desktop, or with a laptop at a park bench downtown in a wireless zone, might search for texts at the Library of Congress or images at the Louvre, join a webcast voice conference with a cell phone by VoIP, or listen to a podcast of a college course from Stanford University or Massachusetts Institute of Technology (*podcast* was declared Word of the Year for 2005 by the *New Oxford American Dictionary*).

In the Field

The convergence of a variety of technologies is most easily examined in Europe, Australia, North America, and the economically advanced areas of Asia. For example, the state of Maine (see Curtis, 2003; *Maine and Apple Sign Contract*, 2005) and a number of school districts in the United States are attempting to provide K–12 students with laptops (see the collection of case studies in Cook, 2002) or with a totally digital school setting where laptops replace print textbooks. The intention of the latter, according to the superintendent of the Vail Unified School District in Tucson, Arizona, in the United States, was "to truly change the way that schools operated" (Baker, 2005, p. 20). Educational publishers, national science institutes, art museums, and other organizations provide databases and other types of content on the Web for these paperless schools. For example, students may study full-text rulings of the U.S. Supreme Court in social studies classes or explore science hands-on by sharing data collected from local areas with children—and scientists—worldwide (see *The GLOBE Program*, n.d., which is sponsored by U.S. and European scientific institutions).

Debate still rages over the value of one laptop per child. For those interested in reading a blow-by-blow account, Toy (n.d.), a middle school principal in Freeport, Maine, weblogged (blogged) about the Maine experiment with seventh and eighth graders on an almost daily basis as it impacted his school. Students carried the laptops on field trips to collect biology data, word-processed essays, designed stage sets for plays, took notes in classes, created slideshow presentations, connected to the Internet for resources, and so on. Although some parents objected to the price tag on the initiative, claiming the money could have gone to other, better uses, the Maine project was renewed in 2006 for 4 more years. Many other schools and universities around the United States have since moved forward with similar initiatives, including the increasingly widespread use of cell phones and iPods to deliver curricular content at universities, for example, at Georgia College and State University (2006), Duke University (n.d.), University of California, Berkeley (Regents of the University of California, 2002–2006), and Stanford University (n.d.). The MIT Media Laboratory (n.d.), with research supported by major private Internet companies, is working on a US$100 laptop to be distributed to schools around the world directly, via purchase by governments. The lab sees this laptop initiative as "a technology that could revolutionize how we educate the world's children" (¶ 1). The tiny laptop with a convenient carrying handle would be wireless and powered by a hand crank or solar cells. According to Nicholas Negroponte, cofounder of the MIT Media Laboratory, "laptops are both a window and a tool: a window into the world and a tool with which to think. They are a wonderful way for all children to *learn learning* through independent interaction and exploration" (OLPC, n.d., ¶ 2).

At Empire High School in Arizona, laptops are replacing textbooks. Students download from Internet subscription services various materials that can be tailored to the individual reader. They use online groups and message forums to stay in touch with the teacher and each other after school hours. One challenge, unexpectedly, is familiarizing students with academic, rather than just social, computing (CBS Broadcasting, 2005). Providing anywhere-anytime access in virtual space with wireless laptops, cell phones, and iPods meets several conditions for optimal learning: offering enough time and immediate feedback, working at an optimal level of stress, and supporting autonomy.

A totally accessible virtual universe is breathtaking in scope and readily achievable in the not-so-distant future. Even as total access becomes a reality, questions remain about pedagogical appropriateness and educational value. Certainly in tertiary and adult education, there is widespread use at the macro-level of course management systems (CMSs) to distribute classes online. Learning is also often enhanced through the use of reusable learning objects (RLOs), which may be distributed impersonally, for example, video lectures, lesson plans, and a wide array of course materials (for the university level, see MIT *OpenCourseWare* [Massachusetts Institute of Technology, 2002–2007] and MERLOT, 1997–2006; for K–12, *eThemes* [eMINTS & the Curators of the University of Missouri, 2003–2006]; for teacher training, see WGBH Educational Foundation, 2006). At the micro- or highly personal level, enormous numbers of cross-cultural, transnational collaborations among students, even in the elementary grades, are taking place through e-mail and Web-based projects (see, e.g., Gaer, 2007; other chapters in this volume), communal blogs (e.g., Dieu, Campbell, & Ammann, n.d.), and exchanges such as those fostered by the GLOBE Program (n.d.), mentioned earlier. In point of fact, students may take courses and full degree programs anywhere, anytime if they have access to the Internet.

The One-Computer Classroom—Smart and Smarter

Jewel (2006) describes several community service CALL activities for high school students, such as creating posters and presentations. These can be executed by students in small groups, sharing a single computer or limited computer lab time and taking advantage of built-in templates that come with typical word-processing and slideshow software. The one-computer classroom, however, gets smarter and smarter. In a town or school district with wireless Internet access, that single computer can offer the same kinds of distributed learning, free resources, and global exchanges as any top-grade lab. It will, however, demand more planning and better scheduling of time. Almeida d'Eça's (2005) Web page of resources links to a number of activities, including e-mail exchanges, voice mail, and Web projects, that may be accomplished with a single laptop by schoolchildren. Her middle school students in Portugal work in small groups at specified times to complete CALL activities or brainstorm and compose messages as a whole class using the laptop hooked up to a projector. Other classrooms report using video cameras and free editing software to create multimedia projects or even webcasts from their classrooms (other chapters in this volume describe these activities in more detail). Teachers using one computer with their classes generally report the added advantage of group work in scaffolding language and developing higher social and thinking skills as students learn how to share what they have and achieve goals together (see Almeida d'Eça, 2006; Gromik, 2006b).

Whether one computer or many, the types of hardware and software are similar:

- Good memory and high processing speeds are necessary for photo, audio, and video projects.
- If your school cannot afford a computer projector, use a TV monitor connected to your single laptop for whole-class instruction.
- Microphones and earphones are desirable for good audio quality and for the sake of more peace in the classroom or lab during voice chat or pronunciation practice.
- A webcam might be a good investment, because it adds life to text or voice chats, and prices are generally well below $100.

- Video cell phones are increasingly affordable and may be used to create short video clips to insert in slide presentations.

- A digital camera, while relatively expensive (US$200–$300), can create both still photos and short videos for student projects.

- A CD or DVD burner is useful for saving memory space on your hard drive, carrying projects home to work on, and distributing completed projects to friends and family.

- A flash memory drive (US$10–$50) may serve the same purpose and can fit on a keychain.

- Internet access is, of course, extremely valuable.

- However, students may also create projects with their own photos, artwork, and homemade videos, and display them to the local community through Microsoft PowerPoint (2007) or a comparable free program, such as OpenOffice Impress (a component of the OpenOffice.org Suite, 2005).

- To make movies, free software such as Windows Movie Maker (2007) and iMovie (for Apple; 2006) are often loaded with the computer, or are readily downloadable. Operation is almost intuitive, but user groups and help files are available online as well.

- Good-quality audio, graphics, and presentation software—useful for electronic portfolios, task-based content projects, and collaborative presentations—is likewise free or nearly free and downloadable online.

The smart classroom can offer students word processing, video production, and a digital studio for projects; the smarter classroom can put students and projects online for collaborative exchanges with other learners around the world.

Perhaps the most common entry to the world of CALL for most teachers is their own personal computer or a single laptop handed out just to instructors. By experimenting with their own computer, it is thought, teachers will become aware of the advantages of technology and get involved in planning for computer use in their lessons. In reality, few teachers have that kind of free time. Perhaps the best use that can be made of a solo computer is to bring it into the classroom and let students experiment with it, teaching each other and the instructor as they proceed. Reading about various technology uses and various lab spaces is not the same as seeing them in action, however. WGBH Educational Foundation (2006) has produced excellent free teacher training videos online that demonstrate a variety of ways to use different technology settings and may be viewed as self-paced study. Preferably, a group of teachers in one school or several schools online together could use the videos as a communal professional development project (see chapter 18 and Appendix A for other professional development options).

Examples and Discussion

Virtual Learning Environments

While many instructors use *blended* approaches—classes that are partly online with, for example, phone, e-mail, and/or virtual office hours in a chat room—smart classrooms can also exist wholly online. A variety of CMSs allow the teacher to create a virtual learning environment (VLE) that performs most of the functions of classroom interactions in cyberspace. While many top-level universities are able to afford a relatively expensive CMS, such as Blackboard (2005), any teacher may start a free *Yahoo! Group* (Yahoo!, 2007e). Designed specifically for educational uses, Moodle (2006) is an open-source VLE that is free if installed on a school's own server, or available for a relatively modest fee when hosted at the Moodle server. A Moodle VLE provides space to store and view lectures in the form of documents or presentations, threaded forums where students may be assigned to specific groups or topics for discussion, a glossary of terms or references created by the instructor, an archive of good Web links found by students and the teacher, journal or blog spaces, a variety of quiz options (e.g., MCQ, Y/N, short answer), surveys and peer assessment of documents online, an event calendar, tracking of individual student activity and access time, and so forth. Whereas the more expensive CMSs also offer, for example, video or webcam-enhanced chats, Moodle has devoted user groups to assist the new user and extensive online documentation, including slide presentations and sample Moodles where teachers can experiment with different types of online courses and content. *Moodle for Language Teaching* (n.d.; managed by Tom Robb and others) contains discussion forums with ideas for teaching through the VLE, debate over the philosophy of constructivism, and so on. (Free registration with Moodle is required to access sample Moodles.)

As teachers become familiar with blended learning, it becomes easier for them to envision how typical course elements of the traditional land-based classroom may be converted to online equivalents. Table 4-1 gives a rough idea of how this translation might work. (See Schramm & Mabbott, 2006, for a fuller discussion of the elements they considered in converting their teacher training courses into a VLE.)

Given the kinds of universal access contemplated around the world, the use of a CMS seems almost a necessity. To get started with virtual learning, the teacher can experiment with free sites, such as *Tapped In* (TI; SRI International, 1995–2004; see Figure 4-4) and *Yahoo! Groups* (YGs; Yahoo!, 2007e). TI offers any teacher a virtual office with whiteboard, space to store resources, and text

Table 4-1. Course Elements and Their Online Equivalents

Course Elements	Cyber Equivalents
Syllabus	Web page, downloadable document, calendar with e-mailed reminders
Lecture	Documents, slideshow with multimedia accompaniments, whiteboard, guided Web tour, lecture notes posted to Web site for reference
Whole-class discussion	Class bulletin board or forum with e-mail delivery options
Small-group discussion	Instant messaging and live chat, group bulletin boards or topic-based forums with e-mail delivery options
Office hours	E-mail, text and/or voice chat, with or without webcam
Study groups	E-mail, private chats, or forums (students-only), with or without webcam
Presentation of student work	Multimedia chat with slideshow, whiteboard, and guided Web tour; uploaded documents
Peer review of work	Wiki or blog, chat with multimedia enhancements, discussion forums
Quizzes, exams, papers	Online interactive quizzes, timed essay questions online, uploaded/downloaded documents
Attendance, roll taking, assessment	Tracking of access and time on task, scoring functions, electronic portfolios

chat. Templates may be easily accessed to decorate the office and make it a welcoming but academically oriented space. Numerous and long-standing teacher user groups hold weekly or monthly chats to provide the opportunity to exchange ideas about using the VLE with K–university students. In addition to extensive help files, live walk-throughs of the environment with knowledgeable guides are held regularly. Once the teacher has become accustomed to the online environment, it is only a short step to creating a YG. Yahoo! allows

Figure 4-4. The Author's Virtual Office at Tapped In

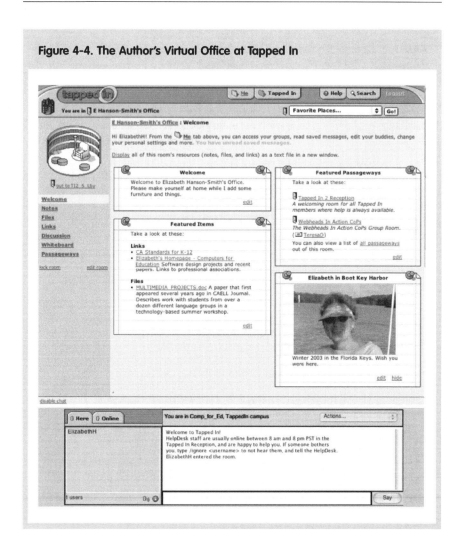

anyone to start a group that includes space to store pictures, files, and links to Web sites; a threaded e-mail discussion list that may be accessed on the Web or received as a daily digest; database and poll features; built-in voice and text chat functions; and easy-to-use templates to personalize the group. The TESOL association's CALL Interest Section has been using TI and YGs for several years as the basis for their annual (January–February) Electronic Village Online, free workshops and discussion groups for teachers around the world (see Hanson-Smith & Bauer-Ramazani, 2004, for a description of typical offerings).

Needs Assessment—Community Planning

As mentioned earlier, it is extremely difficult for one teacher or several teachers on their own to start building a lab, whether physical or virtual, wireless or wired, even if they have had an introduction to technology in their education classes. Beyond self-help, there are several important steps to instituting a program with pedagogically sound uses of technology.

Step 1: Consultation

If the school or district is building or upgrading a lab or undertaking technology use for the first time, it is important to get input from all players, including parents and students. Parents need to know why money is being spent on computers, and computer-using teachers are far better equipped than lab technicians to give them the answers. Eighty-seven percent of U.S. children age 12–17 use the Internet, and half of them go online every day (Rainie & Hitlin, 2005, p. 1). Schools may need to find a way to match that rich virtual life, although pundits such as Oppenheimer (author of *The Flickering Mind*, 2003) feel that technology reorients youngsters to have short attention spans and to put little effort into attaining excellence (Fost, 2005). Even though most computer-using teachers have found the opposite to be true—youngsters work overtime and outside of class to achieve perfect presentations and Web projects—these kinds of issues must be raised with the school community. Computer-using teachers are well aware of the pedagogical issues at stake and need to be consulted in planning for new labs or new technology uses.

Step 2: Needs assessment

A community needs-assessment plan would allow for public hearings and involvement of the business community, perhaps opening the door to donated technical support and funding for a lab. Strong and Kidney (2004) stress the importance of involving the end users of technology and describe a collaborative, needs-based approach as classrooms were renovated at a Canadian university. (Interestingly, their article seems to focus on items such as the podium and data projectors, intimating a preference for information distribution, rather than collaborative learning.) More creative examples of planning are afforded by the Classrooms of the Future project in Britain (Crown, 1995–2007). As of 2005, each of the 12 funded educational regions had performed its own needs analysis and come up with pilot projects both varied and inventive. Most sought input from pupils as well as the adult community. To begin the lab design process, teachers and administrators might consult the classroom design guidelines that many universities post to the Web. However, caution should be taken to seek only the most recent documents because technology changes rapidly. Among such resources for lab and curriculum planning is *Collaborative Facilities* (Trustees of Dartmouth College, 2004), a Web site sponsored by a consortium of U.S. universities that are collecting and organizing information about such facilities to assist institutions with implementation. Web visitors can take a virtual tour of the facilities by clicking on links on the Web site.

Step 3: Community building

At the personal level, educators planning on integrating a computer lab or wireless technology into their teaching must find other computer-using teachers to share their problems, successes, and solutions. Often this is best achieved through online communities of practice. As mentioned earlier, TESOL's CALL Interest Section offers free online sessions every January and February to teachers around the world who want to find out more about technology and best practices in CALL (see Hanson-Smith & Bauer-Ramazani, 2004). Often these sessions build into longer-lived communities, such as *Real English Online* (Marzio & Hanson-Smith, 2003), for video-using teachers and students; *Dekita.org: EFL/ESL Exchange* (Dieu, Campbell, & Ammann, n.d.), for international blogging collaborations for K–adult classrooms; *Learning With Computers* (Baya, Bellusci, & Hillis, 2005), a year-round group that recycles a technology skills syllabus every 4 months; and perhaps the best-known in the cyber world, *Webheads in Action* (Stevens, 2007), a long-standing community of practice in CALL. These communities help teachers get started with technology, but even better, provide long-term emotional and pedagogical support as teachers experiment with new technologies with their students (for more on communities of practice, see Hanson-Smith, 2006a; chapter 18 in this volume). Nothing is better than to have a real teacher just an e-mail away who can answer a question, provide cautionary advice, join in distance collaborations, and celebrate one's triumphs with a class.

Conclusion

It should be evident from this chapter that computer spaces and places come in all sizes and shapes. However, of utmost importance is planning for the kinds of instructional uses that are intended. Although teachers should be involved in decisions about places and spaces to use technology, they are often given little choice. They may still find the means to use their lab or computers flexibly. Table 4-2 indicates some ways to get the most out of specific settings.

Ertmer, Addison, Lane, Ross, and Woods (1999), in examining teachers' beliefs about technology, found three levels of use:

1. supplement outside of the curriculum
2. reinforcement to current curriculum
3. facilitator to an emerging, more student-centered curriculum (cited in Scrimshaw, 2004, pp. 5, 16)

Table 4-2. Settings, Tools, and Activities

Settings	Tools and Activities
Traditional or flexible lab; CMS	Self-access exercises and materials, record-keeping system, direct instruction with electronic whiteboard, word-processed composition, network and/or Internet for group work and projects
Voice/audio lab	Headsets, microphones, and soundproofing; software for pronunciation and speaking practice; network and/or Internet for listening/speaking collaborations
Internet/wireless lab, cafe, cell phone, iPod, laptop, or home computer	E-mail and Web-based exchange projects; data mining and sharing for researched projects; text, voice, and video chat and messaging; personal and collaborative wikis, blogs, and Web sites; VLEs; anywhere-anytime learning with lecture recordings
One computer station in a classroom	All activities and tools shared, turn taking, team building

Not surprisingly, Ertmer et al. also found that unless challenged by new experiences and training, teachers were likely to continue at the level of technology use where they felt most comfortable, depending on prior beliefs about classroom practice and teacher roles (summarized in Scrimshaw, 2004, p. 16). Teachers should feel comfortable in the knowledge that their technology-enhanced environments support the kinds of instruction they want to undertake; however, they also need to be flexible enough to seize the new pedagogical opportunities that the cyber life offers.

Explorations

1. Explore the lab and technological tools your school possesses. What kind of configuration does the technology offer? What kinds of tasks might students be able to accomplish using this configuration?

2. Interview teachers who regularly use the lab and/or technology setting offered by your school. What kinds of activities and projects do they have students perform in the lab? What other kinds of activities might they like students to have access to?

3. Looking at Table 4-1, note ways that teachers in your school might expand their uses of freely available technology. What are some of the advantages and disadvantages of online equivalents to traditional land-based teaching?

4. Explore online some of the freely available content delivery systems, RLOs, chat rooms, and education-oriented tools mentioned in this chapter. For example, you might join *Tapped In* (SRI International, 1995–2004), set up your own virtual office, and invite colleagues or others in your class to join you for a text chat.

5. What kinds of technology do you use frequently? iPod? Cell phone? Wireless laptop? Visit some of the sites mentioned in this chapter (e.g., the *Duke Digital Initiative* [Duke University, n.d.]) to find out how students use such tools to access content and collaborate with partners online.

PART II

Authentic Audience

Chapter 5 ⊡

Theory and Research:
Audience, Language Use,
and Language Learning

Bill Johnston

Focus

Theoretical and applied linguists and language teaching professionals have long recognized the importance of audience in the study of language. A consideration of audience has been central in at least two areas: language use and language learning. For the purposes of this chapter, I argue that the only necessary criterion for the authenticity of an audience is whether or not the message is being read or listened to for its meaning. This definition proves instrumental in analyzing the usefulness of computer-mediated communication (CMC) for language learning.

Background

Audience and Language Use

In linguistics, it has long been known that the nature of the audience and, specifically, the nature of the speaker's relation to that audience have a crucial effect on the forms of language chosen to encode the message. A simple and widespread example is the choice of second-person pronoun. Many languages have a T/V distinction (R. Brown & Gilman, 1960), that is, they have formal and informal (or intimate and nonintimate) forms of the second-person pronoun, such as *tu* versus *vous* in French. These are sometimes called *referent honorifics* (Levinson, 1983, p. 90). In other languages, address forms are more complex: Japanese and Korean, for instance, have intricate addressee honorific systems whereby the identity of the person spoken to affects not only the choice of pronoun used to refer to the addressee but also other lexical and morphological choices. In other languages, like Dyirbal, *bystander honorifics* are used when certain parties (e.g., taboo relatives) are witnesses to a conversation (Levinson, 1983, p. 90). In each of these cases, the nature of the audience has a direct and structured impact on the language produced. In fact, linguistic messages are influenced by addressees in a wide range of subtle and not-so-subtle ways. Within sociolinguistics, it is known that variation in audience accounts for a great deal of social and stylistic variation, and a number of theoretical approaches take some notion of audience as a central construct.

A. Bell (1984), for example, offers the concept of *audience design*, a notion clearly related to that of *recipient design* proposed by Sacks and Schegloff (1979) for conversational analysis. Bell takes as his axiomatic starting point the idea that persons respond mainly to other persons; that is, speakers take most account of hearers in designing their talk. He argues that variation in linguistic style can best be explained by variation in audience; he proposes a nested model of players in speech situations in which *audience* constitutes a scale from addressee through auditor and overhearer to eavesdropper.

Another theory in which the role of audience is central is Giles' speech accommodation theory (Giles & Smith, 1979; Thakerar, Giles, & Cheshire, 1982). Giles' basic claim is similar to Bell's: that speakers adjust their language according to who their interlocutor is. Giles' theory differs in that he argues that this adjustment involves either convergence (moving toward the addressee's style) or divergence (deliberately sounding different from the addressee). In Giles' theory, convergence and divergence can be explained largely by reference to social identity and membership in a class or another social group.

Finally, notions of audience have featured prominently in many postmodern approaches to language and communication. Bakhtin (1986, p. 95), for example, points to the *addressivity* of language, meaning that any language addresses a particular listener and by the same token contains the anticipation of its own response. He also states that "every word is directed toward an answer and cannot escape the profound influence of the answering word that it anticipates" (p. 280). For Bakhtin, the dialogical character of language in use means that audience is a fundamental part of the very structure of language.

This notion is reflected in other postmodern work that emphasizes the *situated* nature of texts (e.g., Green & Meyer, 1991), that is, the fact that the writing and reading of texts do not take place in a vacuum but are located in a very specific social and cultural context. Every reading of a text, for example, is conducted by a particular reader in a particular place in space and time. Thus, there is no such thing as an objective, decontextualized meaning of a text; each reading is unique, so each new reader constructs the meaning of a text afresh. In this way, the audience is crucial in the process of creating meaning.

To sum up, language scholars working in a variety of fields (e.g., sociolinguistics, pragmatics, literary studies) are in accord that the nature of audience and, specifically, the speaker's relation to the addressee are central concerns in describing and understanding features of language use.

Audience and Language Learning

Just as they generally acknowledge that audience is a fundamental part of the way language is used, so a wide range of specialists working in disparate areas connected with the acquisition and teaching of second and foreign languages agree on the importance of audience in the learning of languages. These specialists include both researchers in the field of second language acquisition (SLA) and scholars and practitioners focusing on second language education.

In first language acquisition, even hard-line nativists (those who follow Noam Chomsky in believing that the ability to learn language is innate, forming part of the human biological endowment) acknowledge that babies need proper interlocutors to provide the necessary input for the innate *language acquisition device* (Pinker, 1994) to go to work. Studies have suggested, moreover, that passive input, such as that provided by television, is not sufficient for language acquisition to take place; acquisition requires person-to-person interaction, for example, between parent and child.

In first language acquisition, however, some scholars have argued that such interaction plays a secondary role and that, even when input is severely limited, children still have a natural drive to learn language, just as they have a natural tendency to learn to walk (Pinker, 1994). In SLA, on the other hand, there seems to be more agreement that interaction—that is, the availability of authentic audience—is a necessary (though perhaps not sufficient) condition for learning (Spolsky, 1989). A well-established line of research in SLA, often labeled *interactionism* in surveys of the field (R. Ellis, 1994; Lightbown & Spada, 1994), claims that interaction is a crucial prerequisite to acquisition (e.g., Long, 1983; Long & Porter, 1985; Pica, 1987; Pica, Young, & Doughty, 1987). To simplify, the basic argument is that interaction provides opportunities for the negotiation of meaning; for enriched, suitably modified, and negotiated input; and for enhanced output (for further discussion, see chapters 2 and 11; for a pedagogical application of this work, see Ernst, 1994). Interestingly, sociocultural theory, which is often seen as standing in opposition to interactionism (see, e.g., Duff, 2000), also emphasizes the need for interaction in language learning (see, e.g., Lantolf & Thorne, 2006).

This research is rooted in a belief that audience is a crucial factor in the acquisition of the second language—specifically, that the availability of an authentic audience affects the rate and extent of language learning. In other words, audience is not merely an important element in language use; it is also a vital part of language learning.

Audience in Language Teaching

In what might loosely be called *traditional* language teaching—approaches such as grammar translation, audiolingualism, and the like—little or no real audience exists for the linguistic production of the learners. When they write, it is for "an audience of one" (Murray, 1982, p. 40). When they speak, it is generally only in the presence of classmates and the teacher; the substance of the message is either completely immaterial (e.g., in the case of drills and rote exercises) or secondary to the grammatical form (e.g., real-life questions that are intended to determine whether the learner has mastered a particular morphological or syntactic structure). Schmidt (Schmidt & Frota, 1986), for example, tells of his sense of frustration in his own learning of Portuguese in Brazil when his teacher insisted that he answer the question, "Are you married?" with the factually incorrect "yes" because "we are practicing affirmative answers" (p. 243).

The recognition of the importance of audience in language and language learning eventually led to a reevaluation of the question of audience in language teaching. Although in different ways, a broad range of methodological approaches and techniques of language teaching have incorporated issues of audience into their underlying philosophy and pedagogical practices. For the purposes of brevity, I focus on three such approaches:

1. *whole language*—In whole language approaches to language teaching, the question of audience has been central. Part of whole language's insistence on *real* language use (Rigg, 1991) has resulted from a reappraisal of the audience for students' writing and oral production (for a parallel in reading, see, e.g., Edelsky's [1991, p. 77] distinction between "reading" and "not-reading"). In the whole language class, instead of writing for the eyes of the teacher alone, students write compositions for classmates, students in other classes, parents, and members of the community. Furthermore, an important part of the writing process is the writer's awareness of the audience; consideration of the actual or potential audience and its possible reactions forms an important part of feedback on and revisions of successive drafts of compositions.

2. *process writing*—In the domain of writing pedagogy, in ESL as well as in mainstream education, a prominent movement in recent years has been the process approach, whereby the focus of writing instruction is not simply the finished product but the process of brainstorming, writing drafts, revising, gathering feedback, and organizing all the procedures that real writers in the real world use all the time (Emig, 1977; Raimes, 1983, 1991). A major part of the process writing approach is an emphasis on treating one's writing as something to be read by a real audience (Beach & Liebman-Kleine, 1986). Considerations of audience, then, play a significant role in the development of the text.

3. *English for specific purposes* (ESP)—Finally, a narrower understanding of audience emerges from the approach to writing taken within the tradition of ESP. Certain scholars in ESP were concerned that process writing focused too much on writing as expression and thus failed to address adequately the particular expectations of specialist disciplines (Horowitz, 1986; A. M. Johns, 1986; see also Belcher, 2006; Hinkel, 2006). ESP, then, evinces what Raimes (1991) calls a *focus on the reader* in a different way. Here the idea of audience is associated with that of the discourse community within which particular texts are generated. This approach has tended toward a more prescriptive, norm-focused pedagogy and a view of second language writers as outsiders needing to follow preestablished rules in order to be accepted by the academic community.

Thus, as mentioned previously, by different paths the concept of audience has found its way into many approaches and areas of language pedagogy, in particular into the teaching of writing.

The Meaning of *Audience* in Language Learning

The differences referred to in the previous section may be more significant than they seem at first, as they indicate alternative understandings of what exactly *audience* is in language teaching. Kirsch and Roen (1990) point out that even within composition studies there are at least two divergent understandings of what *audience* refers to:

> The meanings of "audience" . . . tend to diverge in two general directions: one toward actual people external to a text, the audience whom the writer must accommodate; the other toward the text itself and the audience implied there, a set of suggested or evoked attitudes, interests, reactions, conditions of knowledge which may or may not fit with actual readers or listeners. (Park, cited in Kirsch & Roen, 1990, p. 14)

The former understanding is clearly that of the ESP camp; the latter is associated with the process writing approaches outlined in the previous section.

The more one analyzes the nature of audience, the more complex the picture becomes. Kroll (1984), for example, draws a three-way distinction among audience as "target receiver" (the intended audience of the writer), "needy reader" (one who wants to extract specific information from the text), and "constructive participant" (for whom reading is a social act; p. 183). The contributors to McGregor and White's (1990) volume point out that the way audiences of various kinds receive and interpret messages is never entirely predictable, yet it is a crucial part of linguistic interaction.

In the area of language teaching and learning, further complications arise. Second language learners are often at best marginal members of relevant discourse communities; furthermore, they may have differing notions of *audience* either in the sense of actual readership (what Ede & Lunsford, 1984, call the *addressed audience*) or the audience they create through their own texts (Ede & Lunsford's *invoked audience*). Limitations in their command of linguistic style in the target language may make A. Bell's (1984) notion of *audience design* difficult for them to implement. Finally, as Widdowson (1990) points out, second and especially foreign language classrooms tend to be somewhat artificial places by nature; this fact may mean that notions of audience in a classroom context need to be considered and evaluated in their own right.

The truth, of course, is even more complex than any of these analyses. *Audience* in reality is both imagined and real. It is interested in both information and attitude; it is both social and individual. Language learners are sometimes like native speakers and sometimes not. Rather than conclude in any definitive way, I end this section with a set of questions to guide a consideration of audience in relation to language teaching and learning in particular situations:

- To what extent can speakers or writers control or predict who the audience for their linguistic production will be? To what extent can the speaker or writer be said to know this audience? How immediate is the audience in time and space?

- How much shared knowledge can speakers or writers assume? To what extent can speakers or writers count on the cooperation of the audience?

Examples and Discussion

Authentic Audience

The notion of *authenticity* is commonly invoked in language learning (Breen, 1985; chapter 8 in this volume), yet the field's understanding of its meaning is to a large extent purely intuitive. What authenticity might mean in terms of audience and what an authentic audience might be merit some discussion.

Most language teaching professionals agree that it is desirable to aim for authenticity in the classroom: to use authentic texts and materials, encourage real conversations, and find genuine purposes for language use. Yet, as Widdowson (1990) points out, authenticity is a slippery concept in pedagogical terms, above all because "meanings are achieved by human agency and are negotiable: they are not contained in text" (p. 45). Thus, in the case of audience, authenticity really dwells not in the audience itself but in what the audience chooses to do with the text. In light of this, I offer a single criterion to determine whether an audience is authentic:

> An authentic audience is an audience that is concerned exclusively with the meaning of the speaker's message.

This criterion discounts the teacher as audience insofar as the teacher is really interested in what forms the learner can produce in nativelike ways. When teachers are indeed interested in the meaning of what their students write and say, then they may be seen as an authentic audience. This criterion also automatically excludes all evaluators of tests, examinations, and so on.

Of course, other criteria might be proposed. For example, an authentic audience might be said to be the audience that a native speaker would have when speaking or writing in the same context. Yet the audience for many native-speaker texts may itself not be authentic (native speakers also take exams); in other cases, the audience may not be well defined. For example, if I, as an adult, pick up and read a magazine intended for 4- to 6-year-old children, do I constitute an authentic audience? I suggest that the definition given in the previous paragraph, which takes into account the intentions of the audience as much as it does those of the speaker or writer, includes as a de facto subset those cases legitimately embodied in native-speaker audiences.

Authentic Audience and Computer-Mediated Communication in ESL

The emergence of computer-based technologies and new forms of communication quite clearly has radically altered the state of affairs in language teaching in terms of authentic audience (Murray, 2000). In this section I explore the various ways in which computer technology is affecting the conception of audience in language teaching and learning and the significance this has for the field. I touch on issues that are explored in more detail in the other chapters in this book.

The size of the audience available to learners has increased dramatically

A common complaint of ESL and especially EFL learners is that it is hard for them to find native speakers to interact with. The development of computer-mediated forms of interaction, such as e-mail, electronic discussion groups, chat rooms, multiuser domains, weblogs (blogs), and wikis, has vastly increased the potential audience. Learners are no longer restricted to their physical geographical location. Along with this change is an increase in the range of potential interlocutors, who may be of any age, background, and so on.

The nature of the new audiences is hard to judge

Previously, in spoken and written interaction, the audience was either unknown and remote (in the case of writing) or immediate and visible (in the case of speaking). Now audiences can be invisible but immediate (Anderson, 1994). Interactants in text-based chat rooms, for example, respond in real time to each other's contributions, as in face-to-face interaction, yet the additional paralinguistic information available in the latter—eye contact, accent, tone of voice, proxemics—is either totally absent or is provided through linguistic means only. Participants have no knowledge of their interlocutors other than what the latter say (or, more accurately, write). Such a situation creates the need for radically new conceptualizations of audience.

Electronic audiences are authentic audiences

Whatever else may be said about audiences in computer-mediated interaction, clearly these audiences are by and large focused on the meaning of messages rather than on their form (Solomon, 2003). Thus, by the definition I offered earlier, they constitute authentic audiences for the linguistic production of learners.

Computer-mediated interaction is intensely language based

Some observers have claimed that society is shifting from *logocentrism* (a reliance on language-based communication) to *iconocentrism* (communication primarily by images). Ironically, much computer-mediated interaction, whether by e-mail, in a chat room, or Voice over Internet Protocol, is intensely grounded in language and language alone. As mentioned in the preceding section, without visual cues to provide additional information, participants must judge their interlocutors based entirely on what they write; likewise, a participant's own presentation of self relies completely on what that participant writes. Thus, communication is language based to an even greater extent than before. This change offers new and exciting possibilities for language learners; it also presents a tough challenge to them because they cannot use many of the compensatory communicative strategies (Tarone, 1977) that learners customarily draw on.

Written and spoken forms of language are converging

Studies of e-mail and other forms of electronic communication (e.g., Naumann, 1995; Uhlirov, 1994; see also Murray, 2000) have found that the forms of language used in this medium occupy a middle ground between conventional written and spoken forms. The language of e-mail, for instance, is less formal than other written language because it is written with greater speed and less attention to detail (e.g., spelling mistakes are tolerated) and because it is generally private rather than intended for large audiences; yet because it is written rather than spoken and because of the distance between sender and receiver, e-mail retains some qualities of written language (e.g., absence of fillers and repetition, less use of indeterminate reference, use of more complex forms of subordination and relativization). This *intermediate* language also presents new challenges to language learners already struggling with variations in genre and style in the target language.

The distinction between hearers and eavesdroppers is less clear

A problem with much language learning, especially in the receptive skills, is that the learner is often obliged to take on the role of eavesdropper rather than that of hearer. Prerecorded tapes in listening tasks, for example, relatively rarely address the learners themselves; more often the content of the tape is something like a conversation that they hear only because it is on the tape. Although it would be more tenuous, a similar argument could be made about reading.

In many computer-based forms of communication, the distinction A. Bell (1984) draws among addressees, auditors, overhearers, and eavesdroppers is significantly eroded. On electronic discussion lists, for example, anyone may read the messages that are posted. Although some lists (e.g., managed lists) involve gatekeepers who determine which messages are sent in the first place, the gatekeepers generally do not attempt to control who the recipients are. Likewise, in all but the most repressive societies, access to the World Wide Web is spectacularly uncontrolled. Thus, it is easier for learners to become an authentic audience themselves and, in this domain at least, to transcend the status of eavesdropper.

New conventions are emerging

Partly in response to some of the problems identified above, electronic communication has begun to produce its own set of conventions for interaction (Cathcart & Gumpert, 1994; Naumann, 1995). Examples include the emoticons used in e-mail and the elaborate stage directions, often abbreviated, found in contributions to chat rooms and the like. These new conventions again present a challenge to second language learners trying to interact effectively with the unseen electronic audience, and they suggest a useful role for instruction.

Conclusion

The issue of audience in language learning and teaching is highly complex. In a variety of ways, audience has been seen as crucial in both language use and language learning. At the same time, language learners are potentially disadvantaged both in their understanding of audience-related issues and in their productive capacity for audience design in target language contexts.

CMC offers new opportunities and new challenges to learners. Although the size and range of potential audiences have increased dramatically, and although learners also have a greater chance of becoming an authentic audience themselves, language learners must become familiar with new conventions and new conditions if they are to participate effectively in these new forms of communication.

Explorations

1. Think of your current or potential students. Consider the students' ages, their English proficiency levels, and the size of the class. Decide on two different CMC tools appropriate to these students. What are three of the most practical ways for them to encounter an authentic audience? What are advantages and disadvantages of each?

2. How can CALL contribute to providing an authentic audience for your students? Discuss the guidelines that might be necessary for finding and using an authentic audience as part of class projects.

3. What kinds of problems might arise for language learners when they attempt to be good interlocutors or an audience in a text-based CMC environment? What kinds of provisions might the teacher make to anticipate and overcome these problems?

4. Audience design differs, depending on the teaching/learning context (e.g., different types of CMC tools, audience size, number of interlocutors, purpose of the teaching or learning situation). Decide on an appropriate lesson for your students, and then design the target audience that would best fit your lesson. Explain your reasons, and share your idea with your classmates.

5. Seek out and join an online community for professional development (see chapter 18 and Appendix A for ideas). As you develop lessons, invite community members to become an authentic audience for your students' performances.

Chapter 6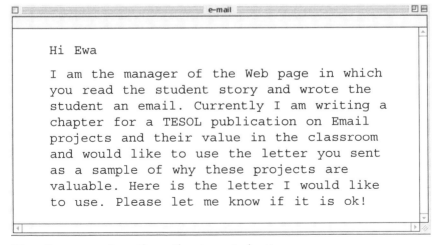

Classroom Practice:
E-mail and Web Projects

Susan Gaer

Focus

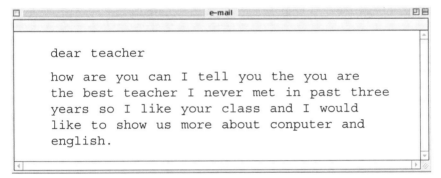

dear teacher

how are you can I tell you the you are
the best teacher I never met in past three
years so I like your class and I would
like to show us more about conputer and
english.

(E-mail message by Israel Carmargo, ESL student)

Hi Ewa

I am the manager of the Web page in which
you read the student story and wrote the
student an email. Currently I am writing a
chapter for a TESOL publication on Email
projects and their value in the classroom
and would like to use the letter you sent
as a sample of why these projects are
valuable. Here is the letter I would like
to use. Please let me know if it is ok!

(E-mail message from the author to a student)

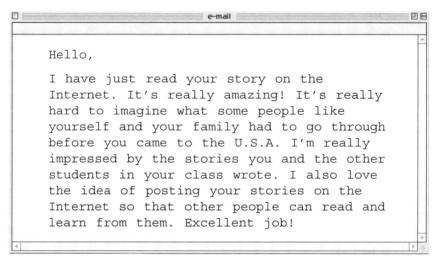

Hello,

I have just read your story on the
Internet. It's really amazing! It's really
hard to imagine what some people like
yourself and your family had to go through
before you came to the U.S.A. I'm really
impressed by the stories you and the other
students in your class wrote. I also love
the idea of posting your stories on the
Internet so that other people can read and
learn from them. Excellent job!

(E-mail response to a student's story on the Internet)

Each of these messages represents an authentic voice speaking to an authentic audience in order to accomplish real purposes. E-mail and other kinds of Web-based projects

- give learners opportunities to interact and negotiate meaning
- give learners authentic tasks to perform
- expose learners to varied and creative language and encourage learners to produce it
- give learners enough time and feedback
- guide learners to attend mindfully to the learning process
- help learners work in an atmosphere with an ideal level of stress and anxiety
- support learner autonomy

The most profound effect of such projects, however, is that they provide an authentic audience for the language learner. As defined by Johnston, in chapter 5 of this volume, whether an audience is authentic or not depends on "whether or not the message is being read or listened to for its meaning" (p. 61).

In this chapter I first explain the differences between the Internet and the World Wide Web, describe e-mail as a process, and explain weblogs (blogs) and wikis, which naturally develop an authentic audience easily on the Web. I then discuss the value and uses of these tools on the Internet.

Background

The Internet is a vast system involving a multitude of computers, and it is rather hard to navigate without tools. Some Internet tools include software with which to send e-mail and use the Web (the multimedia version of the Internet). You can connect to the Internet by contracting with a commercial carrier (an Internet service provider [ISP]), through a university or through a school district or other community system. Most public libraries and many coffee shops now have Internet access as well.

E-mail addresses consist of a name plus information about the account (Figure 6-1). For example, my e-mail address is *sgaer@yahoo.com*. My account name is *sgaer*, my account is with Yahoo! and it is an Internet account. The last three letters, called the *domain name suffix*, tell what kind of service the account holder is affiliated with: the government (*.gov*); an educational institution (*.edu*); as in my address, a commercial provider (*.com* or *.net*); or a multitude of other organizations. (For a list of domain name suffixes, see *Techdictionary.com*, 2006.)

With an Internet account you can send e-mail to anyone who is also connected to the Internet. You can attach and receive letters, photographs, video clips, and sounds. E-mail messages are usually text-only files, and any computer or word processor can read them, regardless of what kind of computer and platform created them. However, the attachments usually contain a document, photo, or video, and you will need the appropriate program to be able to access it.

Electronic Discussion Lists

Imagine asking a question and being able to receive hundreds of responses to that question in a few seconds. Discussion lists, often referred to by the type of software that manages them (e.g., Listserv, Listproc, Majordomo), make this

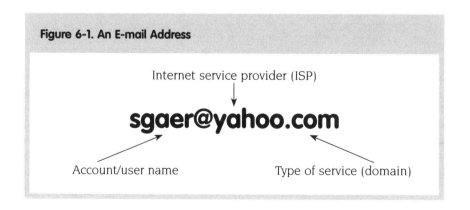

Figure 6-1. An E-mail Address

Internet service provider (ISP)

sgaer@yahoo.com

Account/user name   Type of service (domain)

possible. Lists are valuable for discussing issues, asking questions, and giving and receiving information. Basically, a discussion list is similar to a mass mailing. A message is posted to a certain address via e-mail, and everyone on the list is then sent the message to read and respond to at their leisure.

Discussion lists connect groups of people with similar interests. To participate in a list, you must first subscribe to it, which is usually free of charge. Messages posted to a list are sent automatically via a server to every member of the list. Some electronic discussion lists are very small, and some are huge; the larger the list, the more messages generated. To stop messages from coming into a mailbox, you must *unsubscribe* from the list. Each discussion list has its own rules for subscribing and unsubscribing and its own etiquette. Messages describing these ground rules are usually sent to you automatically when you subscribe.

Lists are related to a certain topic of particular interest to the group of people who have subscribed, such as community college ESL or ESL literacy issues, and many lists are related to language learning. Students can benefit from lists in a variety of ways, which are described later in the chapter, but as a teaching professional you also may want to sign up for one or more lists in order to stay current in your field.

One of the major ESOL lists for teachers is TESL-L. Founded in 1991, it is supported by a grant from the United States Information Agency. The list has the following branches, reflecting the wide variety of teachers' interests, but to join any of the branches, you must first become a member of TESL-L (see Appendix B for directions):

- TESLCA-L—TESL and technology
- TESLFF-L—fluency first and whole language pedagogy
- TESLIE-L—intensive English programs, teaching, and administration
- TESLJB-L—jobs, employment, and working conditions in the TESL/TEFL field
- TESLMW-L—material writers
- TESP-L—teachers of English for specific purposes

Several options available to subscribers, described briefly here, determine how and if you receive messages from the list. The functions and instructions are described in the information you receive when you sign up with any list. The volume of mail you receive may be enormous, so you may want to set the main list to the *index* (or *daily digest*) or, at times, the *nomail* function. Under the *index* option, you receive only the titles of messages; you may then automatically receive only those you select. Under the *nomail* function, you remain a list member, but you do not receive messages from the list. You can begin to receive messages again by activating the *mail* function. You can examine the archives for older messages. Warschauer (1995) provides further information about the organization and goals of TESL-L; see Appendix B for instructions on joining TESL-L and its sublists and for information on other lists for teachers.

Electronic Groups

Learning is enhanced when it is a team effort. Good learning is collaborative and social, not competitive and isolated (see Chickering & Ehrmann, 1996, ¶ 14). Electronic groups are online work areas for people and teams to collaborate on some shared task. The group areas can be public or private depending on user settings. Groups send e-mail to your box only if you request it, and most groups have an area to examine messages, photos, and documents on the Web. There are public groups that anyone can join; private groups joined by invitation only; and moderated groups, which anyone can join but in which the group owner reads all messages before posting. Some of the most popular group software includes *Yahoo! Groups* (Yahoo!, 2007e), *Google Groups* (Google, 2007c), and MSN *Groups* (Microsoft, 2005).

One of the most active, if not largest, groups as of this writing is Webheads in Action (based in *Yahoo! Groups*; see Stevens, 2001–2007). There are currently more than 500 members and more than 50 messages each week. According to its home page,

> this group comprises participants in events convened under the auspices of TESOL EVOnline (Electronic Village). Participants meet informally throughout the year but more formally between January and March to help each other learn about forming and maintaining robust online communities through hands-on practice with synchronous and non-synchronous text and multimedia CMC (computer mediated communication) tools. (¶ 1)

Blogs and Wikis

As of this writing, the newest collaborative tools are blogs and wikis. A *blog* (Web + log) is a journal (or newsletter) that is frequently updated and intended for public consumption. Blogs contain the writings of an author (usually in reverse chronological order) and comments posted from blog readers. A *wiki* is a type of Web site that allows users to collaborate on the Internet. The name is a shortened form of *wiki wiki*, which is from the native Hawaiian language meaning something *quick* or *fast*, encompassing the idea that wikis are quickly and easily updated and edited. The order of entries may be changed easily, and internal links to additional pages may be added. While a blog primarily represents the personality of the author, a wiki represents the personality of the group. Although blogs have been used a great deal by language teachers and students, the wiki potential, in my opinion, has yet to be fully harnessed for ESOL.

Christine Meloni (personal communication, February 25, 2006), at Northern Virginia Community College, collected the following comments from students, illustrating how useful blog-based collaboration can be in a composition class. Students mention the convenience of writing to each other at any time, the importance of blogs in getting to know each other, the archival power of a written record of comments and discussion, and the usefulness of online peer audiences in error correction.

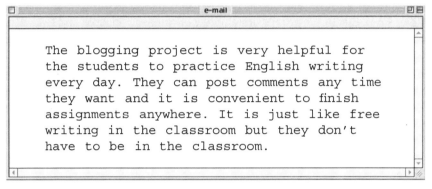

The blogging project is very helpful for the students to practice English writing every day. They can post comments any time they want and it is convenient to finish assignments anywhere. It is just like free writing in the classroom but they don't have to be in the classroom.

(Tuangrat)

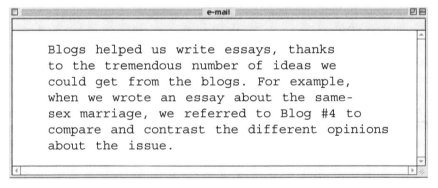

Blogs helped us write essays, thanks to the tremendous number of ideas we could get from the blogs. For example, when we wrote an essay about the same-sex marriage, we referred to Blog #4 to compare and contrast the different opinions about the issue.

(Anis)

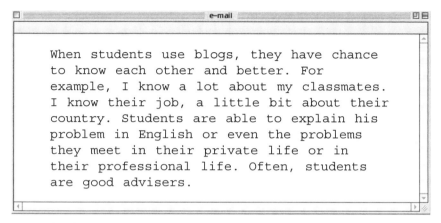

When students use blogs, they have chance
to know each other and better. For
example, I know a lot about my classmates.
I know their job, a little bit about their
country. Students are able to explain his
problem in English or even the problems
they meet in their private life or in
their professional life. Often, students
are good advisers.

(Jean Claude)

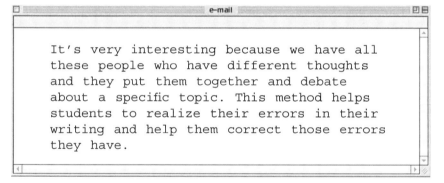

It's very interesting because we have all
these people who have different thoughts
and they put them together and debate
about a specific topic. This method helps
students to realize their errors in their
writing and help them correct those errors
they have.

(Juan)

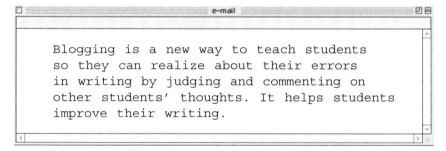

Blogging is a new way to teach students
so they can realize about their errors
in writing by judging and commenting on
other students' thoughts. It helps students
improve their writing.

(Juan)

The largest wiki is *Wikipedia* (n.d.), a free, wholly online encyclopedia with over 4 million articles that anyone can edit and contribute to in a great variety of languages. In the field of ESOL, Tom Robb has developed a collaborative project using a wiki called Famous Personages (*Welcome to the Famous Personages Project*, n.d.). Although originally Robb had to update a Web page as students wrote new articles, now his students write the articles and are able to add them to the wiki themselves. As more teachers and students start to see the value of collaboration via the Internet, more wikis for language instruction and practice will be developed.

Examples and Discussion

Why Should Students Use the Internet?

E-mail, electronic discussion lists, electronic groups, collaborative blogs and wikis—all benefit learners by serving as learning networks among nonnative speakers of different ages and cultural backgrounds. Internet communication through these various tools can help teachers and learners create many of the conditions for optimal learning environments by

- enhancing self-esteem by empowering both the teacher and the student. According to the U.S. Department of Education and SRI International (1995), "both the increased competence they feel after mastering technology-based tasks and their awareness of the value placed upon technology within our culture, led to increases in students' (and often teachers') sense of self worth" (¶ 7).

- accommodating different learning styles and empowering learners regardless of physical challenges or social and cultural differences (Berge & Collins, 1995)

- encouraging and motivating students to become involved in authentic projects and to write for a real audience of their peers instead of merely composing for the teacher (Berge & Collins, 1995)

- promoting critical thinking because students move from being passive learners to participants and collaborators in the creation of knowledge and meaning (Berge & Collins, 1995), making learning relevant by teaching students the skills they need when they are most ready to learn them

- allowing learners to participate cooperatively in the educational process, as in the following e-mail, written to an instructor while she was absent due to jury duty:

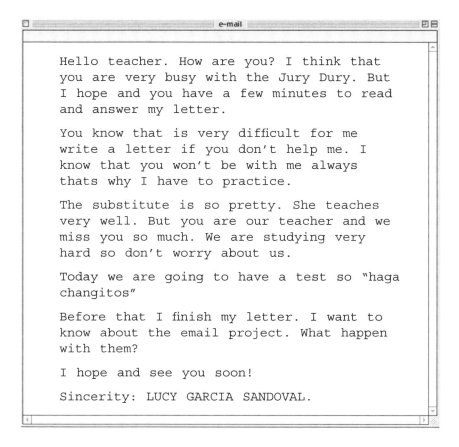

Hello teacher. How are you? I think that you are very busy with the Jury Dury. But I hope and you have a few minutes to read and answer my letter.

You know that is very difficult for me write a letter if you don't help me. I know that you won't be with me always thats why I have to practice.

The substitute is so pretty. She teaches very well. But you are our teacher and we miss you so much. We are studying very hard so don't worry about us.

Today we are going to have a test so "haga changitos"

Before that I finish my letter. I want to know about the email project. What happen with them?

I hope and see you soon!

Sincerity: LUCY GARCIA SANDOVAL.

Although at a modest level of accomplishment thus far in the learning process, Lucy is using conscious processes to analyze her progress and her needs. Even though part of the purpose of the e-mail message is to practice letter writing, as expressed in the second paragraph, the message is also filled with authentic communication ("We are studying very hard so don't worry about us.") and contains a real request for information ("What happen with them?"). Throughout, an authentic voice speaks to a real audience and expects an authentic reply.

How Can Students Learn to Use the Internet?

Using e-mail

The following is an outline of a process I have used for teaching e-mail to adult immigrant students at Santa Ana College School of Continuing Education in Santa Ana, California.

- *acquiring basic computer literacy* (1 week)—Students learn how to use the mouse, keyboard, and word processor by typing in exercises from their textbooks or doing peer or group dictations
- *learning about e-mail* (1 week)—Students learn what e-mail is and how it works. The class sets up an e-mail account and sends a letter to a collaborating teacher.
- *getting an e-mail account* (2 weeks)—Students learn to use the local e-mail system and are taught the steps involved in signing up for individual e-mail accounts. In classes with only one computer linked to the Internet, the students are grouped, and the groups rotate until all the students have accounts. Student assistants (peer tutors—students who seem to learn computer skills quickly or have some knowledge of computers) help the groups.
- *using e-mail* (until the end of the semester and beyond)—Students start by e-mailing the teacher and each other. As they become accustomed to using e-mail, students are assigned various tasks to help them write to a keypal (see the next section for ways to find keypals). Students need to learn how to write a letter to a person they do not know, how to ask questions, and how to use information in a letter when replying to it (i.e., conscious *scaffolding*; see chapter 11 in this volume). For this reason, students are asked to save all their letters so that the teacher can help them continue with the communication if a problem arises.

Students can get a free e-mail account from any number of sources. The most popular are *Gmail* (Google, 2006), MSN *Hotmail* (Microsoft, 2007c), and *Yahoo! Mail* (Yahoo!, 2007f). These free accounts, however, are not commercial free and tend to receive a great deal of *spam* (unsolicited e-mail). *Gaggle* (Gaggle.Net, 2006) is a moderated e-mail system designed especially for students. Although there is advertising, all of the advertisers are screened to make sure that the ads are appropriate for younger learners. Teacher feedback about advertisers is always welcome and, for a reasonable yearly fee, schools have the option of an advertising-free subscription.

Finding keypals

One way for students to find keypals from around the world is to join an electronic discussion list. Just as teachers have their own discussion lists, the Student List Project (Robb, n.d.-b) specializes in cross-cultural discussion and writing practice for college, university, and adult students in English language programs around the world. There are currently twelve forums:

1. Introductions
2. Group Projects

3. Teen Talk

4. Living in a new country

5. General Chat

6. Culture & Society

7. Current Events around the World

8. Learning English

9. Business English

10. Movies

11. Music

12. Sports

To use the lists, students must have individual e-mail accounts. For a description of the Student List Project and instructions for joining, see Robb (n.d-b.) and Appendix B.

Students can also connect to another classroom or school site and find keypals at that specific location. With *ePALS* (1996–2007), the teacher decides what area of the world to focus on and finds a group to collaborate with via e-mail, chat, voice, or video. Teachers of adult students can find partners for e-mail exchanges, collaborative blogging, and cross-cultural project exchanges at *Dekita.org: EFL/ESL Exchange* (Dieu, Campbell, & Ammann, n.d.).

If a language learning classroom has only one Internet account, students can still post messages to a particular individual by specifying the name in the subject line. If students have their own e-mail accounts, they can write private messages back and forth, work on a collaborative project such as a book review, or discuss their global locations, creating a truly authentic audience for their work.

Keypalling and blogging projects allow for authentic communication between and within different cultural groups. One benefit of a cross-cultural keypal exchange on the Internet is that students from nonnative-English-speaking backgrounds can communicate with native speakers of English without the communicative pitfalls of pronunciation or accent (see, e.g., Chen & Pauchnick, 2005). Exchanges can also be cross-lingual, with each side practicing the other's native language. Intergenerational communication can also form bonds between the young and old because e-mail is independent of sound and age.

Keypalling for language learning

Keypalling and blog exchanges can be rather free-form. This section explains how to maximize the pedagogical value of e-mail and Web-based correspondence. (To simplify the discussion, I refer to these activities generally as *keypalling*.)

The following process gets students started in keypalling:

1. prekeypalling activities

    -   Find another class or several other classes that are willing to be keypals.

    -   With the other teacher(s), decide on a topic that is relevant to each class's curriculum, and formulate questions for students to answer in their letters.

2. keypalling

    -   Have the students write individual letters in a text file, making sure to include their partner's and their own first and last names.

    -   Develop a grid of partners.

    -   Have the students send letters to the participating class.

    -   As the students receive letters from the participating class, have the students respond.

3. postkeypalling activities

    -   Begin the cycle again. (See Almeida d'Eça, 2006, for more on keypalling.)

If students have their own e-mail accounts, management is much simpler, but keeping students focused is a little more difficult. Students who have their own e-mail accounts must learn how to send and receive messages independently. To ensure that the students stay on task in the messages, you can assign a summary or report based on their conversation topics. Such an assignment can also help students reflect on and self-evaluate their work. This process is simpler in a Web-based exchange (e.g., with blogs or wikis). Because of the public nature of the medium, teachers and peers can quickly make comments on students' work.

Once students are familiar with computers and the technical aspects of e-mail or posting comments to a blog or wiki, the teachers of two or more classes can collaborate on assignments and arrange for students with key-pals at different schools—perhaps in different countries—to collaborate on a cyber project. The following are examples of keypal assignments used in an academic setting:

-   *reading journals*—Instead of keeping a reading journal for you, students can write their journal to other students. They might write to each other about the same book or about two different books. Two students reading the same book can collaborate on a review to submit to an online blog or Web site (see Carnicero, n.d., for more on student book reviews in a text and audio blog).

- *authentic literary interactions*—Students can write reviews for *Amazon.com* (1996–2007) or join an author-led reading group at *Barnesandnoble.com* (1997–2006).

- *authentic information search*—Students find a Web site that interests them and ask the developer of the site questions in an e-mail. For example, during a discussion of voting, my students read about the Los Angeles voter registration rate. A student from Mexico wanted to know what the voter registration rate was in Mexico. He found the Web site of a Mexican newspaper, e-mailed a journalist, and got the information.

- *collaborative WebQuests*—A WebQuest is "an inquiry-oriented activity in which most or all of the information used by learners is drawn from the Web" (Dodge, n.d.-a, ¶ 2). Imagine the possibilities as groups of students create WebQuests based on research or cultural knowledge. WebQuests are beginning to be used widely for language and culture learning, an excellent example of which is *Culture Quest* (H. Lynch & Tennille, n.d.). WebQuest templates and examples can be examined at Dodge's (n.d.-b) main site or filled out interactively online with *QuestGarden* (Dodge, 2007).

Creating online projects

Writing to an authentic audience demands that teachers create authentic tasks that will spark meaningful exchanges. Assigning projects for students to complete through online collaboration can provide the necessary spark.

Getting started

In online projects, either individual or collaborative, students use e-mail to obtain information from other participants or use the online environment as a means of publishing classwork for others to read. Projects help students develop language skills because they involve the creation of a product collaboratively (for more on project-based learning, see chapter 13 in this volume). Completed projects can be displayed on the Web and thus become an authentic form of publication.

The *Email Projects Home Page* (Gaer, 2007; see Figure 6-2), supported by the Outreach and Technical Assistance Network, lists current and completed projects that are offered worldwide. At this site, prospective teachers and students can see what types of projects are currently in progress and get ideas for their own. Among the many projects accessible from the *Email Projects Home Page* are the following:

- *Intergenerational Project*—Parents share traditional cultural practices with their children.

- *Annotated Booklist*—Students summarize books they have read for pleasure or books they read with their children.

- *International Home Remedies*—Students write descriptions of home remedies for various ailments.

- *Cookbook*—Students prepare a recipe, write it up, and post it.

- *Virtual School Visit* (facilitated by David Rosen and Susan Gaer)—Students develop a Web page describing their school and location. They are then matched up with another school whose students read their description and ask questions.

Several other Web sites offer examples of the wide variety of student projects available online (see also chapters 7 and 14 in this volume) and places to find exchange partners:

- *Student-Teacher Writing Pages* (n.d.)—a list of sites for student writing projects by Steve Schackne

- *Theme Tourism* (n.d.)—podcasts produced by teachers and students of Turismo Sant Ignasi, part of the University of Ramon Llull in Barcelona, Spain

Figure 6-2. The Email Projects Home Page

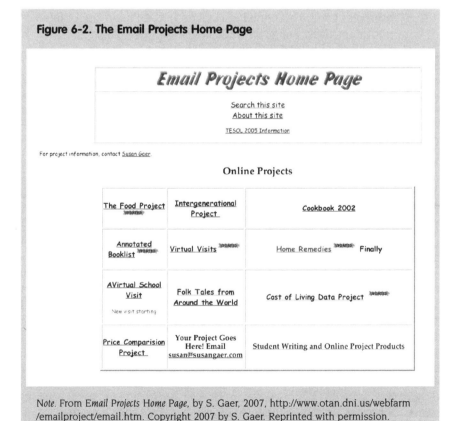

Note. From *Email Projects Home Page*, by S. Gaer, 2007, http://www.otan.dni.us/webfarm /emailproject/email.htm. Copyright 2007 by S. Gaer. Reprinted with permission.

- CAE B's *podcast* (n.d.)—discussions by students in Argentina and the United States about culture and personal preferences through photos, audio, and text in a blog
- ESL: *Student Projects*—a lengthy list maintained by *The Internet* TESL *Journal* (1995–2007b)
- *Blue Web'n: A Library of Blue Ribbon Learning Sites on the Web* (AT&T Knowledge Ventures, 2006)—a compendium of projects for all content areas with suggestions for how teachers can get started
- *The Global Schoolhouse* (Global SchoolNet, 2000a)—a virtual place to meet teachers hosting projects in schools throughout the world
- *Intercultural E-mail Classroom Connections* (IECC; Mighty Media, 2007)—a place to find online exchanges and collaborative projects, originally facilitated by Craig Rice, Bruce Roberts, and Howard Thorsheim at St. Olaf College
- *Dekita.org: EFL/ESL Exchange* (Dieu et al., n.d.)—classroom teachers seeking collaboration among their students; includes the best work of ESL/EFL students on the Web

Participating in an online project

To complete an online project, complete the following steps:

1. Choose a project that fits your curriculum guidelines. Write to the teacher coordinating the project; indicate your interests in detail so that a match can be found.
2. Have your students find and examine some projects on the Web.
3. Depending on your students' level, develop a model for them to follow, or guide them in developing a model that will help them conceptualize the steps involved in completing the project.
4. Allow plenty of time for communication with your collaborating teacher and classroom to finalize the project design and curricular area.
5. As students complete their sections of the project, make sure the correspondence between the collaborating teachers and classes highlights the progress made.
6. Send the completed project to the coordinating teacher, or post it on the appropriate Web site.

For more examples of other types of projects, see the several Classroom Practice chapters in this volume. Figure 6-3 shows the International Home Remedies project (Gaer, 2006) from the *Email Projects Home Page* (Gaer, 2007). Students may play interactive games related to health and the body, and add their own class projects to the list at the site.

Figure 6-3. The International Home Remedies Page

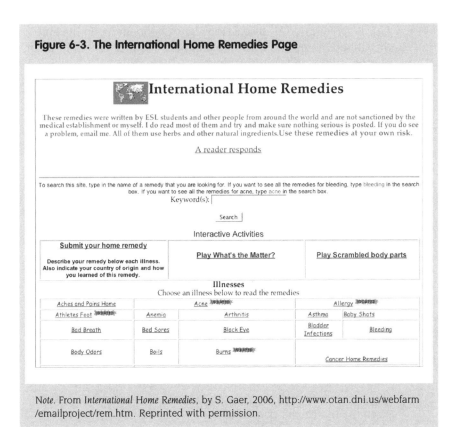

Note. From *International Home Remedies*, by S. Gaer, 2006, http://www.otan.dni.us/webfarm /emailproject/rem.htm. Reprinted with permission.

These are more specific directions to join the International Home Remedies project at the *Email Projects Home Page*:

1. Print out a model entry by choosing one of the illnesses and clicking the mouse on the >PRINT button of your browser.

2. Use the model to explain to students the key components of a good remedy.

3. Have students decide on a problem for which they would like to write a home remedy.

4. In small groups, have the students read and discuss the remedies already posted for that problem (see Figure 6-3).

5. Have students write their remedy using examples from the Web site as models.

6. Using peer correction techniques, have the students revise their writing. Optionally, correct some of their work yourself.

7. Have the students return to the project and click on >Submit Your Home Remedy. This brings up a Web form to complete.

8. Have the students copy the information they have written onto the form in the appropriate places, either by retyping or by copying and pasting if their work is word-processed.

9. Have the students submit their work by clicking on >Submit.

Online projects are enjoyable for students, they foster language learning as students collaborate on the development of the project, and they are driven by the necessity of writing to an authentic audience of peers on the Internet. In the case of my students, as a result of writing and posting on the Web, they have improved their cultural and cross-generational understanding and increased their tolerance for others. Publishing student work on the Web allows others to read and understand the day-to-day life of the ESL/EFL student. Some of these stories have had a great impact on readers from around the world. The benefits are evinced by the following two responses that students received about their writing:

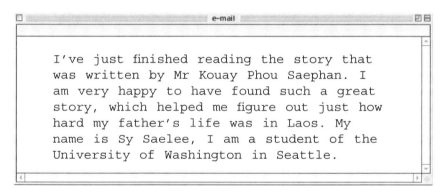

I've just finished reading the story that was written by Mr Kouay Phou Saephan. I am very happy to have found such a great story, which helped me figure out just how hard my father's life was in Laos. My name is Sy Saelee, I am a student of the University of Washington in Seattle.

```
┌─────────────────────────── e-mail ───────────────────────────┐
│                                                               │
│  Dear Vladimir,                                               │
│                                                               │
│  I got interested in your story because you                   │
│  and I have some things in common. For one,                   │
│  we both have Russian first names; my name                    │
│  is Ivan. I also come from Latin America                      │
│  (born in Ecuador) and am an immigrant to                     │
│  the U.S. I've lived here most of my life                     │
│  and, two years ago, became an American                       │
│  citizen, something I am particularly proud                   │
│  of.                                                          │
│                                                               │
│  I would like to congratulate you on your                     │
│  progress in English and your determination                   │
│  not to let personal hardships deter you                      │
│  from persevering in your education. I am                     │
│  glad you are a resident of my country and                    │
│  encourage you to someday contribute to the                   │
│  betterment of others who find themselves in                  │
│  the circumstances you have found yourself                    │
│  in during your stay in this country. God                     │
│  bless you.                                                   │
│                                                               │
└───────────────────────────────────────────────────────────────┘
```

Conclusion

Electronic discussion lists, group lists, keypals, and Web-based projects can promote reading, writing, listening, and speaking skills in English by providing an authentic audience for students' output, as recommended in chapter 5 in this volume. These projects also help students develop computer literacy and Internet skills as they use the computer for real purposes. E-mail, Web-Quests, blogs, wikis, and the resulting projects can be used with students at any grade level and any English proficiency level. For more information about creating tasks and projects in the Internet environment, see other chapters in this volume.

Explorations

1. Explore some of the electronic groups and e-lists discussed in this chapter, and design a keypal project for your students so that they can interact with an authentic audience. Would you use an electronic group or an e-list? What would be the reasons for using each? With whom would your students be connected and why? What would the requirements of the assignment be? How would you assess the results?

2. Search the Web for sites that meet your students' learning objectives and provide ways for them to interact with an authentic audience. (Several starting points are listed in this chapter, chapter 7, and Appendix B.) Make an annotated list of your favorite sites, or use *Filamentality* (AT&T Knowledge Ventures, 2007b) to save and share your favorites.

3. Develop and describe an interclass project using the Web. How will students interact with this audience? What kinds of help will they need from the teacher or technical personnel? How will the project attain closure? Share your project plans with classmates or your working group. What would be some of the advantages and disadvantages of a class-to-class project?

4. Explore some of the educational blogs and wikis mentioned in this chapter. What is the difference between a blog and a wiki? What kinds of projects are teachers using them for? Which one do you feel is more appropriate for your students and why?

5. Explore *The WebQuest Page* (Dodge, n.d.-b) and *QuestGarden* (Dodge, 2007). How would you set up teams to create a collaborative WebQuest? Individually or in a group, find some of the materials you would need, and begin work on your own WebQuest, reporting back to your class or colleagues.

Chapter 7 ▟

Critical Issues: Resources for CALL

Elizabeth Hanson-Smith, Joy Egbert, and Jim Buell

Focus

An 8th grade science teacher, Ms. S, retrieves her MP3 player from the computer-connected cradle where it's spent the night scanning the 17 podcasts she subscribes to. Having detected three new programs, the computer downloaded the files and copied them to the handheld. En route to work, Ms. S inserts the device into her dash-mounted cradle and reviews the podcasts, selecting a colleague's classroom presentation on global warming and a NASA conference lecture about interstellar space travel [for possible use in her class].

A few doors down the hall [at Ms. S's school], veteran English teacher Mr. P is reviewing a new batch of student wikis. In an effort to help the students become better communicators, he never provides study guides for tests, instead relying on students to construct their own study resources using their team wikis. He rewards teams that create the most useful/popular study guides.

Mr. P begins adjusting the volume on the microphone that hangs from his classroom ceiling. Today's discussion about *The Grapes of Wrath* will be recorded and posted in an audio file as a class podcast, as are all significant class presentations and discussions. Students, parents, community members, and other educators subscribe to his podcast programs. In fact, on the other side of town, Mrs. B, the parent of one of Mr. P's students, is listening to a podcast classroom conversation about a science fiction short story the students recently read.[1]

Just as learners need many modes and sources of input, they require many ways to produce language and the tools and resources to share what they

---

[1] From "A Day in the Life of Web 2.0," by D. Warlick, 2006, *Technology & Learning*, 27(3). http://www.techlearning.com/showArticle.php?articleID=193200296. Copyright 2006 by NewBay Media. Reprinted with permission.

have learned or created. The land-based and electronic resources for computer-enhanced language education are amazingly rich and diverse. Whether you like to provide a great deal of guidance for students or prefer to set them free to discover and learn for themselves, there are hundreds of online and offline resources to choose from, including thousands of language-specific and general-interest World Wide Web sites and software that might have just the information teachers and students are looking for.

This chapter examines representative samples of a variety of CALL resources in the form of Web sites and tools as well as software packages. It also looks at

- the kinds of problem-solving activities that engage teachers and learners
- ways that CALL resources help English language learners work together and support each other
- ways that teachers can guide students toward their learning goals using these resources.

Background

Although no single educational methodology unites computer users, and although no one point of view unites all teachers of ESL/EFL, the eight conditions for optimal learning environments that form the framework of this text encourage teachers to

- give learners experience in and foster their appreciation for multiple perspectives
- embed learning in realistic and relevant contexts
- encourage ownership and a voice in the learning process for learners
- embed learning in social experience
- foster the use of multiple modes of knowledge representation
- foster awareness of the knowledge construction process (Honebein, 1996, pp. 11–12)

As seen throughout this volume, ESL/EFL teachers are using the Web and other CALL resources to create optimal learning conditions for their students. Even without teacher involvement, electronic resources can give students immediate access to a world of authentic language samples, tasks, and audiences. But it is up to teachers to help learners by structuring activities and projects that promote authentic and meaningful interaction with these materials and with each other. With the right mix of resources, instruction, and opportunities for local and distant collaboration, learners even in foreign language settings can overcome the constraints imposed by narrow textbook-based study and break into the real world of English language interactions. In particular, for students with access to the necessary technology, the Web offers unprecedented opportunities to communicate unencumbered by geographic limits, whether the locus of communication is one to one, one to many, or many to many.

The resources mentioned in this chapter, and throughout the volume, are organized into the appendixes at the end of this book. This chapter introduces some types of Web sites and software and mentions just a few of the many examples worth exploring.

Examples and Discussion

World Wide Web Resources

Many of the sites mentioned in this chapter are maintained by classroom ESL teachers, whereas others are set up by language programs, small- and medium-scale software design firms, and students themselves. However, one of the most important aspects of good educational use of the Web is to develop a critical stance toward the material you will be examining. In an age of information overflow, perhaps the most significant questions about any medium are, "Why are they telling me this?" "What use is it to me?" and "How does this fit in with what I already know?" These questions are particularly crucial in a medium that has no editors—anyone with a computer and an Internet connection can put up a Web page, and anyone else in the world can locate it through an electronic key-word search. All Web sites, even those recommended by other language teachers, should be used with care and a degree of skepticism. Because many Web sites require registration (usually to prevent casual spam attacks), you should also examine carefully the privacy statements on any site to be sure that an e-mail address is not going to be used for junk mailings. Most reputable Web sites offer an *opt out* option and an *unsubscribe* link in every e-mail addressed to the user.

Links to professional development for teachers

Most professional organizations now maintain frequently updated Web sites, for example, TESOL and its CALL Interest Section, which sponsors the yearly Electronic Village Online. (See Appendix A for full contact information for a number of educational sites useful for teachers.) At any of the professional association Web sites, you may join the organization, link to catalogues of publications for sale or subscription, obtain information on conferences, and read online papers and electronic journals. Some organizations, such as MERLOT (1997–2006), offer tools and reusable learning objects, such as lesson plans and syllabi, as well as community-building opportunities with other computer-using teachers. *The* LINGUIST *List* (1989–2006) contains many links to Web sites and resources for a number of different languages. *The Linguistic Funland* (Pfaff-Harris, n.d.-b) collects teacher resources, such as information on teaching and learning, jobs, scripts to improve your Web page, links to teacher training institutions, and so on. *The Linguistic Funland* also sponsors the ESL-*Loop* (Pfaff-Harris, n.d.-a; see the next section for more information). *Tom's Page*, by Robb (n.d.-a), creator of the Famous Personages in Japan Project, has excellent guides for teachers (e.g., what podcasting is and how to use it), as well as links to his own projects and papers and various educational Moodle (2006) communities for those interested in experimenting with an online learning environment. Many journals in the field of language teaching and learning are wholly online, including *Language Learning & Technology* (2007), *The Internet TESL Journal* (1995–2007a), and many others that can easily be found by conducting an Internet search. (See Appendix A for full contact information for a number of educational sites that are useful for teachers.)

Links to exercises and activities for student practice

Lesson plans, content-based units, and opportunities to practice the skills of writing, listening, speaking, grammar, and test taking are all abundant on the Web. Although many teacher-made sites exist, they are apt to go in and out of existence as teachers change jobs, schools, and interests. Some of the most stable and enduring are mentioned here (see also the sites discussed in other chapters and Appendixes C and D).

- *Dave's ESL Cafe* (1995–2007) has many interactive features, such as online quizzes and a bulletin board called Graffiti Wall. The site is especially useful for beginners, but has many links for teachers as well.

- *Interesting Things for ESL Students* (Kelly & Kelly, 1997–2006) offers hundreds of free exercises, games, and activities of all types for English and Japanese learners, including grammar, listening practice with podcasts, crossword puzzles and Hangman, and listening based on Voice of America broadcasts in Special English. The site is organized by level, by skill type, and alphabetically.

- Opp-Beckman's (1995–2005) OP*Portunities in ESL* features a huge list of projects developed for international programs in Thailand, Africa, and Egypt; specific lesson plans; links to exercises; and so forth. It is particularly rich for business English for specific purposes and writing at more advanced levels (e.g., adult, college).

- *Volterre-Fr: English and French Language Resources* (WebFrance International, n.d.) is a comprehensive exercise and resources site for learning English or French.

- *English Online: EFL/ESL Resources* (Hanson, 2000–2006) is rich in exercises, many created with Hot Potatoes (Arneil & Holmes,

2006), and links to sites useful to English language teachers and students.

- *Randall's ESL Cyber Listening Lab* (R. Davis, 1998–2006) offers hundreds of listening exercises and a study guide for teachers and independent learners.

- *The ESL Loop* (Pfaff-Harris, n.d.-a) is a webring of sites that offer exercises and activities, as well as links to sites such as *StudyCom English for Internet* (Winet, n.d.), where students can work with an online tutor for free.

- The Test of English as a Foreign Language (TOEFL), the Test of Spoken English, and the Test of Written English are among the most important hurdles for would-be international students at U.S. colleges and universities. The Educational Testing Service (ETS; 2006a) Web site can help demystify these important tests by providing thorough familiarity with the test procedures. ETS also offers practice questions at its TOEFL *Practice Online* site (ETS, 2006b).

Search engines

Among the most useful general tools for teachers and students alike are the many search engines that let users find nearly any site on the Web through key-word searches. You may want to write out a list of likely search terms ahead of time and type in different combinations as individual words and as phrases until your search results in the kinds of links you are looking for. As you find sites, be sure to bookmark them in your browser, or add them to a *Filamentality* (AT&T Knowledge Ventures, 2007b) list for future reference. Although *Google* (2007a; see also *Google Scholar* [Google, 2007f] for academic searches) and *Yahoo!* (2007a) are among the most popular engines, there are many others (including those that produce visual maps, such as *KartOO* [KartOO Technologies, n.d.]) that may be more appropriate for visually oriented learners than text-only engines (see Figure 7-1).

Links to print publications on the Web

Thousands of nonelectronic periodicals and books, many of which address issues in language learning and CALL, have made their way online. Indeed, some publishers and booksellers (e.g., *Amazon.com*, 1996–2007), even post entire books or chapters of books on the Internet in the hope of attracting sales. It might seem strange to give something away in order to sell it, but experience is beginning to show that it works—reading on-screen and printing out are both just inconvenient enough that people who find something they like on the Web often buy the paper version, too. The growing number of publications available online is especially good news for the many teachers and learners who live far from well-stocked English-language bookstores and

Figure 7-1. A Search for "Grammar Exercises for English"

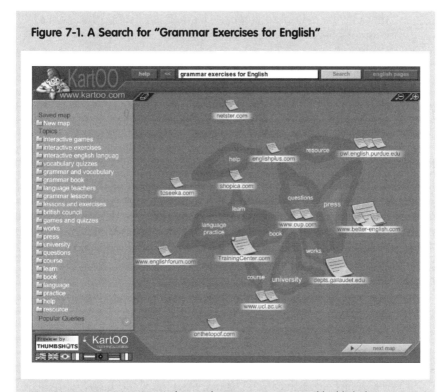

Note. Mouse-over animations indicate relations among sites and highlight key features, such as "language practice." From *KartOO*, by KartOO Technologies, n.d., http://www.kartoo.com/. Copyright by KartOO Technologies. Reprinted with permission.

magazine shops. The following sites are good sources for extensive reading and/or professional development:

- *Project Gutenberg* (2007) offers the complete text of several hundred classic works that are copyright free and thus in the public domain.

- Academic papers by individuals in portable document format (PDF) are increasingly easy to find: search by author and title.

- Many local newspapers, such as *The Mercury News* (San Jose Mercury News, 2006), offer a great deal of their content for online readers in quite a few languages. Some encourage reader interaction through weblogs (blogs) and letters-to-the-editor columns online.

- Cable news sources, such as CNN.*com* (Cable News Network, 2007), offer continuously updated news stories in text with video support that may be helpful to language learners and support sustained content-based teaching. CNN.*com* has versions in many world languages.

- A number of sites offer the lyrics to music and/or poetry, as well as poetry recitations, some with video. For example, *Poemar* (Moutinho, n.d.) offers works in Portuguese, and *Poem Present: Readings and Lectures* (University of Chicago, n.d.) presents work in English by contemporary U.S. poets.

Media-rich content-based learning

Many teachers use the Web as a place to explore content-rich issues and to showcase their students' learning. Chapter 9 in this volume deals with content-based learning extensively and mentions many sites to find authentic content on the Web (see Appendix C for a list of multimedia content sites). Among those Web sites offering a combination of teacher tools and resources, pedagogically sound student activities, and rich multimedia content, the most notable are the following:

- MIT *OpenCourseWare* (Massachusetts Institute of Technology, 2002–2007) offers a great deal of free course content online, including video lectures and syllabi.

- Television and cable stations also deliver free content online. In the United States, some of the best of these are *DiscoverySchool.com* (Discovery Education, 2006a); *History.com* and *Biography* (A&E Television Networks, 1996–2007b and 1996–2007a, respectively); and PBS *TeacherSource* (Public Broadcasting Service, 1995–2006), which links to television programs like NOVA and *Frontline*, and offers particularly good content in the sciences. PBS boasts more than 3,000 lesson plans, which may be used in conjunction with the television shows or solely with the videos and other materials online.

- The larger radio stations also have Web sites, such as the *British Broadcasting Corporation* (BBC; 2006), *National Public Radio* (NPR; 2006), and VOA: *Voice of America* (n.d.), which are excellent resources for listening and writing, and they come equipped with lesson plans and other teacher resources. With streamed radio on the Internet, students can listen to the programs and follow up with the lessons from anywhere in the world. BBC and VOA also have webcasts in languages other than English.

- Television and cable news channels (e.g., CNN [see Cable News Network, 2007]) offer extensive video and text archives as well as up-to-the-minute breaking news stories. Most have blogs or opportunities to write to the editors or producers of the shows, and many are adding education tools and lesson plans to help educators incorporate television programs into their classrooms (see, e.g., C-SPAN *Classroom* [National Cable Satellite Corporation, 2007]).

- *ThinkQuest* "inspires students to think, connect, create, and share" (Oracle Education Foundation, n.d.-a, ¶ 1), encouraging 21st-century skills in a problem-based learning context with a wide range of activities supporting various aspects of the curriculum.

Many content sites have excellent search engines to find content by topic and student grade or level, and ways for teachers to store the lessons and resources they have created at the site itself.

Tools for creative projects and collaborative learning

Chapter 6 in this volume deals extensively with e-mail and Web-based exchanges, and Appendix B lists many places to find exchange partners. Chapters throughout this volume mention the astonishing range of tools now available on the Web to foster project-based learning and class-to-class, group-to-group, or student-to-student exchanges: blogs, audioblogs, wikis, videologs, media-supported voice and text chat rooms, and so on (see Appendixes B and D). These tools support what is often called *Web* 2.0, the socially communicative version of the Internet (see Warlick, 2006, and the Focus section of this chapter). An especially good ESL/EFL example of the new combinations of media coming online is the *absolutely intercultural!* (n.d.) podcast, billed as "the first podcast in the world to deal with intercultural issues" (¶ 1). The show combines photos, documents/text (including lesson plans), and a *Frappr!* map (Rising Concepts, 2007; with pinpoints to indicate locations of community members) with audioblogs, a podcast feed, and space for student comments on intercultural matters (see Figure 7-2). Teachers from countries around the world participate with their students.

Free, downloadable tools, such as Audacity (2006) for audio recording or a screen recorder (e.g., CamStudio, 2005) to create a video of mouse movements on your desktop, make for excellent enhancements to slide presentations or instructional video that students can make for each other. Your learners might also enjoy finding free, downloadable background music in *jamendo* (Zimmer, Kratz, Gérard, & Roelants, n.d.) or creating their own music to upload and share. They can use Groupboard (Group Technologies, n.d.), a multiuser chat, whiteboard, and voice conferencing system, to draw their own pictures (see Figure 7-3) or *Gliffy* (n.d.) to create graphs and charts. Many students find that learning simple HTML is quite easy and that it is rewarding to create their own Web pages at one of the many free Web site providers or on their school server. W3*Schools* (Refsnes Data, 1999–2006b) is one of many sites that provide tutorials on aspects of Web page creation in all the major Web development languages.

Figure 7-2. *absolutely intercultural!* **Podcast**

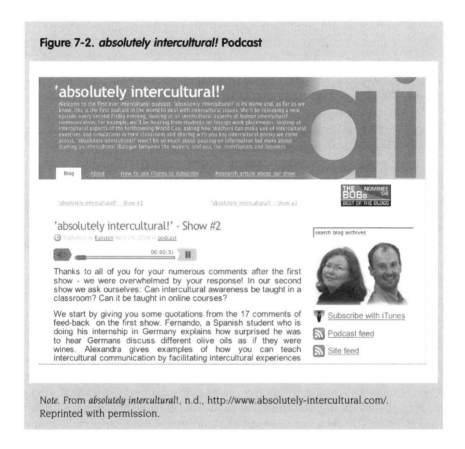

Note. From *absolutely intercultural!*, n.d., http://www.absolutely-intercultural.com/. Reprinted with permission.

Schools and programs

Higher education is making use of the Web in nearly every area imaginable. Learners in every field will find it worthwhile to visit *World Lecture Hall* (University of Texas at Austin, 2006), the premier archive of links to Web-based university courses. Almost all universities around the world have Web sites with extensive information, as do intensive English programs in English-speaking countries. To visit the sites of U.S. universities and 4-year colleges, see the links at *College and University Home Pages—Alphabetical Listing* (DeMello, 1995–1996). You can also use a search engine to find institutions in specific cities and towns around the world.

Guides for teachers

What use do you and your students have for the Web? That question has a world's worth of answers, as this volume demonstrates. But with so many possibilities, how can you know which to choose? Four sites are especially relevant for educators who favor a social constructivist approach, which is

Figure 7-3. *Groupboard* Demo With Drawing Experiments and Chat

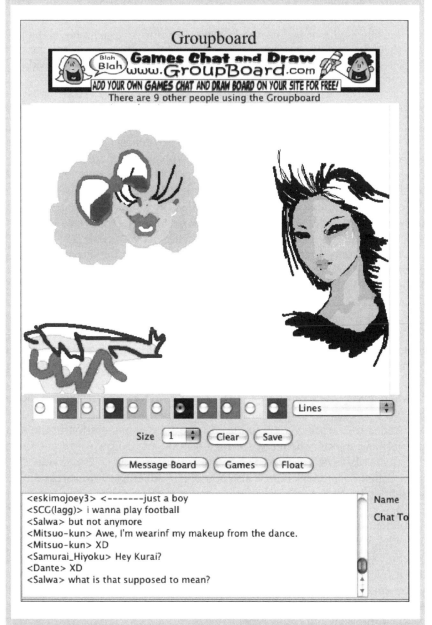

Note. From *Groupboard*, by Group Technologies, n.d, http://www.groupboard.com/. Reprinted with permission.

centered on content-based and group-project-based discovery learning that fulfills all of the conditions for optimal learning environments. In *Harnessing the Power of the Web: A Tutorial*, Global SchoolNet (2000b) states:

> The Internet has made the world smaller. Of particular significance is the ability for students, teachers and researchers to use the web as a tool for interaction, collaboration, distance education, cultural understanding and cooperative research—with peers around the globe. (¶ 1)

The tutorial describes how to design and deliver Web-based projects and how to find and join exemplary projects with partners around the world.

Apple Learning Interchange (Apple Computer, 2007) offers numerous examples of ways that Pre-K–12 educators can connect with peers and create curriculum-based content lessons. A vast media collection at the site includes videos of teachers describing students' projects, student-made videos, reusable learning objects (e.g., photographs and audio files contributed by classes around the world), and documents containing classroom-based research and further descriptions of more extensive student projects.

The Western Michigan University English Education Program (2003) provides free online streaming videos of their series *Teaching English Through Technology*. Topics include Classroom Websites and Content Learning and Building an E-Community, among a dozen or so others. The program is "dedicated to preparing teachers to excel in technological settings" (¶ 2). For community college and adult education teachers, *Getting Results* (WGBH Educational Foundation, 2006) provides current information for collaborative learning with technology in a free but professionally produced video-based format online.

Annenberg Media's (1997–2006) *Learner.org* offers free streaming video lessons that exemplify the teaching of such varied subjects as social studies for Grades K–2, writing communities for Grades 3–6, integration of the arts with other subjects, chemistry for high school, and so on. The Annenberg videos are also available free by satellite and for sale on DVD and videocassette. Annenberg Media's site is also notable for adhering to Web accessibility guidelines for those with disabilities, and a number of the videos concern pedagogy for the disabled. Annenberg Media also produces free short-term seminars for international teachers.

What all these sites have in common is an overarching vision that situates technology in the context of optimal learning environments, where teachers assist learners in locating, understanding, and creating meaningful content while encouraging communication with authentic audiences in authentic tasks. (See chapter 18 in this volume and Appendix A for more resources for personal professional development.)

Software

In addition to the Internet and mobile computing, a great number of desktop resources support language and content learning and teaching. This section outlines software that can help teachers create optimal language learning environments by supporting the eight conditions and 21st-century skills outlined in chapter 1. The majority of sample software packages listed here include multiple modes and multimedia, providing access for a wide variety of learners. Some of the software packages intended for specific groups of learners can also be used with other levels or ages if their use is carefully designed. Most of the programs mentioned here come with exceptional teacher and technical support and suggestions for on- and offline tasks. Although a great variety of student software packages is available, care must be taken to choose those that provide the most flexibility and the greatest possibility of relevant curricular integration. Because many schools around the world may be using older computers, and because good software is often eventually updated or moved to a Web-based version, we include some older software in our suggestions.

Teacher support software

A good deal of software and other hard-copy resources are available to help language teachers manage their classrooms and prepare instruction, including the following:

- The Essential Word Worksheets software (in Essential Tools for Teachers Classroom Suite, 2001) helps teachers build their own worksheets or use or adapt premade worksheets.

- Teacher resource kits by Teacher Created Materials provide all-in-one templates, exercises, and tutorials to help teachers and students learn and use common software packages for authentic purposes. Offerings include TechTools Resource Kits for Microsoft PowerPoint, Microsoft Word, Inspiration, Hyperstudio, and KidPix, and multitool kits for curriculum activities, including a set for middle school language arts (Curriculum Activities Using the Computer, 2001).

- Primary Power Pack (1998; which includes Puzzle Power and Jigsaw Power) from Centron Software has many language-based puzzle formats that both teachers and students can use to create vocabulary exercises.

- Grade Machine (2005) and other grading programs allow teachers to easily calculate grades and keep track of attendance.

Content-free software

Software tools that do not have any preset content and can be employed for any number of language and content learning tasks include the following:

- The Microsoft Office suite (2007), which includes Excel, PowerPoint, FrontPage, and Word, is used widely around the world. It offers help in many formats and languages, and the individual programs can be used for anything from writing letters to giving a multimedia presentation. Templates to create newsletters and other kinds of projects in these applications (and comparable templates for AppleWorks, 2004, for Macintosh computers and for the multiplatform OpenOffice.org suite, 2005) may be downloaded free from the Web. *Google Docs and Spreadsheets* (Google, 2007b) offers a word processor and spreadsheet that are used entirely online.

- Desktop-based geographical information systems (GIS) that students can access for interesting mapping and instruction-giving tasks include Google Earth (2007), a free, downloadable multiplatform software that uses satellite and 3D imagery.

- With book-making software like Storybook Weaver Deluxe 2004 (2004) and Imagination Express (e.g., Destination: Ocean, 1995; Destination: Rain Forest, 1995), any learner can be an author.

- Scaffolded movie-scripting software such as Hollywood High (1995) and Hollywood (1995) helps students develop an understanding of speech.

- The Print Shop (2006) and other desktop publishing software support student language and content learning by providing templates and content for holiday cards, posters, flyers, and more.

- Graphical organizer packages such as Inspiration (2006) and Kidspiration (2006) help learners make semantic maps, story plots, and essay outlines.

- Presentation packages such as Kid Pix (2006) are versatile, and learners of all ages can learn to use them quickly and easily.

- TimeLiner (2001) software is bilingual (English and Spanish) and provides support for essay and story plotting and learning about sequenced events.

- Movie-making software such as iMovie (2006; for the Macintosh) and Windows Movie Maker (2007) lets learners edit videos they have taken with a digital camera, cell phone, or video camera.

Content-based software

Software with preset content is most often used at the K–12 level, but some of the following high-quality programs have also been used very successfully with adult learners.

- Math Mysteries (2000) and Fizz and Martina's Math Adventures (2000) are engaging multimedia programs for the one-computer classroom that help students understand mathematical operations and the process of solving word problems while having fun doing math.

- Other simple and popular math programs include Sunburst's Lemonade for Sale (2001) and Splish Splash Math (2001). Many of Sunburst's content-based programs provide effective, context-based practice with 21st-century skills in basic numeracy, science, text-based literacy, and social studies while at the same time supporting student language learning.

- Science Court (2006) uses the basic premise of a popular television courtroom drama to help students solve problems and learn language and content. This package is intended for the one-computer classroom.

- Microsoft Encarta (2003) and other electronic encyclopedias offer information in accessible multimedia format that can be used in any language-learning project. Although many of these packages are migrating online, electronic encyclopedia software still exists for all ages and levels of learners.

21st-century skills

Some software packages specifically address the thinking and communication skills that learners need to survive (see chapter 1 on 21st-century skills). Some contain content; others are content-free. Such programs include the following:

- With CmapTools (2005), users can input text and change the colors of graphics and text to show different categories of reasoning such as objections, reasons, and claims.

- eKidSkills (2003), a free software package, is intended for students ages 7–13 and includes sections called Getting Organized, Learning New Stuff, Doing Homework, and Doing Projects—all of which focus on critical thinking.

- BrainCogs (2002) helps students to learn, reflect on, and use specific learning strategies across a variety of contexts.

- Choices, Choices (1997) and Decisions, Decisions (2001) are packages that help school-age learners make good decisions. Many titles are available in each set.

- Reason!Able (van Gelder & Bulka, 2001) provides scaffolds such as advice from Socrates for students who are trying to answer a question or prove a claim.

Language practice software

There is an abundance of drill-and-practice software, much of it available from software archives such as those listed in the next section. However, language practice software that also has engaging content and/or contextualized grammar or vocabulary exercises is much harder to find. A few such programs are listed here.

- In Grammar for the Real World (1998), learners take on roles at a newspaper to work with grammar.

- Pearson Education's (2003–2007) Focus on Grammar CD-ROMs, which accompany texts by the same name, feature highly contextualized grammar practice with interactive activities and an extensive teacher apparatus. Focus on Grammar is one of the few grammar programs to deal with voice and register.

- I Spy Treasure Hunt (2001), I Spy School Days (2000), and I Spy Spooky Mansion (1999) are intriguing vocabulary treasure hunt programs that keep learners focused and on task. Although each program has a theme, the language consists of isolated, discrete words and phrases within the theme. Teachers may therefore want to incorporate this software into other tasks to contextualize the vocabulary. Each program also has a problem-solving aspect.

- Usborne's Animated First Thousand Words (2004) emphasizes crucial survival vocabulary and presents it to learners in a variety of games and puzzles set around themes.

- The Oxford Picture Dictionary Interactive (Shapiro, Adelson-Goldstein, Hanson-Smith, & Fella, 1999) offers the vocabulary of the classic adult dictionary in animations and provides engaging games to practice listening and speaking the words, a built-in recorder for dialogues, and a word processor that links to the dictionary pictures for writing help.

- Live Action English Interactive (2006), also for adult learners at the low-intermediate level, uses Total Physical Response techniques in computer-based activities and short narratives with a special emphasis on verb forms and sequence of tenses.

Software publishers and distributors often make available online demos or sample screens from their products. They also provide worksheets, lessons, and advice to help teachers use and adapt their products effectively.

Software reviews and information

Locating useful software is not always easy, but there are a variety of options for finding out if a software package will be useful for a specific classroom. In addition to asking colleagues, attending technology conferences, and reviewing a trial copy of the software, there are the following options:

- Members of the TESLCA-L discussion list (see TESL-L, n.d.) provide rapid responses to any query about software (and most other CALL-related issues; see also the technology interest sections of many of the professional associations mentioned in Appendix A).

- A popular searchable resource is *Download.com* (CNET Networks, 2007), which has links to tens of thousands of shareware, freeware, and demonstration programs, along with software reviews and feature articles (see the >Home & Education link). In addition, ZDNet (CNET Networks, 2006) has almost 50,000 downloadable programs and features reviews and white papers. The education-oriented U-M *Software Archives* (2000) is dated, but parts of it are still alive.

- *Essential Teacher* (TESOL, 1996–2006a), TESL-EJ (1994–2007), CALICO Journal (2007), *Language Learning & Technology* (2007), and other magazines and journals also offer software reviews. Reviews of software for languages other than English may be found by searching for the specific language; for example, the Chinese Language Teachers Association (2006) has reviews of CALL for Chinese.

Lesson plans

An efficient way to use software and the Internet in classrooms is to access tested lesson plans available on the Web. Many sites offer plans in which technology can be integrated; others make available plans that are already enhanced with technology or that are useful in introducing technology to students. The following are a few sources of lesson plans online:

- IATEFL Poland's (2002) Computer Special Interest Group
- The Technology Applications Center for Educational Development (TCET, 2001)
- *DiscoverySchool.com* (Discovery Education, 2006a)
- *Technology Lesson Plans for ESL Teachers* (n.d.)
- *Teaching Tips* (Haynes, 1998–2006)

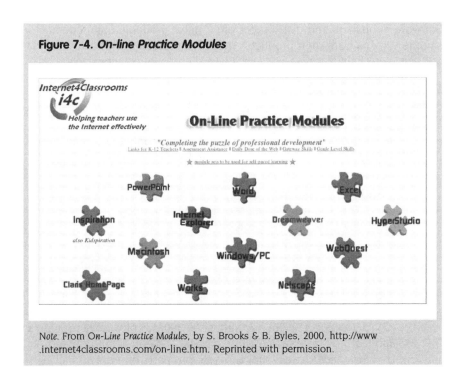

Figure 7-4. On-line Practice Modules

Note. From *On-Line Practice Modules*, by S. Brooks & B. Byles, 2000, http://www .internet4classrooms.com/on-line.htm. Reprinted with permission.

- *Technology Lesson Plans* (Banville, 2004–2007)
- *Internet4Classrooms* (S. Brooks & Byles, 2000), which offers interactive quizzes for a variety of common software applications (see Figure 7-4)

The lesson plans cover a range of topics, from current events to grammar, and apply a variety of Web sites and software packages. Not all of them are right for all contexts, but teachers can adapt the plans to involve students in effective goal-oriented learning.

Conclusion

The organizations and products mentioned in this chapter are only a small number of the numerous resources available both on- and offline to the language teacher working in a computer-enhanced environment. By far the most important resource is colleagues, who can be reached through electronic discussion lists, Web searches, online communities, or many professional organizations (see chapter 18 and Appendix A). Discussion among computer-using educators promises to continue to be a rich source of information and sharing about technology resources far into the future.

Explorations

1. Which Web site do you use most to support your teaching? Which do you use as part of your lessons? Why? Share your favorites with your classmates or working group, and, if possible, try them out together in a lab setting.

2. Choose one of the software resources from this text (see also chapter 12 and Appendix E for more suggestions) that might be appropriate for your students, and find reviews that have been written about it. Do the reviews make you want to try the package? Why or why not? If possible, obtain a copy or demo lesson from the software, and try it out with your students. Observe your students using the software to find out what kinds of language learning or acquisition may be taking place.

3. Do a simple Google search for a language skill. Then click on and learn about the >ADVANCED SEARCH option, and look for the same language skill. What is the difference in outcomes of these searches? Explore further some of the resources you have found. You may wish to collect all of your results in a social Web archive, such as *Filamentality* (AT&T Knowledge Ventures, 2007b), where they can be referred to easily by everyone.

4. Search one or more of the lesson plan sites mentioned in this chapter for a technology-enhanced lesson suitable for your context. What did you find? How does the lesson meet the conditions for optimal learning environments? Download or print the lesson and try it out, if possible, sharing the results with your classmates or colleagues.

5. Review the resources that you currently use in your classroom (or, if you are not currently teaching, those of a friend or colleague). What language, content, and skills do they support? Are 21st-century skills included? If not, how could they be? Look for software or Web resources that might enhance this aspect of the learning environment (see chapters 3 and 20 for more ideas on resources). Share your results with classmates or colleagues, and include them in your Filamentality list.

PART III

Authentic Task

Chapter 8

Theory and Research: Investigating Authenticity

Carol A. Chapelle and Hsin-min Liu

Focus

Most teachers and researchers believe that learners best acquire the target language by engaging in *authentic* tasks. Egbert (2005) defines an authentic task as "one that learners perceive they will use outside of class in their real world or that parallels or replicates real functions beyond the classroom" (p. 6) and claims task authenticity to be one of the conditions for optimal classroom language learning. If authenticity is defined on the basis of what learners perceive, how are teachers, material developers, and researchers to tell whether or not CALL tasks are authentic?

In the previous edition of this volume, this chapter on authenticity (Chapelle, 1999) discussed two ways that researchers can evaluate authenticity: evaluator's judgments about features of the CALL tasks and empirical investigation of learners' performance. Neither of these methods took account of learners' perspectives, but over the past 10 years, additional conceptual and empirical developments have occurred. Researchers have begun to examine learners' perspectives on authenticity of CALL tasks. In addition, authenticity has been placed within a broader framework for CALL evaluation, which provides a means of weighing other important conditions for learning along with authenticity in the evaluation of a specific CALL task.

We begin this chapter with a brief discussion of authenticity in language learning materials and explain implications for research on the authenticity of CALL tasks—research that includes the researchers' judgments and learners' perceptions of task authenticity as well as investigation of learners' performance. We place authenticity within a larger framework for evaluation of CALL and draw conclusions from theoretical perspectives and empirical evaluation of CALL authenticity.

Background

Defining Authenticity

Researchers concerned with language teaching have highlighted the importance of authenticity of learning materials for second language acquisition, and authenticity as a positive attribute of materials is also reflected in professional discussion of CALL. Whether CALL professionals are discussing a WebQuest on the Internet, an activity in a chat room, or a multimedia program, they are likely to describe one positive attribute as its "authenticity." Researchers in language assessment have gone beyond discussing authenticity to develop empirical approaches for the study of authenticity that are useful in the evaluation of CALL.

Widdowson (1979) argues that exposing learners to texts extracted from real life does not necessarily lead to the real-life or near-real-life engagement between learners and texts. He uses the term *genuine* to refer to real-life extracted language as an absolute quality and reserves the term *authentic* to refer to the learners' engagement of strategies for making sense of language in context during a communicative activity. A genuine text is not necessarily authentic to any particular learner; authenticity can result from learners making sense of the text as they normally process it in a real-world context. Widdowson's characterization of authenticity poses a challenge for those who refer to CALL activities as categorically authentic: According to him, authenticity is a relative quality that depends on how learners process the language of the activity. In this sense, a CALL activity cannot in and of itself be authentic or not.

Second language researchers attempt to create authenticity by designing *communication tasks* in which learners are required to interpret and construct meanings (Pica, Kanagy, & Falodun, 1993). Functional meanings are implicated as learners simulate talk that works toward objectives used in the real world—for example, deciding on a class schedule through conversation with classmates or finding the most efficient transportation to the art museum through querying a tourist information person. The research methods associated with task-based learning include discourse analysis describing the language that learners use while they work toward solutions to the problems that tasks set out (R. Day, 1986; Gass & Madden, 1985; Pica, 1994), but in this research the focus is on particular episodes that suggest that learners are attending to language. Authenticity is assumed through task design.

With the intention of systematizing the investigation of authenticity, Bachman (1991) and Bachman and Palmer (1996) outline a framework of task characteristics that has become a mainstay for the study of language assessment tasks. The framework identifies a number of factors that are important for describing aspects of tasks:

- setting
- test rubric
- input
- expected response
- relationship between input and response (Bachman & Palmer, 1996, pp. 43–60)

Setting includes physical setting, participants, and time on task. Intended to guide task designers and judgmental authenticity analysis, task characteristics do not necessarily address Widdowson's concern about the learners' perception or the SLA researchers' methodology of examining performance.

Working on tests of language for specific purposes, Douglas (2000) attempted to include the test taker's perception on authenticity. He points out that context "is not simply a collection of features imposed upon the language learner/user, but rather is constructed by the participants in the communicative event" (p. 43). That is, "what really counts in the communicative performance of a language user is not the external context *per se* but how the speaker interprets the contextualization cues present in the communicative event" (Douglas, 2004, p. 25). This way, context becomes the result of the interaction between situational cues, interlocutors, and their internal interpretation of those cues. Investigating the internal interpretation of context by language users, according to Douglas, is the way to reveal the effect of context in this interaction. His research does so through qualitative analysis of performance and examinees' reflections.

Also examining the authenticity of assessment tasks, Lewkowicz (2000) argues that one way to investigate test takers' interpretation of context cues is through investigation of their performance. Authenticity of performance refers to the authenticity of the language elicited from test takers during test taking. The response is important because with open-ended questions, such as essays or oral interviews, test designers do not control the outcome: Test setters can try to match the test characteristics in terms of situational authenticity and interactional authenticity when setting the test, but the extent to which the outcome is authentic will be determined by the test taker. In addition, it is possible that test takers conceive the input of a test as highly authentic but the outcome as of limited authenticity. Lumley and Brown's (1998) analysis of interview discourse found this to be the case, demonstrating that this analysis of performance could reveal insights about authenticity.

These combined perspectives from researchers concerned with language teaching, second language acquisition, and language assessment provide some guidance for the investigation of authenticity of CALL tasks. We have synthesized these perspectives to reformulate the two approaches to investigating CALL task authenticity that were introduced in the first edition of CALL *Environments*. The first approach describes ways of evaluating task authenticity, and the second approach shows how performance authenticity can be investigated.

Evaluating Task Authenticity

Evaluation of task authenticity is a process of estimating correspondences between a pedagogical task and tasks in the domain of interest. This process requires a framework suggesting points of comparison to be made by the evaluator. We therefore outline such a framework for CALL tasks and show how it can be used for an authenticity analysis of a role-play task in a multimedia CALL program and how it has been used as a basis for gathering learners' perceptions about multimedia CALL activities.

The framework for evaluating the authenticity of CALL tasks described by Chapelle (2003) is based on task frameworks in second language assessment, second language research, systemic functional linguistics, and empirical studies of CALL use. It includes features relevant to language acquisition and technology-mediated environments. As shown in Table 8-1, the features, which describe the topics and actions included in the task, the task participants, the mode of communication, and the evaluation of performance, can be defined for both CALL tasks and tasks outside the classroom to identify areas of similarity and difference in a systematic way. The framework provides a principled basis for task designers and researchers to make judgments about the degree of similarity between a CALL task and a task outside the classroom.

Examples and Discussion

Judgments About Authenticity

In order to investigate how authenticity can be judged in CALL, Liu (2005) analyzed CALL tasks based on a framework containing features of situation. The CALL tasks were in Longman English Interactive (LEI; Rost & Fuchs, 2004), a multilevel, CD-ROM-based general English learning program. It provides video, audio, animations, and extensive practice activities. Level 3 (Intermediate) LEI, which was used in the study, claims to facilitate learners' development of essential language skills and real-world communication strategies. It is organized into three four-unit modules, and each unit contains a variety of instruction for listening, speaking, grammar, vocabulary, and reading.

An analysis of the role-play task and the comparison with its corresponding real-world task are displayed in Table 8-2. This speaking role-play task was chosen from a unit about making and responding to requests in the workplace. The role-play is a typical task in multimedia materials; it asks the learner to play one role in a conversation and to take turns with the video character, whose turns are not contingent on the content of the students'

Table 8-1. Features and Corresponding Questions for Analyzing CALL Task Authenticity

Task Features		Questions for Analysis
Topics and actions	1. Goal	Is the task communicative? Is there one or more than one possible outcome? Is the conveyance of information necessary for reaching the goal?
	2. Topics	What is the content? Is it personal or nonpersonal? Is it field specific or general? How precisely is the topic defined?
	3. Process	What are the learners engaged in—in everyday terms (e.g., listening to a lecture)? How can the processes be characterized as a genre?
	4. Cognitive complexity	How cognitively complex is the topic? How cognitively complex are the processes?
	5. Location	Where are the participants located as they work on the task?
Participants	6. Identity	Who are the participants?
	7. Interests	What are their interests with respect to language learning?
	8. Technology experience	What is their experience in using technology?
	9. Group size	How many participants are there?
	10. Relationships	What is the relationship among the participants?

(Continued on p. 116)

Table 8-1 (continued). Features and Corresponding Questions for Analyzing CALL Task Authenticity

Task Features		Questions for Analysis
Mode	11. Modes	What are the modes of language use?
	12. Length and duration	How long are the tasks and texts?
	13. Pressure	How quickly must the language be processed?
Evaluation	14. Importance of correctness	How important is it to complete the task and do it correctly?
	15. Eminence of evaluation	How will the learners' participation be evaluated?

utterances. The corresponding task in the real-world context is defined as following and giving instructions in the workplace. The analysis of the real-world office task is based on reports of research investigating oral workplace communication, discourse/conversation structure, and requests as speech acts (Boden, 1994; Carnevale, Gainer, & Meltzer, 1991; Charles, 1996; Crosling & Ward, 2002; Garcez, 1993; Gimenez, 2001; Gumperz, 1982; J. Holmes, 2004; Jacoby, 1998; Louhiala-Salminen, 2002; Schiffrin, 1994; Tacey, 1975). These discourse analyses of workplace communication can inform judgment about CALL task authenticity by focusing the teacher on features known to affect communication.

The analysis in Table 8-2 reveals the complexity of an authenticity analysis. It should also be apparent that the CALL task is neither completely authentic nor inauthentic. Instead, the analysis points out areas in which the task is more or less authentic. It also provides a basis for development of questions that might be posed to CALL developers, teachers, and learners to guide an empirical evaluation of the authenticity of the CALL task.

Learners' Perceptions of Authenticity

Liu (2005) began with such a framework to develop a questionnaire that would help gather data on learners' perceptions of authenticity. Recognizing the multiple perspectives on the study of authenticity, Liu defines this aspect

Table 8-2. Analysis of LEI Role-Play

Feature of Task	Analysis of Role-Play Task in LEI	Analysis of Corresponding Task in a Real-World Office
1. Goal	Simulated communicative task	Communicative task
	More than one possible outcome	More than one possible outcome
	Conveyance of information is not necessary for reaching the goal	Conveyance of information is necessary for reaching the goal
2. Topics	Work; requesting help and refusing to help with a work project	Work; getting work-related things done through talk
	Personal/nonpersonal; not specified/restricted	Mostly nonpersonal, some personal
	Field specific	Field specific
	Content topic (situation) is not clearly defined	For the most part, topic is precisely defined
3. Process	Role-play with simulated characters to complete conversations on computer; practice using requests by actually producing them in a conversation format	Conversation with real person who has real needs
	Semi-interactive dialogue	Conversation
	Listen to the character (prompt), read direction, record response using the model or learners' own words, listen to pre-prepared feedback	Listen to the interlocutor, respond, receive feedback, respond to feedback
4. Cognitive complexity	Topic is unclearly defined, yet straightforward	Topic complexity varies depending on job/project
	Takes practice to become familiar with the process, but it is not cognitively complex	Process is mostly straightforward

(Continued on p. 118)

Table 8-2 (continued). Analysis of LEI Role-Play

Feature of Task	Analysis of Role-Play Task in LEI	Analysis of Corresponding Task in a Real-World Office
5. Location	Computer lab or any place where a computer can operate	Varied; can be anytime during the day and at any place
6. Identity	Amy and Talia (simulated characters from the course video), an English language learner, and a researcher (as a facilitator)	Varied; boss/employee, colleagues with higher/lower status, worker, customer, clients, and so on
7. Interests	Only the English language learners (ELLs) have interests in improving their speaking ability	Varied; interests are pragmatically oriented to getting work done
8. Technology experience	ELLs generally are familiar with technology and feel comfortable with it	Varied
9. Group size	One real person, two simulated characters, one facilitator	Varied
10. Relationships	No real relationship; simulated relationships are not specified	Varied, yet power relationships are apparent
11. Modes	Reproduced aural spoken language	Live aural or oral spoken language
12. Length and duration	Three turns, each with one short sentence Duration varies depending on ELLs; pauses during conversation range from 5 seconds to 30 seconds	Conversation and sentence length vary Duration varies depending on the complexity of job content; pauses need to be short

(Continued on p. 119)

Table 8-2 (continued). Analysis of LEI Role-Play

Feature of Task	Analysis of Role-Play Task in LEI	Analysis of Corresponding Task in a Real-World Office
13. Pressure	Moderate rate of speech input; no time pressure for processing the input, and learners can replay the prompt input as many times as they like	Moderate to fast rate of input speed; the language must be quickly processed
14. Importance of correctness	Not very important; depends on students' motivation because the performance is not scored and feedback is not provided	Very important; clear and mutually beneficial understanding are necessary for completion of job tasks
15. Importance of evaluation	None (unless facilitators announce additional evaluation)	Immediately evaluated by the interlocutor(s)

of authenticity as "the extent to which learners perceive the test task as corresponding to the [target language use, or TLU] task" (p. 41). This approach looks at the correspondence between tasks across domains from learners' perspectives; Bachman and Palmer's (1996) task characteristics framework was used as a basis for the investigation. Liu used their framework to investigate learners' perceptions of four tasks in LEI and found that learner perception also provides useful information for investigating authenticity.

In the study, a total of 15 questions with a seven-point Likert scale (with choices from *very close to* to *very different from*) were distributed right after each CALL activity (see Appendix 8-A for the actual questions). The questionnaire asked how participants rated each characteristic of each LEI task relative to the real-life TLU situation. For example, for investigating the characteristics of setting, this question was asked:

> As you were doing these questions, was there enough information about the location and how it looked to picture yourself in the conversation there in real life?

For the characteristics of the simulated participants, the question was

> Do the people in these questions seem like people you might encounter in real life?

For characteristics of content, the question was

> Is the topic of the questions one you would be likely to encounter in real life conversation?

The questions were designed in a way that allowed learners to do the evaluation regarding the authenticity of tasks across domains.

The findings from the questionnaire revealed considerable variation across the judgments of five learners. Such variation made it difficult to draw a single conclusion about the degree of this aspect of task authenticity. However, the relative authenticity of a task is evident when the results are examined across tasks. Tasks rated consistently high by most students across many of the features might be considered the most authentic; tasks that received ratings with greater variation across characteristics might be considered less authentic. It seems that students vary in their ability to perceive authenticity in tasks intended to correspond to tasks outside the classroom, perhaps because they lack imagination to relate it to the real world, or they lack the knowledge that such a relationship was intended by the task developers.

Jamieson and Chapelle (2006) attempted to assess authenticity with fewer questionnaire items in a larger, quantitative study. Rather than probing specific areas of similarity and difference between the CALL tasks and the language use situation, they assessed learners' perceptions of the authenticity of LEI tasks using a four-point Likert-type scale with the following questions about general correspondence between the tasks and the target language use situation:

> How much were you able to use what you had learned in the LEI lessons while outside of the classroom?

> For each part you worked on, how often outside of the classroom did you see or hear what you studied?

Multiple samples of students' responses on these two questions were obtained by asking students to respond once for each of the six sections of LEI that they had worked on (a total of 12 questions) each time they worked on LEI. The responses were averaged across time and added across items for a total possible score of 48 (four-point Likert scale x 12 items).

The mean value for 208 students' perception of authenticity was a score of 31 (which is more than 50% of the total possible score of 48); however, significant differences were found in the perceptions of students in different classes, as shown in Table 8-3. Except for the classes in Japan (JAP1–3), the mean scores for all groups fall in the 30s, which is interpreted as *good* on a scale of *excellent*, *good*, *weak*, and *poor*. The scores of the three classes in Japan are lower than those of the other classes. The mean score of 16.77 for JAP1 would be interpreted as *poor* authenticity, and the mean scores of 26.25 for JAP2 and 20.49 for JAP3 are interpreted as *weak*.

These two studies demonstrate ways that CALL task authenticity can be estimated by taking into account the learners' perceptions, thereby reflecting the definitions of authenticity given by Widdowson (1979), Egbert (2005), and Douglas (2000, 2004). The research assessing learners' perceptions reveals both individual variation and variation across groups when learners are asked about the correspondence they perceive between tasks and language use beyond the task.

Evaluating Performance Authenticity

Performance authenticity requires analysis that goes beyond learners' perceptions to examination of their performance. Empirical research methods for evaluating second language tasks have evolved from second language classroom research methods of the 1980s, which to a large extent abandoned the evaluation of language instruction by measuring learning outcomes in favor of the investigation of classroom processes (Allwright & Bailey, 1991; Chaudron, 1988; R. Day, 1986; Gass & Madden, 1985). Second language classroom researchers found that the most revealing way to document the processes occurring in a language classroom was to describe the language of the classroom participants. Such data can be analyzed in terms of the authenticity of classroom language relative to language used outside the classroom.

To evaluate performance authenticity, Liu (2005) gathered data on her participants' use of the role-play task in LEI. Example 1 shows the performance of a student, Chen, in a role-play with Amy. Amy is the LEI character shown in the video, and Chen is sitting at the computer playing the role of a coworker. Chen is able to develop a conversation by responding to Amy's turns. However, Chen maintains a second conversation (or think-aloud; shown in italicized text in parentheses) with the researcher who is sitting next to him. The second conversation consists of an analysis of how the role-play dialogue is progressing. In Chen's first turn (Line b), he thinks and then comes up with a question for his coworker. The analysis begins as soon as he has spoken; he wonders if the computer recorded his comment, so he then needs to return to the conversation in the role-play by repeating the question. Amy's response fits as a response to what Chen said, and Chen continues by asking another question (Line d). This receives a response from Amy, however, that Chen sees as inappropriate. Chen therefore returns to his analytic commentary: "She responded me this way, so do I have to change my previous request?" Chen changes his request to a form that fits the response, and then listens

Table 8-3. Authenticity: Reliability and Descriptive Statistics From Questionnaire Items for 12 Classes

		1 UCC1 A	2 UCC2 B	3 UCC3 C	4 NAU D	5 LAG1 E	6 LAG2 E	7 JAP1 F	8 JAP2 G	9 JAP3 H	10 THAI1 I	11 THAI2 I	12 CHILE J
								Class					
N	Valid	22	17	20	8	22	25	14	33	12	20	11	4
	Missing	0	1	3	0	1	2	0	2	2	1	1	0
Mean		**33.31**	**32.15**	**35.38**	**33.37**	**30.97**	**31.78**	**16.77**	**26.25**	**20.49**	**36.91**	**38.14**	**35.03**
Median		34.41	36.66	36.96	32.85	30.83	31.75	14.76	26.30	20.70	38.00	39.50	34.56
Std. Deviation		7.23	11.34	7.23	4.16	6.611	6.65	6.20	4.92	6.76	5.09	6.44	4.62
Minimum		10.50	11.33	18.00	26.08	19.67	15.25	12.00	14.44	12.00	20.00	24.00	30.00
Maximum		45.00	47.00	45.08	38.60	42.00	41.50	30.35	37.37	33.33	43.33	45.50	41.00
Reliability		.86	.88	.97	.94	.97	.96	.99	.97	.98	.85	.78	.96

Note. From *Empirical Evaluation of CALL Use for ESL Students' Learning Processes and Outcomes* (TIRF Priority Research Grant) (p. 11), J. Jamieson and C. A. Chapelle, 2006, Birmingham, AL: The International Research Foundation.

to Amy's response and is apparently satisfied. He pauses to think of another request, which he does.

Example 1: Chen

a) Amy: Hi Chris what can I do for you?
b) Chen: [pause 13 sec] Would you give me a cup of coffee? Thanks. (*Did it record? Not loud enough right? Decide to record again.*) Hi Chris, um could you give me a cup of coffee, thanks.
c) Amy: Sure.
d) Chen: [13 seconds] Um, um, could you also give me the schedule of today's work?
e) Amy: No, not at all, anything else?
f) Chen: (*She responded me this way, so do I have to change my previous request?*)
g) Would you mind give me um the today's work schedule?
h) Amy: No, not at all, anything else?
i) Chen: [long pause, 30 seconds] (*I can't think of anything to ask. . . .*) Could you also help me to set the appointment with Sandy? Thanks.

The dual conversation is characteristic of many of the conversations that were collected in this study of performance authenticity. Example 2 (Line d) also illustrates how Chen narrates his reflection on what he said when the response did not fit. After the one instance of analysis, the subsequent conversation continues smoothly.

Example 2: Chen

a) Talia: Say Alex . . . could you check some background information for the Nick Crawford story?
b) Chen: Sure, no problem . . . anyel anyel else?
c) Talia: Oh, really? Well, can you do it later this afternoon?
d) Chen: (*Oh, so I have to change my previous one, listen again the first prompt*) Um, sorry, but un . . . now I got the other things I need to do.
e) Talia: Oh, really? Well, can you do it later this afternoon?
f) Chen: Um, sorry, but I'm afraid I can't do that for you this afternoon.
g) Talia: Oh. Ok. Well, have fun tonight!
h) Chen: Thanks. See you later.

In Example 3, in contrast, Wen has some initial difficulty in putting himself into the role-play, and throughout this exchange, he is much more oriented to his conversation with the researcher than with Amy in the role-play.

Example 3: Wen

a) Amy: Hi Chris what can I do for you?
b) Wen: ([laugh] . . . *so you can record your own answer . . . so do I have to ask her question? You need to listen and follow direction and record your response, oh so I have to speak and record* . . . [long pause] . . . *what could I request? Anything? Or should I say what was said in the model? I can't remember . . . play the second*

time. So weird. . . . Speaking to a computer . . . [long pause] . . . *figuring how to control the record button . . . play the third time, try out the record button, was it recording? Yes, you can stop it by clicking it again.*)

c) Wen: Coffee please. (*ok, I've done the first request.* [laugh])

d) Amy: Sure.

e) Wen: (*uh . . . let me think* [pause, clears throat] Then leave my office right now.

f) Amy: No, not at all.

g) Wen: Oh (*I did it wrong*). Do you mind leaving my office right now?

h) Wen: Please shot the door [laugh].

These three examples illustrate the specific language involved and how the learners' performance is enacted in the role-play. Second language researchers can analyze learner language from a number of different perspectives. From the perspective of authenticity, one might wish to look at the pragmatic functions that make up the conversations, the linguistic characteristics (e.g., the lexico-grammatical characteristics of the language), the quantity of language that the learner is exposed to and is able to produce, the nonlinguistic moves and forms, and the medium. Using these categories, an analysis of the authenticity of these conversations can be carried out as shown in Table 8-4.

The analysis summarized in Table 8-4 shows some similarities and differences in the performance one finds in the CALL task and in the office. The primary difference is that the actual office communication is characterized by greater variation on all of the points of comparison. However, other important differences include the use of language for reflection in the CALL task and its use for making requests and refusals. Moreover, the nonlinguistic cues and moves are different because of the use of the mouse to move the conversation forward and the computer display; the computer interface adds an additional layer to the medium of communication in the CALL task that is not present in many office communication tasks. However, just as there are differences between the simulated conversation and the real one, there are also similarities in each of the categories. In short, performance in the simulated conversation is neither authentic nor inauthentic. Instead, it has some characteristics at both ends of the authenticity continuum.

Authenticity in CALL Evaluation

Most CALL researchers and teachers would argue that authenticity alone does not fully characterize valuable CALL tasks. Chapter 1 outlines eight conditions for successful language learning, only one of which is involvement in authentic tasks. Focusing specifically on CALL, Chapelle (2001) defines six guiding criteria for CALL: language learning potential, meaning focus, learner fit, authenticity, positive impact, and practicality. Like empirical methods for evaluation of authenticity, these qualities of CALL materials can be used

Table 8-4. Analysis of the Three Conversations: Chen and Wen With Computer

Feature of Performance	Example 1	Example 2	Example 3	Real-Life Office Conversation
Pragmatic functions	Requesting services and information **Reflection**	Refusing requests and explaining **Reflection**	Requesting services and information **Reflection**	Requesting and refusing requests
Lexico-grammatical characteristics	Short utterances with polite requests (e.g., *would you*)	Short utterances with polite refusal (e.g., *I'm afraid*)	Short utterances with polite requests (e.g., *do you mind*)	Utterance size and politeness degree may **vary**
Quantity	Short turns and conversations	Short turns and conversation	Short turns and conversation	Turn and conversation size may vary
Nonlinguistic moves and forms	Visual cues from **information displayed on computer screen**—a picture and a set of written directions **Mouse clicks**	Visual cues from **information displayed on computer screen**—a picture and a set of written directions **Mouse clicks**	Visual cues from **information displayed on computer screen**—a picture and a set of written directions **Mouse clicks**	Visual cues from inter-locutor's physical presence **or audio/text only**
Medium	Oral language **with computer interface**	Oral language **with computer interface**	Oral language **with computer interface**	Oral and **written** language

Note. Points of difference are indicated in bold.

to guide empirical research and make informed judgments about tasks and activities.

Such research needs to grapple with the issue of how to gather sufficient amounts of evidence that could be used to support an overall evaluation of a particular CALL activity or series of activities. For example, Jamieson and Chapelle (2006) included in their questionnaire not only 12 questions about authenticity, but also questions designed to provide evidence about other characteristics of CALL. Evidence about each of the criteria was obtained through teacher questionnaires and phone interviews as well as through student questionnaires. In short, the idea is to seek evidence about other qualities in addition to authenticity, and then to integrate the findings into a general perspective about the appropriateness of the CALL tasks for particular learners (for illustrations of this type of evaluation for language assessment, see Chapelle, Jamieson, & Hegelheimer, 2003; for CALL, see Jamieson, Chapelle, & Preiss, 2005).

Conclusion

Chapter 8 in the first edition of CALL *Environments* (Chapelle, 1999) described two ways of analyzing authenticity of CALL tasks—one based on teachers' judgments of the relationship between the second language task and the tasks that learners might encounter outside the classroom, and the other based on observation and analysis of the language that learners engage in during task performance. Ten years later, we present a more complex view that comes from multiple perspectives on authenticity, methods for evaluating authenticity, and the place of authenticity in an overall judgment of appropriateness. Authenticity continues to be an important concern in CALL tasks. The following three conclusions can be drawn about the role of authenticity in evaluating CALL materials:

1. *Authenticity* has more than one meaning. It can be assessed through the judgments made by task designers, teachers, and students. Multiple perspectives are needed to make reasoned judgments about the degree of authenticity of CALL materials. A framework containing task features believed to influence performance is helpful for guiding judgments and constructing instruments for gathering judgments about authenticity.

2. Authenticity results from an interaction between the materials and the situation in which CALL is used. Therefore, CALL users should examine critically the claim that authenticity is an inherent characteristic of CALL. For example, Butler-Pascoe and Wiburg (2003) connect CALL with communicative language teaching

by pointing out that "technology extends the communicative classroom to provide authentic tasks and audiences for English language learners locally and globally" (p. 47). Such claims about the categorical value of CALL based on its authenticity are questionable in view of a context-related definition of authenticity.

3. Authenticity is only one characteristic of appropriate CALL tasks; it should not be considered as the sole criterion for the value of CALL. Instead, judgments and data about authenticity should be weighed along with other criteria such as language learning potential. All of these characteristics are context dependent and therefore worthy of investigation across the contexts in which CALL tasks might be used.

In this chapter, we have discussed the conceptual basis of authenticity and provided illustrations of how this construct has been operationalized in two studies. But this research is only beginning, and much more research is needed in order to understand authenticity in CALL across different learners and contexts. In our view, such research would be well worth the time spent because as computers and the Internet come into increasing use in the classroom, the potential of CALL tasks for achieving authenticity is of great interest to all language teachers.

Appendix 8-A: Questions for ELLs on Authenticity of Tasks

Directions: Compare the questions you did with a real-life conversation. Please circle a number to indicate your opinion and explain your answer.	Very close to real-life conversation				Very different from real-life conversation		
1. Do you understand the purpose and procedures of doing the task based on the info given?	7	6	5	4	3	2	1
2. As you were answering these questions, was there enough information about the location and how it looked to picture yourself in the conversation there in real life?	7	6	5	4	3	2	1
3. Do the people speaking in these questions seem like people you might encounter in real life?	7	6	5	4	3	2	1

4. Do you think there could be a purpose for answering these questions in real life, apart from learning English or testing your English ability?	7	6	5	4	3	2	1
5. Is the topic of the questions one you would be likely to encounter in real-life conversation?	7	6	5	4	3	2	1
6. Would you encounter this type of task format in real-life conversation? Task 1—Multiple-choice questions about a short dialog in English	7	6	5	4	3	2	1
Task 2—Role-play with a character, follow the direction, and record your response	7	6	5	4	3	2	1
Task 3—Drag-and-drop items to respond to the listening prompt	7	6	5	4	3	2	1
7. Do you think the speaker gave any information about how he/she felt about the topic in the way he/she talked about it?	7	6	5	4	3	2	1
8. Do you hear the pronunciation, vocabulary, & grammar like that in the questions in real life?	7	6	5	4	3	2	1
Would you use English like that in these questions in real life conversation?	7	6	5	4	3	2	1
Do the questions require you to use other kinds of knowledge in addition to your English knowledge to respond to it?	7	6	5	4	3	2	1
9. In real life, people talk to different people in different ways depending on their social relationship (for example, student-teacher, boss-employee, etc.). In responding to these questions, how important was social relationship to the way you responded?	7	6	5	4	3	2	1
10. Is this type of conversation complete and realistic?	7	6	5	4	3	2	1
11. Is the problem you had to solve in answering these questions one that you might have to solve in real life?	7	6	5	4	3	2	1

12. Do you think the language ability required for answering these questions is similar to language ability required for participating in a conversation of a similar situation in real life?	7	6	5	4	3	2	1
Is the way your English is being evaluated in these questions similar to how people might judge you in real life situations?	7	6	5	4	3	2	1

Explorations

1. Before you read this chapter, how did you define authenticity? Has the chapter changed your understanding of authenticity? If so, how? Keeping in mind the three conclusions at the end of this chapter, formulate a working definition of authenticity that can be used when examining CALL materials. Share your discoveries with your team or working group. As you read further in this volume, you might want to weblog (blog) or journal further ideas about the role of authentic and semi-authentic materials in the language classroom.

2. Using the Bachman and Palmer (1996) framework from this chapter, create a chart identifying the setting, test rubric, input, expected response, and relationship between input and response for a classroom task that you have devised or observed. What do your observations say about the authenticity of the task? Compare your chart with those of classmates or colleagues.

3. Use the criteria in Table 8-1 (see also Table 8-2) to examine a CALL task. How does this framework assist teachers and researchers in evaluating authenticity? Is there anything missing from this framework that you can add? Discuss the framework and your conclusions with classmates or colleagues.

4. Students' idea of task authenticity often differs from their teacher's. Devise and administer a survey for your students (or those in a classroom you are observing) about the authenticity of a task or lesson unit. What do their perceptions tell you? Share your survey with your community.

5. Plan an action research project that investigates authenticity in a language learning classroom. Brainstorm ideas for your project with others beforehand. Write up your results, and discuss them with your team or working group.

Chapter 9

Classroom Practice: Content and Language

Elizabeth Hanson-Smith

Focus

When Argentinian and U.S. students took part in a collaborative international tandem exchange, these are the kinds of comments they left in their weblog (blog) of the experience:

> How to describe the experience we had last week is quite complex.
>
> The project we are doing is an amazing idea in order to learn the language in another way. To my mind, that's very important to know how to communicate correctly in English with other people, especially if they are from abroad. This opportunity that we had was a perfect occasion to do it!
>
> We were able to do something that, I think, not many students would ever do. Luckily, I and my classmates could do it! We talked with Spanish students from the USA. We exchanged opinions about many different and interesting topics.
>
> In my personal case, I talked with Lucia, Maya and Daniel who were really talkative and knowledgeable. They were interested in very controversial and well-known topics, such as kidnappings, the policies of Hugo Chavez and what people all around the world think of him. Luckily, I knew something about these topics and I could help them a bit in their final projects.
>
> That's not all; we also talked about our daily routines and customs. We were able to spot how different we are as regards social customs! But these won't prevent us to keep in touch and help each other when there's a need; and why not. . . . .making some new friends. . . . ha!
>
> It's highly important to realize that this opportunity is unique and that we must take profit from it!
>
> To sum up, I reckon this was a spectacular experience. I was able to take advantage from it and to learn that the most important part of learning a language is to know how to communicate with it! (Denise, posting on CAE B's *Podcast*, n.d.)

The U.S. and Argentinian students shared their respective cultures and current events in Latin America, the subject of the U.S. students' research papers. In addition to audio, photo, and text contributions (see Denise's posting in Figure 9-1), they placed free Internet phone calls using Spanish and English. Such exchanges, as described later in this chapter, are taking part all over the world as the Internet's capability for free communication grows. Although early CALL teachers found the computer lacking in the ability to respond to and interact with humans in natural language, the Internet's ability to carry voice and video is highly motivating. With careful planning by the teacher, learners can master the language structures and content they need in collaboration with authentic local or global audiences.

This chapter explores some of the sustained content projects that students are engaging in, particularly those that involve the use of CALL tools and

Figure 9-1. Denise Describes Her Experiences in a Tandem Exchange With Photo, Recording, and Text Message

Play   send to a friend | (8) Comments | Download | Permalink

Denise
May 02, 2006 06:28PM

How to describe the experience we had last week is quite complex.
The project we are doing is an amazing idea in order to learn the language in another way. To my mind, that's very important to know to how to communicate correctly in English with other people, especially if they are from abroad. This opportunity that we had was a perfect occasion to do it!

Note. From CAE B's *Podcast*, n.d., http://caeb2006.podomatic.com/. Reprinted with permission.

environments to create an optimal setting for collaborative language learning. With the best applications, the technology becomes a virtually invisible servant to the students' goals and their expanding store of knowledge.

Background

Brinton, Snow, and Wesche (2003), Chamot and O'Malley (1994), and Nunan (2001), among many others, have emphasized that a curriculum constructed around tasks and content-based instruction (CBI) can provide significant practice that is more motivating than skill-oriented drills. Extending this notion, a special-topic issue of TESOL *Journal* in 2001 discussed the then-emerging issue of *sustained content language teaching* (SCLT), that is, a "focus on the exploration of a single content area" with a "complementary focus on L2 learning and teaching" (Murphy & Stoller, 2001, p. 3). The TESOL *Journal* issue included a range of applications at various levels: sourcebooks (collections of authentic texts) in intensive English programs, sheltered instruction for school subjects, and adjunct university courses. In addition to elementary and secondary education, many institutions worldwide offer courses combining sustained content and language (often referred to as English for specific purposes, or ESP).

Even if you are not a content teacher or do not have ESP learners, if students study a particular content area of immediate interest to them (e.g., a community issue, local effects of global warming, cross-cultural diversity), they can engage in the challenges of thinking through language, as in the CAE tandem project. As this chapter demonstrates, SCLT simultaneously addresses several of the issues raised in chapter 8 concerning *authenticity* and valuable CALL tasks. SCLT also emphasizes higher cognitive processes, as learners work collaboratively with complex structures, organization of materials, and new vocabulary and ideas over an extended period of time. As experienced teachers know, learning itself can become a highly motivating adventure, particularly in a communicative, collaborative, content-based classroom. A further advantage for the teacher is the potential for cognitive complexity (see Part VI, Intentional Cognition), both in studying content and in performing the tasks that can be based on it. Kennedy (2006) of the GLOBE Program refers to such content-based tasks as both hands-on and "minds-on" (p. 84).

For the purposes of this chapter, I group SCLT, CBI, and ESP together when I discuss SCLT, although of course each has certain differences in approach. These approaches have the advantage of using language about the content, or *field-specific vocabulary*, as well as the language to engage in and complete operations with the content (e.g., group work, portfolio and presentation creation). I also refer to *authentic texts*, that is, written or spoken materials not created specifically for language learners. Generally, *prepared authentic texts*, that is, authentic materials with appropriate linguistic and semantic assistance built in, are preferable at the high-intermediate level and above, but new-comers to a language need texts written by teachers or materials developers specifically for their level. Web sites like *Learning Resources* (Literacyworks.org, 1999–2004), which has archived news items written in simplified English with accompanying exercises for learners, or Voice of America's *Special English* (n.d.) items (i.e., spoken more slowly and with a lower vocabulary level) for listening practice can be invaluable for learners studying a content area. DVD players that can slow down playback without distorting sound are also useful for learners watching authentic video. Later in this chapter, I discuss various tools to prepare texts and materials for language study as students use them online.

A significant element in SCLT is *collaboration*. This might be as simple as weekly e-mail exchanges (see chapter 6) or as complex as sharing data collected locally with real scientists around the world, as in the GLOBE Program (n.d.; described in further detail later in the chapter). This is the kind of computer-enhanced teaching that diSessa (2000) speaks of as enabling "a new increment of intellectual power" that allows children to learn with "pleasure and commitment" (p. ix). SCLT lends itself well to *social learning*, or "collaborative knowledge-building" (Stahl, 2000, p. 70) along *constructivist* lines. In a cyclical pattern, learners share personal comprehension, articulate their understanding in words, negotiate differing perspectives, and clarify meanings through argument and discussion (Stahl, 2000). The teacher who is unfamiliar with how groups interact collaboratively would do well to explore some of the literature about team dynamics, such as Duncan and Szmuch's (2000) article on building rapport in groups. The *Getting Results* site (WGBH Educational Foundation, 2006) offers an online, self-paced video course to prepare teachers to create a collaborative learning community in class and use technology in a hands-on, task-based, cooperative way. Although specifically targeting community college teachers, the examples and resources could be applied to all levels and could be conducted at a land-based site as a multiweek exploration by a group of instructors.

Keeping in mind three major concerns—use of authentic materials, preparation of materials for language learning, and collaborative knowledge building—the remainder of this chapter discusses examples of SCLT in a variety of content areas. The resources and tools suggested are simply the tip of a very large iceberg.

Examples and Discussion

Content Resources

Much of the software described in the first edition of CALL *Environments*, such as Steck-Vaughn's Violent Earth or Edmark's Imagination Express, is available only in remainder lists and has not been recoded for newer versions of Windows and Macintosh operating systems. If you have older computers, or have retained a copy of an earlier operating system, the software is a real bargain and may still be appropriate as a curricular supplement at a workstation. Given the exciting, free resources on the Internet, however, current software is less likely to offer content choices than in the past, unless it comes packaged with your textbook. Of great help in enriching the curriculum are Web sites that provide a wide variety of resources—not just texts, but elaborated, standards-based lesson plans with supporting video, photos, graphics, language exercises, and tasks to encourage collaborative SCLT. (A selection of important content sites is found in Appendix C.) For particular content areas, reading and conducting searches in electronic journals is helpful in finding appropriate sites. Many teachers also build their own content sites with reusable learning objects (e.g., Dodge, n.d.-b; MERLOT, 1997–2006). Contributing to such projects is a rewarding experience.

Curricular Projects and Collaborations

A number of worldwide collaborative projects are based on the standards and curricula of elementary school. One of the most prominent of these is the GLOBE Program (n.d.) for science education, sponsored by various U.S., European, Japanese, and Argentinean government and educational agencies and managed by the University of Colorado's University Corporation for Atmospheric Research. Students in elementary and secondary schools take part in collecting samples and making observations about their local environments. They then share the data with scientists and partner classrooms around the world. GLOBE has materials specifically developed for English language learners, and because of its international components, there are opportunities to use a variety of languages in authentically communicative tasks. GLOBE also has topics in music and the arts (for further details, see GLOBE *Program*, n.d.; Kennedy, 2006).

A more free-form type of collaboration covering many content areas, the eTwinning program (European Commission, 2004) partners schools throughout Europe in a variety of long-term (one week to a full school year) curricular projects, for example, creating a joint Web site to learn more about a foreign language or culture. The partner schools or classrooms themselves negotiate the type of project they wish to undertake, using the examples of models and themes offered at the eTwinning Web site. Some schools undertake a whole-school initiative: Each classroom connects to a partner in a different country and presents its findings on the topic to the whole school at the end of the year. Topics include "Crossing the Cultural Divide," "We musn't forget" (a cross-generational project based on interviews of living survivors of European history), and "From Earth Day to Green Week in Tandem" (English and French), culminating in participation in World Environment Week. (Resources for locating collaborative partners can be found in Appendix B, with additional examples of projects in Appendix D.)

Collaborative Class Projects

Outside of these large curricular projects, an individual teacher seeking a partner classroom can visit *Dekita.org: EFL/ESL Exchange* (Dieu, Campbell, & Amman, n.d.), which serves as a clearinghouse for international collaborations. *Dekita.org* publishes regular brief reports on projects and activities. These exchanges, like the one cited at the beginning of this chapter, are based on *weblogs* (blogs), which appear in chronological order and can contain text and multimedia. Their primary uses have been for individual journals or freewriting and self-reflection as part of an electronic portfolio. However, the *comment* function makes them an opportune vehicle for peer response, peer editing, shared data collection, and other forms of social collaboration. Although usually only the teacher reads a journal, a blog can be read and commented on by the whole class or the whole world. A teacher can also create a blog specifically for group or whole-class interaction by giving all members the password so that any of them can add items. In audioblogs, such as those found on *podOmatic* (2007), the comments may be voice recordings as well as text. *Videoblogs* (vlogs; see, e.g., *Odeo* [Obvious, n.d.]) add a further dimension, and some, like *BlogCheese* (2006), can record directly online with a webcam, thus avoiding the uploading of huge video files. Part of the excitement of online exchanges occurs when students see their work in the public environment of the Web and receive comments from others around the world. One such exchange, the *Young Caucasus Women* (n.d.) project, engaged university-level women in Georgia, Azerbaijan, and Armenia in thinking about the culture of Central Asia and ways to strengthen democracy in these relatively new republics. International guest "speakers" prompted discussion on a wide range of themes with thoughtful questions, and participants responded on an almost daily basis in the course blog.

Internet Environments for SCLT

This section discusses tools that enable collaborative SCLT, with a variety of actual classroom uses. More tools for collaborative CALL can be found in Appendix D.

Text chats are often the easiest way to get started with content collaborations, whether globally or within a classroom. Exchanges among chatters are much faster than e-mail (see the discussion of keypalling in chapter 6), and thus may be better for intermediate and higher level students than for beginners. In the area of literature, Akayoglu (2005), in Bolu, Turkey, created a series of live text chats for student-led discussions about two short stories, and EFL teachers from various countries also participated. The students, who were language teachers in training, discussed character, plot, setting, and how the stories might be used for language teaching. By spacing out the discussion over several days, with a maximum of seven students per group, Akayoglu could ensure that every class member had a chance to "speak." For the following reasons, text chat organized around a content area is a better language learning environment than simple face-to-face group discussions in class, where the teacher cannot be everywhere at once:

- Chat is saved as a text archive, which enables the collection of detailed data about who responds to questions and how often.

- The chat archive can be used to decide which language items to address.

- The teacher can intervene to encourage every member of the group or class to participate so the best talkers cannot dominate the group.

- A set agenda of target questions or topics and teacher supervision means the group cannot easily get off track.

- Text messaging allows time for lower level students to compose their thoughts before responding.

Invited outside "speakers," as in Akayoglu's literature class, are an easy way to provide an authentic audience for SCLT projects. Other literature collaborations might include book reviews, poetry writing, and the creation of a play (see, e.g., "Kitikula," a student radio play, in Klemm's [2006a] *Schoolmaster's Blog*).

Voice and/or video chat can be incorporated by using a CMS tool such as Acrobat Connect (2006; formerly Macromedia Breeze), which allows small classes to see and hear each other as they write, view Web sites together, watch a slideshow presentation, and write on an interactive whiteboard. For example, González's (2006) English for Architecture class used text and voice chat with presentation software to explore Modernism in Valencia. Grouped into teams, the architecture students prepared for their live oral presentations with a jigsaw reading task in which each student shared information from a variety of text and Internet sources in successive groupings. The accuracy of the teams' final reports depended on each team member's research skills. The student teams then created Microsoft PowerPoint (2007) presentations using photos of buildings. They presented their findings to a live audience of EFL teachers who asked impromptu questions during the text and voice chat. The presentations were similar to the authentic tasks students might perform as part of a design team in an architecture firm: Each group member spoke during a specific part of the presentation, and the teams responded to live questions from the audience. This type of presentation resolves some of the problems surrounding the use of authentic tasks, as described in chapter 8. González (2003) warns that collaborative, task-oriented chat requires careful planning, but she finds it very useful for team projects and the development of content knowledge. She recommends practicing with the chat tool well beforehand to ensure that technical issues are resolved early. Voice chat supported by a webcam is a natural extension of the international chat concept and makes an authentic audience even more real.

Blogs, vlogs, podcasts, and other Web sites with media capability are excellent free substitutes for elaborate Web conferencing systems. These online tools provide a place for visitors to leave a text, voice, and/or video comment. Yeh's (2006) English for Advertising students in Taiwan were placed in teams to create mini video commercials in English. They came up with fictional products, such as Burp Cola and Ooh La La Deodorant. Their videos were then uploaded for critique by peers at *podOmatic* (2007), a media blog site. Yeh's intention in this project was to have students understand the appeal of advertising from the inside out and to work in design teams, as they might in the field of advertising. Like González, Yeh invited EFL teacher colleagues to view and comment on the videos. Video can be created with simple devices like the digital camera and cell phone, and sound recordings can be made with free tools such as Audacity (2006) or at the podcast site itself. Thus, students can become engaged creatively with a minimum of struggle with the technology.

Word-processing software, Web page editors, and *presentation programs* (e.g., Microsoft PowerPoint, 2007; Presentation in AppleWorks, 2004) are commonly available in educational settings and can be inspiring for students. They have added value when used for service learning. Jewell (2006) describes a project in which her high school students created educational posters for an antidrug campaign and brochures on a community issue. Hanson-Smith (1997) describes teaching HyperStudio (2005) to junior high and high school students as they used the program in teams to create presentations about their cultures and cross-cultural friendship. Students can also use these tools to learn about their local surroundings or research global concepts. With *MagazineFactory* (Finnish National Board of Education, n.d.), students can collaborate internationally in writing an online multimedia magazine about their content topic. Soos (2001) describes a number of collaborative multimedia projects in elementary school supported by a modest level of technology. He states that "perhaps the most meaningful learning occurs when students realize that each specific decision made by the group directly affects their future activity as a group" ("Collaboration Among Students," ¶ 3). Of great importance for the success of such projects is assigning each student responsibility for a particular role on the team: editor, webmaster, graphics designer, research coordinator, and so forth.

WebQuests help students learn how to use search engines effectively and to organize the content of their research. For adult students, especially those in an academic track, research plays an important role in content learning, and electronic resources dominate research. In WebQuests the teacher can have a high degree of control over what sites students visit to read and gather information, thus providing a measure of security and privacy. The original WebQuest site (Dodge, n.d.-b) has numerous examples of completed quests that teachers can borrow from, and *QuestGarden* (Dodge, 2007) provides an online template to create a quest from scratch. *LanguageQuests* are WebQuests developed with a specific orientation toward instructed second language acquisition (see Koenraad, Westhoff, Pérez Torres, & Fischer, 2004–2007, for a description of the LQuest project in German or English). Presentations of quests, as with the projects mentioned earlier, can take place in class or online.

Wikis, another important collaborative tool, are Web pages with an editing tool that can be manipulated online like a word processor. While blogs are arranged chronologically, wikis can be organized hierarchically and support internally linked pages. Hence, they are perhaps even more appropriate for developing content-based projects (see, e.g., PB*wiki* [PBwiki.com, 2007], *Wiki-spaces* [Tangient, 2006]). Without having to learn HTML, students can contribute collectively to their knowledge store at a collaborative wiki by adding entries, comments, notes, links, photos, graphics, and so forth to a password-protected site. Commenting, revising, and editing all play a role in content learning. (For more on the additional value of wikis in school assessment and curricular planning, see Figure 9-2; University of Southern California, 2006.) Baya (n.d.), for instance, uses a wiki in her teacher education course to allow students to quickly share ideas, beginning with brainstorming about what makes an ideal teacher, then creating a chart about ways to handle a classroom, and finally giving feedback on each other's presentations on famous figures in education. The wiki space gives all students the opportunity to share and develop needed information. If students have little experience with technology (or if they fear technology), they can e-mail entries to her so that she can copy and paste them into the wiki (Baya, 2006). To facilitate projects such as Baya's, several wikis are now available in the form of online word processors (e.g., *Zoho Writer* [AdventNet, 2006]; *Google Docs and Spreadsheets* [Google, 2007b]).

Digital video provides a cognitively demanding way to create, display, and archive an SCLT project. Gromik (2006b) feels that video creation and editing present a significant means to become media literate in the digital age. He describes a process by which student teams plan a video with storyboards, film the content, and present their work to peers either at an awards night or on the Internet. A number of sites (e.g., *YouTube*, 2006; *Odeo* [Obvious, n.d.];

Figure 9-2. Wiki Contributions

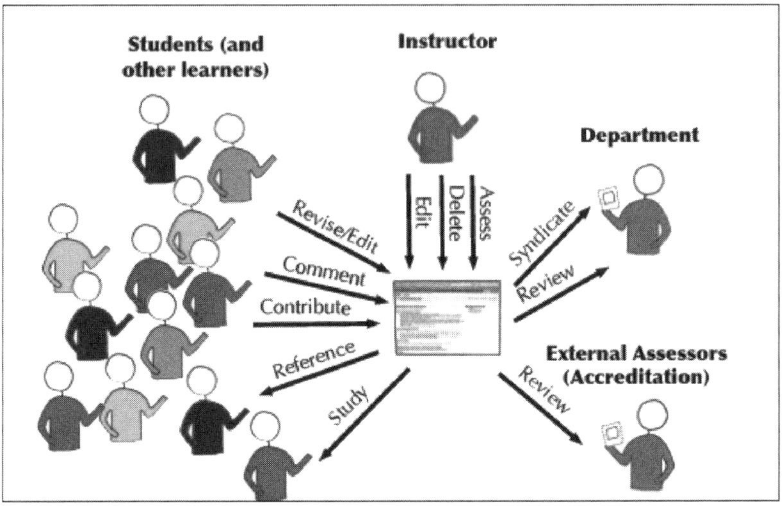

Note. From *What Is a Wiki?*, by the University of Southern California, Center for Scholarly Technology, 2006, http://www.educause.edu/ir/library/pdf/ELI0626.pdf. Copyright 2006 by the the University of Southern California, Center for Scholarly Technology. Reprinted with permission.

Internet Archive, n.d.) offer free space to post videos online where others can review and comment on them. In addition to selecting appropriate content, students will need to learn how to manipulate digital cameras and video-editing software (much of which is free). These tools, however, are easy to use, and sites such as *MightyCoach.com* (Root, 2000–2003) offer free training for many types of video-editing software. Typical projects might include interviewing a local celebrity, demonstrating a complex process, exploring a famous local site, or examining community issues. For example, one of Gromik's student teams filmed at a local park and museum, walking through the location, interviewing the curator, and speaking about the significance of the place. Students had to plan the pathway through the process, master the video tools and design, research the site, edit the product, and present it to the other teams—all cognitively complex tasks. (For examples of K–12 students using video in such projects as electronic portfolios and content presentations, see Springfield Public School District 186, n.d.; for instructions on how to compress and upload files to a widely used blog, see Høier & Hoem, n.d.)

Using Collaborative Learning Tools for Output

To create successful projects with Internet tools (see also Appendix D) you will need to do the following:

Experiment with software and applications. Though most applications have help files, many with graphics and even video support, you may need to write your own simplified directions at a level appropriate to your students. Students are often quick to experiment with tools, and you will soon find "experts" among them who can be encouraged to help others (and you). A screen-recording tool can make a *screencast*, a video of mouse movements on the desktop with a voice recorded over, possibly the easiest way for students to learn a new application—and teach it to others.

Incorporate collaborative activities. Figure out which types of collaborations will help students increase their understanding of the subject matter. More advanced students can participate in voice chat, now a part of many course management systems, including *Yahoo! Groups* (Yahoo!, 2007e). Such aids as a Know–Want to Know–Learned (KWL) chart can help shape useful discussion, whether in class or online, as can blogs and wikis to make notes and brainstorm ideas rapidly and collaboratively. Partner teachers and schools can be found at the collaborative sites mentioned earlier (see also Appendix B), but joining a community of practice (see Hanson-Smith, 2006a) will guarantee reliable guest speakers from among global colleagues.

Determine what kind of language support will be needed. As suggested in the sampling of sites in Appendix C, there are many resources for SCLT lesson plans and teaching ideas online; however, teachers often need to prepare authentic content Web sites and documents for use with language learners at the appropriate input level. Although some software and Web sites for native-speaking youngsters may also work for older students, care should be taken that adult students do not find them insulting. The teacher should take the following steps:

- Research carefully the sites to be used, following several different paths through content material to see if it is really appropriate for your learners. Whereas experienced Web users tend to ignore flashing ads and sexual promotions, these may disqualify a site from use with youngsters or members of traditional cultures.

- If translation or glossing is needed, use *VoyCabulary* (Voyager Info-Systems, 1998–2004), which creates pages with hyperlinks to a user-selected dictionary. Another useful tool, *Babel Fish Translation* (Overture Services, 2006), translates blocks of text pasted in from a document or Web page. If you are working in a lab setting, you may wish to open these tools before students begin reading. They may need help in jumping back and forth between the dictionary or translator and the page containing the text they are trying to read.

- For advanced students, an online concordancer like *The Compleat Lexical Tutor* (*Lextutor*; Cobb, 2006) lets them look up how a word is used in context or find a dictionary definition. Sevier (2006) provides several sample lessons for using *Lextutor* to study field-specific grammar and vocabulary in a content genre.

Prepare pre- and posttests or quizzes for vocabulary and grammar. Incorporating this type of assessment encourages students to be attentive to the language of the passages they read. Extensive reading in a content area may provide excellent input, but students need heightened awareness or *noticing* in order to transform input into uptake (for more on attention, noticing, input, and uptake, see Schmidt, 2001; chapter 11 in this volume). You may wish to use Hot Potatoes quiz software (Arneil & Holmes, 2006), which generates cloze passages from reading texts and visually supported vocabulary quizzes of various types, including crossword puzzles—a good way to make students aware, for example, of the conventions of definition in a subject genre. Hot Potatoes is free on a share-and-share-alike basis, while *Quia Web* (Quia, 1998–2007) is a fee-based online quiz generator that can quickly provide short tests as well as create calendars, grade books, and a variety of activities. Discovery Education's (2006b) *Teaching Tools* include free quiz and puzzle makers. Student answers are e-mailed to the instructor. *WebGapper* (K. Robinson, n.d.) turns any Web page into a fill-in-the-blank exercise on the fly.

Decide on final products. Project-based learning is a natural fit with SCLT, and this volume offers many ideas for extensive projects (see, e.g., chapters 6, 13, 27 in this volume). Other ideas can be found at sites on the PBL *Web Ring* (San Mateo County Office of Education, 1997–2002). The *Problem-Based Learning* site (University of Delaware, 1999) has a clearinghouse of sample syllabi, lesson plans and projects, and links to many other resources for use at the university level. Though definitely not for ESOL without some language support, many of the projects can be adapted while making use of the content resource sites the lessons suggest.

Decide how formative and summative assessment will proceed. Rubrics should be determined well in advance of students' undertaking a creative project, research paper, or WebQuest (Dodge, n.d.-b), and students should have input into their creation. Electronic or paper portfolios can be produced to demonstrate how projects developed and what responsibility each group member took. A Multimedia Project Scoring Rubric is available at the *Multimedia Project* site (San Mateo County Office of Education, 1997–2001), as are customizable rubric makers at RubiStar (ALTEC & University of Kansas, 2000–2006). Where lengthy, multidisciplinary, and collaborative projects are involved, it is always wise to have intermediary checkpoints or multiple drafts so students can see progress in their understanding and language output, take up new directions as needed, and recharge their batteries.

Decide how final products will be presented. Publication of student work for an authentic audience is desirable, as it gives significance to and provides motivation for the effort of completing a project. Publication may take many forms, and often the content area under study will indicate an authentic publication mode (e.g., a slide presentation for a business study, a science fair display for chemistry). In collaborative SCLT, projects may possess the additional value of replicating authentic tasks, as described by Yeh (2006) and González (2006), as well as Susser (2006), who explored creating tourist Web sites and travel brochures with his English for tourism class.

Conclusion

With the wide variety of tools and free space available for uploading, saving, and displaying projects, electronic-enhanced SCLT becomes an inspiring means to authentic learning. To bring this excitement to the classroom, teachers need only start small—even one shared computer can be the entree to group projects, a class magazine, and slide presentations. Add the Internet, and the potential to find and converse with an authentic audience is multiplied many times over. School districts and government agencies offer free training in the most useful tools (e.g., *Openweekends* [KnowPlace, n.d.]). As Egbert (2005, pp. 76–77) cautions, however, students should be fully engaged in understanding the opportunities afforded by the technology, for example, by brainstorming the types of projects they can create. And the goal of learning language must be foremost when planning SCLT.

Explorations

1. In your work group or individually, select a content area that might be used with language students or that you use already with your students. Explore resources on the Web and/or in software. Collect your Web links at *Filamentality* (AT&T Knowledge Ventures, 2007b) or at a wiki or blog so that others may contribute to them. (For examples of a technology-oriented blog, see Hanson-Smith, 2004–2006; Lister, 2005–2006.)

2. Explore some of the lesson plans in your selected content area at *Discovery.com* (Discovery Communications, 2006), *Nova* (WGBH Educational Foundation, 1996–2006), *BBC* (British Broadcasting Corporation, 2006), or another content site that has preplanned lessons. How well do these lessons meet the needs of second language learners? What kinds of preparation would you need to do to use the sites and activities presented?

3. In teams or individually, visit the *WebQuest Page* (Dodge, n.d.-b) and look at examples of quests in the foreign languages category. Then go to *QuestGarden* (Dodge, 2007), register, and create a quest of your own to teach language and content together.

4. Visit the L*Quest: LanguageQuest* (Koenraad et al., 2004–2007) assessment page and use the rubric to analyze your WebQuest. What are the strengths and weaknesses of your quest from the language learners' point of view?

5. Try *VoyCabulary* (Voyager Info-Systems, 1998–2004) and/or B*abel Fish Translation* (Overture Services, 2006) using a language you are learning. Or try the >QUICK LOOK-UP concordance feature at Cobb's (2006) *Compleat Lexical Tutor.* How helpful would you find these aids in reading Web pages?

Chapter 10

Critical Issues: Limited-Technology Contexts

Senem Yildiz

Focus

Ms. Polat is an EFL teacher at a high school in the heart of Istanbul, the largest and richest city in Turkey. She is young and enthusiastic and strikes one as a person open to innovation. However, her attempts to incorporate CALL into her practice have been futile so far because of the limiting context in which she works. For example, the Turkish Ministry of National Education granted two computer labs to her school 2 years ago, with 20 computers of the latest technology in each lab. However, she reports that these labs have not been used even once since they were built because the ministry does not allow the equipment to be used without expert technology staff. The ministry promised to assign such staff to the school 2 years ago but has failed to do so. The school administration is unwilling to use the labs since it does not want to undertake the financial responsibility in case something happens to one of the computers. Now, instead of the labs, teachers use only the one technology room at the school that has a computer and a projector for teacher or student presentations. Meanwhile, the computers in the labs continue to collect dust and become obsolete.

For many teachers, this school vignette will sound familiar. Limited computer use in a school equipped with the latest technology is not new to many classroom teachers. Factors such as a lack of trained personnel, resistance to the use of computers, an inflexible curriculum, and an uncooperative administration put the best technology beyond the reach of many students in schools where technology is indeed available.

Background

Today, although computer technology is the fastest-developing information and communication tool all over the world, it still remains a more Western phenomenon and divides the rich from the poor around the world. The *digital divide*, a commonly used term indicating the socioeconomic gap between communities in terms of access to computers and the Internet, has captured the attention of politicians and scholars throughout the world and has been acknowledged as a social problem. Chinn and Fairlie's (2004) analysis of computer and Internet penetration in 161 countries during the 1999–2001 period shows that computer and Internet access rates in developing countries were 1/100th of that of North American and European countries. Their more recent analysis of the 1999–2004 period, however, shows that computer and Internet access rates were increasing rapidly in developing countries (Chinn & Fairlie, 2006). While in 1995 there were only 6 computers per 1,000 people and four Internet users per 10,000 people in developing countries, by 2004 there were 3.7 computers per 100 people. The percentage of Internet users also rapidly increased to 6% by 2004. Despite this rapid expansion, most developing countries had substantially lower rates of computer and Internet access than developed countries (see Table 10-1).

The World Summit on the Information Society (2005, ¶ 8) reports that while there were 429 million Internet users in G8 countries (Canada, France, Germany, Italy, Japan, Russia, the United Kingdom, and the United States), there were 444 million Internet users in the rest of the world combined. The report also revealed that there were still 30 countries with an Internet penetration of less than 1% (¶ 8).

Table 10-1. Computer and Internet Penetration Rates

Location	Computers per 100	Internet users per 100	Population (000s)
World	12.24	13.65	6,359,891
Developed countries	56.64	51.83	983,477
Transition countries	11.89	13.98	403,681
Developing countries	3.68	5.95	4,972,734

Note. Adapted from *The Determinants of the Global Digital Divide: A Cross-Country Analysis of Computer and Internet Penetration* (p. 33), by M. D. Chinn and R. W. Fairlie, 2004, Santa Cruz: University of California, Santa Cruz, Santa Cruz Center for International Economics. Copyright 2004 by M. D. Chinn and R. W. Fairlie.

The inequitable distribution of computer technology around the world inevitably leads to a widening digital gap between schools in developed and developing countries. Even within countries, there are large discrepancies in the access to and use of computers and the Internet based on factors including school size, locale, and financial status. For instance, in the United States—where 99% of all public schools have Internet access—the ratio of students to instructional computers with Internet access is higher in schools with the highest poverty concentration (5.1:1) than in schools with the lowest poverty concentration. Also, 54% of the poorest schools made computers with Internet access available to students before school, compared with 82% and 80% of schools with the two lowest categories of poverty concentration (National Center for Education Statistics, 2005). In addition, the initial findings of *Learning a Living: The Adult Literacy and Life Skills Survey* (Veenhof, Clermont, & Sciadas, 2005; conducted in 2003 in Bermuda, Canada, Italy, Norway, Switzerland, the United States, and the Mexican state of Nuevo Leon) also revealed large divides in access to and use of information and communications technologies (ICT). Difference in income was found to be the most influential factor in predicting access to and use of ICT. The differences stand out especially between the second, third, and fourth quartiles of income (Veenhof et al., 2005, p. 183).

Traditionally, limited technology contexts have been associated with the lack of computer hardware, software, and Internet access. However, limited-technology CALL contexts also include all physical, educational/institutional, and philosophical constraints upon the integration of computer technology into practice. Warschauer (2002) argues that the word *access* needs to be redefined because the common definition is based on ownership or availability of a device such as a computer, but the meaning of the word can harbor more than that. He claims that access exists in gradations, rather than in bipolar opposition. He goes on to state that

> the actual purchase price of a computer is only the small part of what can be considered the *total cost of ownership*, which includes the price of software, maintenance, peripherals, and, in institutional settings, training, planning, and administration . . . not to mention the price of replacement hardware and software due to corporate-planned product obsolescence. ("Models of Access," ¶ 1)

Warschauer labels the necessary resources for ICT access as physical, digital, human, and social, claiming that the presence of each of these resources contributes to the effective use of ICT. Egbert and Yang (2004), in a different take on limited-technology contexts, draw attention to the good and bad use of computer technology in the foreign/second language classroom, with the implication that bad use of computers can lead to a limited-technology environment.

In this section, the factors that can cause limited technology access are categorized as physical, educational, and philosophical. As Warschauer (2002) argues, the categorization of reasons or resources is completely arbitrary, but it provides a framework for talking about these issues.

Factors That Create Limited Technology Environments

Physical factors

Many teachers work in conditions where the availability and maintenance of computer technology, including hardware, software, and access to the Internet, fall short of expectations. The reason for this shortfall is that the total cost of ownership of computer technology in an educational institution goes beyond the purchase cost of hardware and is seldom included in technology planning. Once the computers and related software are purchased and installed, additional funding is required for planning, training, maintenance, support and upgrading, recruiting technology support personnel, and providing opportunities for training and professional development. Failing to understand the total cost of ownership for integrating computer technology into education and naïvely believing that providing hardware and software will be the end of expenditures often lead to obsolete technology, frustrated teachers, and, finally, failure to achieve the desired results. Nonprofit organizations, such as The Consortium for School Networking (CoSN), help institutions in the United States understand the total cost of ownership of technology through projects such as *Taking TCO to the Classroom* (n.d.). This particular project aims to help school teachers and administrators understand and detail "the Total Cost of Ownership (TCO) involved when they build a network of computers and wire their classrooms to the Internet" (*Taking TCO to the Classroom*, n.d., ¶ 3).

When integrating computer technology into the curriculum, the barriers that first come to mind are mainly physical:

Lack of hardware. This includes computers, printers, and other peripheral devices. The lack of financial resources to fund the cost of hardware is the most traditional cause of limited-technology contexts.

Lack of software. This includes operating systems, generic applications, and specialized and subject-specific software, such as packages for language skills. Catching up with the latest software is a challenge because existing software can go out of date within 1 or 2 years, and versions with more capabilities come on the market.

Lack of resources for infrastructure. Computers require ergonomic furniture, cabling, new room arrangements, and sustainable maintenance and continuous upgrading of systems as components become obsolete. Failing to provide these resources results in broken connections, jammed printers, and software that does not run on an outdated computer or, conversely, on an upgraded computer.

Slow or unstable Internet connections. Even in the age of wireless Internet connections, many schools around the world still have only erratic electrical connections, and school buildings may be so old that it is almost impossible to establish an infrastructure.

Educational factors

Even when computer hardware and software are available for teachers, there are educational factors that can constrain their use.

Teacher resistance. Successfully incorporating computer technology into classroom practice is a complex task that requires technical and pedagogical knowledge. Many teachers are not motivated to gain this knowledge, largely for two reasons, the first stemming from teachers' lack of training and education in this field. J. J. Poole and Moran (1998) argue that in many schools computers are collecting dust rather than being used and that the source of this problem "lies in limited and/or inadequate staff development—not in funding, the time to provide training, or the ability to learn on behalf of the teacher" (p. 1). Currently, many teacher education institutions attempt to prepare student teachers through computer literacy courses in which basic applications and integration strategies are taught. However, research shows that these preservice courses and subsequent in-service training for practicing teachers have little impact on their attitudes, and the transfer from these courses to classroom application is very limited (Moore, Morales, & Carel, 1998). Yildirim, Kocak, and Kirazci's (2001) study of 592 basic education school teachers in Turkey shows that teachers often do not feel competent to use computers, even though almost 66% of respondents had training or prior experience with computers. One reason for this failure is the paucity of support teachers receive later when they actually attempt to incorporate technology into their teaching. (For more on this problem and possible solutions, see chapter 18 in this volume.)

The second reason for teachers' resistance to technology comes from their beliefs: Many teachers are not convinced of the benefits of computer technology. Y. Lam's (2000) case study of second language teachers, for instance, describes teachers who never used the computer lab even though they had full access to it. Brickner (1995) argues that barriers to teachers' implementation efforts are both extrinsic and intrinsic. Extrinsic factors include lack of access to equipment, lack of time for planning, and insufficient support. Intrinsic factors include teachers' beliefs about computers, their teaching approaches, and unwillingness to change. Brickner claims that it is relatively easier to change extrinsic barriers by providing more resources, but changing intrinsic barriers is more challenging because it requires changing belief systems and teachers' institutionalized routines (p. xvii).

Overcrowded classrooms. In schools around the world, it is not uncommon to have 60 or more students in a class. In this context, students far outnumber computers, which results in several students sharing one computer. Yet for students to work productively, they should all be able to see the monitor and have enough space to move around and take notes. Studies show that in 2001, while the average ratio of computers to students was 1:9 in the United States (Cattagni & Farris, 2001), it was 1:35 in Portugal (James, 2001) and even higher in developing countries.

Inflexible curriculum. Unfortunately, many schools, even those rich in technology, cannot rebuild their curricula to integrate the use of new technologies. Even if they wanted to, they are usually mandated to cover a preset curriculum imposed by the local or regional government and are severely limited in terms of budget and staff training to fulfill the demands of the government. Although much educationally sound software is being developed, obtaining software that meets students' needs and fits into the existing curriculum, especially in EFL contexts, remains difficult. Searching for and finding software that supports major curriculum goals, is consistent with existing materials (mainly the textbooks), and is in line with the teacher's approach to teaching—all these are complex and challenging tasks. Guha (2003) lists barriers to integration of computer technology by teachers that include an overwhelming number of educational software titles and Web sites, a small percentage of high-quality software and Web sites, the lack of titles that match curriculum provided by the state and districts, the lack of incentives or support from states and districts to preview software, and the lack of time to prepare and try out software and Web sites.

Lack of institutional support. In many schools, teachers who are eager to incorporate computer technology into their practice face institutional constraints, such as uncommitted administrators or colleagues, insufficient technical support, lack of time for professional development, and very little personal return for hours of work. Despite the recent acceleration of interest in computer-assisted instruction, many school administrations hesitate to encourage teachers to explore new approaches for fear of falling behind the preset curriculum and other schools, and failing to meet state requirements and the demands of parents, students, and other teachers. W. R. Thomas (1999) suggests that "administrators do not appear prepared for their emerging role in technology, and their lack of understanding and resources sometimes creates barriers to change and improvement" (p. 3). In many cases, school administrators and teachers look for shortcut prescriptions, using whatever technology is immediate and available and has the face validity of technology integration into education. Teachers buried under administrative duties in addition to their regular teaching load can rarely afford to spend time investigating the use of computer technology for improved instruction and professional development.

Philosophical factors

Although computers hold the potential for improving learning and developing the higher order skills of critical thinking, analysis, and scientific inquiry, their mere presence is no guarantee of better academic achievement. Neither equipping schools with cutting-edge technologies nor connecting schools to the Internet can promise more effective instruction and improved student achievement.

Believing in the myth of an immediately better education because of the mere existence of the latest technologies, many governments, local administrations, and schools themselves have made substantial investments in technology. For example, between 1991 and 2000, the expenditures on developing information technology infrastructure in local school districts and classrooms in the United States surpassed $19 billion (Market Data Retrieval, 1999, as cited in Slowinski, 2000). In Turkey, the Turkish Ministry of National Education and the nongovernmental Turkish Information Technology Services Association have joined together to increase the number of computers in schools through the Supporting the Computer Assisted Instruction campaign, which asks the Turkish people for financial support to supply 1 million computers to educational institutions (only 1 out of 71 students in Turkey currently has the opportunity to use computers at school). Another recent initiative, the MONE Internet Access Project, undertaken by the Turkish Ministry of National Education (2004), cost nearly US$30 million and aimed to provide high-speed Internet connection to 43,000 schools by the end of 2005. Although these initiatives are based on good intentions and provide a good start, they are not sufficient to improve the quality of education. Unless the computers purchased through these programs are used appropriately, these initiatives are doomed to have very little, if any, return on investment. What might easily be overlooked here is that a school with even the highest quality and latest technology is just another school with lots of hardware if the computer use is not based on solid pedagogical understanding and strong instructional guidance.

Limited Technology Contexts in CALL

Research reveals that although the availability of computers is the first step for successful integration of computers into education, being rich in technology is not crucial for improved learning. For instance, Knutson (2000) conducted a study of 142 second- and third-grade students in California, half in high-technology classrooms and half in limited-technology classrooms. The goal of this study was to investigate the effects of classroom computers on student achievement. Although both quantitative and qualitative data from this study suggest that computer technology does have a positive effect on student achievement, the results of the analysis also show no statistically significant differences in student achievement between students in high- versus limited-technology classrooms. What seems to count is the *use* of technology rather than its availability: Becker's (1994) study of exemplary and other computer-using teachers reveals that not only do exemplary teachers have access to computers, but they also teach in an environment that helps them to be better computer-using teachers. For example, their districts provide relevant and broad-ranging staff development activities, they teach smaller classes, and they teach where many other teachers also use computers. Also, they are better prepared to use computers well in their teaching, and they make greater demands on available resources. Becker points out that economic advantages may not be of great importance once the basics are in place:

> We could have found that exemplary computer-using teachers dispropor-tionately taught at elite private schools or at public schools serving wealthy communities, or that they disproportionately taught high-achieving and high-ability students in gifted programs. But that was not the case. Exem-plary teachers in our study taught in a representative range of communities, schools, and classrooms; but they taught in schools and districts where resources had been used to nurture and support the kind of teaching practice we classified as exemplary. ("Summary and Conclusions," ¶ 4)

The rest of this chapter presents what administrators and superintendents can do to manage limited-technology CALL contexts in their institutions and what language teachers can do to use the available equipment to its full potential in their classrooms.

Examples and Discussion

How Can Administrators Manage CALL Contexts With Limited-Technology Resources?

Provide sustained technical support and budget for maintenance

Problems occur when schools allocate funding for the purchase of hardware and software while neglecting foundational support, maintenance and upgrad-ing, and skilled technicians. Brody (1995) points out that "helping technology users while they are actively engaged with technology at their work location is probably the most meaningful, essential and appreciative support that can be provided" (p. 137). For example, many language teachers find using technology in the classroom a terrifying experience when one or more of the devices does not work, spoiling their perfectly prepared lesson plan. Another frustrating experience for teachers is to find that an excellent software pack-age that fits into the curriculum and their lesson objectives does not run on the outdated computers. Having 30 students waiting impatiently, wondering why the technology does not work, can shake teachers' confidence, embarrass them, and eventually discourage technology use. When such problems occur, immediate support from expert personnel should be available for teachers.

Administrators should consider how they will establish professional help before they start setting up computer labs. Doing so will help to accurately estimate and reduce the total cost of ownership. CoSN, a nonprofit organization that aims to improve successful technology use in K–12 education in the United States, offers such help free of charge. Some major computer companies, such as Hewlett Packard and Apple Computer, also provide guidelines to reduce the total cost of ownership (see Appendix A).

Provide opportunities for adequate teacher training

An important component of technology use is providing teachers with continuous in-service technology training programs that take into account teachers' current interests and needs and supplement their strengths. It is also important to acknowledge that teachers need time to understand and acquire technology skills and ways to incorporate them into their classroom teaching. When these training programs include pedagogical training in addition to technical training, they tend to have more successful results.

Several professional organizations that emphasize CALL and teaching organize annual symposiums, publish journals, offer discussion lists, and provide occasional training programs for teachers. Some examples include TESOL's Principles and Practices of Online Teaching Certificate Program and the TESOL CALL Interest Section's free Electronic Village Online. Others are listed in Appendix A, and additional means of support for teacher education in CALL are mentioned throughout this volume.

Have and share a vision, mission, and goals

School administrators should have a vision of what is possible through the use of computer technology, and they should formulate goals related to how technology can be used to support best practices in foreign/second language instruction. In the United States, almost every school district has a technology plan in place, which typically specifies a 3- to 5-year vision of which hardware, software, and networking capabilities will be purchased and how teacher training, technical support, and maintenance will be funded. Integrating technology into the curriculum, continuously evaluating the impact of technology on teaching and learning, and reviewing and updating the plan should also be part of this vision.

How Can Second/Foreign Language Teachers Cope With Limited-Technology Contexts?

The most important reasons for the underexploitation of computer technology where it is available stem from some general misconceptions about computers and the frustrations that teachers experience with technology use in limited contexts. It is true that it takes a great deal of sustained effort on the part of the teacher to successfully and effectively incorporate computers into classroom teaching, especially in limited-technology contexts; however, with some strategic and pedagogic planning and implementation, the impacts of these constraints can be minimized.

Learning Point Associates offers a series of publications (several of them free) on technology in education. These thorough and theoretically sound resources can help teachers detail their vision for technology use and then find out how best to make it happen. Perhaps the most useful of these is *Teacher Education and Technology Planning Guide* (Fulton, Glenn, & Valdez, 2004), which provides questions that can serve as an "assessment, discussion guide, and planning and decision support resource" (p. 2) for anyone who is interested in the classroom integration of computer technology.

Understand the role of computers in foreign/second language instruction

The computer is an instructional tool just like any other tool that aids learning; it is not a teaching methodology in itself. However, computers are very capable and powerful tools that hold a remarkable potential to improve and enhance language learning in numerous ways. The transition from being merely a tool to being a great support in language learning lies in the teacher's full understanding of foreign/second language learning theories and how computers with their unique features can be used strategically to implement and build on these theories.

Many scholars have listed optimal classroom conditions for second language learning to occur based on second language acquisition research (chapter 1 in this volume; R. Ellis, 1986; K. Johnson, 1995; Meskill, Mossop, & Bates, 1999b; Savignon, 1991). According to Warschauer and Healey (1998), the unique features that support these conditions are multimodal practice with feedback, opportunities for individualization in a large class, pair and small-group work on projects, collaboration or competition, a variety of resources available and learning styles used, opportunities for exploratory learning with large amounts of language data, and real-life skill building. Teachers who understand these conditions and specific features can use computers to create an optimal language learning environment in their classrooms.

Engage in continuous professional development

Current trends in language teaching emphasize process rather than product, integrated language skills, a wealth of authentic input, communication, and development of higher order thinking skills such as problem solving and critical thinking. Computer technology can support these teaching approaches and help teachers make use of resources to their full extent. However, research shows that even though teachers employ computer technologies, they use them to complement traditional teaching methods rather than enhance students' problem-solving and critical-thinking skills (Galloway, 1996; Smerdon et al., 2000; Strudler, McKinney, & Jones, 1999). For continuous professional development, teachers can attend local and international conferences, seminars, and workshops; participate in relevant discussion forums; and follow recent publications in the field. Language professionals can find a thorough list of resources in Appendix A, including resources for program development, software lists, and ideas for using technology and studying technology for personal professional development. (See chapter 18 for more ideas on continuous professional development.)

Plan ahead

Planning ahead of time the goals of the lessons, the procedures to be used during class time, the instructions to be given to students, and the type of assessment to use gives the teacher time to check the available resources and see whether and how technology can help to achieve these goals. Early planning also gives the teacher time to consult technical support for the incorporation of technology. Given that the computer lab might be available for a class only at certain hours of the day or week, the teacher may prefer to prepare hard-copy handouts and distribute them to students before class to avoid wasting precious computer time. For instance, in the lesson before implementing an online treasure hunt activity in the computer lab, the teacher can spend time telling students what they will be doing and distributing hard-copy instructions to be reviewed. Another example would be to use an archived news broadcast on a predetermined topic from a Web site such as *Learning Resources* (Literacyworks.org, 1999–2004; Figure 10-1). Students can take notes on the content while they watch and listen to it as many times as they want during class time. Once the computer lab time is over, students can individually or in pairs prepare a report to share with their peers.

Make informed software choices

Choosing appropriate software for learning purposes is of the utmost importance in the productive use of technology. Teams of teachers can convene and select software based on such factors as pedagogical appropriateness, ease of implementation, technical knowledge of the staff, and constraints on resources. Language teachers should develop software and Web site selection criteria based on their curricular objectives and their approach to language teaching. A number of the Web sites listed in Appendix A offer guidelines for the evaluation and use of software.

Use technology to save time

The computer's potential effectiveness for language instruction is remarkably high due to its unique features of interactivity and the capacity to access and control a wide range of media including text, video, photos, images, sound, and graphics. Some things cannot be done without computers in the language classroom. For instance, in an EFL setting, it would be very difficult to have access to a wealth of authentic audio and visual materials within seconds without a computer and Internet connection. Although giving immediate feedback to 30 students in a classroom would be beyond the teacher's capacity, an interactive Web site or software can do that easily. In addition, certain

Figure 10-1. *Learning Resources*

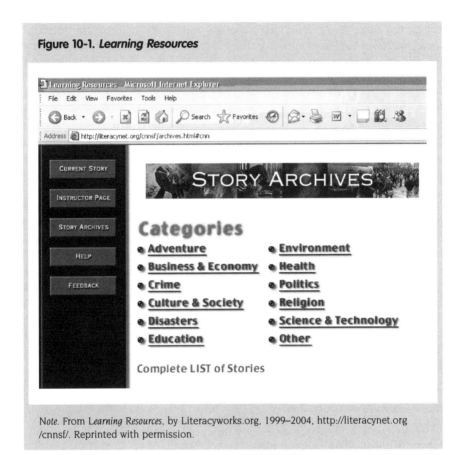

Note. From *Learning Resources*, by Literacyworks.org, 1999–2004, http://literacynet.org /cnnsf/. Reprinted with permission.

Web sites and software programs cater to different learning styles; students can hear and see the language and have a hands-on experience all at the same time. For instance, via Storybook Weaver software (2004), students write and illustrate their own storybooks, and they can review hundreds of images and scenery combinations. In addition to writing their own stories, they can add relevant sounds and music. Completing such a task with computers is a relatively rapid and engaging experience, and it can hardly be achieved in a technology-free classroom.

Students also enjoy interactive Web sites such as action mazes, in which learners are given a scenario and as a result of their choices are faced with the next phase of the story. For an example, see *The Evil Landlady Action Maze* (M. Holmes, n.d.). While such learning environments can provide learners with authentic tasks, reasons to mindfully attend to them, control over their learning, enough time, and immediate feedback opportunities, they also encourage students to practice problem-solving and critical-thinking skills.

Equally important, they save teachers time that would otherwise be spent developing materials and tasks.

Know what technology to use and when

Teachers can also cope with limited technology by making more effective use of whatever is available. In some cases, a lesson can be conducted equally successfully in a traditional classroom environment without computers. Teachers should review the content, objectives, and procedures of their lessons to see whether they need the computer to conduct them. If there is no need to use the technology, that is, if a textbook or any other immediately available material can do the same job, then the teacher may not need to take the time and trouble to use the computer. Similarly, if each student does not require a computer to complete the task, then the teacher can use other configurations.

For instance, if there is only one computer in a classroom, and no computer lab is available, that computer (especially if it is connected to the Internet as well as a projector) can be used for a variety of different activities such as displaying notes, reviewing information, demonstrating software or a Web site, or presenting student projects. Stevens's (2003) Web site *Language Learning Techniques Implemented Through Word Processing* presents ideas for using a word processor to carry out grammar exercises, review information, and develop computer skills. Most of the activities can be completed on one computer and involve the whole class. Similarly, Reason!Able software (van Gelder & Bulka, 2001; a trial version can be downloaded from the Web) features reasoning and critical-thinking activities that could easily involve whole-class discussions with the help of one computer and a projector. Other one-computer activities include the following:

- a *simulation center*, using software such as Decisions, Decisions (2001), where students take on roles to examine fundamental historical and social studies events and ideas

- a *communication station* where, through the use of a microphone and a webcam connected to the Internet, students can communicate with a class on the other side of the world. Godwin-Jones (2005) offers a thorough list of emerging technologies in this area as well as possible activities.

- a *learning center* where a whole class can solve a crossword puzzle that they see on a large screen or add a sentence to an incomplete story by taking turns

- an *information center* through which the class can visit the official Web sites of countries or cities as they study specific cultures, Web sites about authors as they work on novels, or weather sites as they learn about climate

- a *virtual whiteboard* attached to a single computer, which can help students get started with keyboarding, navigating a menu bar, and learning file/folder conventions

Make adaptations to achieve communicative goals

Even old software based on simple drill exercises or a Web site designed for practicing grammar can be adapted by the teacher to promote interaction and creative language production. Egbert and Yang (2004) offer concrete suggestions about how to design an activity that makes grammar drill software or fill-in-the-blank questions optimal language learning tools through pair work and a little adaptation. Their suggestions are based on quickly transforming these discrete-item questions or exercises into information-gap or jigsaw activities.

Provide cooperative work opportunities

Classrooms with fewer computers than students can be seen as a limited technology environment, but such a situation also may very well be used as an advantage in the foreign/second language classroom. The limited number of computers requires students to work cooperatively, and a clearly defined and communicative task can involve them in meaningful and engaging interaction. Free Internet activities such as WebQuests (Dodge, n.d.-b) and low-cost software like Storybook Weaver Deluxe (2004), TimeLiner (2001), Neighborhood MapMachine (2003), and Inspiration (2006) can be used cooperatively. For instance, two or three students sharing one computer can create maps of their own neighborhoods, other communities, or imaginary places with Neighborhood MapMachine, while at the same time reading, interpreting directions, and writing descriptions. These software options help the teacher use content in language instruction and integrate all four language skills. They provide learners with opportunities to interact meaningfully, produce creative language, and work in an atmosphere of ideal stress while maintaining control over their learning.

One caveat for the EFL teacher in classes where students share the same native language, however, would be to ensure that students interact in the target language among themselves. Another point that the teacher should pay attention to is that all students in groups can see the monitor clearly and have enough space to take notes as they carry out the discussion.

Always have a Plan B in case technology does not work the way it is supposed to

Never underestimate the complexity of computer technologies, and always remember the probability that one or more of the devices may not work the way they are supposed to. Having a second plan that does not involve technology, such as bringing a hard-copy handout, an adapted technology-free version of the activity, overhead projector transparencies, or a completely different activity to be used as a substitute, will save the teacher many anxious moments.

Conclusion

The reasons for limited-technology environments in foreign/second language classrooms are numerous. Only the most obvious ones and some suggestions as to how to cope with them have been discussed in this chapter. However, because computer technology is continuously developing, there will always be factors that put schools, classrooms, teachers, and students behind or make their contexts limited in some way. The important thing for teachers to understand is not what you *cannot* do with the available equipment but rather what you *can* do with it, and how this enhances the effectiveness of language teaching and learning.

Explorations

1. In what ways is your teaching context limited in CALL? Which one of these limits is actually due to the lack of computers? Discuss with your classmates or working group possible ways to overcome these limitations.

2. Find organizations, associations, or community groups in your area that provide support and a venue for sharing experiences regarding CALL. How might they help in overcoming the barriers you face in integrating CALL into your teaching?

3. Do you have a vision for the purchase and use of technology in your classroom? If so, what are the foremost criteria on which it is based? If not, draft a vision with the help of classmates or your working group.

4. Outline your priorities in selecting hardware and software. You might organize your list by cost. Explore the resources your teaching institution might have that could be diverted to technology purchases. What kinds of justifications could you make to encourage more or better technology use in your teaching setting?

5. Find and explore three free-access Web sites that you could use with your students, either in a lab or at a one-computer station in your classroom. What kinds of adaptations would you need to make to provide language support and overcome limited access when using these sites?

PART IV

Exposure and Production

Chapter 11 🔳

Theory and Research: Interaction and Awareness

Lloyd Holliday

Focus

Learning a language is about somehow internalising a very complex set of interlocking systems that allow the user to produce and interpret novel but culturally acceptable utterances in appropriate situations. To produce or understand such utterances, the language user or learner has to interact with other users of the language. No matter to what degree human beings are genetically programmed to acquire languages, they need to interact with language environments (and that means with language users) in order to learn, acquire, or become language users. This interaction is not a simple process of identifying labels for things in the environment. A word is not an independent, preexisting item that transparently refers to a preexisting object or action. And one cannot learn a second language (L2) by simply substituting new names for the first language names for things. Nor can a person learn a language by being filled up with knowledge about the rules of a language. People may learn the rules of physics or chemistry, but they do not use that knowledge to produce the chemicals reacting in their bodies, which make them living organisms. Knowing the rules consciously is not how human beings produce the chemical reactions that sustain their lives.

In the same way, knowing about a language does not turn people into language users and producers; being taught the grammar rules of a language does not turn them into speakers of a language. To have learnt a language means to have become an interactive language user and indeed a lifelong learner of that language, constantly updating one's knowledge of and ability to use the language as it changes and partaking in an increasing repertoire of *speech events* (Hymes, 1962/1968, 1972). To become a proficient user of a language or a participant in communicative exchanges in the L2, the learner has to actively interact with other speakers in the L2. In a way, it is like being eased into a workplace situation: feeling your way, learning the new rules of the job, and getting to know the quirks of your colleagues and bosses in the new situation so that you can be fully accepted as a new member of that society; or in language learning terms, becoming a fully accepted, functioning member of a new *speech community*.

A key component of modern second language acquisition (SLA) theory is therefore the study of these interactive processes and the nature of the interaction between the learner and the L2 that most facilitates language learning, and how that interaction can be encapsulated in *structured language learning* environments (e.g., the classroom, self-access centres, CALL and information technology [IT] networks). Research into *input, uptake, negotiation of meaning, negotiation of form, noticing, awareness,* and *consciousness* provides insight into what this interaction looks like and how much of it is necessary for learners to be successful. This chapter explores some of these studies and how their conclusions can affect planned language instruction in the classroom or lab.

Background

Input in its broadest sense can refer to all the target language that the learner is exposed to and that potentially provides the learner with knowledge about the target language. (The term *input* is not intended to mean knowledge about the language in the form of direct teaching about grammar rules.) The origins of research into input from the interactionist perspective commenced with Ferguson's (1971) concept of *foreigner talk* as a specific register of simplified input used by native speakers when talking with L2 learners. Having studied the structural characteristics of foreigner talk discourse, Hatch (1978a, 1978b, 1983) proposed a *discourse model* of SLA and suggested that by using conversational strategies in interactions to negotiate input, language learners are creating their own language-learning syllabus (Snow, 1972) or *comprehensible input* (Krashen, 1978, 1980, 1985). Krashen's *monitor model* proposed that acquisition is a process relying totally on innate factors in the human brain and that deliberately learned language knowledge cannot become acquired knowledge. Although most SLA theorists have no problem with the relatively obvious concept that comprehensible input is necessary for SLA, many differ from Krashen in that they stress the additional necessity for negotiation during interaction to generate comprehensible input and the necessity of deliberate attention to feedback about output.

Interactionists developed the concept of *negotiation of meaning* by borrowing several constructs that had previously been developed in the fields of ethnomethodology and conversational analysis (Garfinkle, 1967; Schegloff, Jefferson, & Sacks, 1977): *other-correction, self-correction, repair, feedback channel, side sequences,* and *negotiation.* J. Schwartz (1980) described repairs in learners' conversations as "a process of *negotiation* [italics added], involving speakers conferring with each other to achieve understanding" (p. 151).

During interaction, both learners and their native-speaker interlocutors have opportunities to check the comprehensibility of their own messages, as well as request clarification, confirmation, or reiteration of each other's messages to achieve mutual comprehensibility.

Pica, Young, and Doughty (1987) confirmed that negotiations of meaning (i.e., *adjustments*) during native speaker–nonnative speaker conversations result in *comprehensible input*. Comprehensible input is the result of input modified by the native speaker at the request of the learners as they negotiate to complete tasks. Interactionists have not claimed, however, that modified comprehensible input is the only factor that leads to acquisition. Swain (1985) pointed out that *modified comprehensible output* is also a necessary requirement for complete native-speaker-like acquisition of the target language and has subsequently examined in greater depth this process of negotiation of meaning in *language-related episodes* (Swain & Lapkin, 1998), showing that they play a role in *uptake*, or language learning. Several studies since have added to the suggestion that in addition to a focus on comprehensible input, a *focus on form* (E. Day & Shapson, 1991; Lightbown & Spada, 1990; Trahey & White, 1993) is required for the acquisition of some linguistic features.

This call for a focus on form and output led during the 1990s to a research emphasis on the learner and the learning process. Some research following the interactionist perspective took a closer look at *intake* or *uptake* (see Lyster, 2001; Lyster & Ranta, 1997). Such research has shown that noticing corrections or *recasts* is often not useful in the classroom because they are not taken up very easily by learners, who appear to be unaware of the correction or of the reason for the correction in their own output. These findings imply that some form of explicit focus of attention is needed for learning to take place. Parallel to and responding to this line of enquiry, some researchers focused on *consciousness* and *noticing* (P. Robinson, 1995, 2003; Schmidt, 1990), and others on how learners may accomplish their language development through the use of language learning strategies (see chapter 15 in this volume).

Meanwhile, another line of debate generally referred to as the *universal grammar* (UG) approach to language acquisition (following Chomsky, 1965) argued that mere exposure to the language to be learnt, or *primary language data* (as it is called by B. Schwartz, 1993), is needed for SLA to occur. The degree and availability of UG in SLA for the parameter setting required has been discussed at length. In a short chapter such as this, I am unable to present all the twists to these various arguments, but the key debate in SLA is about the degree of deliberate learning versus implicit, unanalysed knowledge (the *interface debate*) required for L2 language development (R. Ellis, 1993, 1994, 2001). Current thinking suggests that the following are necessary:

1. both *implicit* and *explicit learning* (DeKeyser, 2003; N. C. Ellis, 2002a, 2002b, 2005), aided by input and enhanced by instruction (Rutherford & Sharwood Smith, 1985; Sharwood Smith, 1981, 1993)

2. *integrative processing* (Izumi, 2002), a term from cognitive psychology, which refers to how learners integrate connections or structures among several kinds of stimuli

3. *learner-generated elaborations*, by which students generate their own examples of targeted concepts or language structures (see Huang, 2006, for a full review)

Discussion and Examples

If one accepts the *weak interface hypothesis* (R. Ellis, 2001) that some focus on form via instructional intervention or design is necessary for SLA (Long, 1991), then the purpose of the debate is to discover the answers to two questions:

1. How much should the learner's attention be drawn to explicit items in the input and output?

2. How is this best achieved, that is, through the teacher's direct intervention or through indirect intervention by developing language learning tasks that create the conditions for noticing of various kinds to happen?

Focusing a learner's attention on form in input can be achieved through various types of negotiation of meaning or input enhancement, including glosses (which are easily accomplished in CALL environments), various visual effects to highlight text (e.g., colour, subtitling, cartoon bubbles, mouse-over text highlighting or revealing hidden text), or sound effects (e.g., volume, pauses, change of pitch). However, focusing attention on form in output is slightly more complex, especially in CALL because the learner's new and unpredictable output has to be reacted to and possibly in real time (e.g., in a conversation). The basic theoretical premise has always been that through a cognitive comparison between their non-target-like forms in the output and the target-like forms presented either in model texts or acceptably rephrased output, learners would restructure their interlanguage to incorporate the newly learnt information about the L2 forms and to accommodate a more target-like L2 system.

To facilitate such noticing and restructuring, Wajnryb (1990) put forward a method called *dictogloss*, in which learners had to reconstruct a dictated passage or one they could access only momentarily. During their reconstruction of the text, students first negotiated the forms of the target text with their peers in a group activity and later compared their completed texts with the original under guidance from the teacher, thus encouraging cognitive comparisons. While observing such lessons in a classroom, I have overheard students arguing about whether the tense form of the main verb had to be *present* or *past* or *present perfect* because the event was supposed to have occurred after or before another event described in the text (see Holliday, 1994). During the reconstruction process, the students were thus pushed by the dictogloss method to explicitly consider the form of their output and relate it to meaning and, after the task, to make a comparison between the form-meaning relationships of their output and the target text. Other types of text reconstruction tasks have been developed (see, e.g., Huang, 2006; Izumi, 2002) to promote learner-generated elaborations in which the reconstructed text may be more closely related to the learner's background knowledge to stimulate deeper processing. The learner is asked to compare and comment without peer negotiation on the differences between their constructed text and the target text. It remains to be seen how much explicit intervention and guidance by a teacher is necessary to obtain the optimum amount of noticing of form and hence in-depth processing and retention of learning or acquisition.

The application of the findings from the research on SLA to CALL is important because computers influence the environment in which learners are exposed to the target language; as such, all these factors—input, output, and noticing—need to be taken into account when designing multimedia language learning products, such as CD-ROMs, and computer-mediated communicative language tasks. Unfortunately, a great number of programs have been written that do not make use of the computer for the best language pedagogy and that do not exploit the potential of computers to achieve desirable pedagogies that previously were impractical in classrooms. There is no doubt that computers can be used for task-based activities that focus on form, but very often the type of focus is no better than a paper-based grammar drill with photo or video illustration, and the ways that computers may be uniquely able to focus attention on form are ignored. The way in which human beings develop cognitively, that is, build a fully functioning language system in the brain that matches the target language systems used by other speakers, needs to be taken seriously in developing Internet- and computer-based language learning support systems.

In addition to CALL activities in which learners interact with multimedia programs, learners can interact authentically with other speakers of the target language via networked computers on the Internet. As an example, Holliday (1995a, 1995b, 1996, 1997) attempted to describe the use of computers in Internet-mediated communication for language learning using *e-mail lists*. It is possible that the repetitive nature of some e-mail, in which writers often tend to comment on one another's messages, may generate distributional cues to syntax similar to those described by Holliday (1993). One of the possible advantages of having asynchronous conversations in writing mediated via computers is that the productive output is available not merely in a linear speech stream to learners, but in a fixed, written medium available for comparison. Whether this facilitates the learner's ability to focus on unknown forms and accelerates their language acquisition needs investigation.

It has been argued that language mediated via computer is an impoverished *nonstandard variety* that cannot supply learners with suitable L2 input. Holliday

(1998) examined the quality of a large corpus of L2 learner output in e-mail from the SL-Lists for L2 learners (Robb & Holliday, 2006) and compared this corpus with two genres from Biber's (1988) corpus, namely personal letters and telephone conversations, using 32 of the 67 linguistic features that Biber uses in his analysis to profile the discourse characteristics of various genres. By comparing the learners' output with an established native speaker corpus, Holliday was able to demonstrate that, by and large, the e-mail messages of L2 learners do provide other L2 learners with grammatical target-like input of a range of language features similar to those used by native English speakers in comparable genres. In the e-mail messages of English language learners, the frequency of use of various linguistic features that characterise genres or styles appears to coincide with those for telephone conversations and personal letters. Differences in frequency can be explained, first, by the medium of e-mail English that is written but more interactive than letters and thus approximates more closely conversations that are not face to face and, second, by the fact that the addressees are in fact largely unknown to the writers in e-mail lists. Holliday (1998) commented that

> overall there seems no reason to believe that the use of English features in computer mediated communications via email are skewed from norms of use by first language speakers of English. And thus there is no reason to believe that second language learners do not benefit from the practise of producing output in email messages nor that they cannot benefit from these same messages as second language input. (p. 144)

However, it must be noted that although such e-mail lists do not have a built-in design to feature feedback on the learner's output, they do provide learners with a context for authentic communication in a common L2, which seems to boost learners' self-esteem and motivation (Holliday, 1995b). More recently, Robb and Holliday (2005) compared the e-mail messages of L2 learners using a traditional listserver and the threaded-message bulletin boards of Moodle (2006) and came to the conclusion that

> the intimacy and communicativeness created by the messages on Moodle as opposed to Listserv may lead to a more tightly knit "speech community" willing to communicate with one another and thus make use of opportunities to write in the target language more frequently and also pay more attention to the responses, leading to greater learning or acquisition. (p. 7)

Since the earliest days of CALL, there has also been an interesting use made of computer corpora of the target language in L2 instruction (Garton, 1996; Tribble & Jones, 1990). A recent example is the use of a Web-based concordancer to teach collocations (T.-P. Chan & Liou, 2005). Learners can also use such IT resources to focus on form in authentic L2 material as needed for their understanding of input and production of comprehensible output.

In a fascinating article, Cobb (n.d.) presented a renewed call for the use of computers in L2 reading by making use of such networked resources. Blogs are another resource that provides an environment for L2 input and output. The modern IT specialist, who is well informed by the latest theories and empirical research findings, should be able to devise learning environments that take these language learning possibilities, strategies, ways of noticing, and the necessity for depth of processing into account.

Now more than ever, it is possible to cater to students' individual needs in terms of cultural background, proficiency, readiness to learn, learning styles, and congruency with special interests and background knowledge, by using multiple networks of choices and paths in an online environment. Yet sometimes such interfaces appear more daunting to users than useful, as they get lost in an intractable maze of network links. Another innovation now more generally available, wireless networking, coupled for example with video-enabled cell phones and personal digital assistants (PDAs), can also be used to provide synchronous real-time streaming video that allows learners to see immediately the real-time world of their interlocutors and their speech events and cultures. It is also possible to make use of wireless networks and PDAs to provide personalized *instant feedback* on learner output or respond to learner *requests for clarification* or information. Again, such technology can retard rather than speed up the process of communication, so care must be taken to use it intelligently in instructional environments. Resources such as podcasting (Stanley, 2006) also make useful adjuncts to providing authentic, immediate, and relevant listening materials for language learning. Particularly interesting are recent developments that allow authentic interactive webcasting (Lebow, 2006). How such a wealth of information can be tamed to provide focused noticing is yet an open question.

Conclusion

To summarise, with the Internet and CALL, teachers should use the medium of learning to provide learners with

- opportunities for human interaction to negotiate meaning
- opportunities to hear/read modified comprehensible input
- opportunities to produce/write modified comprehensible output
- input that allows for a focus on target features of the L2 and a wide range of authentic Englishes, both spoken and written
- possibilities for optimal feedback on output via either synchronous or asynchronous networking

On the other hand, there are also factors that research into input and output has cautioned teachers to be careful of in multimedia environments. For instance, the less context, the more linguistic coding is required. In other words, if the situation and the nonverbal signals are not rich in clues about the message, the speakers need to use more language to make their message clear. Conversely, too much context in interactive multimedia may detract from, rather than promote, an increased attention to form because learners will not need to focus on language to understand the message or interact with the program.

Also, in CALL activities, links or windows offering corrected versions of learner errors (i.e., modified comprehensible input about errors in the learner's production) may not be a particularly useful teaching strategy. Research has shown that learners often simply acknowledge such signal modifications to their output and that these modifications do not lead to learners' further production of modified comprehensible output. Such acknowledgements may not be sufficient to allow for the depth of processing that will ensure that this feedback leads to cognitive restructuring of the learner's interlanguage.

There are many different arguments about which interactive processes are absolutely necessary for language acquisition. I take the view that interaction in a social and verbal sense is necessary whether the L2 is learnt in a second or foreign language environment and whether under naturalistic or classroom-instructed conditions. I also take the view that L2 learners can acquire a language through various levels of conscious attention to the language and that, to achieve success, the language available in the environment needs to be enhanced or organised in such a way that learners can indeed make use of this input at various levels of attention, leading to acquisition and automaticity in performance.

Explorations

1. Record by logging to disk the *input* supplied by a multimedia language teaching program, the *output* supplied by learners while using the program, and all *interactive* responses or *feedback* given by the program or users. Print out this log and examine it to see how many instances of negotiation of meaning you can find. Look for a sequence that contains (a) an utterance indicating nonunderstanding followed by (b) a turn taken indicating a response to this signal of nonunderstanding. Try to see whether the signals of nonunderstanding by the program or other users encourage the student to produce modified comprehensible output and to what extent such modified output is target-like and/or understood by the program or users the second time round. Also, examine the interactions to see whether the program is able to supply modified comprehensible input if the student signals or displays noncomprehension. Draw some conclusions about the value of the program from an interactionist perspective. Is it better for supplying the learner with input or for pushing the student to develop more target-like use of language?

2. Alternatively, you can do the previous task using the logs of a real-time chat session online between language learners or between language learners and native speakers. Such logs can be obtained, for example, during MOO sessions, Voice over Internet Protocol (VoIP) calls using Skype, or chat or instant messaging software, but you must alert participants to the fact that you are logging their conversations, and you need to obtain their permission.

3. Look at the recorded archives of an established e-mail list to see whether anything comparable to negotiation of meaning occurs between e-mail messages (i.e., regard the e-mail messages as extended turns taken by different speakers). Are learners pushed to modify their output in e-mail messages? Can learners obtain modified comprehensible input from e-mail messages?

4. Look at a CALL software program or an online L2 learning environment; try to determine how the program may encourage *noticing* or *awareness* of the L2 forms and their relationship to meaning. Discuss whether this feature is aligned with any of the SLA theories about the psycholinguistics of processing language for acquisition. If possible, keep a record of your students' use of such a program over a period of several months. Do you find any changes in their habitual uses of forms targeted by the program/environment?

5. In examining the archives of a voice or text chat, do you notice any evidence of a *speech community*? That is, do you find speakers/writers using particular words, phrases, or grammatical structures that do not appear in your particular dialect of English? Are nonstandard variations common? What general conclusions can you draw about the speakers' usages?

Chapter 12

Classroom Practice: Language Knowledge and Skills Acquisition

Deborah Healey

Focus

As language professionals, we are concerned not only with the knowledge that learners need to meet their needs but also with what we can do to best organize curricula and environments to help learners achieve their goals. Both fluency and form are important, whether learners just want to read in English to keep up with trends in their fields, need English to pass an exit test from high school or college, or want to succeed in school or work while in an English-speaking country. Technology can be used to enhance a teacher's repertoire, create a motivating learning space, and provide language information. This chapter focuses on how technology can help teachers and learners use language information for language acquisition. In teaching, language information is often categorized by skill area—reading, listening, writing, speaking, and the foundations of vocabulary and grammar—so this chapter uses that organizing scheme.

I use CALL *material* here to refer to software as well as Internet-based resources and activities. *Software* refers to programs either delivered from a central server or downloaded onto an individual computer, but not programs or activities that are solely Web-based. (For a list of CALL software, see Healey, 2006.) *Internet-based material* includes Web sites; programs delivered over the Web (e.g., with Flash, Shockwave, Java, and the like); software employed directly on the Internet; and *computer-mediated communication* (CMC) tools, such as online discussion, chat, instant messaging, text and audio or video weblogs (blogs), and podcasting.

Background

Many current uses of CALL are based on constructivist views of human learning. Constructivism is the concept that learners create knowledge for themselves most effectively with structured assistance (or *scaffolding*) as needed from more knowledgeable partners, be they human or digital, and that such knowledge creation takes place best in problem-solving or task-based environments. Current constructivism owes much to earlier work by Vygotsky (1978) and Dewey (1897). The autumn 2002 issue of TESOL *Journal* explored ways that CALL can be used in constructivist classrooms and learning spaces; work by Warschauer (1997, 1999) is also notable in this respect.

Current views of second language teaching emphasize both *fluency* and *form* (Doughty & Williams, 1998; Schmidt, 1995). Learners also need exposure to language data in authentic contexts (chapter 8 in this volume; Krashen, 1982). Tandem learning environments, online discussion, chat, and other Internet-mediated group interactions offer authentic contexts for language use (see related chapters in the Authentic Audience and Authentic Task sections in this volume). At the same time, research shows the the benefit of a "focus on form" in order for "uptake" to occur (R. Ellis, Basturkmen, & Loewen, 2001, p. 314). Highlighting of key words (Jourdenais, Ota, Satauffer, Boyson, & Doughty, 1995); use of graphics and sound with text (Kumar, 2004); and gap-filling exercises (Vandergrift, 1999), perhaps with audio or video input as well as text—all these can help focus learner attention on salient features. Miscommunication with a computer or an online language learning partner can also be an incentive for attention to form (Lewis & Walker, 2003; Von der Emde, Schneider, & Kotter, 2001).

Multiple exposure is another important element in language learning, especially with vocabulary (Folse, 2004). Multimedia's ability to offer the same information in multiple channels (text, graphics, audio, video) provides an effective approach (R. C. Clark & Mayer, 2003; Mayer & Moreno, 1997, cited in Kumar, 2004). Multiple exposure can also come through focused practice and with *data-driven learning* (T. Johns, 1991). Concordancing—seeing a target word or structure in a number of different sentences—is increasingly informing how teachers think about grammar and how they teach grammar and vocabulary (Conrad, 2000). Learners can use a concordancer themselves to construct and test their own definition or rule (Bowker & Pearson, 2002; C. Hall & Lee, 2006; Sevier, 2006).

Whereas some language learning takes place within highly structured, high-tech course management systems, or with occasional access to computers in a class or lab, a great deal of language learning also takes place outside the classroom in informal learning settings. Homes and cybercafés may provide access to Internet-based language information and tools for learning. Both inside and outside the classroom, a teacher can play a large role in setting the stage for learning and helping learners make sense of their own experience. Teachers can help guide learners to material that is at an appropriate difficulty level and is appropriate to their goals, interests, and individual learning styles; and teachers can encourage both repeated and higher level interaction with the language information that learners encounter. The remainder of this chapter revolves around best practices—how best to use CALL material in a constructivist way, in what settings, with what sorts of learners, and with what additional effort on the part of the teacher.

Examples and Discussion

Very few language courses, much less natural language acquisition settings, build one skill or proficiency area exclusively. Some CALL material is specifically designed to enhance multiple skill areas. These *comprehensive programs* typically have readings with audio and video clips; pre- and postreading and listening exercises; a mechanism for students to listen, record, and playback the recording to compare themselves to a model; grammar explanations; grammar and vocabulary exercises; and some form of electronic record-keeping so that learners can see what they have done and where to go next. Some comprehensive programs are designed to fit Council of Europe curricula or are aligned with state-mandated benchmarks for primary and secondary education in the United States (e.g., English Discoveries, 2005; Odyssey, 2006). Others take a more topical focus, often on vocational education, business, or traveler's language. Most of the heavily audio- and video-enriched programs are on stand-alone CD-ROM or DVD, but others can be delivered either online or via software loaded onto a computer. For example, ELLIS Academic (2003) is a comprehensive CD-ROM-based program; PEAK *English* (Distance Learning, 1998–2005) is one of many online English language course providers; and DynEd offers its comprehensive programs (e.g., First English, 2006; New Dynamic English, 2006) in a hybrid online/CD-ROM format.

Comprehensive programs can be very useful in a *self-directed learning* setting. They provide material in multiple modes, a path through the material, and record-keeping so that learners can see their progress. Assessment is based on multiple-choice or other fixed-response exercises rather than on productive ability, with a few exceptions. Automated writing and speaking assessment technologies are maturing and will probably be incorporated into future programs. Programs that include interaction with other learners, for example, with discussion boards or chat, are likely to keep the learner's interest and create a real-world connection. Without this type of person-to-person interaction, learners easily grow weary of the same interface and activities over an extended period of time. Other risks in extensive use of comprehensive programs include overdependence on a one-size-fits-all solution and merely plugging second language learners, often immigrant children, into the computer without offering other options for language learning or interaction.

Learning Through Reading

D. Freeman and Freeman (2004), Rorschach and MacGowan-Gilhooly (1993), and Krashen (1982) see *extensive reading* as the cornerstone of becoming a better reader and at the heart of language acquisition overall. Even those who eagerly read in their first language find it challenging to learn to read a second language. Those who never liked to read have a more difficult road to tread. CALL material can help in two major ways: by making reading more engaging through use of multiple media and scaffolding in the form of glosses and grammar explanations; and by offering instruction and practice to help readers read more quickly, focus their attention, predict, and recall what they have read.

Engage the reader

Reading aloud to children is a time-tested technique in early literacy development. Parents hold children in their lap, and teachers hold up *big books* to show children the text as they read aloud. *Talking books* on the computer similarly offer the combination of sound and text. Software-based books highlight the text that is being read, as is the case with Just Grandma and Me (n.d.; good for all ages) and Arthur's Teacher Trouble (n.d.; targeting K–6). The better talking books highlight phrases rather than individual words, further encouraging good reading practices. Some also offer clickable objects that move or speak, enriching the story line. Interactive readings are also available online; *On-Line Stories* (Tancock, n.d.), for example, lists Web sites with interactive readings for K–12. The free stories do not have the range of activity that the software programs provide, rarely highlighting as they read or providing clickable objects.

Hypertext documents can also provide scaffolding for readers in the form of concept maps; illustrations; vocabulary, grammar, and cultural glosses; and links to related information. For example, *The Intersect Digital Library* (Center for Electronic Studying, 1999–2001) provides online readings with graphics and study guides. *Wikipedia* (n.d.) is a hypertext encyclopedia with glosses and illustrations, primarily text and graphics based.

Other types of CALL material also encourage repeated and extensive reading. *Whole-text deletion exercises*, such as in The Authoring Suite (n.d.), replace every word in the text by dots or blanks, and students guess words to fill in the text. Such exercises are engaging when learners work with a partner or small group. The learning comes both from using context to predict meaning and from repeatedly reading the text in order to fill in gaps left after the obvious words are guessed. When learners choose to peek at the whole text, it stays on the screen a relatively short time. The speed effect encourages faster eye movement, develops skimming skills, and provides a repeated reading opportunity.

Simulations with extensive text also encourage reading. In SimCity (2003), for example, the task is to create a city that survives and prospers. Students working as a class or small group take roles within the simulation, such as police chief, city planner, mayor, and so forth. The program asks players to make the decisions necessary to successfully create and run a city, and it gives them information in a variety of categories. Because there are time limits within this simulation, students need to skim the on-screen information quickly and accurately to find facts relevant to their role. A simulation that uses longer readings helps students work on scanning to decide whether a specific reading deals with a topic they need to know about. Extensive material to read, a time limit, and some element of competition can motivate students to read faster and more efficiently. (See Using a Simulation for Reading; for more information, see chapter 26 in this volume.)

WebQuests (Dodge, n.d.-b) offer another project-based approach to reading for information. Like a simulation, a WebQuest is based on group work that requires each person to perform a task or role. The teacher provides the framework for the activity, a rubric for the final project, and Web links for the information that the learners need in order to complete their task. Successful completion of the task requires both extensive and repeated reading to be sure the information is adequate and correct. In a WebQuest, reading is a means to an end, not an end in itself, making the effort less visible and more enjoyable. (See the QuestGarden [Dodge, 2007] Web page for interactive templates and examples of quests.)

Focus on specific reading skills

Some CALL material is designed to focus on specific reading skills, including developing basic literacy, increasing reading speed and accuracy with details, finding main ideas, skimming, and scanning. Large packages, such as Reading

---

Using a Simulation for Reading

1. Plan short sessions with specific tasks based on the simulation.
2. Assign groups, and let students choose designated roles within each group.
3. Have small groups of students use one computer or a computer pod to play the simulation.
4. Problem solving: At the end of the specified time, have the students save the game at its current state and discuss their understanding of the scenario with the whole class.
5. If you wish, ask student groups to swap stations, or have them continue at their own station, swapping roles.

Horizons (2006) and Odyssey (2006), offer a staged series of activities to improve reading. They also support practice in most other skills, including vocabulary, grammar, listening, and speaking. These two programs are designed for schoolwide rather than individual purchase and use.

Supplementary material for basic literacy is widely available and generally inexpensive. This includes material for alphabet and phonemic awareness (e.g., audio plus text), orthographic skill building (e.g., handouts to print, *kinesthetic activities* online), stories that build on limited and reused vocabulary, and the like. For child literacy, Web sites, freeware, shareware, and inexpensive software abound. A couple of good sources for child literacy material online are *LiteracyCenter.net* (Literacy Center Education Network, 1999–2006) and *Reading Is Fundamental* (2006). Some good adult literacy sites and material can be found at *AdultEdTeachers.org* (Outreach and Technical Assistance Network, n.d.) and *Skillswise* (British Broadcasting Corporation, n.d.-a).

Computers are particularly helpful for *speed-reading practice*, taking advantage of the computer's ability to provide timed tasks. Whereas the freeware program Reading Acceleration Machine (Pavur, 1999) is just for speed-reading practice, other speed-reading programs, such as eyeQ (2002) and RocketReader (2006), work on training the eye to move quickly and reading in phrases by focusing on more than one word at a time. These programs work well as a supplemental activity in a one-computer classroom or in a self-directed learning setting. Useful features include the ability to add texts in order to customize the activity to learner needs and a record-keeping function to track learner progress.

Teachers taking a constructivist approach can choose to have learners contribute their own texts and exercises to reading activities. Hot Potatoes (Arneil & Holmes, 2006) is an easy-to-use *authoring program* that allows both teachers and learners to create reading exercises that can be timed or untimed; include graphics; and offer multiple-choice, short-answer, or gap-fill exercises. When learners choose texts and create exercises for each other, they have a chance to test their own knowledge. The teacher can also encourage questions that require higher order thinking skills rather than just recollection of details.

Learning Through Listening

Listening is complex. Listeners process both *bottom-up* (from sound to meaning) and *top-down* (from expectation to sound). Elements of listening include the listener forming expectations about the interaction; decoding the speech stream into meaningful chunks; and considering the setting, the relationship between speaker and listener, and the expected response (Dunkel, 1991; Rost, 1990). Whether or not the speaker and listener are speaking to each other directly, there is an interaction between the sound, interpretation, and reaction or response (P. W. Peterson, 2001).

Morley (2001) calls for listening activities that are relevant in content and use, transferable or applicable outside the immediate lesson, and task oriented. P. W. Peterson (2001) stresses the importance of activating students' background knowledge (*schemata*) for top-down processing, practicing bottom-up processing to encourage automaticity, and teaching specific listening strategies. CALL material for listening falls into two basic categories: material that makes listening more engaging and comprehensible (better top-down processing), and material that offers focused listening practice (bottom-up processing and strategy use).

Engage learners in listening

The Internet offers a wide array of potentially engaging, real-world listening material, especially for adult learners. News Web sites (e.g., BBC [British Broadcasting Corporation, 2006]; CNN.*com* [Cable News Network, 2007]) offer audio, often video, and related text. Text and related graphics help evoke and build background knowledge before listening. Adult beginners can read a news story in their own language first, using an online newspaper or an online translator (e.g., *Babel Fish Translation* [Overture Services, 2006]) to get the gist of the story. The online translation is not particularly good, but it does provide context. For children, the audiobooks mentioned earlier in the Learning Through Reading section provide visual context. Children's stories in multiple languages may be found online as well. Activating schemata plays a substantial role in comprehension (Mendelsohn, 1995), so getting the gist of a story in their first language initially can make the same story more comprehensible when learners hear it in their second language.

Finding sites that are age- and proficiency-level-appropriate to learners is just the first step. Teachers also need to create *activation and follow-up activities*, encourage skill building, and tie all the activities to the curriculum. *Randall's ESL Cyber Listening Lab* (R. Davis, 1998–2006) is an exceptional listening site for English language learners because it provides a range of audio and video by English proficiency level and pre- and postlistening activities. Advanced learners can take advantage of downloadable video and exercises from Sorsa's (2003) *English Insight* page, which contains television broadcasts (recorded with permission), so they are rich in real-world content. The segments on controversial topics lead easily into thought-provoking questions that can encourage interest in listening more than once, deeper processing, and greater comprehension. Using audioblogs allows the teacher or students to record a short clip based on a reading, upload it for distribution via the Web, then have others add audio comments. (See Using an Audioblog for Engaged Listening.)

Encourage focused listening

The comprehensive CALL programs mentioned earlier generally ask listeners to find the main idea and recall supporting details. Test preparation software, for tests such as the Test of English as a Foreign Language and the Test of

Using an Audioblog for Engaged Listening

1. Organize topics by brainstorming possible themes with the class. Suggest a provocative question or an issue related to class readings, or invite a fellow teacher as a "mystery" guest to talk about where they live and their local customs.

2. Select a blog provider, such as Blogger (Google, 1999–2006), podOmatic (2007), or WildVoice (Equicast Media, 2006), and create a template for student contributions. All students receive the password to post recordings to the site. Students will need to download audio software such as Audacity (2006) if they are recording on a Windows computer.

3. Set appropriate deadlines for completed contributions, and require a minimum number of comments on others' contributions. Decide how much written text should accompany each post.

4. Offer comments on student contributions, modeling correct expressions and speaking to the content.

5. Follow up at the end of each posting period with in-class discussion of the topic, based on students' contributions.

English for International Communication, also includes finding the speaker's point of view, guessing the setting, figuring out who the speakers are, and the like. The mp3 files at *Interesting Things for ESL Students* (Kelly & Kelly, 1997–2006) provide listen-and-repeat activities of highly specific items, such as irregular verb conjugations (many as jazz chants or songs), in a format that may be saved to a computer or iPod for anywhere-anytime listening. With discrete listening items, the teacher can make the activity more communicative by encouraging students to think about follow-up questions that they might ask in a face-to-face discussion, offering ways to incorporate the items into conversation, and helping learners practice note taking.

Audio or video chat provides an opportunity for learners to listen and respond. Because chat operates in real time, discussions may be under a certain amount of time pressure and do not cross time zones easily. As the ability to incorporate audio and other media into asynchronous (not real-time) online discussion expands, learners will be less pressured to speak quickly and will have time to respond thoughtfully. Audioblogs such as *podOmatic* (2007) and video sites such as *Hellodeo* (Odeo, n.d.) give learners time to think before posting (for examples of focused audio- and videoblogging, see Yeh, 2006, n.d.). With any technology, learners need to be given tasks that require listening for details and that help them formulate clarification questions.

A different approach to using technology to enhance listening and note-taking skills was developed by the Center for Electronic Studying at the University of Oregon. A set of wireless-linked laptops are set up with collaborative writing software, such as ACE (2006), or linked to a collaborative writing Web site, such as *Writeboard* (37Signals, n.d.). The learners see the note taker's computer screen on their own computers and watch as that person takes notes. This setup provides a way to help learners understand the thought process that goes on while skilled note takers listen to a lecture. The teacher can also watch what learners do as they take notes, providing a better idea of student weaknesses in listening comprehension and note taking.

Learning Through Writing

Just as reading is best improved by reading, writing is best improved by writing. There is strong evidence of the benefits of word processing in encouraging longer writing and more revision for both first and second language writers (Bangert-Drowns, 1993; Daiute, 1985; Phinney, 1988), associated in part with the ease of revision, the motivation provided by writing on a computer, and the reduction of anxiety about writing. Writers need to communicate with their readers, which includes having a sense of audience and writing to the expectations of that audience, using peer review effectively, and revising and editing as needed rather than assuming that once is enough.

Engage learners in writing

Writing is rarely easy. Writing is even more difficult when learners are struggling to find a voice in a second language and may not see the point in the process anyway. One of the great benefits of using e-mail and online discussion is that students, even in EFL settings, can see the point in writing in the target language, especially if it is the only language they can use to communicate with their online partner. Doing an interesting group project with someone in another town or halfway around the world is an authentic reason both to write and to use the target language (see Steps to a Successful Classroom Exchange; see chapters 9 and 12 in this volume for more on writing exchanges and the value of blogging).

Broadening the audience base can also enhance motivation for taking the time to edit and revise. Class projects can be put in a public space, such as a newsletter (possibly created using a Microsoft Word [2007] template) distributed in the library or published by students on the Web. Students can participate in e-mail lists (see the *Student List Project* [Robb, n.d.-b], organized by topic and language level) or Web-based discussion groups (such as those at *Dave's ESL Cafe*, 1995–2007), many of which have an audience of thousands. Even posting a message to a class discussion group gives the sense of an audience "out there" rather than one that consists only of the teacher. People may get only 15 minutes of fame, but they are still pleased to have it, and most people are quite motivated at the thought of being read publicly (for more on e-mail projects, see chapter 6 in this volume).

Steps to a Successful Classroom Exchange

1. Find online exchange partners through a community such as IECC (Mighty Media, 2007; e-mail exchanges—especially good for K–12), *eTandem* (Brammerts Ruhr-University Bochum, 2005; bilingual exchanges), or *Dekita.org*: EFL/ESL *Exchange* (Dieu, Campbell, & Ammann, n.d.; blog-based exchanges for adult students).
2. Negotiate curricular topics and decide upon projects.
3. Decide on the number of exchanges and the venue or tools to be used (e.g., e-mail, online discussion, text chat, Web pages, blogs).
4. Decide on evaluation rubrics for projects.
5. Decide how projects will be presented.

Focus on specific writing skills

Writing is the result of more than just feeling motivated. Better communication can be achieved by defining and visualizing an audience, using peer review, and revising and editing one's own work. Online discussion spaces such as *Nicenet* (1996–1998, 2003) and *Yahoo! Groups* (Yahoo!, 2007e) provide ready-made Web sites that classes can use. Teachers or students can set up blogs through providers such as *Blogger* (Google, 1999–2006) for another type of interactive writing. Sites with easily editable Web pages called *wikis* are also used for writing practice online (teachers can create their own at PB*wiki* [PBwiki.com, 2007]). Any and all of these can be helpful for skill building if the teacher assigns specific types of activities and guided writing (see other chapters in this volume for more specific assignments).

CALL material can help learners acquire knowledge about audience, voice, conventions, and usage. Software such as The Report Writer (2003) prompts learners with information about organization, grammar, and style as they create business and technical documents. Learners can also look up information about specific writing skills at online writing lab sites such as *The* OWL *at Purdue* (The Writing Lab, The OWL at Purdue, & Purdue University, 1995–2006). Some online labs allow learners to write in with their questions about grammar and rhetoric, and a tutor at the other end responds. (For information and advice on starting your own OWL, see Rilling, 2006.)

Simulations and WebQuests can be interesting routes to writing for an audience, especially in English for specific purposes contexts. Learners can create charts and graphs of information they have collected, for example, in a business simulation or Web search, and then explain the chart in writing as they would for an actual business report. They can use presentation software like Microsoft PowerPoint (2007) to create an on-computer slideshow with a related handout. Giving a talk to a large group through computer projection is an incentive to focus on form in the text on the slides and in the handouts.

Peer review provides another type of audience. When both the writer and the reviewer are anonymous, the reviewer may be more open to asking questions and giving a critical response. On the other hand, having the opportunity to respond to the reviewer extends the communication between writer and reader. Where the Internet is available, comments posted in online discussion sites, blogs, or wikis are an excellent means to share papers rapidly while allowing teachers to check participation of all members of a peer-review group. Peer review works well with online and/or tandem exchanges, as described earlier.

Teachers also engage in communicating with writers, typically by writing comments in the margin. When a learner sends his or her writing to the teacher electronically, it is easier for the teacher to have a more extensive dialogue with the learner. Some word processors have the electronic equivalent of Post-it notes, with the advantage that the note can expand in size to fit the length of the comment. If the teacher wants to encourage dialogue, the writer can be asked to add a response directly onto the comment. Comments in Microsoft Word (2007) can be relegated to the footnote area (so as not to intrude on the text), show up in a balloon in the margin, or pop up when the mouse moves over an area that has a comment (see Figure 12-1).

Other real-world tools for writing can assist language learners as well. Online dictionaries (both translating and same-language) and thesauruses are widely available, as are style and grammar checkers. These can be waiting in the background for the writer to invoke as needed. Beginning-level writers are unlikely to have the language skills to make effective use of such

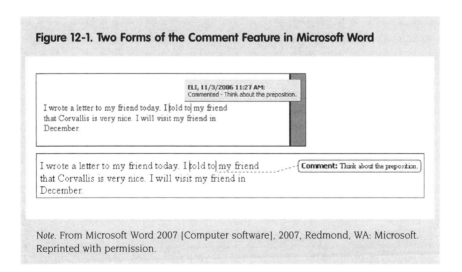

Figure 12-1. Two Forms of the Comment Feature in Microsoft Word

ELI, 11/3/2006 11:27 AM:
Commented - Think about the preposition.

I wrote a letter to my friend today. I told to my friend
that Corvallis is very nice. I will visit my friend in
December.

I wrote a letter to my friend today. I told to my friend
that Corvallis is very nice. I will visit my friend in
December.

Comment: Think about the preposition.

Note. From Microsoft Word 2007 [Computer software], 2007, Redmond, WA: Microsoft. Reprinted with permission.

references, but writers at high-intermediate and advanced levels can benefit greatly from getting the word they need just when they need it. Writers are much more likely to avail themselves of such tools if they are instantly available, rather than having to break a train of thought to cross the room and pick up a reference book.

Learning Through Speaking

Incorporate speech-recognition software

A significant enhancement in commercial software for language teaching is *speech recognition*, the ability of the machine to process spoken input and make some sort of response. A number of DynEd's products, for example, include evaluation of answers to questions, grammar exercises, and dialogues through speech recognition (see Harris, 2006, for a description of speech recognition in such programs). English on the Job (2006), software for adult education and workplace literacy training, provides an assessment of how closely the learner's response matches the written text in a dialogue (see Figure 12-2).

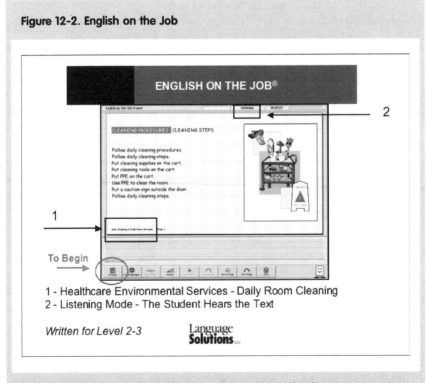

Figure 12-2. English on the Job

ENGLISH ON THE JOB®

1 - Healthcare Environmental Services - Daily Room Cleaning
2 - Listening Mode - The Student Hears the Text

Written for Level 2-3

Language Solutions

Note. From English on the Job [Computer software], 2006, Lake Elmo, MN: Language Solutions. Reprinted with permission.

Computer games that use speech recognition offer *consequence-driven* speaking practice. These games are designed for native speakers, so this option is for users who are relatively proficient. If the game-playing user cannot be understood by the computer, bad things can happen to a character in a game. Unlike a human interlocutor, the game character does not just mutter polite phrases and hurry off when communication breaks down. If the program fails to respond after repeated attempts, the main outcome is frustration on the part of the learner. The best results in terms of language learning, of course, occur when the consequences of being misunderstood in a computer game are striking enough to be memorable.

Using commercially available *speech-to-text* programs like Via Voice (2003) and Dragon Naturally Speaking (2006) can also provide consequence-driven speaking practice. After a "training" period, the software is ready to listen to and transcribe what the speaker says. Advanced speakers with pronunciation that deviates substantially from what the program expects are most able to benefit. A program such as these is generally unable to interpret accents strong enough to cause miscommunication, so the text it produces is the program's best guess, which is often gibberish. The speaker has to shift from a focus on fluency to a focus on form in order to get the computer to transcribe appropriately.

Encourage fluency in speaking

Even without speech-recognition capability, one thing CALL material can do well is to set up an environment that encourages learners to speak. Simulations such as Where in the World Is Carmen Sandiego? (2002) and the Decisions, Decisions series (2001) create a microworld in which learners operate in the target language. The simulated world can take on a life of its own, making communication within that context feel authentic. Simulations often require reading, note taking, writing, and group discussion, making simulations a well-rounded vehicle for language acquisition. (See Crookall & Oxford, 1990; Egbert, 2005, for more details on using simulations, both with and without a computer; see also chapter 19 in this volume.)

Another approach is to have learners create their own scripts, whether for role plays, advertisements, digital movies, or podcasts. Learners have to think about speech and communicate with each other as part of the decision-making process while they create and edit the scripts, then during the acting itself. Editing software for digital movies comes with both Macintosh (iMovie, 2006) and Windows (Windows Movie Maker, 2007) operating systems. Podcasts have an audio (and increasingly video) focus, but can incorporate some graphics and text. Audioblogs easily put together text, graphics, and audio. Audacity (2006) is free audio software that makes the technical side of creating audioblogs simple, leaving the focus on creating good digital audio content.

Working on simulations and creating digital movies are interactions that generally take place in the classroom. Independent learners can create an environment for practice with audio and video chat, as discussed earlier in the Learning Through Listening section. A *tandem learning* setting (Brammerts Ruhr-University Bochum, 2005) pairs people who want to learn each other's language by directly communicating with each other. Most tandem learning has taken place through e-mail and text chat; however, as high-speed Internet connections become more widespread, so do video and audio chat possibilities. Just as with other activities, having a challenging and engaging task is a key factor in what can be learned from the experience. Fortunately for beginners, multimedia chat usually allows the learner to avoid a complete communication breakdown by falling back on typing text. And although creating podcasts is a good group activity, it is certainly something that an individual can do also. Online podcasting (e.g., with *podOmatic*, 2007) requires considerable practice beforehand for a polished product, but is very useful for focused speaking practice. Self-evaluations and written comments from other students—and a global audience—can be posted directly to the audioblog or podcast site. (See Yeh, 2006, for her advertising students' online video commercials; and n.d., for examples from an EFL speech class.)

Encourage accuracy in speaking

Fluency is the first goal of many people who want to improve their speaking, but accuracy also plays an important role in oral competence. Pronunciation is one area in which the computer's ability to repeat as often as the learner desires is a great asset. Besides infinite patience, a computer can bring multiple modes of displaying information for the learner. Most pronunciation programs use animated graphics and, in the case of software, video clips to show a speaker's mouth. This allows the learner to stare far longer and more directly than is comfortable with a human interlocutor. Figure 12-3 shows a screen shot from ELLIS Master Pronunciation (part of the ELLIS Academic suite, 2003).

All pronunciation programs and many online pronunciation sites allow learners to listen to a model, record themselves, and then play back their speech to compare it to the model. Unfortunately, most people have a hard time listening to and analyzing their recorded speech to figure out how it deviates from the model. Software programs have tried to address this difficulty by offering some form of visual feedback. Some programs, such as Sona-Speech II (n.d.) and BetterAccent Tutor (n.d.), use contour diagrams to show pitch and intonation in phrases or short sentences. The results are lines, so they are relatively easy to compare. See Figure 12-4 for an example of visual feedback.

Other software uses speech recognition to determine closeness of fit between the learner's repetition and the model, then uses graphic representations, such as an arrow on a target, a child on a swing, or pins knocked over in a bowling lane, to show how close the user is to the modeled target.

Figure 12-3. ELLIS Video of the Mouth

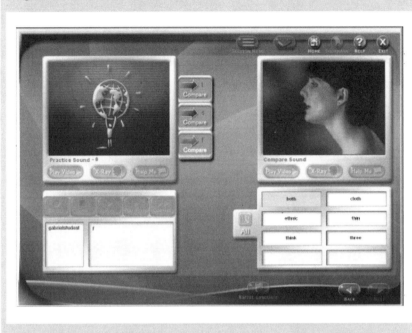

Note. From ELLIS Academic (Version 3.0) [Computer software], 2003, Salt Lake City, UT: ELLIS. Reprinted with permission.

Learn to Speak English (2003), for example, has a meter that indicates where learners' speech falls on a "tourist" to "native" continuum. The software works only with single words or very short snippets of speech, so although it helps learners focus on form in discrete sounds, it does not provide a very realistic learning experience for natural speech.

Building Foundations in Vocabulary

In *Vocabulary Myths*, Folse (2004) asserts that even though vocabulary practice has largely fallen out of favor in communicative classrooms, it is still an essential basis for communication. Gestures only go so far, and only work in face-to-face (or video) communication. The extensive reading called for by Krashen (1982), D. Freeman and Freeman (2004), and others is an effective way to build vocabulary, but when a reader understands no more than 1 word in 20, trying to read a book is an exercise in frustration. Memorizing decontextualized vocabulary in lists may make some learners feel as if they

Figure 12-4. Real-Time Pitch Feature From Sona-Speech II

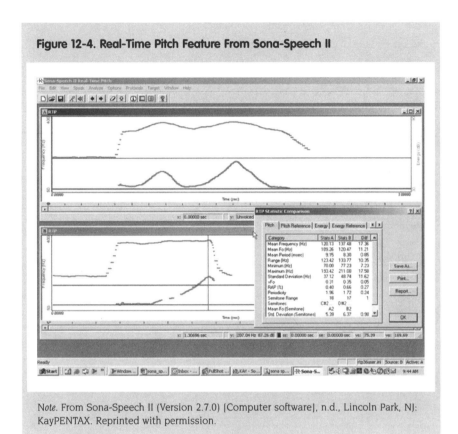

Note. From Sona-Speech II (Version 2.7.0) [Computer software], n.d., Lincoln Park, NJ: KayPENTAX. Reprinted with permission.

are expanding their vocabulary, but there are better approaches to take. Vocabulary learning generally progresses from

- initial recognition ("I know I've seen that word before, but I don't know what it means") to

- recognizing the word as part of a *semantic map* ("I know it's related to this concept, but I don't know exactly what it means") to

- use in a *structured context* (such as a gap-fill from a list) to

- creative, independent use in speaking and writing

CALL tools can give learners control over vocabulary study, allowing them to choose which words to look up, when to do it, and how long to spend on it.

At the recognition level, well-designed programs can help learners fit a word into a semantic category. Software that incorporates graphics and sound, such as the Oxford Picture Dictionary Interactive (Shapiro, Adelson-Goldstein, Hanson-Smith, & Fella, 1999), can be especially helpful in evoking background knowledge and creating multiple connections in memory to the new word. Most learners make their own word lists for studying vocabulary, with varying degrees of success. Some vocabulary programs, such as SuperMemo (2004), take traditional word lists and flashcards to a new level by creating practice sessions that introduce new words and recycle previously practiced words in a systematic way. At the higher end of the price range, the Kurzweil 3000 (2006) offers a complete array of vocabulary study tools that include user-defined word lists and vocabulary journals, glossaries, the ability to insert one's own texts, and adaptive technologies to assist learners with disabilities.

Learning individual English words does not promote accurate usage; only learning in context, with the words that commonly precede and follow (*collocations*), encourages accuracy. The *data-driven learning* approach (T. Johns, 1991) provides learners with language data and lets them draw their own conclusions about usage. For example, the difference between *by* and *for*—a question that often arises with Spanish speakers—can be difficult to turn into a rule. A *concordancer*, a program that has a large collection of text and a search function, can be of help. When queried about the use of *by* and *for*, the concordancer searches its large textbase, finds all the occurrences of these words with leading and following context, and presents those examples to the learner (see Figure 12-5, an example from *The Compleat Lexical Tutor* [Cobb, 2006]).

Figure 12-5. Concordance of *for* From *The Compleat Lexical Tutor*

```
east Asian kingdom.    Britain's plans to press Russia for a definite cease-fire timetable was announced in Londo
heme will be continued with the Balkan strings playing for a dinner the Byron Harveys will give in the Racquet cl
h the Castro regime from the Communist bloc by working for a diplomatic detente and a resumption of trade relatio
e Mayor visited Mr. Buckley at the Bronx leader's home for a discussion of the situation. Apparently he believes
ociation, followed that by announcing plans last night for a door-to-door fund drive throughout their subdivision
ng moderate inflation".   The economist does not look for a drastic switch in the budget during this recovery an
andler who figures to be in the middle of Oriole plans for a drive on the 1961 American League pennant, held the
from Paris, and Mr. Kennedy asked Stevenson to search for a face-saving way- for both Paris and Tunis- out of th
mliner, City of San Francisco, stopped in Ogden, Utah, for a few minutes. Sports Writer Ensign Ritchie of the Ogd
on orders for corn A28 0630 6   pickers.   Except for a few months in late 1960 and early 1961, retail farm
n its sessions last week, liberal Democrats were ready for a finish fight to open the sluice gates controlled by
rmer Vice-President Richard M. Nixon in Detroit called for a firmer and tougher policy toward the Soviet Union. H
back. You must also wear a car coat.    The wardrobe for a foreign bomb is a little expensive. But we couldn't
a new word into international diplomacy with his call for a fresh approach to the problem of peace "at the summi
n bonds.    The bond issue will go to the state courts for a friendly test suit to test the validity of the act,
0  4   boost revenues.    Result is a better prospect for a full payoff by bonds that once were regarded as high
signs. Occasionally she deserts the simple and elegant for a fun piece simple because "It's unlike me".  A29 0230
no democratic institutions and precious little freedom for a generation, and all alternative leadership has been
o the entertainment A32 1060 4   of our guests".   FOR A GOOD MANY SEASONS I've been looking at the naughty
istration should find it does not need the $28 million for a grant-in-aid program, a not unlikely conclusion, it
dministration could not say why $28 million was needed for a grant-in-aid program.   The effectiveness of the go
he courageous actions of President Kennedy". He called for a greater attraction of industry and a stop to the pir
ime his heart, Lucille Ball, can come along. And watch for a headline from this pair any time now. A16 1170  9
there seemed to be feeling that evacuation plans, even for a high school where there were lots of cars "might not
Commissioner Eugene A. Gillis.   Petitions asking for a jail term for Norristown attorney Julian W. Barnard
s tackle Richard Stafford, who is undergoing treatment for a leg injury suffered in the Raiders' 38-7 loss to Tex
sing for faculty families, particularly for those here for a limited time. A24 0530  1     Employes of Pawtuck
```

Note. From *The Compleat Lexical Tutor*, by T. Cobb, 2006, http://www.lextutor.ca/. Reprinted with permission.

As learners look through the examples, they start to draw their own conclusions about when and where to use a specific word or structure. Most concordancers allow the learner to select which textbase to search, which lets learners see how words are used in different ways in different styles of writing or speaking. Using a concordancer works best with advanced learners who can understand the sentences presented to them well enough to see the differences in meaning. A concordancer makes a good addition to an online reference collection in a one-computer classroom, in a lab, or at home. A free online concordancer, *The Compleat Lexical Tutor* (Cobb, 2006), has many suggestions for activities with students and even a quick concordancer on the front page. The Web site *Grammar Safari* (University of Illinois at Urbana-Champaign, n.d.) explains how to turn any search engine into a concordancer, and C. Hall and Lee (2006) suggest more ways of doing search-engine-based concordances. To use a browser as a simple concordancer, see the next section, Building Foundations in Grammar.

Vocabulary work can also be on a need-to-know basis. With an online dictionary, learners can peruse a CD-ROM encyclopedia, a Web page, or another electronic document and have access to definitions and often graphics, sound, video, and example sentences for unfamiliar words during the process of reading or writing. Having a dictionary a keystroke away means that a reader's train of thought does not have to be completely broken by going to get a paper dictionary, then thumbing through to find the word in question—a process that may take so long that readers forget what they were looking for.

Building Foundations in Grammar

Discrete-point drill and practice has its place, particularly with learners who prefer to go from rules to data rather than vice versa. If nothing else, it gives some learners a sense of security to get answers right (in much the same way that some learners enjoy doing workbook drills). Still, far more than just workbook-style drill is possible on the computer, and more is required in order to achieve the automaticity and accuracy in grammar needed for effective communication. Frustration with explicit grammar teaching may have been what motivated Krashen's (1982) emphasis on acquisition rather than learning. However, proponents of focus on form (R. Ellis et al., 2001; Schmidt, 1995) argue that relying solely on indirect learning is not the most efficient approach. A blend of content, task, and form activities, such as readings or discussion with a follow-up cloze, can be very effective in calling learners' attention to grammar in context (Leeman, Arteagoitia, Fridman, & Doughty, 1995).

Hypertext with grammar glosses, such as EnglishNow! (2006) for Spanish speakers, lets learners open a grammar window to see a gloss of that point in the video or text—a sentence, phrase, or word—in terms of the grammatical structures used. This might be thought of as *just-in-time* grammar: Learners get what they need to know only when they request it. Such programs tend not to have elaborate grammar explanations, however, so teachers may want to direct students who want more information to other sources.

A concordancer (described earlier in the Learning Through Vocabulary section) offers a way for learners to explore grammar and discover rules by seeing multiple examples of a specific usage in context, such as *-ing*, *-ly*, or *so*. Even without a concordancer, though, learners can see how words are used by taking advantage of the >FIND function in most word processors and Web browsers. (See Using a Browser for Simple Concordancing.)

The very stupidity of the computer can be another incentive to pay attention to form. With a *conversation simulation* like ELIZA (now online in several versions; see *Eliza, Computer Therapist* [Manifestation.com, 1999–2006), the computer processes what the learner types in and responds according to specific key words and structures. If the student's grammar is off, the computer's response will likely be unsatisfactory or nonsensical. Although not notably accurate in flagging grammatical problems, such programs help raise the learner's consciousness about form.

Collaborative writing online can be another incentive to pay attention to form. If learners are trying to do a joint project and the grammar of one or more of the partners creates miscommunication, the other(s) will encourage attention to grammatical detail, usually by requesting clarification. If the collaboration takes place in real time, readers can ask for clarification on the spot, and meaning can be negotiated in an immediate way. Students are more likely to engage in such *scaffolded negotiations* if teachers encourage them to do so. When a task requires a clear sense of who, what, where, when, and why—such as writing a guide to the city that includes historical details—then grammar will follow.

Using a Browser for Simple Concordancing

1. Preselect two texts online (or ask students to use a target text and their own paper) and the target item to be explored.
2. Have students open the texts in their browser or word processor and click on >FIND, inserting the target item.
3. Have students copy and paste the sentences where the item is located into a word-processor document, highlighting the target word or phrase they have chosen.
4. Have students discuss their findings in small groups and attempt to formulate a general rule or principle of usage for the item.
5. Show the whole class an example of the sets of sentences found for further discussion.

Conclusion

Dede (as cited in Feldman, 2004) describes technology as an *amplifier* for learning that "lets you learn the content faster and lets you master the skills more deeply" (¶ 3). Amplifiers can be both positive and negative. Technology can help put control over learning into students' hands, provide multiple ways of acquiring knowledge that speak to multiple intelligences, and build connections between people separated by time and space. CALL material can bring into any classroom not only extensive reference material and cultural artifacts like newspapers and movies, but also people. Technology can offer multimodal comprehensible input, learner control, and the incentive for language learning that person-to-person contact brings. However, technology can also limit a learner's choices by blocking access to information, rigidly controlling the learner's path through material, presenting errors of fact with the assurance of truth, and confusing superficial online interaction with deep interpersonal connection.

C. Jones (1986) puts this dilemma into perspective in reference to an earlier generation of CALL with an article titled "It's Not So Much the Program, More What You Do With It." As teachers, we need to be aware of what technology can do to and for our learners, and we must do our best to ensure that it is used well, to help learners achieve their goals. CALL material is only as effective in encouraging knowledge acquisition as learners and teachers shape it to be.

Explorations

1. Examine a syllabus to see where technology could be used to enhance learning if time and money were no object. Now take a second look, this time from a low-budget perspective. What differences do you see in terms of expected learner activities and learner outcomes? What adjustments might you make for a one-computer setting or limited lab time? Do your students have additional options for technology access?

2. CALL material needs to fit the teacher as well as the learner. In looking at the types of material in this chapter, which do you see fitting your teaching style best? Why? Formulate a plan that might help a teacher become more familiar with CALL resources, pedagogies, and technologies.

3. Most if not all of the CALL material in this chapter can be used to improve learner knowledge in a variety of skill areas. Take one example activity from those suggested in the chapter and see how many different skill areas it could address.

4. Classroom-based research is a great resource for CALL practitioners. Think about how you could examine the effectiveness of a particular use of CALL material in the classroom. Describe the students who would participate and the questions you would explore. What kinds of activities would students perform? With what goals? What would the teacher's role be? If you currently have a classroom, try out a classroom research project with your students.

5. Many schools, especially in the primary grades, are very concerned about safety on the Internet. If you had to convince an administrator to allow you to use the Internet in your language class, what arguments would you use to allay parental and administrative concerns?

Chapter 13 ⊞

Classroom Practice:
Tasks for Collaborative Learning

Elizabeth Hanson-Smith

Focus

At the beginning of her university's term, Petring (2006) assigned her ESL students in Canada to look at the weblogs (blogs) teachers created as experiments in the TESOL CALL Interest Section's Electronic Village Online. She writes with enthusiasm about her students discovering the variety in these blogs, and her testimonial reflects the sense of wonder that the Internet seems perpetually to inspire, as well as the truly global reach of this communicative tool:

> They absolutely loved the journey to all of your countries. Let's see . . . Anita, the guys loved listening to you sing in Slovenia and when they saw your picture several of them were ready to drop English and start learning Slovenian. Isabel—one student was so surprised to discover the beautiful architecture in Brasilia. JoAnn—what fun they had when your pictures opened them to Google Earth [2007]. Anna (Russia) they adored your daughter's big blue eyes. Uwe—a number of them enjoyed listening to your book blogs. Claudia—the students enjoyed the variety of images you uploaded. Anna (Ukraine)—one of my students immigrated from Ukraine 12 years ago so he was very happy to see your blog . . . and I could go on and on. It was such a joy watching them discover the blogs all of you made and to think that they may have future interactions with you or your students!

Chapter 11 in this volume describes language acquisition or, perhaps more accurately, language development, as a complex process involving far more than a passive exposure to input. The active negotiation of meaning, comprehensible output, and the cognitively based restructuring of the learner's interlanguage appear to play important roles in the development of fluency and accuracy. Blogs, as described by Petring, are just one of many types of multimedia that are readily available for these purposes. As computer software has evolved into the elaborations of multimedia, the teacher has had to face a crucial question: How can the CALL environment best provide both (a) exposure to language (input) in a variety of modes and representations and (b) opportunities for interaction or negotiation with the language (output) in a variety of modes?

Background

Multimedia in a CALL environment means that input from written texts may be enhanced by pictures, graphics, animation, video, and sound as well as hyperlinks to other, explanatory texts, pictures, and so on. Likewise, video and other visuals, as well as a scrolling or highlighted text, may support audio. Multimedia on the computer allows students almost complete control of the number of word or phrase repetitions, the amount of nonlanguage media support, a choice of other languages for bilingual glossing, and instant replay from any point in an audio or video presentation. Likewise, students may respond to multimedia stimuli not just by hitting a key or button but by producing answers in the form of text, audio, and even video.

Although multimedia may be touted as a feature of many highly passive drill-and-grill software programs, computer-using teachers who have made the leap beyond this type of CALL soon find that a task- or project-based approach (also referred to as *problem-based learning, experiential learning,* or *activity-based learning*) is one of the most satisfactory means to ensure an optimal learning environment with multimedia technology and the Internet. The publication of R. Ellis's (2003) volume on task-based learning marks the continued interest in and significance of this approach to teaching languages over the past several decades (see Laborda's [2003] review). For the purposes of this chapter, I treat *task-based* or *project-based learning* (PBL) in both *authentic tasks* (projects or activities that students might complete as part of their career, service learning, or education generally) and semi-authentic or *realistic tasks* (those that imitate the types of activities students will face in the workforce or daily life; see chapter 8 in this volume for more on authenticity). Although Krashen (1982) has noted that the study of language forms or grammar can in itself be a type of input, I exclude from consideration here tasks or activities that are solely related to language exercises or to unfocused, conversational e-mail or chat exchanges, however valuable these activities may be for practice. Authentic tasks must have sufficient complexity to call upon students' higher cognitive processes and demand that they stretch their language skills and engage their imaginative powers. (See chapter 11 in this volume for more on the need for cognitive and emotional engagement.)

Ideally, tasks or PBL in an optimal language learning environment as described in chapter 1 of this volume involve the following:

1. seeking out, synthesizing, and analyzing information in order to comprehend or create higher order knowledge expressed in varied and creative language

2. interaction, that is, the use of language, both input and output, supported by the students' need to know and the scaffolding effects of communication

3. collaboration as a group or team in which specific roles are assigned and knowledge is networked, thus readily facilitating the previous two processes

4. guided assessment, both formative and summative, that includes time for individual reflection and peer evaluation in addition to the teacher's feedback

The role of the teacher in PBL is to devise tasks that encourage language learning or development, motivate students by tapping into their personal interests, and help learners reflect on their achievements. Multimedia in CALL and the Internet are ideally suited to the kinds of challenges that inspire students to grow and learn with what diSessa (2000) characterizes as "pleasure and commitment" (p. ix). This chapter looks at some of the literature supporting the use of social learning and offers examples of successful PBL taken from many levels of language achievement and a variety of CALL environments.

The social aspect of working in groups and collaborating on projects demands communication, and thus peer-to-peer interaction forms a significant element of authentic tasks. Dewey (1938/1963), Piaget (1972), Vygotsky (1962, 1978), and the writers who promulgate activity-based learning and *constructivism* (e.g., J. Brooks & Brooks, 1993; J. S. Brown, Collins, & Duguid, 1989; Wheatley, 1991; Williams & Burden, 1997), support the notion that learners are most effective when they are engaged in communication with others as they study and actively explore subject matter or content and attendant processes together. (For a concise definition of *constructivism*, see Southwest Educational Development Laboratory, 1999.) Although teachers might not go as far as Siemens (2004a), who espouses the view in his discussions of *connectivism* that learning *is* networking, PBL lends itself especially well to authentic tasks that focus on communicative activities, rather than linguistic structures (see Nunan, 1989a, 1993). It may be considered an expression of *situated learning* (see Lave & Wenger, 1991), in which students in an educational community develop expertise and competencies while performing authentic activities in a *zone of proximal development* (Vygotsky, 1987). Of particular interest for further reading beyond the scope of this chapter is Stahl's (2000) work on *collaborative knowledge building*. For the teacher just beginning to work with groups or teams in class, Duncan and Szmuch (2000) provide a brief introduction to some ways to create group rapport.

Among many authors reporting on the efficacy of tasks and PBL for language development in conjunction with technology are Müller-Hartmann (2000), who looks at students reading literature and exchanging e-mail to learn about culture; González (2006), who helps architecture students create live online presentations that replicate the type of team projects they will undertake during their careers; and Land and Greene (1999), who emphasize the importance of metacognitive and goal-driven factors in Web-based tasks. Two prestigious research institutes, SRI (Challenge 2000 Multimedia Project, funded by the U.S. Government Office of Technology; see Penuel & Means, 2000) and RAND (New American Schools study; see Berends, Bodilly, & Kirby, 2002), have conducted long-term evaluation projects supporting the value of PBL. C. Richards (2005) provides an excellent discussion of how the design of Internet-based projects can support effective language learning, including an informative chart comparing traditional lesson design with PBL design. His article is based on four case studies extending from easy or low-level technologies to more complex project designs that teachers may quickly adapt in their own classrooms, depending on their level of comfort with technology. J. W. Thomas (2000) offers an extensive survey of quantitative research on PBL and its relationship to school reform and scholastic achievement.

Examples and Discussion

This section is organized by the degree of difficulty or complexity of technology used in the tasks, so that teachers may begin with simpler types of technology-based projects and add more complexity as their own technological know-how advances. Often they will find that their students, many of whom are already adept at using such technologies as an iPod or a video camera, will bring their own digital competencies to bear on enhancing a task.

Types of Multimedia Projects

Word-processor templates

Jewell (2006) describes word-processor templates to create newspapers, magazines, brochures, or informational posters in a school setting. Templates exist in most common word-processing software or may be downloaded from their respective sites online. Students gain oral practice by devising interview questions and meeting with local community leaders or experts online to obtain information. Such projects combine well with WebQuests (Dodge, n.d.-b; discussed in more detail later) and are useful in service learning, in which students' activities may benefit the community around them. Learners use writing and editing skills to create the final product, which might be a poster, newsletter, or magazine. Visual design elements, photography, and printing form part of the knowledge base, and topics such as school events or community issues (e.g., violence, drug abuse) offer authenticity.

Multimedia presentations

Presentations with software such as Microsoft PowerPoint (2007) or Apple-Works' (2004) Presentation may be used as culminating projects to organize and present what has been learned in any classroom task. Students use oral skills both in creating the slideshow collaboratively and in presenting to a live audience (e.g., peers, parents, the larger school or community) or online with webcasting software that can incorporate such media. Presentation software can also incorporate video and audio media created by students (see, e.g., Al-Othman, 2004; Hanson-Smith, 1997; P. G. Taylor, 2006, who describes the use of hypermedia in art education as producing genuine critical thinking and deep learning experiences). PowerPoint presentations have become a typical activity in business workplaces, and thus learning presentation technology and the attendant visual design and oral presentation skills has a significant authentic basis. The following list describes the types of presentations that my middle school and high school ESOL students worked on during a summer program. Their design teams (see Figure 13-1), crossing almost a dozen languages and 5 years' difference in ages, brainstormed ideas for their projects and where they would look for resources, as well as negotiated who would perform which task within the project. An important motivational element was the presentation of completed projects to an audience of family and friends.

- *hometown magazine*—Students research interesting facts about the city they live in. Output might be a Web page like those produced by Tom Robb's students for restaurant reviews (*Welcome to the Kyoto Restaurant Pages!*, n.d.).
- *jobs and careers*—Students research the minimum wage, housing costs, and job prospects in their area, interviewing prospective employers.
- *where to find it*—Students create a multimedia guide to their school or their community, perhaps including a treasure hunt game.
- *multimedia journal*—Art and graphics come to life as students record interviews.
- *school newsletter*—Posted on the Web, it can be updated cheaply and easily and makes a good international advertising tool for intensive programs (see TOPICS: *An Online Magazine for Learners of English* [Peters & Peters, 1997–2006]).
- *cross-cultural friends*—Students research typical greetings and social expressions in their own language and that of the target country. Internet search engines make it easy to find language and video sites.

- *travelogue*—Students research their home country or town as a place to visit. For examples of unusual travel videos that might be used as models, see *TurnHere* (n.d.).

- I-*search*—Students negotiate with the teacher to research a subject they have a genuine interest in; the project can be adapted to any level (see Macrorie, 1988; for updates, examples, and adaptation to elementary school students, see C. Bowen, 2002). Structured Internet-based searches can follow the WebQuest model (Dodge, n.d.-b) described later in the chapter.

- *curriculum exchange*—Teachers from classrooms in different parts of the world help students decide on complementary projects (see Almeida d'Eça, 2006, for an example of such an exchange between students in Portugal and Florida). The GLOBE Program, for instance, sponsors hundreds of exchanges, mainly in the sciences (see Kennedy, 2006). To find adult education exchange partners, visit *Dekita.org: EFL/ESL Exchange* (Dieu, Campbell, & Ammann, n.d.).

E-mail keypal projects and writing collaborations

These are among the simplest kinds of communicative exchanges to organize. Keypals are much like pen pals, but without the lengthy wait for postal delivery across oceans. Aside from planning fruitful exchanges, perhaps the most difficult aspect is to locate the appropriate level of class or course to engage in writing. One of the longest-running exchanges, the *Email Projects Home Page* (Gaer, 2007; see chapter 6 in this volume), was designed originally for adult beginners with an emphasis on cross-cultural exchanges. These can be a good entry point to PBL for students without much computer access and for teachers with little PBL experience. For more experienced students and teachers, many of the "e-mail projects" now involve Web-based as well as keypal exchanges, and the multimedia projects suggested earlier make good jumping-off points to engaging peers around the world: Classes send each other their projects and discuss both process and product as cultural artifacts.

In one such exchange, C. Taylor and Weser (2005) used a combination of e-mail, voicemail, blogs, a *Flickr* (Yahoo!, 2007b) page for photos of the teams in Japan and Brazil, and *Google Docs and Spreadsheets* (Google, 2007b) for joint online compositions. Both *Friends and Flags* (Eini & Bryant, n.d.) and *The Global Schoolhouse* (Global SchoolNet, 2000a) are sites focused on K–12 schools and cross-cultural exchanges in international collaborations. For adult learners, *Dekita.org: EFL/ESL Exchange* (Dieu et al., n.d.) is a totally advertisement-free, education-oriented blog space where classroom teachers can find each other for cross-cultural Internet exchanges, whether simple or elaborate. Appendix B provides a list of curricular exchanges.

Figure 13-1. Organization of Design Teams for Multimedia Projects

Team Leader
- clarifies and maintains organization
- enforces deadlines

Graphic Designer
- creates flowchart of project
- supervises media layout and/or print or Web page design elements

Information Manager
- handles software and researches software problems
- masters technical manuals

Research Coordinator
- serves as content expert
- works with librarian or teacher to help teammates with paper or Web searches

Editor
- is responsible for writing quality
- consults with teammates on writing problems and with teacher for help
- maintains product standards

Public Affairs Person
- schedules interviews
- makes appointments with outside consultants as needed
- reports to the outside world as needed

Process Observer/Recorder
- observes and records processes
- reports observations back to team and class

Note. See Hanson-Smith, 1997.

Simulations and role-playing games

Whether with software or online, simulations and role-playing games provide students with not only the opportunity to explore a rich, simulated environment containing objects and the vocabulary of common actions, but also excitement, suspense, and a sense of adventure. Most classroom teachers are familiar with such standard simulation software as The Oregon Trail

(1991, 2001; available in several versions, with numerous sites offering additional information and related games) and SimCity (Classic [Electronic Arts, 2006] can be played online for free, and there are many other Sim products, including an ant farm). Sid Meier's Civilization II (1997; still available used, and with a huge online fan base) replicates a number of famous cruxes in world history. A free, downloadable version, Freeciv (2007), has multilingual support (see Figure 13-2; see chapter 9 in this volume for more on content-based software).

Although most online multiplayer or massive multiplayer simulations are filled with exotic creatures, blood, and gore, some ESL/EFL teachers are in the process of developing rich settings appropriate for language learning, such as Second Life: EduNation (Consultants-E SL, 2004–2007; see chapter 19 in this volume). To use simulations successfully for language development, teams of students with designated roles should explore the environment, and beforehand the teacher should walk through various parts of the software or

Figure 13-2. *Freeciv*

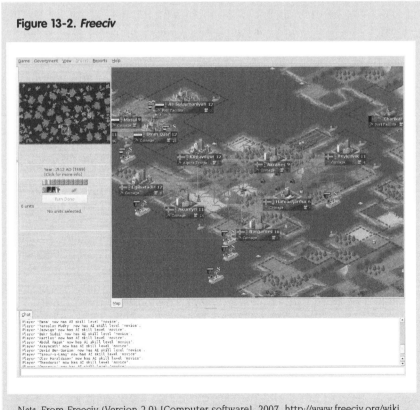

Note. From Freeciv (Version 2.0) [Computer software], 2007, http://www.freeciv.org/wiki/Main_Page. Reprinted under GNU General Public License.

online habitat in order to guide students, create help files (or cheat sheets), and anticipate the kinds of language to be practiced in advance of play. Simulations usually also have a text chat function, so students may discuss their adventures as they explore; they can either gather in triads at one computer or work together from several stations in a networked lab or over the Internet, depending on the software involved.

Once they are familiar with the concept of simulations, higher level learners might enjoy creating their own, as did graduate humanities students in Alberta, Canada, who studied hypermedia narrative by developing a game module themselves using Neverwinter Nights (2006; see Gouglas, Sinclair, Ellefson, & Sharplin, 2006). Bioware, the maker of Neverwinter, produces other games and has links at its site to additional examples of educational uses. (For more about simulations and games for ESOL, see chapters 12 and 26 in this volume.)

WebQuests

WebQuests, a form of research project designed specifically for use on the Internet, have become almost synonymous with PBL (see Garry, 2001). They involve online research, metacognitive skills, and rubric-based assessment. Dodge's (n.d.-b) WebQuest page offers many premade quests, and his *Quest-Garden* (Dodge, 2007) provides a template for creating your own quests or helping student teams create quests for each other. WebQuesting coordinates well with an I-Search (Macrorie, 1988) or Know–Want to Know–Learned (KWL; Ogle, 1986) approach, in which students first determine the basis of their own knowledge or experience with a subject, and then build on that prior knowledge to research what others have done. Generally, a WebQuest sets forth a scenario or problem to be solved, describes a specific task, and lays out the steps to accomplish that task. Students may be organized to work individually or in teams. The teacher may determine in advance what Web sites the students will visit, or make a Web search engine part of the activity. The quest concludes with a rubric or checklist so that students may judge how well they have completed all parts of the task, and it usually suggests how to conduct further research. The tasks in a quest may be highly controlled, which might be more appropriate for young learners or beginners, or open-ended for advanced or older students. For examples of recent WebQuest projects developed at an Electronic Village Online session, join the Yahoo! Group *Creating WebQuests* (Emmert, 2005) and explore its links and files. (See several other chapters in this volume for more on WebQuests.)

Web-page creation

Creation of Web pages has already been mentioned as a way to present multimedia projects to the world. The skill can be readily learned with the many free editors, templates, and tutorials available online (e.g., HTML *Tutorial*

[Refsnes Data, 1999–2006a]). Typical projects that students have completed include the creation and maintenance of a school Web site or newsletter, which might offer a calendar of community events, a message from the principal, interviews, and even an interactive discussion forum (see, e.g., any of the nearly 60 school newspapers linked at Yahoo!'s [2007c] K–12 pages). Web pages are an excellent means to present a completed project, and both word-processed and presentation software documents may be quickly converted to Web pages using their >SAVE AS . . . WEBPAGE functions. *ThinkQuest* (Oracle Education Foundation, n.d.-a) offers an educational Web page creation contest that may inspire students to higher achievements.

Weblogs

Weblogs (blogs) and collaborative blogging are slightly more difficult than static Web pages and may require some knowledge of HTML conventions. They can replace journals, freeing teachers from the burden of lugging home paper notebooks, and they can allow peer comments online. Blogs are an excellent means to keep an e-portfolio, which includes reflection on work during a project, and a summative evaluation of the final product. *Social blogging* or *wikis* allow all members of a group or class to comment and contribute media such as photos, videos, or audio in a password-protected Web environment. For example, as part of the European Centre for Modern Languages BLOGS Project, a group of students blogged about their school field trip to France, taking turns as reporters to interview French learners about their experiences (see *Paris-Normandy* 2005, 2005). Their parents avidly read and commented on the students' experiences, thus creating excellent cross-generational communications. A. Davis (2006b) describes a blog where at-risk students comment on their readings in U.S. history. She believes that asking good questions pushes students to "think harder," and she offers a list of comment starters for use in thoughtful blogging (A. Davis, 2006a). *The Weblog Project* (Montemagno, Good, & Stella, n.d.) provides numerous videos of blog producers, explaining what a blog is and why one should use it, and links to typical types of blog projects. Hetherington (2006) offers instructions for setting up a classroom social blog. *Dekita.org: EFL/ESL Exchange* (Dieu et al., n.d.), mentioned earlier, is an excellent resource for finding collaborative educational blogs. Teachers should keep in mind, however, that students need focus and structure to use blogs effectively for language learning.

Live chat and podcasting

Live chat and podcasting add audio elements to the blogosphere. The equipment and preparation for successful multimedia blogging are somewhat more complex than the projects mentioned earlier, demanding, for example, installation of a desktop recorder (e.g., Audacity, 2006) and headsets, or a digital video camera; however, the kinds of tasks are commensurately more intricate and can include, for example, a regular weekly radio show for a school, community-based projects, and inventive classroom activities, such as the following:

- *podcast book reports*—Students practice composition and oral skills by including a written review, a photo of the cover, and the reading of a typical passage (see Klemm, 2006b, for a teacher's example).

- *serialized radio play*—Klemm (2006a) also podcasts plays written and produced by his English class in Germany. The productions are then broadcast over the local community radio station. He reports that one such play won a prestigious award from the state's Media Board. A bonus is that the radiocasts helped others in the town practice listening to English.

- *voice exchange online*—In a cross-cultural Skype (2006; a free Voice over Internet Protocol tool) exchange at *WorldBridges* (n.d.; a free webcasting site devoted to teaching and learning), Al-Othman and Zeinstejer (2005) prepared students for a live oral exchange between Kuwait and Argentina using asynchronous blog exchanges beforehand, and then followed up afterward with more exchanged writing. A simple task to start podcasting might be the type of holiday- or event-related activity produced by Costa's (2006) students using *podOmatic* (2007), an interface so simple that students need virtually no instruction. They recorded messages about the meaning of Valentine's Day, then decided to have the instructor add a poll where peers and visitors to the site could vote on which message they thought best expressed the day's meaning. In the spirit of the day, students also included links to or clips from their favorite romantic songs.

- *podcasting for speech and pronunciation*—Yeh's (n.d.) speech class students in Taiwan use *podOmatic* (2007) to record their speeches formally, then comment in writing more informally. Instead of carrying around bundles of cassettes and a recorder, the instructor can go online from any computer at her own convenience, listen, and immediately make either a written or oral comment on the speeches.

Video

Video created by students can involve an extensive variety of higher order planning, scripting, visual design, and collaboration skills, thus appealing to students with a wide range of learning preferences. Gromik (2006b) believes that video production, particularly video editing, develops the skills that are crucial for students to have in the digital age, and he regularly teaches a course in EFL and the foundations of video literacy. Some of his students' productions may be viewed at *filmedworld.com* (n.d.) and *Sendai Museums* (n.d.; see Figure 13-3). He helps students formulate their own topics and storyboard their scripts before they begin filming. Typical topics include visits to historical sites, interviews with community members, debates, drama, what-if history, and so on.

Other types of task-based projects, listed from simpler to more complex, include the following:

- *grammar or vocabulary skits*—B. Morris (2006) places students in groups of four to produce four 30-second videos in which they take turns as director, sound recorder, and actors to illustrate the target language item. Student-created short videos explaining grammar are viewable at Drury's (n.d.) site. Technology such as webcams, digital still cameras (most of which can take short videos), or video-capable cell phones are perfect for such nano productions, but the planning and execution of even a short video can require higher level cognitive skills and extensive language practice.

- *digital storytelling*—Personal experiences, social issues, and authentic contemporary topics seem especially appropriate to the video medium (see N. Paul & Fiebich, 2005, for the elements of digital storytelling). For example, a small group of Hernández-Márquez's (2006) advanced students at the Centro de Investigación

Figure 13-3. Hachiman Jinja: Student Video of a Hand-Washing Ceremony

Note. From *Sendai Museums*, n.d., http://sendai-city-tourism-tohoku-university.blip.tv /file/55530. Reprinted with permission from N. Gromik.

en Docencia Económicas in Santa Fe, Mexico City, created a series of interviews dealing with Mexican immigration into the United States. For other models of student video, students might visit the archive of local, high-quality but amateur-produced videos at *Video Nation* (British Broadcasting Corporation, n.d.-b).

- *videoblogs* (vlogs)—Storage of video online, where students can share, compare, and write about their videos, is becoming increasingly available, as server costs decrease. *Ourmedia* (n.d.), *YouTube* (2006), and *Vimeo* (2006) are popular sites for uploading and storing files, and tagging them for future cross-referencing and research projects. Password protection and word-identification security protect students from spam and interlopers, but teachers must still be careful not to expose students to pornography. Thus, access to vlogs might best be limited to adult students. Some vlogs (e.g., *BlogCheese*, 2006) are webcam based and allow video comments from other users.

- *video contests online*—Competitions for learners of all ages (for current lists, search online for "video contest") may inspire student groups to push for the best while providing an authentic audience.

Planning PBL Projects

To assist students in any of these multimedia projects, teachers need to plan the PBL task carefully. Generally, educators agree on several crucial design elements (see, e.g., D. L. Schwartz, 1998): *scaffolding* (both of tasks and of social collaborations), *goal setting*, and *formative assessment*. The use of technology, however, and the additional preparation needed for language learning indicate several further considerations:

Assemble the technology tools. What kinds of applications will be needed to produce and edit files? Some of these are quite expensive; others are free, requiring only that you download from the Internet and install. Will the school's technical support staff allow such downloads? Will you need special passwords to access and install the applications? Will students need video cameras, computer lab time, and Internet access (and at what speed)? Headsets (earphones and microphone) may be crucial in a noisy lab and are often demanded by an application's interface.

Ensure that students can use the tools easily. Most sites have their own help or frequently asked questions (FAQs) pages, but you may need to rewrite these into step-by-step instructions with simpler language that is appropriate for your students' level. However, the newer the technology, the easier it is to manipulate. As I explored a new digital still camera, for example, I discovered by accident that it would take relatively lengthy movies with sound just by pressing a button. If you or your students have only an older camera, you could benefit from a site like *Bubbleshare* (2004–2006), which allows you to add audio files to still photos and present them as a slideshow with sound. *BlogCheese* (2006), on the other hand, lets you post video that you record directly online with your webcam. With the convergence of technologies (see chapter 29 in this volume), students are becoming ever more adept at using and repurposing tools. For example, one teacher recently reported that his 15-year-old had figured out how to use a digital camera to make a phone call on the Internet.

Explore in advance the sites that students will use to create, store, and share their work. Security and protection of student privacy is invaluable. For younger students especially, it may be important to have your school's technology staff reserve space on your institution's own server to archive student work. Conversely, the exchange of information and products with other schools around the world can add a significant element of authenticity and commensurate motivation. Most blog sites now allow either public or private modes of sharing so that you can control access and offer password-protected entry only to other classes that are your collaborative partners. You should practice with the online tools yourself in order to know exactly how the sites function and what difficulties might arise while students are using them.

Outline all the steps that students will take. Experienced Internet-using teachers often create instructional pages with detailed directions, as Costa (2006) did for the Valentine's Day project. If you are using the WebQuest format, *QuestGarden* (Dodge, 2007) offers online templates for building the task; the teacher can closely direct the research process (often the best method with younger learners) or encourage more advanced students to create their own projects. Having learners view a number of Web sites with projects similar to those they will create should stimulate their receptivity to PBL and inspire creativity. Simply letting students loose on the Internet seldom results in a good production. In using media projects with students, I require periodic team reports in outline form that help me (and the students) keep track of their progress.

Scaffold the language used. Much of the language learning benefit of PBL comes from students interacting with each other as they plan, produce, and present their projects. Have students practice appropriate communication strategies, preparing them for new content vocabulary that they will encounter and for the terminology of appropriate discourse (e.g., taking turns, interrupting politely, suggesting, offering advice). Online dictionaries and thesauri such as *Freedictionary.com* (2006), or a Web tool such as *VoyCabulary* (Voyager Info-Systems, 1998–2004; which makes words on any Web site into links to the dictionary the user selects), will prove very helpful as students work through Web sites intended for a native-speaker audience.

Scaffold the collaborative experience. Students also need guidance and assigned roles so that every individual feels responsibility for the process and ownership of the final product. For online collaborations, student preparation for cultural differences can be an important part of the learning experience. The teacher also needs to spend some time finding and consulting with an appropriate exchange partner so that both sides are targeting compatible and appropriate goals. (See Suparp, Todd, & Darasawang, 2006, for research on the scaffolding used by Thai English language learners while playing a simulation.)

Offer multiple evaluation strategies. Students benefit greatly from being encouraged to examine their own processes and strategies while they are in the midst of the task. One means to encourage formative self-evaluation is to build that expectation into the task itself. In the podcast activity mentioned earlier, Yeh (n.d.) requires that students leave self-evaluative comments about their speeches and that learners listen to and comment on each other's podcasts. The audioblog format lends itself well to this type of learning activity, and the evaluative comments provide additional speaking and listening practice. Because these projects are creative activities, they may at first glance appear to be difficult to grade. Teachers should prepare a detailed rubric with the specifications for successful completion of a project and include such aspects as contributions to the team effort, amount and quality of communication, and so on. Links to many kinds of rubrics, including downloadable worksheets, can be found at *Rubrics* (Rollins, 2001). *RubiStar* (ALTEC & University of Kansas, 2000–2006) is a free online tool, organized by subject matter and by type of project, that teachers can use to create a wide variety of rubrics to print and even store on the Web.

Conclusion

PBL activities are exceptionally rewarding for students and can promote optimal language learning practice—both input and output—because they stretch the students' creative and imaginative powers. With the ever-increasing presence in daily life of digital technologies, "educators have noted the emergence of new forms of literacy and the need for educational institutions to revise their curricula and modes of functioning in order to better prepare students for life outside of school" (Parks, Huot, Hamers, & Lemonnier, 2003, p. 28). Students must become digitally literate and deploy technology not only as a means to further their own education, but to earn them a place in the workforce of tomorrow. Less often discussed is the notion that collaborating in teams to complete PBL activities replicates authentic workplace practices, where social skills are as important as factual knowledge. For the classroom teacher facing the more immediate and crucial problems of student engagement and motivation, PBL—particularly when combined with the resources of the Internet—provides the answer to the problems of adequate input and interaction.

Explorations

1. Visit any of the sites in the PBL *Web Ring* (San Mateo County Office of Education, 1997–2002) that are appropriate to your students' level. Explore the variety of projects and tasks and how they are organized. Report back to your group or class on findings of interest.

2. Experiment with the presentation software on your computer (if you do not have a professional program like Microsoft PowerPoint, 2007, download a free program at *Opensource.org* [Open Source Initiative, 2006]). Practice creating templates; adding transitions; and inserting graphics, audio, and video files. As you work, take notes on what you discover, and create a brief handout that could be used by English language learners to master the software.

3. Start a blog of your own to keep a record of your professional growth or teaching practices that worked. (Remember that failed experiments are good learning experiences, too.) What kinds of tips and assignments would help your students use a blog for language practice?

4. Visit some of the podcasting sites mentioned in this chapter. Experiment with creating your own audio recording using, for example, *podOmatic* (2007), or for a more polished performance, a free recorder, such as Audacity (2006). How difficult would it be for your students to access and use the Internet for aural-oral tasks?

5. View some of the online video and vlog sites mentioned in this chapter. (For a more extensive list of resources, see Hanson-Smith, 2006c.) If you have a digital camera, webcam, or video-equipped cell phone, experiment with recording and uploading short videos. Formulate some video projects that you might use with your students, for example, digital storytelling or a grammar skit. Be sure to create an evaluation rubric for the project using one of the templates suggested in this chapter.

Chapter 14 ⊟

Critical Issues:
Creativity and CALL

Keun Huh

Focus

What is creativity?

Is creativity teachable?

Are language and creativity related?

In what ways can language learners be more creative?

Can computer technologies enhance the creativity of language learners?

Can student creativity be fostered in CALL classrooms?

Teachers who are interested in creativity often ask these questions. However, little research and few texts address creativity in the areas of language learning or CALL. In fact, the link between creativity and language is crucial in that language is one of the most important reflections of creativity (Davies, 1998). In addition, creativity is a much-valued asset in today's outcomes-focused world. Therefore, it is important to discuss the links between language and creativity and the development of tasks to enhance both language learning and creativity. This chapter discusses the need for teaching creativity in language classrooms and ways of integrating creativity instruction into CALL.

Background

The Need for Teaching Creativity in CALL

As the world changes ever more quickly and technologies continue to change and evolve at a rapid pace, language students need skills to address the changes in effective ways. They must be helped to respond and adapt to changes rather than being trained to approach a task in a single way. They must actively interpret and organize the information they are given, fitting it into prior knowledge or revising prior knowledge in the light of what they have learned. In other words, the abilities to think about a problem and respond to it creatively need to be taught in language classrooms. Technology can assist in this endeavor.

To respond appropriately and actively in a variety of situations, what skills do language learners need to develop and learn? What opportunities should language teachers provide for students? Exposing students to learning environments that provide opportunities to think creatively and express their thoughts in the target language may be one solution; creative thinking skills and language skills should be integrated into language learning environments. However, before that can happen, teachers must understand what is meant by creativity.

Generally, *creativity* is defined as imagination, the ability to generate novel and valuable ideas, a thinking process that involves several stages (e.g., preparation, incubation, illumination, verification), or the product created by using several thinking skills (e.g., fluency, flexibility, originality, elaboration). Most scholars in the area of creativity believe that it can be developed if the environment supports it (Torrance, 2000; Torrance & Safter, 1990; Treffinger, Young, Selby, & Shepardson, 2002). They also believe that content can be learned more economically and effectively if students are taught in creative ways that make use of creative thinking skills (Millar, 2002; Torrance, 1972, 2000).

In language learning, creative thinking can benefit students by helping them see a problem or phenomenon from various points of view and by offering them greater freedom of expression. For example, some studies have reported that bilingual children express their thoughts more than monolingual children (Hakuta, 1985, 1986; Hakuta & Diaz, 1985) because bilingual people can express the same ideas in different ways and view tasks or problems from more than one perspective. This implies that language teachers can increase English language learners' (ELLs) potential language skills by providing opportunities to promote their creativity. In fact, it is not necessary to wait until ELLs acquire a specific level of fluency to teach creative thinking. Because there are no skill prerequisites or right or wrong answers in creative thinking, all students can respond successfully. In addition, ELLs can increase their autonomy when given the opportunity to express their feelings and opinions without any strict rules or restrictive discipline.

Preparing ELLs to be more creative individuals imposes new and challenging demands on language teachers. However, CALL teachers can systematically promote new kinds of learning—for example, how to think creatively and apply creative abilities for solving problems in and out of school—by capitalizing on the special advantages of computer technologies. Although whether computer technologies can be considered good or bad for creativity depends on how the computer is used, researchers have found that computer technologies have enormous capabilities to contribute to the creativity of learners. Jamieson-Proctor and Burnette (2002), for example, found that computers increased both the speed and efficiency of learners' mental efforts and intellectual development. Other research findings also support the idea that computer technologies contribute to teaching and learning in ways that promote cultural and social learning and interactivity in communication (see, e.g., Wheeler, Waite, & Bromfield, 2002; Zellermayer, Salomon, Globerson, & Givon, 1991). Computer use can change the focus of teaching and learning toward creativity. Namely, if the technology is well integrated, CALL environments may foster the creativity of students and help them enhance their language acquisition and make adaptive responses to complex, novel, and dynamically evolving situations.

The following section introduces the role of CALL in supporting creativity, creativity resources, and examples of creative CALL activities or creativity-enhanced CALL tasks. In addition, learning environments that expose students to more creative language learning opportunities are addressed.

The Potential Roles of CALL in Supporting Creativity

Generating input

In general, one of the major powers of CALL is to introduce new types of input that lead to a richer language learning environment. In addition, CALL provides better, more focused, and more individualized input than many other learning media (Lightbown & Spada, 1994; Pennington, 1996). Computer software and Internet-based programs can offer practice targeting an individual's specific level and subject-matter specialty, and adaptive programs can respond to learner feedback to offer challenges at an individually appropriate level. Computer-based modes of teaching can also increase the variety and diversity of learning opportunities and enrich the quality of the learning experience for the individual learner. Both software and Internet sites can help the learner enter a simulated environment, for example, the undersea world at *DiscoverySchool.com* (Discovery Education, 2006a), where content is offered in visual and auditory sensory modes as well as text. These extended input opportunities may positively affect the creativity of language learners.

In addition, CALL can provide several other input advantages that support language learners' creativity. For example, the great amount of comprehensible information received through computer technologies such as the World Wide Web helps expand ELLs' fluency in thinking and language skills, while offering the means to test what is understood with immediate feedback. By capitalizing on the special advantages offered by a computerized environment, language teachers can make it possible to systematically promote creative foci of learning.

Supporting interaction

Flexible thinking can be encouraged by expanded opportunities for comprehensible input in social-interactive CALL environments, such as e-mail exchanges, bulletin boards, and chat rooms. CALL activities such as interactive software programs and online communication can also promote the creativity of language students by situating them in a more learner-centered environment that increases their attention to active learning. An environment that provides relatively fewer restrictions on their interaction or conversation topic is an important condition for developing creativity by increasing learner autonomy. Through social exchange, students can become aware of their language usage and forms as they read and listen to the way others use language (see Peyton, 2000, for a case study of scaffolding). The teacher can also play a direct role in facilitating students' creative thinking by suggesting collaborative writing activities at a wiki, using interactive online whiteboards for brainstorming, or drawing programs to visualize concepts.

Facilitating creative output

CALL also supports learners in generating language output that reflects creative thought. Clearly, language production in the development of a second or foreign language has a crucial role in providing learners with the opportunity to use language effectively. In particular, when language learners receive a variety of opportunities to produce target language output, such as digital storytelling or video production, they are more likely to increase the quantity and quality of their learning outcomes (see examples in chapter 13 in this volume). Huh (2005) found that ESL students who participated in creative tasks using a computer-mediated communication (CMC) tool increased their language outcomes as the communication proceeded. The frequency and quantity of their outcomes in the electronic discussion forum increased, and their messages showed that the degree of their thinking became deeper and more creative as the communication progressed.

Learning Environments for CALL and Creativity

The learning environment is crucial to enhancing both language learning and creativity development. Creativity researchers agree that, through instruction and practice, all people can develop and improve creative thinking skills. Evidence indicates that creative thinking comes naturally to most children and that creativity can be further developed by a creative environment and a focus on learning (Torrance, 2000; Treffinger et al., 2002). To support such growth, teachers must establish conditions for the development of creativity (Amabile & Tighe, 1996; Csikszentmihalyi, 1996; McCoy & Evans, 2002; Sternberg & Williams, 1996; Torrance, 2000). Contexts that are conducive to creativity must reflect the following qualities:

- exploration
- openness
- learner autonomy

- risk taking
- reflection
- flexibility
- sensitivity to valuing the endeavors of individual learners

These conditions for creativity overlap with those for effective CALL environments (Spolsky, 1989; chapter 1 in this volume). The supporting literature for both areas shows that when students are provided with tasks in supportive environments where they can be motivated and comfortable, and when they have enough time and feedback, exposure to the target language, and autonomy, they have more opportunities to learn creativity as well as language. Therefore, by embracing these conditions, CALL teachers may contribute to enhancing both language learning and creativity development.

The Role of Teachers in Fostering Creativity in CALL Classrooms

As economic and social changes continue at a rapid pace worldwide, the CALL paradigm has changed to deal with an ever-larger amount of information and the increasing need for teachers and learners to communicate across languages and cultures. Language teachers' roles have also changed with the times so that teachers have become one source of language information rather than the sole source. Effective, creative teachers are facilitators of learning, and their strategies include the following:

- finding, selecting, and offering information in a variety of ways based on what students must learn in order to meet their diverse needs
- creating an enjoyable, meaningful, and effective learning environment
- preparing tasks that encourage students to be creators of language and ideas rather than passive recipients
- having an open-minded attitude toward students' ideas and considering the students to be active participants in learning (J. D. Brown, 1997)
- being aware of and using a variety of materials as a facilitator, a supporter, or "a co-inquirer in an intellectual enterprise" (Zamel, 1987, p. 710) to improve students' language and thinking skills
- knowing how to teach learners to interact with the materials effectively

In other words, the teacher's role is a key element to success in a flexible language classroom that supports the development of creative thinking in language learners (Corpley, 2001; Crozier, 1999; Huh, 2005).

Moeller (2002) asserts that teachers are responsible for finding and using the technology that would best fit their students. In other words, whether students are able to produce desired outcomes using computers largely depends on their teachers' level of preparation (for more on this issue, see chapter 18 in this volume). Teachers, therefore, need to be not only sensitive to students' needs but also flexible in choosing and using CALL materials in order to attain the goal of enhancing language and creativity learning in CALL.

Examples and Discussion

Tools and Activities for Computer-Enhanced Language and Creativity

There are many ways to integrate creativity into CALL activities. In this section, examples are categorized by tool type. A creative CALL task does not necessarily mean one that is entirely focused on creativity. Rather, it is better explained as any CALL activity that stimulates or supports creative thinking. The tools used in these tasks are crucial: Various software programs can increase opportunities to develop language learners' creative thinking skills, such as originality, flexibility, and imagination. Web-based resources are also available for learners to generate, express, and test their ideas online; finding information in order to support, challenge, inform, and develop ideas is an important element in the process of using creative thinking. In addition, communication technologies can help language learners think creatively by making connections with other people, projects, information, and resources. Many additional ideas can be found in chapter 5 of Egbert's (2005) CALL *Essentials*.

Software Applications

Word-processing software

Many teachers use creative writing activities to promote language production and creative thinking. Giving learners a choice of topics can promote creativity, and language learning can be developed by background readings, discussion, and sharing. For example, a writing prompt might say, *Imagine what your life would be like if you lived 1,000 years ago*. After some study of the past, students would use their creative thinking to complete the task by imagining their roles and lives. A group brainstorm, for example, at a collaborative class weblog (blog) or wiki, or in the classroom itself, would help students share their imaginary scenarios and inspire new ideas. They then would type their insights using word-processing software. During this process, they could use online dictionaries or thesauri to find new vocabulary or search additional Web-based resources to learn more about life in the past. Peers could use the comment function in the word-processing software to focus on language and or creativity in responding to the author.

Authoring and productivity software

Authoring software offers various tools for students to use in creating their own works, such as stories, reports, and slideshows combined with clip art, personal artwork, digital images, and sounds. Packages such as Inspiration (2006) and the Imagination Express series (e.g., Destination: Ocean, 1995; Destination: Rain Forest, 1995) can support creative thinking development and language learning by providing opportunities for idea generation. Students also can use drawing software such as Microsoft Paint (see Microsoft, 2007a) or an online virtual whiteboard, such as *Groupboard* (Group Technologies, n. d.) to create pictures of imaginary places or to design their own creatures on the computer. In a simulated online environment, such as *Second Life: EduNation* (Consultants-E SL, 2004–2007), students may create a whole world, sharing its development and exploration with others in a chat window (for more on virtual learning environments, see chapter 26 in this volume). These same tools allow teachers to create learner-appropriate tasks at different levels of fluency and creativity. Authoring software makes it possible to extend learning opportunities by providing various activities for language learning and creative thinking.

Problem-solving software

The most popular CALL creativity tasks are brainstorming and problem solving with the aid of the computer. Problem solving is one of the most effective ways to foster language learners' creative thinking abilities while enhancing language skills. Many researchers in the area of creativity believe that problem solving itself is creative and that creativity is better understood if placed within a problem-solving structure (Guilford, 1976; Hinton, 1968; Torrance, 2000). *ThinkQuest* (Oracle Education Foundation, n.d.-a) provides many kinds of puzzles and thinking activities to encourage creative abilities, as does *The Internet TESL Journal* (1995–2007a). In CALL, skills for seeking a solution to a problem can continually improve while a language learner works with challenging tasks that require creativity in the target language.

Problem-solving software programs such as the ClueFinders series may help teachers design CALL lessons that provide creative thinking opportunities. For example, in ClueFinders 4th Grade Adventures (1999), students are asked to interpret maps and search for clues about mysterious scrolls. While engaging in the tasks, students have opportunities to think flexibly and originally as they practice and learn language content and skills such as vocabulary, reading comprehension, grammar, and spelling. Moreover, students can test their assumptions about different cultures and geographies while working in a particular environment (e.g., ancient Egypt, a volcanic island, a rain forest).

Presentation software

Presentation software such as Microsoft PowerPoint (2007) and Apple's Keynote (2006) enables learners to present and celebrate their work with a range of audiences from a classroom of peers to Web site viewers. Using presentation software, students can publish work from all areas of the curriculum, including language learning products, produced alone or with classmates. The process of designing, creating, and presenting multimedia in the target language expands students' awareness of their work process, outcome, and audience. In addition, students can practice their creative thinking throughout the processes of brainstorming ideas, creating the title and content, and designing the format. Students can use Ultimate Writing and Creativity Center (n.d.) as a publishing tool for school or personal projects. The software makes it easy for students to transform their own stories into multimedia presentations. Language learners can embellish on words and ideas using images, music themes, and font colors while creating various products such as Web pages, book reports, greeting cards, or banners.

Web-Based Resources

User-created Web resources

In recent years, a number of Web sites created by language teachers and educational organizations offer resources that can be used for creativity-integrated CALL lessons. These include *ThinkQuest* (Oracle Education Foundation, n.d.-a) and *DiscoverySchool.com* (Discovery Education, 2006a), mentioned earlier, as well as blogs, photoblogs, and podcasting sites for the creation of radio plays and digital storytelling. Language learners can also participate in inquiry activities, such as WebQuests (Dodge, n.d.-b), which require both language leaning and creative thinking (for more on creativity in language learning, see chapter 20 in this volume). In addition, students can create their own Web sites where they can publish a wide variety of creative work, such as scanned images of their own art work, stories and poetry they have written, and sound files of their songs. Web publishing enhances language learning and promotes creative thinking not only by allowing students to publish content but also by requiring students to think about design issues and solve other problems that arise in the creation of Web pages. Tutorials and tips for publishing student-made Web pages can be found at the Web sites listed in Table 14-1.

The Web as a shared space

In a CALL task carried out with creativity training in mind, teachers must allow students to demonstrate not only the processes of development, manipulation, and evaluation of their work, but also a growing awareness of the potential creativity in each other's work. Students have opportunities to consider different perspectives by sharing each other's learning products. The Internet can become a shared space where ELLs are motivated by having real audiences from all over the world. In this space, all students' pieces can be modeled for each other. Moreover, a Web publishing activity provides collaborative

Table 14-1. Resources for Student-Made Web Pages

Personalizing Web pages	*Designing an Autobiographical Webpage Using FrontPage 2003* (n.d.) Directions for a common Web editor
Creating a school Web site	*Tips for Developing School Web Pages* (Payton, 1997–1999) Design and how-to directions
Integrating the Internet into the classroom	*Collaborate 1: With One Person or Classroom* (Payton, n.d.) Integrating the Internet into the curriculum
Publishing Web pages on a school Web site	*Internet Assignment: Publishing Webpages* (Gibbs, 2006) Sample Web publishing instructions
Learning HTML code basics	*Vance's e-Zguide "10+ steps to creating simple HTML files"* (Stevens, 2005) A primer for writing code

learning experiences that help students expand their range of thinking and communication skills (see, e.g., the podcasts, blogs, and student Web pages described in chapter 13 in this volume). Like many other sites, the *ThinkQuest Library* (Oracle Education Foundation, n.d.-b) provides an opportunity for students to publish their collaborative work. The site also offers examples of work created through the collaboration of students from around the world. It provides rich, innovative online learning resources for students of all ages on a wide range of educational topics.

The process of Web publishing provides many opportunities for language learners to improve their creativity by

- thinking about a topic intensely
- communicating and developing ideas
- shifting ideas from one to another domain
- evaluating their work and the work of others

In addition, students can take increased responsibility for their work, which in turn can help the revision process. By using all the learning opportunities of a Web publishing experience, language learners have unique and exciting motivation to create and celebrate their achievements.

Existing resources

In addition to creating their own Web-based resources, teachers and learners can use existing resources to promote creative thinking and language learning. For example, at *Little Explorers* (Enchanted Learning.com, 1996–2006), an online picture dictionary, language learners can visualize or elaborate their thoughts with the aid of pictures, maps, and diagrams. They can also use their creative thinking skills by participating in games and art activities at English language television Web sites such as CBBC (British Broadcasting Corporation, 2007) and PBS *Kids* (Public Broadcasting Service, 1995–2007). These sites also offer stories and enjoyable activities that teachers can use to design creativity tasks. For example, teachers can have students create their own e-cards, adding messages and decorating them with graphics.

Sites for virtual libraries and museums also provide valuable resources to enhance language and creativity in teaching and learning. For example, the *Virtual Library Museums Pages* (J. Bowen, 2006) provide numerous links to an eclectic collection of art galleries and virtual museums worldwide. The Metropolitan Museum of Art (2000–2007a) site includes an Explore & Learn link that gives children new and intriguing ways to see art with detailed information about an artist or collection. For example, children can make their own drawing using four kinds of tools after learning about Van Gogh's drawing techniques. The site also provides opportunities to read a short version of Van Gogh's biography (Metropolitan Museum of Art, 2000–2007b) with visual aids.

Accessing such sites provides language learners with opportunities to learn about art, history, and culture in the target language and to create their own products (for more about such content sites, see chapter 9 in this volume). To use these sites effectively in language classrooms, teachers must evaluate the purpose of the Web site and adapt the use of the resource to best meet instructional goals. (For other sites and tasks, see the Classroom Practice chapters in this volume.)

WebQuests

A WebQuest is an inquiry-based task activity in which most or all of the information used by learners is drawn from the Web. Although many teachers employ them for content learning, participating in a WebQuest is also an effective way to develop language learners' creativity through problem solving. Not many of the vast number of quests have been built specifically with language learners in mind (see Dodge, n.d.-b); however, teachers can fairly easily create a WebQuest task using the templates at *QuestGarden* (Dodge, 2007). Teachers create specific instructions and give each student a particular role. Evaluation rubrics are developed to keep students aware of their learning process and objectives. Because a major goal of creativity teaching in CALL involves effectively promoting and sustaining student creativity, teachers must consider whether the WebQuest activity is engaging and meaningful enough for their students and whether it provides an open-ended dimension for the exploration of ideas. Then teachers must carefully watch students' task process and check whether students can and are willing to express their ideas, a very important indicator in creativity development. With careful planning by the teacher (and perhaps the students), students can enhance their creativity along with language skills while participating in WebQuest activities.

CMC

CMC is broadly defined as human communication via computers. CMC includes various media—e-mail, discussion boards, chat rooms, instant messaging—discussed in other chapters throughout this volume. CMC can enhance learning both linguistically and socially, but it is also a powerful tool when used to enhance the teaching process. Having learners engage in communicative tasks using chat, e-mail, and instant messaging functions affords opportunities for learners to negotiate meaning (see chapters 1 and 6 in this volume; Sotillo, 2000) and to resolve communication breakdowns (Blake, 2000; Toyoda & Harrison, 2002). In addition, CMC moves language learning classrooms toward learner-centered communication, which according to Sotillo (2000), gives students "empowerment, autonomy, equality, and enhanced critical thinking skills"; it also encourages "greater participation by people in subordinate positions," including "shy students and the physically challenged" (pp. 83–84).

CMC can promote creativity by accelerating the learning process and the development of creative thinking skills (Loveless, 2002; Shneiderman, 2002a). In one-on-one interaction, language learners can receive personal feedback and increase both the quantity and the quality of the communication. With more opportunities, as in a peer group chat, learners can generate more ideas and produce more meaningful work, involving them more mindfully in the interaction. In short, CMC can increase learner motivation by providing language learners with a less threatening means to communicate than in a face-to-face class, where one speaker (or the teacher) may dominate the conversation (see chapter 13 in this volume; Kern, 1996; Ushioda, 2000).

CMC collaborations include keypal exchanges and videoconferences. In addition, the learning environment offered by a multi-user object-oriented domain (MOO) or multi-user domain (MUD), and platforms such as Moodle (2006) or Blackboard (2005), can help expand creative thinking when it is used for writing and interacting with other learners. CMC thus facilitates work on meaningful projects (Barson, Frommer, & Schwartz, 1993), including those that encourage student creativity. During discussions, teachers can ask meaningful questions to help learners develop their imagination and their skills in flexible idea generation, fluent expression, and detailed explanation. Teachers can also encourage the use of "what if," "suppose," and "imagine" types of questions to help learners support the creative thinking of their peers.

Virtual reality/virtual environments

Like the physical spaces in which software and Web resources are made available to promote learners' creativity, virtual learning environments can provide experiences for creative activities and promote creativity (Bullinger, Müller-Spahn, & Rübler, 1996). In particular, a multi-user virtual environment encourages language learners to reflect on a particular theme, generate new ideas, and jointly contribute thoughts. Schwienhorst (2002) notes that virtual reality (VR) allows greater self-awareness, support for interaction, and real-time collaboration.

In fact, VR and computer simulations could potentially extend across the entire language curriculum, enabling students to immerse themselves in historical events and foreign cultures and explore them firsthand. The collaborative features of VR support this process, while also providing a creative atmosphere and comfortable environment that support the expression and visualization of ideas. The collaborative learning experience in VR is a good way to spark creative breakthroughs, providing a way into knowledge creation for all students. In other words, students can acquire agency over their own thoughts while they interact with others. (See the earlier discussion of *Second Life: EduNation* [Consultants-E SL, 2004–2007], a VR environment designed by and for educators and language students; see also chapter 26 in this volume.)

Conclusion

It is apparent that computer use can offer opportunities for students to learn language and creativity at the same time. The CALL resources discussed in this chapter (and the many others available) can be used to support the conception and development of tasks that directly support the creativity of language learners. However, to be effective, such tasks must be built on a thoughtful and well-informed task design (for more on task design, see chapter 13 in this volume). When creative thinking is supported in the CALL classroom, language learners' creative and linguistic potential will be awakened and transformed to tap its real power.

Explorations

1. What opportunities for creative thinking can language learners have in real-time (synchronous) interactive network environments (e.g., chatting, MOOs)? How are the opportunities different from or similar to those in asynchronous contexts? How do opportunities in synchronous CMC environments differ from those in asynchronous environments? Compare, for example, linguistic interaction, attitude, learning processes, and outcomes. Create a chart to detail your conclusions.

2. What are the gains and losses that hypertext materials provide in the creative thinking of language learners? Explore a Web page or software application with multiple hyperlinks, such as *Little Explorers* (EnchantedLearning.com, 1996–2006), making a note of the path you take through the program. Do you return to the same point each time? Explore other options or linked sites. From your notes, what conclusions can you draw about the use of hypermedia?

3. Keeping in mind the definition of creativity—the ability to generate novel and valuable ideas, a thinking process involving several stages, or a product created by using several thinking skills—discuss how teachers can create or improve supportive CALL environments for the creativity development of language learners in your particular teaching situation.

4. Try a free online group drawing board, such as *Groupboard* (Group Technologies, n.d.), with a friend or classmate, using it to analyze a weekend trip or a proposed lesson plan. How can you take best advantage of different colors, fonts, sketches, and text chat? Discuss your working session to determine if you generated more or better ideas using the various media.

5. Explore the Web site *Educational Uses of Digital Storytelling* (University of Houston System, 2005). Be sure to examine the >Goals and Objectives and >Examples links. You may also wish to download some of the software tools suggested, like the free Microsoft

Photo Story (2004). Create a story, either individually or with your working group, by applying some of the genres and suggestions on the site. Share your story with your class. What kinds of things did you discover about the creative process in completing this project?

PART V

Time and Feedback

Chapter 15

Theory and Research: New Emphases of Assessment

Chin-chi Chao

Focus

Assessment, as a form of feedback, is a critical component of the language learning classroom, but most former language students still remember the nightmarish assessments in which they took part. My memories of foreign language learning include long lists of vocabulary words and multiple-choice, fill-in-the-blank, and discrete-item tests. Every week I took at least one vocabulary test, which normally included a long list of lexical items. The teacher would stand in the front of the classroom, carefully and slowly uttering the foreign words one by one. The girl sitting next to me would write furiously on her paper, but, unable to think of anything to write, I could only stare at the white piece of paper. I was supposed to spell all the words correctly in less than 2 minutes, but the words did not ring a bell in my mind because they were completely out of context; it was extremely difficult to spell them correctly. The best strategy that I could think of for learning the words was to use mnemonics, but remembering 10–20 different mnemonic devices was also difficult! The teacher assessed our communicative competence by having us recite memorized paragraphs, articles, and dialogues word for word.

Most of the assessment methods used in my foreign language learning years involved no skills other than memorization and test-wiseness, that is, picking up an answer based on the clues revealed by how the question was structured. Other people's experience with language learning and assessment might have been better than mine, but many are probably like me in believing that there must be a better way to conduct assessment. Just as the computer has brought about many new possibilities in other aspects of life, it might also bring about new ways of conducting assessment in the language learning classroom.

Background

The Purpose of Assessment

To discuss how the computer might change the way language learners are assessed requires an understanding of why assessment is necessary. Most teachers would probably say right away that the purpose of assessment is to document students' achievement. But why do teachers want to document students' achievement?

First, employers want to know how well teachers teach and how well students learn. *Employers* in a broad sense include the head of the educational institution, the board of the school corporation, the ministry of education, and other offices or personnel that have the power to decide on language education policies. For these entities, the most useful kinds of information result from comparing different groups of teachers and learners based on discrete criteria. In English language teaching, the Test of English as a Foreign Language (TOEFL; see Alderson, 2000; Alderson & Hamp-Lyons, 1996; Hamp-Lyons, 2000) is one of the instruments most often used for this purpose. Communicative skills are often assessed with the ACTFL Oral Proficiency Interview (OPI; see Buck, Byrnes, & Thompson, 1989; for an overview of the OPI, see Yoffe, 1997) and some newer approaches, such as having the test takers work on cooperative tasks. For the convenience of comparison and for an assessment to be objective, standardized questions as well as carefully observed procedures for administering these tests are absolutely necessary. The test constructors have to be very careful about obtaining high reliability and validity ratios, and language learners have to outperform a large number of others to be considered favorably and to honor their teachers.

On the other hand, the teacher, the learners, and the learners' families also want to know how well the teacher and the students perform. For this purpose, however, comparisons among students or teachers are not necessary. What teachers need is information that shows a learner's strengths, weaknesses, and progress (or lack of progress) in learning so that appropriate instructional support can be provided. For teachers, as opposed to employers, in other words, assessment has instructional purposes. For such purposes, the goals of classroom assessment are to help learners

- move ahead and improve
- gain familiarity with the content being taught
- become aware of their own position in the learning process
- fine-tune their understanding of the target language and culture
- set goals for the next stage of learning

The classroom assessments that language teachers use often consist of self-developed, discrete-item questions with a focus on lexical or grammatical knowledge. Many teachers also include functional language-use assessments such as oral interviews with students. However, to accomplish the goals listed, assessment must

- be integrated into the classroom activity
- be learner centered
- guide the learner toward improvement
- encourage reflective and conscious learning

Assessment has to focus on the learning process itself, not the product. The information collected should cover all facets of language learning, including grammar and lexical knowledge and use, learning strategies and styles, and communicative competence. Perhaps assessment can also provide teachers with some data on which to base a learning diagnosis. Useful forms of assessment might include projects, portfolios, cooperative tasks, and even self-assessment tools.

Having begun the chapter by describing a situation in which only one kind of learning and assessment was used, I emphasize that it is not my intention to say that language learning classrooms and curricula should exclude memorization activities, vocabulary testing, or discrete-item questions. Most standardized and objective tests are efficient sources of information that help teachers understand a student's mastery of structural and functional knowledge in relation to other learners. Even though there are many problems associated with standardized tests, they are still widely used and are efficient for administrative decision making. However, no single assessment tool can tell teachers everything about the learner and the learning process (Chapman & King, 2005; Woodward, 1994); what is important is to understand the reasons for using a particular type of assessment and to use one that can generate useful information. In other words, teachers need to know which assessment method to use in which contexts, for which audience, and for which purposes (see Table 15-1).

New Emphases of Assessment

The kind of classroom assessment that I experienced during my language learning years is most often used to assess lexical, grammatical, and structural knowledge similar to what the paper-based TOEFL assesses. (The newer generation of the TOEFL Internet-based test takes a more integrated approach in which, for example, the writing section requires the test taker to understand a lecture in a video.) This type of assessment, perhaps the most common type of achievement test in ESL/EFL classrooms, has a few shortcomings:

- The test questions appear out of context.
- The test does not require students to use the language as it appears in normal, everyday life.

Table 15-1. Overview of Second Language Testing and Assessment

	Formal testing	Classroom assessment
Audience	Educational institutions, administration, researchers	Teachers, learners, parents
Purposes	Support administrative decisions by comparing group achievement or identifying a learner's relative position in a group	Support learning and facilitate instruction by identifying each learner's strengths and weaknesses
Forms: Assessment of grammatical or lexical knowledge	Standardized tests (e.g., paper-based TOEFL)	Teacher-created, discrete-item tests
Assessment of functional language	Tests of communicative competence through interviews (e.g., ACTFL OPI, 1986; performance assessments)	Tests of language knowledge as a functional whole, including grammar and lexical knowledge; observation of learning strategies and styles, communicative competence and general learning problems, problem solving through projects, portfolios, tasks, and self-assessment tools

- The test may not show a complete and correct picture of the learner's proficiency level, strengths, and weaknesses.

According to Spolsky (1989), functioning well in a second language requires the coordinated and integrated use of not only linguistic knowledge of structural forms but also functional abilities and general proficiency. To help learners become fluent language users, then, teachers need not only to address the problems with structural form that knowledge assessment can reveal but also to use other evaluative methods to assess learners' growth in the integrated use of the target language. This idea is the basis of and rationale for a recent shift in the emphases of assessment in communicative second language learning.

A trend in educational assessment that has been observed in classrooms of all subject areas (see, e.g., Farr, 1992; Haney & Madaus, 1989; Hudson, 2005; Marshall & Drummond, 2006; Moya & O'Malley, 1994) incorporates five principles:

1. integration rather than isolation

2. learner autonomy rather than teacher control

3. guiding rather than mere grading

4. critical thinking rather than test-wiseness

5. process as well as product

Examples and Discussion

How Teachers Engage With Assessment for Learning

Embedded in these new emphases of assessment is the most current educational philosophy: Learners should take responsibility for their own learning in context-embedded social interaction. According to this philosophy, all classroom activities are to bring about mindful and reflective learning on the part of the learners. Assessment as an important part of classroom activities is no exception. The following scenario describing Mr. White's class exemplifies the five principles.

Learner profile. Mr. White's ESL students in the United States are 18–22 years of age. Their proficiency in the target language is intermediate, which means that they can use English fairly well in everyday situations. The students are from different countries and have varying native language backgrounds. Most of them have college degrees and are preparing for graduate study in the United States as the next stage of education. Their length of stay in the United States ranges from 6 months to 1 year.

The activity. Using Web pages that they design and create in teams, the students are to introduce one aspect of the city that they are now living in to prospective students from around the world. The aspect can be food, customs, school life, traffic, or any topic that they think a new or prospective international student would be interested in knowing about. The class has two weeks to complete the project.

The students agree that they will use a friendly tone in their Web pages, as if they are talking to a friend face-to-face. After they have finished creating the Web page, each of the student teams will do an oral presentation in class in the target language, stating the rationales for their designs; a question-and-answer session will follow.

Criteria for assessment. Mr. White and the class jointly create an assessment rubric for the project. The students will critique each other's work based on this rubric. Grades will be determined as follows:

- language accuracy: 30%. The class decides that accuracy of language is very important. The students will especially attend to the way future tense (e.g., *You will see* . . . , *You will need to* . . .) and subjunctive mood (e.g., *If you have trouble, be sure to* . . .) are used. For the Web page, correct spelling is a must.

- presentation: 30%. Presentation includes the way information is displayed on the Web, in the oral presentation, and in the question-and-answer session.

- richness and usefulness of the information provided: 25%

- feedback to classmates: 20%

Learners are encouraged to cooperate with and support each other in carrying out the project. All students are to use the rubric to evaluate their own work and to give feedback to other members of the class. Mr. White will also evaluate the students' work and, as necessary, provide suggestions using the rubric.

Student tasks. The students are responsible for the following tasks:

1. Students decide on a topic to work on. They need to reflect on their own experience of living in the city and possibly talk to friends who have experienced coming to a new country.

2. Students search for information on the topic in the local library or other information sources (e.g., local government databases, the Internet). A great deal of reading is involved, leading to discussion and decisions about which information to use.

3. Students design and develop the Web page, with attention to key grammatical structures and vocabulary. Help with computer skills comes from peers as well as from an aide provided by Mr. White.

4. After feedback from Mr. White and peers, students revise the Web pages as necessary; they examine other class members' work and give feedback.

5. Student teams present their Web pages to the class and conduct a question-and-answer session.

Teacher's role. The following are the teacher's responsibilities:

1. During the development stage, Mr. White forms the student teams, guides the students, and helps solve problems with (not for) them. When the students can solve problems by themselves, Mr. White stands aside, carefully observing their activity. From time to time, he may encourage them or provide help with and feedback on

language, Web page development, research strategies, and project ideas and direction, but he lets the students make decisions for themselves. Outside class, he maintains contact with individuals and teams through e-mail.

2. During the presentation, Mr. White ensures that the discussion flows smoothly (e.g., by helping with timing), helps students facilitate discussions or form questions and answers, and provides feedback.

3. At the end of the activity, Mr. White conducts a class discussion in which students reflect on the process of this activity. He asks questions about how they performed; what problems they had; and what Mr. White, the class, or an individual student could have done to make the project better.

4. Mr. White writes a descriptive report of each student's achievement, strengths, and weaknesses based on the rubric as well as the effort that he observed in class and in e-mail interactions.

I now look more closely at how to implement the five principles of assessment listed earlier.

1. Integration rather than isolation

The concept of integration includes two ideas:

1. Language should be seen as an integrated construct, and its use and assessment should be treated as such.

2. Assessment should be part of the classroom activity rather than something set aside to do separately.

Many educators believe that language is no longer language if it is not maintained and treated as a whole. As the framework for this volume does, Gomez, Parker, Lara-Alecio, Ochoa, and Gomez (1996) suggest that language assessment should always be situated in a meaningful, realistic situation over extended periods of time and within a range of social situations involving two-way communication. This list sounds daunting, but with careful project management, integration is possible.

For example, Mr. White's Web page project involves integrated use of the target language in a context that is meaningful to students. The language is used as a whole construct; students read in order to select appropriate content for their project, write in order to present their thinking on the information presented, speak in order to inform the audience of their rationale and design, and listen in order to understand questions asked during the presentation. The students also use English when they negotiate the rubric, give and receive feedback and support, and consult Mr. White for ideas and various kinds of help. Even the reflection at the end of the activity is a meaningful use of the target language in context. In other words, language use itself is not the purpose of the activities; rather, language serves as a tool for real-world purposes, just as it does in everyday life.

As for the second point, that assessment itself should be made an integral part of normal classroom activities, Rivers (1973) describes how testing can be a part of learning:

> The test is, as it were, a source of information or a set of instructions that enables the learner to keep up his efforts till he has matched the criterion, testing and retesting to see how close he is coming to the desired performance. Each time he falls short he makes a further effort to reach the criterion; each time he achieves his aim he moves on to the next phase of activity. In this way, the testing is an integral part of the learning process. (pp. 3–4)

The process that Rivers describes has the overriding intention of helping learners improve and fine-tune their own learning. To do so, learners must be engaged and reflective. For an assessment activity to implement this principle, its design has to be based on a learning goal. Pearson and Berghoff (1996) have shown that the appropriate interweaving of assessment and teaching can encourage students to participate actively in their own learning. Herschensohn (1994), H. D. Brown (2004), and others also suggest that assessment should be consistent with classroom procedures: It should measure growth and breadth, and use authentic language materials and a variety of evaluation techniques.

However, because the goal of instruction is often embedded in the activity, students may find it difficult to see the goal and therefore to reflect on it. Mr. White may choose to discuss the goal when negotiating the rubric with his students. A rubric or a list of evaluation criteria is helpful both in his assessment of the learners and in the students' self-assessment. Both parties should understand and agree on how the final product will be evaluated (Tuttle, 1996). In the process of developing the project, Mr. White should emphasize the goals and objectives through feedback and discussion. He should also take debriefing as another opportunity for students to become conscious of their weaknesses, appreciate their strengths, fine-tune their understanding, and move ahead in the learning journey.

2. Learner autonomy rather than teacher control

Because assessment is part of learning, and learning is basically a very personal endeavor (i.e., no one can really make people learn if they do not want to), it should follow that learners' autonomy must be honored in assessment, too (for a discussion of autonomy, see chapter 25 in this volume). Teachers should therefore respect students' opinions regarding the structure of the assessment and leave room for students to show their individual strengths. Portfolios containing an ongoing evaluation of student progress, self-assessments, and peer reviews are a means of empowering and motivating students in this way (H. D. Brown, 2004; Newman & Smolen, 1993).

In Mr. White's Web project, the students are given many opportunities to exert control over their learning. For example, in creating the assessment rubric, students negotiate with him to determine the weight of such criteria. They have a say in the items on which they are to be evaluated. In addition, based on their own experiences, students can decide on the project theme that they feel is the most urgent for newcomers. Students also have to make many design and development decisions in the process of the activity, including the kind of feedback that they will give to their peers. They help each other learn new computer skills and acquire language knowledge. Furthermore, the question-and-answer session during the presentations is another opportunity for the students to "control" the class—if Mr. White is willing to leave the floor open to them.

Empowering students, however, is not an easy thing to do from either the teacher's or the learners' perspective because both must change their attitudes and the way they interact with each other in conventional class-rooms. In providing opportunities for learner control, Mr. White has to be willing to give up the traditional authority that teachers enjoy. As described in the scenario, Mr. White still has many critical roles to play in the assess-ment process. He needs to probe and guide the students, encourage them, provide help and feedback, sustain interaction with them by e-mail, retain the management of the classroom, facilitate discussions, organize learning events, and write detailed descriptive reports on the learners based on his careful observations. If Mr. White is not willing to share some of the classroom authority and support learner-centeredness, the students will not be able to assume responsibility for their own learning.

Empowering students involves some hidden concerns. For example, some students might not appreciate the opportunity to have so much power or might not have enough experience to handle it, and Mr. White might find it difficult to stand aside and watch the students make their own way at a very slow pace. He should explain to students the importance of having them take on some of these responsibilities and provide the kind of support that is helpful to them. He should also show them that he is there to support them whenever necessary in becoming independent learners. His actions and attitudes must be consistent and definite; Mr. White himself needs to be mindful when giving feedback and interacting with the students. Following these assessment principles and supporting learning in a learner-centered project is an art that has to be learned. Fortunately, with the convenience of e-mail, the interaction between teacher and student can be more frequent and more timely, and it can allow more time for careful thinking.

3. Guiding rather than mere grading

In the scenario, Mr. White is to give a descriptive report of each student's achievement, strengths, and weaknesses at the end of the activity. These descriptions should help the learners and their parents understand the learning that took place more clearly than numbers and letter grades could, and each report should also indicate a concrete direction for future improvement. This step supports the idea that assessment is a part of learning.

In fact, the teacher's guidance is not limited to the final report. In the scenario, Mr. White does not just give the students questions and let them struggle in the dark; he is always present to help and guide them. Because assessment is part of the learning process, appropriate feedback during the process is critical. Bonk and Cunningham (1998) have identified 10 ways of providing guidance:

1. modeling
2. coaching
3. scaffolding and fading (gradually reducing the scaffold)
4. questioning
5. encouraging student articulation and application
6. pushing student exploration
7. fostering student reflection
8. providing cognitive task structuring
9. managing instruction through feedback and reinforcement
10. giving direct instruction only when absolutely necessary (p. 39)

Guiding emphasizes leading students to reach a decision by themselves. Students must not only be required to do the task well but must also be shown how. Guidance should lead every student to be successful and allow the assessment to contribute to learning.

For large classes such as Mr. White's, general guidelines, job aids, or graphic organizers may be useful in guiding students in the development process. Students should also be encouraged to help each other. A good support system that has been successfully built up within a class promotes good interaction among class members and leaves the teacher free to work with those who need more help.

Appropriate feedback generally cannot be prepared ahead of time, and giving just-in-time guidance certainly takes some planning and management skills. The CALL classroom provides some help with this. For example, the use of e-mail keeps the interaction between the learners and the instructor immediate, rapid, and secret. The learners do not feel the threat of exposing their weaknesses to the rest of the class, and the instructor and the learners are encouraged to maintain constant interaction with each other. In addition, computer databases can keep records of the teacher's interaction with each individual, which certainly can help to make guidance efficient and effective; keeping records in a database makes it easy for Mr. White to compose descriptive reports. In addition, because work produced on the computer is generally easy to change, the learners are more likely to revise and improve their work in response to feedback. Feedback is then much more useful to the learner than if the computer is not available for projects and assessments.

4. Critical thinking rather than test-wiseness

As mentioned earlier, traditional methods of assessment, such as standardized multiple-choice or fill-in-the-blank tests, often encourage test-wiseness; students who can figure out what the logic of test questions is or what is in the teacher's mind can accurately guess the correct answer. What students learn is how to appear smart without rigorous study and thinking. Students waste reflection on approximating what other people (especially the teacher) think rather than seek real and meaningful understanding for themselves.

Teachers need to design tasks well enough that there is little room for test-wiseness and a great deal of demand for critical thinking during the assessment. *Critical thinking*, generally defined as the ability to interpret, analyze, evaluate, infer, explain, and self-regulate (reflect), is often related to the concept of problem solving (see chapter 3 in this volume). It can also be defined as the ability to think about one's thinking in such a way as to recognize its strengths and weaknesses and, consequently, the ability to recast the thinking in an improved form (R. Paul, 1995). The biggest difference between test-wiseness and critical thinking skills is that tasks requiring critical thinking leave room for creative problem solving, self-assessment, and deeper understanding of the use of the target language. Many times, there may be more than one correct answer to an assessment task that requires students to think critically about solutions to real-world problems and use the target language creatively. Browne and Keeley (1990) offer a detailed explanation of critical thinking skills. In addition, the Questioning Kit (McKenzie, 1997), which distinguishes 18 question types, is a good resource for any teacher who would like to ask thought-provoking questions during assessment tasks.

In Mr. White's Web project, students have little need for test-wiseness but many opportunities to use reflective and conscious thinking skills. When students decide on a theme for the project, they need thinking skills to read, analyze, select, and organize the information. Because accuracy is weighted heavily during evaluation, the students have to consciously monitor their own language use, especially in the area of structural forms. The feedback provided to other class members also demands good critical thinking skills. The most obvious opportunity for reflection is the class discussion at the end of the activity. Students are asked to reflect on how they did, what problems they had, and what they could have done to make the project better. This is a time for students to evaluate their use of language, learning strategies, learning styles, communication skills, and many other factors related to the project and to language learning. Mr. White can also give his own feelings, experiences, and observations at this time. It is important to show that the purpose of the debriefing and reflection is improvement, not criticism. If the class has been interacting quite well in the process of carrying out the project, a friendly and supportive classroom atmosphere can be expected, and reflection is more likely to be useful and helpful to class members.

All kinds of computer tools can promote the goal of encouraging learners to think critically. For example, word-processing tools automatically highlight typographical or spelling errors as they are typed. While writing for assessment, students should be encouraged to try to correct these errors themselves before looking at the suggestions provided by the software. The prompt and the immediate feedback provided by the software help students become aware of the mistakes they most often make and encourage students to make a conscious effort to avoid these errors. In this way, the requirement to correct their own spelling errors could contribute to students' awareness, learning, and improvement rather than just function as a means of assessment.

5. *Process as well as product*

In the past, most classroom assessment methods strongly emphasized the product of instruction, that is, what the student could produce after instruction. More recently, the process, that is, how the student accomplishes the task, has become more important in evaluating students' achievement. The concept of *process* is most used in writing instruction, in which students, whether with each other or with the teacher, brainstorm writing topics; draft pieces; share and confer on writing; and revise, edit, and publish (for a review of techniques for assessing the writing process, see Hurley & Tinajero, 2001; Rotta & Huser, 1995). In the workshop atmosphere in which these steps occur, reading, writing, and speaking are often integrated and support each other. Process-oriented activities and assessment in fact work very well in projects that require students to use computer applications such as authoring or presentation software (see chapters 16 and 17 in this volume).

Again, putting the focus on the learning process leads to more concern about how students think, solve problems, reflect on their own learning, and set the next goal. A process orientation encourages learners to think and to reflect constantly; students are guided to think deliberately and modify before coming to any decisions on their actions. An emphasis on process also fosters the deliberate integration of critical thinking functions, such as abstracting, generalizing, defining, and comparing. These processes allow learners to make an evaluation or judgment and not to respond purely intuitively or without a basis for connecting ideas constructively (Schön, 1983). Reflection, which is important as a means to focus on the learning process, thus assists understanding, develops self-awareness, enhances the ability to analyze, encourages deeper thinking, and promotes independence (Miller, Tomlinson, & Jones, 1994).

An assessment that encourages reflection during the learning process does not require that students be corrected or perfect during the first attempt at a task. It is an excellent result if students can do a task perfectly, but the experience is also useful if students can think for themselves about what they did well, what they did not do well, why they did certain tasks well or poorly, and what they should do to make the work better the next time. Being aware of what decisions one makes during the task and of why and how one makes them is a critical factor for self-improvement and is greatly valued in the new assessment paradigm.

In the new assessment paradigm, process as the support of learning becomes the focus of attention. The purpose is not to label students by the work they produce but to understand what difficulties they have so that the necessary help can be provided. And that is also why teachers should value learner-centeredness; guidance rather than instruction; critical thinking; reflection during the assessment; and the integration of language use, instruction, and assessment.

How the Computer Helps

The five new emphases of assessment discussed in this chapter apply to learning environments with and without the computer. However, with the help of the computer, educators now have more tools than ever to create language learning assessments that fit the new emphases of integration, learner control, guided learning, critical thinking, and process orientation. Authoring software, word processors, presentation software, video and graphics software, spreadsheets, and database applications all allow learners to create new information for assessment purposes in an authentic, meaningful, and holistic way.

The thinking skills required for integrated projects are much more varied than those required for traditional pencil-and-paper, discrete-item tests. In the process of creating, the teacher and the learners can see the development of thoughts easily. The teacher can give learners guidance and feedback with the expectation that the learners will take advantage of the ease in making corrections that the computer allows. Communication tools such as e-mail and instant messaging can promote interaction among learners as well as between teachers and learners. In addition, with the convenience of tracking functions and database software, teachers can now easily trace each student's language learning development, making it easier to provide personal help, feedback, and descriptive reports. In fact, all of these functions can now be seen in *automated writing evaluation* software (AWE, or automated essay scoring; Warschauer & Ware, 2006), a program currently being tested that allows composition creation and self-regulated learning with the mediation of machine- and teacher-generated evaluation and feedback. The result is an environment that supports learning, which is exactly the purpose of classroom assessment.

Conclusion

This chapter has presented recent emphases in educational assessment. The ideas of integration rather than isolation, learner autonomy rather than teacher control, guiding rather than mere grading, critical thinking rather than test-wiseness, and process as well as product help teachers focus on promoting better learning from second language classroom assessment. The convenience of computers gives teachers more tools than ever before to make these ideas work.

As seen in Mr. White's Web project, these principles do not dictate the use of any particular form of assessment. Mr. White's project is just one example that employs several computer tools. Many different projects and tasks based on these tenets of classroom assessment can be designed around the computer (for practical ideas about implementing these principles in the CALL environment, see chapters 16 and 17 in this volume). I certainly hope that if I learn a new language, I can avoid the assessment nightmare I experienced in learning English. I also hope that my instructor understands that classroom assessment is a part of the learning process that belongs, at least in part, to me as a learner and that it should be treated as such.

Explorations

1. Reflect on the last test you took. What did you take away from the process? Compare your responses and feelings about the testing situation with others in your work group.

2. Have you ever had an experience like the one Chao describes in her opening narration? How will you avoid making students feel the way she did? Make notes of specific ideas and share them with your work group.

3. What barriers to authentic assessment exist in your current or future teaching context? How will you overcome them?

4. Find a release copy of a language learning test at your school or on the Web. Analyze some of the questions, explaining what you think the questions test and why you think so.

5. Find or create a lesson for your classroom. Use Chao's principles as a guide to develop assessment(s) that meet the goals she lays out for classroom assessment.

Chapter 16

Classroom Practice:
Practical Classroom Assessment

Joy Egbert

Focus

Learners need both enough time to complete their tasks and sufficient feedback to succeed. Classroom feedback has many components; traditionally, teachers might think of feedback as providing answers to learners' questions or making a qualitative statement such as "You're right" or "That's good." However, if feedback is seen as information that helps the learner understand just-completed tasks or assists with present or future tasks, then assessment that gives information to the learner is an important type of feedback in the language learning classroom.

Background

Assessment includes three complementary elements that can help learners succeed: (a) the assessment of process (as mentioned in chapter 15 in this volume), including the metacognitive, cognitive, and procedural operations learners use as they complete the task; (b) the evaluation of progress or outcomes (in other words, determining where learners were and where they are now); and (c) evaluation of instruction (as described in chapter 15). In computer-assisted language classrooms, technology can also play two overlapping roles in the process of assessment. First, the computer can play the role of an integrated tool that supports the assessment of what happens during or as a result of CALL tasks. In this case, the technology is used not directly as an assessment tool but as support for activities that are assessed. Second, the technology can be used to prepare or perform the assessment, as, for example, in computer-based testing.

Many guidelines for large-scale *outcomes testing* are related to legislation, such as the U.S. No Child Left Behind Act and the Common European Framework for education across the disciplines, including language learning.

Standardized tests, such as the Test of English as a Foreign Language or the Test of English for International Communication, have normed items and systematic procedures for writing, revision, and review of items so that results can be compared across large numbers of students. However, most of this chapter focuses on the classroom assessment process because the literature contains far less about this area than about outcomes testing. The techniques mentioned here are only a few of the many possibilities for providing feedback in the language learning classroom; these tools and activities should be used not in isolation but in conjunction with each other because none of them can fully do the job of demonstrating learners' knowledge and skills.

The general principles of assessment remain the same regardless of what tool students are using to learn—whether they are reading from a book or from the computer screen, or speaking into a stand-alone microphone or into a video camera hooked up to a computer. This chapter presents practical ideas for assessing learners' process and progress in the CALL classroom using the following guidelines, which are based on the principles discussed in chapter 15 in this volume:

1. Assessment takes place in multiple contexts.

2. Both process and outcomes are assessed.

3. Assessment is spread out over time.

4. The method of assessment fits the content and method of what is taught.

Examples and Discussion

Testing

Testing has been the most common way for teachers to evaluate student outcomes or products in the language classroom, and much has been written about how and why to use tests. Cloze, multiple-choice, true-false, and fill-in-the-blank tests are very popular evaluation tools, used to test discrete grammar points and specific vocabulary items, to check reading and listening comprehension, and to evaluate other discrete linguistic tasks. As noted in chapter 15, there are advantages and disadvantages to using these types of tests in the classroom. They can be used in multiple contexts, and retesting can take place over time, but it is difficult to see learners' processes from this kind of outcomes testing. However, by adding a section that asks students to explain their answers, teachers can make learner processes more apparent and create fairer tests. Teachers also need to make sure that the teaching and testing match, that is, that testing helps measure outcomes based on the goals set for the task or activity and that the test is appropriate to the method through which the learning took place.

For example, in teaching vocabulary from authentic texts, it would probably be invalid to test learners' knowledge of vocabulary through an uncontextualized multiple-choice or fill-in-the-blank test. A more useful way might be to ask the learners to do a verbal report using an authentic reading passage, as outlined in Scenario 2. If, on the other hand, the learners have studied grammar items using drill-based grammar software, a drill-like test would be appropriate. As another example, if students are to choose their own topics for the creation of a Web page, employing integrated skills as in the scenario in chapter 15, it would probably not be profitable to give students a standardized test on discrete vocabulary items.

Creating tests that match teaching and learning methods and that actually do test what teachers want to test is a very difficult task even for seasoned educators. Although technology cannot really help in the design and content of tests, computers can make the administration of tests easy. Various computer-based testing software exists to help teachers construct and score tests that students can take on the computer; teachers and students can receive scores instantly. *Adaptive testing* software allows the teacher or student to set the initial test level and allows students to progress through various levels of self-testing as they show their competence at one level. Adaptive testing software programs are available from many Internet-based software archives (see Appendix E) and are becoming more common over time. For example, GO Solve Word Problems (2006) employs adaptive leveling.

Verbal Reporting

One goal of an activity in the language learning classroom is to help students learn how to think about how they learn, for example, how to approach unfamiliar vocabulary in context or how best to approach problematic situations. *Verbal reporting*, one component in a powerful set of assessment tools available to teachers, helps learners understand their metacognitive and cognitive processes and helps teachers understand where students are in this skill development process. In verbal reporting, students speak or write; it has also been called a *think-aloud protocol*. During verbal reporting, the teacher is assessing how learning is taking place (the process) rather than what specific items have been learned (the product).

Verbal reporting can take a variety of forms and can be used to assess learning that takes place at the computer. The computer can also be used as part of the assessment, as, for example, in Scenarios 1 and 2.

Observation

Teachers observe their students all the time. In fact, many teachers do it constantly but barely give it a thought; others consider observation a valu-

Scenario 1: *Oral Reporting*

During a project that involves finding information on the World Wide Web about rain forests, Ms. Rivera asks her students to use Web directories, which are indexes of topics covered by a site, rather than search engines, in which only key words are entered. Having observed several students experience trouble performing the same operations during other assignments, she wants to check on the processes that students are using to find information from the index and make hypertext links. Ms. Rivera sits next to Maya, one of the students who seemed to have trouble previously, and asks her to describe her process as she performs the task. Ms. Rivera finds out that although Maya knows the names of all of the letters of the English alphabet, she has an incomplete grasp of alphabetical order. Ms. Rivera develops lessons to help Maya and her classmates with this essential skill.

Scenario 2: *Written Reporting/Journaling*

One of the goals of the week has been to help students discover ways to uncover the meaning of unfamiliar words through the use of context clues. To assess students' progress with the concepts involved in using context clues, at the beginning of the week Ms. Howard asks the students to read a passage that she has provided and to write in their electronic journals their thoughts and processes when they come to words that they do not know (she has modeled this process for the students prior to this assignment). During the week, the students work on a variety of exercises emphasizing the use of context clues. At the end of the week, Ms. Howard assigns a reading passage with several new words and asks the students to complete another written report in their electronic journals. She accesses the journals and compares the two reports to determine what progress the students are making toward the goal of applying the strategy she has taught. She can then prepare further lessons based on the information collected from this assessment.

able way to assess students. *Observation* is one of the most reliable tools for determining how students are progressing in class and can be purposefully employed to gather information about a wide variety of learners' abilities, skills, and competencies. Observation over time, in a variety of contexts, helps teachers understand their students' needs in ways that they cannot with one-shot assessment methods such as tests. Observation is integrated into the language lesson and is most profitable when done with guiding questions in mind. Teachers may even prepare a formal or informal checklist to guide their observations in the classroom. For example, teachers might compile from their resources a short list that includes the characteristics of good language learners and gather useful data about learners by observing over time which of these characteristics they display.

Although technology can play a role in observation, the computer itself cannot "observe" in the true sense of the word. However, in tandem with video or audio recording, technology can make it easier for the teacher to record what is going on in class and to have a chance to observe and reflect on the classroom outside of class time. Computer technology might also capture aspects of students' performance that otherwise might be overlooked. Scenario 3 suggests one way to use observation.

Written and Oral Retelling

How well do students understand what they read or listen to? Can they understand the rhetorical devices? Do they grasp the main ideas, the key subtopics, and the subtle nuances of a text? Can they use the text's structure to help them gather information about what they read or hear? Teachers may try to answer these questions with a test that involves comprehension questions,

---

Scenario 3: Observation

Based on his observations of learners in group work over the years, Mr. Long has put together a checklist of what learners need to do in order to achieve the language goals of group tasks. These actions include active participation, clear preparation, the use of the vocabulary of turn taking, and others. During a computer-assisted problem-solving task in which students must unanimously decide how to proceed in the software program, Mr. Long walks around the classroom mentally checking off students who are meeting the goals in the checklist and noting those who do not seem to be employing one or more of his guidelines. Mr. Long repeats this procedure over the course of the first several weeks of class, determining which students need more assistance in working successfully on this type of task.

perhaps with short-answer or fill-in-the-blank items, but this type of test has several crucial disadvantages in this context. Because a discrete-point test cannot easily cover an entire reading passage, it is difficult to tell from this type of evaluation where the students are having difficulties in comprehension and what students really understand of the passage as a whole.

Retelling, an assessment tool that has been around for a very long time but has not been the focus of much recent attention, can provide a holistic idea of what students understand and why they do not understand certain things. In retelling, students write or tell what they remember in their own words, including main ideas and relevant details, without looking back at the reading or listening to the text again. For oral retelling, which requires the teacher to meet with individual students, Brozo and Simpson (1995) suggest that the teacher use a checklist to record the kinds of ideas that the student mentions in the retelling, whether they are main ideas, significant details, or insignificant details (for more on checklists, see chapter 17 in this volume). The teacher might also note whether significant vocabulary from the text has been used appropriately. Reading or listening instruction can then center around the skills that the student needs to improve. A more detailed analysis of the retelling might involve audiotaping the learners' responses.

Computer technologies can help with this assessment process in several ways, such as by presenting a passage through text or audio within a limited time frame and not permitting learners to look back at it. The computer could then provide a place for students to record their retelling orally or in writing. Such a system could be created fairly easily using any of the authoring software mentioned in this chapter, such as Hot Potatoes (Arneil & Holmes, 2006). Scenarios 4 and 5 use retelling for classroom feedback. Note that in

---

Scenario 4: Written Retelling

Using a Hot Potatoes (Arneil & Holmes, 2006) exercise, Ms. Campion has presented students with a brief reading passage dealing with immigration, a subject that they have been exploring in class. She has created the timed reading activity so that the reading speed is at 150 words per minute, the curricular goal for speed at the students' level. After the students read, Ms. Campion asks the students to use the open-ended answer box provided in the program to retell the passage in their own words. From this exercise, she finds that some of the faster readers need help understanding how to find main ideas and some of the slower readers need to focus less on details. After discussing these points with her class, she creates lessons to assist all of the learners in gaining the skills they need to meet the reading goals of the course.

Scenario 5: Oral Retelling

For her part in a group project, Hai's assignment is to write a summary of Dr. Martin Luther King, Jr.'s "I Have a Dream" speech, and she asks her teacher for assistance in finding computer-based resources. Mr. Chen shows Hai how to use *MSN Encarta* (Microsoft, 2007b), which contains a video clip of the speech. Mr. Chen knows from recent verbal reports that Hai's metacognitive processes for listening have been improving and decides to take this opportunity to assess her understanding of the speech. Mr. Chen sits beside Hai as she listens to parts of the clip and asks her to retell what she understands of the passage during periodic breaks. Mr. Chen sees that, although Hai does not understand the nuances of the speech, she is applying the skills that have been practiced in class and is making a concerted effort to be a good listener. He discusses Hai's progress with her and encourages her to continue applying the skills she is learning.

each of these scenarios retelling is not used in isolation but instead adds information about students to a growing set of assessments compiled in a variety of ways.

Graphical Organizers

The use of *graphical organizers*, especially for content-based activities and lessons, is becoming more popular as alternative methods of assessment take hold in language classrooms. Graphical organizers, including Venn diagrams, grids, pictorial representations, tree diagrams, tables, charts, figures, concept maps, and webs, help teachers see how students understand the relationships between concepts, ideas, and words.

Graphical organizers can be constructed by students or teachers, either freehand, by using a simple electronic graphics or presentation package such as Microsoft PowerPoint (2007) or Kid Pix (2006), or even by using a simple word processor (see Figure 16-1). For older students, the free *Gliffy* (n.d.) Web site has fairly complex flowchart and diagram builders.

As Scenario 6 shows, software can be used during the assessment of tasks.

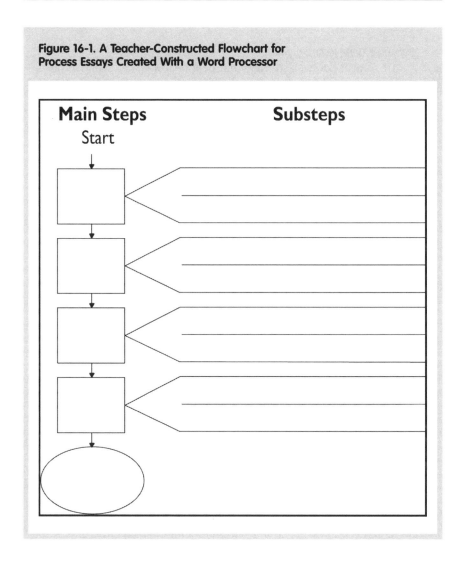

Figure 16-1. A Teacher-Constructed Flowchart for Process Essays Created With a Word Processor

Role-Plays

Many language teachers employ *role-plays* and *simulations* to provide learners with language practice, but few use them as the effective assessment tools that they can be. Role-play can be used (a) to prepare students to deal with issues before doing a task (e.g., assess prior knowledge and competence) or (b) to demonstrate an understanding of the basic concepts of a completed task, as in Scenarios 7 and 8. The teachers in these scenarios could evaluate students on the basis of the outcomes of the activities and assign a letter

Scenario 6: Graphical Organizers

Dr. Flinker believes strongly that peer review is a critical component of assessment both to help writers assess themselves and to give peer reviewers exposure to others' writing. During the writing and revising stages of his unit on process essays, Dr. Flinker routinely has his learners review other students' essays using graphical organizers as their comment sheets. During this process, each student sends an essay via e-mail to another student for review. The peer reviewers either use a flowchart template that Dr. Flinker has created (see Figure 16-1) or create their own flowchart that shows what they understand as the steps in the process described in the essay. Breakdowns in the process are signaled by broken arrows, and missing steps are signified by a blank shape. The author, the peer reviewers, and Dr. Flinker can clearly see where the essay does not work and which areas need to be clarified. During the next round of reviews, all of the interested parties can see where changes have occurred and what still remains to be done.

Scenario 7: Role-Play

Dr. Mickuleski will soon start a content-based unit on U.S. culture. One of the topics that she will include in the unit is prejudice and discrimination, and she will use the Decisions, Decisions: Prejudice (2001) software as a learning tool. First, she needs to find out how much her students already know about the topic, including vocabulary, content knowledge, and appropriate grammatical structures, so that she can accurately plan the type and content of lessons. She gives her students cards asking them to act out a situation in such a way that the other students can guess what it is. For example, one student is asked to portray how it might feel to see a bumper sticker denigrating her home country, and another is asked to show how it might feel to be an immigrant coming through Ellis Island alone. Through the portrayals and the audience's responses, Dr. Mickuleski can judge where students might have a gap in knowledge and what their related experiences have been, and she can start to develop her plan for the unit.

Scenario 8: Role-Play With Simulation

Students have been asked to consider the current situation in the simulated town that their group has built using SimTown (1995). There is a water shortage in their town, the food supply is low, and unemployment is high. The town's limited funds can be used to solve only one of these problems for the time being. Students role-play different members of a town council, each with a different set of priorities and an individual agenda. As a member of the town council, each student must present a recommendation for the use of the limited funds at the next council meeting.

One of the goals for this project, and one emphasis of the teacher-directed parts of the activity, has been to help students understand good decision-making processes. To assess whether her learners have integrated good decision-making skills into their metacognitive repertoire, Mr. Jones asks the learners to describe aloud the process they use as they formulate their recommendations during the role-play. The students use computer-based audio or video software to record their choices and their thought processes as they consider their options. Mr. Jones can then listen to these recordings and decide which, if any, concepts need to be reinforced. After the town council has made its decision, the class discusses the problem-solving process in which they have participated.

grade to individual students, but they choose instead to use the opportunity to explore students' learning processes and to use the assessments as feedback to students and as a basis for developing lessons focused on the students' needs.

Academic Journals

To obtain accurate information about students, teachers need to help some students overcome a reluctance to demonstrate ignorance in front of the class or provide a way for everyone to participate equally. *Academic journals* are one way of obtaining more information than outcomes testing can provide. A subset of or complement to communications-based dialogue journals (Peyton, 1990a), academic journals contain information based on course content. Students summarize, write questions, tell what they do not understand, explain how a lecture or an experience relates to what they have read, or respond to a statement about their writing. Students can write in their academic journals as a 5-minute exercise at the beginning of class, or the teacher can assign a question to be answered in the journal as homework. Students can complete their journals electronically in a variety of ways, such as a word-processed document sent by e-mail, a weblog (blog), or a Moodle (2006) area (using the computer as part of the assessment), or they can write about a computer-assisted task in which they participated (assessing an activity supported by the computer), as in Scenario 9.

A computer-based outcomes test alone cannot provide Mr. Crider with the same kind of information that a variety of assessment measures can. The additional measures greatly enhance his understanding of the problems his students are having with prepositions.

Self-Assessment

The teacher should not be the only member of the class to use assessment results to help students learn. Students themselves can be taught not only to assess themselves but also to take advantage of ongoing assessment in the language classroom. There are many tools that teachers can use to help learners gain information about their own processes and progress toward their goals; these same tools can provide teachers with a variety of information about learners. For example, at the beginning of a unit or lesson, learners using a pretest-posttest model can note what they know at the beginning of a lesson and what they want to know by the end. At the end of the unit or lesson, learners can look back at the pretest and note what they now know and whether or not they have learned what they wanted to learn. They can also note why they may not have learned it. (For another version of this type of self-assessment, see the Know–Want to Know–Learned chart described in chapter 17 in this volume.)

Scenario 9: Academic Journal

Mr. Crider's class has just completed a unit on prepositions, and in addition to giving a standardized computer-based test and having the students perform role-plays, Mr. Crider asks students to explain by writing in their electronic academic journals what they understand about preposition use in English. He expects that, because his students know that only he will read their messages, they will be open about what they do and do not understand. He provides feedback to the students via e-mail, answering questions and explaining the kinds of problems that he reads about. He will use the information that he obtains from the journal entries to integrate information about prepositions into future lessons.

Scenario 10: Self-Assessment With Projects

Students in Ms. Gunawan's class have been using the authoring software HyperStudio (2005) for a variety of assignments during the school year. Ms. Gunawan has asked teams of students to build an assessment tool that will measure how well their classmates have mastered HyperStudio. The tool may take any form on which the team members agree. At the completion of this task, Ms. Gunawan has the teams exchange assessment tools and complete whatever task the tool demands. The tool creators then comment on how well the assessed team performed. Ms. Gunawan then has the teams do a self-assessment, indicating what skills and knowledge they needed to build their assessment tools in the first place. Both the teacher and the students have several ways to see not only what students think was important to learn about the program but also how well they progressed toward these goals.

Alternatively, students can be asked how much they think they understood of a reading or a lesson, or they can construct an assessment tool for the lesson, administer the assessment to each other, and then evaluate how successful the tool was. These and many other methods can be used in the language classroom to help students learn how to help themselves. Computers can play a central role in self-assessment, as in Scenarios 10 and 11.

As explained in chapter 15, it is important for students to have a hand

Scenario 11: Self-Assessment With Tests

After previewing grammar software that students will use throughout the session as a complement to their in-class work, Mr. Jessop and his students develop the outline for a pretest that he will create. The students note the kinds of questions that should be asked, the topics about which they should be asked, and the format of the questions. After Mr. Jessop creates the test using test-making software, he and the class check to make sure that the test has the correct content and format. The students then take the test. At the end of the session in which they study with the software, students take the test again. In class discussion, they note why the test does or does not accurately reflect their grammar knowledge and explain how they would change the test to make it reflect more accurately what they think they know.

in their own assessment. With computer technology, teachers can help learners control their learning by involving them in the process of ongoing assessment.

Portfolios

Portfolio assessment, addressed briefly here, is another way to involve students in their own learning (for additional discussions of portfolio assessment, see chapters 15 and 17 in this volume). There seems to be a great deal of confusion among language educators about what should go into a portfolio, how it should be used, how it should be graded, and who should see it. Fortunately, many texts and other guides are available to assist teachers in using portfolios successfully in different situations. However, the *what*, *how*, and *who* of the portfolio are up to the teacher, the students, or both. It is important first to have a goal for the assessment and then to decide what it will contain. There is no minimum set of requirements, nor is there a set of standard guidelines that must be followed.

Portfolios can be used in any number of authentic ways. For example, if the portfolio is meant to measure a student's outcomes across a school year, it can be a compilation of the student's products, including tests, quizzes, and final drafts of papers. If the goal is to assess a student's progress or process, the portfolio can include multiple drafts of essays with self-assessment reflections, exercises and activities leading up to a test, and so on.

If necessary, the students and teacher can compose a formal rubric (see the next section) to help them assign a letter or number grade to the portfolio. This rubric could include, for example, five critical skills or concepts that students must show they have mastered, whether the skill is accuracy in using English articles or a clear understanding of the water cycle. For bilingual education students, the portfolio could be developed in either language so that progress in content area studies can continue in spite of language difficulties.

Regardless of the goal of the portfolio, technology can help students organize and present their work. Electronic portfolios, created with simple presentation software such as Kid Pix (2006), HyperStudio (2005), and Microsoft PowerPoint (2007) are easy to save and revisit, save storage space, are more durable than paper portfolios, and integrate computer skills throughout the process of building the portfolio. Electronic portfolios, for example, in a wiki such as PB*wiki* (PBwiki.com, 2007) or software packages such as those listed previously, can contain links to Web pages and other electronic documents created by the students and can include audio and video clips to give a more holistic view of a student's performance than a collection of papers in a folder. (For more on e-portfolios, see chapter 17 in this volume.)

If e-portfolios are not an option, technology still has a role to play in portfolio development. Students can use word-processing software to record their reflections about their work; they can print e-mail messages and include them in the portfolio to demonstrate a variety of concepts such as brainstorming, revising, and assistance-seeking strategies; and they can incorporate screen-shots from software packages used in class in explanations of the activities that they have completed and the learning that has occurred.

Rubrics as an Aid in Assessment

The techniques and methods already mentioned are only a few of those that teachers can use to meet the goals and employ the principles of ongoing assessment. The techniques can be used informally or systematically, depend-ing on the objective of the assessment. In both cases, *rubrics* can help quantify the results of these assessments when necessary.

Rubrics, in forms such as checklists or charts, can be used to assess CALL projects that might not have standard outcomes, such as multimedia portfo-lios and other computer projects (e.g., building a Web page, participating in a group simulation). Rubrics can also be used to formalize observation, retelling, and the other techniques mentioned in this chapter. Rubrics come in many shapes and sizes; some specify the exact criteria for successful completion of each objective and assign grades for each level of performance, and others are more holistic, informal lists of expectations. Teachers might use the rubric in Figure 16-2 as they observe students' spoken grammar during group work. The rubric in Figure 16-3 could be used for a group presentation.

Rubrics aid the teacher and students in clarifying goals, organizing les-sons and tasks, and assessing the extent to which students have met the goals during the lesson or task. (For more details about rubrics, see chapter 17 in this volume.)

Figure 16-2. Simple Rubric for Spoken Grammar

	Alone	With help
Forms sentences		
Uses past tenses		
Uses future tenses		
Forms simple sentences		
Forms complex sentences		
Errors prevent comprehension	_____ Yes	_____ No

Figure 16-3. Presentation Evaluation Form

I. Delivery
Planning: Prepared and rehearsed presentation but did not write it in detail or read it from a script
Voice: Used appropriate volume, pace, articulation, pronunciation, variety, and verbal "noise"
Participation: Promoted and managed effective audience participation

1 .... 2 ....3...........4 .... 5 ....6...........7 .... 8 ....9...........10

II. Visual Aids
Appearance: Used simple, clear, large, easily seen, consistent, spell-checked, and error-free aids
Use: Aligned and focused aids, did not block aids, pointed to screen, and replaced aids quietly and carefully

1 .... 2 ....3...........4 .... 5 ....6...........7 .... 8 ....9...........10

III. Organization
Structure: Evidenced logical flow, clear introduction, agenda, body, conclusion, and summary
Transitions: Used smooth, logical, and informative transitions between speakers or sections
Audience awareness: Tailored speech to audience's needs, wants, knowledge, and skills
Time management: Used time effectively; stayed within the time constraints

1 .... 2 ....3...........4 .... 5 ....6...........7 .... 8 ....9...........10

IV. Quality
Support: Addressed relevant issues and provided support for major points
Accuracy: Demonstrated sound, in-depth understanding of relevant issues
Creativity: Presented materials in an innovative, interesting manner

1 .... 2 ....3...........4 .... 5 ....6...........7 .... 8 ....9...........10

V. Teamwork
Collaboration: Showed evidence of individual participation, group understanding, and agreement
Cooperation: Showed support for all team members

1 .... 2 ....3...........4 .... 5 ....6...........7 .... 8 ....9...........10

Conclusion

Assessment is an important but often overlooked component of feedback in the language learning classroom. Standardized tests, although useful in specific contexts, often do not account for the kinds of task-based activities that occur with and around the computer in the CALL classroom. This chapter has described practical ways to assess the processes that students use while engaged in computer-assisted activities as well as the outcomes of these activities. It has also mentioned the role of computer-based testing and adaptive testing as an integrated part of the assessment process. Many more assessment techniques can be used in a variety of ways in the CALL classroom; the point is that, whether in a CALL environment or not, language teachers must consider the assessment of both process and product as an integral and ongoing activity in their classrooms.

Explorations

1. How can teachers fit authentic assessment into their daily routines?

2. Making sure that the method of assessment fits the content and method of what is taught means that standardized tests generally cannot be authentic. How can teachers deal with this conundrum when their students are required to attain a certain level on standardized tests?

3. Find and take an adaptive test on the computer or online. Make notes as you work, describing the process and your thoughts while taking the test. How can you apply these ideas to your classroom?

4. Choose a technology-enhanced lesson that you have created or discovered (for ideas on where to find lessons, see chapters 7 and 12 in this volume). Decide how you could best assess both process and product in this lesson. Justify your choices.

5. Search the Web and find two rubric creators (see chapter 17 in this volume and Appendix D for help with finding resources). Test each one by creating a rubric for a lesson of your choice. Explain which rubric creator is more useful, and justify your decision.

Chapter 17 🔲

Classroom Practice: Assessing Instructional Goals

Dafne González and Rubena St. Louis

Focus

The end of the 20th century marked a change in the way language, language learning, and the language learner were conceived by teachers as well as students. As national boundaries receded under the effects of globalization, emphasis on the structural nature of language as form shifted toward a view of language as communication. Continuing research into the areas of motivation, cognition, multiple intelligences, individual learning styles, and learning strategies (see Reid, 1998) has led to reassessment of the roles that students and teachers play in the learning process. The increasing use of technology and the penetration of the Internet into the four corners of the globe have opened up a wide range of new possibilities and a shift in paradigm for language learning and teaching. Teacher-centered classrooms have begun to make way for those in which students participate in classroom decision making, goal setting, and selection of objectives and materials. Teachers are also beginning the slow and sometimes painful process of ceding power to students, who are thus being given the opportunity to take more responsibility for their own learning.

These dramatic changes have led, and must lead, to a reassessment of the role of evaluation in the language classroom. *Alternative assessment* has given students the opportunity to take control of their own learning. In this chapter, we consider the advantages of alternative assessment and the different ways in which it can be implemented in blended and online courses.

Background

Evaluation Versus Assessment

Evaluation has been part of the language learning and teaching process for centuries, and its purpose has been that of collecting data to be used in making sound decisions about classroom teaching and learning. Traditionally, many teachers have looked at evaluation as a way of testing a learner's knowledge of a particular aspect of language at a specific point and time. So students often hear of the weekly vocabulary *quiz* or grammar *test* or even the TOEFL *exam*. Aebersold and Field (1997) state that these are the words usually associated with traditional evaluation. In standardized as well as classroom testing, multiple-choice items tend to be used (O'Malley & Valdez Pierce, 1996) along with true-or-false and open-ended questions. This type of assessment is dictated and controlled by the teacher, who maintains a position of power in the classroom with regard to when, what, and how language is evaluated.

However, teachers have found that the results from these traditional types of tests do not paint a true picture of student performance because they fail to adequately cover the range of objectives and the diverse manner in which they are accomplished through work carried out in the classroom. They do not take into consideration each student's individual learning styles, types of intelligence, aptitudes, and cultural values—all of which influence the language learning process; neither do they reflect the prior knowledge and cognitive strategies that a student may use to accomplish a task. Furthermore, traditional exams often must place language in an unnatural or *inauthentic* context and not within the social and communicative setting in which it is really used. Other factors (e.g., the surroundings in which the tests are administered, students' emotional and physical condition) can also affect learners' performance, thereby giving an inaccurate picture of their knowledge and ability (Genesee & Upshur, 1996). Thus, although traditional types of exams tend to evaluate a product at a certain point, they cannot show the learning process that leads to a given product. But a different view of evaluation can: alternative assessment.

As language learning and teaching do not exist in a bubble, immune to changes from the outside world, the definition of evaluation must change to keep in line with current trends. At present, evaluation is seen as intimately linked to psychological, social, cultural, environmental, and political factors. The emphasis is not only on what students learn, but also on how they learn (Nunan, 1999), and there is a move toward making students aware that they are responsible for their own learning (Benson & Voller, 1997). Seen in this light, students have an important role to play in their own evaluation, and they should work with the teacher to determine not only the procedures to be included in assessment, but also the weight and importance of each of the aspects to be considered (K. Smith, 2000). Just as learning is an ongoing process, so too should its evaluation reflect procedures; this in-progress feedback can give teachers the information they need to help them make correct decisions about student learning. Alternative assessment, which "reflects student learning, achievement, motivation and attitudes on instructionally-relevant classroom activities" (O'Malley & Valdez Pierce, 1996, p. 4), encompasses all of these aspects.

Alternative assessment deals with collecting data that show how students deal with, process, and complete tasks within a specific time frame, thus allowing the teacher to have a general view of the student's academic performance over a period of time. This type of assessment is in contrast to traditional evaluation, which looks at the student's academic performance at one specific moment. With alternative assessment, language can be seen as a whole, not fragmented into different skill areas, but as a communicative tool used by the learner as an active participant in the interaction. As opposed to the psychological constraints of an exam situation, alternative assessment includes varied data collection methods to trace the learner's social, cognitive, and academic development:

- samples of student work in traditional or e-portfolios

- teacher observation of the student's performance in the classroom during normal interactions

- project work (e.g., WebQuests [Dodge, n.d.-b])

In turn, tracing the student's progress through an extended activity cycle or set of procedures helps the teacher determine instructional possibilities and future goals.

Another important aspect of alternative assessment is *self- and peer evaluation*, whereby students reflect on and critically evaluate not only their own learning processes and performance, but also that of their classmates. Murdoch University (see R. Phillips & Lowe, 2003) considers this learning activity to be part of its official evaluation scheme. The reflective process involved in self- and peer evaluation develops critical thinking skills, encourages student autonomy, increases student motivation, promotes a positive attitude toward learning, and implies a new view of teacher and student roles (Hansen, 1998; O'Malley & Valdez Pierce, 1996; Sinclair, McGrath, & Lamb, 2000). Students become part of the instructional process, rather than a passive consumer of it.

Alternative assessment can also promote *collaboration* that helps students prepare for work in their future professional field. To this end, when teachers assess collaborative activity, as in a student-generated project, Angelo and Cross (1993) stress that goals and objectives should be clearly defined at the beginning of the assignment to focus the activities and tasks and to lay down the criteria for evaluation. Students should be made aware of their individual responsibility toward the group, the importance of accepting negative as well as positive feedback, the active role they should play in solving any problems that might occur, and perhaps most important, the fact that all participants should be treated fairly and with respect. Group work also develops critical thinking and builds research, organizational, and writing skills. By using alternative assessment, the teacher is not only evaluating language skills but also allowing students to use other skills that will be of equal importance in the future. The real-life situation is felt more keenly than if traditional assessment had been used.

Alternative assessment takes into consideration both the process and the product of student learning. Further, it does not exclude traditional types of exams, but rather adds more varied methods of collecting data. If, as Genesee and Upshur (1996) state, the essential bases of evaluation are information gathering, interpretation, and decision making based on the information obtained, then the more varied the information teachers receive, the better equipped they will be to make the right decisions when developing their language teaching curriculum.

CALL-Based Versus Face-to-Face (f2f) Assessment

Technology has always been a key tool for learning, and it has kept up with the trends in language testing. As early as the 1970s, students used computer programs to practice grammar through drills (e.g., CALIS from Duke University [no longer available]). More recently, they have done so through interactive CDs and the World Wide Web, in a format that was also generally used for traditional testing. For standardized testing, many universities have item banks where tests are generated randomly (e.g., the ESL Placement Examination at the University of California, Los Angeles [Henning, 1986]; the item bank at the language department of the Simón Bolívar University [Champeau, Marchi, & Arreaza, 1994]). Computer-adaptive language testing (CALT) selects standardized items from a databank based on the responses given by the student. Students are tested until their proficiency level has been reached, thus avoiding questions too far above or below their level. Students can work on items at their own pace and are not pressured by the psychological constraints of the f2f testing environment. With CALT, feedback is immediate, allowing students to see the areas in which they made errors and so making them aware of the work to be done in the specific area. If the bank contains enough items, there is a lower chance of students becoming acquainted with the questions. Also, unlike humans, machines are very precise and accurate when marking and reporting results. The disadvantage is that the infrastructure needed and the high program costs take this option out of the hands of the individual classroom teacher.

However, the Internet has placed within the range of classroom teachers a number of resources that can be used for authentic assessment. Not only can videos and recordings be found on the Internet, either from news or organizational sites, but a number of educational sites also offer source materials. Authentic language in authentic settings allows testing that is much more in keeping with the communicative nature of language. Moreover, there is a greater chance of being able to tap into individual student learning styles, capture students' attention, and feed their interests with up-to-date topics, so that learning occurs even when they are being evaluated, an extremely difficult task to accomplish in an f2f classroom.

Once the material has been found, online software can be used to generate different kinds of exercises for testing: multiple-choice, multiple-correct, matching, drag-and-drop, short-answer, and open-ended questions. The answers can also be programmed so that, as in CALT, student receive immediate feedback. Software allows students to be evaluated anywhere, anytime, for instance, by podcast or cell phone, again removing the constraints of traditional pen-and-paper testing. Some programs like *Quia Web* (Quia, 1998–2007) even generate statistics that can be useful for further decision making about instructional goals. Computer-mediated communication tools, such as text and voice chat, weblogs (blogs), wikis, forums, podcasts, and virtual environments, can also be integrated into class activities that can be evaluated according to specific criteria. Just as new dimensions are opening up with alternative assessment, so, too, is technology giving teachers a wide range of synchronous and asynchronous means of communication that can be manipulated by both the teacher and the student and used to show the authentic and communicative nature of a living language.

Examples and Discussion

Some typical assessment strategies include contracts and e-portfolios, which can be used to evaluate classroom activities alongside assessment tools such as checklists, rubrics, and Know–Want to know–Learned (K-W-L) charts. These will each be discussed in further detail.

Contracts in Language Learning

Dickinson (1987) first defined a contract as an agreement between a learner and a tutor or a learner and himself or herself, and since then, the concept of contracts has grown to include how the individual will meet specific instructional objectives, what will be learned, how objectives will be met, the time period for completion, how the student will self-evaluate, and how the teacher will assess student learning. As a result, contracts can be said to help students learn how to manage their learning process. Figure 17-1 shows the basic steps needed in drawing up a learning contract.

As the flowchart in Figure 17-1 indicates, contracts involve the active participation of students as well as teachers. Students' individual learning styles, needs, and views with regard to goal setting, resources needed, and time available for achieving goals, as well as the type of evaluation to be used, are

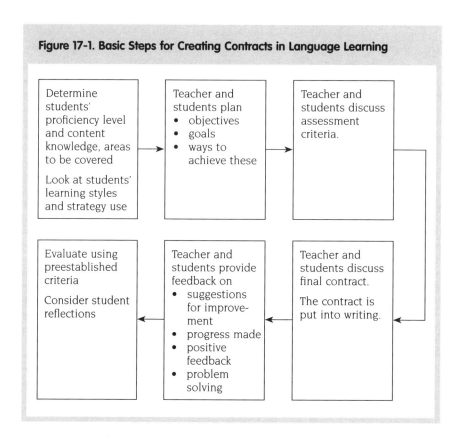

Figure 17-1. Basic Steps for Creating Contracts in Language Learning

essential factors. The use of rubrics and checklists, which ensure that students and teachers know what is being evaluated and the criteria for evaluation, is also important. Feedback on student progress can be given through checklists, rubrics, and observation forms as well as in discussions with students using chat or meetings in virtual rooms. Students should also be encouraged to evaluate their own work and the learning process through reflection on what they have achieved, any new perceived needs, and how these should be met. This self-monitoring will help them make the necessary changes to their work plan. Evaluation of the final product should be performed using the preestablished criteria, and students should include reflections on their performance, perhaps using a blog, and what they learned during the period.

Learning contracts can thus be seen as both a teaching strategy and an assessment tool geared toward self-directed learning. By allowing students to negotiate their work plan based on what they perceive as their needs, teachers share the decision-making process in the classroom. Doing so gives students a sense of control over their learning, which is reflected in a greater responsibility toward their work and higher motivation and interest in learning (St. Louis & Pereira, 2003). Contracts also give students the opportunity to choose the types of activities they would like to have assessed. Students are assessed not just on selected activities, but on the criteria established by specific rubrics (González & St. Louis, 2002). Alternative assessment contracts are geared toward individualized learning. However, activities that foster collaborative learning through group work should be included:

- *Vocabulary games* created with programs such as *Quia Web* (Quia, 1998–2007), Makers Pages (n.d.), or Hot Potatoes (Arneil & Holmes, 2006) can generate different kinds of exercises, in addition to multiple-choice and true/false, such as drag-and-drop (which involves eye and hand movement), matching, and Hangman (see Kelly, 2003b). Images and audio can be added as well, to appeal to different learning styles.

- *Research activities* in the form of WebQuests (Dodge, n.d.-b; *Filamentality* [AT&T Knowledge Ventures, 2007b]) set the task processes and clearly describe the outcomes expected. Students must use critical thinking and organizational skills to complete their project. These activities can also be enriched by the use of multimedia and collaboration.

- *Oral presentations* for a foreign audience live online or videotaped and uploaded to a Web site motivate students to give their best performance (González, 2005), whether individually or in groups. Self- and peer evaluation through blogs and forums where other people can leave comments is also a plus. Students realize that they have an authentic audience and not just the classroom teacher interested in giving a grade.

- *Process writing* using blogs or wikis allows students to receive feedback from their teacher and their peers.

- *Class preparation* in English for specific purposes courses involves students preparing a class as if they were professionals already working in the field. Students must research their topic and can use Internet resources to present as varied and interactive a class as possible. As in real work situations, teams are often the best option.

- *Videocasts* or *streaming videos* taken from Web sites (e.g., *Real English* [The Marzio School & Real English, 2007]) offer dictation or listening comprehension with interactive pre- and postactivities prepared using online exercise software such as *Quia Web* (Quia, 1998–2007), Makers Pages (n.d.), Hot Potatoes (Arneil & Holmes, 2006), and *Script-O!* (The Reading Matrix, 2000–2005). (See Appendix D for more testing tools.) The variety of exercises that can be generated with these free software products can appeal to different learning styles.

- *Podcasting* and *audioblogging* can be used for short oral presentations, interviews, and reflection on readings and videos. (*PodOmatic*, 2007, is an example of an audioblog site.)
- *Storytelling* using Microsoft Photo Story (2004), Windows Movie Maker (2007), iMovie (2006), or *BubbleShare* (2004–2006) to enhance photos with written texts, music, animation, and voiceover allows students to inject their personality into the activity and use all the senses.
- *Multimedia exams* and *quizzes* can be generated by students (individually or in teams) and teachers using the software mentioned previously.
- *Chat sessions* held while working on projects may be used to evaluate turn taking, negotiation of meaning, and other more subtle forms of communication in an authentic context (González, 2003).
- *Online jigsaw readings* present each student with a different piece of the reading or aspect of a project, and groups must work together and share information to complete the activity (see González, 2006, for a fuller description of jigsaw reading).

These are but a few of the different kinds of activities that can be included in the contract and used with resources and applications found on the Internet.

Alternative Assessment Instruments

Considering the variety of activities and the subtasks needed for their completion, teachers and students must have a clear idea of what is to be evaluated and how to do so. In alternative assessment, validity and reliability are maintained through the use of instruments that include checklists, rubrics, scales, and inventories.

Checklists delineate factors, aspects, components, criteria, and/or dimensions of a task, or properties that should be taken into consideration while it is being carried out (Scriven, 2005). Advantages of using checklists include having a list of criteria that ensure that no important aspect is forgotten, that all students and tasks are evaluated equally, and that the same criteria are available for subsequent reevaluation (Stufflebeam, 2000). A well-designed checklist reduces both the Rorschach effect (the tendency to see what one wants in the data) and the halo effect (being carried away by a highly valued factor; Scriven, 2005), thus ensuring better objectivity and credibility in the evaluation process. In addition, the large amount of data received from checklists makes them excellent diagnostic tools that can help the teacher determine if individual and course instructional goals are appropriate.

Checklists (see Table 17-1) are essential in the planning stages because the information about what is required of students allows them to plan their course of action in terms of resources, time and material, level of performance, and the final product expected. Students and teachers can also monitor and evaluate the learning process at any stage before getting to the final product.

Figure 17-2 is an example of a checklist created to give qualitative feedback to students working collaboratively in a chat to complete a task (González, 2004). This checklist can be used while the students are chatting or later with the chat log or recording. The following criteria are used:

- *helping*—The teacher observes the students offering assistance to each other.

- *listening*—The teacher observes the students working from each other's ideas.

- *participating*—The teacher observes each student contributing to the project.

Table 17-1. Types of Checklists

Type	Characteristics	Example
Laundry	A list of items that should be taken into consideration, with *yes* or *no* indicating presence or absence of item	"To do" list
Sequential	Items placed in strict hierarchical order, with one step dependent on the other	Steps in experiments
Weak sequential	Order of the items important only for physiological or efficiency reasons	Job requirements
Criteria of merit	Complete and concise items based on criteria with an assigned numeric value; criteria should be clear, comprehensible, applicable, and measurable	Oral presentation

Note. Adapted from *The Logic and Methodology of Checklists*, by M. Scriven, 2005, Western Michigan University, http://www.wmich.edu/evalctr/checklists/papers /logic&methodology_oct05.pdf

Figure 17-2. Qualitative Feedback Checklist for a Chat Session

Chat # 1   Date: Topic of discussion:

Scoring: Never—Sometimes—Always

Skills	Helping	Listening	Partici-pating	Per-suading	Ques-tioning	Respecting	Sharing
Group 1							
Group 2							
Group 3							

- *persuading*—The teacher observes the students exchanging, defending, and rethinking ideas.
- *questioning*—The teacher observes the students interacting, discussing, and posing questions to all members of the team.
- *respecting*—The teacher observes the students encouraging and supporting the ideas and efforts of others.
- *sharing*—The teacher observes the students offering ideas and reporting their findings to each other.

Rubrics give samples against which the performance is judged; they are used for tasks that involve oral or written production. (A number of online rubric generators, such as *RubiStar* [ALTEC & University of Kansas, 2000–2006] and *teAchnology: Rubrics* [n.d.], may be found in Appendix D.) Although general rubrics can be formulated to cover multiple tasks, it is important that they be used with the specific tasks and goals of instruction to be evaluated (National Capital Language Resource Center, 2003–2004). Students can check their performance at any time against the standards and expected outcomes established in the rubric, and this feedback allows them to correct any weak areas and plan the strategies that they should use to improve them (see Table 17-2).

Rubrics, however, are not always useful for classroom evaluation because they might not provide students with enough information on their performance. Analytic rubrics provide teachers and students with more information about the learner's strengths and weaknesses; however, they have been criticized for

Table 17-2. Types of Rubrics

Type	Characteristics	Use
Holistic	• Uses 4- or 6-point scale ranging from *needs work* to *excellent* • Considers language as a whole • Scores student's best performance	Large-scale composition testing
Analytic	• Uses categories representing different dimensions of student performance • Allows each category to be graded separately and added to final score	Evaluating written work, looking at content, organization, vocabulary, grammar, and mechanics

not giving a more holistic assessment of the learner's performance (National Capital Language Resource Center, 2003–2004). Figure 17-3 shows an example of an analytic rubric used to assess students' participation in group chat meetings (González, 2004).

K-W-L (Know–Want to know–Learned) charts are an inventory (see Figure 17-4) that allows the teacher to assess the depth of students' prior knowledge of a topic while making students aware of the cognitive and metacognitive strategies they can use to enhance learning. Students activate their prior knowledge through the use of pictures, key words in a text, or charts. They then make predictions based on this information and categorize the data to be used. Students fill in the last column with information they have learned. Adaptations to this basic chart have been made by Campbell Hill, Ruptic, and Norwick (1998), who include a fourth column, *further wanderings*, in which students write questions that have emerged as a result of their research, thus giving added incentive to continue exploring the topic. Teachers can use K-W-L charts to assess students' oral production, participation in class discussions, and ability to focus on the topic or work in groups. K-W-L charts also allow teachers to rethink their lessons based on where students are weakest or strongest. (For further information, see Saskatoon Public School Division, 2004.) The K-W-L chart can be posted to a Web page or sent to students via e-mail for them to complete and post to their e-portfolio (see Figure 17-4).

Rubrics, checklists, and K-W-L charts are but a few of the different assessment instruments that can be used in alternative assessment. Quite a few Web sites provide other types of instruments that teachers can use to personalize their evaluation process, for example, *Curriculum Bytes* (Prairie Land Regional Division #25, 2004). A number of these sites are included in Appendix D.

Figure 17-3. Analytic Rubric

	Excellent (5 points each)	Very Good (4 points each)	Satisfactory/Good (3 points each)	Needs Improvement (2 points each)
1. Participation related to technical aspects	Student actively participates in discussion with moderator and other participants.	Student asks and answers questions from moderator and other participants.	Student asks and answers questions from moderator.	Student answers questions posed by moderator.
2. Participation related to content	Student actively participates in discussion with moderator and other participants.	Student asks and answers questions from moderator and answers questions from other participants.	Student asks and answers questions from moderator.	Student answers questions posed by moderator.
3. Use of content vocabulary	Student makes good use of most of the new content area vocabulary.	Student uses properly some of the new content area vocabulary.	Student barely uses the new content area vocabulary.	Student makes no use of new content area vocabulary.
4. Demonstration of content knowledge	Student demonstrates full knowledge of content.	Student is at ease with content; fails to elaborate fully.	Student is uncomfortable with content; demonstrates basic knowledge.	Student does not have grasp of information; cannot answer questions about the content.
5. Social engagement	Student actively participates in nontechnical/academic topics voluntarily.	Student incorporates some nontechnical/academic topics in conversation if asked.	Student socializes a little (e.g., offers greetings).	Student restricts his or her participation to technical and academic aspects.

Note. From Dilemas de la evaluación del aprendizaje de Inglés con Propósitos Específicos a través de soportes electrónicos: Estudio de un caso [Dilemma in the evaluation of English for specific purposes through electronic supports: A case study], Unpublished doctoral dissertation, Universitat de València, Spain, by D. Gonzalez, 2004.

Figure 17-4. K-W-L Chart

What I know	What I want to know	What I've learned

Rubrics and checklists can be used when evaluating WebQuests, podcasts, chats, chat logs, and activities in blogs and wikis. They are extremely useful in the latter because, without actually physically correcting the product, the teacher can note the different areas in which students have improved or those that need work. The teacher can either e-mail the information or embed it as a link in the student's blog or in the course Web site. Students then use this linked reference to find and correct their mistakes. Over a period of time, this type of information can serve as an indicator of students' overall progress. Rubrics and checklists are crucial to guiding students in the process of self- and peer evaluation. For generating your own rubrics, see Figure 17-5.

Creating checklists or rubrics may appear to be a lengthy process, but doing so becomes almost second nature if they are used consistently throughout all your courses. Bear in mind that different skills can be assessed through one activity, and not all activities and tasks need to be evaluated. When designing the evaluation instrument, remember that the different skills needed for carrying out each activity should be listed, as should the objective to which each refers. Assign a mark for each component so that the total sum for each is equal to the total percentage assigned for the activity. Finally, remember to include students in the decision-making process, listen to their ideas, and incorporate their ideas in the evaluation instrument.

Portfolios are collections of complete works organized in systematic form. They have been used by artists and architects for many years to showcase the best examples of their work. The concept has been adapted by educators as a learning and assessment tool that includes reflection on and self-evaluation of work the student considers as representative or as fulfilling learning objectives. Portfolios can also include peer evaluations and the teacher's comments.

With the implementation of blended and online learning, *e-portfolios* or *web-folios* have begun to be used for assessment. Webfolios are static pages whose functionality is derived from the inclusion of hyperlinks, whereas e-portfolios are dynamic pages that include student work (Batson, 2002). E-portfolios should allow the addition of the self- and peer evaluations. They

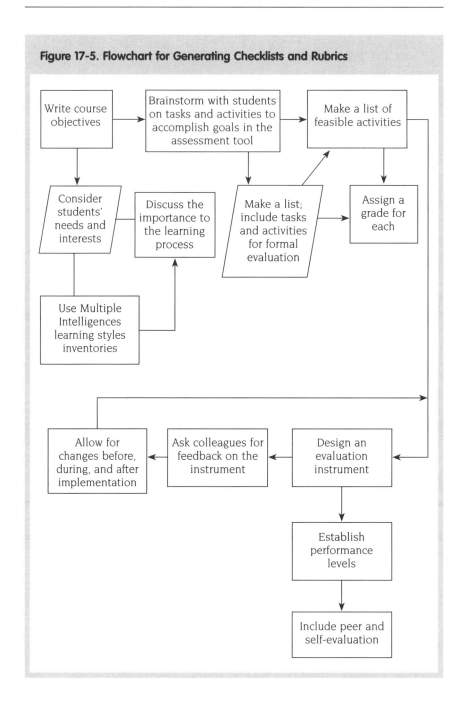

Figure 17-5. Flowchart for Generating Checklists and Rubrics

generally include the notion of a digital resource (personal artifacts, instructor comments) demonstrating growth, allowing for flexible expression (i.e. customized folders and site areas to meet the skill requirements of a particular job), and permitting access to varied interested parties (parents, potential employers, fellow learners, and instructors). (Siemens, 2004b, ¶ 3)

Because alternative assessment is a dynamic process that promotes the use of metacognitive strategies, e-portfolios fit well with student-centered teaching approaches, and each stage in their creation contributes to students' lifelong learning:

- collecting and saving artifacts that represent success and growth
- selecting those artifacts that show the achievement of objectives
- reflecting on work done
- evaluating growth
- setting learning goals to overcome gaps in the learning process
- making work available for peer and teacher feedback (Barrett, 1999–2000)

E-portfolios can be created on a CD, on a static Web page, or in an interactive space where peers and teachers can leave feedback, such as a guest book, blog, forum, voice board, wiki, videocast, or videoblog (see Tosh & Werdmuller, 2004, for a discussion of blogs as e-portfolios). Formatted portfolio applications, both commercial and free, are available on the Web (see Appendix D). However, for security and convenience, it is preferable to provide space on the school's own server. Wikis are ideal for e-portfolios because they can be password protected. They allow students to post and organize their work where they can receive teacher and peer feedback, and no knowledge of HTML is required. Whatever format is used to create an e-portfolio, the essentials are to formulate the objectives clearly and to provide self-reflection on the selected activities. E-portfolios, as a cumulative record of work, can present the teacher with multiple views of the instructional process as seen through the eyes of the students throughout the course of a term.

Conclusion

We have briefly summarized the main characteristics of alternative assessment and its importance for assessing instructional goals in situations where the student is the center of the learning process. We have also suggested the combination of contracts; Web-based activities evaluated with criteria clearly established in rubrics, checklists, and inventories; and reflective e-portfolios used to implement alternative assessment in Web-enhanced, blended, or wholly online courses. These types of assessment allow for sufficient time and feedback to the language learner and lay the groundwork for growth in autonomy.

However, when using alternative assessment, teachers lose power and control, and more work is involved—preplanning, correcting drafts, providing ongoing feedback—and students may not be used to taking responsibility for their learning. To overcome these problems, a change of paradigm is necessary. As suggested throughout this volume, learning is not information transfer, and students are not passive recipients of information. Teacher training in this new vision of the assessment process is needed. Modeling, coaching, and scaffolding should be considered as follow-up activities for training sessions. Teachers as well as students need to be aware of the importance of the learning process. Furthermore, the validity of assessment in blended and online courses has been questioned by administrators and teachers who see quantitative exams as the only reliable source of evaluation; they are afraid that students will cheat in the online exams. Formative and summative evaluations that take place throughout a course, with the help of alternative assessment techniques and instruments, such as those suggested in this chapter, are crucial for e-learning. A well-formed assessment plan will help teachers and administrators see that they have nothing to fear.

Explorations

1. Thinking of your own educational context, would you use any of the alternative evaluation strategies suggested in this chapter? Which ones? Why?

2. How would you involve your students in the design of any of the assessment instruments you use? How could you best make use of this involvement as part of the instructional process?

3. How can you best give your students opportunities to reflect on their learning process? Explore some of the learning tools, such as rubrics, checklists, and K-W-L charts, suggested in this chapter.

4. How would you include self- and peer evaluation in your assessment plan? How would you use that evaluation to revise your instructional processes?

5. Given the resources of your instructional context, what Web tools would you incorporate into your assessment plan? How would you prevent students from cheating?

Chapter 18

Critical Issues: Professional Development

Philip Hubbard

Focus

Of all the areas of language teaching, CALL is perhaps the one most in need of regular professional development. This is due to three reasons:

1. Many teachers do not establish sufficient foundational competencies during their initial training.

2. The hardware and software applications change so rapidly that existing skills and knowledge soon become obsolete.

3. The technology and technical support vary widely across teaching settings, and even within the same institution they may undergo radical changes with little notice.

All of this means that teachers must be constantly engaged in learning and relearning in order to make the most out of the technology available to them.

This chapter provides an overview of issues in CALL professional development and explores resources and strategies for maintenance and growth in this critical area. It addresses the topic primarily from the perspective of the practicing classroom teacher; however, its content is clearly relevant for those in teacher preparation programs as well, who will soon be out on their own in the field. Other stakeholders, notably teacher educators and language program administrators, can also profit from an examination of the need for professional development in CALL and the resources mentioned here. This chapter considers the following points:

- What are the foundational CALL competencies for the field as a whole?

- How do teachers determine their individual objectives?

- What are effective learning processes for reaching those objectives?
- What are some examples of resources and model strategies for professional development?

Background

Proficiency in CALL is increasingly becoming part of the repertoire of skills expected of ESOL teachers in the 21st century. Recent job listings attest to this fact, showing that some expertise in CALL is necessary or desirable for many advertised positions. For example, a search of TESOL's (1996–2004) online job list in October 2005 yielded 56 entries with the proportions listed in Table 18-1. Given that these job listings are quite limited in detail, many that did not explicitly list CALL expertise as desirable in a candidate might nevertheless consider it a positive factor.

How well are teachers being prepared for positions such as these? TESOL's directory of teacher education programs in the United States and Canada (Christopher, 2005) provides an interesting snapshot of the present state of preservice CALL training, at least within those two countries, because the directory listings include specifications of the required and optional courses for each institution. Table 18-2 extrapolates the proportions of CALL mandated by the 172 master's programs listed in the directory.

Admittedly, such a count does not accommodate programs that include a significant technology component in content courses with other names, but there is no evidence that such a practice is widespread yet. Given these

Table 18-1. Representative TESOL Job Listings

	n	%
Did not mention CALL or technology	34	61
Mentioned CALL or technology	22	39
General or specific CALL or technology expertise required	15	27
CALL as desirable or preferred qualification	7	12

Note. N = 56. From TESOL *Career Center*, by TESOL, 1996–2004, http://careers.tesol.org/. Accessed October 29, 2005.

Table 18-2. Technology Offerings in TESOL Master's Programs

	n	%
Indicated no CALL or technology course offerings	109	63
Listed one or more courses in CALL or technology training	63	37
Required a course in CALL or technology	22	13
Offered a course in CALL or technology as an elective	41	24

Note. N = 172. From *Directory of Teacher Education Pprograms in* TESOL *in the United States and Canada*, by V. Christopher (Ed.), 2005. Alexandria, VA: TESOL. Copyright 2005 TESOL.

data, one can conclude that the majority of teacher preparation programs in the United States and Canada may be providing nothing in the way of structured training in the use of technology for teaching and learning languages, presumably leaving teachers to fend for themselves.

Proficiency in CALL, as in other areas of language teaching, includes two steps: (a) building foundational competencies and (b) updating, upgrading, and adapting that foundation based on changes in technology, language teaching approach, and current teaching context. Unlike many other areas of professional development, foundational competency for CALL does not seem to be present for many practicing teachers (Kessler, 2006). Thus an additional challenge, to teachers as well as educators who implement professional development workshops, courses, and programs in CALL, is to recognize the need to build that foundation.

Discussion and Examples

I identify three central issues in CALL professional development:

1. What are the foundational CALL *competencies* for a teacher? That is, what standards should the field provide?

2. How does a teacher determine what the objectives of professional development should be for him or her individually?

3. What are the means for reaching those objectives? In other words, what are effective ways to learn CALL and sustain that learning?

In this section, I address each of these questions briefly and explore some directions for resolving them. However, it should be noted that these issues are evolving as the technology evolves, are quite complex, and are undoubtedly contentious. Thus a quick overview is as far as this chapter will go.

Foundational Competencies

There are currently no fieldwide standards for what an ESOL or other language teacher should know and be able to do with computers. In fact, given the rapid changes taking place in technology and the enormous variety in terms of computer facilities and support in teaching settings, it is clear that any statement of desired qualifications for the profession as a whole would have to be at a very general level. As noted in the introduction, for many teacher preparation programs the position seems to be that a teacher does not need to know anything about computers.

Promulgating technology standards for teachers could provide both motivation and some direction to teacher education programs to improve this situation. TESOL has a long history of developing other standards in the field of ESOL (see the >PROFESSIONAL ISSUES menu at the TESOL [1996–2006c] Web site for information on current standards and ongoing initiatives). Although at the time of this writing TESOL has not produced a set of standards addressing technology, progress is being made: In early 2006, the TESOL Standards Committee appointed a project team to begin developing sets of technology standards for students and teachers.

Other organizations have also made progress on technology standards. A widely accepted model has emerged from the International Society for Technology in Education (ISTE). ISTE has laid out technology standards for teachers and students in K–12 contexts through its National Educational Technology Standards (NETS) initiative, which addresses the following six areas:

1. technology operations and concepts
2. the planning and design of learning environments and experiences
3. teaching, learning, and the curriculum
4. assessment and evaluation
5. productivity and professional practice
6. social, ethical, legal, and human issues (ISTE NETS Project, 2000–2005a)

Though of course not specific to language teaching, the NETS for teachers nonetheless provide a good starting point, especially in the area of technical proficiency. And the American Council on the Teaching of Foreign Languages (ACTFL) is an official partner in the NETS initiative. Additional details for each of the six areas are available at the ISTE NETS Project (2000–2005a) page, which also has a >TEACHER PROFILES link to detailed performance profiles for technology-literate teachers in the areas of general preparation, professional preparation, student teaching, and first-year teaching.

Individual Objectives

Although a growing body of standards provides targets for professional development in the language teaching community as a whole, Pettis (2002) observes that "commitment to professional development must be ongoing and personal" (p. 394). Beyond the role of professional organizations and government institutions to promote standards and offer avenues for meeting them, teachers have an individual responsibility for the maintenance and growth of their own CALL proficiency.

The listing of performance profiles on the ISTE site is one place to start in determining individual objectives for the practicing teacher. Teachers can match their proficiencies and areas of need to those profiled. Teachers may also self-assess their CALL instructional skills using other means, such as the *Learning With Technology Profile Tool* (Learning Point Associates, 1997).

An alternative approach can be found in a recently developed role-based framework providing areas of consideration for generating and evaluating the content of CALL teacher education initiatives (Hubbard & Levy, 2006). That framework begins with two assumptions: (a) what one needs to know and be able to do depends on the role one is assuming at any given time, and (b) roles may be defined to a large degree by the expressed, or perceived, expectations of those affected by the individual. Continuous, dynamic changes in CALL mean that role specifications are somewhat fluid (often fuzzy, in fact), and rather than being developed top-down and universally for language teachers, these roles are closely tied to the social and educational setting in which they are embedded. This role-based framework recognizes the relatively constant *institutional roles* of preservice or in-service classroom teacher, CALL specialist, or CALL professional, and the more flexible *functional roles* of practitioner, developer, researcher, and trainer (see Figure 18-1).

With respect to institutional roles, I focus here on a discussion of the parts of Figure 18-1 that relate to the primary audience for this chapter: *preservice* and *in-service classroom teachers*, including the relatively new category of *online teacher* for whom technology is the sole medium of interaction with the student. CALL *specialist* and CALL *professional* refer to expanded roles both in and out of the classroom setting. In the CALL specialist role, an individual would be expected to possess deep knowledge and a wide range of skills in a given CALL domain, such as pronunciation, writing, or lab direction. As a CALL professional, the individual would have both breadth and depth across several CALL domains. It is worth noting that these expanded roles are all too often informal and uncompensated (Kessler, 2006), as in cases where administration and colleagues expect someone whose formal institutional

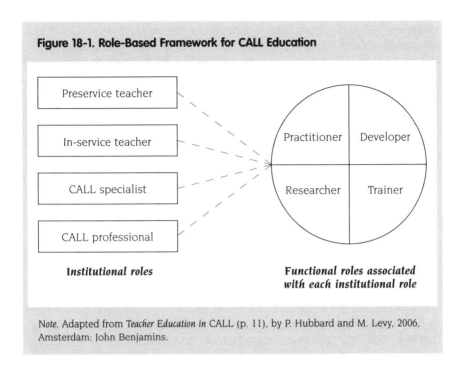

Figure 18-1. Role-Based Framework for CALL Education

Preservice teacher

In-service teacher

CALL specialist

CALL professional

Institutional roles

Practitioner | Developer

Researcher | Trainer

Functional roles associated with each institutional role

Note. Adapted from *Teacher Education in* CALL (p. 11), by P. Hubbard and M. Levy, 2006, Amsterdam: John Benjamins.

role is *classroom teacher* to provide CALL expertise to others freely in addition to their existing workload.

I explicitly emphasize multiple functional roles here because a professional teacher is more than just a classroom "technician" who "performs certain acts with skill and becomes more skillful as time goes on" (Ur, 2002, p. 389). As D. Freeman (1998) observes in arguing to expand the roles of teachers, "teachers are seen—and principally see themselves—as consumers rather than producers of knowledge. Other people write curricula, develop teaching methodologies, create published materials, and make policies and procedures about education that teachers are called upon to implement" (p. 10). Freeman goes on to urge teacher education programs to emphasize the importance of the teacher as researcher to sharpen and expand instructor effectiveness. By specifying these differing functional roles, the framework in Figure 18-1 makes clear that professional language teachers using technology are not just practitioners serving as conduits for the work of others, but are also expected to be creative researchers and developers. The framework additionally fore-grounds the functional role of *trainer*. In that role, the teacher's responsibility is to ensure that students have appropriate technical competence along with a repertoire of effective strategies to link CALL applications, activities, and tasks to their language learning objectives.

Within each of the functional roles, Hubbard and Levy's (2006) framework also formalizes distinctions between knowledge and skill and between technical and pedagogical areas of CALL. In doing so, it emphasizes the importance of a solid technical foundation for all pedagogical roles in CALL. Brief definitions for these domains can be characterized in greater detail when linked to specific institutional and functional role combinations (e.g., in-service teacher as practitioner), as suggested in Table 18-3.

With respect to professional development, it is possible for a teacher to use the role-based framework as a guide in addressing the following questions in both the technical and pedagogical domains for each function:

1. What do I currently know, and what am I able to do? (knowledge or skills acquired formally or informally)

2. What do I need to know, and what do I need to be able to do? (as required by current position or mandated by applicable standards)

3. What do I want to know, and what do I want to be able to do? (professional growth or expansion of role to specialist or professional)

It is well beyond the scope of this chapter to suggest a detailed list of all the technical and pedagogical knowledge and skills needed by classroom teachers. However, Table 18-4 presents an example for one area: the use of WebQuests

Table 18-3. Role-based Framework for Classroom Teachers

Technical Knowledge	Technical Skills	Pedagogical Knowledge	Pedagogical Skills
Systematic and incidental understanding of the computer system, including peripheral devices, in terms of hardware, software, and networking	Ability to use technical knowledge and experience both for the operation of the computer system and relevant applications and in dealing with common problems	Systematic and incidental understanding of ways of effectively using the computer in language teaching	Ability to use knowledge and experience to determine effective materials, content, and tasks, and to monitor and assess results appropriately

Note. Adapted from *Teacher Education in CALL* (p. 16), by P. Hubbard and M. Levy, 2006, Amsterdam: John Benjamins.

in language learning. Dodge (n.d.-b) originally designed WebQuests as exploratory projects to support analysis and synthesis of information drawn from Web resources, especially to foster research and critical thinking skills. In language classrooms, they have the additional advantage of leading students to interactions with authentic online material (see Godwin-Jones, 2004, for an overview of WebQuests for language teaching). Table 18-4 indicates some of

Table 18-4. Examples of Skills and Knowledge Required for a WebQuest Overlaid Across the Functional Roles of a Classroom Teacher

	Practitioner	*Developer*	*Researcher*	*Trainer*
Technical Knowledge of . . .	Basic search options, e.g., how to use *Google* (Google, 2007a) or *Yahoo! Answers* (Yahoo!, 2007d)	Advanced search engine options; Web page creation	Options for recording student searches/ interactions	Search engine options; mastery from student side
Technical Skills to . . .	Find desired lessons and present them to class; format online lessons	Find useful new sites; lay out and upload Web pages; create online lessons	Implement technical end of research design	Troubleshoot student hardware/ Internet problems
Pedagogical Knowledge of . . .	Lesson types/ activities that use Web searches; links to learning objectives	Core concepts of WebQuests and links to objectives; content sources	How research results may lead to curricular changes	The range of student needs and techniques for meeting them
Pedagogical Skills to . . .	Identify and select material; integrate it into effective class lessons	Adapt existing WebQuests or develop new ones to meet local needs	Select and interpret student project data to evaluate success	Identify and implement appropriate training techniques

the knowledge and skills needed in each functional role to teach WebQuests to language learners.

Hubbard and Levy's (2006) framework provides only a rough guide. In practice, individual objectives will likely be determined over time and perhaps with some guidance from others.

Whatever the process, it is important to identify the necessary knowledge base and skill set and to target both technical and pedagogical expertise. Although in settings with high levels of support much of the technical expertise may be provided by others, a foundation in the appropriate knowledge and skill areas is still helpful, and understanding the pedagogical component is always going to be the individual teacher's responsibility.

Learning Processes

The previous two sections focused on the content of professional development. The final set of issues involves the processes for reaching identified professional development objectives and how a teacher chooses among them. This section looks briefly at several alternatives.

Formal training in CALL exists in, for example, workshops at conferences, institutional courses, and certificate programs consisting of multiple courses. Increasingly, workshops and courses are available online, and engaging in an online learning environment itself typically enhances technical and pedagogical knowledge and skills. The advantages of formal training are that it is more likely to be systematic, presented by an expert, and acceptable for fulfilling continuing education requirements. The limitations are that formal coursework may not be readily available or well suited to the individual (too easy or too challenging), and unless there is organized follow-up, some of the skills and knowledge may disappear before ever being used. Further, unless the workshop or course description is sufficiently detailed, a teacher may discover that the content is not a good match for his or her teaching situation for either technical or pedagogical reasons.

Situated learning is one way to address some of the limitations of formal instruction. As noted by Egbert, Paulus, and Nakamichi (2002),

> it is not due to a lack of confidence or interest in CALL that teachers do not use CALL activities; rather, it is due to a lack of time, administrative or curricular restrictions, or lack of resources. The findings point to the need for more contextualized instruction directly related to the teaching environments in which language teachers will be practicing. (p. 122)

Egbert (2006) argues convincingly that teacher education in CALL will be most effective when the technology is situated in the realities of the classroom and students. She presents a set of concepts from situated learning theory focusing on authenticity in context, activities, and assessment; access to expert performances; experiences with different perspectives; and ample opportunities for collaboration, reflection, and scaffolding. She demonstrates how these can be incorporated into a CALL course and notes that for preservice teachers in particular, detailed case studies can be used to capture some of the essential character of situated learning. As a concept, situated learning is not limited to formal courses. An individual learning independently should be even more aware of the need to link his or her professional development in CALL to the immediate teaching environment.

Project-based learning refers to learning through the experience of constructing something, for example, developing a Web site. Debski (2006) provides a rationale for utilizing project-oriented learning in CALL courses and describes the development and implementation of a student project in such a course at the University of Melbourne, where participants created a Web site and online community to prepare foreign students for their arrival in Australia. Whether within a formal course or not, project-based learning provides links to the real world as well as enhanced motivation associated with creating a useful product, such as a WebQuest, a Web site, or a set of online language exercises—all projects that provide a concrete setting where teachers can develop appropriate knowledge and skills while producing valuable learning materials for their students.

Mentoring, in the informal sense of learning by doing with the support of a more expert associate, has long been an established means of acquiring both technical and pedagogical expertise. Since its inception, TESOL's CALL Interest Section has been a group in which informal mentoring takes place during the TESOL convention, especially during the open hours of the Electronic Village, a dedicated computer lab at the convention where teachers can try new software and visit Web sites with volunteer advisors present. Meskill, Anthony, Hilliker-VanStrander, Tseng, and You (2006b) provide a rationale for mentoring in CALL and describe an innovative project at the State University of New York, Albany, where doctoral candidates in the institution's teacher education program and practicing classroom teachers simultaneously mentor preservice teachers. As discussed in the following paragraph, mentoring is also a common characteristic in communities of practice.

Collaborative learning with one's colleagues is another well-established route for professional development. Collaboration may take place with one or more coworkers, perhaps in the context of a project that serves the local program, or in larger, often widely distributed groups known as *communities of practice* (CoPs). Examples of both in nontechnical areas can be found in the fourth volume in TESOL's Professional Development in Language Education series (Murphey & Sato, 2005). Kolaitis, Mahoney, Pomann, and Hubbard (2006) describe a collaborative effort at a community college ESL program where a group of faculty that had been using CALL in their courses for a number of years decided to implement a learner training project to help students develop strategies for using ESL software more effectively. Hanson-Smith

(2006a) provides an overview of both the rationale for and implementation of CoPs in the CALL domain. She notes that CoPs can provide a mechanism for teachers to maintain and upgrade their CALL proficiency as well as alleviate the isolation of individuals from other technology-using teachers, an all-too-common occurrence in settings where there may be only one CALL-oriented instructor in a language program or even an entire institution.

As should be clear from this discussion, the learning processes and environments described here are not mutually exclusive, and combinations of them are likely to provide the best match for an individual's professional development trajectory.

Resources and Strategies

This section reviews a number of avenues for CALL professional development. These range from formal in-service training in the field to informal initiatives engaged in independently or with others. Before looking at these resources, however, it is worth considering two general strategies for engaging in professional development. Egbert (in press) offers a useful procedure for producing an individual technology learning plan. Teachers first list information about their current technology proficiency and use, then reflect on that information to identify potential areas of improvement, and finally produce three or four goal statements. For each goal, teachers lay out the means for achieving the goal, a target time for completion, and a means of tracking progress toward the outcome. A second strategy, following the project-based approach mentioned previously, is to begin by identifying a single technology project to integrate into an existing language course and then to learn the technical and pedagogical skills needed to complete that project through the resources noted in the remainder of this section. Whether considered individually or with collaborators, building professional development around a concrete, practical project is likely to enhance motivation and lead to deeper learning.

CALL *degrees and certificates*

A few universities around the world offer advanced degrees in CALL and related areas for those seeking to become CALL professionals. A partial list can be found at the EUROCALL *Postgraduate Courses* page (Riley, 2006). Certificates relating to technology and language learning are also available from various institutional sources as well as from the TESOL association. These certificates typically require completion of a set of courses, and although they are not generally given the same sort of official recognition that some TESL/TEFL certificates are (e.g., the Cambridge Certificate), they do provide teachers with validation of significant professional education in CALL. For example, a comprehensive program offered by the Monterey Institute of International Studies consists of 10 short courses: The first 4 are required, and the remaining 6 are chosen from a list of electives (see Monterey Institute of International Studies, 2006).

The TESOL association offers professional development in online teaching through its Principles and Practices of Online Teaching Certificate Program (TESOL, 1996–2006b). The program is taught entirely online both for practical reasons and to give teachers experience with the same learning environment their students will use. It offers certification following successful completion of a required foundation course and five elective courses.

Individual courses

As noted in the introduction, although the majority of master's degree programs in TESL/TEFL do not provide dedicated CALL courses, some programs do. Depending on the institution, these may be open to teachers who are not enrolled in the degree program, or through continuing education or extension programs. Sometimes CALL courses are offered in an online format so that teachers outside the immediate area can participate. Bauer-Ramazani (2006) describes one such course in detail. A teacher considering this option should find out as much as possible about the course content since there is such a variety of conceptions of CALL and approaches to teaching it. Also, as noted earlier, professional development in CALL requires both technical and pedagogical knowledge and skills; one or the other may represent the individual's greater need.

Workshops

Workshops are short courses, sometimes no longer than a few hours, that are aimed at presenting practical information and in some cases providing hands-on experience. Workshops are presented at a number of venues: teaching institutions, conferences, and even internally in some language programs. In 2002, TESOL's CALL Interest Section began offering the Electronic Village Online, preconvention workshops conducted online. These 6-week, all-volunteer virtual workshops in January and February are free; information on upcoming sessions can usually be found at the TESOL CALL Interest Section Web page in December. (For a description of typical workshop sessions, see Hanson-Smith & Bauer-Ramazani, 2004.)

However, teachers should be aware of two problems associated with workshops. First, even a well-designed workshop may provide content that is not a good fit to the individual's functional role, skill level, or knowledge. Second, most workshops are not designed to include follow-up, and it may be difficult to find the time and the resources to implement the material once the workshop is over. To be most effective, a workshop should have immediate value, and ideas should be implemented as quickly as possible.

Professional organizations and interest groups

CALL organizations provide some of the best resources for furthering professional development, and there are a number of regional and international associations to choose from. Some of the more prominent, in addition to TESOL, are listed in Appendix A. In addition to these, some national organizations and TESOL affiliates have technology interest groups. Teachers should check the local affiliates of professional organizations for technology-oriented interest groups.

Professional journals

Several refereed journals devoted to technology in language learning (some associated with the aforementioned organizations) provide major resources:

- CALICO *Journal* of the CALICO professional organization—All issues from 1983 onward are available online to members.
- *ReCALL*, the journal of the EUROCALL professional organization— Back issues from 1996 to 1999 are available free online.
- *Language Learning & Technology*—This free online journal is devoted to theory and research in CALL and related fields.
- CALL EJ *Online*—This free online journal deals with research and practice in CALL and related fields.
- *Computer Assisted Language Learning*—This journal is dedicated to uses of computers in language teaching, learning, and testing.
- *System*—This journal is devoted to educational technology and applied linguistics in foreign language teaching and learning.

Books

In addition to the present volume, several recent texts provide an introduction to CALL:

- Beatty (2003) presents CALL from an applied linguistics perspective and includes historical and research perspectives with practical teaching examples.
- Butler-Pascoe and Wiburg (2003) build from a communicative language teaching base and connect technology to contemporary ESL theory and practice.
- de Szendeffy (2005) offers pedagogical rationales for CALL activities without much reference to theory or research, but provides the strongest technology focus.
- Egbert (2005) begins with classroom conditions and uses practical examples and quotations from other teachers to lead readers through the process of thinking about how to integrate

CALL, guided by principles from second language acquisition (SLA) theory and research. She includes a chapter on teacher development with a number of useful recommendations, perhaps the most valuable of which is to learn "to search the Web efficiently and effectively" (p. 154).

- Hanson-Smith and Rilling (2006) present practical examples of CALL in a variety of settings. Each chapter specifies the relevant SLA and communicative language teaching theories and includes discussion questions and research activities.

All of the preceding texts offer helpful, practical information, examples, and resources to teachers. Other recent books presenting a somewhat more academic overview of CALL are valuable to teachers looking for more depth: Chapelle (2003), Ducate and Arnold (2006), Fotos and Browne (2004), and Levy and Stockwell (2006). A list of other technology-oriented books published by TESOL can be found under the >Publications link at TESOL's (1996–2006c) home page. Another good source of books is the reference list in this volume.

Communities of practice

CoPs within the CALL domain are groups of language teaching professionals who work toward mutual support in the pursuit of a shared interest. These can be formal groups within professional organizations, mentioned previously, or informal and independent groups open to all interested parties, such as the Webheads in Action, founded by Vance Stevens (see Stevens, 2007). Hanson-Smith (2006a, 2006b) provides details about the Webheads and other CoPs in the CALL and ESOL context. Some CoPs are organized around specific technologies, such as ESL/EFL Student Video Production (Gromik, 2006a) or Hot Potatoes Users (2006).

Web sites for professional development

For those with reliable Internet access, the Web offers the most convenient means of professional development. A good place to start is the set of resource links on the TESOL CALL Interest Section home page (see TESOL CALL-IS: *Make the Connections*, n.d.). In addition, many other sites can be found by conducting a Web search or looking up references in published works. One project deserving particular mention is the ICT4LT (Information and Communications Technologies for Language Teachers; ICT4LT Project, 1999–2006), whose Web site is a collaborative effort by a number of CALL experts from Europe under the editorship of Graham Davies. It provides material for a comprehensive introduction to the uses of technology in language teaching and offers a fair amount of depth in selected areas, all free if used online. Its 16 training modules, offered in several major European languages, are divided into basic, intermediate, and advanced levels of technological knowledge, with a separate module on assessment. The site also includes a rich set of links to other resources and is updated regularly. Another resource worth exploring is Teaching and Learning Languages Enhanced by New Technologies (TALLENT Project, 2000), which offers free, in-service training modules in five languages, developed by experts from 11 European universities under the sponsorship of the European Commission.

In addition to the aforementioned sites focusing on technology in language learning, there are others in the general education area worth exploring. Besides the standards documents already mentioned, NETS *Resources* (ISTE NETS Project, 2000–2005b) has content area standards (including for foreign languages), rubrics, forms (e.g., for software evaluation), software listings, and a technology glossary. The NCRTECH *Lesson Planner* (Learning Point Associates, 2001) leads teachers through a series of questions to develop coherent, standards-aligned curriculum units that include technology. The Education World (1996–2007) Web site includes a rich section on technology integration, highlighted by a selection of "techtorials" covering a range of topics of value to teachers. *Getting Results* (WGBH Educational Foundation, 2006) has produced a series of videos to guide community college teachers in using technology.

Conclusion

As with learning a language or any other topic on your own, the key elements to professional development are motivation, access to appropriate content, and a plan. Motivation can come from many sources, but as mentioned earlier, motivation will perhaps best emerge from engaging in a project relevant to your local teaching context. Content is widely available through the publications and Web sites noted previously. As for a plan, the following are a few suggestions for those embarking on professional development:

- If you are still in a degree program, take advantage of any available courses to build sound technical and pedagogical foundations for the future. Technology is likely to play an increasingly important role in your language teaching career.

- Explore constantly. Look at some of the resources described here, in the appendixes, and in other chapters of this volume to get an idea of the range of possibilities for using technology in language teaching and a sense of the knowledge and skills necessary to realize them. Keep a list of Web sites, activities, and lesson concepts that interest you, along with your reactions to them as you go through the exploration phase. Take some time before you make your plan to reflect on options, especially if you are relatively new to CALL.

- Try to identify one specific topic for further exploration by reflecting on your current teaching and focusing on some area in which you believe technology could lead to more efficient or effective learning for your students.

- Start small to keep the professional development objective manageable.

- Find local collaborators if possible; it is usually easier to maintain progress if someone else is sharing the experience. If local collaborators are not available, look for support through an appropriate online professional group or CoP.

- Get to know your local technology infrastructure, including the physical environment, hardware, software, networking, and support personnel.

- When working with colleagues or technical support personnel, try to get them to show and tell you what they are doing rather than just doing it for you if the skill or knowledge they possess is potentially useful to your development.

- Throughout, keep a reflective journal or weblog (blog) of the experience and review it regularly for information and inspiration. Continue to explore and share what you have found with interested colleagues.

Educators often cite the need for lifelong learning for teachers (e.g., Pettis, 2002; Ur, 2002), and nowhere is this need felt more strongly than in the area of technology because it is the domain of language teaching that changes most rapidly. Busy working professionals may find it challenging to develop and maintain their CALL competencies, but the payoff for meeting that challenge is substantial, in both personal and professional terms. Language departments and programs that recognize the added value such development offers, and that provide the appropriate resources to support it, will almost certainly find that investment worthwhile. Whatever a teacher's current stage of knowledge and skill, whatever preparation he or she may have had in the past, professional development in CALL is an area deserving serious and ongoing attention.

Explorations

1. Think of an instance in the past year when you had a computer problem of some sort that took some time to resolve. How was it finally fixed? By whom? If you did not fix it yourself, would you be able to do so in the future? Did you learn anything valuable that might transfer to other scenarios?

2. Using the chart in Table 18-4 of this chapter, perform a self-evaluation of your technical knowledge and skills relative to a particular aspect of language teaching, such as teaching composition or reading: What do you know and what can you do?

3. Visit the TESOL CALL Interest Section Web site (TESOL CALL-IS: *Make the Connections*, n.d.). Explore the various links and note which ones you find useful and why.

4. Visit the ICT4LT Web site (ICT4LT Project, 1999–2006) or *Getting Results* (WGBH Educational Foundation, 2006) for adult or community college teachers. Survey the material you find there, and select one module or video to look at in some depth. Try to connect the information you discover with your own teaching setting. If possible, use a suggestion you find there for a class activity.

5. This chapter mentioned the value of situated learning and project-based learning in several places. Think about a CALL-oriented project that would be useful either in your current teaching situation or an anticipated one whose setting you can clearly imagine. Outline a plan for the project, noting some of the technical and pedagogical knowledge and skills you will need to realize it. You may wish to refer to some of the projects noted in many of the other chapters in this volume. As a follow-up, consider the different knowledge and skills you will need in the various roles of practitioner, developer, researcher, and trainer for the project you envision (see Table 18-4 for examples).

PART VI

Intentional Cognition

Chapter 19

Theory and Research: Language Learning Strategies

Chin-chi Chao

Focus

Because English is associated with positive career prospects in Asia, there is an unfailing zeal for learning the language among Asian students. Naturally, one of the most frequently asked questions for any EFL teacher here is "How can I learn English?" Students, parents, colleagues from other disciplines, and people from all walks of life are interested in a good answer to this question. Books about learning English are everywhere, and they are always on the top of bestseller lists. A colleague of mine says that a good answer to the question is simply "Why don't you just go ahead and learn it?" Behind this comment is the assumption that people can learn a language if only they take action to find ways that work for them.

Teachers definitely need to have some understanding of language learning strategies before it is possible to make sound suggestions when asked the question about how to learn a language. In contexts where technology is employed, it is also necessary to understand the strategies that learners can apply to the tools embedded in language learning software so that the tools chosen can be used fruitfully by learners. In addition, teachers must keep in mind that computer tools could encourage students to develop habits that are not conductive to language learning; thus, awareness of potential problems is critical. In short, for effective learning through CALL, students and teachers alike must be aware of language learning strategies and their use.

This chapter takes the reader on a journey toward an understanding of language learning strategies in computer-supported language learning environments. The discussion starts with findings from earlier research that focused on successful learners and what less successful learners might learn from them. Later in the chapter, I focus on systems of strategy categories and learning strategies in computerized learning environments. To encourage the proper use of learning strategies, I identify two types of strategy instruction: (a) taking on a *training model* and (b) creating a *culture of language learning.*

Background

Good Learners

Research into language learning strategies started in the 1970s with the investigation of how good learners learn a language. Researchers attempted to derive useful strategies by documenting what good learners do, mainly through *self-report methods* such as questionnaires and journals. The assumption was that if unsuccessful language learners could be taught what successful learners do, it would be possible to help them improve their performance. Researchers such as Naiman, Frohlich, Stern, and Todesco (1978/1995) and Rubin (1975) have provided well-known lists of good learner strategies. For example, based on insights into good learners' cognitive processes, Rubin states that a good language learner

- is a willing and accurate guesser
- has a strong drive to communicate, or to learn from communication
- is often not inhibited. He [or she] is willing to appear foolish if reasonable communication results. He [or she] is willing to make mistakes in order to learn and to communicate. He [or she] is willing to live with a certain amount of vagueness.
- is prepared to attend to form in addition to focusing on communication. The good language learner is constantly looking for patterns in the language.
- practices
- monitors his [or her] own and the speech of others. That is, he [or she] is constantly attending to how well his [or her] speech is being received and whether his [or her] performance meets the standards he [or she] has learned.
- attends to meaning. He [or she] knows that in order to understand the message, it is not sufficient to pay attention to the grammar of the language or to the surface form of speech. (pp. 45–48)

Although such lists are mostly speculative, and research with good learners has not supported many of these strategies (H. D. Brown, 2000), I have found that the language learners I know are often very interested in obtaining such lists. The reason given by learners is often that it is interesting to see what other people do with the same language learning task, especially if they have been successful at the task. What is more, learners often get motivated about language learning by just reading or hearing about strategies or tips. However, whether they actually adopt the new strategies is a different issue. As Pressley, Levin, and Ghatala (1984) have found, learners have the tendency to stick to tried and tested strategies even if they know for sure that there are alternatives.

Systems of Language Learning Strategy Categories

With so many strategies available, researchers have developed systems to categorize them. Oxford (1994) points out more than 20 categorical systems available for language learning strategies, including systems based on successful learners, psychological functions, linguistic practices, language skills, and learning styles. Taking all the systems together, some researchers (e.g., H. D. Brown, 2000; Jamieson & Chapelle, 1987) contend that there are basically three major kinds of learning strategies: metacognitive, cognitive, and socioaffective. *Metacognitive* strategies "involve planning for learning, thinking about the learning process as it is taking place, monitoring of one's production or comprehension, and evaluating learning after an activity is completed" (H. D. Brown, 2000, p. 124). Metacognitive strategies can be further subdivided into the categories of planning, monitoring, and evaluating. *Cognitive* strategies are mental processes that learners use to acquire, sort, remember, and use information. Finally, *socioaffective* strategies include getting a message across, practicing the language with the resources at hand, and cooperating with others.

Oxford's model, presented in her seminal 1990 book, *Language Learning Strategies: What Every Teacher Should Know*, has been adopted widely for teaching and research. Language learning strategies in this model are divided into *direct* and *indirect* strategies, with direct strategies being mnemonic, cognitive, and compensational and indirect strategies being metacognitive, affective, and social. The Strategy Inventory for Language Learning (SILL; Oxford, 1990, pp. 293–300), based on this model, has also been adopted for research projects and utilized by many classroom teachers to help learners identify their strategies. Table 19-1 shows the strategies discussed in Oxford's model as well as some sample computer-supported activities that could provide opportunities for using the strategies.

CALL researchers have also attempted to develop systems for strategies used with multimedia courseware or computer-supported collaborative tasks. For example, in a study examining strategies used by experienced adult foreign language learners with multimedia courseware, Ulitsky (2000) categorized the learners' strategies into four types. The first type is *general learning strategies*, including organizing and planning for learning, regulating or fine-tuning learning, and dealing with frustrations and challenges. The second type is *medium-specific strategies*, which learners used to exploit the multiple modalities offered by the computer. The third type is *content-specific strategies*, which learners used to apply prior knowledge. The final type is *context-specific strategies*, which were used when learners sought outside resources.

rd's (1990) Strategy Categories and puter-Enhanced Activities

Strategy Categories	Corresponding Strategies	Supportive CALL Activities
Mnemonic	Creating mental linkages, applying images and sounds, reviewing well, employing action	• Using courseware that has components such as drill and practice, games, and exercises (e.g., Rosetta Stone, n.d.) • Using a dictionary Web site such as OneLook (n.d.) to define words • Developing a concept map for new vocabulary with software such as Inspiration (2006) • Using Google Image Search (Google, 2007d) to look up new words and view their corresponding images
Cognitive	Practicing, receiving and sending messages; analyzing and reasoning; creating structure for input and output	• Engaging in computer-mediated communication activities or projects such as an iEARN (n.d.) collaboration • Talking with a Web robot such as A.L.I.C.E. (A.L.I.C.E. AI Foundation, n.d.)
Compen-satory	Guessing intelligently using clues, overcoming limitations in speaking and writing	• Talking with native speakers in chat rooms or through synchronous videoconferencing
Meta-cognitive	Centering learning by overviewing and linking with already known materials, paying attention, delaying speech production to focus on listening, arranging and planning learning, evaluating learning	• Using an alarm function and an online calendar to remind oneself of appropriate times to work and to rest • Checking understanding with online exercises and feedback • Listening to online radio programs or podcasts

(Continued on p. 299)

Table 19-1 (continued). Oxford's (1990) Strategy Categories and Supportive Computer-Enhanced Activities

Strategy Categories	Corresponding Strategies	Supportive CALL Activities
Affective	Lowering anxiety, encouraging oneself, taking emotional temperature	• Keeping a language learning diary using a weblog (blog) or wiki
Social	Asking questions, cooperating with others, empathizing with others	• Supporting a community online • Asking for help from online communities in a way similar to *The Diary Project* (1998–2003)

Note. Adapted from *Language Learning Strategies: What Every Teacher Should Know* (pp. 15–22), by R. Oxford, 1990, Boston: Heinle & Heinle.

M. Smith (2000), in investigating factors influencing collaborative language learning tasks on the computer, also discovered additional strategies necessary for computer-supported collaborative learning tasks. Because computers and network technologies are becoming integral parts of language instruction, the necessity to add new categories can be expected. One such strategy category is *resourcing*, which deals with how learners utilize computer tools and functions.

Resourcing

Resourcing, a term coined by O'Malley, Chamot, Stewner-Manzanares, Kupper, and Russo (1985), refers to the way learners use software's built-in language learning tools or online help functions as a kind of cognitive strategy (Liu, 2000). Chapelle and Mizuno (1989) focused on software that claimed to encourage learner-centeredness and found that there was usually an assumption that learners would choose to use explanations provided by the computer at the right time, at the right frequency. Learners were also expected to modify their answers based on the feedback message and to determine the right time to quit the program based on their performance. Investigating five strategies that adult ESL learners applied to spelling and dictation material, including two cognitive strategies (resourcing and practice) and three metacognitive strategies (self-monitoring, self-management, and self-evaluation), Chapelle and Mizuno found that most learners actually did not use all of these strategies optimally.

When learners use the tools provided by software, they use them in very limited ways. Within all the studies on resourcing, first language (L1) translations were the most popular comprehension aids consulted by learners (F. L. Bell & LeBlanc, 2000; J. N. Davis & Lyman-Hager, 1997; Laufer & Hill, 2000). F. L. Bell (2005) confirmed that adult language learners reading authentic second language (L2) texts on the computer overwhelmingly prefer bottom-up lexical types of resources rather than top-down, nonlexical aids. Furthermore, learners consulted more visual resources than L2 glosses. Interestingly, none of the studies found differences in comprehension no matter which resource type or resourcing strategy was adopted. Laufer and Hill also found that extensive use of glosses does not correlate with vocabulary retention.

So far, the only consistent finding across many studies is that L1 translation is the most preferred resourcing strategy that language learners use on the computer. The fact that learners use very limited computer functions suggests that many do not automatically know how to use computers to learn a language, particularly in a situation in which they are expected to direct their own learning (Ulitsky, 2000; for more on the problem of autonomy, see Robb, 2006).

Problematic Strategies With Computers

Computers provide useful tools for language learning, but they may also encourage learners to develop habits and strategies that are not conducive to effective language learning. For example, many computer users have already found that the automatic spell-check function in word-processing software seems to have a detrimental effect on spelling ability. Likewise, depending too much on typing can cause some students' handwriting to deteriorate. Chat room conversations, with their emphasis on speedy and oral-like written communication, have been found to lead to the attitude that sloppy spelling, poor punctuation, and pidginized language use are justifiable. Language educators often need to remind learners of the possible damaging sociocultural consequences.

There are actually wider effects of computer use on learning strategies and attitude in general. Research in the United States on Generation Y (people born between 1982 and 2002) has found that those who possess an information-age mindset tend to hold the following beliefs:

- Computers are not technology. They are simply a part of life.
- The Internet is better than TV.
- Reality is no longer real. What you see most often is fake.
- Doing is more important than knowing.

- Learning more closely resembles Nintendo than logic. Trial and error is the strategy to use.
- Multitasking is a way of life.
- Typing is preferable to handwriting.
- Staying connected is essential.
- There is zero tolerance for delays.
- Consumer and creator are blurring. (Oblinger, 2003, p. 40)

Based on this mindset, the new generation of language learners may have already developed some strategies that are not helpful to language learning or learning in general. For example, in order to be quick, they may use trial-and-error as the major strategy for tackling online exercises instead of trying to figure out the principles operating behind the language. With experience-based learning preferences, they may also lack the patience necessary for reading long passages or feel reluctant to take the long path necessary for developing writing proficiency. It is important for teachers and learners to be aware of the pitfalls and challenges associated with computers. It is also necessary to consider how to best help the new generation of learners develop effective language learning strategies.

Examples and Discussion

Research about learning strategies reveals patterns of strategy use and helps to advance understanding of the processes that learners use to learn. Such understanding naturally leads to attempts to train or encourage less successful learners to use strategies more effectively (e.g., H. D. Brown, 2002; Chamot, Barnhardt, Ei-Dinary, & Robbins, 1999; Chamot & O'Malley, 1994). This section discusses two ways to encourage strategy use: (a) strategy training and (b) fostering a culture of learning.

Strategy Training

Strategy training should be learner centered, providing sufficient opportunity to develop learners' awareness and strategies as autonomous language learners. Among all that is known about good learner strategies, one thing is clear: Successful learners use strategies more appropriately than unsuccessful learners. They know very well when to use which strategies. Consider the following:

- Successful language learners tend to select strategies that work well together in a highly orchestrated way, tailored to the requirements of the language task (Chamot & Kupper, 1989, cited in Oxford, 1994).

- Successful language learners "are skilled at matching strategies to the task they were working on, whereas less successful language learners apparently do not have the metacognitive knowledge about task requirements needed to select appropriate strategies" (Chamot, 2005, p. 116).

These two statements show that what matters is context, not strategies per se. Which strategy is appropriate to what context has a lot to do with, for example, the demands of the task facing the learner, the resources available to the learner, or the inspiration derived from watching how other people go about learning. Learners therefore need to develop the ability to reflect, to observe, to pay attention, and to use resources more creatively and appropriately. Teachers must encourage learners to generate their own strategies through interaction with the world around them, not based on one perfect successful-learner model, which, according to Naiman et al. (1978/1995), does not exist.

This context-based attitude is taken by strategy textbooks (e.g., H. D. Brown, 2002). Brown starts with the notions that not all learners have the same preferences for learning and that it is important for learners to know themselves well. He discusses learning styles and affective issues; mental, linguistic, and cultural aspects of learning; individual and group strategies; and test-taking techniques. Questionnaires help learners understand their own preferences for learning. Brown places strong emphasis on promoting self-understanding and developing strategies based on each learner's unique context.

Fostering a Culture of Language Learning

Another way to encourage effective use of language learning strategies is by fostering a culture of learning. Nowadays having appropriate resources to learn a language such as English in an EFL environment is generally not a problem. The issue is how to help learners become aware of the opportunities around them and to make good use of these learning opportunities and resources. Encouraging learners to control their own learning is the concern of researchers studying autonomous language learning (Benson, 2001). Effective language learning environments encourage students to take control of their learning and to develop personal meaningfulness in language learning.

Donato and McCormick (1994), inspired by sociocultural theory, maintain that language learning strategies are *situated activities* generated from a culture of learning and are the by-product of mediation and socialization that novices depend on to develop into competent members of a *community of practice*. To encourage such a culture of learning in a college-level conversation course, the researchers engaged students in self-assessment, goal setting, and strategy use through the mediation of a portfolio in which the learners selected items and collected evidence of their own language development. A reflection journal every 3 weeks and an end-of-semester metareflection allowed the learners to be involved in a critical dialogue with themselves and the teacher about their own strategy use and performance. The researchers found that, as the course developed, the learners' goal setting and strategy use changed from general and vague to focused and precise, indicating that the learners were engaging in "reflective construction of language learning strategies" (p. 463), rather than merely operating as consumers of other people's learning directives. Students also became critical of their own strategy use as they engaged in research-like activities investigating problems in their learning experiences. This study shows that classroom culture, developed by a "mediated, dialogic cycle of self-assessment, goal setting, and strategy elaboration and reconstruction" (p. 463), is a promising tool to encourage autonomous and appropriate strategy use.

I have observed similar development at a university language center in Taiwan. The center, having a large collection of language learning materials but few learners who utilized them, developed a program to encourage autonomous language learning and increased use of the facility, mainly through informal study groups. Learners have been encouraged to propose topics for study groups, some of which include 'The Frontline of TOEFL" and "Be Friends With *Friends*" (the popular U.S. sitcom). The topics show that the themes suggested by language learners *for* language learners can be creative and designed with the interests and sensibilities of a peer group in mind. When five to seven students sign up for a topic, the study group is ready to start. The group is encouraged to function as a learning community in which all members have the obligation to contribute to the collective learning achievement of the group and to support each other in the program. Each group develops its own rules to regulate learning. For example, when a member misses a meeting, he or she may be asked to prepare handouts for one extra episode of *Friends* for the whole group. This way, even punishment can be related to language learning.

The program is highly learner controlled, and the center trusts that the groups have the ability to monitor and regulate their own learning. There is little teacher interruption in the process; however, if help is needed, teachers are always approachable. It is only at the end of the semester that groups are required to hand in a portfolio to show that the group and each individual made good use of the time in the program. For those learners who have attended all of the meetings during the semester, a certificate is awarded.

In a follow-up interview, students in the program spoke reflectively about their language learning experience. They were clear about ways to improve their learning, and they showed an appreciation of the opportunity to learn in a supportive community, even though the program was not part of the formal language curriculum. It was clear that developing a culture of language learning has encouraged these students to make use of the learning opportunities around them. Having observed the encouraging results and the learners' satisfaction with the program, I am convinced that this is a useful model for encouraging autonomous language learning.

Conclusion

In the process of evolving from identifying successful learners' strategies to developing systems to categorize strategies, CALL researchers have investigated strategy use, or resourcing, related to the computer. These researchers have identified "new" strategies and some possible negative influences of computer use on language learning. New information continues to become available (see, e.g., Chamot, 2005, for more on language learning strategies; Murray, 2005, for more on technologies for second language literacy).

An obvious emphasis in the literature is that language learning strategies are goal oriented and context related, aiming to raise learners' awareness of the resources around them and to develop their ability to use the resources appropriately. Researchers have recognized the contextualized nature of strategy use and have begun to explore learner identity and the sociocultural implications of strategy use (Pomerantz, 2001). It is important for researchers and teachers to consider the particular context in which the learner and the learning task are situated. Researching and encouraging strategy use through fostering a culture of language learning, similar to that described in Donato and McCormick's (1994) study, are promising in this respect.

When a learner asks how to learn a language, a clear interest exists. Teachers can encourage and strengthen that interest by helping learners identify a course of action that he or she can take to learn or to practice using the target language on a regular basis. Key principles for teaching strategies and the examples of ways to develop a culture of language learning provided here can be a starting point.

Explorations

1. Chao speaks of two different models: (a) *training* and (b) creating a *culture of language learning*. What are some critical differences you see in these two approaches to encouraging strategy use?

2. Observe language students in front of computers, and note the kinds of strategies they use. Compare your notes with others in your work group or class. What can you learn about your students from this activity?

3. Design a language learning activity that aims to foster a culture of learning using the computer and network resources available to you locally.

4. Find and take a learning styles test online (e.g., *Free Learning Styles Inventory* [Advanogy.com, 2003]). What is your learning style? How accurate do you think the test is? How will knowing your own preferences help you design effective instruction for others?

5. Design a teaching module for language learning strategies using the computer and network resources available to you locally.

Chapter 20 ⊞

Classroom Practice: Critical Thinking

Levi McNeil

Focus

When I enter the building of the English department at my university in Seoul, South Korea, I hear loud echoes coming down the hall. As I make my way down the hall, I distinguish the sounds as people speaking English, and when I glance into the room from which the noise is coming, I see the teacher standing in the front of the class, leading the orchestra of sound. She says, "How are you today?" and the students repeat, "How are you today?" Then, she follows with a higher-pitched, "I am fine, thanks, and you?" and the students promptly imitate. The class proceeds in this nature, with the teacher frequently stopping to expand upon grammatical features of the recited phrases. At the end of class, she announces that the material on the midterm exam will be three self-selected dialogues from chapters 2 through 6.

It is 2 a.m., and 20-year-old Hye Sun is sitting in her room with a piece of paper in her hand. The piece of paper contains the three dialogues she will be tested on for her midterm exam. Hye Sun is to memorize the dialogues verbatim. For every word she omits, her instructor will deduct points. She studies for days, memorizing the dialogues. She goes to take the final and finds that she can remember most of the words, but not all of them.

This situation is not uncommon in today's teaching of English as a second or foreign language, as some teachers rely on the traditional strategy of memorization. In fact, decades ago, most language learning classrooms incorporated rote learning using grammar translation and audiolingual methods. A mimicry and memorization (mim-mem) activity, like the one in which Hye Sun and her classmates were participating, would have been the norm. Today, language pedagogy has moved in the direction of engagement with the target language, stepping away from memorizing the "facts" of language and toward "using" the language. More recently, language educators have concluded that, in order to develop target language competency, learners need to know the facts and use of the language and also need to be challenged to use high-level thinking strategies when thinking in the target language. In other words, they need to think critically with and about language.

In this chapter, I briefly examine the evolution of critical thinking and how it has come to be used in classrooms. I present a definition of critical thinking along with a characterization of its subparts, followed by a description of critical thinking and critical thinkers, teachers' roles, computer applications, the Internet, and critical thinking software. I offer examples of how to promote critical thinking skills in CALL classrooms.

Background

Although *critical thinking* as an aspect of language education is somewhat new to the field, it has been a key component of education in the minds of well-known philosophers and educators for quite some time. As far back as the Golden Age of Athens, Socrates emphasized critical thinking as he began to invite others to ask questions about decisions passed down from officials. In the past century, critical thinking has resurfaced, and John Dewey deserves much of the credit for this. Dewey (1933) and his idea of *reflective thinking* brought critical thinking into the classroom by emphasizing that there are reasons and implications for individuals' beliefs. Building on Dewey's ideas, teachers began to view critical thinking as a set of thinking skills, and it was from this premise that teachers began to teach critical thinking as skills.

The development of critical thinking in the classroom can be traced to Bloom's (1956) *Taxonomy of Educational Objectives*. It is from this taxonomy that educators became cognizant of different levels, or hierarchies, of thinking that are active when processing and learning information. From the 1960s to the 1990s, Freire (2004) urged teachers to adopt critical thinking in order for students to force social change. He felt that education in its current form was merely *training* not *educating*, because of the handing down of specific content knowledge and "facts," and that in order to educate, a teacher must "not only teach his or her discipline well, but he or she must challenge the learner to critically think through the social, political, and historic reality within which he or she is a presence" (p. 19).

Today, the call for teaching critical thinking is growing louder. Facione (2006) notes that critical thinking is essential in becoming liberated and that without good critical thinking, "people would be more easily exploited not only politically but economically" (p. 19). As teachers, we prepare language students for the real world, and in order for them to make wise decisions, we must help them acquire and refine analytic skills.

Critical Thinking Skills

Analytic skills are the first facet of what is currently considered critical thinking. Scriven and Paul (2004) define critical thinking as "the intellectually disciplined process of actively and skillfully conceptualizing, applying, analyzing, synthesizing, and/or evaluating information gathered from, or generated by observation, experience, reflection, reasoning, or communication, as a guide to belief and action" (¶ 1). Critical thinking utilizes higher order thinking skills, the final three levels of Bloom's (1956) taxonomy (analysis, synthesis, and evaluation). These thinking skills include

- making inferences
- comparing
- comparing and contrasting
- analyzing
- making supporting statements
- decision making
- ordering
- evaluating
- creating groups
- investigating
- experimenting (A. Johnson, 2000, pp. 46–48)

Many of these skills are implicit in the conditions for optimal language learning described in chapter 1, particularly the negotiation of meaning, the production of varied and creative language, mindful attendance to the learning process, and learner autonomy.

The teaching of critical thinking generally follows one of two approaches. In the first, a direct approach to critical thinking serves as lesson content, the focus of tasks, or its own course. This approach focuses on the teaching of specific skills explicitly without a defined content area. The second approach, immersion, has a content area as a base, and certain topics in the selected discipline serve as material to explicitly teach critical thinking skills. Both approaches have benefits, but the second allows skills to be integrated with authentic problems and content. Cawelti (1995, cited in Heydenberk & Heydenberk, 2000) explains that "students will better learn and use critical thinking skills and strategies if these skills and strategies are taught explicitly in the context of content knowledge with attention to their [various] appropriate applications" (p. 9). Furthermore, some research indicates that critical thinking skills in one area do not completely transfer to a different area. In this view, skills are inherent in certain disciplines, and as such, they should be taught within those disciplines, not outside of them. General critical thinking courses may be too simplistic in believing that thinking skills in one domain are relevant in another (McPeck, 1990). (For more on teaching language through sustained content-based learning, see chapter 9 in this volume.)

Discussion and Examples

One strategy for teaching critical thinking in a language learning classroom is Socratic questioning. In this method, the teacher asks questions to narrow and define the terms and reasoning that students give for answers. There are no planned responses by students, thus a teacher cannot plan what will be said. Often there is no "right" answer to the problem; the goal of critical thinking is to look at problems from varying angles and come up with more than one possible answer (and thus, more language). Table 20-1 presents types of Socratic questions and exemplary questions within those types.

Many other strategies, including the following, can be used to support critical thinking:

- Aid students in information-processing skills.
- Model thoughtfulness in problem solving.
- Allow sufficient time for students to respond and reflect.
- Accept original and unconventional views.
- Examine open-ended social problems.
- Study controversial issues.
- Engage students in debates.
- Use materials that hold contradictive views.
- Analyze propaganda techniques. (Shiveley & VanFossen, 2001)

Learning critical thinking skills takes practice, and teachers should create an environment in which students are invited to take risks.

Affect in Critical Thinking

In addition to the skills component of critical thinking, students' disposition toward being critical is equally important. Superior skills or knowledge do not separate good thinkers from the rest; it is their thinking disposition (Beyer, 1995; R. L. Smith, Skarbek, & Hurst, 2005). Characteristics of a strong critical thinking disposition include

- seeking clarity
- being open minded
- keeping well informed

Table 20-1. Questioning Strategies

Strategy	Examples
Conceptual clarification What exactly are students thinking or questioning?	*Why do you take this stance?* *What exactly are you saying?* *Does this relate to other concepts you spoke of?*
Probing assumptions Do the students have presumptions?	*Are there any other assumptions?* *Are you assuming . . . ?* *What factors aided in the formation of those assumptions?* *How can you support or disprove that assumption?*
Probing rationale, reasoning What is the support for the claim?	*What makes this happen?* *How do you know this?* *Can you give more evidence to me?* *What are some examples of that?*
Questioning viewpoints What is another valid viewpoint?	*Have you considered this point of view . . . ?* *Does this seem reasonable?* *Can you think of another way to look at this?* *What makes . . . necessary?* *Who would this help?*
Probing implications What are the outcomes?	*What would change?* *Are there any negatives that can come from this view?* *In what ways could . . . be used to . . . ?*
Questioning the question Turn the question on its head.	*Why ask that question?* *Do you think there are any reasons why I asked this question?*

Note. Adapted from *Socratic Questions*, by Syque, 2002–2007, http://changingminds .org/techniques/questioning/socratic_questions.htm.

- being sensitive to the feelings of others
- desiring intellectual autonomy
- having independence of mind
- maintaining a sense of objectivity
- remaining skeptical
- respecting clarity and precision in others
- being fair minded (adapted from Beyer, 1995; Heydenberk & Heydenberk, 2000; R. L. Smith et al., 2005)

There are ways to cultivate language learners' thinking dispositions; teachers can begin by using language associated with thinking. For example, D. Adams and Hamm (1996) suggest that teachers use the words *hypothesis*, *reasoning*, *theory*, and *evidence* when communicating with the class. Tishman, Jay, and Perkins (cited in R. L. Smith et al., 2005) advise teachers to model critical thinking, utilize peer interactions, and explicitly explain culturally relevant skills and ideas. For example, teachers might model essay outlining by questioning the class about which items go first or second in reverse order of importance so that the most important is last. Or they might encourage the class to use Venn diagrams to show interconnecting relationships among their ideas.

Skills and disposition are reoccurring themes in definitions of critical thinking. In cultivating proficient critical thinkers, language teachers support opportunities for students to perform the activities suggested by the Foundation for Critical Thinking:

- Raise vital questions and problems, formulating them clearly and precisely.

- Gather and assess relevant information, using abstract ideas to interpret information effectively and come to well-reasoned conclusions and solutions, testing them against relevant criteria and standards.

- Think open-mindedly within alternative systems of thought, recognizing and assessing, as need be, their assumptions, implications of ideas, and practical consequences of lines of thought.

- Communicate effectively with others in figuring out solutions to complex problems. (Scriven & Paul, 2004, ¶ 8)

The Role of the Teacher

The role of a teacher focusing on critical thinking skills is that of facilitator. The students must feel free to voice opinions and take stances, and the teacher needs to allow them enough intellectual room so that they develop their own logic rather than relying on the transmission of the teacher's knowledge. Although while teaching critical thinking the teacher must step back from conversations and debates, he or she must recognize cues as to when to intervene and keep the exchange of students' ideas constructive and flowing. The idea is to promote a student-centered classroom that places the construction of knowledge in the hands of the students. Discussing the role of the teacher in a thinking-based classroom, Anderson and Speck (2001) state that "teachers are facilitators who scaffold instruction to facilitate students' growth while the students assume more ownership and responsibility for their learning" (p. 10).

Computers and Internet Technologies

Computers and Internet technologies have become increasingly powerful tools in supporting critical thinking instruction (T.-W. Lee, 2002). Computer use facilitates critical thinking because it can supply resources to challenge claims. For example, if someone says that school-aged children watch 4.7 hours of television per day, students can quickly research this information on the Internet to determine its accuracy. Having ready access to information helps students refute or adopt claims made by others. Furthermore, learners can perform searches to find specific examples within a topic. For example, a teacher may inform students about the differences in pronunciation between native English speakers from England and the United States. The teacher could then ask students to find and listen to audio clips of each pronunciation style and compare the samples for themselves. Computers are advantageous because they allow learners to be interactive. In transforming the classroom to a student-centered environment where learning is viewed as an active process, computers enable students to move from being passive absorbers of knowledge to active participants in knowledge construction while doing so in ways that lower their affective filter. For example, using e-mail and word processors offers students the chance to plan, taking time to reason and construct their output instead of being put on the spot to respond to a question.

T.-W. Lee's (2002) study suggests that computer literacy is crucial to using technology's power. Teachers should be familiar with six basic computer applications in order to provide students with computerized critical thinking tasks: databases, spreadsheets, word processors, presentation tools, communication tools, and Web browsers. With an understanding of what these are and the potential that they have, teachers can help students use the computer as a tool to connect ideas.

Software

Teachers can develop many exercises, activities, and tasks by combining language and content achievement standards, critical thinking skills, and computer applications. In addition, for institutions that have the financial resources, critical thinking software programs can be purchased. There are certain advantages to using software, particularly because the preorganized material of the programs offers a clear structure. Many of the critical thinking programs allow teachers to bring data in from outside sources, and they come ready-made with charts, diagrams, and mind maps to help organize data. Countless programs are available, and the list changes and grows quickly. Increasingly, software is being delivered over the Internet, either as a supplement to CDs and DVDs, or as a stand-alone.

Some software is specifically designed for language learning. If a software package is not designed for language purposes, it could still be used if the teacher selects critical thinking software that contains language appropriate for the learners' proficiency levels. Here are a few of the software packages available:

- Inspiration Software has three programs, spanning kindergarten to Grade 12. The software promotes critical thinking through visuals, organization, collecting data, and making connections among data.

- Rationale (2006; formerly Reason!able) is designed, according to its Web site, to help students organize thoughts, present strengths and weakness in arguments, and learn the theory of reasoning and argument using visualization modes. A free trial is available.

- Mind Benders (n.d.) are CD-ROMs based on books by Anita Harnadek. They include activities and games that employ deductive reasoning skills for students in Grades 2–12. Students are taught logic, mental organization, and reading comprehension skills.

- Thinkin' Things Collection 1 (1995) helps develop problem-solving and critical thinking skills in young children but may also be useful for adult oral language practice.

- The Critical Thinking Company sells software bundles in the subject areas of Logical Thinking and Language Arts. The Logical Thinking bundles are designed for Grades 2–12, and the Language Arts for Grades 3–12. The Language Arts bundles provide training with grammar, reading, and puzzles.

The Internet

With limited resources to buy critical thinking software programs, many teachers look to the Internet. The Internet is ideal for utilizing multiple resources and real-world data, but as with other forms of media, it can expose students to inaccurate information. D. Lynch, Vernon, and Smith (2001) note that students find it hard to distinguish between "cybertreasures" and "cybertrash" (¶ 1). Students often take Internet claims at face value. Paris (2002) identified two reasons for the acceptance and use of Internet information: (a) students are unaware of the ease of publishing Web sites, and (b) they trust the authors of Web sites as "authorities." For students to think critically about the resources they use, they can answer these four questions:

- *What is the domain?* The last three letters of a Web address can help sort the good from the bad. Web sites ending in *.gov, .edu, .org,* and *.mil* are generally considered better than those ending in *.com* and *.net.* The latter can be published by anyone, and thus accuracy could be an issue. However, some commercial *.com* and *.net* sites have been set up by professional journals and teachers. Sites must be examined on a case-by-case basis.

- *Who is the sponsor or page owner*? Read the mission or vision statements (sometimes found in the "About us" page) to determine the sponsor's or owner's point of view or ideology. Also, there should be ways to contact the sponsor or owner of the Web site.

- *Who is the author*? Who actually wrote the content of the page (as distinguished from the Web page designer, programmer, or service provider)? If there is information about an author, search citations to confirm the information, or contact the sponsor to request information about the author.

- *When was the page posted or last updated*? Web sites are often not kept current, so it is wise to look at the date that information was last posted. Dating is especially important for topics about which content may change rapidly. (Adapted from D. Lynch et al., 2001)

A Critical Thinking Disposition

One activity that can be undertaken to create a strong critical thinking disposition would be to examine the lives of good critical thinkers. For instance, students could research Abraham Lincoln's life, hardships, and achievements. While studying these topics, the students could be asked to identify aspects of Lincoln's character and why he might be considered a critical thinker. While working on vocabulary development, teachers could help students recognize and use adjectives to describe people and their dispositions. Here are some possible steps for such an activity:

- Students search the Internet to find three famous people they admire. They list the reasons they admire the famous people, including the adjectives listed on the Web pages that describe them. (The *History.com* [A&E Television Networks, 1996–2007b] and *Biography* [A&E Television Networks, 1998–2007a] Web sites might be useful in this search.)

- Students tell the teacher the names they have selected, and these are written on the board along with adjectives, related behaviors, characteristics, and dispositions. The teacher makes a diagram showing the items listed, linking the famous people with certain adjectives and dispositions.

- Students identify characteristics that great thinkers have in common, using a paper or software chart to note adjectives that will be the focus of subsequent lessons.

- Students follow up by researching and writing a report explaining, with the use of the focal adjectives, why the selected person

can be considered a great thinker. (Adapted from Heydenberk &
Heydenberk, 2000)

Online Research to Develop Thinking Skills

At the Filamentality *Activity Formats* Web page (AT&T Knowledge Ventures,
2007a), a number of outstanding activities have been created to integrate
higher order thinking skills into Internet activities. This section outlines a
unit on the topic of pollution to demonstrate a few of these activity formats.
It is important to note that activities need not be consecutively sequenced;
they can be done in any order and on different topics. Each activity discussed
here includes a short description and a how-to section.

Hotlists of related Web pages provide an abundance of information from
varying viewpoints on various aspects of a topic. For example, the teacher
provides a set of Web pages (it is important to use Web pages, not Web
sites, so that students go to the exact place instead of surfing around Web
sites trying to find a specific page) that deal with causes of pollution, types
of pollution, ways to stop pollution, things affected by pollution, companies
and their products that are polluting, donations made by the companies that
pollute, and jobs that the companies create. As an exploratory activity, students list the information they find from different authors on a spreadsheet,
using the topics (e.g., causes of pollution) as column headings. At the end
of class, the students e-mail their spreadsheet to another student, and they
compare and contrast the information they collected, noting the similarities
and differences of their findings. From the similarities and differences, the
teacher constructs vocabulary-building activities by incorporating terms and
phrases (e.g., *recycle, ozone, emissions, greenhouse effect*) that are commonly seen
within the topic of pollution. (The teacher could use Kelly's [2003a] *Online
Quiz Generator*, for example, to quickly make a vocabulary quiz based on the
pages the students have found.)

The teacher uses *Filamentality's* features (AT&T Knowledge Ventures, 2007b;
see *Filamentality* >START A NEW PAGE; registration is required) to create a hotlist
with accompanying addresses that is directly available on the Internet. Students visit the teacher's *Filamentality* page (a separate page may be created for
each class or group of students) to link directly to the resource.

Treasure hunts are designed for students to develop more background
knowledge and understanding of a topic. To begin a treasure hunt, the
teacher provides a minilesson on question construction and question
response. The teacher preselects 10–15 Web pages that contain answers to a
number of specific questions, the types of questions that were the focus of
the minilesson. If working with higher-proficiency-level students, the teacher
could have each student compile his or her own pages, write accompanying
questions, and have other students answer the questions. The Web pages

can include video and audio clips, readings, or virtual museum tours. The questions call for answers that are contradictory. For example, one question might be *What country emits the most greenhouse gases*? On one of the given Web pages, the answer is the United States, and on another Web page, it is India. This contradictory information can be used to set the stage for future searches. After the students have answered the questions, the teacher poses a question of greater scope. For the pollution example, this question could be *Can the world ever be pollution free*? Considering the data they have collected and sorted on spreadsheets, the students make a table on a word processor outlining whether they believe the world could ever be pollution free. Once the students have completed the tables, they present their reasons, expressed in writing or orally depending on which skill the teacher wants to emphasize. When the students express their opinions, it is a good time to ask Socratic questions, giving practice both for question construction and critical thinking approaches to the information they have uncovered.

Teachers and students can use the free, online, interactive forms at *QuestGarden* (Dodge, 2007) to create their treasure hunts as HTML documents in the form of WebQuests. Dodge (n.d.-b) provides examples in many areas, including language teaching. The Filamentality *WebQuest Overview* page (AT&T Knowledge Ventures, 2007c) also links to many examples of the genre for a variety of purposes.

Subject samplers are Web pages that narrow the focus on a topic. Students are asked to form an opinion based on their own perspective of the information presented. As the Filamentality description puts it, "rather than uncover hard facts (as they do in a Treasure Hunt), students are asked about their perspectives on topics, comparisons to their experiences, and their interpretations of artworks or data" (AT&T Knowledge Venture, 2007a, "Subject Sampler Example," ¶ 1).

The treasure hunt described earlier ended with students separating reasons for and against the question *Can the world ever be pollution free*? With the subject sampler, the teacher introduces two video clips that have "authorities" speaking on each side of the issue. While students view the video clips, the teacher can focus on listening skills. Dictation exercises from the native speakers on the videos could easily fit into a subject sampler. After working on specific listening skills, the students watch the videos again and form their opinions on the issue at hand. Once they have formed their opinions, the students make an outline of ideas supporting their opinions.

In a variation of this activity, students might also create their own videos or podcasts presenting the *pro* and *con* sides of the debate (see Gromik, 2006b). In an audioblog, students could comment on each other's oral speaking skills as well as on the content of the debate (see Yeh, n.d., for an example of student debates in an audioblog).

Scrapbooks expose students to a variety of media concerning the selected topic. Once the students have selected a stance on the issue of the world being pollution free, the teacher asks them to find clip art, pictures, and images on the Internet that visually represent their ideas. (*Google Image Search* [Google, 2007d] may be a good place to start such a search.) The students then integrate the imagery into a Microsoft PowerPoint (2007) presentation. Later, the students present their projects to the class. While the students present, listeners receive oral and visual representations, and the teacher helps presenters with pronunciation. Building on the earlier focus of question formation, the teacher asks students to formulate Socratic questions for each other so that they can practice forming questions and the presenters have more opportunities to think critically and to speak in the target language. Following the presentations, the class has a final open discussion about the possibility of a pollution-free world as students examine the differing viewpoints associated with the question.

Conclusion

For years, critical thinking has been a central idea in the field of education, but not until fairly recently has it been thought of as applicable to the language learning classroom. Yet language students are required to make decisions on a daily basis, and teaching critical thinking skills can help them make those decisions effectively. The teaching of skills is vital in the effective use of critical thinking, but teachers must not forget the importance of a critical thinking disposition. Teachers should be sure to model such a disposition and use terminology that fosters the development of a solid disposition.

Additionally, teachers need to create a safe classroom environment where students are not fearful of making mistakes; taking risks and sharing opinions must be options that are made readily available to students. Using technology to teach critical thinking adds features to the learning experience that keep students interested and aids in their skill development. While incorporating the Internet into lessons, teachers should take measures to safeguard learners from undesirable sources by showing students how to assess the reliability of the Web sites they are viewing. With or without ready-made software and Web sites, teachers need to teach critical thinking, not just for the potential economic benefits, but also for learners' general quality of life.

Explorations

1. Were critical thinking skills taught as part of your language learning or general academic experiences? If so, in what situations and how? If not, why not?

2. How might culture play a role in whether and how such skills are taught? Do you think the direct approach to teaching critical thinking would work better than immersion? Why or why not? Provide some examples from your own experiences to share with your team or working group.

3. What critical thinking skills do your students (or potential students) have, and which do they need to develop or practice? Design or find an assessment to evaluate your students' skills in this area. Discuss your findings with your class or working group.

4. Choose a lesson plan that you have used or will use and add Socratic questions where appropriate. Model critical thinking for your students using these questions. Reflect on how this addition changes the lesson, and share your lesson plans with your class or working group.

5. Depending on the technological skills and language levels of your students, create a hotlist or subject sampler lesson with *Filamentality* (AT&T Knowledge Ventures, 2007b) for a specific content area. Have students work in teams and share their findings with class presentations. If possible, use different lessons with different classes of students. What works best, and why?

Chapter 21

Critical Issues: Visuality

Gina Mikel Petrie

Focus

As an educator who often asks students to use technology, it is valuable for me to remember the first time that I sat before a computer. I was at a friend's house in the fall of 1983, and he had just gotten a computer. As I watched, he fiddled with it in some mysterious way, and it hummed to life. He then walked out of the room for a few minutes, during which time I was drawn to the black screen. It was saying something to me, or at least, it *seemed* to be saying something to me. The screen was black except for the following:

A:/

I stood motionless, unsure what to pay attention to. My eyes did not know what to make of the letter/symbols on the screen any more than they knew how to make sense of the black space surrounding them. I did not know how to react, what to say (or, rather, *type*), which buttons to push, or in what order. A new space had opened up to me, but I did not know what was expected of me there. What was significant and what was to be ignored was unclear.

My print literacy had prepared me to pay the most attention to the single letter on the page. (But was the computer saying *Ahhhhh* to me? I wondered.) This literacy also prepared me to predict that the other symbols carried meaning, but I had no idea how to read or interact with a colon and a slash. Hesitantly, I typed "Hello," resorting to greeting the computer.

Nothing happened.

When my friend returned to the room, he found my attempt at communication amusing. He hit the >Enter button and then typed something just as illegible to me as the computer's original message. As I watched my friend's fingers fly over the keyboard and the computer screen change in response, I reflected on the gap between us: He knew how to read the screen and how to interact in this new space, but my literacy background had in no way prepared me for what I found there.

Background

In our profession, language educators have had enough time to grow comfortable with computer technologies and, consequently, enough time to forget the intricate comprehension abilities that are called upon when we enter electronic environments. Language learners bring with them a variety of background experiences and knowledge, which may or may not match up with what is called upon to comprehend an electronic text. Like me in 1983, they may not know how to respond or how to read the space that lies before them when they view a computer screen. Before that computer screen, students are asked to carry out a different type of discourse than that found any other place. They are asked to develop a new way of seeing, a new way of interpreting symbols and space. In short, they are asked to develop what Goodwin (1994) calls a *professional vision*—a way of paying attention to certain elements and suppressing attention to others.

Language educators and researchers have, of course, long paid attention to the linguistic elements in learners' environments. For example, classroom discourse around academic topics—*cognitive academic language proficiency* (CALP), a term coined by Cummins (1970)—has been investigated in terms of vocabulary and grammar. Grigorescu and Dwyer (2005) have investigated the academic vocabulary students are expected to master across the K–12 curriculum and have channeled this information into frequency-based word lists for several grades. In addition, important gains are being made in understanding how grammar forms vary across different areas of the curriculum (Byrd, 1998). As a result, teachers have at their disposal information regarding the grammar forms students need to acquire in order to comprehend the content in social studies or biology, for example. Thus, the linguistic elements of academic discourse have received attention.

Yet a view of discourse as social practice invites the consideration of more than simply the linguistic elements in the communication (Gee, 1992). Discourse extends beyond the linguistic structures people use to express their meanings and includes ways of thinking and behaving (Gee, 1992). More than vocabulary and grammar structures needs to be considered. Given the increasing importance put on the visual in the greater culture (Stephens, 1998), it is logical to consider its role in the discourses teachers ask learners to take part in. However, the visual has largely gone without investigation, despite Goodwin's (1994) proclamation that

> a theory of discourse that ignored graphic representations would be missing . . . a key element of the discourse. . . . Instead of mirroring spoken language, these external representations . . . organize phenomena in ways that spoken language cannot. (p. 611)

Therefore, failing to include the visual in investigations of any discourse—including that which takes place in electronic environments—is a significant oversight.

There are cues that the visual plays a significant role in people's lives. Horn (1998) points out that people have increasingly begun to use visual language during communication. Researchers such as Chesebro and Bertelsen (1996), Stephens (1998), and Mirzoeff (1999) have reported on the cultural impacts of the growing use of images for communicating. Detailed investigations about how the grammar of images operates have been reported as well, most notably through the work of Kress and van Leeuwen (1996). The electronic technologies people use to communicate usher in a heightened visuality (Chesebro & Bertelsen, 1996; Mirzoeff, 1999; Stephens, 1998). This growing general awareness of the use and impact of the visual simply needs to be turned in the direction of CALL.

The visual is not without mention in language teacher education texts, but these instances are based on limited views of its role. Texts frequently used in teacher preparation programs, such as those by Lightbown and Spada (1994), Cary (2000), H. D. Brown (2000), and D. E. Freeman and Freeman (2001), all recommend such visuals as photographs, line drawings, realia, gestures, and other paralinguistic cues as a form of assistance for struggling language learners. These authors view the visual as a scaffolding device capable of providing temporary aid to an English language learner (ELL). When the learner no longer needs the assistance, it can be removed. The visual is simply a tool, according to this perspective. Its use in classrooms would appear straightforward considering the lack of information provided about specific ways to use the visual with language learners. Its outcome would appear simple considering that these texts assume that the use of image automatically leads to more comprehensible input (Krashen, 1988). Ultimately, this perspective limits the visual element to the equivalent of a training wheel on a child's bicycle—removed and put away when the child is capable of independent bicycle riding. Authors of teacher education texts fail to see that the visual may be far more than a scaffold. Rather, it is an essential permanent element in the discourses that learners take part in. Researchers such as H. D. Brown (2000) have at times appeared on the verge of this recognition. Brown suggests that the broader realms of communication including the visual may be just as crucial to language learning and teaching as any of the specific words uttered or written. Certainly, this may be true of electronic discourse.

It may be helpful to consider, for example, *Starfall* (Starfall Website, 2003), a Web site meant to help children build literacy skills. Although the Web site was not intended for use by second language learners, many educators use it with this group. Teaching and learning are built upon the routine of constructing the unknown on what is already known. This Web site demonstrates that visual literacy is actually necessary to be part of the greater electronic discourse that learners are exposed to in CALL. To gain access to the linguistic, learners need to have a background in the visual.

The visual in electronic environments is not merely a tool, as many teachers of language learners appear to believe (as reported in Dexter, Anderson, & Becker, 1999; Karchmer, 2001; Meskill, Mossop, & Bates, 1999a; Petrie, 2003). Rather, it is a symbolic system that must be learned. There is nothing inherently transparent about the abstract symbols that people use to communicate in electronic environments. Therefore, the visual needs to be taken into consideration in order to truly extend what is known about scaffolding reading experiences for language learners (Fitzgerald & Graves, 2004) to the electronic text. Electronic text is the world of the visual (Chesebro & Bertelsen, 1996; Mirzoeff, 1999); language educators and researchers need to heed such advice as Burmark's (2002), who suggests in the title of her book that they "learn to see, see to learn." Electronic reading is truly different from *ink reading* (Meskill et al., 1999) and requires focused attention from language educators such as that provided by Abilock (n.d.), who created an online tutorial think-aloud procedure for electronic reading that takes the visual into account.

People learning a second language at the same time as they are mastering the visual literacy of electronic texts in the language may face extra challenges. Written languages differ in the reading processes that are used to decipher text and lead to different assumptions about how text is to be read (Birch, 2002). For example, for someone who has learned to read print text from left to right, interpreting an arrow pointing to the right as a way to move forward through an electronic text comes easily. However, it might appear counterintuitive to someone who has learned to read print text from right to left. In addition to possible low-level transfer of reading processes (Birch, 2002) that learners may bring with them to electronic reading, learners may also bring different cultural interpretations of the use and meaning of space (Levinson, 2003).

Examples and Discussion

There are many issues to consider when reflecting on the visuality of the environments that students encounter in electronic texts. Discussion of a number of these will hopefully prompt heightened awareness in teaching and an increase in research in the area of visuality in CALL.

New Meanings

Language learners experience symbols in electronic environments for which they may have assigned previous meanings. It has been noted recently that language learners struggle with print reading in content areas in part due to the double meanings assigned to vocabulary items. For example, in mathematics, everyday words such as *table* and *foot* suddenly take on the discipline-specific meanings of a way to visually demonstrate data and a unit of measurement (Heinze, 2005). Learners encounter new meanings for words they are already familiar with in science as well, when they encounter vocabulary such as *mass* and *matter* (Lindgren, 2002). In addition, learners experience this double meaning when they are asked to assign new meanings to symbols in electronic environments that they have previously known through print literacy. For example, when reading print text, learners come to understand that underlining indicates emphasis. However, in electronic texts, underlining indicates that a word or phrase is a doorway to another text or another part of the text—a link (Petrie, 2003). In print texts such as surveys, an X in a box means I *choose this option*; whereas an X in a box on an electronic document (often in the upper right corner) means I *choose to end this option*, closing the window. In addition, the + and − symbols, interpreted as mathematical symbols in print texts, suddenly take on the meaning of *zoom in* and *zoom out* in electronic texts, allowing readers to increase or decrease the size of images.

Learners also encounter a wide range of meanings for visual symbols across electronic texts themselves. These differences are noticeable when comparing the ways that electronic texts indicate to readers where they are in relation to the different discourse elements of the text. In print text, as readers' eyes move around the page, there is very little to symbolize the location of their attention unless they place a finger on the spot. In contrast, electronic documents provide this information—a point of focus within the document—through a variety of visuals. On the *Google Maps* Web site (Google, 2007e), tabs listing three map views appear on the screen; the tab matching the view the reader is currently using is bolded. Color change and use of geometric shapes is used on the *Phonetics: The Sounds of American English* Web site (University of Iowa, n.d.). The text at the site is categorized according to different pronunciation elements such as place of articulation and phoneme. A change in color indicates which point of articulation within the text is currently being read; a box appears around a phoneme to indicate which one is being referred to in the text currently on the screen.

Besides indicating *you are here* to a reader through various symbols, electronic texts reflect possible movement to another area of the text. When the cursor sweeps across or rests on a button on the *Math Magician* Web site (n.d.), the button grows larger in comparison to the other buttons, reflecting that the reader appears to intend to go to this area of the text. And if the curser moves across the hand at the bottom of the screen pointing to the right, the hand begins to jiggle, indicating to the reader: *judging from your cursor placement, you are about to go here*. While these visual symbols—increasing size and movement—indicate a reader's possible intention to move to another area of text at the *Math Magician* site, they carry a different meaning at *Starfall* (Starfall Website, 2003). Here, these indicators are used to encourage readers to follow a certain path within the site. When both a left-pointing and a right-pointing arrow appear at the bottom of a page, the right-pointing arrow is larger, persuading readers to click on it and thus forward through the text. In addition, animated stars sometimes appear around the right-pointing arrow, further drawing attention to this option for movement through the text and visually communicating *go here*.

Certainly, there is great promise in increasing language learners' discourse competence (Hymes, 1972) in comprehending electronic texts by making them aware of these visual indications of location, possible intention to move, and suggestion for a path through the text. However, the variety of meanings that a visual symbol can take on in electronic environments and the disparity in symbol meaning between print and electronic environments pose a challenge for language learners. CALL researchers can address this challenge by articulating a visual grammar for electronic texts, much as Kress and van Leeuwen (1996) developed a grammar of visual design for print texts. Language educators can apply the same attention to the visual symbols that students are expected to comprehend as they do to print elements when these symbols support students' bottom-up processing (Carrell, Devine, & Eskey, 1988).

Panoramas

Another phenomenon learners encounter in electronic environments is the presence of entirely visually communicated data in the form of a panorama, a 360-degree view from one physical location. These panoramas provide a view of places as if the viewer were actually able to visit the location. Upon opening the video, a still shot of the place appears, and the viewer uses the mouse to move the view to the left or the right in a seamless vision of turning around. If viewers want to draw closer to or pull back, they use the *zoom in* or *zoom out* tools. Examples of panoramas can be found at the *Virtual San Francisco Tower* Web site (National Air Traffic Controllers Association, n.d.) and the *Windsor Castle Virtual Tour* Web site (British Broadcasting Corporation, n.d.-c).

It may appear that such visual data as panoramas are instantly transparent, offer language learners no challenges, and, therefore, do not deserve attention from language educators. However, a reflection on how teachers effectively handle visual phenomena in face-to-face classrooms highlights a disparity. A recent development in the area of supporting ELLs' comprehension of social studies concepts is the use of artifacts (van Borssum, 2005). Teachers use artifacts to support student learning by providing a series of questions for students to answer so that they experience, reflect upon, and express ideas about the artifacts. Teachers often draw upon the questioning strategies used at museums when viewing a painting or an object (van Borssum, 2005). Simply viewing an object does not lead directly to learning; rather, it is the scaffolding questions provided by teachers that encourage students to develop new understandings. Likewise, if language learners are to fully exploit such visual data as panoramas in electronic texts, they may need similar guidance from their teachers to lead them to the strategic competence (Hymes, 1972) that will allow them to think through what they are seeing.

Digital Video

An additional consideration for language learners encountering electronic texts is the presence of digital videos and the particular type of literacy these may bring with them. Many cultures have changed in terms of how information is communicated, moving from oral to print to electronic communication (Chesebro & Bertelsen, 1996). Each of these communication channels places different demands on the people who give and receive messages. Although electronic communication is extremely prevalent in the modern world (Mirzoeff, 1999), other forms of literacy are present as well. The existence of multiple patterns of communication can be explained by considering that, as new technologies are developed, so are new pathways of using these technologies to communicate. The previous pathways for communication have not simply been abandoned, though; they often continue to be used in a slightly morphed *residual* form (Ong, 1978) alongside the newer paths for communication. Although true oral communication—communication not impacted in any way by the other forms—has largely disappeared, a form of oral communication, *residual orality*, persists (Ong, 1978). The classroom is one place where residual orality continues to exist; teachers carry out essentially oral performances as regular parts of their instruction (Brent, 2005). Despite the many cultural changes that have occurred, "teaching has remained, above all, a performance art that unfolds in real time" (Brent, 2005, "What Is 'Teaching' Anyway?" ¶ 2).

Evidence of the presence of residual orality exists in such examples as Rhodes' (2006) *Chalk 'n Talk: The Old Fashioned Way to Teach*. When language learners choose a grammar point from this list, a video begins in which Rhodes stands before a whiteboard explaining the grammar point and offering examples. Learners witness his visual communication through his oral teaching performance. Other literacies are fused with this orality, too: The teacher stands before and refers to a whiteboard covered in print; the video screen offers the electronic feature of clickable names of exercise types (e.g., *matching*, *cloze*; see Figure 21-1) that open exercises in an adjacent window in order to practice the concepts presented in the video. *Chalk 'n Talk* is an excellent example of the coexistence of all three literacies (oral, print, and electronic) made possible with video in electronic environments (see Figure 21-1).

It is worthwhile for language teachers and researchers to recognize the value of digital video and to prepare learners to encounter a range of literacies. To authentically prepare learners to comprehend and interact in a variety of communication contexts, a wide range of input types must be provided. If learners intend to take part in a variety of literacies—oral, print, and

Figure 21-1. Multiple Literacies at *Chalk 'n Talk*

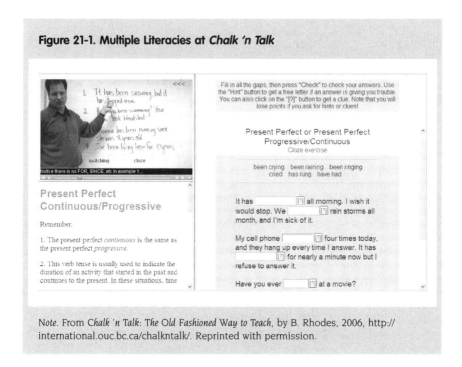

Note. From *Chalk 'n Talk: The Old Fashioned Way to Teach*, by B. Rhodes, 2006, http://international.ouc.bc.ca/chalkntalk/. Reprinted with permission.

electronic—then teachers must provide exposure to these in the curriculum or learners must seek them out for themselves. Teachers can effectively prepare learners with elements for sociolinguistic textual competence (Hymes, 1972), such as understanding the purpose of a text and developing expectations regarding how information will be delivered before encountering a print text. Likewise, teachers must prepare learners for the comprehension demands they will encounter across the literacies found in digital photos and video.

Content and Learner Roles

A couple of final elements to consider regarding the environments learners encounter with CALL are the way that information is provided visually and the roles that learners play in procuring that information. Just as textbooks present information in a variety of conceptual patterns (T. W. Adams, 1989), electronic environments often provide these visually as well, including *cause and effect, steps in a cyclical or linear process, broad statement supported by evidence*, and *ways of classifying*. Various Web pages linked from NOVA's *Interactives Archive* (WGBH Educational Foundation, 2007) provide examples of each of these. For example, *Destroy the Castle* (WGBH Educational Foundation, 2000c) is a type of microworld (Papert, 1993) in which readers can manipulate factors and receive feedback about cause and effect. Readers make choices to design and place a trebuchet with the goal to destroy a castle in the background. After making all of his or her choices, the reader sets the trebuchet into motion and watches where the projectile lands. The reader can consider this feedback and make different choices with another attempt.

In addition, a wide range of processes is demonstrated visually. At *Inside the Jet Stream* (Groleau, 2001c) and *Build a Rice Paddy* (WGBH Educational Foundation, 2000b), readers click on right-pointing or left-pointing arrows to move forward or backward through the steps in a process that are demonstrated visually and accompanied by an explanation in text. At *Engineer a Crop: Transgenic Manipulation* (PBS Online & WGBH/Frontline/NOVA, 2001), readers learn which steps in the process to carry out chronologically by manipulating the mouse. At *Illuminating Photosynthesis* (Groleau, 2001b), readers visually put into motion and witness a cyclical process when they click on the different elements at work (in no particular order).

Visual evidence of a concept is provided with video at the *Bicycle-Wheel Gyroscope* Web page (WGBH Educational Foundation, 2000a). Readers are simultaneously presented with text that explains how forward motion resists side-to-side motion and a video of a woman demonstrating the concept with a bicycle wheel. At the *Dig and Deduce* Web page (Groleau, 2001a), readers locate archeological artifacts and drag them to a box to be interpreted. Readers are visually shown different ways to classify the artifacts. At one site, tools are visually rearranged to demonstrate type and then again to show chronology.

One thing for teachers and researchers to note is the *sociocultural roles* that learners play when they view these visual demonstrations. The Web sites described earlier offer differing ranges of actions that readers are allowed to or required to take to procure visual information, ranging from the most constraining (merely clicking on arrows to move forward or backward) to the least restraining (being able to make choices that may or may not lead to a successful result). W. S. E. Lam (2000b) examined the sociocultural roles that learners play in electronic environments such as threaded discussions, instant messaging, and designing personal Web sites. Lam found that these roles appeared to lead to greater language gains for the central learner in the study. However, the roles students play in viewing online visual demonstrations deserve attention as well. Perhaps more research and heightened awareness of students' roles in a range of visual environments will lead to more informed choices about which electronic environments to enter. In addition, teachers should prepare learners to comprehend and interact in such environments by sharing with students the roles that they will be expected to play.

Conclusion

Considering visuality in CALL is significant because it is likely that second language learners have to put far more effort into interpreting the visual nature of electronic environments than native-speaking students whose background knowledge and assumptions are more aligned with those of electronic text creators. Kress and van Leeuwen (1996) explain that the people who communicate

> make their messages maximally understandable in a particular context. They therefore choose forms of expression which they believe to be maximally transparent to other participants. On the other hand, communication takes place in social structures which are inevitably marked by power differences, and this affects how each participant understands the notion of "maximal understanding." Participants in positions of power can force other participants into greater efforts of interpretation. (p. 161)

Language educators are in a position of power in their classrooms. They can choose to provide struggling learners with better access to communication through scaffolding, essentially anticipating student needs for interpreting the visual. On the other hand, they can fail to investigate the visual characteristics and challenges inherent in the electronic texts their students encounter, ignoring the need to assist students. Just as general educators are beginning to consider how to scaffold spoken and written language so that ELLs are able to comprehend content and further acquire language proficiency (see Fitzgerald & Graves, 2004), language educators should become aware of student needs as they experience visuals in electronic texts. Scaffolding techniques regarding reading and interacting with the visual should be developed so that language learners gain full access to the new spaces that open up to them on their computer screens.

Explorations

1. Locate a Web site written entirely in a language with which you are not familiar. Move around the Web site, noting the choices you make as you do so. How do the visual symbols work? What are you able to transfer from your own base knowledge of visual electronic literacy? What works in an unexpected way?

2. Examine a lesson plan that you have used with language learners to prepare them to carry out a challenging print reading. Note the strategies that you included to assist learners in grasping the meaning of the text. Reflect on how you prepare students to carry out electronic reading assignments. What visual items or design elements in a Web page or software might be unfamiliar or cause reading difficulties? Do you employ similar top-down and bottom-up strategies? If so, why? If not, why not?

3. Locate a print text and an electronic text on similar subject matter that you could use in your curriculum. Compare the ways that meaning is conveyed in the texts linguistically and visually. How would your teaching of the two types of texts differ from each other? (See Hanson-Smith, 2003, for more information about reading electronically.) Consider your own attitudes about visual and linguistic communication. Do you value one more than the other? If so, why? How do your attitudes affect how you teach literacy skills to language learners?

4. Interview your students in order to learn about the first language visual print literacies that they bring with them to your classroom. How does this affect what they expect to find on the electronic screen when they read English? Which symbols are they familiar and unfamiliar with? Help them develop a grammar of visual design that you can use together. (If you are in a working group, develop with your group a grammar of visual design to use with students in your institution.)

5. Write down some predictions about what your students already know or assume about electronic texts. Then investigate what they actually know. Direct individual students to an electronic text they

have not previously accessed. Ask each student to think aloud about their choices and assumptions as they move through the site (see Abilock, n.d., for more on think-aloud design). Compare these findings to your predictions about what the students would know or assume. If you do not have any students, examine electronic documents (e.g., electronic presentation or slideshow, Web site, word-processed document with clip art) created by language learners. What do they reveal about the learners' visual literacy knowledge? How do the linguistic and nonlinguistic elements interact to make meaning?

PART VII

Atmosphere

Chapter 22 🔲

Theory and Research: Classroom Atmosphere

Bill Johnston

Focus

Perhaps the greatest truism in early 21st-century education is "There has to be a good atmosphere in the classroom." When all is said and done, this belief may be one of the most important ways in which values in education have changed over the past 100 years or so: Whatever changes in content and curriculum have occurred, educators now recognize that fear, coercion, punishment, threats, and other forms of negative psychological manipulation do not represent the best way of going about educating people.

What is true for education in general, of course, is also true for language teaching. The central importance of affective factors in language learning, including appropriate stress and anxiety levels and a good classroom atmosphere as one of the eight conditions for optimal learning, is noted in chapter 1 in this volume. Spolsky (1989), too, included motivation/affect as a crucial element in the equation for second language acquisition (SLA).

Yet in the field of language learning and teaching, little theoretical or empirical work has investigated what exactly classroom atmosphere is and what exactly about it ought to be good. This omission is a pity, because even though teachers highly value good classroom atmosphere, confusion often exists over how best to realize it in class. Perhaps precisely because good classroom atmosphere is taken as a universally understood principle, the concept has not been critically examined, and teachers do not have a common language in which to discuss and think about the central issues.

The aim of this chapter, then, is to offer the beginnings of a vocabulary with which to address the question of what *good classroom atmosphere* means and the related issue of the teacher's roles and responsibilities in creating such an atmosphere in the ESL/EFL class. My emphasis is on atmosphere as it relates to technology and specifically to computer-assisted learning, but most of what I present in this chapter applies to classroom atmosphere in general.

Background

Stress and Anxiety: Focus on the Individual

In the 1960s and 1970s, a fair amount of research tried to identify the exact influence of certain affective factors, like stress and anxiety, on language learning. Researchers looked at a range of affective and personality factors in SLA, including anxiety, introversion-extroversion, motivation, attitude, degree of risk taking, and self-esteem. (For reviews of this literature, see R. Ellis, 1994, pp. 479–523; Larsen-Freeman & Long, 1991, pp. 172–192; MacIntyre & Gardner, 1991.) One classic study in this vein is that of Guiora, Beit-Hallahmi, Brannon, Dull, and Scovel (1972), who investigated the effect of progressively increasing doses of alcohol on second language pronunciation. Their findings, however—that small doses of alcohol improved pronunciation—have been called into question, for example by R. Ellis (1994, p. 519).

In fact, this literature as a whole has not really fulfilled its promise and has been less prominent in the field since the early 1980s, even though the topic is clearly an important one. Although certain general conclusions were possible—for example, that anxiety was indeed "an important factor in L2 acquisition" (R. Ellis, 1994, p. 483)—taken as a whole, the studies have produced "mixed results" (p. 482). Parkinson and Howell-Richardson (1990), for example, found no correlation between anxiety and rate of improvement in a study of adult ESL learners in Scotland, whereas MacIntyre and Gardner (1991) report that in some studies anxiety was positively correlated with language learning; that is, more anxious learners learned more.

Anyone who has experienced a language learning situation knows that R. Ellis (1994) is right to say that anxiety plays an important role. Yet the studies he reviews are problematic in a number of ways, not because they are wrong to focus on anxiety but because they do so in ways that distort basic truths of the situation.

Above all, in the aforementioned surveys of research, anxiety was included in a group of other affective and personality variables, such as motivation, attitude, extroversion, and self-esteem. The underlying assumption is that, like the other variables, anxiety is an inherent characteristic of the learner (in the same way as aptitude or intelligence is). In reality, however, anxiety is obviously likely to vary considerably and to be, to a large extent, a product of a given situation (e.g., relations with a teacher or peer, the stress of exams) rather than a personality constant. Indeed, many theories of stress are transactional in nature in that they take into account the interaction between personality and stressful events or situations (*stressors*) found in the outside world (see, e.g., Lazarus & Launier, 1978). Linked to these problems is the fact that the studies assume anxiety to be an individual trait; they focus on the state of individual learners and pay scant attention to the social setting.

An additional problem is that the relation between, for example, anxiety and language learning is conceived in terms of simplistic, linear, causal relations. Such an approach belies the complexity of the language learning situation, a complexity that any practicing teacher knows only too well. Furthermore, in the tradition of quantitative social scientific research, investigators have attempted to quantify and measure anxiety in numerical terms, and, as with any form of psychometric measurement, researchers cannot be entirely sure that what they are measuring is what they intend to measure.

Nevertheless, this research at least has put affective notions such as stress and anxiety on the table, acknowledging their importance and making them part of the *educational conversation* (Garrison & Rud, 1995) in ESL teaching. It is unfortunate that the problems I have listed have seemed insurmountable and that new ways have not yet been found to look at these old and enduring issues. In fact, given the way the research tradition described here has largely petered out (although see, e.g., Elkhafaifi, 2005; Gregersen & Horwitz, 2002), new research in this area is urgently needed.

The Class as Community

In contrast to the focus on the individual that characterized the research on anxiety outlined in the previous section, other approaches to teaching methods and to conceptualizing the language classroom have emphasized the class as group and, further, as community. For example, Egbert, Hanson-Smith, and Chao (chapter 1 in this volume) name "opportunities to interact and negotiate meaning" as the first of eight conditions for optimal language learning. In addition, the themes of cooperation, collaboration, and class as community are found in approaches as diverse as the Silent Way (Gattegno, 1972), Community Language Learning (Curran, 1976), whole language (e.g., Rigg, 1991; Weaver, 1990), cooperative learning (D. W. Johnson, Johnson, & Smith, 1991), communicative language teaching (e.g., H. D. Brown, 1994), sociocultural approaches to learning (e.g., Norton & Toohey, 2001), constructivism (Lave & Wenger, 1991), and critical pedagogy (e.g., Norton & Toohey, 2004).

Although these various approaches obviously differ considerably in many aspects, the idea of community tends to be realized in the classroom in similar ways: students collaborating on tasks, an emphasis on cooperation rather than competition, students learning from other students, peer feedback on written and oral assignments, and a sense of the class as an audience for students' work. In general terms, community means respect for all students and for what each one brings to the class, more active student participation (i.e., engagement) in the class, and recognition of the importance of collaboration in a learning situation.

The aforementioned classroom conditions are admirable goals or ideals. In addition, although they have not always been implemented, they represent a general tendency in many educational settings and have made classrooms less stressful places. In many educational and sociopolitical contexts, however, other forces have continued to militate against the widespread adoption of a cooperative approach to teaching. In thinking about the role of community and its influence on classroom atmosphere, teachers must be aware of these forces and recognize practical and perhaps theoretical limitations on the extent to which language classrooms can rely on community as a factor in promoting student growth.

Three practical limitations in particular present themselves. One is that, even in many situations in which collaboration and cooperation are prized over solitary work, strong remnants of the latter remain—for example, grading tends to be done individually. When it is not—for instance, when a grade is awarded to a group as a whole—students often perceive this practice as inequitable.

The fact that students often want to be assessed individually leads to a second, related point. The broader context in which collaborative teaching takes place is often opposed to this form of teaching. Systems as a whole (e.g., programs, schools, universities) are generally set up in ways that favor individualism and competition over community and cooperation. In my experience, many teachers who have elected to take a whole-language approach have found themselves relatively isolated within their schools and at odds with the prevailing values and methods supported by the administration and the other teachers. This barrier in itself is an insufficient reason not to pursue cooperation in learning, but it is a factor that teachers must take into account when trying to introduce cooperative modes of working as a way of enhancing the classroom atmosphere. In addition to these systemic constraints, many language learners, especially those from cultures in which education focuses on discrete individual accomplishments, are consciously and often volubly opposed to alternative forms of assessment.

The third major limitation on the notion of classroom as community is crucial to acknowledge: In its traditional use in fields such as anthropology or sociology, the term *community* refers to groups of people who live together for extended periods of time. Geertz (1973), for instance, talks of a community as a group of people who "grow old together" (p. 53). Yet this idea does not really apply to classrooms. In the U.S. educational system, the longest any group of learners stays together is usually 1 year, and that happens only up to sixth grade (around the age of 12). After that, classes become even more fragmentary groupings of learners, who may come together for an hour or two a day and may stay in this configuration for a year. At the tertiary level, even these parameters are curtailed. A typical college class meets perhaps three or four times a week over 15 weeks. Unified cohorts of students such as those found in central European secondary and tertiary education systems are rarely encountered in the United States. ESL classes are generally no exception: For example, two intensive English programs with which I have had extensive contact offer courses that run for 7 weeks and 10 weeks respectively. Furthermore, because of their diverse backgrounds, ESL learners have even less in common with each other than students from a single culture. When it comes to virtual communities in distance education, a sense of community is even harder to achieve (as mentioned by several authors in Henrichsen, 2001).

Under such conditions, speaking of community in the conventional sense is rather difficult. Rather, these groups more closely resemble the kind of *instant communities* sociologists have observed springing up in the United States (e.g., in retirement communities). People in the United States are particularly skilled at this kind of group formation, perhaps because of the high level of mobility found in U.S. society. People brought up in other cultures (as ESL students by definition always are) may find the process of community building more difficult given the inherent time constraints.

Additionally, permanent communities have a broad range of interests and concerns in common and extensive shared knowledge that they can draw on. Language classes, on the other hand, bring together people who may have little in common other than their desire or need to learn the target language—and they may have widely differing reasons, motives, and interests even in that sphere. The language class could be said to create a *desert island situation*, in which a small number of people with little in common are thrown together by little more than chance and for a limited period of time.

In fact, the typical getting-to-know-you games that many teachers play in the first few classes are arguably a response to the difficulty of forming a sense of community in such a transient situation. Teachers are, in a way, acknowledging the desert island situation. One wonders, though, how non-native speakers feel about these attempts to create instant, ersatz communities in the precious time they have available to learn the language.

Finally, the desire to talk about the class as a *community of learners* (an axiomatic phrase of the whole-language movement) also reflects something of a romanticized notion of community—that the community is an "unalloyed good" (Noddings, 1996, p. 245). This is not always the case. Communities can be indifferent to their members; they can be constraining and conservative, and sometimes downright unsupportive. Research in group theory (e.g., Hare, Blumberg, Davies, & Kent, 1994; Witte & Davis, 1996) demonstrates clearly that in small-group interactions, conflict, power struggles (or, technically, "power exertion" [Scholl, 1996, p. 138]), and attempts to impose agendas are the rule rather than the exception. F. A. Morris and Tarone (2003), for example, document harmful interpersonal conflict in language learning activities that require collaboration. Thus, the equation of *community* with *cooperation* may also be misleading. (For a fascinating critique of whole language from the perspective of the orthodoxies of classroom interaction that it engenders, see Tobin, 1995.)

The Teacher's Responsibilities

The problems and limitations outlined in the previous section raise a critical question: What are the teacher's responsibilities in establishing and maintaining a desirable classroom atmosphere? This question is no less important for rarely being addressed directly in the literature on language teaching.

H. D. Brown (1994), one of the few writers to give prominence to affective issues, says that the teacher needs to create a "warm, embracing climate" (p. 255) and that "all second language learners need to be treated with affective tender loving care" (p. 22). He makes certain recommendations for teachers, including the following for teachers working with young children: Help your students laugh with each other at various mistakes that they all make, be patient and supportive, and elicit as much oral participation as possible from students (p. 93).

H. D. Brown (1994) proposes a set of affective principles for teaching, including the following:

- The fragility of *language ego* in the second language must be recognized.

- Learners' *self-confidence* is a crucial element in ensuring their success.

- For success, learners must be able to *take risks*.

- The language learner's encounters with the *culture* of the target language are a vital part of the language learning process. (pp. 22–26)

Finally, Brown argues that group work promotes a positive affective climate for learning (p. 174).

Other writers on language teaching methodology (e.g., Nunan, 1989b) and classroom interaction (e.g., Malamah Thomas, 1987) also mention such matters but tend to relegate them to the categories of "affective-humanistic activities" (Nunan, p. 241), perhaps in line with Oxford's (1990) identification of affective strategies as one of the six categories of learning strategies. Nunan and others who have written about language teaching methods (e.g., J. C. Richards & Rodgers, 1986) take what might be termed an *instrumental* approach to what teachers do in classrooms. In this view, teachers' work is technical in nature and aimed primarily at making students learn faster and more efficiently. Affective techniques are simply one way of doing so. A similar focus can be seen in much research in language classroom discourse, which has often tended to focus narrowly on language learning issues (e.g., J. K. Hall & Verplaetse, 2000).

An alternative position, however, is that teaching involves much more than influencing the cognitive processes of students. According to this position, teaching is first and foremost a *relational* activity. The relations between teacher and student and among students are the foundation of all that goes on in classrooms; learning springs from these relations. Thus, so-called affective factors in fact represent the very core of teaching and learning.

Such a view of teaching is set out by Noddings (1984) in general education, and Johnston (2003) in language teaching. According to Noddings, at the core of the occupation of teaching is the relation between teacher and learner, which she characterizes as a *caring relation*. Yet her account of this relation goes far beyond the warm and fuzzy caring and sharing that was supposed to occur in the humanistic classroom. Rather, Noddings recognizes "human encounter and affective response as a basic fact of human existence" (p. 4). In other words, affective issues are not an add-on that will help students learn better, but a fundamental part of what is happening in the classroom.

Noddings (1984) describes the caring relation as comprising two unequal persons, whom she designates as the *one-caring* and the *cared-for.* The archetypal relation of this kind is mother-child; the teacher-student relation is comparable. The central characteristic of the one-caring is what Noddings calls *engrossment*—"I must see the other's reality as a possibility for my own" (p. 14). Engrossment refers to the ability of the one-caring (the teacher) to see things from the perspective of the cared-for (the student). In an example significant for teachers, Noddings talks of a math teacher with a student who is not doing well in her class. Noddings suggests that rather than saying, "I must help this poor boy love mathematics," teachers should put another question to themselves: "How would it feel to hate mathematics?" (p. 15). Likewise, ESL teachers, instead of asking, "Why can't this student form questions properly?" might ask themselves, "What does it feel like to have difficulty with question formation in English?"

The notion of the caring relation as Noddings (1984) describes it offers a number of advantages in terms of thinking about classrooms and the teacher-student relation. First, it captures the unequal power and status inherent in the relation without making this imbalance the central issue. Second, it recognizes the potential conflict in the way a class, with its many students, can make competing demands not just on the teacher's time but on his or her emotional resources. Third, it emphasizes the relational nature of teaching and indicates that, whereas the primary responsibility lies with the one-caring (the teacher), the cared-for (the student) also has a part to play in the relation. Finally, it acknowledges that, because of the "uniqueness of human encounters" (p. 5), it is not possible to talk in general terms of a "universal caring" (p. 18); rather, "to care is to act not by fixed rule but by affection and regard" (p. 24), and thus teachers' relations with different students will themselves be different.

At the same time, the particular character of language teaching means that some features of the caring relation are peculiar to the language classroom. Above all, the practice of engrossment is more difficult because the teacher must cross profound cultural, social, and linguistic boundaries in seeking to understand the student's perspective. Indeed, a typical ESL class, with students from different native cultures, may evidence multiple sets of boundaries of this kind. Engrossment is not impossible, of course, but the imaginative leap is much harder with students from different cultures than with students from one's own country or culture.

One central pedagogical point that emerges from Noddings's (1984) theory is that teaching is not and cannot be a technical and mechanistic activity that relies on generalized knowledge generated by research. Learning takes place from the point at which a particular student finds himself or herself at a given time, and can best be facilitated if the teacher focuses on the learner, not the material. As Noddings says, "the learner is infinitely more important than the subject" (p. 20). This statement should give considerable pause to any teacher who has ever worried about "covering the material." Noddings argues that the teacher can help make real learning take place only from the attempt to engage with specific learners at the point where they find themselves.

The rationale that Noddings (1984) has developed clearly has major implications for classroom atmosphere. Above all, it suggests two things. First, each group of learners is unique, just as each individual learner is unique; therefore, the resulting relations between teacher and student will also be unique. In other words, a teacher's human response to each class will differ; overall guidelines may be of some use, but classroom atmosphere will depend on the particular relations in a particular setting. Given the diversity of ESL classrooms, differences between classes are likely to be dramatic.

Second, the teacher plays a specific role in developing a desirable classroom atmosphere. By Noddings' (1984) account, the teacher-student relation is two-sided, and therefore part of the responsibility lies with the student (in other words, the teacher is not 100% responsible for the atmosphere in the class). However, the unequal nature of the relationship between the one-caring and the cared-for—an inequality all the more marked for learners from authoritarian cultures, who are accustomed to having less voice in educational settings—means that it is primarily the teacher's job to attempt engrossment, to see things from the perspective of the students, and to nurture learning from that perspective. Classroom atmosphere depends largely on the teacher's ability to meet the students where they are and to lead each student to greater knowledge and skills in ways that are best for that student (Noddings, 1984).

Examples and Discussion

Optimal Learning Conditions

As mentioned earlier, one much-overlooked truth in education is that stress in itself is not necessarily a bad thing. Psychologists (e.g., P. L. Rice, 1987) talk about *eustress*, a desirable form of stress that leads to heightened alertness, improved performance, and greater engagement with whatever one is doing. In fact, it has long been known that with an increase of stress, performance levels constitute an inverted U-shaped curve (see P. L. Rice, 1987, p. 19). As stress increases, performance increases proportionately—to a point. When stress becomes too great, performance falls and continues to fall as stress increases further.

Perhaps the clearest framework in which to develop and convey this idea is psychologist Csikszentmihalyi's (1990, 1996, 1997a) notion of *flow* (see also van Lier, 1996). The basic concept of flow is that optimal experiences (which in educational settings are intimately linked with optimal learning) take place in a zone that lies between anxiety and boredom; that is, as in the relation of stress and performance, some stimulation—what Csikszentmihalyi (1990) calls *challenge*—is required for an optimal experience to be attained. (For more on the concept of flow, see chapter 23 in this volume.)

Flow, however, is a dynamic process. As an example, imagine Akiko, a student learning ESL. Akiko has a low level of ability, so activities or tasks requiring a low level of skill (e.g., simple linguistic and pragmatic actions like giving her name or ordering coffee in a coffee shop) provide the right level of challenge for her. At this point, an increase in the level of challenge (e.g., making small talk at a party) will lead to anxiety or frustration. Conversely, if the level of skill required by different tasks remains the same but Akiko's command of English improves, the result will be boredom. What she needs is an activity that requires greater skill and represents a greater challenge. This activity may be writing a short personal letter or having a brief conversation about a movie she has seen. As Akiko's fluency and vocabulary develop even more, appropriate kinds of activities will be located further along the flow channel.

Csikszentmihalyi (1990) has documented accounts of flow experiences recounted by a wide range of people and involving a huge variety of activities, including reading, raising children, rock climbing, playing professional football, dancing, and appreciating art. From these instances, he observes that flow experiences typically contain at least some of the following elements:

1. They occur "when we confront tasks we have a chance of completing" (p. 49).

2. People can concentrate on what they are doing.

3. The task undertaken has clear goals.

4. There is immediate feedback.

5. People act "with a deep but effortless involvement that removes from awareness the worries and frustrations of everyday life" (p. 49).

6. People have a sense of control over their actions.

7. Concern for the self vanishes, yet "paradoxically the sense of self emerges stronger after the flow experience is over" (p. 49).

8. People's sense of the passage of time is temporarily altered: Time seems to pass more quickly.

Summing up, Csikszentmihalyi says, "the key element of an optimal experience is that it is an end in itself" (p. 67).

These elements of flow are remarkably consonant with the eight conditions for optimal language learning outlined in chapter 1. Four points of similarity are particularly noteworthy. First, Csikszentmihalyi's (1990) emphasis on tasks that can be completed, that have clear goals, and during which there is adequate feedback is reflected in Condition 5 ("Learners have enough time and feedback to complete the task"; addressed in Part V of this volume). Second, the effortless involvement and absence of concern for the self that Csikszentmihalyi writes about seem to be another way of describing the *mindfulness* (Zellermayer, Salomon, Globerson, & Givon, 1991) discussed in chapter 18. Third, Csikszentmihalyi's mention of control is clearly equivalent to Condition 8, which concerns the importance of learner autonomy (discussed in Part VIII). Lastly, at a more general level Condition 3, regarding authentic tasks (see Part III), seems to echo Csikszentmihalyi's overall point about optimal experiences constituting an end in themselves.

Clearly, as van Lier (1996) has also suggested, Csikszentmihalyi's (1990, 1996, 1997a) model of flow provides a wonderful stimulus for thinking about classroom atmosphere and the classroom experiences of language students. Although it would be unreasonable to expect to replicate flow experiences for all students all of the time (or even for most of them, most of the time) as an ideal and a goal, the previously mentioned description of flow offers certain guidelines for the design of language teaching activities. Preliminary research by Egbert (2003) indicates that flow does indeed provide a valid and useful framework for thinking about interaction in language classrooms.

Csikszentmihalyi (1990) argues that it is no accident that many flow experiences occur in activities such as games and sports:

> What makes these activities conducive to flow is that they were *designed* to make optimal experience easier to achieve. They have rules that require the learning of skills, they set up goals, they provide feedback, they make control possible. They facilitate concentration and involvement by making the activity as distinct as possible from the so-called "paramount reality" of everyday existence. (p. 72)

Yet at the same time, Csikszentmihalyi notes that flow can be achieved in "an almost infinite range" (p. 6) of activities.

Put briefly, Csikszentmihalyi's (1990) challenge to language teachers is to create activities for students that push them to perform better and better without overreaching themselves. Language learning, surely, is a skill like those Csikszentmihalyi describes. He suggests that to maximize positive stress, activities need to have clear rules and clear goals, offer rapid feedback, be clearly delineated, allow the students to feel in control, and, above all, have a purpose. Additionally, and crucially, Csikszentmihalyi's emphasis on student control supports Noddings's (1992) argument that learning must be related to the individual and the individual's stage in his or her own development. Each person's flow channel looks different; the design of learning experiences needs to recognize this fact. With these principles in mind, Csikszentmihalyi suggests, teachers have a chance of providing an optimal learning experience for their students.

Computer Anxiety

For CALL environments, one form of anxiety requires close examination: *computer anxiety* (G. S. Howard, 1986), or the fear (distrust, dislike) of technology. Other terms for this concept, used with more or less precision, include *computer phobia* (Davidson & Tomic, 1994) and *technostress* (Weil & Rosen, 1997).

The notion of computer anxiety continues to figure in research on CALL. For example, Wolfe and Manalo (2004) look at computer anxiety in relation to computer-based forms of testing internationally, and Matsumura and Hann (2004) discuss the impact of computer anxiety on students' feedback preferences and academic writing performance. It seems that, despite growing access to and use of computers, this anxiety remains a persistent factor in computer-assisted forms of learning. The concept has not been examined in detail in the field of language learning; in other fields, however, notably psychology, management, and to a lesser extent education, some attempt has been made to pin the concept down; to ascertain how many people it affects, to what extent, and in what ways; and finally, to consider what to do about it.

Weil and Rosen (1997) refer to a range of studies and surveys suggesting that 30–80% of people report some sort of anxiety about using computers. Given the notorious problems associated with self-reported data and survey research, a large part of this variation is probably related to research methods. Nevertheless, the results suggest strongly that computer anxiety is a widespread phenomenon, and most scholars agree that it will not go away. (The 11-year gap between the books by G. S. Howard, 1986, and Weil and Rosen, 1997, would seem to support this premise.)

What exactly is computer anxiety? It covers a range of negative attitudes, beliefs, and emotions concerning computers in general and one's own interaction with them in particular. Recurrent issues in the literature include

- confusion caused by computer jargon
- a sense of being left behind as everyone else turns to computers

- a fear that learning computer skills is too difficult

- a fear of making mistakes that cannot be corrected later

- a more generalized anxiety about the role of computers in everyday life

- the everyday hassles of computer use, such as crashes and the loss of data

- the dehumanizing effect of computers

- a feeling of lack of control (Dukes, Discenza, & Couger, 1989; Hudiburg, 1989, 1990; Kernan & Howard, 1990; Marcoulides, 1989)

Computer anxiety, then, appears to be a complex, pervasive, and persistent phenomenon.

G. S. Howard (1986) suggests that psychological resistance to computers is both deep-seated and rather vague; as such, it may be difficult to affect. On the other hand, guided experience under the right conditions can address what he calls *operational anxieties* concerning the actual use of the computer. In other words, actually using computers in an environment where help is available may go some way toward dealing with this part of the problem (see chapter 23 in this volume).

G. S. Howard (1986) also acknowledges the usefulness of being aware of one's feelings about computers. This theme is taken up by Weil and Rosen (1997), whose book, interestingly enough, was shelved in the self-help section of my local bookstore. Weil and Rosen stress the importance of the computer user's taking control, including carefully reflecting on the computer's purpose and the purposes for which the user needs it. Such reflection clearly relates to the theme of autonomy running through this book (see, e.g., chapter 25 in this volume).

A third, contrary position is taken by Yeaman (1993). He claims that "computer anxiety is a label that blames the victims," and he challenges the "myths of computerism" (p. 19)—pointing out, for instance, that the biggest obstacle to learning about computers is not computer anxiety but restricted access to computers. He argues that computer anxiety is a perfectly normal (not pathological) reaction to computers as they are presented and used in society. Finally, he lays the blame squarely at the feet of those who design the software and hardware with their often "opaque and mysterious" (p. 23) technologies.

In any case, computer anxiety is clearly a force to be reckoned with. In the language classroom, the elements of computer anxiety are compounded by language problems and may be exacerbated by cultural unfamiliarity with a range of features of software, from the language of commands to the iconography employed. Like it or not, computer-assisted learning adds computer anxiety to the other sources of anxiety and stress that learners may be experiencing.

Computers and Classroom Atmosphere

This chapter has focused mainly on classroom atmosphere in general with the aim of considering how research and theory in this area might affect CALL. It is instructive to turn this question on its head and ask, "How is the use of computers in education likely to affect classroom atmosphere?"

Speculation on this topic is rife. Here I draw on a single study because of the rich material it offers. Schofield (1995) conducted a yearlong qualitative study (one of the best and most thorough empirical investigations available) of the use of computer technology and computer-aided instruction in a number of classes in a large urban U.S. high school. The following were her research questions:

1. What is the effect of the instructional use of computer technology on students and on social processes?

2. How does the social context in which computers are used for instruction shape their use? (p. 8)

Although the study is complex and reveals a great number of interesting facts, Schofield's overall findings include the following:

- Computer use "enhanced student enjoyment of, interest in, and attention to classroom activities" (p. 192). Schofield speculates on the reasons for this and reports research suggesting that "computers are motivating to the extent that they increase challenge, control, curiosity, and fantasy that allows for personalization of one's work" (p. 196). Note that the themes of challenge, control, and individualization echo the earlier discussion of the work of both Noddings (1984, 1992) and Csikszentmihalyi (1990, 1996, 1997a) as well as the conditions for language learning presented in chapter 1.

- With increased use of computers came a change in the role of the teacher "from that of the expert who presented information . . . to that of a coach or tutor" (Schofield, 1995, p. 201) assisting students.

- In some classes, peer interaction increased when computers were used. However, this change was not as widespread as has been claimed elsewhere in the literature (p. 207). In some cases, the use of computers did not have a demonstrable influence on interaction. In others, interaction was competitive rather than cooperative. Additionally, girls who developed an interest in computers found themselves socially isolated and even ostracized (p. 208).

- On the subject of the influence of computers on education, Schofield found that computer use increased "the disparity between the *haves* and the *have-nots*," in that, for example, "the academically more advanced students had more access to computers than did their peers" (p. 214). Schofield notes that this tendency has been observed in many other settings (p. 215).

- Generally, there was a failure in this school setting to realize the "transformative potential of computers" (p. 217), for example, in enhancing individualized instruction, fostering collaboration, promoting critical thinking skills, and connecting the classroom with the real world outside. Schofield says that this, too, is "not an idiosyncratic finding" (p. 217). Speculating on the causes of this failure, she suggests that relevant factors include the fact that teachers' values are often in conflict with the views of proponents of computers in education (p. 219). Furthermore, the traditional classroom format (e.g., lecture-style teaching) is at odds with computer-based teaching (p. 221). Finally, standardized tests have a strong tendency to "inhibit the innovative use of computer technology" (p. 222).

Taken together, Schofield's (1995) findings provide fascinating food for thought about the use of computers in schools and other educational settings. Her overall conclusion is twofold: (a) computers inevitably affect classroom atmosphere ("social processes," p. 8) in varying and unpredictable ways, and (b) existing social and political structures in turn shape computer use in educational contexts.

Conclusion

In this chapter I have offered a vocabulary and a set of concepts that might help open a dialogue on classroom atmosphere in language teaching. I suggest that, although stress and anxiety clearly play a role in language learning, thinking of them as individual traits or states may not be helpful, for they are critically linked to contextual features. On the other hand, although collaboration and community in the language classroom are admirable goals, there may be significant practical and theoretical constraints on the extent to which they can be realized.

Perhaps paradoxically, although I question the validity of the notion of *community*, I propose Noddings's (1984) notion of the caring relation as the best way of conceptualizing the teacher's role in establishing, promoting, and maintaining a desirable classroom atmosphere. Her work suggests that classroom atmosphere may most usefully be thought of not in general terms but in light of relations between the individuals concerned. Further, classroom atmosphere may depend to a large extent on teachers' abilities to perceive the learning situation from the perspective of their students.

Noddings's (1984) emphasis on the individual learner and on the teacher's response to that learner's unique situation is echoed in Csikszentmihalyi's (1990, 1996, 1997a) concept of flow, which I put forward as a way of capitalizing on the positive elements of stress in promoting an optimal learning experience. The principle of flow offers a provocative framework for teachers striving to provide the best possible learning experience for each of their students; it is also remarkably close to the conditions proposed in chapter 1.

Finally, computer anxiety is a force to consider in the language classroom. Schofield's (1995) detailed study of the impact of computing on learning and social relations in a high school supports the notion of the social component of stress and anxiety and suggests strongly that classroom atmosphere and computer-assisted learning will affect each other in ways that are as profound as they are unpredictable. Specifically, her study supports the emphasis on individualization and learner control that is noted by Noddings (1984, 1992) and Csikszentmihalyi (1990, 1996, 1997a) and is a major theme of this volume.

Explorations

1. What aspects of technology are motivating to you personally? What aspects of technology use are most motivating to your learners? Do these aspects contribute to second language acquisition? What aspects dampen learners' motivation? Do you and your students share the same interests in technology? Share your ideas with classmates or your working group.

2. Visit a multiuser object-oriented domain (MOO). Make note of how specific features of the MOO might affect the atmosphere in a language learning classroom. Would your students find role-playing a motivating factor? What might be the advantages and disadvantages of using a virtual environment for your learners? Share your findings with classmates or colleagues.

3. Describe to your team a task you might have students do in the CALL classroom. Brainstorm ways that you can tell when your students are experiencing the appropriate amount of stress. What can you do to help them experience the optimal amount of stress? Revise your task to meet the needs of a successful atmosphere.

4. How can teachers help students experience *flow* while studying and learning in the classroom? Develop a proposal for an action research study in which you will find out when and how students are optimally stressed. Beforehand, you may wish to brainstorm the kinds of signals that will help you determine if a condition of flow is occurring.

5. Examine your technology-enhanced instruction from the perspective of H. D. Brown's (1994) set of affective principles outlined in this chapter. Share your discoveries with your team or colleagues.

Chapter 23 🔳

Classroom Practice: Learner Engagement

Bill Snyder and Selin Alperer-Tatlı

Focus

From his home, a Turkish student engaged in a Web-based independent study English course sends an e-mail to his teacher about his recent explorations of the Web:

> I liked this site very much. While you read, the computer times the activity and when the time is over, the passage disappears. This really made me excited and concentrate more on the task. Also, when you answer the questions, an informative box appears above the answer, which helps the reader to find out where he has made a mistake and to understand the passage better, and what's fascinating, I'm doing all these by myself. (Pekel, 2002, p. 47)

Meanwhile, in the United States, a future Spanish teacher talks about the network-based initiative that has her interacting by computer with a native speaker in order to improve her language skills:

> [Networked Collaborative Interaction] is a challenge but with the help from my Spanish partner, I managed to use my limited Spanish knowledge to discuss different types of tasks with her. I liked the way I was challenged. It pushed me to go forward in my ability to find different ways to express myself. (L. Lee, 2004, p. 93)

And a student of Chinese in Australia rhapsodizes over his work in the language laboratory with sound files made by his teacher:

> Now I don't care about others in the lab. I just did [the sound file task] again and again. (Jiang & Ramsay, 2005, p. 55)

These learner voices suggest some of the possibilities of how learners can engage in tasks, as well as some of the possible sources of engagement (e.g., *informativeness*, *control* by the learner, *challenge*) and possible outcomes of engagement (e.g., emotional involvement, greater concentration, resistance to distraction, willingness to persevere, autonomy).

Learner *engagement* refers to "how involved learners are in the material they study and in the learning process itself" (Young, 2003, p. 1) and is not only the precursor and the product of motivation to begin a learning process but also the will (volition) to continue in that process. A variety of research supports the idea that more complete engagement in instructional tasks leads to greater learning (Dörnyei, 2001; R. Ellis, 2000; Laufer & Hulstijn, 2001; Schallert, Reed, & Turner, 2004). Engagement provides a nexus for examining ways to develop self-regulation in learners and to improve learning outcomes in tasks (Schallert et al., 2004).

In this chapter, we provide an overview of *flow theory*, specify how that theory relates to engagement in tasks, and explore aspects of task engagement about which the theory may provide insight. We then look at the implications of flow theory for implementing CALL tasks and conclude by highlighting its importance in CALL teacher education.

Background

The application of CALL has been premised in part on the potential of technology to lead to greater learner engagement in instructional tasks through the unique opportunities it creates. In her criteria for evaluating the appropriateness of CALL tasks, Chapelle (2001) includes the category *learner fit*, which she defines as "the amount of opportunity for engagement with language under appropriate conditions given learner characteristics" (p. 55). *Learner characteristics* covers the linguistic and nonlinguistic individual differences of learners, including, for example, language level or various personality factors. The *amount of opportunity for engagement with language*, then, arises from how well the design of any CALL task relates to those learner differences. Thus, engagement should be seen as an experience of the individual learner in his or her relationship to the task being performed.

Such positive outcomes as represented earlier by the student quotes in the Focus section are not consistently the case for learners participating in CALL courses. Ware and Kramsch (2005), for example, explore in some depth the gradual disengagement of a student participant in a German-English telecollaboration project caused by misunderstandings that may have been reinforced in part by the distance of the technology-based communication. Other studies of CALL projects (Belz, 2002; Stepp-Greany, 2002; Ware, 2005) have indicated similar outcomes for some students. The positive quote from L. Lee (2004) mentioned earlier is balanced in her article by reports of other students' frustrations in the networked collaborative initiative she researched. Results from both Stepp-Greany (2002) and Bordonaro (2003) suggest that even when students are positively disposed to technology-based instruction, their levels of engagement may differ and result in different levels of willingness to continue with CALL instruction.

These mixed results, in some cases coming in the same study, point to the individual nature of engagement in instructional tasks. They also confirm a truth generally recognized within the field of CALL: Technology alone does not produce engagement and learning, but the pedagogy applied in the use of technology can (Egbert, 2005; Kern & Warschauer, 2000; Salaberry, 2001; Warschauer, 1997). CALL tasks may require a high level of engagement from learners (Ware & Kramsch, 2005), and thus, one purpose in designing CALL tasks should be to maximize engagement for the greatest number of learners.

Unfortunately, there has been little research so far on student engagement in the tasks employed in CALL pedagogy that might provide helpful insights into how to achieve this goal. The student quotes at the beginning of this chapter are anecdotal accounts from studies with purposes other than exploring learner engagement. Chapelle (2001) reviews a number of obstacles to research on the linguistic and nonlinguistic aspects of engagement, suggesting potentially fruitful paths to follow, including analysis of student behaviors while engaging in CALL activities. However, although studies that look at student behaviors in CALL may suggest ways to explore engagement, looking at behaviors alone may mislead researchers regarding what is happening psychologically for learners (Hwu, 2003). There is a need for approaches to engagement from a student perspective, looking at their views on the experience of participating in CALL activities.

Flow Theory

Egbert (2003) has pioneered the use of flow theory for exploring learner engagement in CALL tasks. The primary focus of flow studies has been to explore the quality of subjective experience that causes behavior to be intrinsically motivating. Research concerning the existence of flow experiences and the conditions associated with them in educational settings has illuminated learners' emotional states while being engaged in language learning tasks. Moreover, these studies have supported the existence of a systematic relationship between emotional states and cognitive functioning (Larson, 1988; MacIntyre, 2002). Despite being limited, the investigation of flow theory in language-oriented classrooms has shed light on the significance of autonomy-promoting contexts, motivating tasks, and teacher roles in inspiring flow in learners.

Flow theory holds that intrinsically motivating experiences result in an improved psychological state during total engagement in an activity (Csikszentmihalyi, 1975, 1990, 1997b; Csikszentmihalyi & Csikszentmihalyi, 1988; Egbert, 2003; Tardy & Snyder, 2004). Csikszentmihalyi describes this state of mind as an experience of *flow*. Flow is characterized by feelings of enjoyment and satisfaction, referred to as *optimal experience*, wherein individuals become so absorbed in the activity that the distinction between the self and the activity becomes unclear (Csikszentmihalyi, 1997b; Deci & Ryan, 1985). Such intense focus during the activity, in effect, may cause people to lose their self-consciousness and experience a sense of transcendence.

While experiencing flow, people are usually not concerned with the consequences of their performance. Instead, the enjoyment of doing the activity provides an intrinsic reward that promotes the desire to stay involved in the task. Flow experiences are characterized by feelings of enjoyment, interest, happiness, and satisfaction. Therefore, flow by its very nature is said to be an *autotelic experience* in which people engage in an activity for its own sake even when the task is perceived as difficult or dangerous. The perfect balance between the challenges afforded by the activity and the individual's available skills is believed to contribute to this optimal experiential state.

Flow theory holds that intrinsically rewarding experiences characterized by this optimal state ultimately result in increased performance. Because the activities that produce flow are intrinsically motivated, "a person in flow should be able to function at his or her best" (Larson, 1988, p. 150). In other words, the autotelic nature of flow-conducive activities enables individuals to be at the peak of their performance and productivity. Consequently, flow may possibly contribute to optimal performance and learning (Csikszentmihalyi, 1990, 1997b; Egbert, 2003, 2005; Larson, 1988; Tardy & Snyder, 2004).

Flow has been extensively studied in relation to involvement in activities such as sports, dancing, reading, art, music, and computer games (Csikszentmihalyi, 1975, 1990; Csikszentmihalyi & Csikszentmihalyi, 1988). Csikszentmihalyi (1993) points out that such activities are specifically designed to facilitate flow; however, he further claims that "almost every activity has the potential to produce flow" (p. 189). In fact, studies investigating flow in everyday life have revealed that flow experiences are reported more frequently in work and study than in leisure, provided that the necessary conditions for flow are embedded in the activity.

Conditions of Flow

Flow theory holds that some preconditions must exist for enhanced experiences to occur:

1. a balance between challenge and available skills
2. focused attention and concentration
3. learner interest
4. a sense of control (Csikszentmihalyi, 1997b; Egbert, 2003)

Other correlates of flow might include clear task goals, immediate feedback on the task, "a lack of self-consciousness," and the perception that time passes more quickly (Egbert, 2003, p. 502), as well as a deep sense of enjoyment in the activity. However, Jackson and Marsh (as cited in Egbert, 2003) claim that lack of self-consciousness and loss of a sense of time are not universal prerequisites for flow.

The balance between challenge and skills is cited as one of the most important conditions among the factors that contribute to the emergence of flow (Csikszentmihalyi, 1975, 1988, 1990, 1997b; Deci & Ryan, 1985; Dörnyei & Otto, 1998; Egbert, 2003; Tardy & Snyder, 2004; van Lier, 1996; Wilkinson & Foster, 1997). Enjoyment from the task is ultimately experienced if learners feel that their available skills and the challenges offered by the task are in optimal balance. This balance, in turn, leads to improved performance on the task, and the learner feels motivated to face new challenges (Csikszent-mihalyi, 1988, 1997b; Egbert, 2003). This view suggests that optimal balance is not static, and therefore flow can be sustained only if the level of challenge is continually adjusted to match learners' increasing skills (Csikszentmihalyi, 1997b; Egbert, 2003). If the task presents learners with challenges that are too much above or below their skill level, flow is replaced by feelings of boredom or anxiety (see also the discussion of flow in chapter 22 in this volume).

Focused attention and concentration on the task are also essential for the emergence of flow (Csikszentmihalyi, 1997b; Egbert, 2003). Many second language acquisition studies have emphasized the important role of attention in learning (Crookes & Schmidt, as cited in van Lier, 1996; Schmidt, as cited in Egbert, 2003; Skehan, 1998). In relation to flow theory, Csikszentmihalyi (1990) also views attention as a "distinctive feature of optimal experience," with an individual's attention so absorbed by the task that "the activity becomes spontaneous, almost automatic" (p. 53). Thus, such full concentration on the task produces flow, with the activity becoming an intrinsic reward in itself. Although much research has emphasized conscious attention to language, many subjects who have reported experiencing flow maintain that "unintention-ally focused attention" (Egbert, 2003, p. 504) was essential for the occurrence of flow (Deci & Ryan, 1985; Egbert, 2003).

Because flow theory is concerned with the affective dimension of motiva-tion, learner interest as an emotionally arousing factor has received attention in the research. Schneider, Csikszentmihalyi, and Knauth's claim (as cited in Dörnyei & Otto, 1998) that there exists a negative correlation between academic environments and motivation has been supported by students' identification of most academic tasks as being boring and uninteresting. However, it has been revealed that topics that were of interest to learners were positively correlated with engagement, enjoyment, and focused attention (Abbott, 2000; Schiefele, 1991; Schraw, Flowerday, & Lehman, 2001). These findings further support *self-determination theory*, wherein involvement in activities that interest individuals is believed to direct intrinsically motivating behavior (Deci & Ryan, 1985). Interest that leads to flow could result from tasks that are meaningful to learners, that are authentic, and that offer them choices in the activity (Egbert, 2003).

The fourth precondition for flow is the need for individual control. It has been pointed out that *autonomy-supportive environments* in which learners enjoy some degree of freedom are more likely to create conditions for flow than controlling environments (Abbott, 2000; Benson, 2001; Deci & Ryan, 1985; Noels, Pelletier, Clément, & Vallerand, 2000; Pelletier, Séguin-Lévesque, & Legault, 2002; Ryan & Deci, 2000; van Lier, 1996). One role of immediate feedback in tasks may be to help learners regulate the level of challenge in the task and thus control their engagement in it. The intrinsic need for control does not imply control over the environment, but rather the need to have a choice and consequently be self-determining (Deci & Ryan, 1985). The inherent need for self-determination, in effect, motivates individuals across cultures to seek and engage in new challenges, which is thought to be essential for the occurrence of flow (Egbert, 2003).

Flow in Language Learning

Larson (1988), exploring high school students' subjective experiences while they were working on a research paper for an English class, observed that disorder in emotional states such as overarousal (anxiety) or underarousal (boredom) could adversely affect students' motivation, cognitive processing and attention, and quality of work. Conversely, optimal arousal, defined as an experience of enjoyment or flow, has the potential to enhance cognition as well as "clear attention and command over one's thoughts" (Larson, p. 167). The relationship between optimal arousal and writing performance was also supported with Larson's conclusion that "enjoyment as both cause and effect contributes to creating and sustaining flow in writing, [and] that the conditions that create enjoyment and that create good writing are closely related" (p. 170). Although enjoyment per se is not dependent on high-quality performance, the optimal conditions that could facilitate the experience of enjoyment can yield valuable insights into establishing desirable classroom environments.

A recurring issue emphasized in research studies exploring flow in language learning settings is the autonomy afforded to learners. In autonomy-supportive contexts, learners are observed to function with increased intrinsic motivation and greater task engagement that are likely to be accompanied by feelings of interest, enjoyment, satisfaction, and pleasure (Abbott, 2000; Larson, 1988; Tardy & Snyder, 2004). Furthermore, flow is believed to enhance "optimal experiences," whereby learners "push themselves to higher levels of performance" (Csikszentmihalyi, 1990, p. 74) when the learning environment is autonomy supporting. Drawing on Csikszentmihalyi's concept of flow and the conditions associated with its occurrence, one could conclude that learning environments in which autonomy grants learners choice and control over tasks (Abbott, 2000; Larson, 1988) seem more likely to create flow experiences. (For more on autonomy, see chapter 25 in this volume.)

Content-based tasks, for example, may contribute to the development of intrinsic motivation to learn (Egbert, 2003; Grabe & Stoller, 1997; Tardy & Snyder, 2004). Grabe and Stoller suggest that content-based activities that "generate interest in content information through stimulating material resources and instruction" (p. 12) can lead to flow in language classrooms. Content-based activities can also enhance greater intrinsic motivation by exposing students to "contextualized language experiences within content learning" (Tardy & Snyder, 2004, p. 121), by allowing students to personalize the content information and communicate for real purposes and by providing students "a fair amount of choice in thematic content" (p. 121). (For more on content-based tasks, see chapter 9 in this volume.)

Discussions of flow in learning environments suggest that flow can exist in language classrooms (Abbott, 2000; Egbert, 2003; Larson, 1988; Tardy & Snyder, 2004; Wilkinson & Foster, 1997) and that teachers can contribute to the occurrence of flow states in learners by creating environments and designing tasks that might stimulate optimal experiences.

Examples and Discussion

CALL Tasks and the Conditions of Flow

Learners can become engaged by any task, even if others think of it as boring and repetitive. As Chapelle's (2001) concept of learner fit suggests, whether and when engagement occurs depends on the interaction between each learner's individual qualities and the nature of the task. Flow theory suggests that tasks that are more effective at creating conditions for engagement are

- structured around interesting content and activity
- designed to be flexible, that is, allowing learners to control the difficulty of the task, their level of participation, and the focus of their attention
- designed to provide feedback on performance to learners

Both learner-computer interaction and computer-mediated communication (CMC) tasks may be more likely than non-CALL tasks to meet the conditions for engagement because the use of technology can allow learners to personalize tasks to a greater extent than in an ordinary classroom (Egbert, 2003).

But because engagement is interactive and contextual, it is impossible to say that any particular type of CALL task will lead to engagement. Egbert (2003) conducted the only study so far to look specifically at engagement in language learning from a student perspective, and she found that two superficially similar Internet chat tasks produced different levels of engagement in learners. However, pedagogical differences in the tasks resulted in differences in challenge, control, interest, and focused attention. One student reported that previous experience with the first chat task made the second one easier, suggesting that the level of challenge in the latter task was reduced. Egbert points to an important difference in the structure of the two tasks, with students having more control over the chat interaction in the first task, whereas in the second, the interaction was more structured and more controlled by the learner's chat partners. Egbert's description of the tasks suggests that their content may have made a difference in the learners' motivation, with the first chat task focused on "artists and general questions" and the second on "dietary habits" (p. 508). Finally, the second chat task was subject to an interruption that may have broken the attention of some learners. The results should make it clear that it is not the use of chat itself that makes the task engaging or not, but rather how the pedagogical task invoked in using chat is designed and perceived by the learners. We now offer four pedagogical suggestions that can help make a CALL task more likely to result in engagement for more learners: aligning the use of technology with task purposes, providing choices to support learner control of the task, promoting interaction in tasks, and providing learner training.

Aligning Technology and Task

Tasks can interest learners and focus their attention without necessarily helping them achieve learning goals. It is important that the use of technology in tasks be designed to help learners focus on language in ways that move them toward specific learning goals. Levy (2006) points to the different effects of CMC technologies on how learners distribute attentional resources:

> If the goal of the task is to promote a focus on meaning and fluency one would choose a CMC technology that is compatible with that focus, most likely a synchronous technology. Alternately, if the goal of the task were a focus on form, in terms of either accuracy or complexity, an instructor would want to choose an asynchronous CMC technology or to instigate a post-synchronous CMC activity which focuses on form. As MOOs [multiuser object-oriented domains] support both synchronous and asynchronous communication, it may in fact be possible to realise a cyclic approach to attention to meaning as well as form within a single online environment. (pp. 7–8)

Levy is stressing here that the technology is separate from the task and that a particular technology's affect on task outcomes must be considered in task design. With the appropriate technology employed in relation to task purposes, students' attention will be drawn to the object of learning.

In tasks described by Levy and Kennedy (2004), audio chat and its transcripts were used to set up the *cyclic approach* to attention mentioned previously. Audio chat was embedded in project work in order to give the chats purpose beyond simply being a free speaking activity. The synchronous nature of the audio chats provided opportunities for learners to work on "fluency, negotiation and getting the message across" (p. 54), whereas the chat transcripts were used later for form-focused activities undertaken with the teacher or other students. Schwienhorst (2003a) details the evolution of relationships among technology, task design, and task purpose when a tandem-learning project moved from being e-mail-based to MOO-based. He points out "three areas in which a combination of technology and pedagogy will affect reflective processes" (p. 439) with the use of MOOs. The technology will in some cases

- "pressure" learners to reflect in particular ways (e.g., reviewing screens in the MOO)

- provide "affordances" that learners are likely to make use of in reflection (e.g., opportunities for mutual correction of errors)

- offer "potentials" for reflection that learners might make use of only when guided to them by the teacher (e.g., chat transcripts; pp. 439–440)

Providing Choice

Alperer (2005) shows that the provision of choice has a significant effect on learners' engagement in task, in particular on their interest in the task and sense of control of the task. Creating opportunities for engagement and flow in learner-computer interaction involves using the computer technology to let learners control the task and establish the appropriate level of challenge for themselves. Pekel's student (2002; cited at the beginning of the chapter) found the use of the computer for timing online reading activities and controlling access to a text challenging and exciting. The way technology regulated his participation in the task and provided feedback pushed him to try to improve his performance.

A. Taylor, Lazarus, and Cole (2005) report the results of a study examining the use of drop-down menus with lexical and grammatical models in frames to support writing in German. With the drop-down menus, learners could decide individually when to consult the models to solve different problems in their writing and "to think through something on the screen," working "at their own pace, with support" (p. 448). The design of the menus allowed learners to focus their attention on the problem they were solving by isolating the process on the screen, something that paper approaches to writing cannot do. The teacher and the learners reported that the drop-down menus gave learners more opportunities to be creative in their writing, pushing them to extend their vocabulary and use of grammatical structures. One student is reported as saying, "Making a sentence—it's a challenge for everyone. But it's a challenge that with the drop down menus can be met because the drop down menus set it out" (p. 448). These menus also supported greater student engagement in the writing task, evinced not only in the video recordings of their activity in class, but also by the increased creativity of student output.

Technology can provide support to individual learners in deciding not only when and where they need it, but also how they will use it, allowing the learners themselves to create the learner fit of a task. Extending the earlier discussion of process and product differences in the use of chat, Hoshi (2002) reported on Japanese learners of English who made a similar distinction in purpose between different types of chat groups. The learners saw native-speaker chat rooms as sources of input and an archival record to study for features of language, that is, for *product*; chat rooms for learners were sources of output and *process*, places where they could practice, possibly anonymously, in a community of fellow learners with whom they had much in common. Learners' perceptions of differences in chat environments and their ability to determine how they would use chat might make a difference in their willingness to engage in it and learn from it.

Promoting Interaction

Alperer (2005) found that giving students the opportunity to work in groups and interact with each other had a positive effect not only on learners' interest and sense of control of tasks, but also on their attention to the task. CMC tasks may be thought of as inherently interactive because they involve multiple parties linked by the computer, sharing information; however, there is much room for variation in the nature of the interactions (e.g., synchronous versus asynchronous, one-to-one versus one-to-many versus many-to-many) across different CMC technologies (e.g., e-mail, text chat, voice chat, video chat, cell phone) and different tasks. Synchronous and asynchronous CMC tasks involve different kinds of interaction, and a number of factors may impact the success of these interactions in terms of learning, including the match between participants in interest and proficiency (see, e.g., Stockwell & Levy, 2001). Yet numerous studies across different permutations of CMC suggest that the use of technology can promote a wider range of participation in discussion and greater equality among group members (Warschauer, 1997). Even though participation and equality have not been linked empirically to greater engagement in tasks, these results imply that there is a connection.

Although learner-computer interaction tasks are generally assumed to be solitary activities, in classroom contexts they can be structured to allow interaction among learners by having them work collaboratively before shared screens (Egbert, 2005). Jeon-Ellis, Debski, and Wigglesworth's (2005) study of learner interaction in developing Web pages as part of project-based French instruction shows how interaction focused the learners' attention and created increased opportunities for learning the target language. In A. Taylor et al.'s (2005) study, although students were intended to be working individually on their writing, they helped each other in a variety of ways that showed engagement in the task and supported learning:

> Video data revealed how much verbal interplay there was between those sitting near each other; they checked hypotheses, short-circuited dictionary use through asking those near them and, in one particular case, a student assumed the role of teacher and tutor with his neighbor. He leaned over, operating the partner's mouse, to illustrate where all the past participles were, carefully checking each sentence and gently correcting an error in the formation of one past participle. (pp. 446–447)

Learners taking over the task in this way is a sign of their engagement (Tardy & Snyder, 2004), and the teacher should encourage such interaction when it occurs.

Providing Learner Training

Csikszentmihalyi (1975) suggests that the experience of flow "depends on a very delicate balance between being in control and being overwhelmed" (p. 64). For learners to maintain this balance, it is essential that teachers provide learner training regarding the technology and the tasks learners are asked to do. Learner control of the learning process is seen as the basis of learner autonomy (Benson, 2001). Hubbard (2004) argues that learners in CALL classes may not be prepared to take control of their learning without training specifically aimed at helping them with the technologies they will be using:

> Most students will profit from some formal, sustained training in how to take *operational* competence in a given computer application and transfer that into *learning* competence. We should not release our students into powerful learning environments unprepared: It is our responsibility as teachers to see that they are able to make informed decisions about how to use computer resources effectively to meet their learning objectives. (p. 51)

Hubbard (2004) suggests that general training should cover the appropriate use of semantic-oriented technologies (e.g., captioning systems, translation programs), various forms of CMC, how to select and exploit authentic materials on the Web, and the appropriate use of tutorial software. Learners also need to learn how to match the demands of the task to the technology; how to make good choices from options available to support their learning; and when and how to work effectively with their teacher, classmates, and other interlocutors to succeed in achieving task goals. This kind of training is necessary because the engagement is not a result of the nature of the task itself, but more the result of the learners' ability to structure their participation in the task (Csikszentmihalyi, 1975, 1990). See chapter 18 in this volume for more on the need for teacher training in technology to support appropriate student uses.

Conclusion

It will be the job of CALL teachers to implement the aforementioned suggestions and to match technology to task purposes, provide choices for learners, support interaction, and, most important, provide the necessary training to learners to support engagement and autonomy, and thereby, learning. Many of the chapters in this volume point to the kinds of tasks and activities that provide these features, but teachers must be reflective in their use of technology:

> The existence of new technology and the desire to exploit it place teachers and learners in a labyrinth of opportunities, challenges, imperatives, and expectations. What is required to negotiate ways out of this maze are meaningful and productive practices that help teachers monitor, reflect, and prepare for their classroom specific experiences. (Towndrow, 2005, p. 507)

Towndrow advocates a professional development program for teachers that helps them "identify and assess their roles" (p. 511) as implementers of tasks and sees this as requiring that teachers be able to think about the design of tasks in all their aspects, including the affective.

What flow theory provides teachers is a vocabulary and a way of thinking about the affective nature of tasks that can help them in attending to what does and does not work in their classrooms. Operationalizing engagement in terms of challenge, attention, interest, and control provides a way to analyze CALL task design and dissect CALL task implementation. Bringing about discussion of tasks in these terms in CALL teacher education will provide a basis for improved practice by increasing teacher awareness and flexibility. As Tardy and Snyder (2004) put it,

> discussions of flow can provide valuable opportunities for teachers to become more aware of how different tasks affect them and their students. Teachers can be helped to develop a sensitivity to classroom moments in which they perceive authentic involvement and learning to be happening, and to adopt flexibility when appropriate, following those moments to their conclusions rather than rigidly adhering to a plan. Reflection on flow can be presented as a way to help develop these particular abilities. (p. 124)

The teachers who are able to do these things will be the teachers who are most able to provide support to students as they begin to work with technology in their learning and to help them "attend mindfully to the learning process" (Egbert, 2005, p. 7).

Explorations

1. Reflect on a time when you experienced flow. What were you doing? What was the outcome of the experience? Make a note of your recollections and share them with your classmates or working group.

2. In what formal or informal ways do you determine learner fit in your classroom? Make a chart of these ways and share it with your classmates or working group.

3. Reflect on the age, personal preferences, language level, and challenges and skills your students possess. What is most likely to engage learners in your classroom? Why? Share your findings and discuss possible ways to overcome obstacles to flow.

4. Review a lesson plan that you have used or might use in your classroom. How does it provide choice, promote interaction, and afford learner training? How does technology support the goals of the task and learner engagement? Share your lesson with your classmates or working group.

5. Teacher engagement and flow have been posited by Tardy and Snyder (2004) to be central to learner engagement and flow. Make a list of tasks that are the most engaging for you, and review how you might use this information to improve student engagement. In particular, you might explore what kinds of computer uses provide engagement.

Chapter 24

Critical Issues:
Culturally Responsive CALL

Birgitte Gade Brander

Focus

From the perspective of an educator and former preschool teacher, I always remind the student teachers and in-service teachers I work with that teaching and learning are holistic phenomena—they involve teaching the whole child. To be able to teach the whole child and ensure academic success, it is important for teachers to understand the students' cultural, linguistic, and ethnic backgrounds. But being culturally aware of students' backgrounds requires training, self-reflection and -evaluation, and cultural responsiveness on behalf of the teacher. I recall an incident when I was observing an in-service seventh-grade teacher teaching corrective reading by means of both classroom teaching and CALL. The majority of the students in the classroom were second language learners (native Spanish speakers learning English). The day I was present, the students were reading a story in English, and as I observed, I wondered whether the students really liked the story because not all students seemed equally engaged in the reading and listening activities. I was sitting next to one of the kids in the classroom who was doing the corrective reading exercise on the computer. As I read over the student's shoulder I suddenly stumbled over several baseball terms (e.g., *dugout, umpire*) that were unfamiliar to me. Because I am an ESL learner myself, not knowing the key words caused me to miss the meaning of the story entirely. At the same time I noticed that the Spanish-speaking student sitting next to me also paused as he reached the sentences with the baseball terms. I could tell that he, too, was confused and obviously did not know what these baseball terms meant. The meaning was lost on him, and he lost interest in reading because the teacher did not offer any help. The teacher had taken for granted that all of the Mexican American students in her class understood the story (in particular the references to U.S. culture and baseball) because they lived in the United States. The teacher had not provided any definitions for the students, and because the majority of the students did not comprehend the story, there was not a lot of discussion. This situation highlights the critical issue that is addressed in this chapter—failing to take cultural and linguistic differences into account when teaching all students, including culturally and ethnically diverse students.

Because language, identity, culture, and education are deeply intertwined (J. Banks, 2001), teachers have to be able to apply pedagogical and instructional practices that respect and support the cultural and ethnic differences among the students in their classrooms; to do so, they must also understand that there are different perceptions of cultural diversity and that these perceptions affect the student-teacher relationship in language learning.

Perceptions of cultural diversity are varied. Some educators see culture from a *deficit* perspective, reflecting a belief that supports the mainstream culture as the norm while deviations from the norm are viewed as dysfunctional or in some way inferior (Ford, Howard, Harris, & Tyson, 2000). Opposed to the cultural deficit model, the cultural *difference* model sees different cultures, ethnicities, and languages as positive assets. Educators working under the difference model acknowledge and accommodate students by making curriculum and instruction compatible with the students' cultures and backgrounds.

This chapter supports the cultural difference model of CALL; it encourages CALL educators and researchers to consider cultural, linguistic, and ethnic aspects of technology use. It emphasizes that, when using computers in language learning, it is crucial that teachers not employ a "color-blind" ideology that ignores the cultural differences among students. Teachers often use this ideology assuming that they are treating all students equally, but what they really are doing is ignoring the students' cultural and racial differences (Ladson-Billings, 1994) and thereby failing to accommodate the diversity of all learners. Those students whose cultural capital differs from that of the computer classroom presentation designed experience inherently unequal treatment given that they do not share the same relational association to the curriculum and instructional practices.

This chapter discusses concepts of culture and technology and explores the literature that addresses culture and language, *culturally responsive* teaching, and how such teaching can be situated in CALL. The final section presents examples of culturally relevant teaching in virtual classrooms.

Background

Computers are bringing new dimensions and insights into education and language learning. The interactive structure of language learning classrooms using computers challenges teachers and researchers to examine and consider the *cultural contexts* of their classroom learning environments, particularly where Internet-mediated communication is employed, because the Internet is a medium that can facilitate interactions among people of many cultures

(Brander, 2005). Even within self-contained classrooms, the computer is a tool that can be used to facilitate teacher and student interactions and help teachers learn about students and their communities. However, very little research has investigated cultural variables in CALL or in incorporating culturally responsive teaching into the CALL context (Brander, 2005). A focus in this area can contribute to cultural understanding and accommodation of language learners' cultures and thereby more effective second language learning.

Culture and Language

Culture influences all aspects of teaching language learners because languages are always situated in cultural contexts. Willinsky (1998) states that language and cultural differences fix people to given places in the world by situating them through their identities, heritages, and traditions. The perception that culture and language are interchangeably linked is supported by Tavares and Cavalcanti (1996), who believe that culture learning should be placed on an equal footing with language learning. Foreign languages are acquired through social, cultural, and linguistic interactions during which meaning is negotiated (Chapelle, 1997). Language is linked to people's cultural learning experiences and provides them with skills that allow them to communicate and interact with other people. Culture frames the world in terms of where people live, their values, beliefs, epistemologies, and social behaviors. Even within a culture, there are different systems and symbols that only some members are familiar with and that become a frame of reference for identifying with that particular group of people (J. Banks, 2001; Burniske & Monke, 2001; Grant & Lei, 2001).

In the same vein, some CALL researchers (Chapelle, 1997; Gray & Stockwell, 1998; Tam, 2000; Warschauer, 1996a) argue that educators should apply technology to enhance *intercultural awareness*. This can be done in environments where learners are encouraged to engage in dialogue with other students and the teacher, are supported in cooperative learning, and can be involved in real-world situations (Weasenforth, Biesenbach-Lucas, & Meloni, 2002). However, teachers must make cultural awareness an explicit expectation for students, otherwise it may not happen.

In their study of Japanese and Australian learners, for example, Gray and Stockwell (1998) examined how intercultural awareness can be enhanced by using the Internet for language learning. However, in this language learning e-mail exchange, the Japanese students' cultural differences and understandings in discourse and interaction—which are very different from those of the Australians—were not apparent. For example, in the Japanese culture, interactions, wishes, and needs are not expressed openly. Rather, each party attempts to understand and anticipate the needs of the other even before anything is said. In a face-to-face classroom setting, the Australian language learners would have been confronted with these cultural differences; however, the language learners in Gray and Stockwell's study did not address intercultural problems of any kind, and the researchers did not go into detail about the importance of cultural awareness.

Because culture, language, and discourse are factors that are interchangeably linked, it is important that cultural issues and conflicts are brought forward and addressed—even in CALL. Cultural differences influence the discourses and interactions that take place online (even if the cultural differences are not implicitly expressed in terms of language and culture). In many cases, teachers are unaware of how aspects of students' cultures and languages affect the interaction styles and communication online. To avoid problems that can result from such a lack of awareness, it is important for teachers to be aware of cultural differences among students. It is therefore vital for teachers to take the time to learn about their students and provide resources and strategies to create supportive, culturally responsive, and understanding classroooms.

Culturally Responsive Teaching

Culture influences how people make sense of the world, how they interact, communicate, learn, and so on. That is why language learning cannot take place in a setting where teachers devalue or reject the students' cultures (Nieto, 2000). Effective teaching must make learning meaningful to all students, and to be meaningful it must consider culture, or be culturally responsive. By examining the development of social and cultural competencies in CALL, computer-using teachers and researchers can understand how students' prior knowledge and cultural communities facilitate or interfere with language learning in a virtual environment. Understanding can also help teachers build essential bridges between students' prior knowledge and experiences and the language concepts and content to be learned.

However, considering CALL from a culturally responsive teaching perspective can be complex and challenging because teachers must learn to accommodate all language learners and make the learning meaningful to all students. As part of a culturally responsive teaching philosophy, teachers need to be able to create "an environment in which students can acquire, interrogate, and produce knowledge and envision new possibilities for the use of that knowledge for societal change" (C. A. Banks & Banks, 1995, p. 157) and, I would add, for cultural understanding. In other words, educators need to understand and accommodate students' communicative strategies and instructional practices in their native languages and cultures in order to reinforce effective language learning. It is therefore important for CALL teachers and researchers to consider the following when applying a culturally responsive perspective:

- What is culture, and how does it affect teaching and learning in CALL?
- What are the students' backgrounds, cultures, and epistemologies?
- What do teachers know about the students' cultures, and how can they find out more?
- What steps can teachers take to engage in self-reflection, for example, examining their own attitudes toward different racial, ethnic, social class, and gender groups?
- How can the students' cultural backgrounds be used as scaffolding for teaching and learning in a CALL context?
- Is the teaching culturally responsive in terms of curriculum goals and material?

In the 1970s, Gay identified different ways to develop multicultural content specifically aimed at improving and establishing the interest and motivation for learning among diverse students. These included making clear connections between school, home, and community (Gay, 1975, as cited in Gay, 2000). Culturally responsive teaching involves a sociocultural consciousness on the teacher's behalf that recognizes, among other things, the different ways that students perceive the world, interact with each other, and approach learning. To be responsive, teaching and learning processes should be structured in ways that encourage students to negotiate their own meaning based on their cultures, dispositions, attitudes, and approaches to learning (Gay, 2000; Villegas & Lucas, 2002). Furthermore, culturally responsive teaching should build on students' prior knowledge, language skills, and beliefs.

According to Gay (2000), culturally responsive teaching is about how the teacher makes "learning encounters more relevant to and effective" for students (p. 29), which involves

1. acknowledging the legitimacy of the cultural heritages of different ethnic groups, including students' dispositions, attitudes, and approaches to learning, as worthy content to be taught as part of the standardized curriculum

2. building meaningful bridges between home and school experiences as well as between abstractions and lived sociocultural realities

3. using a broad variety of instructional strategies that support different learning styles

4. teaching students to acknowledge and praise their own and each others' cultural heritages

5. incorporating multicultural information, resources, and materials within all subjects and curriculum (p. 29)

Culturally responsive teaching affects the language learning process; hence, the goal is to accommodate language learners' cultural values, inter-action and communication skills, encoding and decoding skills, and first language skills (Cummins, 1987).

In culturally responsive classrooms, it is important that teachers "employ ongoing and systematic assessment of student abilities, interests, attitudes, and social skills" (Montgomery, 2001, p. 7) as part of the cultural assessment. However, students will become more involved if they are able to take part in their own evaluation and assessment and thus are able to reflect on their own learning outcomes. *Self-assessment* and *critical self-reflection* are important components for culturally responsive teaching and are dependent on how well teachers critically reflect on their teaching styles, assumptions, biases, and personal attitudes, and how each of these affects students of different ethnicities and cultures (T. C. Howard, 2003). Using self-assessment and criti-cal self-reflection in culturally responsive teaching requires that teachers be explicitly aware of what to reflect on and how to ask deep-grounded questions (see Figure 24-1). Self-assessment could, for example, include reflections on the curriculum and instructional programs for teaching students from different

Figure 24-1. Considerations and Questions for Critical Teacher Reflection

1. How frequently do I differentiate instruction?

2. Do scoring rubrics give inherent advantages to certain ways of knowing and expression?

3. Do I allow culturally based differences in language, speech, reading, and writing to shape my perceptions of students' cognitive abilities?

4. Do I create a multitude of ways to evaluate students? Or do I rely solely on individual written responses? How often do I allow for nontraditional means of assessment, such as poetry, rap, and self-evaluations?

5. How often do I plan nontraditional activities, such as Socratic seminars, journaling, student-led conferences and discussions, or cooperative group projects?

6. How will my culture and race influence my work as a teacher with students of color?

7. How do I situate and negotiate students' knowledge, experiences, expertise, and culture with my own?

Note. Adapted from "Culturally Relevant Pedagogy: Ingredients for Critical Teacher Reflection," by T. C. Howard, 2003, *Theory Into Practice*, 42(3), 195–202; and "Teacher Reflection and Race in Cultural Contexts: History, Meanings, and Methods in Teaching," by H. R. Milner, 2003, *Theory Into Practice*, 42(3), 173–180.

racial and ethnic backgrounds, as well as teacher assumptions about interacting and communicating with students and their families.

These questions and reflections are in line with Montgomery (2001), who provides guidelines and strategies for teachers working with students from culturally and linguistically diverse backgrounds. He focuses specifically on how teachers can conduct self-assessment of their own attitudes and practices. He suggests that teachers use different instructional methods and materials to give students opportunities to make relevant connections between the subject matter and the tasks they are asked to perform (Montgomery, 2001). Warschauer (2005) was involved in an aid program to establish English language teaching in Egypt by means of computers, and he suggests that one must be

> cognizant that theory cannot be divorced from practice and that knowledge cannot be separated from cultural context. What seems applicable because we studied it in a course, or used it in our own class, or our own lives, in the US, will take on very different meanings to local actors in different sociocultural contexts. (p. 163)

In particular, Warschauer states that it is extremely important to pay attention to the local context in which one is teaching. His example illustrates the importance of looking critically at the contemporary practices of knowledge acquisition among students within CALL and thus emphasizing students' prior experiences, frames of reference, sociocultural and political contexts, and communities.

Examples and Discussion

Strategies for Cultural Responsiveness

A central element of culturally responsive teaching, as mentioned previously, is to promote student achievement through cultural responsiveness. Some approaches are discussed in the following sections of this chapter. Ladson-Billings (1995), for example, stresses that to promote student achievement teachers need to "empower students intellectually, socially, emotionally, and politically by using cultural referents to impart knowledge, skills, and attitudes" (p. 482). Gay (2000) and Ford et al. (2000) emphasize the following:

- accommodations for different learning styles
- a culturally relevant curriculum
- culturally congruent instructional practice
- culturally sensitive and authentic assessment
- a collective and communal philosophy
- an emphasis on lived sociocultural realities

- a holistic teaching philosophy
- respect for students' primary languages and dialects
- a strong student-teacher-home relationship

Additional strategies are presented in Table 24-1.

Table 24-1. Strategies and Activities for Culturally Responsive Classrooms

Strategy/activity	Comments and implementation of activities
1. Let students know you care	When working in the virtual environment, make yourself visual, and make clear that you truly care about students' welfare.
2. Share the real you	Share your hopes, dreams, and background with students. Too many of them think that the teacher has never walked a mile in their shoes or that teachers did not have to struggle to attain their own goals. Start by telling your story, and then have students tell their stories in the language they are comfortable with (see No. 5).
3. Have high expectations	Do not lower standards or shortchange students, but be willing to gradually bring them up to your expectations. The theory of *small wins* advocates leading individuals to a big goal through baby steps.
4. Keep reminding students of the bigger picture and why what they are learning is important	Tell students constantly what the short-term and long-term benefits are, and connect these to their communities and cultures.
5. Get to know students on a personal level	Do so as early in the school year as possible; you will never look at students in the same way again. You will not only understand them better but also be able to see their potential for academic success and creativity. Use exercises requiring them to complete questionnaires about their likes, dislikes, goals, and dreams; autobiographical writing; partner interviews; reflective journals; and storytelling.
6. Make the virtual classroom experience relevant to the real world	Make the curriculum and activities relevant to students' individual cultures, communities, backgrounds, and knowledge bases.

(Continued on p. 370)

Table 24-1 (continued). Strategies and Activities for Culturally Responsive Classrooms

Strategy/activity	Comments and implementation of activities
7. Use schema theory	Find out what students already know about the topics to be covered, and help them link their prior knowledge to the new information.
8. Use storytelling to arouse students' interest	Tie storytelling to students' lives, the curriculum, and language learning. Find out what they have read and what they would like to read. Encourage them to write original stories, and give them opportunities to share these stories.
9. Showcase students' talents, and give them multiple ways to succeed academically	Give students opportunities to facilitate teaching (allow volunteers to create their own lesson plans about preapproved topics) and create a graphically rich environment (e.g., visuals, graphic organizers, charts, pictures)
10. Use questioning to spark discussion beyond the factual level	*How would you feel if . . . ? Well, that's how the main character felt. What if . . . ?*
11. Encourage students to write letters to authors of books they have read in the language they are learning	This activity gives students a chance to use the language in a real-world setting. Contemporary authors' Web sites and weblogs (blogs) offer the opportunity for authentic communication.
12. Assess students' skills and knowledge in advance	Find out if students have the prerequisite skills and knowledge to be successful in your class. If not, it is your responsibility to fill in as many gaps in their education as you can or ensure that they are transferred to an appropriate level or an intensive program.

Note. Adapted from *Culturally Responsive Teaching: Theory, Research, and Practice,* by G. Gay, 2000, New York: Teachers College Press; and *Through Ebony Eyes: What Teachers Need to Know but Are Afraid to Ask About African-American Students,* by G. L. Thompson, 2004, San Francisco: Jossey-Bass.

Culturally Responsive Teaching in CALL

As educators consider the different cultural and social aspects of CALL, they have to remember that computer and Internet use in many cases does not provide face-to-face interaction between and among students and teachers. This distance makes developing and implementing effective instructional practices and strategies more challenging because certain aspects of people's identities—such as race, gender, social class, accent, and dialect—are hidden in the virtual community (Brander, 2005; Burniske & Monke, 2001). Because these hidden social and cultural dimensions determine how people learn, interact with others, and think, as well as their references and ways of knowing, online curricula and activities have to meet language learners' demands in terms of cultural appropriateness and sensitivity (Warschauer, 1996b). Monke (2001) states that the virtual environment makes it easier to overcome certain social inhibitions and injustices, especially with regard to cultural differences like language, interaction, communication styles, and values. Therefore, in some instances technology combined with culturally responsive teaching can empower students as they create their own safe spaces within the virtual community.

An example of culturally responsive CALL teaching can be seen in Warschauer and Donaghy's (1997) study of a group of Hawaiian language activists and scholars who took advantage of the Internet and other technologies to promote their language. The Hawaiian language, formerly banned as a medium of instruction, was slowly reintroduced into kindergarten and first-grade classes. The language learning programs for children were based on traditional Hawaiian customs and traditions of communication and learning. One of these traditions was an "emphasis on *talking story*, that is, learning through the verbal sharing of personal tales and experiences. Another tradition is that of oral (e.g., chants) and visual (e.g., hula) expression" (Warschauer & Donaghy, 1997, p. 357). The opportunities that technology provided and the support of the virtual community gave the Hawaiian children a chance to express themselves through performance, drawing, and singing in their own language. Technology also provided opportunities for the Hawaiians to establish more cross-cultural ties to other Pacific cultures and communicate with other Pacific peoples in Hawaiian and other Polynesian languages such as Mäori, Tongan, Tahitian, and Samoan.

Suggestions for Technology-Enhanced, Culturally Responsive Teaching

Teachers can employ many strategies to make their technology-enhanced instruction culturally responsive. In addition to the recommendations in this chapter and elsewhere in this volume, many others can be found in books and on the Web.

Choose bias-free tools and materials. Creating culturally relevant pedagogy means choosing tools and materials that are free of bias. CALL researchers and practitioners have to be aware of the attitudes, beliefs, and opinions embedded in software that are grounded in specific cultures. CALL software can be culturally biased because of the cultural and social power structures in the countries where it is published. Culturally biased software can affect student achievement, motivation, and learning—thus making it unusable (Blanchette, 1996; Brander, 2005). For example, the language that is used in CALL software has to be understandable by all users. It should not use words that are understandable only to individuals with a specific cultural heritage in mind (e.g., that of the United States or the United Kingdom). If this is unavoidable, the software product should be clearly marked as to the cultural heritage it presents. Attempts should be made to produce editions of the same instructional product from other viewpoints or to create lesson plans that help students understand the cultural implications of the language in the product.

Use multiple modes and viewpoints. Teachers can promote language student success by incorporating multicultural concepts, issues, and materials into CALL software and curricula. Technology can be employed to increase the relevance of learning (e.g., listening to and creating stories, participating in online discussions). Likewise, teachers should also let students choose their own reading materials

Develop background. One place to start is to develop core vocabulary among language learners. Before students begin to read, they can complete multiple vocabulary exercises based on the most difficult words and important concepts in their coursework. Students can make personal computer dictionaries as an individual vocabulary and spelling resource with drawings and pictures to facilitate understanding. This strategy coincides with best practices in teaching reading.

Teach themes. Another strategy that coincides with best practices for teaching reading is to employ themes within the curriculum; doing so allows the teacher to integrate a variety of language concepts into a specific topic area that draws on students' experiences, interests, and prior knowledge (Haas, 2000). The themes should integrate language, culture, and content into activities that allow students to practice the target language and that prepare them to use it in a variety of contexts. It is important to find out what students already know about the theme(s) that will be covered. This theme-based activity can also be facilitated through providing scaffolded instruction and integrating students into cooperative learning groups. Technology can help by providing a wide variety of theme-based resources, experts from around the world, interactive forums, and opportunities for students to express themselves in their mode(s) of choice. (For more on content and technology resources, see chapter 9 in this volume.)

Conclusion

Becoming an effective culturally responsive CALL educator requires a great deal of self-reflection and an in-depth look at students and their cultures. According to Ladson-Billings (1994), certain themes and guidelines characterize culturally responsive environments. Teachers must

- believe that the whole student (e.g., academic, cognitive, moral, and social-emotional development and skills) must be addressed in the learning environment
- believe that students from different cultures have strengths to be acknowledged and addressed in the virtual learning environment (e.g., incorporate different skills of the students into the curricula)
- seek positive, respectful, and trusting relationships with students
- keep reminding students of the bigger picture and why what they are learning is important

A culturally responsive CALL teacher does not "materialize overnight or without strong intentions" (Ford et al., 2000, p. 417). As educators and researchers within CALL, it is imperative that we challenge the educational system by developing a strong sense of understanding of our own worldviews and root value systems. For culturally responsive teaching to become a foundation of CALL, it is critical that teachers hear the voices of all students—including the diverse student populations whose voices are often silenced.

Explorations

1. Have you ever experienced cultural bias in a language classroom or in other aspects of your life? If so, describe your experience and the possible causes of bias. Suggest possible solutions to the problem.

2. What is your understanding of culturally responsive CALL? Share some examples with your classmates or working group. What general principles will you follow in your classroom in order to be culturally responsive?

3. What activities can teachers incorporate to ensure culturally responsive CALL instruction? Work with your classmates or colleagues to create a list of tasks, materials, and strategies appropriate to creating culturally responsive CALL classrooms.

4. Create a rubric to evaluate a CALL resource such as a Web site or a software program in terms of its cultural responsiveness. Be sure to include cultural, linguistic, and ethnic bias in your criteria. (See *RubiStar* [ALTEC & University of Kansas, 2000–2006] or any of the other rubric makers in Appendix E for help with generating your rubric.)

5. Evaluate a Web site or software package using the rubric that you developed for Exploration 4, and share the outcomes with your classmates or working group.

PART VIII

Autonomy

Chapter 25 ▣

Theory and Research: Autonomy and Language Learning

Deborah Healey

Focus

Autonomy, learner independence, self-direction, self-management—all are used to refer to the learner taking some element of control over his or her learning. The images of autonomous learning can range from fierce independence to lonely isolation and frustration to adult maturity and confidence. Learner autonomy in language learning has often been set in contrast to dependence on the teacher. More recent discussions, however, consider the role of the teacher and the need to encourage teachers to take on aspects of autonomy themselves. Current views of autonomy have also moved away from isolated learning toward *social settings* and *flexible interdependence*. Benson (2002), reflecting on his experience in a self-access setting, takes a broad perspective on autonomy in language learning:

> Autonomy is whatever an autonomous person thinks it is. . . . We are most likely to recognise autonomy in the learners' overall feeling that they are in control of their learning—a feeling that may be independent of what we actually see them doing. (p. 6)

Oxford (2003) has systematized varying perspectives on learner autonomy, drawing from early work by Holec (1980, 1981), Dickinson (1987), Allwright (1990), Pennycook (1997), Rivers (2001), and others. She presents a model of autonomy that contains four interrelated but differing perspectives:

- *technical perspective*—focus on the physical situation
- *psychological perspective*—focus on characteristics of learners
- *sociocultural perspective*—focus on mediated learning
- *political-critical perspective*—focus on ideologies, access, and power structure (Oxford, 2003, pp. 76, 80)

After a brief review of relevant literature, this chapter discusses Oxford's four perspectives on autonomous learning and adds CALL as an element. This discussion not only provides the traditional technical viewpoint, but also enriches the exploration of CALL in autonomous learning through the other three perspectives.

Background

Much work has been done to find ways to encourage autonomous learning. Some issues of concern in the literature relate to the setting, the role of learning styles and strategies, age variables, individual versus group work, control and the locus of power, and the cultural relevance of autonomous learning.

Setting. The Centre de Recherches et d'Applications Pédagogiques en Langues began conducting research on self-directed learning in 1974 at the Université de Nancy II in France. A major focus of this effort has been on teaching learners how to work in autonomous settings, often with explicit instruction. The Open University in the United Kingdom, a center for correspondence courses and distance education, has also been involved for many years in seeking ways to encourage learners to be comfortable with learning independently. Benson's (2001) and Candy's (1991) texts provide comprehensive looks at establishing self-directed learning settings with a focus on adult learners. Regarding CALL, Healey (1995) and Meskill (2002) address some settings for autonomy.

Learning styles and strategies. A number of writers have explored the role of learning styles and strategies, including autonomous learning, in language teaching. Among them are Dickinson (1987), O'Malley and Chamot (1990), and Oxford (2003). The ability to address multiple learning styles has long been cited as an advantage of using multimedia in language teaching and learning, from early work by W. F. Smith (1989) to current CALL overviews, such as those offered by Meskill (2002) and Egbert (2005).

Age. Autonomy is generally seen as a characteristic of adults, although younger learners can also engage in autonomous learning. Dam's (1995) work with teens provides one model of student-directed learning that could be used with younger students. WebQuests (Dodge, n.d.-b), whereby the teacher sets some resources and the structure for the activity and then has learners produce a report or other product, have been used successfully with a wide range of age groups. The level of teacher support can easily vary with the age of the learners.

Individual versus group work. Independence in learning does not mean solitude, and autonomous learners are also part of communities of practice. According to Wenger (1998a), a community of practice defines itself along three dimensions:

- **what it is about**—its *joint enterprise* as understood and continually renegotiated by its members

- **how it functions**—mutual engagement that binds members together into a social entity

- **what capability it has produced**—the *shared repertoire* of communal resources (routines, sensibilities, artifacts, vocabulary, styles, etc.) that members have developed over time ("Defining Communities of Practice," ¶ 2)

The community of practice for a language learner—a learning community—may be other learners, or it may be those who have achieved the level of proficiency or access to which the learner aspires. Oxford (2003) points out that more experienced community members can help newcomers understand the elements of a community of practice and thus be more prepared to become part of it. Stevens (2006b) emphasizes the role of technology in creating and sustaining communities of practice in English language teaching.

Autonomous learning with others is enriched by the connectivity provided by the Internet. Tandem learning projects in particular are designed to encourage learners to teach each other, creating their own learning communities. Studies by Von der Emde, Schneider, and Kotter (2001) and Schwienhorst (2003b), along with the edited volume by Lewis and Walker (2003), offer insights into the types of autonomy and learning enabled in these collaborative projects. The teacher generally plays a major role in establishing a learning environment conducive to learning with others. Teachers can also exploit software to create opportunities for pair and group work. Research has indicated that the task, not the technology, enhances or inhibits extended discussion at the computer (Abraham & Liou, 1991; Piper, 1986).

Control and the locus of power. The locus of power is a key concern in *critical pedagogy.* Freire (1970) and those involved in critical pedagogy (Giroux, 1996; Pennycook, 1997) call for learning that is personally and socially relevant and that leads to greater self-awareness—an approach that fits well with autonomy in learning. The role of the teacher is to help learners see that they have options and to help them achieve their goals. Power inequality is at the heart of concerns about the digital divide. Although not everyone may want to be immersed in technology, knowledge about and access to technology are a source of power in today's world.

Cultural relevance. An additional concern for many authors has been the idea that autonomous learning is a Western concept. This issue forms the basis of Palfreyman and Smith's (2003) edited volume. Various authors acknowledge that certain ideas about autonomy and self-directed learning practices are closely tied to Western beliefs, but Holliday (2003) points out that it is inappropriate to assume either that whole cultures do not value autonomous learning or that the Western model in all its aspects is a goal to be attained. Holliday concludes that educators need to presume "autonomy is a <u>universal</u>

until there is evidence otherwise—and that if it is not immediately evident in student behaviour, this may be because there is something preventing us from seeing it—thus treating people equally as people" (p. 118).

Examples and Discussion

This section applies the four perspectives on autonomy described by Oxford (2003) to CALL environments. The typical approach to autonomy in CALL is what Oxford would describe as a *technical perspective*. Adding CALL to her other three perspectives should provide the reader with a rich and appropriately complex view of autonomy in language learning. The technical perspective on autonomy in CALL environments emphasizes the "how to" of setting and content, which are sufficiently complex to be treated separately.

The Technical Perspective: Issues of Setting

One approach to describing self-directed learning settings is to do so along two different continua: locus of control and type of content (see Table 25-1).

Highly structured learning (Cell A). In highly structured self-directed learning settings, where the teacher structures the learning by fixing the content,

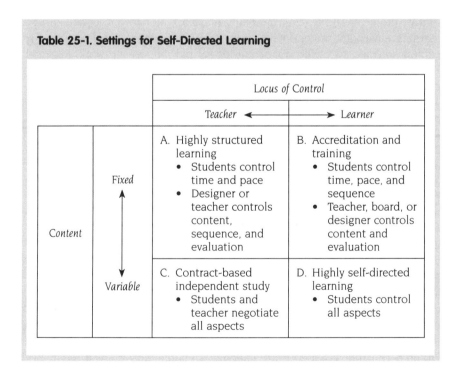

Table 25-1. Settings for Self-Directed Learning

Content		Locus of Control	
		Teacher ← → Learner	
	Fixed	A. Highly structured learning • Students control time and pace • Designer or teacher controls content, sequence, and evaluation	B. Accreditation and training • Students control time, pace, and sequence • Teacher, board, or designer controls content and evaluation
	Variable	C. Contract-based independent study • Students and teacher negotiate all aspects	D. Highly self-directed learning • Students control all aspects

learners working alone or in a group usually control the pace through the material and the time of study. The content and sequence, as well as the form of evaluation, usually come from the teacher or instructional designer. The most rigid form of instruction is the *programmed learning* model that was quite popular in computer-assisted instruction (CAI) circles in a range of fields and was used for language learning in PLATO, a mainframe computer-based courseware system designed in the early 1960s (see PLATO Learning, 2007, for the contemporary version of this system). A good designer builds in ways to account for learner preferences, at least to some extent. Correspondence and many distance education courses follow this model.

Accreditation and training (Cell B). In this setting, learners control the structure but not the content, and a relatively fixed body of content is usually set by an external authority, such as a teacher or accreditation board. This type of setting works best when the body of material to be learned is well defined and learners are able to organize their own learning effectively. The teacher or group that sets the content also typically decides how evaluation will take place.

Much of the current CALL material falls into this category. Learners can choose menu items as well as how often and how long to work on a particular program. In software, context-sensitive help is increasingly offered on demand, giving learners the option to proceed through material at a faster or slower pace, depending on how often help is requested (but see Chapelle & Mizuno, 1989, for problems with demand-based learning in CALL). A language learning course with the usual term deadlines may remove some of the control of pace from the learner, but those constraints are imposed by human demands, not by the language learning technology.

Contract-based independent study (Cell C). The third type of autonomous learning setting is structured by the teacher with variable content. Learners, often working together, generally decide the content, with the teacher serving as a facilitator or guide. The teacher may suggest the route and rate through the material, but the final decision is made jointly or by the learner with an eye to individual learning preferences. Contract-based independent study courses often follow this model, as do many WebQuests. Evaluation is generally negotiated between learners and the teacher-facilitator.

Highly self-directed learning (Cell D). The final type of setting, structured by the learners with variable content, is the most flexible. A teacher is involved only as an optional and additional source of information and guidance, if at all. A research project of the learner's choice would fall into this category, as would certain Open University courses (Nobel, 1980). The learner is responsible for all elements in this setting, including deciding how evaluation will take place. Dam (1995) describes learning groups that successfully operate with this level of autonomy in a self-directed setting. Each group decides its own project, goals, and evaluation. Many tandem learning projects fall into this category. The teacher's primary role is assistant and facilitator.

CALL *and evaluation*. Measurement of success is one arena in which technology can be quite helpful. Individual programs can track not only how learners did on tests, but also how they worked through material, including how long they spent on individual items, words they looked up, help they requested, and guesses they made while doing an exercise. When learners look back to self-assess what they have done, they can see what they worked on and check to see if they now know the words they looked up and the grammar and other rules they asked for help with. A program that tracks reading speed can help learners see their progress over time. By logging user actions, the computer can take some of the record-keeping burden off of learners. Technology can also serve as a reporting medium for self-assessment through regular entries in a learning weblog (blog) or self-evaluation of oral performance through voice mail or a podcast. (See Part V of this volume for more on assessment tools in CALL.)

The Technical Perspective: Issues of Content

Language poses special challenges to learners in that there is no clear path to mastery. Although some work has been done on grammar sequencing (see R. Ellis, 1984; Long, 1987), just about everything else is ambiguous in terms of sequence. Learner goals and learning styles are important factors in content choices. Technology can come into play by helping learners figure out their learning styles with automated questionnaires, then helping match their needs to specific items in a database of available resources. Current multimedia software for language learning can provide for several learning styles, being especially useful for visual (textual and graphical) and auditory learners. Social learners need to make more effort when working in a technology-intensive setting to find people to work with, although Internet connections can help in that regard, for example, in tandem learning and other types of exchanges described elsewhere in this book. With fast, reliable connections, learners can take advantage of real-time, synchronous interaction with multiuser object-oriented domains (MOOs), chat, and instant messaging. Learners can also use the delayed interaction, asynchronous mode of e-mail for peer review of writing and other project work, an option that is especially useful for those whose partners are in different time zones.

In terms of content, multimedia certainly offers the possibility of variation in learning approaches. It is a rare software program that does not have at least two modes: less structured and more structured, practice and test, individual and group, and so on. Most multimedia software also provides information in textual, graphical, and auditory form. Internet-based multimedia has begun to take more advantage of audio and even video elements, although it is still primarily text and graphics based.

The facilitator in an autonomous setting has a substantial role to play in encouraging learners to use a variety of material and methods and explaining how to go about doing so. Although most CALL developers create materials for learners to use individually, better results are often achieved with learners working in pairs. For example, learners spend more time guessing words in a cloze before giving up and checking the answer when they work in pairs than when they work alone (Healey, 1993). The physical layout of the lab or classroom also needs to be conducive to pair work, allowing enough space and chairs at individual machines for learners to work together.

Most CALL programs offer feedback in one way or another. Using a word processor to produce a good-looking printout gives learners an internal sense of satisfaction. At the other end of the intrinsic-extrinsic continuum, a grammar program may keep student records over time and generate a score for the immediate exercise as well as for the learner's work with the program throughout a term. A problem often pointed out with autonomous learning is that students sometimes have trouble seeing the progress they have made or become discouraged when they think about how much further they need to go. Explicit assessment from time to time helps provide those mileposts for learners. Unfortunately, current CALL rarely gives more than a limited snapshot of learner performance on a given task. Unless the material has been customized to meet specific personal goals, it will not give students a sense of where they stand in meeting their overall language learning goals. Facilitators can ask learners to keep records of what they worked on and how they did as a way to self-assess on a more global level. In the Individualized Directed Learning class at Oregon State University's English Language Institute, for example, learners' midterm and final grades depend in large part on the self-assessment they perform based on the records they have kept (Healey, 1992). Self-assessment may also be prompted automatically when students begin to log off from a workstation: They may be asked to make notes and print a local file or reminded to write a blog entry on the Internet.

The issue of barriers to learning from a program design standpoint generally revolves around user-friendliness. A program that regularly fails to work falls into the worst-case category. Programs that require reference to a manual in the target language generally do not work well for language learners, either. Programs can impose barriers to learning when they are cumbersome to use, requiring unnecessary keystrokes or memorization of obscure commands to accomplish basic tasks. Learners who have to struggle just to operate a program are engaged in inauthentic labor—the only struggle necessary should be to meet the reasonable cognitive demands involved in actual language learning.

The Psychological Perspective: About the Learner

Looking at autonomy and CALL through a psychological lens focuses on learner characteristics, most notably motivation and learning preferences.

Self-motivation. Many language learners and teachers come from educational backgrounds in which teachers are expected to control all knowledge in their realm. The pedagogical image is often that of the learner as an empty vessel, waiting to be filled with the teacher's flowing knowledge. Such a background actively discourages learner autonomy. It is often difficult to convince learners who have always been taught this way and teachers who have learned this way that giving some control to learners carries certain advantages. As Oxford (1990) remarks, "just teaching new strategies to students will accomplish very little unless students begin to *want* greater responsibility for their own learning" (p. 10). It sometimes seems like a chicken-and-egg problem: Unless learners have autonomy, they cannot be self-directed, but they may have no interest in autonomous learning until they start to take some control into their own hands.

Many CALL projects, such as WebQuests (Dodge, n.d.-b), can help by providing learners with a structure that gradually gives them more control, thus maintaining their comfort level. Having a public venue for one's work, such as a Web site, blog, or podcast, provides a sense of pride and accomplishment that can further enhance learner motivation.

Independent style. Ideal self-directed learners are always motivated to learn through some internal fire that never needs stoking from a teacher-facilitator. Such people are able to organize their learning independently, knowing when to ask for assistance, but not seeking it otherwise. A former student who had learned an appreciable amount of English just from Beatles songs and a dictionary is an example of such a person; he was, needless to say, quite unusual in both his motivation for learning and his approach. Some Web sites and software offer an index and let learners choose the level that they feel is most appropriate for themselves. When learners can make these kinds of choices, thus having an element of control, learning is often enhanced (Goforth, 1994).

Self-knowledge. Learners who are not very self-motivated and independent in their learning (i.e., most people) need more assistance in an autonomous setting to define and then focus on specific language learning goals. Impossible goals can cause learners to lose heart, but a series of smaller, achievable goals can encourage learners to continue. Simply telling someone to be motivated and independent will not create a personality change; incentives for new attitudes need to be built into the learning setting (Hiemstra & Brockett, 1994). Feedback research by Chapelle and Mizuno (1989) shows that learners are not necessarily good judges of their own skill level, at least in certain areas of language, and may assume they know more than they actually do as a result. Work by Johanesen and Tennyson (1983) indicates that learners given advice about their level of knowledge will practice for a more appropriate time—usually longer—than if they do not have that information. Goforth's (1994) meta-analysis of learner control studies confirms the importance of information given to the learner when the learner is empowered to make decisions.

Some software provides an option for assessment in the areas of instruction it offers, then presents the information customized to the learner's needs. This individualized approach means that, at least within the subset of language that the program deals with, learners can work on an area that fits their skill level. Many programs also track results over time, giving learners a sense of their own accomplishment. Learners who can use Help functions in software, including tools like spelling and grammar checkers in a word processor, can see potential problem areas and choose how to fix them, gaining confidence and control.

Technology and barriers. Technology itself can impose psychological barriers. Many learners are excited by what computers can offer, but others feel anxious and uncertain. They may be threatened by the unfamiliar technology and feel completely lost when a program does not work the way they imagined it would. The self-esteem of older learners in particular may be damaged if they feel that younger learners are more skilled than they are with the technology (especially if the younger learners are also more skilled with the language); such older learners may hesitate to ask for help for fear of exposing their weakness and losing face. Facilitators may need to take extra efforts to avoid such problems and to create a climate conducive to learning, such as being thoughtful in pairing learners for group work and providing extra help sessions to bring learners up to speed with the technology.

The Sociocultural Perspective: Learning Together

Vygotsky (1934/1986) and other social constructivists (e.g., Walker & Lambert, 1995) emphasize the need for interpersonal interaction in order to enhance learning. Vygotsky's *zone of proximal development* is the point in learning at which an individual could benefit from assistance, including exemplary discourse or scaffolding, from a more knowledgeable partner. That partner can be a teacher-facilitator, a fellow student, user-friendly material, or a computer program or other digital resource. Whether or not direct help is provided, the teacher interested in autonomy can design a learning environment that offers encouragement when learners are ready for assistance. (However, for caveats about the potential for hostile community atmosphere and group pressures, see chapter 22 in this volume.)

Wenger's (1998a, 1998b) exploration of learning in communities of practice provides another sociocultural perspective on autonomy. Learning comes from the interaction between experience and competence, which dovetails with Vygotsky's (1934/1986) suggestion of a more skilled partner to assist in a learner's zone of proximal development. Communities of practice are mutually engaged in a joint enterprise that develops a shared repertoire of resources over time (Wenger, 1998a, "Defining Communities of Practice," ¶ 2). A community of practice, generally larger than a pair or small group, can enhance autonomous learning by providing social, psychological, linguistic, and academic support for learning. *Mutuality* is central to Wenger's conception of the community of practice. He points out that even though computers can be used by participants in a community, the computers themselves are not members. Computers do not have true mutuality in engagement, cannot understand a community's shared enterprise, and cannot negotiate meaning to coproduce elements of the shared repertoire (Wenger, 1998b, p. 138). Teachers and learners need to know how to use computer-based tools to support these community functions.

Even though computers are not full members of learning communities, using computers can help learners work together to create a better understanding of language use. Some of the early users of microcomputers in teaching had learners share a computer to work together on a computer-based activity, whether it was a cloze, simulation, or even a grammar drill (Healey, 1995; M. Phillips, 1986). The availability of local area networks provided the capacity for peer editing and commenting on writing in ways that did not require photocopying and did not make the original document unreadable. With e-mail, learners could collaborate on joint projects. One early implementation was the *De Orilla a Orilla* (n.d.) project that began in 1985 to link English- and Spanish-speaking students (see Cummins & Sayers, 1995). This type of collaboration, also known as *tandem language learning* (see Lewis & Walker, 2003, on tandem learning) is designed for pairs of learners with different first languages to teach each other and to practice through conversation and joint projects. With growth in Internet capacity, tandem learning is no longer limited to e-mail. Schwienhorst (2003b) describes a tandem German-English language learning project based in a MOO, a cognitively rich, real-time online environment; Zeinstejer and Al-Othman (2005) describe a tandem blog exchange. (For other tandem exchanges, and the projects involved, see chapter 13 in this volume.)

Internet access for more people at higher speeds has meant more possibilities for online interaction. Text-based MOOs and chat, in which slow typing and overlapping conversations can make communication difficult, are now joined by audio and video chat. Groups like the Webheads (Stevens, 2006a, 2006b) encourage teachers to learn with each other in multiuser text-audio-video communication spaces. González and Almeida d'Eça (2004) explain what it means to be a Webhead: "We explore Web communication tools and share the best ways of using them in our teaching practices, engage with students in virtual classes, collaborate on projects, and participate in conferences as audience and presenters" (¶ 3). The essence of the Webheads group is to foster autonomous learning through communities of practice. A great deal of the activity is synchronous, but there are also extensive logs, archived resources, and e-mail discussion from which learners pick and choose what they want to know about anytime, anywhere.

The Web provides additional opportunities for autonomous learning in groups. WebQuests are designed to offer a structured space for groups to produce various types of projects. Each individual in a group has a role in a WebQuest, and the project can be completed successfully only if everyone collaborates. A WebQuest can be very teacher directed, but it can also be designed to offer guidance and scaffolding to learners as they create understanding of a topic for themselves. The *WebQuest Page* (Dodge, n.d.-b) has scores of models for teachers and learners to use in designing these projects collaboratively. *QuestGarden* (Dodge, 2007) offers templates ready for use by teachers or learners.

The Political-Critical Perspective: Autonomy and Power

Autonomous learning can fit well with elements of critical pedagogy, which calls for learning environments that help learners become more self-aware, take more control over their own learning, and achieve their personal goals. At the same time, autonomy as learner-centeredness is challenged by critical pedagogy. Learner actions and goals need to be seen within a larger political and social context. Critical pedagogy asks learners to realize how what they are studying supports or undermines dominant power structures and to challenge their own beliefs and goals. An important step in taking a political-critical perspective on CALL environments is to realize that technology, like all human artifacts, is not neutral. It can encourage certain ways of thinking and acting and discourage others. CALL materials developers can easily implement materials that require learners to work one-on-one with a machine, to use workbook-style exercises that give instant feedback but require no deeper thought, to see one right answer in exercises, to memorize and repeat after the computer, and to trust what they find online. Such materials mesh with the expectations of many learners. However, the assumptions behind these approaches—that human communication can be replicated in a machine, that language learning is divorced from thinking, that language can be memorized, and that the knowledge of those who post online is greater than the learner's—is challenged in critical pedagogy and made visible.

Technology can also enable broader perspectives and a shift in the locus of power. Using the Internet, foreign language learners are not limited to language data provided by a handful of more skilled, locally available speakers of the target language. Rich language in a variety of media can open the door to critical thinking. In fact, teachers need to keep in mind that whatever they assert can be queried by students using online resources. Advanced language learners can access online news sites from across the globe, which provide somewhat different perspectives on the same events. Teachers can guide less proficient readers to multiple points of view online. Joint projects with students in different parts of the world, such as a recent Kuwait-Argentina cross-cultural blog exchange (Zeinstejer & Al-Othman, 2005), can also be used to create information gaps about what "reality" looks like. To be autonomous, then, learners need to know how to query, find, and question what they find on the Internet, in software, and in print.

Embracing this perspective is not easy. As Oxford (2003) puts it,

> the political-critical perspective shakes us by the shoulders, forcing us to question assumptions and to critique existing power structures. It causes us to think hard about accepting the status quo. It creates an internal (and sometimes an external) struggle. It reminds us that we can critically analyse the discourses that frame our lives, we can create new alternatives for ourselves, and we can challenge our students to do the same. (p. 90)

Conclusion

Teachers bring their own views of teaching and learning to every interaction, in class and out. Similarly, materials developers and programmers embed their views of teaching and learning in what they produce, whether in software or online. Applying Oxford's (2003) four perspectives on autonomy to CALL underlines the multiple facets involved in enabling learners to be self-directed in technology-enhanced environments. Autonomy is more than sitting in a lab with material, more than being motivated to learn, more than having company in one's studies, and more than having choices in terms of topics. Autonomy can be seen as knowing one's goals for learning, preferred ways to learn, and ways to feel motivated, and then creating a learning community that allows one to achieve these goals—in many ways, being able to make adult decisions about learning.

For teachers, being committed to encouraging autonomous learning is more a frame of mind than a technique. Technology can assist or detract; thoughtful use is key. As teachers, we cannot create autonomy in learners, but we can do our best to think about the technical, psychological, sociocultural, and political aspects of learning and how CALL can be used to enable and enhance a learning environment conducive to autonomy.

Explorations

1. Describe CALL environments that you have observed in terms of the settings in Table 25-1. Where do they fall on the continua of locus of control and content?

2. What are your attitudes about learner autonomy? Do you favor one side of the continuum of control or another? Are you an autonomous learner? How might your attitudes about autonomy limit or expand your learners' choices?

3. Are there learner characteristics that you would describe as typical of enthusiastic CALL users? Share your list with your working group.

4. How do different learner characteristics affect learner motivation and independence in a CALL environment?

5. CALL is now used in a wide variety of English language teaching settings around the world. Is CALL used in different ways in autonomous learning settings in different countries? If so, how and why? (Each member of your group might explore CALL in a different country.)

Chapter 26

Classroom Practice:
Virtual Environments

Douglas W. Coleman, Torey Hickman,
and Alexander Wrege

Focus

Suppose you were locked in a room and were continually exposed to the
sound of Chinese coming from a loudspeaker; however long the experiment
continued, you would not end up speaking Chinese. . . . What makes learning possible is the information received *in parallel* to the linguistic input in
the narrower sense (the sound waves). (Klein, 1986, p. 44)

Klein's (1986) Chinese Room thought experiment shows that the input for
learning to communicate, surprisingly perhaps, is not language. Yet, two
decades later, second language acquisition (SLA) theorists almost all continue to accept, by assumption, the idea that input consists of language (see
Coleman, 2005a, 2005b, for a fuller description of this problem). This confusion actually goes back to an assumption made by Chomsky (1964, p. 26)
that "language learning" and "language comprehension" operate by different
"devices" in the brain and that the input for the former consists of well-formed
sentences (and only that). Coleman elaborates on the implications of Klein's
argument, showing that many SLA materials are faulty in design because of
the false underlying assumption that input for learning how to communicate
consists of language, rather than the full range of sensory experience, that is,
the perception of speech and other sounds, of people (e.g., their gestures,
facial expressions), and of objects (e.g., their size, color, shape, location).

The Chinese Room suggests that CALL software that purports to provide
virtual environments can be evaluated in part on the basis of assumptions
made about the nature of input for learning how to communicate, that is,
whether it consists of language or of multisensory experience. As we demonstrate in this chapter, educators cannot assume that all multimedia software
necessarily escapes from Klein's Chinese Room—far from it.

Background

In this chapter, we focus on virtual environments (VEs). By *virtual environment*, we mean a computer-generated environment that simulates, or reproduces, key aspects of external realities in which people communicate. Yngve (1996, p. 130) identifies those aspects as the people themselves, individual relevant objects, the surroundings taken as a whole, and the means of energy flow (e.g., light waves, sound waves). Thus, we do not refer to things like electronic books (which simulate paper books), so-called whiteboard programs (which extend classroom whiteboards across a distance online), computerized quizzes (which simulate paper-and-pencil quizzes), Web delivery of hypertexts (which are often merely a technological extension of the programmed instruction textbooks of old), or Web delivery of foreign language audio and video. We present examples of VE to clarify this distinction.

K. Jones (1982), writing about simulation as a learning tool, says of the term *simulation* that "it is a signpost pointing in the wrong direction, . . . toward artificiality, pretense, feigning, mimicry . . . and so on" (p. 4). The same negative connotations can be applied to *virtual* in the term *virtual environment*. However, just as paper-and-pencil simulations for learning establish what Jones so aptly calls "reality of function" (p. 4) in communication, so can virtual environments. There is functional reality in a simulation (whether paper-and-pencil or VE) when learners treat simulated events as they would the corresponding real events. In a VE, for example, when learners type "Where is the grocery store?" they are not performing a drill on present-tense question formation; rather, they really want to know where the store is so that they can navigate through the VE to get to it.

It is usually assumed that language learning (or acquisition—we intend no endorsement or denial of Krashen's [2003] acquisition-learning distinction) is a means to the end of learning how to communicate. It is often the case that students have learned the grammar and vocabulary of a language, yet we say they have not learned how to put that knowledge to use. On the other hand, if a student learns how to communicate, then all is to the good. Thus, in this chapter, we focus directly on learning new ways to communicate, rather than on the assumed means to that end—second language learning.

Examples and Discussion

This section provides a general overview of the large domain of virtual reality software that is useful to CALL. Some software has been excluded on the basis that it does not fulfill our definition of *virtual reality*.

Early Virtual Environments

Because of limitations in the technology, the earliest VEs were primarily text based. Such text-based VEs were in common usage in ESL and foreign language education during the late 1980s and the years following. A number of them (e.g., Mystery House [see Baltra, 1990]) are described in a collection of papers that appeared in a series of special issues of the journal *Simulation & Gaming* (see also Carrier, 1991; Hubbard, 1991; Jordan, 1992; Mulligan & Gore, 1990; M. Taylor, 1990). A few such programs simulate conversation between the computer and a learner (e.g., Relations, described in Coleman, 1988). By the late 1980s, simulation games were in a period of transition from text to multimedia VEs, which added graphical elements to represent the setting of the simulation, objects, and so on, thus improving functional reality for participants (K. Jones, 1982, p. 7).

Multimedia Environments

Apple Computer's QuickTime (QT; 2006) has remained a popular standard of multimedia content delivery on the Internet as well as on removable media, such as CD and DVD, for a surprising length of time. In 1994, QuickTime Virtual Reality (QTVR) was added to the QuickTime package. It allowed the user to pan up, down, left, and right, and gave the viewer the illusion of being immersed in a scene. Due to the photorealistic nature of QTVR, the product was years ahead of competitors and, for the first time, gave content providers the opportunity to create lifelike immersive environments for the user. The debut product for QTVR was Star Trek: The Next Generation: Interactive Technical Manual (1995), which showcased QuickTime's and QTVR's abilities effectively by meshing traditional text content with self-playing multimedia files to give a narrated video tour and self-guided QTVR tour of the spaceship *Enterprise.* The self-guided tour allowed the user to pan 360 degrees horizontally and 110 degrees vertically. It also used hyperlinked objects: When a user clicked on these objects, image, text, and audio descriptions were displayed.

QTVR has remained of special importance to language teachers who plan to give their students a virtual reality experience. The technology allows for a variety of simulated and realistic immersion exercises. One example is *Around the House* (Wrege & Hickman, 2004), a QTVR Web site created to provide vocabulary training to nonnative speakers of English. In this case, QTVR served as the foundational technology. Wrege and Hickman photographed a house using a fisheye lens on a digital camera and then turned those images into a VE that allowed horizontal and vertical panning. The user can click on objects within the QTVR to hear an explanation accompanied by the text, as well as zoom in to see the object itself up close (see Figure 26-1). A planned extension of *Around the House* includes a treasure hunt setting, in which the user is given an auditory cue to find a certain object and then has to navigate

Figure 26-1. Screen Image of *Around the House*

Note. From *Around the House: A Website for Language Learning*, A. Wrege and T. Hickman, 2004, http://homepage.mac.com/alexander.wrege/qtvr/QTVR/english_home.html. Reprinted with permission.

through the virtual world to find it. At present, guests may visit the Web site and use the Vocabulary Builder module to explore the VE.

A VE that incorporates features similar to *Around the House* is *Mystery at Motel Zero* (Coleman, n.d.). Its panoramic VE, however, uses computer-generated images rather than photographs of actual places and is presented via a freeware Java applet called PTViewer (Dersch, 2001), thus requiring no special browser plug-in (see Figure 26-2). The *Mystery at Motel Zero* Web page includes a detailed lesson plan and instructions for teachers and students accompanying the VE itself. Students, in the role of investigative journalist, solve a mystery by navigating the VE to find clues; after classroom discussion, they write a report in which they present their conclusions about what events must have occurred.

Escape From Planet Arizona (Raskin, 1995), a program created for use in an intensive EFL program for students intending to study in the United States,

Figure 26-2. Screen Image of *Mystery at Motel Zero*

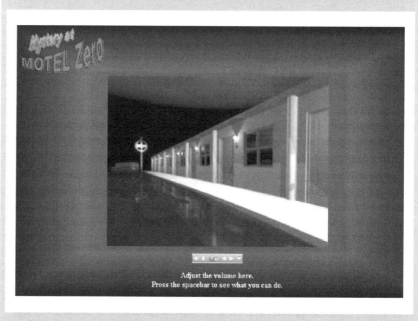

Note. From *Mystery at Motel Zero*, by D. W. Coleman, n.d., http://homepages.utoledo
.edu/dcolema/motelzero. Reprinted with permission.

also used QTVR; however, a variety of other software technologies have also
been used for the creation of CALL programs. TRACI Talk (1997; see Hubbard,
2002), for example, presents an immersive environment via interaction with
three-dimensional (3D) characters. Like several other programs, Planet Arizona
and TRACI Talk incorporate some capability for speech input from the learner
(although they were not intended for pronunciation practice).

Other single-user VEs adapted for CALL include true 3D programs,
which differ from QTVR and other panoramic software technologies in that
they represent objects in 3D space, rather than as flat images in a movable
background. One such VE is the original SimCity (1998), and its many spin-off
products, which uses a bird's-eye pseudo view. CALL use of SimCity is briefly
described by Healey (2006).

SimCopter (1996), another in the Sim family of games, is discussed by
Coleman (2002) as the basis for an ESL composition assignment. In this assignment the original purpose of SimCopter (to fly various missions as a copter
pilot, for example, airlifting accident victims or destroying attacking UFOs)
was bypassed in favor of one supplied by the instructor with the addition of

supporting documents. In teams, students flew the helicopter in search of a predetermined location, and then wrote directions to tell a reader how to get there on foot (see Figure 26-3 for a short lesson plan). Each time the reader came to a literal crossroads in the VE, the clarity of directions had *reality of function* (K. Jones, 1982, p. 4).

Unlike all the examples discussed previously, SimCopter provides a true 3D environment through which the learner can navigate in the person of the helicopter pilot—not only while flying over the city, but also by leaving the helicopter and walking through the city on foot. Unlike image-based VR technologies, such as QTVR, the true 3D technology of SimCopter permits movement not merely from one discrete point of view to another, but smoothly through a simulated 3D space. Thus, programs like SimCopter represent a departure from earlier forms of virtual environments, and their use in CALL begins to hint at previously unseen possibilities in how VEs can provide reality of function in learning new ways to communicate.

We see such possibilities, particularly the expression of culturally appropriate behaviors, both verbal and nonverbal, beginning to be exploited in the Tactical Language Training System (TLTS) developed at the University of Southern California for use by the U.S. Army. Its Mission Practice Environment (W. L. Johnson et al., 2004, pp. 7–8) uses 3D computer game technology that "exploits game design techniques, in order to promote learner engagement and motivation" (p. 2). Tactical Iraqi (2006) is designed to give task-specific lessons in Arabic to members of the U.S. Armed Forces working in the Middle East. Learners are coached in how to communicate (via the Mission Skill Builder, W. L. Johnson et al., pp. 6–7) before being sent out to complete specific tasks within the Mission Practice Environment. Figure 26-4 shows a scene

---

Figure 26-3. Using SimCopter for Giving Directions

1. Each student team is given a unique location to find and assigned roles: pilot, navigator, recorder.

2. Flying in its helicopter, the team finds its target location, taking notes about direction, landmarks, and so forth so that they can give directions on how to get there on foot.

3. Teams then trade directions.

4. They must use the other team's directions to find a location they have never been to. They must do this by walking the game character there on foot, not using the helicopter.

Note. Active Worlds, or any other VR environment with sufficiently detailed scenery, could be used for this type of activity. (For more ideas on teaching with simple simulations, see Hyland, 1993; Figure 26-2; and chapter 12 in this volume.)

Figure 26-4. Screen Image of Tactical Iraqi

Note. From Tactical Iraqi (Version 3.1) [Computer software], 2006, Los Angeles: Tactical Language Training. Reprinted with permission.

during a simulated interaction with two Iraqi men in a cafe (in this image, the user controls the character second from left). An effort has been made to teach not only verbal communication skills but also culturally appropriate actions and nonverbal gestures (two lines of text at the bottom of the screen remind the user of keyboard controls for gestures and other actions). Learners interact with on-screen characters using a speech recognition system of the sort pioneered in programs like TRACI Talk (1997). Learners "speak and choose appropriate gestures in simulated social situations populated with autonomous, animated characters" (W. L. Johnson et al., p. 1). Not only are nonverbal gestures taken into account, but also "cultural norms of etiquette and politeness" (W. L. Johnson et al., p. 2).

Multiuser Environments

In all the VE examples discussed so far, learners may be encouraged to communicate with each other while working in a group in front of the computer; however, the group is located *outside* the environment represented by the computer. Only with the rise of networked computing has another possibility arisen: the multiuser virtual environment or world (MVW). The MVW online has begun to reveal even greater possibilities for creating reality of function by simulating the key aspects of external realities in which people communicate. Among MVWs are *Active Worlds* (1997–2006), *blaxxun* (MobileMultiGames GmbH, n.d.), and *Second Life* (Linden Research, 2006). We discuss *Second Life* in some detail to provide the reader with a clearer idea of what such MVWs provide.

Second Life (SL; Linden Research, 2006) is an online community that provides users with an immersive 3D environment. Like other MVWs, it allows each user (or player) to choose an *avatar*, a 3D character that can interact with its surroundings. SL has a currency, and the user has the ability to purchase objects and property within the virtual environment (Llewelyn, 2005). Although SL was primarily intended to be an online VE where people could meet and engage in text-based conversations, it has evolved into a world within the real world. It has its own power dynamics and celebrities, and is now being used as an educational tool (see, e.g., the *EduNation* island [The Consultants-E SL, 2004–2007] being constructed specifically for teacher training and seminars; see Figure 26-5). Educators have seen potential for SL in their classrooms and have begun to include its components in their classes (see, e.g., Antonacci & Modaress, 2005, for links to videos of sample lessons).

The primary language of SL is English, with most users coming from the United States, Canada, the United Kingdom, and Australia. Users from non-English-speaking countries have also started to join the network and as of today are embracing the official language of SL: English. SL is interesting for second language educators because it gives users the opportunity to interact as if they were immersed in an English-speaking environment. If, for example, a user from France with basic English skills encounters a native speaker of English, the two may decide to go on a virtual excursion together. The native speaker might, for example, point out objects and ask the nonnative speaker to respond to inquiries about them.

Linden Research, the creator of SL, gives teachers the opportunity to purchase land within SL. (Educational areas prohibit sexual innuendo, violence, and a variety of socially proscribed behaviors.) The teacher can then outfit this land to meet certain objectives, depending on the methodology the teacher uses. So-called *direct* approaches to language learning then become possible, for example, Terrell's (1977) Natural Approach or Asher's (1982) Total Physical Response approach, but with the lesson taking place in a virtual, rather than a classroom, environment. Such approaches can work from Day 1 or zero level without students and teachers having a common language ahead of

Figure 26-5. Avatar in *Second Life* at *EduNation*

Note. From *Welcome to EduNation!*, by the Consultants-E SL, 2004–2007, http://www
.theconsultants-e.com/edunation/edunation.asp. Copyright 2004–2007 by the
Consultants-E SL. Reprinted with permission.

time because the VE itself provides appropriate sensory input in parallel to
the sound of speech. Figure 26-6 offers a lesson that might be used with any
relatively complex virtual environment, such as SL or the popular software
Myst (1993).

VIRLAN (n.d.), a project devoted to second language learning, "provides
on-line, real-time, collaborative communication in a virtual reality environment" (Milton & Garbi, 2000, ¶ 11). VIRLAN is designed for children and early
language learners of English, German, Greek, and Finnish. Each language has
its own virtual area—the United Kingdom for English, Greece for Greek, and
so on. Within each country there are towns that can be visited, and in each
town, the user might be given directions to go to a certain building. There
are also areas (e.g., a zoo) where learners can talk about related objects and
content (e.g., animals). Beyond the 3D environment, there are also areas to
practice spelling, a whiteboard to play something like Pictionary by draw-

Figure 26-6. Using Myst (or any set of VR environments) for Persuasive Writing

1. The teacher prepares four saved games of Myst (1993), one for each of the Myst environments. (In a complex online environment like SL, the teacher may send groups of students to different coordinates.)

2. Students are given a scenario similar to that in K. Jones' (1982) Space Crash simulation. However, they are told that their damaged spaceship is within range of four different (apparently) uninhabited planets. They may be marooned indefinitely on whichever one they choose to land; they must choose the one that best insures their long-term survival or their best chance to repair their ship and escape.

3. Students are then permitted to send out a shuttle to explore each of the four planets. They must take notes. (The shuttle has just enough fuel to complete this four-part mission.)

4. They then write a report to their ship's captain proposing which planet they believe the ship should land on.

ing figures, and a picture board area where learners identify and talk about images. Part of the impetus behind VIRLAN was the fact that, as Milton and Garbi note, "you will struggle to find examples of good practice which are applicable to very young learners and near or absolute language beginners. This is a great pity since the vast majority of language learners are both very young and beginners" (¶ 2).

Massively multiplayer online role-playing games (MMORPGs) offer another potential source of VEs for learning how to communicate. Most are costly (a typical MMORPG subscription runs about US$10 per month per individual), and the vast majority are focused on swords-and-sorcery themes, are excessively violent, or both. Quite a few free MMORPGs exist (see the MMORPG. com Web page [Cyber Creations, 2001–2006] and *Play Free Online Games*, n.d.), but those that are not excessively violent or do not focus on obscure themes (and are thus potentially useful for CALL) also typically do not allow users to interact with the VE in great detail; when VEs do not present a monster to kill or a deathtrap to avoid, they serve primarily as elaborate theatrical backdrops for text chat. Worth noting, however, is *WorldForge* (1998–2005), an open-source project aimed at providing tools for MMORPG creators, which allows users "to build complex persistent online virtual worlds" (¶ 2) and has serious potential for future developments relevant to the field of language teaching.

Problems in Applying VEs

The software products for making and hosting VEs permit an MVW designer to provide for complex interactions with individual objects within the environment. However, this feature remains largely unexploited in practice because the designer-educator must (a) have the technical ability to custom-design the environment and (b) realize the importance of doing so. Thus, a common weakness of adaptations of multiuser VEs for CALL is that they become essentially "3D talking-head" environments—text-based chat rooms with pretty pictures.

From the educator's point of view, a second weakness common to all of the examples cited in this chapter is cost. In most cases, the client software (the browser or plug-in required on the user's computer) is free. A temporary visit to one or more virtual worlds may also be free. But having a persistent identity and access to significant features of online virtual worlds in *Active Worlds* (1997–2006), SL (Linden Research, 2006), or any of the major MMORPGs requires a subscription fee. If an educator wants to create a unique VE or run a "closed" world space (one restricted to designated learners), costs can run into the thousands of dollars for a typical-size class—per year.

A third weakness is the problem of time. Busy educators rarely have enough of it to use in designing simulated environments even when the code is free, as in *WorldForge* (1998–2005). The Langland Project (no longer available) was an attempt to circumvent the issue of cost by providing a free, open-source multiuser VE specifically for nonnative speakers to learn how to communicate in English; however, it has made little progress since its inception. Teachers who have seen it demonstrated all too frequently have asked, "But how can students learn language from that?" That this question is being asked—that the ESL community at large has evinced little interest in the use of VEs over the years—puzzles us.

Many readers will ask, "If funding is available, why not simply adapt some current multiuser VEs that were made for other purposes?" Aside from the question of time, this approach has worked reasonably well in some cases. For example, some readers might see our omission of *The Sims2* (Electronic Arts, 2007; an outgrowth of The Sims) as rather glaring. However, this is a purposeful exclusion. A few years ago, one of the authors, Coleman, was shown *The Sims Online* by a colleague at a TESOL convention. The player's character made a plate of food and, when she picked it up and turned away from the kitchen counter, the plate not only moved away in the character's hands, but also stayed on the counter. Notoriously gleeful to see bugs in (other people's) software, Coleman exclaimed, "Look! It's a glitch. It left a copy of the plate on the counter." The colleague explained that she had made a "two-plate meal." The colleague ignored the reply that when one actually makes a two-plate meal, the two plates do not normally occupy the same corner of space-time.

When the colleague demonstrated how her character could go out into the garden to pick tomatoes, Coleman noticed that a basket appeared only at the moment the player's character knelt next to a tomato plant, and that each tomato popped into existence only as the character's hand reached out for it. Readers may be thinking, "But this is nit-picking—we're teaching language, after all." If so, they should consider that precisely because we consider reality to be a quibble and an abstract object (language) to be "the thing," we find ourselves with students who "know language" but can, in reality, communicate only poorly. Note, for example, that whether a person says *a basket* or *the basket* depends on whether the object in question is present or otherwise obvious to whomever the person is conversing with. How does someone learn to properly refer to baskets if they pop in and out of space-time like rabbits out of a hat? When using virtual online or CD environments, regardless of how charming the graphics, the teacher must still be aware of their functional reality.

Conclusion

It is argued that learning a new way to communicate cannot take place at its fullest potential because adults are inhibited when faced with a situation in which they may be subject to the scrutiny of others. All kinds of simulations (including the pencil-and-paper sort) have been shown to be able to remove this major obstacle of potential embarrassment that results from committing errors (Gardner & Lalonde, 1990; K. Jones, 1982, pp. 10–13). A VE can reduce that inhibition. Other frequently discussed advantages of VEs include motivational aspects such as "an appealing environment, the incorporation of educational game-like activities, and most importantly . . . letting learners collaborate actively in the learning process" (Milton & Garbi, 2000, ¶ 11).

Although these are important features that meet many of the criteria for creating an optimal atmosphere (see chapter 22 in this volume), we cannot afford to ignore certain key aspects of human communication. When people communicate face to face, they interact with each other not only via speech, but also via gesture and facial expression in rather complex ways. In addition, a great deal of basic communication is not only situation-bound in a general way, but also *deictic*, that is, referring to specific things in a shared spatial, temporal, and cognitive environment. These particulars are not a side issue, something that happens in addition to language, but a significant part of the communication. We caution the reader to keep in mind that language is not "out there" to be learned. The sound of speech does not "contain" words or grammar or semantic features. In real-world terms, the sound of speech has only frequency and amplitude varying over time. This is why the learner cannot learn how to communicate in Klein's (1986) Chinese Room. As Klein makes abundantly clear, unless learners receive appropriate sensory input in parallel to the sound of speech (or text), they will not be able to learn new ways to communicate. This is the lesson of the Chinese Room, and it points to the very real potential value of VEs.

Virtual worlds for CALL seem to have come a long way from the text-based simulation games of the 1980s. With tremendous improvements in hardware and software capabilities, ever more immersive graphic environments have emerged, from 2D to panoramic scanning to true 3D. The development of the World Wide Web and improvements in network transmission speeds have allowed the creation of multiuser VEs, including MMORPGs. Sadly, however, the greatest potential of multiuser VEs—interaction other than static realities and chat—remains unexploited, not because of technological limitations, but because of theoretical misunderstandings about the nature of input. As Klein (1986) and Coleman (2005a, 2005b) indicate, as long as educators think of the input for learning how to communicate as consisting of language, rather than the full range of sensory experience available to the learner, they will not even try to incorporate the most important features of real contexts into the design of VEs for CALL.

Explorations

1. Why can it be said that the *virtual* in *virtual environment* seems to be, to paraphrase K. Jones (1982), like a signpost pointing in the wrong direction? How does it differ from a typical classroom environment?

2. What is the relevance of Klein's (1986) Chinese Room thought experiment to how people learn to communicate? Is it enough merely to have multiple channels (text, images, audio) to escape from the Chinese Room, or must those channels have specific characteristics? If the latter, what are those characteristics?

3. What are some positive characteristics of multiuser VEs, such as those provided by *Active Worlds* (1997–2006) and *Second Life* (Linden Research, 2006), relative to their use for CALL? What are some weaknesses they typically share? Try a free VE such as *Second Life* to explore its strengths and weaknesses.

4. Go to the *Play Free Online Games* (n.d.) Web page and try a few that are "free to play indefinitely," or find another free MMORPG by using a Web search engine. Evaluate the potential of the MMORPG(s) that you have chosen for use in CALL. Share your findings with your classmates or working group.

5. Sketch out a lesson plan to use with an MMORPG that you have tried. What kinds of help will your learners need? How can you best evaluate their activity in the VE? What pros and cons do you perceive in using the virtual space for language learning?

Chapter 27

Critical Issues: Blended Learning

Aiden Yeh

Focus

I learned a lot from your language and culture class and am still benefiting from it. The skills of critical thinking and computer assisted teaching not only make me a better student but also a better teacher. (Student feedback from Language and Culture class)

Using handouts of Gwendolyn Brooks' eight-stanza poem "We Real Cool" (see Alexander, 2005, p. 60), students enrolled in my Language and Culture class discussed literary style, the meaning of the language used, the social and cultural message, and its relevance to their personal lives (see Yeh, 2005–2006b). I then presented Web pages related to the topic of discussion using a computer, a projector, and the Internet to enhance students' knowledge on the subject. Students read and discussed the text in class, listened to several authors' readings, watched an authentic video online, and used critical thinking skills. In less than an hour, students virtually traveled across the continent to learn how unique an African American poet's manner of reading was—reading each *we* softly and stressing the first two words of each line—and how the same poem could be delivered differently by a White American Boston art student (John Ulrich) without losing the poem's depth and meaning. Ulrich's (n.d.) analysis of his version and interpretation of "We Real Cool" describes how this poem revealed what was going on in his neighborhood and the effect it had on him.

Teaching language, culture, and nonviolent means to social reforms to 50 EFL students in a meaningful, creative, and collaborative way without turning the blended (online and face-to-face [f2f]) class into a circus is a huge challenge, particularly in a learning environment where students are encouraged to take an active role. Blended instructional methods using traditional resources, online technology, and multimedia tools for learning purposes are not new. Students learn something with any of these combinations. However, what students learn is different from how much effort they put into the process of learning. Their effort includes understanding, planning and doing, monitoring, sharing and presenting, and evaluating how they effectively connect the learning objectives with their performance. In other words, for teachers to create an optimal learning environment—enhance students' intrinsic motivation, provide opportunities for interaction, trigger learner autonomy, help achieve students' learning goals, and promote mindful attendance to their own learner processes—it takes more than just a blend of the learning resources available. How teachers design their activities is crucial to the whole *blended learning* process.

In this chapter, I take a close look at learner autonomy in blended learning activities and examine how the conditions for optimal language learning environments are met by a blended environment. In addition, I describe the different components of blended learning and share some examples of task-based projects that I have done with my classes. And I discuss some of the critical issues that teachers encounter in delivering language learning activities in a blended environment.

Background

Intrinsic motivation is the driving force that makes learners want to learn new ways to communicate. The higher the motivation, the more successful they will be in learning a language (in this volume, see chapter 22 on atmosphere and chapter 23 on flow). Motivation is linked to autonomous learning or how much learners take control of their own learning (Boud, 1998, p.17; Fazey & Fazey, 2001, p. 345). To be autonomous, learners need to have the freedom to choose, plan, monitor, execute, evaluate, and take responsibility for their learning (Little, 1991, p. 4; Pintrich, 1999). However, as Healey discusses (chapter 25 in this volume), autonomy should not be misunderstood to indicate that learners are completely independent, whether in the classroom or online. As Sheerin (1997) puts it, "teachers have a crucial role to play in launching learners into self-access and in lending them a regular helping hand to stay afloat" (p. 63). Teachers have to make some adjustments to foster learner autonomy. The teacher is no longer viewed as the sole source of information but is viewed as someone who facilitates learning. The teacher takes a step back and gives students the chance to leap forward and engage in active discussions, presentations, and evaluations, unlike traditional educational classroom methods whereby language teachers focus on rote memorization and activities that students find inapplicable to their current and/or future needs, interests, and expertise.

One of the difficulties that teachers face is how to grab students' attention and enthusiasm in ways that bolster their motivation. Brophy (2004) states that teachers "can help students to appreciate their learning opportunities and to find academic activities meaningful and worthwhile for reasons that include intrinsic motivation and self-actualization" (p. 2). Learning tasks and activities is one of the variables (in addition to recognition and evaluation) that foster student involvement in learning. One example of in-class activity that promotes peer-to-peer interaction is group or pair work. Task-based group or collaborative projects are also ideal for promoting learners' interpersonal and/or social skills (for more on group tasks and project-based learning, see chapter 13 in this volume). Although cooperative learning is desirable in some learning situations, independent work can also facilitate student involvement (e.g., independent research study, individual audio recording of speeches, audio/video podcasts, weblogs [blogs]). The rapid growth of online technologies and the constant changes in advanced multimedia tools give teachers a huge range of options in providing learners with the optimal language learning environment for their specific goals.

The diversity of classroom situations generates different strategies in integrating technology into the classroom. On the other hand, it also brings about new challenges for language teachers and learners in blended environments.

Understanding Blended Learning

Blended learning (also referred to as *flexible learning, e-learning, hybrid learning, mixed learning,* or *combined resource teaching*) is transforming how instructors view education. According to Dziuban, Moskal, and Hartman (2005), "a number of universities are experimenting with blended courses and many see them as offering the best of both instructional worlds" (p. 4). But what is blended? In this section, I discuss the components of blended learning and the factors that make a good blend.

To make blended learning more powerful, educators must start by looking at all components (see Table 27-1) as possible options: physical classroom, Web-based courses, online chat tools, and so on.

The following guidelines should help language teachers in choosing the right blend:

1. Provide opportunities for collaboration.
2. Provide the learning content (e.g., syllabus, lessons) in all the different media types to be used (online and offline).
3. Provide learner support (e.g., technical questions, how-to's, guidelines).
4. Understand all the types of technologies that can deliver learning (e.g., be able to operate multimedia equipment, manage online tools, have technical support at hand).
5. Provide feedback and opportunities for learner self-assessment (see Bersin, 2003; A. R. Brown & Voltz, 2005).

Table 27-1. Blended Learning Components

Components	Traditional/f2f	Online
Teachers' roles Note: Teachers' roles vary depending on the teaching methods used.	• Plan and prepare syllabus and lessons • Teach, model for learning • Control the direction and pace of learning • Evaluate and assess students' performance • Provide feedback and counseling • Serve as facilitator/participant in communicative language activities	• Tutor • Mentor • Coach • Guide • Facilitator, host • Collaborator, observer • Provider of feedback • Provider of technical support • Guide for students, modeler of active learning
Activities/learning modes Note: Communicative approaches are used in "traditional" f2f classrooms also.	• Instructional design • Lectures, discussions • Task-based activities, student presentations • Workshops (writing, listening, speaking, reading), role-play • Kinesthetic activities (e.g., games, Total Physical Response)	*Asynchronous communication* • E-mail, bulletin boards/discussion forums • Blogs, podcasts, moblogs, videoblogs *Synchronous communication* • Chats (text/voice) • Audio/video conferencing

(Continued on p. 408)

Table 27-1 (continued). Blended Learning Components

Components	Traditional/f2f	Online
Learning environments Note: Many "traditional" classrooms take advantage of multimedia tools.	• Traditional classroom • Computer lab • Traditional classroom with multimedia equipment (e.g., computer, projector, VCR, DVD player, video camera)	• Online learning environment (OLE) • Learning management system (LMS) • Course management system (CMS) • Moodle (2006), WebCT (2004), Blackboard (2005), and so on	• Online learning resources (text, audio, video) as source of information for creating and interpreting knowledge • Interactive content: multimedia/ hypermedia, Flash activities, online Hot Potatoes (Arneil & Holmes, 2006) quizzes/tests • Collaborative learning or information applications (e.g., blogs, wikis)
Materials and knowledge management	• Chalkboards, whiteboards, overhead projector screens • Textbooks, books, workbooks, handouts, English or bilingual newspapers or magazines • Audio materials, films, videos, realia • Transparencies, flip charts, visual aids, electronic slideshows	• Locating and accessing resources on the Internet and in electronic libraries • Doing Web searches (e.g., WebQuests [Dodge, n.d.-b]) • Collecting information: filing, saving, retrieving data, uploading and downloading data • Access to file storage and archiving using file transfer protocol (FTP)	

(Continued on p. 409)

Table 27-1 (continued). Blended Learning Components

Components	Traditional/f2f	Online
Media	*Electronic media* • CD, VCR, DVD, CD-ROM, audio cassettes • Overhead projector, LCD projector • Electronic slideshows, computer software *Broadcast media* • Television, radio	*Web-based learning* • Search engines, Web sites (medium for publishing students' original work, creating Web sites, podcasting) • Web-based courses (CMSs) • Online community and user group software, listservers, etc. • Streaming radio, webcasts *Mobile learning* • Laptops, PDAs, mobile phones, MP3 players
Learners	Learners' roles in both traditional and online environments depend on the activities and tasks that they need to complete, their learning styles and personalities, and their cultures. *Note:* The size of the class is an important factor in blending.	

One important aspect of blended learning is its flexibility (D. Clark, 2003, p. 6). Teachers can use free online learning environments (OLEs) such as Moodle (2006) and *Yahoo! Groups* (Yahoo!, 2007e) to make the entire contents and resources of a class available for students to use during class or at home on their own time. This gives students the flexibility to take control of their learning outside the classroom, as well as communicate with each other through the e-lists and forums that such OLEs provide. However, in planning for a blended learning course or class activity, teachers should consider how best to combine the different means or styles of learning—including age, gender, and cultural differences—with instructional design and the media mix. Sheperd (n.d.) explains that a lack of sensitivity to these differences may result in a solution that seems convenient but does not have positive effects on students' learning. Careful selection of components is therefore necessary in a structured and carefully thought-out blend.

Meeting the Conditions for Optimal Learning Environments

Understanding how the conditions for optimal language learning environments (see chapter 1 in this volume) are met by blended environments is another important issue that teachers need to consider when attempting to integrate online technology into the classroom. The eight conditions that form the basis for this volume share pedagogical underpinnings with cognitive and constructivist learning theories, which are also the same principles behind blending learning applications. Savery and Duffy (1995) describe four principles that should be applied to technology-enhanced learning environments based on constructivist views:

1. Learning is an active and engaged process. "Learners are actively engaged in working at tasks and activities that are authentic to the environment in which they would be used" (p. 37; see also chapters 22 and 23 in this volume). This aligns with Conditions 1–3.

2. Learning is a process of constructing knowledge. This aligns with Conditions 6–8.

3. Learners function at a metacognitive level. Learning is focused on thinking skills. Students generate their own strategies for defining the problem and devising a solution. They can gain wisdom through reflection. This aligns with Conditions 6 and 8.

4. Learning involves *social negotiation* (p. 38). Students are able to challenge their thoughts, beliefs, perceptions, and existing knowledge by collaborating with other students and thus assist their cognitive development process. This aligns with Conditions 1 and 2.

The goal of teachers who use technology in the classroom, according to Jonassen, Peck, and Wilson (1999), "is to support meaningful learning and use technologies to engage students in active, constructive, intentional, authentic, and cooperative learning" (p. 7). The examples of blended learning activities in the following section show how to encourage students to use the language for genuine communicative purposes in collaborative tasks, both online and off. The wide range of media formats available online provides a wide variety of learning opportunities. As Gen (2000) argues, it is the responsibility of the teacher to provide "the opportunity, context, and framework in which learning is to take place" ("Implementation of Multiple Intelligences," ¶ 2).

Examples and Discussion

Preparing the Blend

The example from my Language and Culture class, introduced in the Focus section of this chapter, included a range of online and f2f materials and activities. I used video materials online to spark interest in a cultural comparison. After viewing, I presented comprehension questions on a Microsoft PowerPoint (2007) slide in class to help students conduct their small-group discussions. Students then worked on an assigned group project to prepare a paper report and produce a digital photo story. Students were required to choose either their original work or a poem in English or Chinese/Taiwanese, and then they had to create a short video or slideshow with images that would establish the relationship between the message of the poem and how they viewed their own sociocultural environment (see Yeh, 2005–2006b). Details of the assignment, links, and other references to help students get started with their project were posted on the class blog and Yahoo! Group. F2f and online support (e-mail, blogs, and/or Yahoo! Group e-list discussions) were provided when needed. After weeks of preparation, the students proudly presented their work in class using a blend of PowerPoint presentations, photo stories (created and edited using various movie editors), paper handouts, Web sites they had created, and wikis. Students' presentations were filled with powerful words and images with matching music and visuals that touched the soul. Examples of students' exemplary work were published (with students' permission) on the class blog, *Language and Culture* (Yeh, 2005–2006b).

In planning for a blended course of this sort, it is important to examine the traditional and online components available and the tools that you will need. Create a checklist by considering the following questions:

1. Does your school/institution/classroom have the online tools and Internet access that you need to teach your class online?

2. What multimedia equipment/online tools will you use to present an activity?

3. What sort of online activities do you have in mind (e.g., synchronous chat, asynchronous chat)?

4. In an online discussion, are you going to invite guest speakers? If so, how will you find them? How will you arrange for the time and place of the online meeting? (For a more detailed checklist, see Yeh, 2005a.)

5. How will the instructional events you plan fulfill the need for variety and complexity in learning? (See chapter 19 in this volume.)

This list of questions is by no means exhaustive; other issues can arise, depending on the situation and learning environment. The point is to examine closely the factors that can affect the outcome of your blended learning activity. Once you are ready, you can begin by creating a Web page or forming an online group using a free facility (e.g., Moodle, 2006; *Yahoo! Groups* [Yahoo!, 2007e]) or your institution's own CMS. Such OLEs enable the delivery of course materials (e.g., electronic slideshows, word-processed documents, video, audio) and the submission of assignments. The e-mail, instant messages, and chat functions available in OLEs serve as *interactive tools* that allow communication among students and with the teacher. This interactivity shapes the learning environment and affects the way students use these tools. According to Thorpe (2003), "the use of interactive technologies is also increasing the range of learning outcomes achievable through learner support" (p. 208). The kind of support teachers provide students online can be divided into three categories:

1. *cognitive*—Materials and learning resources systematically delivered online through OLEs or Web pages can support and develop learning.

2. *affective*—Students' self-esteem and commitment to the course are enhanced by providing a supportive learning environment.

3. *systemic*—Students find systematic and effective management and relay of information (e.g., syllabus, course requirements, tasks, updates, news related to class activities) easy to learn, use, and understand (see Tait, 2000).

Fostering Language Learner Autonomy Through Blended Learning Activities

To determine how well blended learning activities foster language learner autonomy, teachers need to look at how the activity is to be conducted and the degree of freedom given students during a blended learning activity. An effective activity provides learners the opportunity to choose which learning strategies and skills to use, which materials and tools to use (e.g., posters, presentation software, self-produced video), which resources to use (e.g., readings, online videos), and how to carry out the task on their own or in groups (e.g., organizing oral presentations, writing scripts, filming). What students produce at the end of each task or project reveals their understanding of the subject matter and the nature of the task, their willingness to do the task, and how much effort they exerted in performing it. Learner autonomy can be fostered if teachers are willing to give them the freedom to exercise it, while still offering sufficient guidance to make completion possible (see Robb, 2006). Teachers empower students and enhance learner autonomy by outlining the content to be covered and by providing a variety of ways for students to utilize their skills and intelligence online to select and obtain information and to perform the required tasks. In the Understanding Culture Through Poetry unit of my class, I prepared a rubric that detailed what was expected and posted it to the class blog for easy reference (see Yeh, 2005–2006b), and I provided links on the blog to important resources that student might need so that they could concentrate on the content of their projects.

Using Blogs and Online Word Processors in Research Writing

A blog is a Web-based publication tool. There are plenty of free blog providers, including those that may be mounted at an institution's own server for security and student privacy. (See Appendix D for addresses of many of these providers.) Blog entries can be a combination of written texts and photos (photoblogs), voice (or music) recordings (audioblogs), and videos (videoblogs, or *vlogs*). The variety of formats gives teachers and educators an important avenue for delivering blended learning activities (see Yeh, 2005–2006b, for examples of all of these).

I use blogs to disseminate course content, to provide study support, and to publish students' original essays. In my Research Writing class (see Yeh, 2004–2006), I guided students through the writing process of choosing/ narrowing a topic, writing a research proposal, developing ideas, using resources, defining research methodology, and writing their analysis and conclusion. Students were expected to turn in a 20- to 25-page paper by the end of the course. Pair activities were conducted online and in f2f meetings. In addition to in-class lectures, students spent one to two sessions at the computer lab, where they were presented with the online writing tools that they would use for the course. Students created their blogs at B*logger* (Google, 1999–2006) and posted their ideas, notes, and writings about the research topic. They sent the uniform resource locators (URLs) of their blogs to me via e-mail or posted them on our class blog, which was subsequently pooled and published under the Students' Blogs Index in the sidebar at *Research Writing* SY2006 (Yeh, 2004–2006), the blog where I also collected important resources students might need. Visiting individual student blogs from this central point was simple and fast.

Searching for and finding an online resource or Web page and saving online documents have become easier using online bookmarks. My students created their individual online bookmarks at Web sites such as *Backflip* (1999–2006), *del.icio.us* (n.d.), and *Spurl.net* (Spurl ehf, 2004–2006). I gave students a tour of these Web sites and showed/explained the necessary details: creating an account, creating a main folder and subfolders, and sharing their folders with me so I could have access, in case of problems, to their resource folders and templates. Students did the rest of the job themselves. Weekly updates of their blogs and online bookmarks were done at home.

For longer pieces of writing, students wrote their drafts using Microsoft Word (2007) and uploaded them to *Google Docs and Spreadsheets* (Google, 2007b; formerly *Writely.com*), an online word processor, where other students and I could see the original and the corrections that were made. Providing feedback on student work was quick and convenient because the interface allows the teacher and other users who are given password access to easily edit a document without losing the original. Students could also publish their document to their blogs simply by clicking the >POST TO BLOG link in the >PUBLISH tab. Other online collaborative word processors and document-sharing applications include *Zoho Writer* (AdventNet, 2006), *Writeboard* (37signals, n.d.), *QuickTopic Document Review* (Internicity, 1999–2006), and many others (see Appendix D).

By integrating these online tools into my f2f research writing class, I provide students with opportunities to interact with classmates to comment and give feedback on each other's work at a time and place convenient to their schedules and needs. They have sufficient time to offer appropriate feedback (Condition 5 from chapter 1 in this volume), and I can supervise all changes and comments on documents, something that is not possible in an f2f writing class, where only a brief time may be spent with each peer-editing group or pair. In fact, online collaboration meets all the conditions for optimal language learning outlined in chapter 1 of this volume. Students make authentic use of the target language not only in writing the paper, but also during their online peer editing. The latter gives students time to reflect on each other's work, compare documents and changes in typed fonts enhanced by colors and highlighting (rather than in bad handwriting), and make the necessary edits. These tools provide the teacher ample space to write comments, while clearly specifying in the documents where changes should be made—all without worrying about handwriting. The guidelines I provide, and the applications' help files, support student autonomy, allowing students to work independently and figure out how the applications operate. By successfully creating their blogs, online bookmark pages, and online word-processor accounts, students feel a strong sense of satisfaction.

Writing is difficult for many language learners. For some, it is agony. A friendly online environment for learner support can help alleviate the stress associated with writing. In addition to the encouragement to interact and express creativity in their work, students have time to reflect in their activities in an online environment. Simply by looking at the number of messages posted on their blogs, the number of references they have in their bookmarks, the number of times they have edited their drafts, and the length and quality of their writing, students can readily see how much effort they have invested in their work, review their progress, and determine where further effort is needed.

Using Digital Videos and Podcasting in Speech Training Class

My Professional English Speech Training course introduces third-year college students to the fundamental skills needed for the successful delivery of speeches. The class covers informative, impromptu, and persuasive forms; techniques of public speaking; and pronunciation. I use a speech evaluation rubric to assess their ability to gain attention, establish credibility, organize ideas, effectively use visuals and vocal variety, and so on. Speech drafts, comments, and corrections are sent via e-mail (or uploaded to our Yahoo! Group). According to Tsutsui (2004, p. 377), video recording of students' speeches can significantly enhance postperformance feedback and offers advantages where the traditional method of providing feedback in an f2f class falls short. My students' presentations are recorded for self-evaluation and assessment purposes using a digital video recorder. The video files are then distributed to students by e-mail or, for very large files, via the free online data transfer Web site *YouSendIt* (2007).

With the advent of vlogs, audioblogs, and podcasts, the sharing of audio and video files has never been easier. A *podcast*, a name derived from *iPod* and *broadcast*, is an online audio (usually in MP3 format) and/or video file delivered via Web feed or really simple syndication (RSS; Coggins, 2005). I integrated this technology into my f2f speech class to provide students with opportunities to improve their oral skills by recording impromptu speeches and other tasks that could be done outside the classroom. Podcasting allows students to distribute and share their audio and video files using upload/download functions and to self-evaluate their delivery and pronunciation; as a bonus, podcasting provides students with additional aural source materials for analysis or reaction. (For a sample of student speeches, see Yeh, 2005c.) Our class audioblog created an open venue where students could interact with an authentic audience: I invited several online colleagues to listen to the student productions and comment on them at the blog. In this type of blended setting, students' motivation to improve on their craft is enhanced because they know that other people aside from their classmates will be listening to and/or watching their work. The presence of a real audience (Condition 2 from chapter 1) has positive ramifications for student learning, and therefore it can "stimulate student education" (Stanley, 2006, p. 5). The following is a sample posting that demonstrates authentic communication:

> Thank you for a very clear explanation. You should perhaps know that I listened to your presentation after a very bad night's sleep! Let's hope it

goes better tonight. It should do if I follow your good advice!" (Message posted by a colleague on student's podcast)

I'm sorry that I reply you so late, because I just get ready for the second semester. Thank you for your advice and I really hope these tips do help you sleep well. (Student's response)

The use of audio and video digital recording promotes meaningful learning based on constructivist theoretical principles, which, in addition to encouraging active student engagement, provide learners with the chance to reflect upon their errors and progress (see also Ally, 2004, p. 19). Video in particular is helpful, as one student put it:

I can see my weaknesses when watching video, and also learn from other classmates, because sometimes you wouldn't know your weaknesses when you're doing the presentation. (Student self-evaluation from Speech Training class)

In an f2f class, details of students' speeches may tend to be lost in the rush to get through all the performances. Critiques and reflection may be delayed for several class periods, extending over weeks. Blending online tools with an f2f class allows students far more opportunity for immediate reflection and steady improvement of their own performances. They are also able to verbalize self-criticism, an important part of reflection and self-correction, as demonstrated in this student's words:

I can find out my own problems when I was delivering on the stage including body movements, gestures, and voice could be seen/heard clearly from the video recordings so that I could improve myself and correct the shortcomings that I have. (Student self-evaluation from Speech Training class)

The integration of podcasting technology into the classroom creates an optimal learning environment and promotes the idea that learning does not take place only in the classroom. With podcasting, teachers promote learning mobility and autonomy while providing learner support. Access to authentic materials and audiences provides students with a truly motivating learning experience.

Using Voice Chat Applications

Let's Get Physical! (Yeh, 2004) is a task-based project using Total Physical Response (TPR) that blends multimedia tools (voice and videoconferencing, Microsoft PowerPoint [2007] presentations) with synchronous voice and text chat applications in my f2f teacher education class. The aim of this project for fourth-year college students in the Advanced Listening and Speaking class is twofold: (a) to learn about TPR, that is, how to create and implement a TPR activity for adults while practicing the art of giving instructions; and (b) to foster oral communication skills by giving these nonnative speakers the opportunity to use the language in an authentic situation with native-speaker experts in the field.

The procedure for conducting this activity follows three steps: the pre-chat (one week prior to the event), the chat (warm-up and voice chat activity), and the post-chat. These stages provide the teacher with a framework to incorporate reflection, experimentation, and further reflection, representing the cyclical nature of learning: *plan*, *do*, and *review*. I invited guest speakers (Arnold Mühren in Holland and Dafne González in Spain, both ESOL teachers), who prepared a Web site with a sample lesson plan, a welcome message, and links to online video and other resources (see Yeh, 2004). These materials were used as assigned readings. During the voice chat online, our guests delivered a brief lecture on TPR, including a guided Web tour, while the students watched, listened, and asked and answered questions. One of the issues raised was the limitation of using TPR in adult ESOL education (Mühren, 2003). To challenge this myth, students were then assigned a task-based collaborative project to create TPR activities geared toward adult learners using the examples modeled by our guest speakers. The students' in-class presentations (see Figure 27-1) was the culminating activity in which they put theory into practice while using the target language as the vehicle of communication. By videotaping their presentations and uploading them to the *Let's Get Physical!* Web site (Yeh, 2004), students had the chance to see how they performed during the online chat and during their project presentation.

Providing the opportunity for students to interact with international TPR experts in real time would have been very difficult to arrange in an f2f class.

Figure 27-1. Online Chat and Students' In-Class Presentations for *Let's Get Physical!*

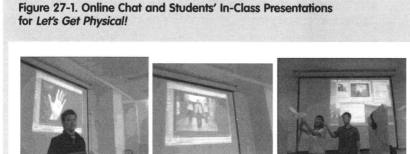

Making Rubber rings

Tai-Chi

Balloon Art

Note. From *Let's Get Physical!*, by A. Yeh, 2004, http://dcyeh.com/sy0304/2ndsem/groupa _projects/tpr/. Copyright 2004 by A. Yeh. Reprinted with permission.

The visuals in the Web pages created for the project and the synchronous, real-time voice interaction also added authenticity to this activity.

When a Blend Goes Bad: Suggestions for Good Practice

In the previous sections, I explored the benefits of blending online technology and multimedia tools with traditional classroom settings and how such integration may affect students' learning. However, it is important to emphasize that it is not only the blend that makes a course different but also how instructors integrate all the necessary elements in designing or planning a course syllabus. Teachers should take into consideration the strengths and limitations of each element. Because there are many variations for blended activities, the pitfalls vary and can be overwhelming. Technical difficulties and other glitches happen when teachers least expect them. These problems, no matter how small, can cause a few setbacks in the overall course plan. The following are the most common pitfalls that occur in a blended learning environment:

1. Ideally, an online chat activity requires collaboration between other teachers, guest speakers, and students. If you have trouble finding a willing partner, you may want to seek support from professional organizations, such as TESOL or the International Association of Teachers of English as a Foreign Language and their respective interest sections, or from online communities, such as *Webheads in Action* (Stevens, 2007) or the *Intercultural E-mail Classroom Connection* (Mighty Media, 2007).

2. Online guests may arrive too early or too late, or they could miss the whole event due to time differences. Use Greenwich Mean Time (GMT) as the basis for time conversion. Use *Time and Date.com* (Time and Date AS/Thorsen, 1995–2006) to create a calendar specifically for the event. Send frequent reminders to all parties.

3. The success of delivering online chats or video also depends on the type of technology you have. A slow Internet connection may cause voice chat program failure. It would be wise to update and test your software or hardware ahead of time.

4. Because students may work on their online assignments independently outside of class, some may encounter difficulty in using the tools. One solution is to provide learner support and Web links to Help pages.

5. Students sometimes forget their user names and/or passwords despite constant reminders from the teacher to write them down. Remind students frequently to jot down important information and keep it in a safe place.

6. The size of the class could also have an impact on the way an online chat is conducted. In a one-computer room, use a projector, speakers, and a microphone so that students can take turns chatting with guests. In large classes, it would be best to divide students into groups. Reserve the computer lab if possible.

7. Teachers may find themselves with uncooperative technical support staff. Be persistent in asking for help. You may need to do things on your own (e.g., use your own tools), but seek out others who share the same commitment to teaching and learning and can offer online support, for example, an international community of practice, such as *Webheads in Action* (Stevens, 2007), which can also help with technology and multimedia tips (see Stevens, 2006a; chapter 18 in this volume).

8. Some educators argue that the Internet and technology in general tend to put less financially privileged students at a disadvantage. However, whether in an EFL or ESL context, there will always be issues regarding equal access to technology. Waiting for equal access to happen would curtail teachers' motivation and creativity in utilizing technological innovations. They should encourage students to make use of available facilities that their schools provide (e.g., libraries, self-access learning centers). Or teachers could bring their own laptop to school and allow students to use it when recording, uploading, or downloading files.

9. Some teachers feel that using blogs, vlogs, and podcasts may result in an invasion of privacy or a violation of copyright. It is important that you explicitly state on your Web site (or in your e-group) that all lecture materials (online or offline) are solely for educational purposes. Personal contents that make either the teacher or students uncomfortable should be avoided, and only password-protected secure sites should be used.

10. Teachers may feel overwhelmed by the amount of information they think they need to know. Those who feel apprehensive about nontraditional means of teaching and learning may find that learning newly coined words or phrases for technology is similar to learning an entirely new language. However, as Sokolik (2006) points out, students have a right to expect that teachers will keep at least minimally up to date.

Technological problems will probably always occur, and as technology keeps on changing, teachers will always have new challenges ahead of them. However, they should keep an open mind and accept possible alternatives to overcoming barriers and narrowing the technological divide. The success of blending multimedia and online technology into the f2f class depends on teachers' willingness to acquire new competencies and their level of awareness of technology's potential and ability to inspire and motivate students. Needless to say, technical training on the use of online tools (e.g., software, platforms, OLEs, e-moderating) is crucial to effective online learning (Salmon, 2000).

Conclusion

> What is becoming increasingly obvious with emerging research is that the new technologies offer excellent potential for adding value to classroom teaching in a large variety of ways. (Felix, 2001, p. 358)

In this chapter, I have explored blended learning's potential for making the learning process meaningful for students. Blended activities can create an optimal learning environment that increases students' level of self-awareness and boosts their motivation. The application of multimedia and online tools provide students with resources for creating their own presentation materials, thus enhancing learner autonomy and reflective, mindful involvement in authentic tasks with authentic audiences—all conditions for optimal learning environments. Blended learning adds versatility and creates a different route to learning and teaching ESOL. Students do not simply learn about the language; they also use the target language as a tool or medium of communication, while practicing the use of technologies that will be important in their careers. Determining the right blend is not easy; teachers should consider all details, both technical and human, and prepare an alternate plan in case technology fails. However, the most important factor is that teachers should be willing to experiment and accept the fact that they might make mistakes along the way until they get the right blend. The teacher's role in blended learning is to be on the brink of exciting, rewarding, but continuous change as new technologies are developed and used in the classroom.

Acknowledgments

I would like to thank Elizabeth Hanson-Smith, Dafne González, Teresa Almeida d'Eça, Chris Jones, Michael Coghlan, and Tanya Viger for their comments and suggestions. The Alado Webheads Portal has been graciously sponsored by Andy Pincon for members of the Webheads online community.

Explorations

1. Yeh expresses the idea that different educational contexts might call for different implementations of blended learning. What does *blended learning* mean for you in your present or potential teaching context? What kinds of facilities and technologies might be available to you?

2. Give two examples of blended learning components (see Table 27-1), and think of an activity that you could use to integrate these components. With your classmates or working group, brainstorm possible technical problems.

3. Can you think of other technical and pedagogical issues that may affect your teaching and/or students' language learning in a blended environment? What solutions to these problems might be found?

4. Explore some of the online tools mentioned in this chapter. How would you arrange your class, whether blended or wholly online, to take advantage of these tools? How would you organize teams for collaborative work?

5. Plan a task-based project in your f2f class that blends multimedia and online technology (see chapter 13 for additional ideas). Choose a combination of language skills and course content on which you want to focus. Explain the reason for your choice of blended learning components, discuss the theoretical pedagogy to be used, and describe how you are going to implement the project.

PART IX

The Future

Chapter 28 ⌐

20 Minutes Into the Future

Carla Meskill

Focus

The year is 2005. It's 2:45 p.m. A high school ESL class is winding down, and students are beginning to pack up to leave their classroom. Thong, age 16, disconnects his 8-1/2-in.-by-11-in. digital notebook computer from the plug on his desk. During this month's 90-minute real-time class, Thong's desk outlet has transferred image and sound files of all class activities to his notebook computer. Thong places the computer in his ergonomic pack, says good-bye to his classmates and teachers, and leaves the classroom.

On the high-speed train that transports him from his class in Albany, New York, to his home on Lake Champlain, Thong takes advantage of the quiet, takes out his computer, opens it on his lap, and spends this time reviewing what occurred in his ESL class.

When his notebook computer pops open, his private tutor (a video image on the computer's screen) greets him and asks how he liked today's class, what he learned, what understandings he gained, and what kinds of questions remain in his mind. Thong indicates that he greatly enjoyed today's activities and that he is interested in reviewing the U.S. courtroom simulation he and his classmates undertook that day. As a previewing strategy, he tests his retention of new vocabulary, structures, and language functions in a dialogue with his online tutor. He then spends several minutes examining the interactional dynamics and accompanying discourse he and his classmates employed in their simulation. He uses zoom, playback, and annotation utilities in conjunction with the numerous files of videoconferences he has had over the past month with field experts and peers around the world and of courtroom scenarios and documents he has carefully included in his personal ESL work database. Using a combination of finger-controlled and voice-generation tools, he edits errors and enhances the video. He then tackles tomorrow's assignment: recast the courtroom simulation by selecting new characters and a new problem and design the outcome. Using video and audio morphing tools, Thong builds his own courtroom simulation. He employs his evolving subject-area and linguistic knowledge and his imagination in conjunction with an extensive database of images and audio options and texts. By the time he arrives at Lake Champlain, a first draft of his version of the courtroom simulation is almost complete. At home, he will eventually plug his notebook computer into the jack in the wall of his room and transmit the completed assignment to his fellow team members and to his ESL teacher's computer for feedback. He then turns to his other high school course work.

This glimpse of the not-too-distant future may inspire awe or skepticism in the late 1990s. However, such technological power is clearly just around the corner. What is less clear is how language teaching professionals can prepare to make the kind of pedagogically grounded use of technology that is depicted here. This chapter explores teachers' preparation for integrating and using instructional technologies, both now and in the future. Central to this discussion is the role of the teaching professional as a mediator of instruction, with technology called into the service of the mediation process. Professional skills—perceptual, technical, and instructional—that are essential now and for the near future are suggested.

Background

Instructional technologies have been in existence as long as the notion of teaching and learning has. Chalkboards, manipulatives, and audiovisual aids have long been standard fare in instruction. Language instruction especially is notoriously resourceful in terms of the kinds of physical objects that are used as illustrations of and catalysts for language. Hardware and software of all kinds have been used to their maximum instructional potential—and sometimes to less than their minimum (Cuban, 1986). What is particularly interesting is the extent to which historical forces affect the adoption of technologies and influence how they come to be used in teaching and learning. The technologies that have become most common to instruction in the past three decades—video and computers—are relevant in this respect.

The "Hand-Me-Down" Syndrome

The technologies used in education very rarely originate there. Teachers borrow them from other sectors that have their own special driving forces: the government, the military, industry, and consumer markets. For example, in recent times the home entertainment industry has supplied education with the videocassette recorder, the videodisc player, the CD-ROM, and the camcorder. They have all become accessible, inexpensive, and extremely easy to use, not in consideration of the needs of, goals for, and beliefs about what constitutes good instruction but because of a vast consumer market. Likewise, the speed of microcomputer processing has grown not in response to the needs, goals, and processes of schools but in response to the requirements of the military, government, business, and entertainment.

This hand-me-down syndrome can be considered both a positive and a negative force in how technologies are used in schools and how they come to influence instruction. The positive side is that teachers reap benefits from other professions' research and development dollars. The negatives are that (a) instructional beliefs, goals, and practices have to be applied to technologies that are designed for something other than teaching and learning; (b) the technology, which was designed for quite a different purpose, may shape teaching and learning; and (c) good pedagogical uses, when they do evolve, take a long time to do so.

The "Because-We-Can" Syndrome

Neither the printing press nor the photocopy machine was invented to be used in schools, yet teachers were quick to appropriate both. Their lasting impact on instructional practice cannot be disputed. One need only walk into any language classroom in the country to witness the phenomenon of the photocopied handout. Like any technology, photocopying can be overused, used poorly, or used to its maximum pedagogical benefit. What is clear is that when photocopying is misused, for example, in creating worksheets simply to keep students quiet and busy, the technology has shaped the instruction, not the other way around.

A contemporary example of this phenomenon comes from a developing country, although such a thing could happen anywhere: Told that the audiotape player was an essential tool in language teaching, a well-meaning instructor recorded and then played back for his students a story using his own voice. Another example might hit closer to home for the TESOL professional. It was not that long ago that teachers used video playback merely as it was designed to be used in consumer contexts, that is, for passive, entertainment-oriented viewing. Teachers had students watch videotapes because they could, not necessarily because of a solid pedagogical rationale. One need only look at the work of TESOL's Video Interest Section to see how far the field has come in providing the needed conceptual work and, in turn, in developing pedagogically grounded uses for this hand-me-down technology.

History shows that there are reasons technologies are used well or poorly. The bottom line is that good use of a new technology requires some conceptual work to retrofit that technology to teaching practice. Using a new approach "because we can" is not good enough.

Examples and Discussion

The Role of Technology in Instruction

The learning and teaching in the ESL scenario at the beginning of this chapter is not that much different from scenarios in ESL classrooms today. The emphasis is on communication, and the bulk of learning is socially mediated. The teacher, who has maintained an ongoing electronic conversation with the group during the month leading up to the real-time, face-to-face session, has employed her knowledge of the individual learners, their interpersonal dynamics, and their current language needs in designing and orchestrating tasks that make optimal use of the face-to-face learning opportunity in the classroom. Student interaction is therefore treated as central. Using her knowledge, her skills, and some very handy electronic tools, the teacher has planned, orchestrated, and facilitated the kind of communicative activities that strike the right chord in the hearts of turn-of-the-millennium TESOL professionals: Students are engaged in constructive discourse. The teacher supports and reinforces critical aspects of that discourse through the appropriate tools.

What role does technology play in this scenario? Certainly not a large, looming one. The technology is instead very quiet and very powerful, used much as technologies are used well now. The hardware is secondary and subservient to the larger goals and social processes of learning. The video storage, playback, and manipulation technologies are pulled into the service of a real-time communicative activity: the courtroom simulation. Before coming to the classroom, students have used technology in collaboratively researching, preparing for, and rehearsing the simulation through videoconferencing and online collaborative tasking that the teacher has designed and orchestrated. The technology provides resources for and a record of what is central to the students' language. Both the students and their teacher are thus empowered by electronic databases, e-mail, and videoconferencing—tools with which they can make greater sense of the language and nuances contained within that record. Teaching and learning continue in this vein when Thong leaves the classroom and is at a distance from the other learners on his collaborative team.

The salient aspect of this scenario is that learning processes are human, not technology, driven. Rather than being involved with technology, students are involved in their learning through negotiations of meaning with one another in electronic contexts—synchronously and asynchronously—and in face-to-face contexts. The teacher is involved in orchestrating and facilitating these processes, not in the cumbersome manipulation of buttons, wires, and peripherals, thanks to a voice-activated control panel that responds to simple commands. The technology serves her need to seamlessly document learning processes, provide individual support and feedback, and engage students in relevant learning activities when they are not in the classroom. Technology complements and enhances these pedagogical processes.

Agency: Who's in Charge?

As expressed by both the language used to talk about computers and the attempt to build software to emulate thinking behaviors, people tend to perceive that the computer can act on its own—that it has powers independent of its user. In short, people attribute agency to a box of plastic parts. Many teachers have been guilty of resorting to "The machine did it!" when something goes wrong and even have thought, "The machine doesn't like me!" when things go really wrong. Much of this tendency to anthropomorphize the computer is due to bad interfaces that cause the user to feel disoriented and not in control (Laurel, 1991; see also chapter 23 in this volume). Interface design is improving, but the attribution of agency to computers continues to present singular and sometimes difficult challenges in conceptualizing their role in instruction.

Risks of the Agency Fallacy

Inadequate interfaces can be very limiting, especially for teachers who are new to computers. First, they fear that the machine will do something unpredictable and irrevocable. This can result in two additional fears for teachers: (a) that they will become forever lost and at the mercy of something they don't understand and (b) that they will look foolish in front of their peers or students.

The fact is, computers are fundamentally dumb. Relative to human intelligence, they will most likely remain that way (Dreyfus & Dreyfus, 1986). The video tutor on Thong's notebook computer screen gives cues and canned suggestions to guide Thong. The tutor's main function is to serve as a record keeper that makes suggestions to Thong from a closed list of possibilities. Selecting from this list is a matter of smoke and mirrors: The tutor cannot perform its function unless Thong and his teacher enter specific information into the tutor and direct it to respond. Likewise, as a communication tool, the computer holds no mystery: It is merely a fancy device for sending and receiving messages. The human communicator is in charge of that which is uniquely human: decision making and communication that is based in thought.

Another risk comes wrapped up in the agency fallacy. When too much power or agency is attributed to the computer, it risks being used as an *electronic babysitter* (Branscum, 1992). The thinking goes something like this: Computers are supposed to be able to teach, so let the computer teach Jorge. Jorge is consequently sent off to the computer so it can teach him something. In this way, both the teacher's time and the student's time are seen as more productive. The idea that computers are good because they free up the teacher is a two-edged sword: True, computers can free the teacher from center stage and allow students some control over their learning, but, particularly for language minority students in mainstream classrooms, computers can also be used as a way to absolve teachers, administrators, programs, and schools from the responsibility for the challenges some students represent.

Traditional kudos for CALL include the message that individualized instruction has merit. So it does, but only when the activity is valued by and integrated into the larger community and learning context (Meskill & Mossop, 2000; Meskill, Mossop, & Bates, 1999b; Meskill & Shea, 1994). In other words, the activity or task that an individual student does with the computer needs to fit into the big curricular and social picture. More specifically, machines need to be cast in the role of mediators, not sources, of learning. Unfortunately, software sales techniques send subtle messages portraying computers as teaching machines that offer solutions to problems. This conception of the role of computers in instruction, in combination with the notion of agency in computers themselves, raises issues that are both prevalent and problematic. These notions reinforce the idea of standardizable instruction delivery rather than the enslavement of technology for larger, human-centered pedagogical purposes.

Revising the Conceptions

The conceptual work needed on the role of computers in ESL instruction can begin with merely taming the beast. Teachers need to understand that the computer is stupid and that, without their skills, knowledge, and humanity, it is little more than a home entertainment system that rewards, punishes, or babysits. Teachers need not feel like unskilled, nonknowers of special formulas or tricks; rather, they should feel empowered by the fact that, given the goals and processes of language teaching and learning, without mediation by smart teachers the machine's role is very limited. Fortunately, new and better interfaces and technical support will eventually help teaching professionals see the soul in the machine as the pile of silicon it truly is. The teacher in the futuristic scenario has no wires, no code, no mystery buttons to push to make her class happen. The interface she uses on her notebook computer could be used by anyone. Happily, the goal of the better, more thoughtful software producers is to eliminate any sense of powerlessness and to promote a sense of what Winograd and Flores (1988) call *at-handedness* in user interface design, meaning that computer interfaces will eventually become so accessible that their use will be as much second nature to the learner as switching on a light or hammering in a nail is.

The second bit of conceptual work is also related to the notion of agency. Historically, instructional technologies have been designed and used based on the transmission model of learning, which sees the learner in a passive or receptive mode and, consequently, sees any learning that takes place as the direct result of teaching (see Figure 28-1). The transmission model thus sees the teacher possessing and purveying knowledge. Many of the media used in instruction—filmstrips, audiotapes, computers—have likewise been conceived

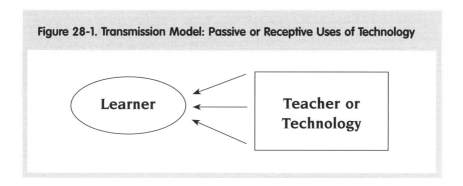

Figure 28-1. Transmission Model: Passive or Receptive Uses of Technology

as conveyances of knowledge. One need only look at the vast number of comparison studies of the use of media—studies that use a classic research design with a control group and a treatment-medium group—to note this prevalent conceptual framework: Learning is seen as the direct result of the medium's actions. Any involvement on the part of the learner is only peripherally taken into account. This concept needs modification if instructional technology is to fit the needs, goals, and beliefs of contemporary language teaching.

The fundamental weakness of the transmission model is that it is based on older notions of teaching and learning. Constructivist, and in the realm of language teaching, communicative schools of thought have since brought a shift away from thinking of the teacher as knower toward the notion of learning as social and collaborative (see Figure 28-2; see also Laurel, 1991). The basic concept of the role of instructional technology, however, has been slower to evolve in a like direction. A sense persists that technology, especially

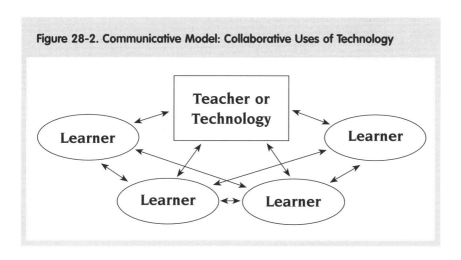

Figure 28-2. Communicative Model: Collaborative Uses of Technology

computers, exerts some power and effects some learning independent of other processes and concerns. Probably the first credo for teachers learning about computers, then, is that *teachers teach; machines don't.* Machines are tools for, not agents of, learning. In a communicative framework, they are at their best when supporting social and collaborative processes. In other words, machines can be catalysts and tools for thinking and communicating. Their use can be integral to learning activities but cannot be their source.

Multimedia Literacy in Language Learning

How do you as a teacher go about evolving pedagogically driven uses for technology in your classroom? A useful starting point is your already extensive knowledge of multimedia. For teachers, adapting computers to language learning can represent a cultural as well as a methodological transition (B. Poole, 1995). Fortunately, understanding multimedia and its potentialities for ESL represents less of a cultural transition than a cultural expansion. First, like it or not, much of the world, regardless of nationality, socioeconomic status, or cognitive ability, is media literate, having lived on a rich, steady diet of popular media from birth. People know how to watch TV and films and listen to the radio. They understand well, but mostly unconsciously, the intricate conventions the media use to inform and entertain.

I define *multimedia literacy* as what teachers already know about media elements and how they can interact to affect language learning. Teachers know, for example, the power of visuals in teaching and learning. Teachers use visuals—both still and moving—frequently in language classrooms, insofar as they are available. Likewise, teachers use charts, diagrams, photographs, slides, and video as tools for many purposes, such as activating schema, providing context within which meaning can be more effectively portrayed and analyzed, stimulating associations, encouraging connections between what is known and what is new, provoking discussion, illustrating, defining, motivating, and clarifying. Teachers also understand the many roles that audio, whether audiotape or audio with video accompaniment, can play. Audio- and videotape bring the target of language study into an accessible and controllable format. It can be the direct object of practice or be used much as visuals are used, for example, to stimulate or illustrate.

What Can Control Over Multimedia Do for Educators?

You know that visual and audio media can be employed in numerous ways and in many combinations as tools for instruction. Your extant familiarity with these elements combined with how you use text in teaching and learning form the basics of multimedia literacy. You need now only add the control and manipulation of these elements, which is becoming ever more feasible with computer-based multimedia technologies.

What does this control gain you as an educator? In the 2005 scenario, the classroom is connected to and managed by a central processing system built specifically to assist in the management of instructional processes. The system facilitates the process of gathering, storing, sharing, and managing background information for the courtroom simulation as well as for the documentation of the activity itself. In preparation for the group activity, the instructor most likely taps into the system to call up visual aids—perhaps video clips of actual court cases or audiovisual samples of the kinds of language students may want to use in their simulation—and to present a searchable database of appropriate texts, possibly based on transcripts of real court cases. In turn, students can save, in a searchable format, a complete audiovisual record of the information gathered and the in-class performance. The simulation was in no way technology dependent, but the enhancement furnished by the technology is called into the service of instruction by virtue of (a) its visual, auditory, and textual elements and (b) streamlined access to and control over that information. As such, this enhancement is not that different from ESL instructors' scavenging a resource room for the tools of their trade—there are just more resources, and they are more at hand.

What about the out-of-class work Thong undertakes on his notebook computer? This work exemplifies the power of controlling and manipulating information—the true hallmark of computers. Note, however, that the material being controlled and manipulated by Thong originated in the social context of his classroom and through online collaboration with his teacher and peers. As such, the material is both human and properly valued when integrated into the larger instructional process.

Human values and instructional integration are critical aspects of instructional technology right now. When examining hardware and software for potential use in the classroom, you can begin by asking

- whether the media elements—aural, visual, and textual—can be used in ways that make sense
- whether the kind of manipulation and control of material is complementary to and translatable to existing classroom contexts
- what adjustments might be necessary in the existing classroom context
- whether the technology is valuable pedagogically, or an instance of the because-we-can syndrome

Where to Begin?

If you want to begin to use some of the new instructional technologies, reading the other chapters in this volume is a good start. Examining exemplary uses of computers and considering whether and how they might be adapted to your own situation serves many purposes, letting you learn from others' mistakes and successes. You can also start with what you know:

- what the needs, goals, and constraints of your teaching context are
- how to learn with and from your students and colleagues
- what the optimal roles are for visual, aural, and textual materials in the instructional process

and believe:

- Machines are servants to your needs and the needs of your students.
- Machines don't teach; teachers teach.
- Machines thoughtfully integrated into classrooms can mediate and support instructional processes.

Is the specific software used important? According to the research of recent years and the experience of long-term computer-using language professionals, the answer is a resounding *no*. Even the most simply constructed software can induce rich constructivist learning if it is used thoughtfully, with communicative principles firmly in mind. The process of considering the adoption of instructional technologies should be grounded in reflective teaching, not in the bells, whistles, and agenda of a given software package. The processes of adopting and integrating software should in effect mirror the kinds of thinking and discourse that teachers orchestrate for their ESL students: Teachers need to talk to one another and share their thoughts and experiences with various media. It is, after all, the negotiation of meaning that instantiates teachers' thoughts and beliefs. Teachers' talk about instruction with, through, and around computers is particular to the technology and becomes a place where meaning is made, a process through which understandings are constructed, and a dialogic space where craft is further crafted. As in other aspects of pedagogical implementation, a supportive administration can do much to assist the dialogic process (see boxed text).

Conclusion

Cast in a role subservient to the goals and processes of language teaching, technologies such as those in the 2005 scenario break away from the transmission model of learning and teaching. Language teachers, however, seem to feel a strong impetus to do something now with the technology currently available. Doing so carries a great deal of both risk and promise. In the ESL classroom in 2005, the craft of teaching and learning will be supported by technology, as long as teachers remember who they are.

A Note to Administrators on Assisting the Pedagogic Dialogue

- Remember that training and adoption require rethinking the curriculum and the act of teaching. This rethinking takes more time than learning which buttons to push.

- Help teachers stay informed. Keeping abreast of the technological tools that are available is a daunting task.

- Encourage teachers to resist the "because-we-can" and "everybody-else-is" syndromes.

- Be aware that software and hardware vendors are selling you hand-me-downs from other sectors and that you therefore will need to retrofit these products by applying good practice to them. This takes time.

- Resist the temptation to buy. Let your teachers select what they need. Support them in discovering what works best for them.

- Don't let buttons and cables get in the way of teaching and learning. A technical support staff on-site is an essential investment.

- Promote the attitude that technology represents opportunity, not imposition.

Explorations

1. Consider Meskill's predictions for 2005 and beyond. Have they come true? How far have teachers come? What do they still need to do?

2. Meskill speaks of the "hand-me-down" syndrome and the "because-we-can" syndrome. Are teachers in CALL still suffering from these false premises? What are the "risks and promises" in current technology use? How do they differ from what Meskill described in 1999?

3. How "multimedia literate" are you? What are your goals, if any, for becoming more literate? Brainstorm goals with your classmates or working group. How will you meet these goals?

4. Conduct action research in an ESOL classroom, asking what area(s) of the language learning curricula could best be supported by available technology. Share your findings with your classmates or working group.

5. Prepare a research proposal to establish the efficacy of computer use for language acquisition. What questions will you ask, and how will you test them?

Chapter 29 ⛿

Afterword: The Future Is Now

Karen Price

Focus

The year is 2010. Yaodong, sitting in his study in Shanghai, has just finished a virtual class at California State University in Sacramento. Yaodong has participated through his mobile phone, which sends both images (including video of himself) and voice. He downloads to his mobile phone the video replay of the Internet voice chat with virtual whiteboard, text chat, and guided Web tour presented by a student team and hosted by his professor in Vancouver. After the quick wireless download is finished, he uses the same phone to project the replay onto an interactive virtual screen, complete with virtual keyboard and mouse, which hangs in space before him. He replays portions of the class, occasionally referring to the closed captioning or checking words in an online speech-to-text bilingual Chinese-English dictionary in another window. As he reads and listens, he exchanges instant messages with other members of his study team, who live in Korea, India, and the United States. Because classes exist anywhere, anytime, students tend to choose them on the basis of sleep preferences and work schedules.

Yaodong's next assignment is to prepare a virtual walking tour of a neighborhood in Shanghai with a local classmate. Because his collaborator could not adjust her schedule to prepare for the class in real time with Yaodong, she walked through the neighborhood earlier that week, leaving StickyShadow text messages, voice messages, and mobile phone pictures for inclusion in their presentation posted virtually for Yaodong outside of her best friend's house, as well as at her favorite climbing tree as a child. Yaodong's location-based mobile phone detects the messages and automatically downloads them to his phone as he passes by each location, so he is able to easily incorporate her content into the live online presentation they will give in the virtual class.

Although it is late, he is so engrossed he cannot stop working. He checks occasionally with other students in the class who will be textually annotating the video tour, inserting comments at relevant points in the video. One classmate has flagged Yaodong's continuing difficulty with a particular pronunciation problem, so he replays the oral presentation he is preparing while referring to an automatically transcribed voice recognition system to check his speech against the machine's recognition of it. When the virtual screen keyboard becomes tedious, Yaodong settles into a comfortable recliner and unfolds a portable keyboard/drawing tablet to transmit text and sketches over the phone wirelessly. His messy handwriting is translated into crisp, clean print. He drops his draft of the presentation into his colleague's electronic mailbox. They will confer about it tomorrow in a live practice session. After a quick message to his girlfriend in Jinan, he turns out the light with a casual wave of his hand that also closes the virtual screen and shuts down his phone.

CALL is no longer limited to desktop computing or students working with laptops. In the scenario imagined here, almost all of the technology is available and being used currently, though probably not all at one time. As this chapter demonstrates, all sorts of digital devices, from mobile phones to video game platforms to digital tablets, can be used for CALL applications. Because many of these devices do not rely on keyboards for input, users interact with the devices in many ways, from gestures to speech. Other emerging technologies involve attaching data such as print, audio, or video to physical objects, linking the digital and physical worlds, thus enabling users to interact with concrete objects.

CALL applications designed for desktop computers and laptops will not disappear. However, a wide array of emerging technologies and stand-alone devices are changing the ways people collect and connect with information and each other, offering new ways for learners and teachers to work with language, multimedia materials, and each other. In this chapter, I survey some of the new communication and information tools developed in fields seemingly unrelated to language learning and language teaching, and I speculate about the desirability and possible transfer of some of these technologies to the more traditional language classroom or distance learning paradigms.

Background

As with CALL applications described elsewhere in this book, the emerging technologies covered in this chapter offer teachers a variety of approaches in the teaching of second and foreign languages. The research reviewed in preceding chapters regarding instructional CALL applications, the use of multimedia, resource-oriented applications, and synchronous and asynchronous communication with other native and nonnative speakers applies to the use of emerging technologies as well as to more traditional applications.

Emerging technologies offer new ways to collect and link information that is harmonious with the shift in teachers' preferences from overtly instructional applications to resource-oriented applications (Meskill, Anthony, Hilliker-Vanstrander, Tseng, & You, 2006a). Although multimedia computer-assisted instructional packages are frequently the subject of research, in a survey conducted by Meskill et al. (2006a), teachers did not cite them as the applications used most frequently. A growing interest in the conceptualization of language learning as a social process is moving many teachers away from the notion of language learning as an input-output process or simply the acquisition of discrete linguistic items (Brouwer & Wagner, 2004).

Several of the technologies discussed in this chapter facilitate new ways and platforms for sharing audio, video, and still photos in two-way communication, either synchronously or asynchronously, with or without location-based information or displays. New multimedia and multiple input-output options can support fully the eight conditions for optimal language learning described in chapter 1, and these options even offer a tangible reality to tasks that could previously be imagined only virtually. The structuring of two-way communication tasks can promote interaction and second language (L2) acquisition (R. Ellis, 2003), although new possibilities described in this chapter for two-way communication require further research.

Unlike traditional CALL applications, some of the technologies presented in this chapter offer ways to link digital information to objects in the real world. Some of these involve interactions through physical movement, for example, visual or audio feedback to dance steps, hand movements, or the touching of a specific object. These types of interactions evoke the approaches of face-to-face instruction using the Direct Method or Total Physical Response (TPR; see Y. S. Freeman & Freeman, 1998; for an insightful approach to the exploration and investigation of how specific media interact with and impact cognition and learning, see Salomon, 1979).

Discussion and Examples

Input Devices

Pentop computers, such as the FLY (see LeapFrog Enterprises, 2001–2006), can scan and store text for subsequent upload to a laptop or desktop computer. Students can scan a word from a restaurant menu or text from a magazine. The word can be viewed on the device's display screen, presented aurally, or instantly translated into a target language. Students may thus have immediate access to a commonly used learning aid—translation—without carrying around a dictionary. Pentop computers intended for use with compatible *electronic paper* transform drawings and handwriting into input, as mentioned earlier in the 2010 scenario. Language students can write a word in their native language and hear the word translated into the target language. If they draw a calculator keyboard and then tap the keys, they hear arithmetical calculations. If they draw a musical keyboard and then tap the keys, they hear the notes.

Display technologies offer many new possibilities. Digital projectors enable more portable, more affordable, and higher resolution large-screen computer projection, even in brightly lit rooms. High-resolution 3D holograms, images projected in the air with such devices as HoloTouch (see 2006) or Heliodisplay (see IO2 Technology, 2005), can be manipulated by touch and may one day replace conventional computer monitors (see Figure 29-1).

Lightweight storage devices the size of a paperback can store the equivalent of hundreds of books on a single unit (e.g., the Sony Reader; see Sony Electronics, 2006; see also E Ink, 1997–2005, for the underlying technology of electronic paper). The text and pictures, with paperlike legibility, can be read at virtually any angle and even in direct sunlight. Public libraries and endeavors such as *Project Gutenberg* (Hart, 2006) offer downloads of e-books compatible with these devices, enabling language students to download books from the Internet and easily carry them around.

3D color printing enables users to create actual objects (based on computer-aided design [CAD] data) with moving parts of different colors made from nontoxic materials. Although these printers were originally developed for rapid prototyping of new commercial products, such as toys and shoes, they are now commonly used in design schools and architectural firms. Although there is now limited use of 3D printing in less specialized educational contexts, it is an example of a technology that ultimately has a place in foreign and second language learning. Educational research comparing the use of objects to pictures indicates the superiority of objects for many students engaged in certain types of tasks, especially those involving comprehension and memory (for a discussion of the need for functional reality in virtual environments, see chapter 26 in this volume). Tangible and portable, these 3D printouts could give language students a new way of reporting and sharing their research and thoughts with other students, just as students use video segments as a way of reporting back to others in the classroom. In the not-too-distant future, teachers may be printing out replicas of real-life objects to accompany vocabulary lessons, and students may be printing out objects from their imagination to write about.

Audio spotlighting is another technology that has potential for language learning and language teaching. Just as a flashlight will cast a focused beam of light, the Audio Spotlight (see Holosonic Research Lab, 1999–2005) directs a focused beam of sound. Only the individual(s) directly in the beam of sound can hear the sound of the audio recording. The Audio Spotlight could be used for simultaneous projection of different streams of audio to one or more students. Although audio spotlighting could be used for managing student behavior by enticing students to stay in their seats to hear a specific audio stream, a more enlightened use might be the elimination of headphones in the traditional language laboratory. For listening practice involving information-gap activities, students could listen to separate streams and then perform movements (as in TPR) or share information to complete a task.

Figure 29-1. Three-Dimensional Holographic Displays From *HoloTouch*

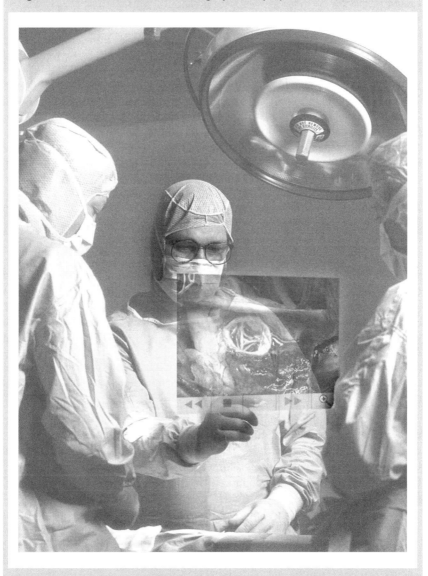

Note. From *HoloTouch*, 2006, http://www.holotouch.com/. Reprinted with permission, per press release notes.

Activity-Specific Devices

Gesture technologies are a good choice for methodologies such as TPR, which ask students to respond physically to verbal commands (Asher, 1969). Motion-sensing mobile phones enable the phone to be used for activities dependent upon specific movements of the phone, just the way some video game controllers, such as those made by Sony and Nintendo, allow players to control a game by making simple, intuitive arm movements instead of pushing buttons. Motion-sensing technology can be used for a variety of games, such as a golf game in which the phone is swung as a golf club or a fishing game requiring the player to swing the handset like a fishing rod. This technology can also be used in games in which the user turns around while holding the phone in order to turn the character on the screen or draws numbers in the air using the handset. Motion-sensing phones or video game controllers might be used to elicit student movements in response to audio prompts, thus giving more authentic realism to tasks and testing. (For more on the importance of authenticity in virtual environments, see chapter 26 in this volume.)

Digital floor mats originally created for dance games used to be found only at video arcades. Now they are used in some physical education programs and are increasingly popular with home video game consoles. Players stand on a single or double mat and strive for speed as they stomp on an arrow or icon in response to real-time instructions from the game. In existing versions of such games, a player's success may depend upon his or her ability to time steps to the rhythm of the song played or to act upon visual instructions in the form of arrows on the screen; however, a CALL application could involve verbal dialogue and visual and audio feedback for listening practice.

Activity-specific devices come in many forms—from wireless boxing gloves to wireless musical batons for aspiring conductors to feedback in the form of a chest plate that vibrates when a player is hit in a virtual game. They enhance a player's experience, giving him or her feedback during a particular physical activity; for language learners, however, they could provide verbal input in the form of encouragement, clues, exclamations, and/or explanations relating to the students' level of accomplishment in performing tasks based on visual and/or aural input.

TileToy (n.d.) is a modular, electronic, open-source game prototype in which players pick up and arrange dynamic blocks that have electronic displays. Each block is individually controllable and can be used to display and transmit information (e.g., a letter) wirelessly on its own or in groups of several tiles. A variety of letter- and word-based activities, from puzzles to language games, could be created for language learners using these physically tactile objects. As explained on the TileToy Web site,

> simple word games can be created where each tile displays a random letter and the players organize the letters into the longest word possible. Numbers and arithmetic characters can be displayed with the player having to

arrange the tiles into a sum to give a specified result. Matching games are yet another way the tiles could be programmed to act as a learning aid. Applications can be developed also to utilize the tiles purely for display purposes to show patterns, animations or even live information. (¶ 4)

The TileToy Web site allows programmers to use and develop the tile code and hardware and share projects (see Figure 29-2).

A *data chip* (the size of a pencil tip), which can be attached to a physical object, makes it possible, for example, to associate audio with existing text or a physical photo. Even short video clips can be stored on the chips. The receptive and productive possibilities for language learners are innumerable for the tagging of objects and may become a means to familiarize new learners with common objects and processes in a classroom, provide signage in a building (e.g., offering directions in the native language for a newcomer), or even add audio or video commentary to specific points in paper text passages.

Figure 29-2. TileToy

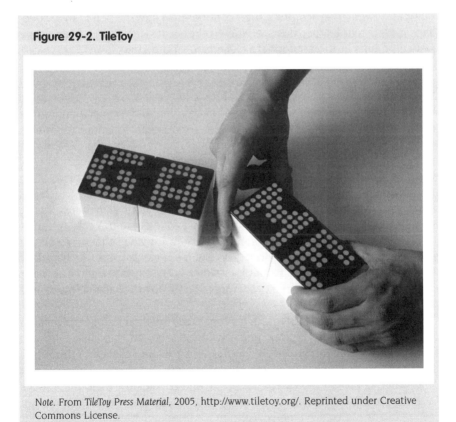

Note. From *TileToy Press Material*, 2005, http://www.tiletoy.org/. Reprinted under Creative Commons License.

Web 2.0

New ways of connecting people and information in time and space is the basis of *Web*. 2.0 (the term was coined by Tim O'Reilly and John Battelle; the first Web 2.0 conference was held in October 2004), which fosters collaboration and participation in ways that are distinctively different from, for example, e-mail and threaded discussions. User-generated content and the notion of users as contributors, not just consumers, is also a key feature of Web 2.0 applications. Threaded discussions have given way to *wikis*, searchable sites that allow users to contribute content and to comment on and edit each other's work in real time. The creation of individual Web pages has given way to sites such as *MySpace* (MySpace.com, 2003–2006), *Flickr* (Yahoo!, 2007b), *Friendster* (2002–2006), and *orkut* (n.d.), which foster social networking and collaborative thinking; people tag photos (on sites searchable by topic or through a link via a pinpoint on a digital map), post comments, edit wikis, and share digital assets to connect with other people.

Web 2.0 is also about aggregating, remixing, and tagging content with tools that are generally free and easy to use. *Click*.TV (n.d.), for example, allows multiple viewers to synchronize their comments at specific points in a video. Once a language learner posts a video, others can view it and attach their own comments at the appropriate place (see Figure 29-3).

Content Creation

An important consequence of the ease in creating and remixing content is a paradigm shift in who can and who does so. Media consumers can now easily be media producers. Software such as Audacity (2006), coupled with a microphone, allows users to easily create audio content. It is almost as easy to create a podcast as listen to one, and unlimited free space for podcasting and videoblogging (vlogging) is available through, for example, *podOmatic* (2007) and *Ourmedia* (n.d.). Many sites, like the nonprofit *Participatory Culture Foundation* (n.d.), are focused on making it easy for anyone to be an Internet-TV broadcaster, striving to make a mass medium for video that works in the same way as weblogs (blogs) do today. Open-source projects, such as *Diva* (Massachusetts Institute of Technology, 2005–2006) for video and *Ogg Vorbis* (Xiph.org, 1994–2005) for audio compression, strive to make software free to the public.

With new tools such as these, content creation is no longer the domain of a few hard-working ESL teachers or developers and publishers. In fact, there is more content on the Web created by users than by authors and developers paid to do so. Research sponsored by the Pew Internet and American Life Project indicated that by the end of 2005, the majority of teens in the United States had created content for the Internet, created a blog or Web page, or remixed online content into an original offering and posted it

Figure 29-3. *Click.TV* **With Video and Comments**

on the Internet (Lenhart & Madden, 2005). The fact that students (younger students, at least) can now easily create content meshes well with current second and foreign language methodologies that value interactions among students and encourage student-generated content. It is estimated that, in many instances, only 30–40% of the content of a course is generated by the teacher or author/developer (Boettcher, 2006), while the remaining content is student generated with guided feedback and revisitation of content. Now that so many people are connected to the Internet, the primary focus of CALL is no longer getting individuals on the Internet, but getting individuals connected to relevant content, which is often created by users, and interacting with content and others in meaningful ways.

Accessing Appropriate Content

In his song by the same title, Bruce Springsteen laments that his cable TV lineup offered "57 channels and nothin' on . . ." The abundance of information and proliferation of applications on the Internet can be overwhelming to those searching for the right software for a particular student or for specific content. B. Schwartz (2004) shows that an abundance of information coupled with many choices is unhelpful to users. One is reminded of the advertisement that asks, "How did 80% of information become 100% useless?"

Socially mediated information (Surowiecki, 2004) can identify content according to a user's personal or social profile. Just as everyone can be more involved in creating content, users can also be involved in evaluating the significance of content. Online communities such as *Gather* (2006) compensate members for publishing content, based upon how interesting the community judges the content. Communities like *Digg* (2006), an online news site, eliminate editors and moderators altogether. Users suggest news links and then vote for the stories that should be promoted to *Digg*. Socially mediated information helps create much more targeted and appropriate search results and determine who the important players are. The bulk of content creation has shifted from expert/developer to ordinary user, resulting in a dramatic increase in content and the realization that high production cost no longer automatically translates into software that users perceive to be the most valuable. Language learners can create their own news feeds, photo journals, video reports, and so on, and through them interact with users around the world.

Search techniques for multimedia have increased in sophistication. Although audio and video materials have been used in language teaching and language learning for many years, the difficulties in locating desired clips, synchronizing audio and text files, and annotating specific moments in multimedia files have made their use very clumsy. However, tagging has transformed the multimedia world. A number of search engines, such as *Singingfish* (1999–2006), index multimedia formats such as Windows Media, RealMedia, QuickTime, and MP3, enabling teachers and instructors to type a word or phrase—the *tag*—that identifies where that lexical string occurs in music, news, movies, sports, TV, and radio files, and then play that segment. (I designed and completed the first such system with an Apple Classroom of the Future Award in 1991 and demonstrated a working prototype at TESOL's 1991 convention.) A step beyond user tags, applications such as *blinkx* (2006), *TVEyes Video Search* (TVEyes, 1999–2006), and *Podscope* (TVEyes, 2006) use speech recognition software to identify the words used in millions of hours of audio, video, podcasts, vlogs, and television content, thus making them far more accessible to the ordinary user and to language learners.

Text-to-audio synchronization, as well as the ability to switch between audio and text versions of media, is also possible in several ways. Synchronized Multimedia Integration Language (SMIL) synchronizes different media streams and can be used, for example, to synchronize text and audio in MP3 files. Microsoft Reader (2003) automatically synchronizes audio-video content for materials accessed on PocketPCs so that readers can hear a passage in audio, then read it in print. Apple also offers teachers and students ways to synchronize audio and text on its iPod (see, e.g., *Sing that iTune!* [Apple Computer, 2006]). For indexing of larger quantities of multimedia at institutions, StreamSage (2004) automatically synchronizes the time codes of words, sentences, lines, or paragraphs in audio-video content to related content in class notes, transcripts, Microsoft PowerPoint (2007) slides, and other multimedia documents. Students may one day be able to access with a single click (or a spoken word) multiple forms of media to enhance their language study, perform research, and annotate their "papers," which will mostly likely be themselves some form of multimedia rather than simply print.

The Evolution of Mobile Phones

Mobile phones have evolved beyond their primary function of voice communications; they are now powerful computers. As Prensky (2005) notes, "even the simplest, voice-only phones have more complex and powerful chips than the 1969 on-board computer that landed a spaceship on the moon" (¶ 1).

Multimedia phones can transmit and receive video, graphics, and sound files; pinpoint the geographical location of mobile phone users; program digital video recorders; and deliver sports and news content. They can connect to sensors to collect data and enable mapping and social networking services for subscribers. Mobile phones can be used for games with Voice over Internet Protocol (VoIP; Internet-based phone service) or videoconferencing over any combination of networks (e.g., Internet, wireless, traditional landline, satellite). Many phones can receive calls while simultaneously accessing and downloading data such as Microsoft Word (2007) and Excel (2007) documents from the Internet. Some come preloaded with, for example, the *Yahoo!* (2007a) portal, giving easy access to e-mail, instant messaging, video on demand, Internet radio, and remote access for programming digital video recorders. Already, many language learners are using VoIP (e.g., with Skype, 2006) to participate in international tandem collaborations (see, e.g., the CAE project described in chapter 13 in this volume).

The hard disk capacity of some mobile phones is now larger than that of many USB backup disks and may soon outstrip the capacity of many laptops. An 8-gigabyte mobile phone has greater capacity than that of most language labs currently utilized in schools and universities. Today's mobile phones commonly include cameras, store documents as well as thousands of tunes, share pictures via e-mail, synchronize playlists and songs from a personal computer (PC), support audio streams to Bluetooth headsets (see Bluetooth SIG, 2006), and offer access to interactive games, high-quality videos, and Web content.

Within 10 years, what people now call the mobile phone may be the only device they use. It will be their phone, wireless terminal, and even desktop computer once it is plugged into a docking station at home or at school. Alternatively, people may use personal media viewers such as Myvu (MicroOptical, 2006), which resemble eyeglasses and enable the wearer to privately see a monitor-like display that appears to be projected several feet away. The future mobile phone, or cellular PC (announced at the Consumer Electronics Show in January 2006), may be a cheaper alternative to traditional PCs and laptops and a better way than laptops to bring Internet connectivity to the people of developing nations: Of the approximately 2 billion mobile phone users in the world today, many of those with conventional desktop or laptop computers cannot afford or do not have an Internet connection.

Meskill's hypothetical student in chapter 28 used a laptop and wireless connections to complete his homework on a train. However, CALL learners can already use other applications with access to Internet-enabled mobile phones and handheld devices.

Peer-to-peer contact is available to students through a variety of channels. VoIP applications have been launched by many service providers (e.g., AOL, Yahoo!, Microsoft), making low-cost phone calls, voice messaging services, and full-screen video conversations between users readily available. Also, many cities, civic groups, and tourism boards offer services that integrate Internet and telephone service, connecting callers with a network of volunteers who answer questions, give advice, and provide language interpretation over the phone. And with the assistance of sites such as *MyLanguageExchange.com* (2000–2006), students can finding a language partner (in some 115 languages) for voice chat by VoIP or voice and text simultaneously using Paltalk (2006).

People can create *voice communities* focused around a particular topic, location, or peer group at sites such as *Radio Handi* (Open Communication Systems, 2003–2006). For the cost of a local phone call, users from landline, mobile, and VoIP phones can post messages or have live group conversations. *Radio Handi* and other sites facilitate the creation of communities of language learners and provide language students with opportunities to converse with other speakers near and far. (See CAE B's *Podcast*, n.d., for an example of a tandem exchange using VOIP; see also chapter 9 in this volume.)

Some of the enormously popular *massively multiplayer online games* (MMOGs) also incorporate VoIP. At *GameComm* (n.d.) and *Vivox* (2006), players can communicate by voice as they play together in real-time online. (For more on the pedagogical applications of simulations and MMOGs, see chapter 26 in this volume.)

Resource-Rich Multimedia With Internet-Enabled Phones

Various *subscription services* are widely available to users. *Mobiedge Radio* (Mobiedge Technologies, 2006), for example, is a *podcatcher* (podcasting client) for mobile phones, which can be used in an offline or online mode; it enables users to download, read, and manage podcasts to which they subscribe. *Mobizines* (Refresh Mobile, n.d.) is a free English-language subscription service that allows users to receive minifile multimedia downloads on topics such as celebrity news and horoscopes. *Everypoint* (2006) delivers sports, news, mobile magazines, mapping, and social networking services to subscribers. Although the bite-sized screen is not conducive to reading substantial text passages, the content delivery of magazines relies heavily on multimedia content and audio. Language learners are increasingly living in a media-rich environment where authentic content can be readily accessed, searched, and researched both aurally and visually (for more on visuality, see chapter 17 in this volume).

Video content for mobile phones and other digital devices is available through many companies, including Google, CBS, and Apple. Some broadcasters create short, 3- to 5-minute episodes specifically for mobile phones; some allow users to purchase or download video originally produced for television or movie theater viewing. Video content can be viewed on handheld devices, beamed to a television for viewing (as suggested by the 2010 scenario in the Focus section of this chapter), or viewed through special personal media viewer eyeglasses, as described earlier.

A number of sites, such as *YouTube* (2006), have over 100 million videos watched daily through streaming files. Other applications, which will no doubt become increasingly common, allow users to send live video across a wireless broadband connection to other enabled handsets so that recipients can see exactly what the other user is viewing in real time. Other real-time video applications involve interactive TV on the mobile phone; with their keypads, users can interact with live broadcasts of sports events, game shows, and reality programs (see, e.g., *AirPlay* [AirPlay Network, 2006]). These types of applications enable language learners to interact with other learners and native speakers in activities that can engage their personal hobbies and passions (for more on the importance of engagement, see chapter 22 in this volume).

In 2005 alone, analysts estimated that 7.5 billion *camera phone* pictures were taken. Research shows that individuals are more likely to take pictures with mobile phones than they are with larger digital cameras. Compared to the use of conventional cameras, pictures taken using a mobile phone are more numerous, more spontaneous, and more journalistic. Using a mobile phone to show pictures—physically passing a phone with images from one individual to another—is common, as is sending images from one phone to another, or blogging and *vlogging* by transmitting media wirelessly.

The creation of communities sharing pictures and videos online, enhanced by *moblogging* (blogging from a mobile device), is rapidly gaining momentum with sites such as *Textamerica* (n.d.), *Buzznet* (2006), and *DropShots* (2007; see Figure 29-4). Language learning communities might be particularly interested in *Flock* (n.d.), a "social Web browser," because its structure would help students simultaneously share media, connect to others, and search Web sites. Sharing pictures related to a specific topic encourages an affective link between photographers and viewers. In the context of CALL, the reaction and subsequent conversation sparked by photographs may create unique opportunities for self-introduction of the student photographer (Reeder, Macfadyen, Roche, & Chase, 2004) and contribute to the shaping of online social contexts (W. S. E. Lam, 2000a). Images generated by students can motivate a cycle of conversational interaction, for example, photos followed by replies or reactions followed by more photos or replies. Images can tell a digital narrative or serve as conversational anchors. They can provoke reactions, record a mood, document a visual reference, or play a role in reminiscing and asking questions (see Figure 29-4).

CALL instructors and researchers should carefully assess the sites selected for moblogging because some interfaces, such as *DropShots* (2007), tend to elicit more textual participation among mobloggers and viewers than others. Clearly, the ease with which students can generate multimedia communication facilitates student involvement, and as O'Dowd (2003) points out, student involvement is key to successful interpersonal and intercultural exchange. (For more on atmosphere and motivation, see chapter 21 in this volume.)

In addition to sharing pictures focused on a specific theme, a variety of *location-based technologies* enable users to post pictures associated with a specific location on a map as long as the user's Internet-enabled device has wireless capability or a Global Positioning System (GPS). Most mobile phones now being manufactured have built-in GPS chips, and in the future, all mobile phones will have location-based services. Location-based technologies allow individuals to interact with content in a physically anchored geographical environment, enhancing the experience of physical exploration with hypermedia.

Software such as Loki (see Skyhook Wireless, 2006), Eye-Fi (see www.eye .fi, 2006), and Socialight (Kamida, 2007; see Figure 29-5) enables users to post text messages or photos associated with a specific location for an individual user or group. Photos associated with locations can be posted online or left to be "discovered" and retrieved at the location where the photo or message

Figure 29-4. Moblogging at *DropShots*

Granna: Aw, she looks so precious - my little angel.
Momma: Oh yeah, watch the videos before... she might be little, but she's got something else on the other shoulder ;-)
Uncle Dave: Eating is hard work!
Auntie Eva: Hey, was someone giving her wine?
Momma: Had to try something to slow her down ;-)
Grandma: That's one way to get her to sleep.
Momma: Whatever works!!

| Enter Name | Enter New Comment | → |

Note. From *DropShots*, 2007, http://www.dropshots.com/. Copyright 2007 by DropShots. Reprinted with permission.

was created, as in the 2010 scenario in the Focus section of this chapter. When a Socialight user reaches the geographical location associated with an image left by someone else, his or her phone vibrates or rings, with notification that a StickyShadow image or message is at that location and can be retrieved.

The U.S. National Park Service now offers location-based mobile phone audio tours, and colleges and universities have developed similar campus orientation tours for newly arrived students. Explanatory audio, pictures, and text can be sent to a mobile phone as the student approaches the associated location. This type of technology is ideal for CALL because students can be asked to leave or retrieve StickyShadows in a specific neighborhood,

Figure 29-5. Sharing Location-Based Pictures and Messages With *Socialight*

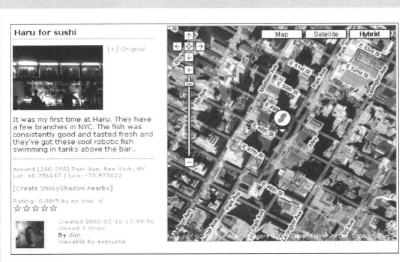

Note. From *Socialight*, 2007, http://socialight.com/. Copyright 2007 by Kamida. Reprinted with permission.

locating physical objects of relevance to a particular theme, historical topic, or personal history (see the suggestions in the 2010 scenario at the beginning of this chapter). In an experiential vein, dozens of mobile-phone-based multiplayer geographical search games exist. Location-based scavenger hunts can require language learners to locate elements and landmarks in a physical location and return with associated StickyShadows. Or, once an individual is in the target location, a StickyShadow message can direct the individual to take a particular action.

Location-based search and navigation applications such as *Earthcomber* (2003–2006a) and Loki (see Skyhook Wireless, 2006) identify and display Web content in proximity to the user's real-time location. *Earthcomber* enables users to create personal travel logs, set up groups for the dissemination of *event maps* for specific events, and find other geographically tagged information important to hikers or sightseers. The resultant screen displays locations near the user. Commercial travel *spot guides*, such as the Moon Metro or Mobile Travel Guide (see Earthcomber, 2003–2006b), let mobile phone users know how far it is to a particular location in real time; a >CLICK-TO-CALL button allows for making reservations at a restaurant or obtaining *Google Maps* (Google, 2007e) directions. Loki users can conduct local searches for a type of location, such as coffee shops or Thai restaurants.

Buddy mapping applications allow users to track the location of friends. Users are able to see where their friends are and connect with others in the same proximity. Some applications, like VITO ActiveTrace (2006), track athletes involved in active sports such as running or skiing, enabling the user's friends to see where the individual is in real time. Other applications, such as Loki (see Skyhook Wireless, 2006), integrate instant messaging and photos tagged to where friends are located on a map. *Social networking applications* that integrate location and hypermedia result in the blurring of online and offline communities and interaction since the messages and images can be retrieved in real time or stored for subsequent review. Extending the social use of technology to the mobile sphere through applications such as buddy mapping may promote and facilitate face-to-face interaction via an initial awareness and meeting of the other through technology.

Regensburg Experience (n.d.), an intriguing project to promote tourism in this medieval town in Germany, combines several features of the previously mentioned applications. It integrates an interactive scavenger hunt with moblogging and the use of motion-sensing mobile phones to interact with targeted landmarks. Visitors wave the motion-sensing mobile phones at landmarked buildings to retrieve "secret" hypermedia messages, use the phones to duel or work cooperatively with other visitors, or use them as wands to "cast a spell" at particular locations. A talking book related to the project is in the works.

Applications such as *Nextcode* (n.d.) or *Mobot* (2006) allow mobile phone users to take pictures of a barcode or image and e-mail it to a server that performs a visual search and then returns a text message comparing prices of the item, customer ratings, or video of the product a few seconds later. Such applications, which use real-world objects as input to trigger other data, may offer intriguing possibilities for future CALL applications. For instance, the U.S. military has attempted to offer soldiers in the field technology that can tag real-world objects; looking through binoculars at a geographical feature, the targeted item is identified in the database, and a resulting lexical tag appears in the viewfinder. Such technology could be used for CALL someday, providing students with words or explanations for locations and objects as they are encountered.

Conclusion

The capabilities of Internet-enabled handheld devices and mobile phones already in the hands of many students and teachers far exceed the capabilities of most CALL technologies in use today. With the widespread use of handheld devices, many students are no longer tied to their PCs to access digital content. Like many emerging technologies created for purposes other than education, "hand-me-down" applications (see chapter 28 in this volume) will undoubtedly enable and inform the future uses of technology in CALL.

Many of the technologies and applications I have reviewed in this chapter are not limited to a particular platform, a specific browser, or a specific device such as a PC or a mobile phone. For example, public libraries commonly offer audio e-book downloads to PCs and handheld devices for their library patrons. Likewise, users can check e-mail on a handheld device, a PC, a wireless laptop, or via a speech synthesizer over the telephone. Not only do applications span devices, but also the same digital information can often be processed in more than one medium. For example, a person might read a text file or Web page on one device and listen to it on another. Or mobile phone users might wish to transmit a voice response to a text e-mail, for example, with *Trekmail* (2002–2006). The possibility of language production and reception in more than one medium and the linking of digital data to real-world objects are exciting new developments for language learners.

Early CALL applications were, of necessity, print and text based. As technology evolved, users were delighted with the possibilities of augmenting print with multimedia. Internet-enabled phones and other handheld devices, with their ease in capturing pictures, video, speech, and audio, coupled with their simplicity in sending this content to other users, however, may reverse the present roles of multimedia and text. The future of CALL may involve the primacy of multimedia, with users delighted by its augmentation with text.

The future has never been easy to forecast. Just as the original notion of the telephone in Europe was for listening to a broadcast of news or weather, mobile phones today are conceived of quite differently from their original purpose, which was to provide mobile voice-to-voice communication. Technologies of the future used to be imagined as replacing teachers, offering exquisitely omniscient expert tutors, or containing huge archives of content. However, it may be that the future will offer a truly learner-centered environment for socially networked users who find it easy to generate and receive content in a variety of media wherever they are located.

Explorations

1. Take a poll of your students or classmates to find out what digital handheld devices they use already. Which of these might you use in language teaching and learning?

2. In your teaching, have you ever used any of the futuristic devices described by Price? Explain which functions of the device facilitated language instruction or learning. What were any disadvantages? Discuss your thoughts with your classmates or working group.

3. Price sketches out a few possible uses of new kinds of technology for language teaching. Imagine a digital device that could enhance language teaching and learning, and imagine how it could be used for a task or activity in or out of your classroom. What would be its chief advantages, and what problems might your students encounter in using it? Share your vision with your classmates or working group.

4. Social mediation may be one factor in determining if a new electronic device may be appropriate for teaching purposes. What kinds of socially mediated technology or Web 2.0 technology do you use currently? What other factors might help determine how useful a tool will be for language learning?

5. Price speaks of students creating content. How might teachers help language learners determine the appropriateness of the content created by others? Brainstorm a list with your classmates or working group.

References

37Signals. (n.d.). *Writeboard*. Retrieved December 8, 2006, from http://www.writeboard .com/

A&E Television Networks. (1996–2007a). *Biography*. Retrieved March 8, 2007, from http://www.biography.com/

A&E Television Networks. (1996–2007b). *History.com*. Retrieved March 8, 2007, from http://www.history.com/

Abbott, J. (2000). "Blinking out" and "having the touch": Two fifth-grade boys talk about flow experiences in writing. *Written Communication*, 17, 53–92.

Abdullah, M. (1998). *Problem-based learning in language instruction: A constructivist method*. Bloomington, IN: ERIC Clearinghouse on Reading, English, and Communication. (ERIC Document Reproduction Service No. ED423550)

Abilock, D. (n.d.). A *"think-aloud" to model reading online*. Retrieved December 19, 2006, from http://www.noodletools.com/debbie/literacies/basic/readstrat/readingstrategies .viewlet/readingstrategies_viewlet_swf.html

Abraham, R., & Liou, H.-C. (1991). Interaction generated by three computer programs: Analysis of functions of spoken language. In P. Dunkel (Ed.), *Computer-assisted language learning and testing* (pp. 85–109). Rowley, MA: Newbury.

Absolutely intercultural! (n.d.). Retrieved November 21, 2006, from http://www.absolutely-intercultural.com/

ACE (Version 4) [Computer software]. (2006). ACE Project Team. http://ace.iserver.ch/

Acrobat Connect Professional [Computer software]. (2006). San Jose, CA: Adobe. http://www.adobe.com/products/acrobatconnectpro/

Active Worlds. (1997–2006). Retrieved December 23, 2006, from http://www.activeworlds .com/

Adams, D., & Hamm, M. (1996). *Cooperative thinking: Critical thinking collaboration across the curriculum*. Springfield, IL: Charles Thomas.

Adams, T. W. (1989). *Inside textbooks: What students need to know*. New York: Addison-Wesley.

Advanogy.com. (2003). *Free learning styles inventory, including graphical results*. Retrieved December 15, 2006, from http://www.learning-styles-online.com/inventory/

AdventNet. (2006). *Zoho writer*. Retrieved December 5, 2006, from http://www.zohowriter .com/jsp/home.jsp

Aebersold, H., & Field, M. L. (1997). *From reader to reading teacher: Issues and strategies for second language classrooms*. Cambridge: Cambridge University Press.

Ahmad, K., Corbett, G., Rogers, M., & Sussex, R. (1985). *Computers, language learning, and language teaching*. Cambridge: Cambridge University Press.

AirPlay Network. (2006). *Airplay*. Retrieved December 30, 2006, from http://www.airplay .com/home.asp

Akayoglu, S. (2005, December 11). Data collection for my MA thesis [Msg 11299]. Message posted to http://groups.yahoo.com/group/evonline2002_webheads/

Al-Othman, B. (2004). A *Web-based students' collaborative project*. Retrieved December 10, 2006, from http://alothman-b.tripod.com/162s4_groupboards04.htm

Al-Othman, B., & Zeinstejer, R. (2005). *The Skype Worldbridges project for EFL in different cultures: Argentina and Kuwait online presentation at WiAOC*. Retrieved December 10, 2006, from http://worldbridges.com/webheads/audio/ritabuthstudents2005-08-22.mp3

Alderson, J. C. (2000). Technology in testing: The present and the future. *System, 28,* 593–603.

Alderson, J. C., & Hamp-Lyons, L. (1996). TOEFL preparation courses: A study of washback. *Language Testing, 13,* 280–297.

Alexander, E. (Ed.). (2005). *The essential Gwendolyn Brooks*. New York: Literary Classics of the United States.

A.L.I.C.E. AI Foundation. (n.d.). A.L.I.C.E. *Artificial intelligence foundation*. Retrieved December 15, 2006, from http://alicebot.org/

Allwright, D. (1990). *Autonomy in language pedagogy* (CRILE Working Paper 6). Cambridge: Cambridge University Press.

Allwright, D., & Bailey, K. M. (1991). *Focus on the language classroom: An introduction to classroom research for language teachers*. Cambridge: Cambridge University Press.

Ally, M. (2004). Foundations of educational theory for online learning. In T. Anderson & F. Elloumi (Eds.), *Theory and practice of online learning* (pp. 3–31). Athabasca, Alberta, Canada: Athabasca University.

Almeida d'Eça, T. (2005). *First steps in experimenting with computers: Resources*. Retrieved November 26, 2006, from http://64.71.48.37/teresadeca/misc/firststepswith computers-refs.htm

Almeida d'Eça, T. (2006). First steps in experimenting with computers. In E. Hanson-Smith & S. Rilling (Eds.), *Learning languages through technology* (pp. 159–174). Alexandria, VA: TESOL.

Alperer, S. (2005). *The impact of choice provision on students' affective engagement in tasks: A flow analysis*. Unpublished master's thesis, Bilkent University, Ankara, Turkey.

ALTEC & University of Kansas. (2000–2006). *RubiStar*. Retrieved December 13, 2006, from http://rubistar.4teachers.org/index.php

ALTEC & University of Kansas. (2000–2007). PBL *checklists*. Retrieved April 17, 2007, from http://pblchecklist.4teachers.org/checklist.shtml

Amabile, T. M., & Tighe, E. (1993). Questions of creativity. In J. Brockman (Ed.), *Creativity* (pp. 7–27). New York: Simon & Schuster.

Amazon.com. (1996–2007). Retrieved April 18, 2007, from http://www.amazon.com/

American Council on the Teaching of Foreign Languages. (1983). ACTFL *proficiency guidelines* (Rev. 1985). Hastings-on-Hudson, NY: ACTFL Materials Center. Retrieved November 24, 2006, from http://www.sil.org/lingualinks/LANGUAGELEARNING/OtherResources/ACTFLProficiencyGuidelines/contents.htm

Anderson, R. (1994). Anonymity, presence, and the dialogic self in a technological culture. In R. Anderson, K. N. Cissna, & R. C. Arnett (Eds.), *The reach of dialogue: Confirmation, voice, and community* (pp. 91–110). Cresskill, NJ: Hampton Press.

Anderson, R., & Speck, B. (2001). *Using technology in K–8 literacy classrooms*. Upper Saddle River, NJ: Merrill Prentice Hall.

Angelo, T., & Cross, P. K. (1993). *Classroom assessment techniques: A handbook for college teachers* (2nd ed.). San Francisco: Jossey-Bass.

Annenberg Media. (1997–2006). *Learner.org*. Retrieved November 30, 2006, from http://learner.org/

Antonacci, D. M., & Modaress, N. (2005). *Second life: The educational possibilities of a massively multiplayer virtual world* (MMVW). Retrieved December 23, 2006, from http://www2.kumc.edu/netlearning/SLEDUCAUSESW2005/SLPresentationOutline.htm

Apple Computer. (2006). *Sing that iTune!* Retrieved December 30, 2006, from http://www.apple.com/downloads/dashboard/music/singthatitune.html

Apple Computer. (2007). *Apple learning interchange*. Retrieved December 1, 2006, from http://edcommunity.apple.com/ali/index.php

AppleWorks (Version 6.2.9) [Computer software]. (2004). Cupertino, CA: Apple Computer. http://www.apple.com/appleworks/

Arneil, S., & Holmes, M. (2006). Hot Potatoes (Version 6) [Computer software]. Victoria, British Columbia, Canada: Half-Baked Software. http://hotpot.uvic.ca/

Arthur's Teacher Trouble [Computer software]. (n.d.). San Francisco: Riverdeep. http://www.riverdeep.net/portal/page?_pageid=353,143803,353_143804&_dad=portal&_schema=PORTAL

Asher, J. J. (1969). The total physical response approach to second language learning. *Modern Language Journal, 53*, 3–17.

Asher, J. J. (1982). *Learning another language through actions*. Los Gatos, CA: Sky Oaks Productions.

AT&T Knowledge Ventures. (2006). *Welcome to Blue Web'n: A library of blue ribbon learning sites on the Web*. Retrieved November 29, 2006, from http://www.kn.pacbell.com/wired/bluewebn/

AT&T Knowledge Ventures. (2007a). *Activity formats*. Retrieved April 18, 2007, from http://www.kn.pacbell.com/wired/fil/formats.html

AT&T Knowledge Ventures. (2007b). *Filamentality*. Retrieved April 18, 2007, from http://www.kn.pacbell.com/wired/fil/index.html

AT&T Knowledge Ventures. (2007c). *WebQuest overview*. Retrieved April 18, 2007, from http://www.kn.pacbell.com/wired/webquests.html

Audacity (Version1.2.6) [Computer software]. (2006). Audacity Development Team. http://audacity.sourceforge.net/

The Authoring Suite [Computer software]. (n.d.). London: Wida Software. http://www.wida.co.uk/noframes/auth.htm

Bachman, L. F. (1991). What does language testing have to offer? *TESOL Quarterly, 25*, 671–704.

Bachman, L. F., & Palmer, A. S. (1996). *Language testing in practice*. Oxford: Oxford University Press.

Backflip. (1999–2006). Retrieved December 29, 2006, from http://www.backflip.com/

Baker, C. (2005, August 22). All-digital school passes first test. *eSchool News*, p. 20.

Bakhtin, M. M. (1986). *Speech genres and other late essays* (V. W. McGhee, Trans.). Austin: University of Texas Press.

Baltra, A. (1990). Language learning through computer adventure games. *Simulation & Gaming, 21*, 445–452.

Bandura, A. (1971). *Social learning theory*. New York: General Learning.

Bandura, A. (1986). *Social foundations of thought and action*. Englewood Cliffs, NJ: Prentice Hall.

Bandura, A. (2001). Social congitive theory: An agentic perspective. *Annual Review of Psychology, 52*, 1–26.

Bangert-Drowns, R. L. (1993). The word processor as an instructional tool: A meta-analysis of word processing in writing. *Review of Educational Research, 63*(1), 69–93.

Banks, C. A., & Banks, J. A. (1995). Equity pedagogy: An essential component of multicultural education. *Theory Into Practice, 34,* 152–157.

Banks, J. (2001). *Cultural diversity and education: Foundations, curriculum, and teaching.* Needham Heights, MA: Allyn & Bacon.

Banville, S. (2004–2007). *Technology lesson plans.* Retrieved March 8, 2007, from http://www.breakingnewsenglish.com/technology.html

Barnesandnoble.com. (1997–2006). http://www.bn.com/

Barrett, H. C. (1999–2000). *Electronic portfolios = multimedia development + portfolio development: The electronic portfolio development process.* Retrieved December 13, 2006, from http://electronicportfolios.org/portfolios/EPDevProcess.html

Barson, J., Frommer, J., & Schwartz, M. (1993). Foreign language learning using e-mail in a task-orientated perspective: Interuniversity experiments in communication and collaboration. *Journal of Science Education and Technology, 2,* 565–584.

Batson, T. (2002, December 1). The electronic portfolio boom: What's it all about? *Syllabus.* Retrieved December 13, 2006, from http://campustechnology.com/article.asp?id=6984

Bauer-Ramazani, C. (2006). Training CALL teachers online. In P. Hubbard & M. Levy (Eds.), *Teacher education in CALL* (pp. 183–200). Amsterdam: John Benjamins.

Baya, G. (2006, June 8). Using wikis with our students [Msg 821]. Message posted to http://groups.yahoo.com/group/learningwithcomputers/

Baya, G. (n.d.). *theoryofeducation.* Retrieved December 6, 2006, from http://theoryofeducation.pbwiki.com/

Baya, G., Bellusci, M. C., & Hillis, M. (2005). *Learning with computers.* Retrieved November 26, 2006, from http://groups.yahoo.com/group/learningwithcomputers

Beach, R., & Liebman-Kleine, J. (1986). The writing/reading relationship: Becoming one's own best reader. In B. T. Petersen (Ed.), *Convergences: Transactions in reading and writing* (pp. 64–81). Urbana, IL: National Council of Teachers of English.

Beale, J. (2002). Is communicative language teaching a thing of the past? *Babel, 37*(1), 12–16.

Beatty, K. (2003). *Teaching and researching computer-assisted language learning.* London: Longman.

Becker, H. J. (1994). How exemplary computer-using teachers differ from other teachers: Implications for realizing the potential of computers in schools. *Contemporary Issues in Technology and Teacher Education, 1*(2). Retrieved January 24, 2007, from http://www.citejournal.org/vol1/iss2/seminal/article1.htm (Originally published in *Journal of Research on Computing in Education, 26,* 291–321)

Belcher, D. (2006). English for specific purposes: Teaching to perceived needs and imagined futures in worlds of work, study, and everyday life. *TESOL Quarterly, 40,* 133–156.

Bell, A. (1984). Language style as audience design. *Language in Society, 13,* 145–204.

Bell, F. L. (2005). *Comprehension aids, Internet technologies, and the reading of authentic materials by adult second language learners.* Unpublished dissertation, Florida State University, Tallahassee.

Bell, F. L., & LeBlanc, L. B. (2000). The language of glosses in L2 reading on computer: Learners' preferences. *Hispania, 83,* 274–285.

Belz, J. (2002). Social dimensions of telecollaborative foreign language study. *Language*

Learning & Technology, 6(1), 60–81. Retrieved December 20, 2006, from http://llt.msu.edu/vol6num1/belz/

Benson, P. (2001). *Teaching and researching autonomy in language learning.* Harlow, England: Pearson.

Benson, P. (2002). Rethinking the relationship of self-access and autonomy. *Self-Access Language Learning, 5,* 3–7. Retrieved December 22, 2006, from http://lc.ust.hk/HASALD/newsletter/newsletterSept02.pdf

Benson, P., & Voller, P. (1997). *Autonomy and independence in language learning.* Boston: Addison-Wesley.

Bereiter, C., & Scardamalia, M. (1987). *The psychology of written composition.* Hillsdale, NJ: Lawrence Erlbaum.

Berends, M., Bodilly, S. J., & Kirby, S. N. (2002). *Facing the challenges of whole-school reform: New American Schools after a decade.* Santa Monica, CA: RAND. Retrieved December 10, 2006, from http://www.rand.org/pubs/monograph_reports/MR1498/

Berge, Z., & Collins, M. (1995). Computer-mediated communication and the online classroom: Overview and perspectives. *Computer-Mediated Communication Magazine, 2*(2), 6–17. Retrieved February 28, 2007, from http://www.december.com/cmc/mag/1995/feb/berge.html

Bersin, J. (2003). What works in blended learning. *Learning Circuits.* Retrieved December 29, 2006, from http://www.learningcircuits.org/2003/jul2003/bersin.htm

BetterAccent Tutor [Computer software]. (n.d.). BetterAccent. http://betteraccent.com/

Beyer, B. (1995). *Critical thinking.* Bloomington, IN: Phi Delta Kappa Educational Foundation.

Biber, D. (1988). *Variation across speech and writing.* Cambridge: Cambridge University Press.

Birch, B. M. (2002). *English L2 reading: Getting to the bottom.* Mahwah, NJ: Lawrence Erlbaum.

Blackboard Academic Suite (Release 7.0) [Web software]. (2005). Washington, DC: Blackboard. http://www.blackboard.com/us/index.aspx

Blake, R. (2000). Computer mediated communication: A window on L2 Spanish interlanguage. *Language Learning & Technology, 4*(1), 120–136. Retrieved December 11, 2006, from http://llt.msu.edu/vol4num1/blake/

Blanchette, J. (1996, June). *The culture of computer technology in education and research: A Canadian perspective.* Paper presented at the Standing Conference on University Teaching and Research in Education of Adults, Leeds, England.

Blinkx. (2006). Retrieved December 30, 2006, from http://www.blinkx.com/

Blogcheese. (2006). Retrieved December 3, 2006, from http://www.blogcheese.com/

Bloom, B. S. (1956). *Taxonomy of educational objectives: Handbook I. The cognitive domain.* New York: David McKay.

Bluetooth SIG. (2006). *Bluetooth: The Bluetooth technology Web site.* Retrieved December 31, 2006, from http://www.bluetooth.com/bluetooth/

Boden, D. (1994). *The business of talk: Organizations in action.* Cambridge, MA: Polity Press.

Boettcher, J. (2006, March). The rise of student performance content. *Campus Technology,* 20–22.

Bolter, J. D. (1990). *Writing space: The computer in the history of literacy.* Hillsdale, NJ: Lawrence Erlbaum.

Bonk, C. J., & Cunningham, D. J. (1998). Searching for learner-centered, constructivist, and sociocultural components of collaborative educational learning tools. In C. J. Bonk & K. S. King (Eds.), *Electronic collaborators: Learner-centered technologies for literacy, apprenticeship, and discourse* (pp. 25–50). Mahwah, NJ: Lawrence Erlbaum. Retrieved December 11, 2006, from http://www.publicationshare.com/docs/Bon02.pdf

Bordonaro, K. (2003). Perceptions of technology and manifestations of language learner autonomy. *CALL-EJ Online*, 5(1). Retrieved January 25, 2007, from http://www.tell.is.ritsumei.ac.jp/callejonline/journal/5-1/bordonaro.html

Boud, D. (1998). Moving towards autonomy. In D. Boud (Ed.), *Developing student autonomy in learning* (pp. 17–39). London: Kogan Page.

Bowen, C. (2002). The I-search with grade 5: They learn! *Teacher Librarian*, 29(2). Retrieved December 10, 2006, from http://www.teacherlibrarian.com/tlmag/v_29/v_29_2_feature.html

Bowen, J. (2006). *Virtual library museums pages*. Retrieved December 11, 2006, from http://vlmp.icom.museum/

Bowker, L., & Pearson, J. (2002). *Working with specialized language: A practical guide to using corpora*. New York: Routledge.

BrainCogs [Computer software]. (2002). Boston: FableVision. http://www.fablevision.com/braincogs/cog_product.html

Brammerts Ruhr-University Bochum. (2005). *eTandem*. Retrieved December 9, 2006, from http://www.slf.ruhr-uni-bochum.de/etandem/etindex-en.html

Brander, B. (2005). Considering culture in CALL. In J. Egbert & G. Petrie (Eds.), CALL *research perspectives* (1st ed., pp. 141–153). Mahwah, NJ: Lawrence Erlbaum.

Branscum, D. (1992, September). Educators need support to make computing meaningful. [Special Edition] *Macworld*, 83–88.

Breen, M. P. (1985). Authenticity in the language classroom. *Applied Linguistics*, 6, 60–70.

Brent, D. (2005). Teaching as performance in the electronic classroom. *First Monday*, 10(4). Retrieved December 19, 2006, from http://firstmonday.org/issues/issue10_4/brent/index.html

Brickner, D. (1995). *The effects of first and second order barriers to change on the degree and nature of computer usage of secondary mathematics teachers: A case study*. Unpublished doctoral dissertation, Purdue University, West Lafayette, IN.

Brinton, D. M., Snow, M. A., & Wesche, M. (2003). *Content-based second language instruction* (2nd ed.). Ann Arbor: University of Michigan Press.

British Broadcasting Corporation. (2006). BBC. Retrieved November 30, 2006, from http://www.bbc.co.uk/

British Broadcasting Corporation. (2007). CBBC. Retrieved April 16, 2007, from http://www.bbc.co.uk/cbbc/

British Broadcasting Corporation. (n.d.-a). *Skillswise*. Retrieved December 8, 2006, from http://www.bbc.co.uk/skillswise/

British Broadcasting Corporation. (n.d.-b). *Video nation*. Retrieved December 10, 2006, from http://www.bbc.co.uk/videonation/

British Broadcasting Corporation. (n.d.-c). *Windsor Castle virtual tour*. Retrieved December 19, 2006, from http://www.bbc.co.uk/history/british/launch_vt_windsor_castle.shtml

Brody, P. (1995). *Technology planning and management handbook: A guide for school district educational technology leaders*. Englewood Cliffs, NJ: Educational Technology.

Brooks, J., & Brooks, M. G. (1993). *In search of understanding: The case for constructivist classrooms*. Alexandria, VA: Association for Supervision and Curriculum Development.

Brooks, S., & Byles, B. (2000). *On-line practice modules*. Retrieved November 30, 2006, from http://www.internet4classrooms.com/on-line.htm

Brophy, J. (2004). *Motivating students to learn*. Mahwah, NJ: Lawrence Erlbaum.

Brouwer, C., & Wagner, J. (2004). Developmental issues in second language conversation. *Journal of Applied Linguistics, 1*, 30–47.

Brown, A. R., & Voltz, B. D. (2005). Elements of effective e-learning design. *International Review of Research in Open and Distance Learning, 6*(1). Retrieved December 29, 2006, from http://www.irrodl.org/index.php/irrodl/article/view/217/300

Brown, H. D. (1994). *Teaching by principles: An interactive approach to language pedagogy*. Englewood Cliffs, NJ: Prentice Hall Regents.

Brown, H. D. (2000). *Principles of language learning and teaching* (4th ed.). New York: Longman.

Brown, H. D. (2002). *Strategies for success: A practical guide to learning English*. New York: Addison-Wesley.

Brown, H. D. (2004). *Language assessment: Principles and classroom practices*. White Plains, NY: Longman/Pearson.

Brown, J. D. (1997). Computers in language testing: Present research and some future directions. *Language Learning & Technology, 1*(1), 44–59.

Brown, J. S., Collins, A., & Duguid, S. (1989). Situated cognition and the culture of learning. *Educational Researcher, 18*(1), 32–42.

Brown, R., & Gilman, A. (1960). The pronouns of power and solidarity. In T. Sebeok (Ed.), *Style in language* (pp. 253–276). Cambridge, MA: MIT Press.

Browne, M., & Keeley, S. (1990). *Asking the right questions: A guide to critical thinking* (3rd ed.). Englewood Cliffs, NJ: Prentice Hall.

Brozo, W., & Simpson, M. (1995). *Readers, teachers, learners: Expanding literacy in secondary schools*. Englewood Cliffs, NJ: Prentice Hall.

Bruce, B., Peyton, J. K., & Batson, T. (1993). *Network-based classrooms: Promises and realities*. New York: Cambridge University Press.

Bruffee, K. A. (1993). *Collaborative learning: Higher education, interdependence, and the authority of knowledge*. Baltimore: Johns Hopkins University Press.

Bubbleshare. (2004–2006). Retrieved December 10, 2006, from http://www.bubbleshare.com/

Buck, K., Byrnes, H., & Thompson, I. (Ed.). (1989). *The ACTFL Oral Proficiency Interview tester training manual*. Yonkers, NY: American Council on the Teaching of Foreign Languages.

Bullinger, H.-J., Müller-Spahn, F., & Rübler, A. (1996). *Encouraging creativity—support of mental processes by virtual experience*. Retrieved December 11, 2006, from http://vr.iao.fhg.de/papers/creativity.pdf

Burmark, L. (2002). *Visual literacy: Learn to see, see to learn*. Alexandria, VA: Association for Supervision and Curriculum Development.

Burniske, R. W., & Monke, L. (2001). *Breaking down the digital walls: Learning to teach in a post-modem world*. Albany: State University of New York Press.

Butler-Pascoe, M. E., & Wiburg, K. M. (2003). *Technology and teaching English language learners*. Boston: Allyn & Bacon.

Buzznet. (2006). Retrieved December 30, 2006, from http://www.buzznet.com/

Byrd, P. (1998). Rethinking grammar at various proficiency levels: Implications of authentic materials for the EAP curriculum. In P. Byrd & J. M. Reid, *Grammar in the composition classroom: Essays on teaching ESL for college-bound students* (pp. 69–97). Boston: Heinle & Heinle.

Cable News Network. (2007). *CNN.com*. Retrieved April 16, 2007, from http://www.cnn.com/

CAE B's podcast. (n.d.). Retrieved November 29, 2006, from http://caeb2006.podomatic.com/

CALICO *Journal*. (2007). Retrieved March 8, 2007, from https://calico.org/p-5-CALICO%20Journal.html

Campbell Hill, B., Ruptic, C., & Norwick, L. (1998). *Classroom based assessment*. Norwood, MA: Christopher-Gordon.

CamStudio (Version 2.0) [Computer software]. (2005). http://www.camstudio.org/

Candy, P. C. (1991). *Self-direction for lifelong learning*. San Francisco: Jossey-Bass.

Carnevale, A. P., Gainer, L. J., & Meltzer, A. (1991). *Workplace basics: The essential skills employers want*. San Francisco: Jossey-Bass.

Carnicero, S. A. (n.d.). *Reading together at Stratford*. Retrieved November 29, 2006, from http://readingtogetheratstratford.blogspot.com/

Carrell, P. J., Devine, J., & Eskey, D. (1988). *Interactive approaches to second language reading*. Cambridge: Cambridge University Press.

Carrier, M. (1991). Simulations in English language teaching: A cooperative approach. *Simulation & Gaming, 22*, 224–233.

Cary, S. (2000). *Working with second language learners: Answers to teachers' top ten questions*. Portsmouth, NH: Heinemann.

Cathcart, R., & Gumpert, G. (1994). Mediated interpersonal communication: Toward a new typology. In R. Anderson, K. N. Cissna, & R. C. Arnett (Eds.), *The reach of dialogue: Confirmation, voice, and community* (pp. 157–172). Cresskill, NJ: Hampton Press.

Cattagni, A., & Farris, E. (2001). *Internet access in US public schools and classrooms: 1994–2000*. Washington, DC: U.S. Department of Education, Office of Educational Research and Improvement.

CBS Broadcasting. (2005). *Laptops are "it" at Empire High: Arizona school goes digital facing benefits and challenges*. Retrieved February 1, 2007, from http://www.cbsnews.com/stories/2005/09/20/earlyshow/living/studyhall/main869425.shtml

Center for Electronic Studying, University of Oregon. (1999–2001). *The intersect digital library*. Retrieved December 9, 2006, from http://intersect.uoregon.edu/

Chamot, A. U. (2005). Language learning strategy instruction: Current issues and research. *Annual Review of Applied Linguistics, 25*, 112–130.

Chamot, A. U., Barnhardt, S., Ei-Dinary, P. B., & Robbins, J. (1999). *The learning strategies handbook*. New York: Longman.

Chamot, A. U., & O'Malley, J. M. (1994). *The CALLA handbook: Implementing the Cognitive Academic Language Learning Approach*. Reading, MA: Addison-Wesley.

Champeau, M., Marchi, G., & Arreaza, K. (1994). Un banco de ítems para medir la habilidad para la lectura de textos en inglés técnico y científico: Un sistema de clasificación [An item bank to measure reading ability in technical and scientific texts: A classification system]. *Argos, 20*, 27–49.

Chan, M. (2003). Technology and the teaching of oral skills. *CATESOL Journal, 15*(1), 51–56.

Chan, T.-P., & Liou, H.-C. (2005). Effects of Web-based concordancing instruction on ESL students' learning of verb-noun collocations. *Computer-Assisted Language Learning, 18*(3), 231–250.

Chapelle, C. A. (1990). The discourse of computer-assisted language learning: Toward a context for descriptive research. TESOL *Quarterly*, 24, 199–225.

Chapelle, C. A. (1995). A framework for the investigation of CALL as a context for SLA. CAELL *Journal*, 6(3), 2–8.

Chapelle, C. (1997). CALL in the year 2000: Still in search of research paradigms? *Language Learning & Technology*, 1(1), 19–43. Retrieved November 24, 2006, from http://llt.msu.edu/vol1num1/chapelle/

Chapelle, C. A. (1999). Investigation of "authentic" language learning tasks. In J. Egbert & E. Hanson-Smith (Eds.), CALL *environments* (pp. 101–115). Alexandria, VA: TESOL.

Chapelle, C. A. (2001). *Computer applications in second language acquisition: Foundations for teaching, testing, and research.* Cambridge: Cambridge University Press.

Chapelle, C. A. (2003). *English language learning and technology: Lectures on applied linguistics in the age of information and communication technology.* Amsterdam: John Benjamins.

Chapelle, C. A., Jamieson, J., & Hegelheimer, V. (2003). Validation of a Web-based ESL test. *Language Testing*, 20, 409–439.

Chapman, C., & King, R. (2005). *Differentiated assessment strategies: One tool doesn't fit all.* Thousand Oaks, CA: Corwin Press.

Chapelle, C., & Mizuno, S. (1989). Students' strategies with learner-controlled CALL. CALICO *Journal*, 7(2), 25–47. Available from https://calico.org/a-458-Students%20 Strategies%20with%20LearnerControlled%20CALL.html

Charles, M. (1996). Business negotiations: Interdependence between discourse and the business relationship. *English for Specific Purposes*, 15, 19–36.

Chaudron, C. (1988). *Second language classrooms: Research on teaching and learning.* Cambridge: Cambridge University Press.

Chen, Y., & Pauchnick, C. (2005). E-*pal connections: Uniting the world!* Retrieved November 28, 2006, from http://henry.sandi.net/staff/cpauchni/Epal%20conf%20pp.ppt

Chesebro, J. W., & Bertelsen, D. A. (1996). *Analyzing media: Communication technologies as symbolic and cognitive systems.* New York: Guilford Press.

Chicago Board of Education. (2000). *Introduction to scoring rubrics.* Retrieved December 13, 2006, from http://intranet.cps.k12.il.us/Assessments/Ideas_and_Rubrics/Intro_ Scoring/intro_scoring.html

Chickering, A., & Ehrmann, S. C. (1996, October). Implementing the seven principles: Technology as lever. AAHE *Bulletin*. Retrieved November 29, 2006, from http://www .tltgroup.org/programs/seven.html

Chinese Language Teachers Association. (2006). *Computer-assisted language learning* (CALL) *software for Chinese.* Retrieved March 8, 2007, from http://clta.osu.edu/reviews/reviews .htm

Chinn, M. D., & Fairlie, R. W. (2004). *The determinants of the global digital divide: A cross-country analysis of computer and Internet penetration.* Retrieved March 9, 2007, from http:// repositories.cdlib.org/cgi/viewcontent.cgi?article=1022&context=sccie

Chinn, M. D., & Fairlie, R. W. (2006). ICT *use in the developing world: An analysis of differences in computer and Internet penetration* (NBER Working Paper No. 12382). Cambridge, MA: National Bureau of Economic Research. Available from http://papers.nber .org/papers/w12382

Choices, Choices (Version 5.0) [Computer software]. (1997). Watertown, MA: Tom Snyder Productions. http://www.tomsnyder.com/products/product.asp?SKU=CHOCHO

Chomsky, N. (1964). *Current issues in linguistic theory.* The Hague, Netherlands: Mouton.

Chomsky, N. (1965). *Aspects of the theory of syntax.* Cambridge, MA: MIT Press.

Christopher, V. (Ed.). (2005). *Directory of teacher education programs in* TESOL *in the United States and Canada.* Alexandria, VA: TESOL.

Chun, D. (1994). Using computer networking to facilitate the acquisition of interactive competence. *System, 22,* 17–33.

Clark, D. (2003). *Blended learning.* Brighton, England: Epic Group. Retrieved February 8, 2007, from http://www.epic.co.uk/content/resources/white_papers/Epic_Whtp_blended.pdf

Clark, R. C., & Mayer, R. E. (2003). e-Learning and the science of instruction. San Francisco: Pfeiffer.

Click.TV. (n.d.). Retrieved December 30, 2006, from http://www.click.tv/

ClueFinder 4th Grade Adventures [Computer software]. (1999). San Francisco: The Learning Company/Riverdeep. http://www.learningcompany.com/jump.jsp?itemID=191&mainPID=191&itemType=PRODUCT&RS=1&keyword=clue+finder

CmapTools (Version 3.8) [Computer software]. (2005). Pensacola, FL: Institute for Human and Machine Cognition. http://cmap.ihmc.us/

CNET Networks. (2006). ZD*Net.* Retrieved November 30, 2006, from http://www.zdnet.com/

CNET Networks. (2007). *Download.com.* Retrieved April 18, 2007, from http://www.download.com/

Cobb, T. (2006). *The compleat lexical tutor.* Retrieved December 6, 2006, from http://www.lextutor.ca/

Cobb, T. (n.d.). *Necessary or nice? Computers in second language reading.* Retrieved December 7, 2006, from http://sitemaker.umich.edu/corpus_analysis_tools/files/computersinl2reading.doc

Coggins, S. A. M. (2005). *Podcast/podcasting/podcasters.* Retrieved December 29, 2006, from http://weblogs.about.com/od/weblogsglossary/g/podcasting.htm

Coleman, D. W. (1988). Simulating conversation with a PARUT. In D. Crookall, J. H. Klabbers, A. Coote, A. Cecchini, & A. Della Piane (Eds.), *Simulation-gaming in education and training: Proceedings* (pp. 67–73). Oxford: Pergamon Press.

Coleman, D. W. (2002). On foot in SimCity: Using SimCopter as the basis for an ESL writing assignment. *Simulation & Gaming, 33,* 217–230.

Coleman, D. W. (2005a, August). *A formal integrated view of speech, gesture, gaze and its implications for learning.* Paper presented at the 32nd annual conference of the Linguistic Association of Canada and the United States, Hanover, NH.

Coleman, D. W. (2005b). Language learning input and input for learning to communicate. LACUS *Forum, 31,* 203–213.

Coleman, D. W. (n.d.). *Mystery at Motel Zero.* Retrieved December 23, 2006, from http://homepages.utoledo.edu/dcolema/motelzero/

Connor, J. (n.d.). *Inequitable literacies: Myths and probabilities.* Retrieved November 24, 2006, from http://www.cdesign.com.au/proceedings_aate/aate_papers/159_connor.htm

Cononelos, T., & Oliva, M. (1993). Using computer networks to enhance foreign language/culture education. *Foreign Language Annals, 26,* 527–534.

Conrad, S. (2000). Will corpus linguistics revolutionize grammar teaching in the 21st century? TESOL *Quarterly, 34,* 548–560.

Consultants-E SL. (2004–2007). *Welcome to EduNation!* Retrieved April 25, 2007, from http://www.theconsultants-e.com/edunation/edunation.asp

Cook, G. (2002). Laptop learning. *American School Board Journal,* 189(7), 12–16. Retrieved November 26, 2006, from http://www.asbj.com/2002/07/0702coverstory.html

Corpley, A. J. (2001). *Creativity in education and learning: A guide for teachers and educators.* Sterling, VA: Stylus.

Costa, C. (2006). *English class' podcast.* Retrieved December 10, 2006, from http://dream team.podomatic.com/

Council of Europe. (2001). *A common European framework of reference for languages: Learning, teaching, assessment.* Cambridge: Cambridge University Press.

Crookall, D., & Oxford, R. (Eds.). (1990). *Simulation, gaming, and language learning.* New York: Newbury House.

Crosling, G., & Ward, I. (2002). Oral communication: The workplace needs and uses of business graduate employees. *English for Specific Purposes,* 21, 41–57.

Crown [Great Britain]. (1995–2007). *Classrooms of the future—progress.* Retrieved March 5, 2007, from http://www.teachernet.gov.uk/management/resourcesfinanceand building/schoolbuildings/sbschoolsforthefuture/futureclassrooms/progress/

Crozier, W. R. (1999). Age and individual differences in artistic productivity: Trends within a sample of British novelists. *Creativity Research Journal,* 12, 197–204.

Csikszentmihalyi, M. (1975). *Beyond boredom and anxiety.* San Francisco: Jossey-Bass.

Csikszentmihalyi, M. (1988). The flow experience and its significance for human psychology. In M. Csikszentmihalyi & I. S. Csikszentmihalyi (Eds.), *Optimal experience: Psychological studies of flow in consciousness* (pp. 15–35). New York: Cambridge University Press.

Csikszentmihalyi, M. (1990). *Flow: The psychology of optimal experience.* New York: Harper & Row.

Csikszentmihalyi, M. (1993). *The evolving self: A psychology for the third millennium.* New York: HarperPerennial.

Csikszentmihalyi, M. (1996). *Creativity: Flow and the psychology of discovery and invention.* New York: HarperCollins.

Csikszentmihalyi, M. (1997a). *Finding flow: The psychology of engagement with everyday life.* New York: HarperCollins.

Csikszentmihalyi, M. (1997b). Intrinsic motivation and effective teaching: A flow analysis. In J. L. Bess (Ed.), *Teaching well and liking it: Motivating faculty to teach effectively* (pp. 72–89). London: Johns Hopkins University Press.

Csikszentmihalyi, M., & Csikszentmihalyi, I. S. (Eds.). (1988). *Optimal experience: Psychological studies of flow in consciousness.* New York: Cambridge University Press.

Cuban, L. (1986). *Teachers and machines: The classroom use of technology since 1920.* New York: Columbia University, Teachers College Press.

Cummins, J. (1970). Cognitive/academic language proficiency, linguistic interdependence, the optimum age question and some other matters. *Working Papers on Bilingualism,* 19, 197–205.

Cummins, J. (1987). *Empowering minority students.* (Teacher Training Monograph 5). Gainesville: University of Florida.

Cummins, J., & Sayers, D. (1995). *Brave new schools: Challenging cultural illiteracy through global learning networks.* New York: St. Martin's Press.

Curran, C. A. (1976). *Counseling-learning in second languages.* Apple River, IL: Apple River Press.

Curriculum Activities Using the Computer: Language Arts [Computer software]. (2001). Huntington Beach, CA: Teacher Created Materials. http://www.teachercreated materials.com/estore/product/3480

Curtis, D. (2003, December 16). The Maine event. *Edutopia*. Retrieved November 26, 2006, from http://www.edutopia.org/php/article.php?id=Art_1119

Cyber Creations. (2001–2006). MMORPG.*com*. Retrieved December 23, 2006, from http://www.mmorpg.com/

Daiute, C. A. (1985). *Writing and computers*. Menlo Park, CA: Addison-Wesley.

Dam, L. (1995). *Learner autonomy 3: From theory to classroom practice*. Dublin, Ireland: Authentik.

Dave's ESL cafe. (1995–2007). Retrieved April 16, 2007, from http://www.eslcafe.com/

Davidson, C., & Tomic, A. (1994). Removing computer phobia from the writing classroom. *English Language Teaching Journal*, 48, 205–213.

Davies, G. (1998, July). *True creativity often starts where language ends*. Paper presented at WorldCALL 98, Melbourne, Victoria, Australia. Retrieved December 11, 2006, from http://www.camsoftpartners.co.uk/worldgd1.htm

Davis, A. (2006a, February 7). Blogging in the schools. *Edublog Insights*. Retrieved December 10, 2006, from http://anne.teachesme.com/2006/02/07#a5172

Davis, A. (2006b, February 22). Thinking about the teaching of writing. *Edublog Insights*. Retrieved December 10, 2006, from http://anne.teachesme.com/2006/02/22#a5204

Davis, J. N., & Lyman-Hager, M. A. (1997). Computers and L2 reading: Student performance, student attitudes. *Foreign Language Annals*, 30, 58–72.

Davis, R. (1998–2006). *Randall's ESL cyber listening lab*. Retrieved November 29, 2006, from http://www.esl-lab.com/

Day, R. (Ed.). (1986). *Talking to learn: Conversation in second language acquisition*. Rowley, MA: Newbury House.

Day, E., & Shapson, S. M. (1991). Integrating formal and functional approaches to language teaching in French immersion: An experimental study. *Language Learning*, 41, 25–58.

De orilla a orilla. (n.d.). Retrieved December 22, 2006, from http://www.orillas.org/welcomee.html

de Szendeffy, J. (2005). *A practical guide to using computers in language teaching*. Ann Arbor: University of Michigan Press.

Debski, R. (2006). Theory and practice in teaching project-oriented CALL. In P. Hubbard & M. Levy (Eds.), *Teacher education in CALL* (pp. 99–114). Amsterdam: John Benjamins.

Deci, E. L., & Ryan, R. M. (1985). *Intrinsic motivation and self-determination in human behavior*. London: Plenum Press.

Decisions, Decisions (Version 5.0) [Computer software]. (2001). Watertown, MA: Tom Snyder Productions. http://www.tomsnyder.com/products/product.asp?SKU=DECDEC

Decisions, Decisions: Prejudice (Version 5.0) [Computer software]. (2001). Watertown, MA: Tom Snyder Productions. http://www.tomsnyder.com/products/product.asp?SKU=DECPJD

Dede, C. (1996). The evolution of distance education: Emerging technologies and distributed learning. *American Journal of Distance Education*, 10(2), 4–36.

DeKeyser, R. (2003). Implicit and explicit learning. In C. Doughty & M. Long (Eds.), *The handbook of second language acquisition* (pp. 313–348). Malden, MA: Blackwell.

del.icio.us. (n.d.). Retrieved December 29, 2006, from http://del.icio.us/

DeMello, C. (1995–1996). College and university home pages—alphabetical listing. Retrieved November 30, 2006, from http://www.mit.edu:8001/people/cdemello/univ.html

Dersch, H. (2001). PTViewer (Version 2.4) [Computer software]. Furtwangen, Germany: Technical University.

Designing an autobiographical webpage using FrontPage 2003. (n.d.). Retrieved December 11, 2006, from http://viking.coe.uh.edu/~smarsh/fp2003/

Destination: Ocean [Computer software]. (1995). San Francisco: Edmark/Riverdeep. http://www.riverdeep.net/portal/page?_pageid=353,184442,353_184443&_dad=portal&_schema=PORTAL

Destination: Rain Forest [Computer software]. (1995). San Francisco: Edmark/Riverdeep. http://www.riverdeep.net/portal/page?_pageid=353,154348,353_154364&_dad=portal&_schema=PORTAL

Dewey, J. (1897). My pedagogic creed. *School Journal*, 54(January), 77–80. Retrieved December 9, 2006, from http://dewey.pragmatism.org/creed.htm

Dewey, J. (1933). *How we think: A restatement of the relation of reflective thinking to the educative process* (Rev. ed.). Boston: D. C. Heath.

Dewey, J. (1963). *Experience and education*. New York: Macmillan. (Original work published 1938)

Dexter, S. L., Anderson, R. E., & Becker, H. J. (1999). Teachers' views of computers as catalysts for changes in their teaching practice. *Journal of Research on Computing in Education*, 31, 221–239.

The diary project. (1998–2003). Retrieved December 15, 2006, from http://www.diaryproject.com/

Dickinson, L. (1987). *Self instruction in language learning*. Cambridge: Cambridge University Press.

Dieu, B., Campbell, A., & Ammann, R. (n.d.). *Dekita.org: EFL/ESL exchange*. Retrieved November 27, 2006, from http://dekita.org/exchange/

Digg. (2006). Retrieved December 30, 2006, from http://www.digg.com/

Discovery Communications. (2006). *Discovery.com*. Retrieved November 25, 2006, from http://www.discovery.com/

Discovery Education. (2006a). *DiscoverySchool.com*. Retrieved November 30, 2006, from http://school.discovery.com/

Discovery Education. (2006b). *DiscoverySchool.com: Teaching tools*. Retrieved December 6, 2006, from http://school.discovery.com/teachingtools/teachingtools.html

diSessa, A. (2000). *Changing minds: Computers, learning, and literacy*. Cambridge, MA: Brandford Book/MIT Press.

Distance Learning. (1998–2005). PEAK *English: The online interactive English school*. Retrieved December 8, 2006, from http://www.peakenglish.com/

Dodd, D. W. (2003, December). Technology 2004: Convergent technologies and the case for VOIP. *College Planning & Management*. Retrieved March 5, 2007, from http://www.peterli.com/archive/cpm/595.shtm

Dodge, B. (2007). *QuestGarden*. Retrieved April 15, 2007, from http://www.questgarden.com/

Dodge, B. (n.d.-a). *Site overview*. San Diego State University. Retrieved November 29, 2006, from http://webquest.sdsu.edu/overview.htm

Dodge, B. (n.d.-b). *The WebQuest page*. San Diego State University. Retrieved November 29, 2006, from http://webquest.sdsu.edu/

Donato, R., & McCormick, D. (1994). A sociocultural perspective on language learning strategies: The role of mediation. *Modern Language Journal*, 78, 453–464.

Dooly, M. (2005, March/April). The Internet and language teaching: A sure way to interculturality? ESL Magazine, 44, 8–10.

Dörnyei, Z. (2001). Teaching and researching motivation. Harlow, England: Longman.

Dörnyei, Z., & Otto, I. (1998). Motivation in action. Working Papers in Applied Linguistics, 4, 43–69.

Doughty, C., & Williams, J. (Eds.). (1998). Focus on form in classroom second language acquisition. New York: Cambridge University Press.

Douglas, D. (2000). Assessing language for specific purposes. Cambridge: Cambridge University Press.

Douglas, D. (2004). Discourse domains: The cognitive context of speaking. In D. Boxer & A. Cohen (Eds.), Studying speaking to inform second language learning (pp. 25–47). Clevedon, England: Multilingual Matters.

Dragon Naturally Speaking (Version 9) [Computer software]. (2006). Burlington, MA: Nuance Communications. http://www.nuance.com/naturallyspeaking/

Dreyfus, F. L., & Dreyfus, S. E. (1986). Mind over machine: The power of human intuition and expertise in the era of the computer. Oxford: Basil Blackwell.

Dropshots. (2007). Retrieved December 30, 2006, from http://www.dropshots.com/

Drury, R. (n.d.). Phrasal verb video dictionary. Georgia Institute of Technology. Retrieved December 10, 2006, from http://web.li.gatech.edu/~rdrury/600/oral/video/dictionary.html

Ducate, L., & Arnold, N. (Eds.). (2006). Calling on CALL: From theory and research to new directions in foreign language teaching. San Marcos, TX: CALICO.

Duff, P. A. (2000). Repetition in foreign language classroom interaction. In J. K. Hall & L. S. Verplaetse (Eds.), Second and foreign language learning through classroom interaction (pp. 109–138). Mahwah, NJ: Lawrence Erlbaum.

Duke University. (n.d.). Duke digital initiative. Retrieved April 15, 2007, from http://www.duke.edu/ddi/

Dukes, R. L., Discenza, R., & Couger, J. D. (1989). Convergent validity of four computer anxiety scales. Educational and Psychological Measurement, 49, 195–203.

Duncan, J., & Szmuch, L. (2000). Rapport with groups. Retrieved December 6, 2006, from http://www.resourcefulteaching.com.ar/articles/rapport_with_groups.pdf

Dunkel, P. (1991). Listening in the native and second/foreign language: Toward an integration of research and practice. TESOL Quarterly, 25, 431–457.

Dziuban, C., Moskal, P., & Hartman, J. (2005). Higher education, blended learning and the generations: Knowledge is power—no more. Retrieved December 29, 2006, from http://www.icindiana.org/events/Summits/it/2005/dziuban_chuck_materials/Knowledge%20is%20Power%20Oct.%2027%202004%20%20Final.doc

E ink. (1997–2005). Retrieved December 30, 2006, from http://www.eink.com/products/index.html

Earthcomber. (2003–2006a). Retrieved December 30, 2006, from http://www.earthcomber.com/

Earthcomber. (2003–2006b). Spot guides. Retrieved December 30, 2006, from http://www.earthcomber.com/comber/catalog/view.do

Ede, L., & Lunsford, A. (1984). Audience addressed/audience invoked: The role of audience in composition theory and pedagogy. College Composition and Communication, 35, 155–171.

Edelsky, C. (1991). With literacy and justice for all: Rethinking the social in language and education. London: Falmer Press.

Education World. (1996–2007). *Techtorials archive.* Retrieved February 28, 2007, from http://www.education-world.com/a_tech/archives/techtorials.shtml

Educational Testing Service. (2006a). ETS. Retrieved November 30, 2006, from http://www.ets.org/

Educational Testing Service. (2006b). TOEFL *practice online.* Retrieved November 30, 2006, from http://toeflpractice.ets.org/

Egbert, J. (1993). *Learner perceptions of computer-supported language learning environments: Analytic and systemic analyses.* Unpublished doctoral dissertation, University of Arizona, Tucson.

Egbert, J. (2003). A study of flow theory in the foreign language classroom. *Modern Language Journal,* 87, 499–518.

Egbert, J. (2005). CALL *Essentials: Principles and Practice in CALL Classrooms.* Alexandria, VA: TESOL.

Egbert, J. (2006). Learning in context: Situating language teacher learning in CALL. In P. Hubbard & M. Levy (Eds.), *Teacher education in CALL* (pp. 167–181). Amsterdam: John Benjamins.

Egbert, J. (in press). *Supporting learning with technology: Essentials of classroom practice.* Upper Saddle River, NJ: Pearson, Merrill, Prentice Hall.

Egbert, J., Paulus, T., & Nakamichi, Y. (2002). The impact of CALL instruction on classroom computer use: A foundation for rethinking technology in teacher education. *Language Learning & Technology,* 6(3), 108–126.

Egbert, J., & Petrie, G. M. (Eds.). (2005). CALL *research perspectives.* Mahwah, NJ: Lawrence Erlbaum.

Egbert, J., & Yang, D. (2004). Mediating the digital divide in CALL classrooms: Promoting effective language tasks in limited technology contexts. *ReCALL,* 16, 280–291.

Ehrmann, S. C. (1995). *Asking the right questions: What does research tell us about technology and higher learning?* Retrieved November 24, 2006, from http://www.georgetown.edu/crossroads/guide/ehrmann.html

Eini, K., & Bryant, J. (n.d.). *Friends and flags.* Retrieved December 10, 2006, from http://www.friendsandflags.org/

eKidSkills [Computer software]. (2003). The KidTools Support System. http://kidtools.missouri.edu/index.php?Content=KidSkillsPrograms

Electronic Arts. (2006). *SimCity classic live.* Retrieved December 10, 2006, from http://simcity.ea.com/play/simcity_classic.php

Electronic Arts. (2007). *The Sims2.* Retrieved April 17, 2007, from http://thesims2.ea.com/

Elias, M., & Tobias, S. (1996). *Social problem solving: Interventions in the schools.* New York: Guilford Press.

Elkhafaifi, H. (2005). Listening comprehension and anxiety in the Arabic language classroom. *Modern Language Journal,* 89, 206–220.

Ellis, N. C. (2002a). Frequency effects in language processing: A review with implications for theories of implicit and explicit language acquisition. *Studies in Second Language Acquisition,* 24, 143–188.

Ellis, N. C. (2002b). Reflections on frequency effects in language processing. *Studies in Second Language Acquisition,* 24, 297–339.

Ellis, N. C. (2005). At the interface: Dynamic interactions of explicit and implicit language knowledge. *Studies in Second Language Acquisition,* 27, 305–352.

Ellis, R. (1984). *Classroom second language development.* Oxford: Oxford University Press.

Ellis, R. (1986). *Understanding second language acquisition.* New York: Oxford University Press.

Ellis, R. (1993). Second language acquisition and the structural syllabus. TESOL Quarterly, 27, 91–113.

Ellis, R. (1994). *The study of second language acquisition.* Oxford: Oxford University Press.

Ellis, R. (2000). Task-based research and language pedagogy. *Language Teaching Research,* 4, 193–220.

Ellis, R. (2001). Introduction: Investigating form-focused instruction. *Language Learning,* 51(Special Issue), 1–46.

Ellis, R. (2003). *Task-based language learning and teaching.* Oxford: Oxford University Press.

Ellis, R., Basturkmen, H., & Loewen, S. (2001). Learner uptake in communicative ESL lessons. *Language Learning,* 51, 281–318.

ELLIS Academic (Version 3.0) [Computer software]. (2003). Salt Lake City, UT: ELLIS. http://www.ellis.com/products/academic/

Emig, J. (1977). Writing as a mode of learning. *College Composition and Communication,* 28, 122–128.

eMINTS & the Curators of the University of Missouri. (2003–2006). *eThemes.* Retrieved November 26, 2006, from http://www.emints.org/ethemes/index.shtml

Emmert, P. (2005). *Creating WebQuests.* Retrieved December 10, 2006, from http://groups .yahoo.com/group/creatingwebquests

EnchantedLearning.com. (1996–2006). *Little explorers: Picture dictionary with links.* Retrieved December 11, 2006, from http://www.enchantedlearning.com/Dictionary.html

English Discoveries (Version 2.12) [Computer software]. (2005). Rosh Ha'ayin, Israel: Edusoft. http://www.edusoft.co.il/en/products/apeed.asp

English on the Job [Computer software]. (2006). Lake Elmo, MN: Language Solutions. http://www.languagesolutionsllc.com/

EnglishNow! (Version 9) [Computer software]. (2006). Nashua, NH: Transparent Language. http://store.digitalriver.com/servlet/ControllerServlet?Action=DisplayPage& Locale=en_US&SiteID=transpar&id=ProductDetailsPage&productID=42017500

ePALS. (1996–2007). Retrieved April 15, 2007, from http://www.epals.com/

Equicast Media. (2006). *Wildvoice.* Retrieved December 9, 2006, from http://www.wild voice.com/

Ernst, G. (1994). "Talking circle": Conversation and negotiation in the ESL classroom. TESOL Quarterly, 28, 293–322.

Ertmer, P., Addison, P., Lane, M., Ross, E., & Woods, D. (1999). Examining teachers' beliefs about the role of technology in the elementary classroom. *Journal of Research on Computing in Education,* 32(1), 54–72.

Essential Tools for Teachers [Computer software]. (2001). Watertown, MA: Tom Snyder Productions. http://www.tomsnyder.com/products/product.asp?SKU=ESSCLA

European Commission. (2004). *eTwinning: School partnerships in Europe.* Retrieved December 2, 2006, from http://www.etwinning.net/ww/en/pub/etwinning/index2005.htm

Everypoint. (2006). Retrieved December 30, 2006, from http://www.everypoint.com/

eyeQ [Computer software]. (2002). Salt Lake City, UT: Infinite Mind. http://www.infmind .com/

Facebook. (2007). Retrieved April 18, 2007, from http://www.facebook.com/

Facione, P. A. (2006). *Critical thinking: What it is and why it counts.* Retrieved December 15, 2006, from http://www.insightassessment.com/pdf_files/what&why2006.pdf

Farr, R. (1992). Putting it all together: Solving the reading assessment puzzle. *The Reading Teacher, 46*, 26–37.

Fasli, M., & Michalakopoulos, M. (2006, October). Interactive game-based learning. *ALT Online Newsletter,* 6. Retrieved November 25, 2006, from http://newsletter.alt.ac.uk/e_article000678809.cfm?x=b8kyLfK,b4bwCj4b

Fazey, D., & Fazey, J. (2001). The potential for autonomy in learning. *Studies in Higher Education, 26*, 345–361.

Fearon, J. (1999). *What is identity (as we now use the word)?* Unpublished manuscript.

Feldman, A. (2004). *The present and future of educational technology: An interview with Christopher Dede.* Retrieved December 9, 2006, from http://knowledgeloom.org/gmott/cdede_intvw.html

Felix, U. (2001). *Beyond Babel: Language learning online.* Melbourne, Victoria, Australia: Language Australia.

Ferguson, C. A. (1971). Absence of copula and the notion of simplicity: A study of normal speech, baby talk, foreigner talk and pidgins. In D. Hymes (Ed.), *Pidginization and creolization of languages* (pp. 141–150). London: Cambridge University Press.

Filmedworld.com. (n.d.). Retrieved December 9, 2006, from http://www.filmedworld.com/page.php?3

Finnish National Board of Education. (n.d.). *MagazineFactory.* Retrieved December 5, 2006, from http://www2.edu.fi/magazinefactory/

Finocchiaro, M., & Brumfit, C. (1983). *The functional-notional approach: From theory to practice.* New York: Oxford University Press.

First English [Computer software]. (2006). Burlingame, CA: DynEd International .http://www.dyned.com/products/fe/

Fitzgerald, J., & Graves, M. F. (2004). *Scaffolding reading experiences for English-language learners.* Norwood, MA: Christopher-Gordon.

Fizz and Martina's Math Adventures [Computer software]. (2000). Watertown, MA: Tom Snyder Productions. http://www.tomsnyder.com/products/product.asp?SKU=FIZFIZ

Flock. (n.d.). Retrieved December 30, 2006, from http://flock.com/

Folse, K. (2004). *Vocabulary myths: Applying second language research to classroom teaching.* Ann Arbor: University of Michigan Press.

Ford, D. Y., Howard, T. C., Harris, J. J., III, & Tyson, C. A. (2000). Creating culturally responsive classrooms for gifted minority students. *Journal for the Education of the Gifted, 23*, 397–427.

Foshee, D. F. (1997). *Planning the smart classroom: A practical primer for designing interactive video learning environments.* Retrieved November 26, 2006, from http://www.ode.state.or.us/initiatives/oraccessnet/resources/classroomPlan.pdf

Fost, D. (2005, August 15). PC or not PC? *San Francisco Chronicle,* pp. E1, E6.

Fotos, S., & Browne, C. (Eds.). (2004). *New perspectives on CALL for second language classrooms.* Mahwah, NJ: Lawrence Erlbaum.

Fraser, B. (1986). *Classroom environment.* London: Croom Helm.

Freeciv (Version 2.0) [Computer software]. (2007). http://www.freeciv.org/wiki/Main_Page

Freedictionary.com. (2006). Retrieved December 10, 2006, from http://www.freedictionary.com/

Freeman, D. (1998). *Doing teacher research: From inquiry to understanding.* Pacific Grove, CA: Heinle.

Freeman, D. E., & Freeman, Y. S. (2001). *Between worlds: Access to second language acquisition* (2nd ed.). New York: Heinemann.

Freeman, D., & Freeman, Y. (2004). *Essential linguistics: What you need to know to teach reading, ESL, spelling, phonics, and grammar.* Portsmouth, NH: Heinemann.

Freeman, Y. S., & Freeman, D. (1998). *ESL/EFL teaching: Principles for success.* Portsmouth, NH: Heinemann.

Freire, P. (1970). *Pedagogy of the oppressed* (M. Bergman Ramos, Trans.). New York: Continuum.

Freire, P. (2004). *Pedagogy of indignation.* Boulder, CO: Paradigm.

Friendster. (2002–2006). Retrieved December 30, 2006, from http://www.friendster .com/

Fujiike, T. (2004). Collaborative interaction in EFL Web-based debates: How do learners develop socially constructed knowledge? *CALL-EJ Online,* 5(2).

Fulton, K., Glenn, A. D., & Valdez, G. (2004). *Teacher education and technology planning guide.* Retrieved December 7, 2006, from http://www.learningpt.org/pdfs/tech/guide.pdf

Gaer, S. (2006). *International home remedies.* Retrieved November 29, 2006, from http://www .otan.dni.us/webfarm/emailproject/rem.htm

Gaer, S. (2007). *Email projects home page.* Retrieved March 1, 2007, from http://www.otan .dni.us/webfarm/emailproject/email.htm

Gaggle.Net. (2006). Retrieved November 29, 2006, from http://gaggle.net/

Galloway, J. P. (1996). How teachers use and learn to use computers. *Technology and Teacher Education Annual,* 1997, 857–859.

Gamecomm. (n.d.). Retrieved March 5, 2007, from http://www.game-comm.org/

Garcez, P. M. (1993). Point-making styles in cross-cultural business negotiations: A microethnographic study. *English for Specific Purposes,* 12, 103–120.

Gardner, R. C., & Lalonde, R. (1990). Social psychological considerations. In D. Crookall & R. Oxford (Eds.), *Simulation, gaming, and language learning* (pp. 215–221). New York: Newbury House.

Garfinkle, H. (1967). *Studies in ethnomethodology.* Englewood Cliffs, NJ: Prentice-Hall.

Garrison, J. W., & Rud, A. G. (1995). *The educational conversation: Closing the gap.* Albany: State University of New York Press.

Garry, A. (2001). Project-based learning just became easy: An introduction to Web-Quests. *Learning Technology,* 3(3). Retrieved December 10, 2006, from http://lttf.ieee .org/learn_tech/issues/july2001/index.html#2

Garton, J. (1996). Interactive concordancing with a specialist corpus. *On-CALL,* 10(1), 8–14.

Gass, S. M., & Madden, C. G. (Eds.). (1985). *Input in second language acquisition.* Rowley, MA: Newbury House.

Gather. (2006). Retrieved December 30, 2006, from http://gather.com/

Gattegno, C. (1972). *Teaching foreign languages in schools: The silent way* (2nd ed.). New York: Educational Solutions.

Gay, G. (1975). Organizing and designing culturally pluralistic curriculum. *Educational Leadership,* 33(3), 176–183.

Gay, G. (2000). *Culturally responsive teaching: Theory, research, and practice.* New York: Teachers College Press.

Gee, J. P. (1992). *The social mind: Language, ideology, and social practice.* New York: Bergin & Garvey.

Geertz, C. (1973). *The interpretation of cultures.* New York: Basic Books.

Gen, R. (2000). *Technology and multiple intelligences.* Retrieved December 29, 2006, from http://www.usdla.org/html/journal/MAY00_Issue/story02.htm

Genesee, F., & Upshur, J. A. (1996). *Classroom-based evaluation in second language education.* Cambridge: Cambridge University Press.

George Lucas Educational Foundation. (2006). *Project-based learning research.* Retrieved November 25, 2006, from http://www.edutopia.org/php/article.php?id=Art_887&key=037

Georgia College and State University. (2006). *Apple + iPods @ GCSU.* Retrieved March 5, 2007, from http://ipod.gcsu.edu/

Gibbs, L. (2006). *Internet assignment: Publishing webpages.* Retrieved December 11, 2006, from http://www.mythfolklore.net/3043mythfolklore/weeks/week02/internet.htm

Giles, H., & Smith, P. (1979). Accommodation theory: Optimal levels of convergence. In H. Giles & R. St. Clair (Eds.), *Language and social psychology* (pp. 45–65). Oxford: Basil Blackwell.

Gimenez, J. C. (2001). Ethnographic observations in cross-cultural business negotiations between non-native speakers of English: An exploratory study. *English for Specific Purposes, 20,* 169–193.

Giroux, H. A. (1996). *Living dangerously: Multiculturalism and the politics of difference.* New York: Peter Lang.

Gliffy. (n.d.). Retrieved December 1, 2006, from http://gliffy.com/

Global SchoolNet. (2000a). *The global schoolhouse.* Retrieved November 29, 2006, from http://www.globalschoolnet.org/GSH/index.html

Global SchoolNet. (2000b). *Harnessing the power of the Web: A tutorial.* Retrieved November 30, 2006, from http://www.gsn.org/web/index.html

The GLOBE program. (n.d.). Retrieved November 26, 2006, from http://www.globe.gov/

GO Solve Word Problems [Computer software]. (2006). Watertown, MA: Tom Snyder Productions. http://www.tomsnyder.com/products/product.asp?SKU=GOSGOS

Godwin-Jones, R. (2003). Blogs and wikis: Environments for online collaboration. *Language Learning & Technology, 7*(2), 12–16.

Godwin-Jones, R. (2004). Language in action: From WebQuests to virtual realities. *Language Learning & Technology, 8*(3), 9–14.

Godwin-Jones, R. (2005). Emerging technologies: Skype and podcasting: Disruptive technologies for language learning. *Language Learning & Technology, 9*(3), 9–12. Retrieved December 6, 2006, from http://llt.msu.edu/vol9num3/emerging/default.html

Goforth, D. (1994). Learner control = decision making + information: A model and meta-analysis. *Journal of Educational Computing Research, 11*(1), 1–26.

Gomez, L., Parker, R., Lara-Alecio, R., Ochoa, S., & Gomez, R. (1996). Naturalistic language assessment of LEP students in classroom interactions. *The Bilingual Research Journal, 20,* 69–92.

González, D. (2003). Teaching and learning through chat: A taxonomy of educational chat for EFL/ESL. *Teaching English with Technology, 3*(4). Retrieved December 6, 2006, from http://www.iatefl.org.pl/call/j_review15.htm

González, D. (2004). *Dilemas de la evaluación del aprendizaje de Inglés con Propósitos Específicos a través de soportes electrónicos: Estudio de un caso* [Dilemma in the evaluation of English for specific purposes through electronic supports: A case study]. Unpublished doctoral dissertation, Universitat de València, Spain.

González, D. (2005). Blended learning offers the best of both worlds. *Essential Teacher, 2*(4), 42–45.

González, D. (2006). Using synchronous communication collaboratively in ESP. In E. Hanson-Smith & S. Rilling (Eds.), *Learning languages through technology* (pp. 11–24). Alexandria, VA: TESOL.

González, D., & Almeida d'Eça, T. (2004). *Becoming a Webhead*. Retrieved December 22, 2006, from http://80.60.224.77/dyg/baw-05/

González, D., & St. Louis, R. (2002). Content-based English for specific purposes course design: The case of English for architecture. In J. Crandall & D. Kaufman (Eds.), *Content-based instruction in higher education settings* (pp. 93–106). Alexandria, VA: TESOL.

Goodwin, C. (1994). Professional vision. *American Anthropologist, 96,* 606–633.

Google. (1999–2006). *Blogger.* Retrieved December 8, 2006, from http://www.blogger.com/

Google. (2006). *Gmail.* Retrieved November 29, 2006, from http://mail.google.com

Google. (2007a). Retrieved March 7, 2007, from http://www.google.com/

Google. (2007b). *Google docs and spreadsheets.* Retrieved March 7, 2007, from http://docs.google.com/

Google. (2007c). *Google groups.* Retrieved November 29, 2006, from http://groups.google.com

Google. (2007d). *Google image search.* Retrieved April 16, 2007, from http://images.google.com/

Google. (2007e). *Google maps.* Retrieved April 16, 2007, from http://maps.google.com/

Google. (2007f). *Google scholar.* Retrieved March 7, 2007, from http://scholar.google.com/

Google Earth (Release 4) [Computer software]. (2007). Mountain View, CA: Google. http://earth.google.com/

Gordon, R. (1998, January). Balancing real-world problems with real-world results [Electronic version]. *Phi Delta Kappan, 79,* 390–393.

Gouglas, S., Sinclair, S., Ellefson, O., & Sharplin, S. (2006). *Neverwinter Nights* in Alberta: Conceptions of narrativity through fantasy role-playing games in a graduate classroom. *Innovate, 3*(2). Available from http://innovateonline.info/index.php?view=article&id=172

Grabe, W., & Stoller, F. L. (1997). Content-based instruction: Research foundations. In M. A. Snow & D. M. Brinton (Eds.), *The content-based classroom: Perspectives on integrating language and content* (pp. 5–21). New York: Longman.

Grade Machine (Version 6.9.5) [Computer software]. (2005). Lynnwood, WA: Misty City Software. http://support.mistycity.com/downloadViewer.asp?RecordID=23287

Grammar for the Real World [Computer software]. (1998). Los Angeles: Knowledge Adventure. http://www.knowledgeadventureschool.com/catalog/grw.aspx

Grant, C. A., & Lei, J. L. (Eds.). (2001). *Global constructions of multicultural education: Theories and realities.* Mahwah, NJ: Lawrence Erlbaum.

Gray, R., & Stockwell, G. (1998). Using computer mediated communication for language and culture acquisition. *On-CALL, 12*(3), 2–9.

Green, J. L., & Meyer, L. A. (1991). The embeddedness of reading in classroom life: Reading as a situated process. In C. D. Baker & A. Luke (Eds.), *Towards a critical sociology of reading pedagogy* (pp. 141–160). Amsterdam: John Benjamins.

Gregersen, T., & Horwitz, E. K. (2002). Language learning and perfectionism: Anxious and non-anxious learners' reactions to their own oral performance. *Modern Language Journal, 86,* 562–570.

Grigorescu, C., & Dwyer, E. (2005, April). A K–12 *academic word list*. Paper presented at the 39th Annual TESOL Convention and Exhibit, San Antonio, TX.

Groleau, R. (2001a). *Dig and deduce*. Retrieved December 19, 2006, from http://www.pbs .org/wgbh/nova/neanderthals/dig.html

Groleau, R. (2001b). *Illuminating photosynthesis*. Retrieved December 19, 2006, from http://www.pbs.org/wgbh/nova/methuselah/photosynthesis.html

Groleau, R. (2001c). *Inside the jet stream*. Retrieved December 19, 2006, from http://www .pbs.org/wgbh/nova/vanished/jetstream.html

Gromik, N. (2006a). ESL/EFL *student video production*. Retrieved March 13, 2007, from http://groups.yahoo.com/group/EVOvideo07/

Gromik, N. (2006b). Meaningful tasks with video in the ESOL classroom. In E. Hanson-Smith & S. Rilling (Eds.), *Learning languages through technology* (pp. 109–123). Alexandria, VA: TESOL.

Group Technologies. (n.d.). *Groupboard*. Retrieved November 21, 2006, from http://www .groupboard.com/

Guha, S. (2003). Are we all technically prepared? Teachers' perspective on the causes of comfort or discomfort in using computers at elementary grade teaching. *Information Technology in Childhood Education* Annual, 317–349.

Guilford, J. P. (1976). Intellectual factors in productive thinking. In R. Mooney & T. Rayik (Eds.), *Explorations in creativity* (pp. 95–106). New York: Harper & Row.

Guiora, A., Beit-Hallahmi, B., Brannon, R., Dull, C., & Scovel, T. (1972). The effects of experimentally induced changes in ego states on pronunciation ability in a second language: An exploratory study. *Comprehensive Psychiatry*, 13, 421–428.

Gumperz, J. J. (1982). *Discourse strategies*. Cambridge: Cambridge University Press.

Haas, M. (2000). *Thematic, communicative language teaching in the K–8 classroom*. Retrieved December 21, 2006, from http://www.eric.ed.gov/ERICWebPortal/contentdelivery/ servlet/ERICServlet?accno=ED444380 (ERIC Document Reproduction Service No. ED444380)

Hakuta, K. (1985). Cognitive development in bilingual instruction. In R. Eshch & J. Provinzano (Eds.), *Issues in English language development* (pp. 63–67). Rosslyn, VA: National Clearinghouse for Bilingual Education.

Hakuta, K. (1986). *Mirror of language: The debate on bilingualism*. New York: Basic Books.

Hakuta, K., & Diaz, R. (1985). The relationship between degree of bilingualism and cognitive ability: A critical discussion of some new longitudinal data. In K. E. Nelson (Ed.), *Children's language* (Vol. 5, pp. 319–344). Hillsdale, NJ: Lawrence Erlbaum.

Hall, C., & Lee, D. S. (2006). Creating "quick-and-dirty" corpora with search engines. *Essential Teacher*, 3(2), 38–41.

Hall, E. (1990). *Understanding cultural differences*. Yarmouth, ME: Intercultural Press.

Hall, J. K., & Verplaetse, L. S. (Eds.). (2000). *Second and foreign language learning through classroom interaction*. Mahwah, NJ: Lawrence Erlbaum.

Hamp-Lyons, L. (2000). Social, professional, and individual responsibility in language testing. *System*, 28, 579–591.

Haney, W., & Madaus, G. (1989). Searching for alternatives to standardized tests: Whys, whats, and whithers. *Phi Delta Kappan*, 70, 683–687.

Hansen, J. (1998). *When learners evaluate*. Portsmouth, NH: Heinemann.

Hanson, G. (2000–2006). *English on-line: EFL/ESL resources*. Université de Franche-Comté. Retrieved November 29, 2006, from http://cla.univ-fcomte.fr/english/index_s.htm

Hanson-Smith, E. (1991). *How to set up a computer lab: Advice for the beginner.* Houston, TX: Athelstan.

Hanson-Smith, E. (1997). Multimedia projects for EFL/ESL students. *CAELL Journal,* 7(4), 3–12. [Available from the author]

Hanson-Smith, E. (2003). Reading electronically: Challenges and responses to the reading puzzle in technologically-enhanced environments. *The Reading Matrix,* 3(3). Retrieved December 19, 2006, from http://www.readingmatrix.com/articles/hanson-smith/index.html

Hanson-Smith, E. (2004–2006). *Virtual=real.* Retrieved December 6, 2006, from http://ehansonsmith.blogspot.com/

Hanson-Smith, E. (2006a). Communities of practice for pre- and in-service teacher education. In P. Hubbard & M. Levy (Eds.), *Teacher education in CALL* (pp. 301–315). Philadelphia: John Benjamins.

Hanson-Smith, E. (2006b). *Community of practice resources.* California State University, Sacramento. Retrieved December 14, 2006, from http://webpages.csus.edu/~hansonsm/CoP_Resources.html

Hanson-Smith, E. (2006c, April). *Video online.* Presentation at CATESOL 2006, San Francisco. Retrieved March 6, 2007, from http://www.geocities.com/ehansonsmi/video_references.html

Hanson-Smith, E., & Bauer-Ramazani, C. (2004). Professional development: The Electronic Village Online of the TESOL CALL Interest Section. *TESL-EJ,* 8(2). Retrieved November 26, 2006, from http://www-writing.berkeley.edu/TESL-EJ/ej30/int.html

Hanson-Smith, E., & Rilling, S. (Eds.). (2006). *Learning languages through technology.* Alexandria, VA: TESOL.

Harasim, L., Hiltz, S. R., Teles, L., & Turoff, M. (1995). *Learning networks: A field guide to teaching and learning online.* Cambridge, MA: MIT Press.

Hare, A. P., Blumberg, H. H., Davies, M. F., & Kent, M. V. (1994). *Small group research: A handbook.* Norwood, NJ: Ablex.

Harris, N. (2006). *Speech recognition: Considerations for use in language training.* Retrieved December 9, 2006, from http://dyned.com/about/speech.shtml

Hart, M. (2006). *Project Gutenberg.* Retrieved December 30, 2006, from http://www.gutenberg.org/wiki/Main_Page

Hatch, E. (1978a). Acquisition of syntax in a second language. In J. C. Richards (Ed.), *Understanding second and foreign language learning* (pp. 34–70). Rowley, MA: Newbury House.

Hatch, E. (1978b). Discourse analysis and second language acquisition. In E. Hatch (Ed.), *Second language acquisition: A book of readings* (pp. 401–435). Rowley, MA: Newbury House.

Hatch, E. (1983). Simplified input and second language acquisition. In R. W. Andersen (Ed.), *Pidginization and creolization as language acquisition* (pp. 64–86). Rowley, MA: Newbury House.

Hayden, D. (2006). *Come visit Wisconsin!* Retrieved November 25, 2006, from http://people.uwec.edu/HAYDENDA/pbl/wisconsinpbl.htm

Haynes, J. (1998–2006). *Teaching tips.* Retrieved November 30, 2006, from http://www.everythingesl.net/inservices/

Haythornthwaite, C., & Kazmer, M. M. (2002). Bringing the Internet home: Adult distance learners and their Internet, home and work worlds. In B. Wellman & C. Haythornthwaite (Eds.), *The Internet in everyday life* (pp. 431–463). Malden, MA: Blackwell.

Healey, D. (1992). Theory and practice in a learning center. CAELL Journal, 3(3), 28–36.

Healey, D. (1993). Learner choices in self-directed second-language learning. Dissertation Abstracts International, 54 (4-A). (UMI No. 9322023)

Healey, D. (1995). Something to do on Tuesday. Houston, TX: Athelstan.

Healey, D. (Ed.). (2006). TESOL CALL Interest Section software list. Retrieved December 9, 2006, from http://oregonstate.edu/dept/eli/softlist/

Heinze, K. M. (2005, April). The language of math. Paper presented at the 39th Annual TESOL Convention and Exhibit, San Antonio, TX.

Henning, G. (1986). Item banking via dBase II: The UCLA ESL Proficiency Examination experience. In C. W. Stansfield (Ed.), Technology in language testing (pp. 69–77). Washington, DC: TESOL.

Henrichsen, L. E. (Ed.). (2001). Distance-learning programs. Alexandria, VA: TESOL.

Hernández-Márquez, B. (2006). Mexican immigration to the USA. Retrieved December 10, 2006, from http://www.youtube.com/watch?v=5hjmuFrT0HU

Herring, S. C. (Ed.). (1996). Computer-mediated communication: Linguistic, social and cross-cultural perspectives. Philadelphia: John Benjamins.

Herschensohn, J. (1994). Balancing assessment procedures in evaluation of foreign language skills. Journal of General Education, 43, 134–146.

Hetherington, M. (2006). How to set up a student centered classroom blog. Retrieved December 10, 2006, from http://mhetherington.net/blogs/?p=8

Heydenberk, W., & Heydenberk, R. (2000). A powerful peace: The integrative classroom. Needham Heights, MA: Allyn & Bacon.

Hiemstra, R., & Brockett, R. G. (Eds.). (1994). Overcoming resistance to self-direction in adult learning. San Francisco: Jossey-Bass.

Hinkel, E. (2006). Current perspectives on teaching the four skills. TESOL Quarterly, 40, 109–131.

Hinton, B. L. (1968). A model for the study of creative problem solving. Journal of Creative Behavior, 2(2), 133–142.

Hofstede, G. (2001). Culture's consequences: Comparing values, behaviors, institutions and organizations across nations. Thousand Oaks, CA: Sage.

Høier, S., & Hoem, J. (n.d.). How to videoblog with Blogger. Norwegian University of Science and Technology. Retrieved December 5, 2006, from http://www.infodesign.no/artikler/Videoblog_with_Blogger_211004.html

Holec, H. (1980). Learner training: Meeting needs in self-directed learning. In H. B. Altman & C. V. James (Eds.), Foreign language learning: Meeting individual needs (pp. 30–45). Oxford: Pergamon.

Holec, H. (1981). Autonomy and foreign language learning. Oxford: Pergamon.

Holliday, A. (2003). Social autonomy: Addressing the dangers of culturism in TESOL. In D. Palfreyman & R. C. Smith (Eds.), Learner autonomy across cultures (pp. 110–126). New York: Palgrave Macmillan.

Holliday, L. (1993, October). A comparison of cross-sentential cues to second language syntax in the negotiated interactions of NS-NNS and NNS-NNS dyads. Paper presented at the Linguistics Symposium, Milwaukee, WI.

Holliday, L. (1994, August). Dictogloss: Opportunities to practise known forms and acquire new ones through student negotiations and teacher support. Paper presented at Victorian Association of TESOL and Multicultural Education (VATME) Practical Mini-Conference on

Promoting diversity in TESOL, LOTE, Multicultural Education and Adult Literacy, Brunswick, Victoria, Australia.

Holliday, L. (1995a, January). *International ESL/EFL email student discussion lists for language practice with a purpose and a peer audience.* Paper presented at the Thai TESOL 15th Annual Convention, Bangkok.

Holliday, L. (1995b). Literacy and networked computers. *Singapore Book World, 25,* 33–150.

Holliday, L. (1996). From CALL to CMC in ESL: Approaching communicative language teaching ideals. In P. Clarkson & R. Toomey (Eds.), *Computing across the secondary curriculum: A review of research* (pp. 141–182). Melbourne, Victoria, Australia: National Professional Development Program.

Holliday, L. (1997, January). *The grammar of second language learners of English email messages.* Paper presented at the 17th Annual Thai TESOL International Conference and the First Pan-Asian Conference, Bangkok.

Holliday, L. (1998). The grammar of second language learners of English email messages. In S. Jager, J. Nerbonne, & A. J. Van Essen (Eds.), *Language teaching and language technology* (pp. 136-145). Lisse, Netherlands: Swets & Zeitlinger.

Hollywood [Computer software]. (1995). Watertown, MA: Tom Snyder Productions/ Grolier. http://www.tomsnyder.com/products/product.asp?SKU=HOLHOL

Hollywood High [Computer software]. (1995). Watertown, MA: Tom Snyder Productions/Grolier. http://www.tomsnyder.com/products/product.asp?SKU=HOLHIG

Holmes, J. (2004). When small talk is a big deal: Sociolinguistic challenges in the workplace. In M. H. Long (Ed.), *Second language needs analysis* (pp. 344–371). Cambridge: Cambridge University Press.

Holmes, M. (n.d.). *The evil landlady action maze.* Retrieved December 7, 2006, from http://www.englishlearner.com/llady/llady1.htm

Holosonic Research Labs. (1999–2005). *Audio spotlight.* Retrieved December 30, 2006, from http://www.holosonics.com/

Holotouch. (2006). Retrieved November 21, 2006, from http://www.holotouch.com/

Holum, A., & Gahala, J. (2001). *Critical issue: Using technology to enhance literacy instruction.* Retrieved November 24, 2006, from http://www.ncrel.org/sdrs/areas/issues/content/cntareas/reading/li300.htm

Honebein, P. C. (1996). Seven goals for the design of constructivist learning environments. In B. G. Wilson (Ed.), *Constructivist learning environments: Case studies in instructional design* (pp. 11–24). Englewood Cliffs, NJ: Educational Technology.

Hoppe, M. H. (2004). Geert Hofstede's cultural consequences: International differences in work-related values. *Academy of Management Executive, 18*(1), 73–74.

Horn, R. (1998). *Visual language: Global communication for the 21st century.* Bainbridge Island, WA: MacroVU.

Horowitz, D. M. (1986). Process, not product: Less than meets the eye. *TESOL Quarterly, 20,* 141–144.

Hoshi, M. (2002). Practices, beliefs and perceptions of Japanese EFL self-access learners toward Internet-based language learning. *CALL-EJ Online, 4*(1). Retrieved January 25, 2007, from http://www.tell.is.ritsumei.ac.jp/callejonline/journal/4-1/hoshi.html

Hot Potatoes users. (2006). Retrieved December 14, 2006, from http://groups.yahoo.com/group/hotpotatoesusers

Howard, G. S. (1986). *Computer anxiety and the use of microcomputers in management.* Ann Arbor: University of Michigan Research Press.

Howard, T. C. (2003). Culturally relevant pedagogy: Ingredients for critical teacher reflection. *Theory Into Practice*, 42, 195–202.

Huang, H. (2006). *Explicit learning or teaching: The effect of self-generated elaborations on EFL in China*. Unpublished doctoral thesis, La Trobe University, Melbourne, Victoria, Australia.

Hubbard, P. (1991). Evaluating computer games for language learning. *Simulation & Gaming*, 22, 220–223.

Hubbard, P. (2002). Interactive participatory dramas for learning. *Simulation & Gaming*, 33, 210–216.

Hubbard, P. (2004). Learner training for effective use of CALL. In S. Fotos & C. M. Browne (Eds.), *New perspectives on CALL for second language classrooms* (pp. 45–68). London: Lawrence Erlbaum.

Hubbard, P., & Levy, M. (2006). The scope of CALL education. In P. Hubbard & M. Levy (Eds.), *Teacher education in CALL* (pp. 3–21). Amsterdam: John Benjamins.

Hudiburg, R. A. (1989). Psychology of computer use: XVII. The computer technology hassles scale: Revision, reliability, and some correlates. *Psychological Reports*, 65, 1387–1394.

Hudiburg, R. A. (1990). Relating computer-associated stress to computerphobia. *Psychological Reports*, 67, 311–314.

Hudson, T. (2005). Trends in assessment scales and criterion-referenced language assessment. *Annual Review of Applied Linguistics*, 25, 205–227.

Huh, K. (2005). *The role of CALL in the language learning and creative thinking development of ESL students*. Unpublished doctoral dissertation, Washington State University, Pullman.

Huitt, W. (2002). Social cognition. *Educational Psychology Interactive*. Valdosta, GA: Valdosta State University. Retrieved November 24, 2006, from http://chiron.valdosta.edu/whuitt/col/soccog/soccog.html

Huitt, W. (2004). Observational (social) learning: An overview. *Educational Psychology Interactive*. Valdosta, GA: Valdosta State University. Retrieved November 24, 2006, from http://chiron.valdosta.edu/whuitt/col/soccog/soclrn.html

Hurley, S., & Tinajero, J. (2001). *Literacy assessment of second language learners*. Boston: Allyn & Bacon.

Hwu, F. (2003). Learner's behaviors in computer-based input activities elicited through tracking technologies. *Computer Assisted Language Learning*, 16, 5–29.

Hyland, K. (1993). Language-learning simulations: A practical guide. *Forum*, 31(4), 16. Retrieved December 23, 2006, from http://exchanges.state.gov/forum/vols/vol31/no4/p16.htm

Hymes, D. (1962). The ethnography of speaking. In T. Gladwin & W. C. Sturdevant (Eds.), *Anthropology and human behaviour* (pp. 15–53). Washington, DC: Anthropological Society of Washington. (Reprinted in *Readings in the sociology of language*, pp. 99–138, by J. A. Fishman, Ed., 1968, The Hague: Mouton)

Hymes, D. (1972). *On communicative competence*. Philadelphia: University of Pennsylvania Press. (Reprinted in part in *Sociolinguistics*, pp. 269–293, by J. B. Pride & J. Holmes, Eds., Harmondsworth, England: Penguin)

HyperStudio (Version 4.5) [Computer software]. (2005). Elgin, IL: Sunburst Technology. http://www.hyperstudio.com/

I Spy School Days [Computer software]. (2000). New York: Scholastic. http://shop.scholastic.com/webapp/wcs/stores/servlet/ProductDisplay_16222_-1_10101_10004

I Spy Spooky Mansion [Computer software]. (1999). New York: Scholastic. http://shop
.scholastic.com/webapp/wcs/stores/servlet/ProductDisplay_27780_-1_10101_10004

I Spy Treasure Hunt [Computer software]. (2001). New York: Scholastic. http://shop
.scholastic.com/webapp/wcs/stores/servlet/ProductDisplay_58838_-1_10101_10004

IATEFL Poland. (2002). *Internet lesson plans.* Retrieved November 30, 2006, from http://
www.iatefl.org.pl/call/j_lesson10.htm

ICT4LT Project. (1999–2006). ICT4LT: *Information and communications technologies for language
teachers.* Retrieved December 14, 2006, from http://www.ict4lt.org/

IDE. (2005). *Great sites for educators: Links archive.* Retrieved November 25, 2006, from
http://www.idecorp.com/bookmark.htm

iEARN. (2004). *MovingVoices: Join in.* Retrieved November 24, 2006, from http://
movingvoices.iearn.org/join.shtml

iEARN. (n.d.). *MovingVoices.* Retrieved November 24, 2006, from http://www.iearn.org/
projects/movingvoices.html

iEARN: *International education and resource network.* (n.d.). Retrieved December 15, 2006,
from http://www.iearn.org/

Illinois Mathematics and Science Academy. (1993–2006). *Problem-based learning network @
IMSA.* Retrieved November 25, 2006, from http://www2.imsa.edu/programs/pbln/

iMovie HD (Version 6) [Computer software]. (2006). Cupertino, CA: Apple Computer.
http://www.apple.com/ilife/imovie/

Inspiration (Version 8) [Computer software]. (2006). Beaverton, OR: Inspiration Software. http://www.inspiration.com/productinfo/inspiration/index.cfm

Internet archive. (n.d.). Retrieved December 5, 2006, from http://www.archive.org/

The Internet TESL Journal. (1995–2007a). Retrieved March 7, 2007, from http://iteslj
.org/

The Internet TESL Journal. (1995–2007b). ESL: *Student projects.* Retrieved April 18, 2007,
from http://iteslj.org/links/ESL/Student_Projects/

Internicity. (1999–2006). *Quicktopic document review.* Retrieved December 29, 2006, from
http://www.quicktopic.com/documentcollaboration/

IO2 Technology. (2005). *Overview.* Retrieved December 30, 2006, from http://www
.io2technology.com/

ISTE NETS Project. (2000–2005a). *Educational technology standards and performance indicators for all teachers.* Retrieved December 14, 2006, from http://cnets.iste.org/teachers/
t_stands.html

ISTE NETS Project. (2000–2005b). NETS *resources.* Retrieved December 14, 2006, from
http://cnets.iste.org/teachers/t_resources.html

ISTE NETS Project. (2000–2005c). *Technology foundation standards for all students.* Retrieved
January 22, 2007, from http://www.cnets.iste.org/students/s_stands.html

Izumi, S. (2002). Output, input enhancement, and the noticing hypothesis. *Studies in
Second Language Acquisition, 24,* 541–577.

Jacoby, S. (1998). *Science as performance: Socializing scientific discourse through conference
talk rehearsals.* Unpublished doctoral dissertation, University of California, Los
Angeles.

Jain, A. (2005, October 13). India's rural majority gets connected. *Financial Times.*
Retrieved November 21, 2006, from http://news.ft.com/cms/s/391a5da6-3bfa-11da-
94fb-00000e2511c8.html

James, E. (2001, January). Learning to bridge the digital divide. OECD *Observer.* Retrieved

December 7, 2006, from http://www.oecdobserver.org/news/fullstory.php/aid/408/
Learning_to_bridge_the_digital_divide.html

Jamieson, J., & Chapelle, C. (1987). Working styles on computers as evidence of second
language learning strategies. *Language Learning*, 37, 523–544.

Jamieson, J., & Chapelle, C. (2006). *Empirical evaluation of CALL use for ESL students' learning processes and outcomes* (TIRF Priority Research Grant: Final Report). Birmingham,
AL: The International Research Foundation.

Jamieson, J., Chapelle, C. A., & Preiss, S. (2005). CALL evaluation by developers, a
teacher, and students. *CALICO Journal*, 23(1), 93–138.

Jamieson-Proctor, R., & Burnett, P. C. (2002). Elementary students, creativity, and technology: Investigation of an intervention designed to enhance personal creativity.
Computers in the Schools, 1(1/2), 33–48.

Jeon-Ellis, G., Debski, R., & Wigglesworth, G. (2005). Oral interaction around computers
in the project-oriented CALL classroom. *Language Learning & Technology*, 9(3), 121–145.
Retrieved December 20, 2006, from http://llt.msu.edu/vol9num3/jeon/

Jepson, K. (2005). Conversations—and negotiated interaction—in text and voice chat
rooms. *Language Learning & Technology*, 9(3), 79–98.

Jewell, M. (2006). Real-world contexts, skills, and service learning for secondary school
language learners. In E. Hanson-Smith & S. Rilling (Eds.), *Learning languages through
technology* (pp. 175–186). Alexandria, VA: TESOL.

Jiang, W., & Ramsay, G. (2005). Rapport-building through CALL in teaching Chinese as
a foreign language: An exploratory study. *Language Learning & Technology*, 9(2), 47–63.
Retrieved December 20, 2006, from http://llt.msu.edu/vol9num2/jiang/

Johanesen, K. J., & Tennyson, R. D. (1983). Effect of adaptive advisement on perception in learner-controlled, computer-based instruction using a rule-learning task.
Educational Communication and Technology, 31, 226–236.

Johns, A. M. (1986). Coherence and academic writing: Some definitions and suggestions for teaching. *TESOL Quarterly*, 20, 247–265.

Johns, T. (1991). Should you be persuaded: Two examples of data-driven learning.
ELR Journal, 4, 1–16.

Johnson, A. (2000). *Up and out: Using creative and critical thinking skills to enhance learning.*
Needham Heights, MA: Allyn & Bacon.

Johnson, D. (1991). *Approaches to research in second language learning.* New York:
Longman.

Johnson, D. W., Johnson, R. T., & Smith, K. A. (1991). *Active learning: Cooperation in the
college classroom.* Edina, MN: Interaction Books.

Johnson, K. (1995). *Understanding communication in second language classrooms.* New York:
Cambridge University Press.

Johnson, W. L., Beal, C., Fowles-Winkler, A., Lauper, U., Marsella, S., Narayanan, S.,
et al. (2004). *Tactical language training system: An interim report.* Retrieved December
23, 2006, from http://twiki.isi.edu/twiki/pub/TACTLANG/ProjectReports/TLTSITS
2004published.pdf

Johnston, B. (2003). *Values in English language teaching.* Mahwah, NJ: Lawrence
Erlbaum.

Jonassen, D. H., Peck, K. L., & Wilson, B. G. (1999). *Learning with technology: A constructivist
perspective.* Upper Saddle River, NJ: Prentice Hall.

Jones, B. F., Valdez, G., Nowakowski, J., & Rasmussen, C. (1995). *New times demand new ways of learning*. Retrieved November 24, 2006, from http://www.netc.org/cdrom/plug_in/html/newtimes.htm

Jones, C. (1986). It's not so much the program, more what you do with it: The importance of methodology in CALL. *System*, 14, 171–178.

Jones, K. (1982). *Simulations for language learning*. New York: Cambridge University Press.

Jordan, G. (1992). Exploiting computer-based simulations for language-learning purposes. *Simulation & Gaming*, 23, 88–98.

Jourdenais, R., Ota, M., Stauffer, S., Boyson, B., & Doughty, C. (1995). Does textual enhancement promote noticing? A think aloud protocol analysis. In R. Schmidt (Ed.), *Attention and awareness in foreign language learning* (pp. 183–216). Honolulu: University of Hawai'i Press.

Just Grandma and Me [Computer software]. (n.d.). San Francisco: Riverdeep. http://www.riverdeep.net/portal/page?_pageid=353,143803,353_143804&_dad=portal&_schema=PORTAL

Kamida. (2007). *Socialight*. Retrieved April 25, 2007, from http://socialight.com/

Karchmer, R. A. (2001). The journey ahead: Thirteen teachers report how the Internet influences literacy and literacy instruction in their K–12 classrooms. *Reading Research Quarterly*, 36, 442–466. Retrieved December 19, 2006, from http://www.reading.org/Library/Retrieve.cfm?D=10.1598/RRQ.36.4.5&F=RRQ-36-4-Karchmer.pdf

KartOO Technologies. (n.d.). *KartOO*. Retrieved November 30, 2006, from http://www.kartoo.com/

Katz, J. E., & Rice, R. E. (2002). Access and digital divide examples. In *Social consequences of Internet use: Access, involvement, and interaction* (pp. 83–99). Cambridge, MA: MIT Press.

Kelly, C. (2003a). *Charles Kelly's online quiz generator*. Retrieved December 16, 2006, from http://a4esl.org/c/qw.html

Kelly, C. I. (2003b). *Flash hangman games for ESL students*. Retrieved December 13, 2006, from http://www.manythings.org/hmf/

Kelly, C. I., & Kelly, L. E. (1997–2006). *Interesting things for ESL students*. Retrieved November 29, 2006, from http://www.manythings.org/

Kelm, O. (1992). The use of synchronous computer networks in second language instruction: A preliminary report. *Foreign Language Annals*, 25, 441–454.

Kelman, P. (1990). Alternatives to integrated instructional systems. *CUE Newsletter*, 13(2), 7–9.

Kennedy, T. J. (2006). Making content connections online via the GLOBE program. In E. Hanson-Smith & S. Rilling (Eds.), *Learning languages through technology* (pp. 83–96). Alexandria, VA: TESOL.

Kern, R. (1996). Computer-mediated communication: Using e-mail exchanges to explore personal histories in two cultures. In M. Warschauer (Ed.), *Telecollaboration in foreign language learning: Proceedings of the Hawaii symposium* (pp. 105–119). Honolulu: University of Hawai'i Press.

Kern, R., & Warschauer, M. (2000). Introduction: Theory and practice of network-based language teaching. In M. Warschauer & R. Kern (Eds.), *Network-based language teaching: Concepts and practice*. Cambridge: Cambridge University Press.

Kernan, M. C., & Howard, G. S. (1990). Computer anxiety and computer attitudes: An investigation of construct and predictive validity issues. *Educational and Psychological Measurement*, 50, 681–690.

Kessler, G. (2006). Assessing CALL teacher training: What are we doing and what could we do better? In P. Hubbard & M. Levy (Eds.), *Teacher education in CALL* (pp. 23–42). Amsterdam: John Benjamins.

Keynote (Version 3) [Computer software]. Cupertino, CA: Apple Computer. http://www.apple.com/keynote

Khalsa, D. K. (2005a). Online learning teams: Impact of socio-cultural dimensions. In G. Salvendy (Ed.), *Human-Computer Interaction International 2005* [CD-ROM]. Mahwah, NJ: Lawrence Erlbaum.

Khalsa, D. K. (2005b). *Support for global project-based learning: U.S. teacher motivation, online training, virtual teamwork, trust and identity.* Doctoral dissertation, University of Maryland, Baltimore.

Khalsa, D. K. (2007). Multicultural e-learning teamwork: Social and cultural characteristics and influence. In A. Edmundson (Ed.), *Globalized e-learning cultural challenges* (pp. 307–326). New York: Idea.

Kid Pix Deluxe 3 (Version 1.1) [Computer software]. (2006). San Francisco: Broderbund. http://www.broderbund.com/jump.jsp?itemID=125&mainPID=125&itemType=PRODUCT&RS=1&keyword=kid+pix

Kidspiration (Version 2.1) [Computer software]. (2006). Beaverton, OR: Inspiration Software. http://www.inspiration.com/productinfo/kidspiration/index.cfm

Kirsch, G., & Roen, D. H. (1990). Introduction: Theories and research on audience in written communication. In G. Kirsch & D. H. Roen (Eds.), *A sense of audience in written communication* (pp. 13–21). Newbury Park, CA: Sage.

Klein, W. (1986). *Second language acquisition.* New York: Cambridge University Press.

Klemm, U. (2006a, January 25). Second show—students' radio play. *Schoolmaster's Blog.* Retrieved December 3, 2006, from http://blog.klemm-site.de/wordpress/?p=13

Klemm, U. (2006b, February 4). Barry Trotter. *Schoolmaster's Blog.* Retrieved December 9, 2006, from http://blog.klemm-site.de/wordpress/?p=25

KnowPlace. (n.d.). *Openweekends.* Retrieved December 6, 2006, from http://knowplace.ca/cgi-bin/mailman/listinfo/openweekends/

Knutson, D. R. (2000). *A quantitative and qualitative study of computer technology and student achievement in mathematics and reading at the second- and third-grade levels: A comparison of high versus limited technology integration.* Unpublished doctoral dissertation, University of Southern California, Los Angeles.

Koenraad, T., Westhoff, G., Pérez Torres, I., & Fischer, O. (2004–2007). Lquest: *Languagequests.* Retrieved December 5, 2006, from http://www.ecml.at/mtp2/LQuest/

Kolaitis, M., Mahoney, M., Pomann, H., & Hubbard, P. (2006). Training ourselves to train our students for CALL. In P. Hubbard & M. Levy (Eds.), *Teacher education in CALL* (pp. 317–332). Amsterdam: John Benjamins.

Kramsch, C., A'Ness, F., & Lam, W. S. E. (2000). Authenticity and authorship in the computer-mediated acquisition of L2 literacy. *Language Learning & Technology, 4*(2), 78–104.

Krashen, S. (1978). The monitor model for second language acquisition. In R. Gingras (Ed.), *Second language acquisition and foreign language teaching* (pp. 1–26). Arlington, VA: Center for Applied Linguistics.

Krashen, S. (1980). The input hypothesis. In J. E. Alatis (Ed.), *Current issues in bilingual education* (pp. 168–180). Washington, DC: Georgetown University Press.

Krashen, S. D. (1982). *Principles and practice in second language acquisition.* Oxford: Pergamon Press.

Krashen, S. (1985). *The input hypothesis: Issues and implications*. London: Longman.

Krashen, S. D. (1988). *Second language acquisition and second language learning*. New York: Prentice Hall International.

Krashen, S. D. (2003). *Explorations in language acquisition and use: The Taipei lectures*. Portsmouth, NH: Heinemann.

Krashen, S., & Terrell, T. (1983). *The natural approach: Language acquisition in the classroom*. Hayward, CA: Alemany Press.

Kremers, M. (1990). Sharing authority in a synchronous network: The case for riding the beast. *Computers and Composition*, 7(Special issue), 33–44.

Kremers, M. (1993). Student authority and teacher freedom: ENFI at New York Institute of Technology. In B. Bruce, J. K. Peyton, & T. Batson (Eds.), *Network-based classrooms: Promises and realities* (pp. 113–123). New York: Cambridge University Press.

Kress, G., & van Leeuwen, T. (1996). *Reading images: The grammar of visual design*. London: Routledge.

Kroll, B. M. (1984). Writing for readers: Three perspectives on audience. *College Composition and Communication*, 35, 172–185.

Kumar, M. (2004). A critical discourse in multimedia design: A pedagogical perspective to creating engaging online courseware. *e-Journal of Instructional Science and Technology*, 7(2). Retrieved December 9, 2006, from http://www.usq.edu.au/electpub/e-jist/docs/Vol7_no2/FullPapers/CriticalDisc_MM.htm

Kurzweil 3000 (Version 10) [Computer software]. (2006). Bedford, MA: Kurzweil Educational Systems. http://www.kurzweiledu.com/kurz3000.aspx

Laborda, J. G. (2003). [Review of *Task-based learning and teaching* by Rod Ellis]. *TESL-EJ*, 7(3). Retrieved December 10, 2006, from http://www-writing.berkeley.edu/TESL-EJ/ej27/r5.html

Ladson-Billings, G. (1994). *The dreamkeepers: Successful teachers of African-American children*. San Francisco: Jossey-Bass.

Ladson-Billings, G. (1995). Toward a theory of culturally relevant pedagogy. *American Educational Research Journal*, 32, 465–491.

Lam, W. S. E. (2000a). Literacy and the design of the self: A case study of a teenager. *Journal of Adolescent & Adult Literacy*, 43, 462–469.

Lam, W. S. E. (2000b). Second language literacy and the design of the self: A case study of a teenager writing on the Internet. *TESOL Quarterly*, 34, 457–482.

Lam, Y. (2000). Technophilia vs. technophobia: A preliminary look at why second language teachers do or do not use technology in their classrooms. *Canadian Modern Language Review*, 56, 389–420.

Land, S. M., & Greene, B. (1999, February). Project-based learning with the World Wide Web: A qualitative study of resource integration. In K. E. Sparks & M. Simonson (Eds.), *Proceedings of selected research and development papers presented at the National Convention of the Association for Educational Communications and Technology*, Houston, TX. Retrieved December 10, 2006, from http://eric.ed.gov/ERICWebPortal/contentdelivery/servlet/ERICServlet?accno=ED436175 (ERIC Document Reproduction Service No. ED436175)

Language Learning & Technology. (2007). Michigan State University. Retrieved March 7, 2007, from http://llt.msu.edu/

Lantolf, J. P., & Thorne, S. L. (2006). *Sociocultural theory and the genesis of second language development*. Oxford: Oxford University Press.

Larsen-Freeman, D. (1986). *Techniques and principles in language teaching*. Oxford: Oxford University Press.

Larsen-Freeman, D., & Long, M. (1991). *An introduction to second language acquisition research*. London: Longman.

Larson, R. (1988). Flow and writing. In M. Csikszentmihalyi & I. S. Csikszentmihalyi (Eds.), *Optimal experience: Psychological studies of flow in consciousness* (pp. 150–171). New York: Cambridge University Press.

Larsson, J. (2001). *Problem-based learning: A possible approach to language education?* Krakow, Poland: Polonia Institute, Jagiellonian University. Retrieved November 25, 2006, from http://www.nada.kth.se/~jla/docs/PBL.pdf

Laufer, B., & Hill, M. (2000). What lexical information do L2 learners select in a CALL dictionary and how does it affect word retention? *Language Learning & Technology*, 3(2), 58–76. Retrieved December 15, 2006, from http://llt.msu.edu/vol3num2/laufer-hill/index.html

Laufer, B., & Hulstijn, J. (2001). Incidental vocabulary acquisition in a second language: The construct of task-induced involvement. *Applied Linguistics*, 22, 1–26.

Laurel, B. (1991). *Computers as theatre*. New York: Addison-Wesley.

Lave, J., & Wenger, E. (1991). *Situated learning: Legitimate peripheral participation*. Cambridge: Cambridge University Press.

Lazarus, R. S., & Launier, R. (1978). Stress-related transactions between person and environment. In L. A. Pervin & M. Lewis (Eds.), *Perspectives in interactional psychology* (pp. 287–327). New York: Plenum Press.

Lea, M., O'Shea, T., Fung, P., & Spears, R. (1992). "Flaming" in computer-mediated communications: Observations, explanations, and implications. In M. Lea (Ed.), *Contexts of computer-mediated communication* (pp. 89–112). London: Harvester Wheatsheaf.

LeapFrog Enterprises. (2001–2006). *FLY pentop computer*. Retrieved December 30, 2006, from http://www.leapfrog.com/Primary/GradeSchool/FLY.jsp?bmUID=1167537883286

Learn to Speak English 9 Deluxe [Computer software]. (2003). San Francisco: Broderbund.

Learning Point Associates. (1997). *Learning with technology profile tool*. Retrieved December 14, 2006, from http://www.ncrtec.org/capacity/profile/profwww.htm

Learning Point Associates. (2001). NCRTEC *lesson planner*. Retrieved December 14, 2006, from http://www.ncrtec.org/tl/lp/

Lebow, J. (2006). Worldbridges: The potential of live interactive webcasting. TESL-EJ, 10(1). Retrieved December 7, 2006, from http://tesl-ej.org/ej37/int.html

Ledlow, S. (2001). *Using think-pair-share in the college classroom*. Tempe: Arizona State University, Center for Learning and Teaching Excellence. Retrieved November 25, 2006, from http://clte.asu.edu/active/usingtps.pdf

Lee, L. (2004). Learners' perspectives on networked collaborative interaction with native speakers of Spanish in the US. *Language Learning & Technology*, 8(1), 83–100. Retrieved December 20, 2006, from http://llt.msu.edu/vol8num1/lee/

Lee, T.-W. (2002). A study of problem-based instructional strategies for technological literacy. *Proceedings of the National Science Council*, ROC, 12(2), 55–63. Retrieved June 19, 2007, from http://nr.stpi.org.tw/ejournal/proceedingD/v12n2/55-63.pdf

Leeman, J., Arteagoitia, I., Fridman, B., & Doughty, C. (1995). Integrating attention to form with meaning: Focus on form in content-based Spanish instruction. In R. Schmidt (Ed.), *Attention and awareness in foreign language learning* (pp. 217–258). Honolulu: University of Hawai'i Press.

LeLoup, J. W., & Ponterio, R. (2003). *Second language acquisition and technology: A review of the research.* Washington, DC: Center for Applied Linguistics. Retrieved January 17, 2006 from http://www.cal.org/resources/digest/0311leloup.html

Lemke, J. L. (1998). Metamedia literacy: Transforming meanings and media. In D. Reinking, M. C. McKenna, L. D. Labbo, & R. D. Kieffer (Eds.), *Handbook of literacy and technology* (pp. 283–302). Mahwah, NJ: Lawrence Erlbaum.

Lemonade for Sale [Computer software]. (2001). Elgin, IL: Sunburst Technology. http://store.sunburst.com/ProductInfo.aspx?itemid=176632

Lenhart, A., & Madden, M. (2005). *Teen content creators and consumers.* Retrieved December 30, 2006, from http://www.pewinternet.org/pdfs/PIP_Teens_Content_Creation.pdf

Levin, J., & Boruta, M. (1983). Writing with computers in classrooms: "You get exactly the right amount of space!" *Theory Into Practice, 22,* 291–295.

Levinson, S. C. (1983). *Pragmatics.* Cambridge: Cambridge University Press.

Levinson, S. C. (2003). *Space in language and cognition: Explorations in cultural diversity.* New York: Cambridge University Press.

Levy, M. (1990). Towards a theory of CALL. *CAELL Journal, 1*(4), 5–7.

Levy, M. (2006). Effective use of CALL technologies: Finding the right balance. In R. P. Donaldson & M. A. Haggstrom (Eds.), *Changing language education through CALL* (pp. 1–18). New York: Routledge.

Levy, M., & Kennedy, C. (2004). A task-cycling pedagogy using stimulated reflection and audio-conferencing in foreign language learning. *Language Learning & Technology, 8*(2), 50–68. Retrieved December 20, 2006, from http://llt.msu.edu/vol8num2/levy/

Levy, M., & Stockwell, G. (2006). CALL *dimensions: Options and issues in computer-assisted language learning.* Mahwah, NJ: Lawrence Erlbaum.

Lewis, T., & Walker, L. (Eds.). (2003). *Autonomous language learning in tandem.* Sheffield, England: Academy Electronic Publications.

Lewkowicz, J. (2000). Authenticity in language testing: Some outstanding questions. *Language Testing, 17,* 43–64.

Lightbown, P. M, & Spada, N. (1990). Focus-on-form and corrective feedback in communicative language teaching. *Studies in Second Language Acquisition, 12,* 429–448.

Lightbown, P. M., & Spada, N. (1994). *How languages are learned.* Oxford: Oxford University Press.

Linden Research. (2006). *Second life.* Retrieved December 23, 2006, from http://second life.com/

Lindgren, J. (2002). Teaching science to English language learners. In H. Zainuddin, N. Yahya, C. A. Morales-Jones, & E. N. Ariza (Eds.), *Fundamentals of teaching English to speakers of other languages in K–12 mainstream classrooms* (pp. 386–405). Dubuque, IA: Kendall Hunt.

The LINGUIST list. (1989–2006). Eastern Michigan University. Retrieved November 29, 2006, from http://linguist.emich.edu/

Lister, S. (2005–2006). *Teaching, training, learning . . . a life-long engagement.* Retrieved February 9, 2007, from http://teacherintraining.edublogs.org/

Literacy Center Education Network. (1999–2006). *Literacycenter.net: The early childhood education network.* Retrieved December 8, 2006, from http://www.literacycenter.net/

Literacyworks.org. (1999–2004). *Learning resources.* Retrieved December 6, 2006, from http://literacynet.org/cnnsf/

Little, D. (1991). *Learner autonomy 1: Definitions, issues and problems.* Dublin, Ireland: Authentik.

Liu, H. C. (2000). Assessing learner strategies using computers: New insights and limitations. *Computer Assisted Language Learning, 13,* 65–78.

Liu, H. (2005). *An investigation of methods for assessing authenticity in computer-assisted language learning and assessment.* Unpublished master's thesis, Iowa State University, Ames.

Live Action English Interactive [Computer software]. (2006). Berkeley, CA: Command Performance Language Institute. http://www.cpli.net/

Llewelyn, G. (2005). *The internationalization of Second Life.* Retrieved December 23, 2006, from http://secondlife.game-host.org/article37visual1layout1.html

Long, M. (1983). Native speaker/non-native speaker conversation and the negotiation of comprehensible input. *Applied Linguistics, 4,* 126–141.

Long, M. H. (1985). Input and second language acquisition theory. In S. M. Gass & C. G. Madden (Eds.), *Input in second language acquisition* (pp. 377–393). Rowley, MA: Newbury House.

Long, M. H. (1987). Instructed interlanguage development. In L. M. Beebe (Ed.), *Issues in second language acquisition* (pp. 113–142). New York: Newbury House.

Long, M. (1991). Focus on form: A design feature in language teaching methodology. In C. Kramsch (Ed.), *Foreign language research in cross-cultural perspective* (pp. 39–52). Amsterdam: John Benjamins.

Long, M., & Porter, P. (1985). Group work, interlanguage talk, and second language acquisition. TESOL *Quarterly, 19,* 207–228.

Louhiala-Salminen, L. (2002). The fly's perspective: Discourse in the daily routine of a business manager. *English for Specific Purposes, 21,* 211–231.

Loveless, A. M. (2002). *Literature review in creativity, new technologies and learning.* Retrieved December 11, 2006, from http://www.nestafuturelab.org/research/reviews/cr01.htm

Lozanov, G. (1978). *Suggestology and outlines of suggestopedy.* New York: Gordon & Breach.

Lumley, T., & Brown, A. (1998). Authenticity of discourse in a specific-purpose test. In E. Li & G. James (Eds.), *Testing and evaluation in second language education* (pp. 22–33). Hong Kong: Hong Kong University of Science and Technology, Language Centre.

Lynch, D., Vernon, R. F., & Smith, M. L. (2001). Technotes—critical thinking and the Web. JSWE *Online (Journal of Social Work Education), 37*(2). Retrieved December 15, 2006, from http://www.cswe.org/publications/jswe/01-2TechNotes.htm

Lynch, H., & Tennille, S. (n.d.). *Culture quest.* Retrieved January 26, 2007, from http://coe .west.asu.edu/students/stennille/st3/webquest.html

Lyster, R. (2001). Negotiation of form, recasts, and explicit correction in relation to error types and learner repair in immersion classrooms. *Language Learning, 51*(Suppl.), 265–301.

Lyster, R. & Ranta, L. (1997). Corrective feedback and learner uptake: Negotiation of form in communicative classrooms. *Studies in Second Language Acquisition, 19,* 37–66.

MacIntyre, P. D. (2002). Motivation, anxiety and emotion in second language acquisition. In P. Robinson (Ed.), *Individual differences and instructed language learning* (pp. 45–68). Philadelphia: John Benjamins.

MacIntyre, P. D., & Gardner, R. C. (1991). Methods and results in the study of foreign language anxiety: A review of the literature. *Language Learning, 41,* 85–117.

Macrorie, K. (1988). *The I-search paper.* Portsmouth, NH: Heinemann.

Maine and Apple sign contract to continue Maine Learning Technology Initiative. (2005). Retrieved November 26, 2006, from http://www.state.me.us/mlte/

Makers Pages [Computer software]. (n.d.). Mellon Tri-College Language Project. Retrieved January 26, 2007, from http://web.archive.org/web/20041010183546/makers .cet.middlebury.edu/makers/index.htm

Malamah Thomas, A. (1987). *Classroom interaction.* Oxford: Oxford University Press.

Manifestation.com. (1999–2006). *Eliza, computer therapist.* Retrieved December 9, 2006, from http://www.manifestation.com/neurotoys/eliza.php3

Marcoulides, G. A. (1989). Measuring computer anxiety: The computer anxiety scale. *Educational and Psychological Measurement, 49,* 733–739.

Marshall, B., & Drummond, M. J. (2006). How teachers engage with Assessment for Learning: Lessons from the classroom. *Research Papers in Education, 21,* 133–149.

Marzio, M., & Hanson-Smith, E. (2003). *Real English online.* Retrieved November 26, 2006, from http://groups.yahoo.com/group/Real_English_Online/

The Marzio School & Real English. (2007). *Real English.* Retrieved April 17, 2007, from http://www.real-english.com/

Massachusetts Institute of Technology. (2002–2007). MIT *OpenCourseWare.* Retrieved April 18, 2007, from http://ocw.mit.edu/index.html

Massachusetts Institute of Technology. (2005–2006). *Diva.* Retrieved December 30, 2006, from http://www.diva-project.org/

Math magician. (n.d.). Retrieved December 16, 2006, from http://www.oswego.org/ocsd-web/games/Mathmagician/mathsmulti.html

Math Mysteries [Computer software]. (2000). Watertown, MA: Tom Snyder Productions. http://www.tomsnyder.com/products/product.asp?SKU=MATMAT

Matsumura, S., & Hann, G. (2004). Computer anxiety and students' preferred feedback methods in EFL writing. *Modern Language Journal, 88,* 403–415.

McCoy, J. M., & Evans, G. W. (2002). The potential role of the physical environment in fostering creativity. *Creativity Research Journal, 14*(3/4), 409–426.

McGregor, G., & White, R. S. (Eds.). (1990). *Reception and response: Hearer creativity and the analysis of spoken and written texts.* London: Routledge.

McKenzie, J. (1997). The questioning kit. *From Now On: The Educational Technology Journal, 7*(3). Retrieved December 11, 2006, from http://www.fromnowon.org/nov97/toolkit .html

McPeck, J. (1990). *Teaching critical thinking.* New York: Routledge.

Meagher, M. (1995). Learning English on the Internet. *Educational Leadership, 53*(2), 88–90.

Mendelsohn, D. J. (1995). Applying learning strategies in the second/foreign language listening comprehension lesson. In D. J. Mendelsohn & J. Rubin (Eds.), A *guide for the teaching of second language listening* (pp. 132–150). San Diego, CA: Dominic Press.

MERLOT. (1997–2006). MERLOT: *Multimedia educational resource for learning and online teaching.* Retrieved November 29, 2006, from http://www.merlot.org/merlot/index.htm

Meskill, C. (2002). *Teaching and learning in real time: Media, technologies and language acquisition.* Houston, TX: Athelstan.

Meskill, C., Anthony, N., Hilliker-Vanstrander, S., Tseng, C., & You, J. (2006a). CALL: A survey of K–12 ESOL teacher uses and preferences. TESOL *Quarterly, 40,* 439–451.

Meskill, C., Anthony, N., Hilliker-VanStrander, S., Tseng, C., & You, J. (2006b). Expert-novice teacher mentoring in language learning technology. In P. Hubbard & M. Levy (Eds.), *Teacher education in CALL* (pp. 283–299). Amsterdam: John Benjamins.

Meskill, C., & Mossop, J. (2000). Technologies use with ESL learners in New York State: Preliminary report. *Journal of Educational Computing Research, 22,* 265–284.

Meskill, C., Mossop, J., & Bates, R. (1999a). Bilingualism, cognitive flexibility, and electronic literacy. *Bilingual Research Journal, 23*(2/3). Retrieved December 19, 2006, from http://brj.asu.edu/v2323/articles/art9.html

Meskill, C., Mossop, J., & Bates, R. (1999b). *Electronic text and English as a second language environments* (Report Series 12012). Albany: State University of New York, National Center on English Learning and Achievement. Retrieved February 20, 2007, from http://cela.albany.edu/reports/meskill/meskillelectronic12012.pdf

Meskill, C., & Shea, P. (1994). Multimedia and language learning: Integrating the technology into existing curricula. In P. Kramer (Ed.), *Proceedings of the Third Conference on Instructional Technologies* (p. 57). Albany: State University of New York, Office of Educational Technology.

Metropolitan Museum of Art. (2000–2007a). *Explore & learn.* Retrieved April 16, 2007, from http://www.metmuseum.org/explore/index.asp?HomePageLink=explore_l

Metropolitan Museum of Art. (2000–2007a). *How Van Gogh made his mark.* Retrieved April 16, 2007, from http://www.metmuseum.org/explore/van_gogh/menu.html

MicroOptical. (2006). *Myvu.* Retrieved December 30, 2006, from http://www.myvu .com/

Microsoft. (2005). *MSN groups.* Retrieved November 29, 2006, from http://groups.msn .com/home

Microsoft. (2007a). *Microsoft Paint overview.* Retrieved April 23, 2007, from http://www .microsoft.com/resources/documentation/windows/xp/all/proddocs/en-us/mspaint_ overview.mspx?mfr=true

Microsoft. (2007b). *MSN Encarta.* Retrieved April 23, 2007, from http://encarta.msn .com/

Microsoft. (2007c). *MSN Hotmail.* Retrieved April 23, 2007, from http://www.hotmail .com/

Microsoft Encarta Premium 2007 [Computer software]. (2007). Redmond, WA: Microsoft. http://www.microsoft.com/encarta/

Microsoft Excel 2007 [Computer software]. (2007). Redmond, WA: Microsoft. http:// office.microsoft.com/excel/

Microsoft Office 2007 [Computer software]. (2007). Redmond, WA: Microsoft. http:// office.microsoft.com/

Microsoft Photo Story (Version 3) [Computer software]. (2004). Redmond, WA: Microsoft. http://www.microsoft.com/photostory/

Microsoft PowerPoint 2007 [Computer software]. (2007). Redmond, WA: Microsoft. http://office.microsoft.com/powerpoint/

Microsoft Reader (Version 2.1.1) [Computer software]. (2003). Redmond, WA: Microsoft. http://www.microsoft.com/reader/

Microsoft Word 2007 [Computer software]. (2007). Redmond, WA: Microsoft. http:// office.microsoft.com/word

Mighty Media. (2007). *IECC home page.* Retrieved January 26, 2007, from http://www .iecc.org/

Millar, G. W. (2002). *The Torrance kids at mid-life.* Westport, CT: Ablex.

Miller, C., Tomlinson, A., & Jones, M. (1994). *Learning styles and facilitating reflection* (Research Report Series: Researching Professional Education). London: English National Board. (ERIC Document Reproduction Service No. ED390991)

Milner, H. R. (2003). Teacher reflection and race in cultural contexts: History, meanings, and methods in teaching. *Theory Into Practice*, 42, 173–180.

Milton, J., & Garbi, A. (2000). VIRLAN: Collaborative foreign language learning on the Internet for primary age children: Problems and a solution. *Educational Technology & Society*, 3(3). Retrieved December 23, 2006, from http://ifets.ieee.org/periodical/vol_3_2000/d04.html

Mind Benders [Computer software]. (n.d.). Coos Bay, OR: Bright Minds. http://www.brightminds.us/series/013/index_h.html

Mirzoeff, N. (1999). *An introduction to visual culture*. New York: Routledge.

MIT Media Laboratory. (n.d.). OLPC. Retrieved November 26, 2006, from http://laptop.media.mit.edu/

Mobiedge Technologies. (2006). *Mobiedge radio*. Retrieved December 30, 2006, from http://mobiedge.ca/index_files/page0002.htm

MobileMultiGames GmbH. (n.d.). *blaxxun*. Retrieved December 23, 2006, from http://www.blaxxun.com/

Mobot. (2006). Retrieved December 30, 2006, from http://www.mobot.com/

Moeller, D. (2002). *Computers in the writing classroom*. Urbana, IL: National Council of Teachers of English.

Molebash, P. (n.d.). *Web inquiry projects*. Retrieved November 25, 2006, from http://edweb.sdsu.edu/wip/

Monke, L. (2001). The global suburb. In R. W. Burniske & L. Monke (Eds.), *Breaking down the digital walls: Learning to teach in a post-modem world* (pp. 131–151). Albany: State University of New York Press.

Montemagno, M., Good, R., & Stella, M. (n.d.). *The weblog project*. Retrieved December 10, 2006, from http://www.theweblogproject.com/

Monterey Institute of International Studies. (2006). *Computer-assisted language learning (CALL) certificate overview*. Retrieved December 14, 2006, from http://language.miis.edu/tdc/call.html

Montgomery, W. (2001). Creating culturally responsive, inclusive classrooms. *Teaching Exceptional Children*, 33(4), 4–9.

Moodle (Version 1.7) [Computer software]. (2006). East Perth, Western Australia, Australia: Moodle. http://moodle.org/

Moodle for language teaching. (n.d.). Retrieved November 26, 2006, from http://moodle.org/course/view.php?id=31

Moore, Z., Morales, B., & Carel, S., (1998). Technology and teaching culture: Results of a state survey of foreign language teachers. CALICO *Journal*, 15(1–3), 109–128.

Morley, J. (2001). Aural comprehension instruction: Principles and practices. In M. Celce-Murcia (Ed.), *Teaching English as a second or foreign language* (3rd ed., pp. 69–85). Boston: Heinle & Heinle.

Morris, B. (2006). Sustainable video production in short-term courses. TESOL *Video News*, 17(1). Retrieved December 10, 2006, from http://www.tesol.org//s_tesol/article.asp?vid=188&DID=5442&sid=1&cid=757&iid=5434&nid=3268

Morris, F. A., & Tarone, E. E. (2003). Impact of classroom dynamics on the effectiveness of recasts in second language acquisition. *Language Learning*, 53, 325–368.

Moutinho, J. (n.d.). *Poemar*. Retrieved November 30, 2006, from http://www.poemar.com/

Moya, S., & O'Malley, J. M. (1994). A portfolio assessment model for ESL. *Journal of Educational Issues of Language Minority Students*, 13, 13–36.

Mühren, A. (2003). *Total physical response* (TPR): An *effective language learning method at beginner/intermediate levels.* Retrieved December 29, 2006, from http://home.planet.nl/~mhren000/tpr/primer_tpr.pdf

Müller-Hartmann, A. (2000). The role of tasks in promoting intercultural learning in electronic learning networks. *Language Learning & Technology, 4*(2), 129–147. Retrieved December 10, 2006, from http://llt.msu.edu/vol4num2/muller/default.html

Mulligan, P. A., & Gore, K. (1990). The immigrants: The Irish experience in Boston 1840–1859. *Simulation & Gaming, 21,* 453–456.

Murphey, T., & Sato, K. (Eds.). (2005). *Communities of supportive professionals.* Alexandria, VA: TESOL.

Murphy, J. M., & Stoller, F. L. (2001). Sustained-content language teaching: An emerging definition. *TESOL Journal, 10*(2/3), 3–5.

Murray, D. (1982). *Learning by teaching.* Montclair, NJ: Boynton-Cook.

Murray, D. E. (2000). Protean communication: The language of computer-mediated communication. *TESOL Quarterly, 34,* 397–421.

Murray, D. E. (2005). Technologies for second language literacy. *Annual Review of Applied Linguistics, 25,* 188–201.

Mylanguageexchange.com. (2000–2006). Retrieved December 30, 2006, from http://www.mylanguageexchange.com/

MySpace.com. (2003–2006). *MySpace.* Retrieved November 24, 2006, from http://www.myspace.com/

Myst [Computer software]. (1993). San Francisco: Broderbund.

Naiman, N., Frohlich, M., Stern, H. H., & Todesco, A. (1995). *The good language learner.* Clevedon, England: Multilingual Matters. (Original work published 1978)

NASA. (n.d.) *The NASA scifiles.* Retrieved November 25, 2006, from http://whyfiles.larc.nasa.gov/

National Air Traffic Controllers Association. (n.d.). *Virtual San Francisco tower.* Retrieved December 19, 2006, from http://www.natca.net/assets/multimedia/gatetogate/SFOtower.mov

National Cable Satellite Corporation. (2007). C-SPAN *classroom.* Retrieved March 7, 2007, from http://www.c-spanclassroom.org/

National Capital Language Resource Center. (2003–2004). *Assessing learning: Alternative assessment.* Retrieved December 13, 2006, from http://www.nclrc.org/essentials/assessing/alternative.htm

National Center for Education Statistics. (2005). *Internet access in U.S. public schools and classrooms:* 1994–2003. Retrieved December 7, 2006, from http://nces.ed.gov/pubsearch/pubsinfo.asp?pubid=2005015

National Institute for Literacy. (n.d.). *Four purposes for learning.* Retrieved November 24, 2006, from http://eff.cls.utk.edu/resources/purposes.htm

National Public Radio. (2006). NPR. Retrieved November 30, 2006, from http://www.npr.org/

Naumann, B. (1995). Mailbox chats: Dialogues in electronic communication. In F. Hundsnurscher & E. Weigand (Eds.), *Future perspectives of dialogue analysis* (pp. 163–184). Tübingen, Germany: Max Niemeyer.

Neighborhood MapMachine (Version 2.0) [Computer software]. (2003). Watertown, MA: Tom Snyder Productions. http://www.tomsnyder.com/products/product.asp?SKU=NEIV20

Neverwinter Nights (Version 2.0) [Computer software]. (2006). Edmonton, Alberta, Canada: Bioware. http://nwn.bioware.com/

New Dynamic English [Computer software]. (2006). Burlingame, CA: DynEd International. http://www.dyned.com/products/nde/

Newman, C., & Smolen, L. (1993). Portfolio assessment in our schools: Implementation, advantages, and concerns. *Midwestern Educational Researcher, 6*, 28–32.

Nextcode. (n.d.). Retrieved December 30, 2006, from http://www.nextcodecorp.com/

Ngeow, K., & Kong, Y. (2001). *Learning to learn: Preparing teachers and students for problem-based learning*. Bloomington, IN: ERIC Clearinghouse on Reading, English, and Communication. (ERIC Document Reproduction Service No. ED457524)

Nicenet. (1996–1998, 2003). Retrieved December 8, 2006, from http://www.nicenet.org/

Nieto, S. (2000). *Affirming diversity: The sociopolitical context of multicultural education*. White Plains, NY: Longman.

Nobel, P. (1980). *Resource-based learning in post compulsory education*. London: Kogan Page.

Noddings, N. (1984). *Caring: A feminine approach to ethics and moral education*. Berkeley: University of California Press.

Noddings, N. (1992). *The challenge to care in schools: An alternative approach to education*. New York: Teachers College Press.

Noddings, N. (1996). On community. *Educational Theory, 46*, 245–267.

Noels, K. A., Pelletier, L. G., Clément, R., & Vallerand, R. J. (2000). Why are you learning a second language? Motivational orientations and self-determination theory. *Language Learning, 50*, 57–85.

Norton, B., & Toohey, K. (2001). Changing perspectives on good language learners. *TESOL Quarterly, 35*, 307–322.

Norton, B., & Toohey, K. (Eds.). (2004). *Critical pedagogies and language learning*. Cambridge: Cambridge University Press.

Nunan, D. (1989a). *Designing tasks for the communicative classroom*. Cambridge: Cambridge University Press.

Nunan, D. (1989b). *Language teaching methodology: A textbook for teachers*. New York: Prentice Hall.

Nunan, D. (1993). Task-based syllabus design: Selecting, grading and sequencing tasks. In G. Crookes & S. M. Gass (Eds.), *Tasks in a pedagogical context* (pp. 55–66). Cleveland, England: Multilingual Matters.

Nunan, D. (1999). *Second language learning and teaching*. Boston: Heinle & Heinle.

Nunan, D. (2001). *Aspects of task-based syllabus design*. Retrieved December 6, 2006, from http://www3.telus.net/linguisticsissues/syllabusdesign.html

Oblinger, D. (2003). Understanding the new students. EDUCAUSE *Review, 38*(4), 36–45.

Obvious. (n.d.). *Odeo*. Retrieved December 5, 2006, from http://odeo.com/

Odasz, F. (n.d.). *Lone Eagle Consulting*. Retrieved November 24, 2006, from http://lone-eagles.com/

Odeo. (n.d.). *Hellodeo*. Retrieved December 8, 2006, from http://www.hellodeo.com/hello

O'Dowd, R. (2003). Understanding the "other side": Intercultural learning in a Spanish-English e-mail exchange. *Language Learning & Technology, 7*(2), 118–144.

Odyssey [Computer software]. (2006). Austin, TX: CompassLearning. http://www.compasslearning.com/technology/

Ogle, D. S. (1986). K-W-L group instructional strategy. In A. S. Palincsar, D. S. Ogle, B. F. Jones, & E. G. Carr (Eds.), *Teaching reading as thinking* (Teleconference Resource Guide; pp. 11–17). Alexandria, VA: Association for Supervision and Curriculum Development.

Ohio Literacy Resource Center. (2006). *Problem-solving introduction.* Retrieved November 25, 2006, from http://literacy.kent.edu/salt_fork/prob_solv/intro.html

OLPC. (n.d.). *Frequently asked questions.* Retrieved November 26, 2006, from http://www .laptop.org/faq.en_US.html

OLPC: *One laptop per child.* (n.d.). Retrieved November 24, 2006, from http://www.laptop .org/

Olson, G. M., & Olson, J. S. (2000). Distance matters. *Human-Computer Interaction, 15,* 139–178.

O'Malley, J., & Chamot, A. (1990). *Learning strategies in second language acquisition.* New York: Cambridge University Press.

O'Malley, J. M., Chamot, A. U., Stewner-Manzanares, C., Kupper, L., & Russo, R. P. (1985). Learning strategies used by beginning and intermediate ESL students. *Language Learning, 35,* 21–46.

O'Malley, J. M., & Valdez Pierce, L. (1996). *Authentic assessment for English language learners: Practical approaches for teachers.* New York: Addison-Wesley.

OneLook dictionary search. (n.d.). Retrieved December 15, 2006, from http://www.onelook .com/

Ong, W. J. (1978). Literacy and orality in our times. *Association of Departments of English Bulletin, 58,* 1–7.

Open Communication Systems. (2003–2006). *Radio Handi.* Retrieved December 31, 2006, from http://www.radiohandi.com/

Open Source Initiative. (2007). *Opensource.org.* Retrieved March 6, 2007, from http:// opensource.org/

OpenOffice.org Suite (Version 1.1) [Computer software]. (2005). Santa Clara, CA: Sun Microsystems. http://www.openoffice.org/

Opp-Beckman, L. (1995–2005). *Leslie Opp-Beckman's opportunities in* ESL. Retrieved November 29, 2006, from http://www.uoregon.edu/~leslieob/

Oppenheimer, T. (2003). *The flickering mind: Saving education from the false promise of technology.* New York: Random House.

Oracle Education Foundation. (n.d.-a). *ThinkQuest.* Retrieved November 30, 2006, from http://www.thinkquest.org/

Oracle Education Foundation. (n.d.-b). *ThinkQuest: Library.* Retrieved December 11, 2006, from http://www.thinkquest.org/library/index.html

The Oregon Trail 5th Edition [Computer software]. (2001). San Francisco: The Learning Company. http://www.learningcompany.com/

The Oregon Trail Classic (Version 1.1) [Computer software]. (1991). Minneapolis, MN: MECC.

orkut. (n.d.). Retrieved December 30, 2006, from http://www.orkut.com/

Ourmedia. (n.d.). Retrieved December 10, 2006, from http://www.ourmedia.org/

Outreach and Technical Assistance Network. (n.d.). *Adultedteachers.org.* Retrieved December 8, 2006, from http://www.adultedteachers.org/

Overture Services. (2006). *Babel fish translation.* Retrieved December 6, 2006, from http:// babelfish.altavista.com/

Oxford, R. (1990). *Language learning strategies: What every teacher should know*. Boston: Heinle & Heinle.

Oxford, R. (1994, October). *Language learning strategies: An update*. Retrieved November 24, 2006, from http://www.cal.org/resources/digest/oxford01.html

Oxford, R. L. (2003). Toward a more systematic model of L2 learner autonomy. In D. Palfreyman & R. C. Smith (Eds.), *Learner autonomy across cultures: Language education perspectives* (pp. 75–91). New York: Palgrave Macmillan.

Palfreyman, D., & Smith, R. C. (Eds.). (2003). *Learner autonomy across cultures: Language education perspectives*. New York: Palgrave Macmillan.

Paltalk Messenger (Version 9.0) [Computer software]. (2006). New York: Paltalk. http://www.paltalk.com/en/messaging.shtml

Papert, S. (1993). *Mindstorms: Children, computers and powerful ideas* (2nd ed.). New York: Basic Books.

Paris, P. G. (2002). Critical thinking and the use of the Internet as a resource. *International Education Journal*, 4, 30–41. Retrieved December 15, 2006, from http://ehlt.flinders.edu.au/education/iej/articles/v4n1/paris/paper.pdf

Paris-Normandy 2005. (2005). Retrieved December 10, 2006, from http://mgsonline.blogs.com/paris2005/

Parkinson, B., & Howell-Richardson, C. (1990). Learner diaries. In C. Brumfit & R. Mitchell (Eds.), *Research in the language classroom* (British Council ELT Documents 133, pp. 115–128). London: Modern English.

Parks, S., Huot, D., Hamers, J., & Lemonnier, F. H. (2003). Crossing boundaries: Multimedia technology and pedagogical innovation in a high school class. *Language Learning & Technology*, 7(1), 28–45. Retrieved April 16, 2007, from http://llt.msu.edu/vol7num1/pdf/parks.pdf

Participatory culture foundation. (n.d.). Retrieved December 31, 2006, from http://participatoryculture.org/

Paul, N., & Fiebich, C. (2005). *The elements of digital storytelling*. University of Minnesota. Retrieved December 10, 2006, from http://www.inms.umn.edu/elements/index.php

Paul, R. (1995). *Critical thinking: How to prepare students for a rapidly changing world*. Santa Rosa, CA: Foundation for Critical Thinking.

Pavur, C. (1999). Reading Acceleration Machine (Version 3.5) [Computer software]. http://www.slu.edu/colleges/AS/languages/classical/ram/ram.html#awds

Payne, J. S., & Ross, B. M. (2005). Synchronous CMC, working memory, and L2 oral proficiency development. *Language Learning & Technology*, 9(3), 35–54. Retrieved November 24, 2006, from http://llt.msu.edu/vol9num3/payne/default.html

Payton, T. (1997–1999). *Tips for developing school Web pages*. Retrieved December 11, 2006, from http://www.siec.k12.in.us/~west/online/index.html

Payton, T. (n.d.). *Collaborate 1: With one person or classroom*. Retrieved December 11, 2006, from http://www.siec.k12.in.us/~west/edu/wwwdo/index.html

PBS Online & WGBH/Frontline/NOVA. (2001). *Engineer a crop: Transgenic manipulation*. Retrieved December 19, 2006, from http://www.pbs.org/wgbh/harvest/engineer/transgen.html

PBwiki.com. (2007). *PBwiki*. Retrieved April 16, 2007, from http://pbwiki.com/

Pearson, B., & Berghoff, C. (1996). London Bridge is not falling down: It's supporting alternative assessment. *TESOL Journal*, 5(1), 28–31.

Pearson Education. (2003–2007). *Focus on grammar.* Retrieved March 8, 2007, from http://www.longman.com/ae/marketing/fog/

Pekel, N. (2002). *Students' attitudes towards independent Web-based learning at Bilkent University School of English Language.* Unpublished master's thesis, Bilkent University, Ankara, Turkey.

Pelletier, L. G., Séguin-Lévesque, C., & Legault, L. (2002). Pressure from above and pressure from below as determinants of teachers' motivation and teaching behaviors. *Journal of Educational Psychology, 94,* 186–196.

Pennington, M. C. (1996). *The power of* CALL. Houston, TX: Athelstan.

Pennycook, A. (1997). Cultural alternatives and autonomy. In P. Benson & P. Voller (Eds.), *Autonomy and independence in language learning* (pp. 35–53). London: Longman.

Penuel, W. R., & Means, B. (2000, April). *Assessing the quality of student learning in multimedia-supported project-based learning.* Paper presented at the American Educational Research Association, New Orleans, LA. Retrieved April 16, 2007, from http://pblmm.k12.ca.us/sri/ReportsPDFFiles/Means.pdf

Peters, S., & Peters, T. (1997–2006). TOPICS: *An online magazine for learners of English.* Retrieved December 10, 2006, from http://www.topics-mag.com/index.html

Peterson, M. (n.d.). *Skills to enhance problem-based learning.* University of Delaware, College of Health and Nursing Sciences. Retrieved November 25, 2006, from http://www.med-ed-online.org/f0000009.htm

Peterson, P. W. (2001). Skills and strategies for proficient listening. In M. Celce-Murcia (Ed.), *Teaching English as a second or foreign language* (3rd ed., pp. 87–100). Boston: Heinle & Heinle.

Petrie, G. M. (2003). ESL teachers' views on visual language: A grounded theory. *The Reading Matrix, 3*(3). Retrieved December 19, 2006, from http://www.readingmatrix.com/articles/petrie/article.pdf

Petring, J. (2006, February 10). My students loved your blogs [Msg 703]. Message posted to http://groups.yahoo.com/group/blog06

Pettis, J. (2002). Developing our professional competence: Some reflections. In J. Richards & W. Renandya (Eds.), *Methodology in language teaching: An anthology of current practice* (pp. 393–396). Cambridge: Cambridge University Press.

Peyton, J. K. (Ed.). (1990a). *Students and teachers writing together: Perspectives on journal writing.* Alexandria, VA: TESOL.

Peyton, J. K. (1990b). Technological innovation meets institution: Birth of creativity or murder of a great idea? *Computers and Composition, 7*(Special issue), 15–32.

Peyton, J. K. (2000). Immersed in writing: Networked composition at Kendall Demonstration Elementary School. In E. Hanson-Smith (Ed.), *Technology-enhanced learning environments* (pp. 99–110). Alexandria, VA: TESOL.

Pfaff-Harris, K. (n.d.-a). *The ESL loop.* Retrieved November 29, 2006, from http://www.linguistic-funland.com/esloop/esloop.html

Pfaff-Harris, K. (n.d.-b). *The linguistic funland.* Retrieved November 29, 2006, from http://www.linguistic-funland.com/

Phillips, M. (1986). *Communicative language learning and the microcomputer.* London: British Council.

Phillips, R., & Lowe, K. (2003). Issues associated with the equivalence of traditional and online assessment. In G. Crisp, D. Thiele, I. Scholten, S. Barker, & J. Baron (Eds.), *Interact integrate impact: Proceedings of the 20th Annual Conference of the Australasian Society for Computers in Learning in Tertiary Education* (pp. 419–431). Retrieved January 26, 2007, from http://www.ascilite.org.au/conferences/adelaide03/docs/pdf/419.pdf

Phinney, M. (1988). Computers, composition and second language learning. In M. C. Pennington (Ed.), *Teaching languages with computers: The state of the art* (pp. 81–96). San Francisco: Athelstan.

Piaget, J. (1972). *The psychology of the child.* New York: Basic Books.

Pica, T. (1987). Second language acquisition, social interaction, and the classroom. *Applied Linguistics,* 8, 2–21.

Pica, T. (1994). Questions from the language classroom: Research perspectives. TESOL *Quarterly,* 28, 49–79.

Pica, T., Holliday, L., Lewis, N., & Morgenthaler, L. (1989). Comprehensible output as an outcome of linguistic demands on the learner. *Studies in Second Language Acquisition,* 11, 63–90.

Pica, T., Kanagy, R., & Falodun, J. (1993). Choosing and using communication tasks for second language instruction. In G. Crookes & S. Gass (Eds.), *Tasks and language learning: Integrating theory and practice* (pp. 9–34). Clevedon, England: Multilingual Matters.

Pica, T., Young, R., & Doughty, C. (1987). The impact of interaction on comprehension. TESOL *Quarterly,* 21, 737–758.

Pinker, S. (1994). *The language instinct.* New York: HarperCollins.

Pintrich, P. R. (1999). The role of motivation in promoting and sustaining self-regulated learning. *International Journal of Educational Research,* 31, 459–470.

Piper, A. (1986). Conversation and the computer: A study of the conversational spin-off generated among learners of English as a foreign language working in groups. *System,* 14(2), 187–198.

PLATO *learning.* (2007). Retrieved April 17, 2007, from http://www.plato.com/

Play free online games. (n.d.). Retrieved December 23, 2006, from http://play-free-online-games.com/

PodOmatic. (2007). Retrieved April 18, 2007, from http://www.podomatic.com/

Pomerantz, A. I. (2001). *Beyond the good language learner: Ideology, identity, and investment in classroom foreign language learning.* Unpublished doctoral dissertation, University of Pennsylvania, Philadelphia.

Poole, B. (1995). *Education for an information age: Teaching in the computerized classroom.* Madison, WI: Brown & Benchmark.

Poole, J. J., & Moran, C. (1998, December). Schools have their computers, now what? T.H.E. *Journal.* Retrieved December 7, 2006, from http://www.thejournal.com/magazine/vault/A2008.cfm

Porter, P. (1986). How learners talk to each other: Input and interaction in task-centered discussion. In R. R. Day (Ed.), *Talking to learn* (pp. 200–221). Rowley, MA: Newbury House.

Prairie Land Regional Division #25. (2004). *Curriculum bytes: Resources.* Retrieved December 13, 2006, from http://www.plrd.ab.ca/sites/bytes/web/resources/links.htm

Preece, J. (2000). *Online communities: Designing usability, supporting sociability.* New York: John Wiley.

Preece, J., Maloney-Krichmar, D., & Abras, C. (2003). History and emergence of online communities. In K. A. Christinsen & D. Levinson (Eds.), *Encyclopedia of community: From village to virtual world* (pp. 1023–1027). Thousand Oaks, CA: Sage.

Prensky, M. (2001). Digital natives, digital immigrants. *On the Horizon,* 9(5), 1–6.

Retrieved November 24, 2006, from http://www.marcprensky.com/writing/Prensky%20-
%20Digital%20Natives,%20Digital%20Immigrants%20-%20Part1.pdf

Prensky, M. (2005). What can you learn from a cell phone? Almost anything. *Innovate*, 1(5). Available from http://www.innovateonline.info/index.php?view=article&id=83

Pressley, M., Levin, J. R., & Ghatala, E. S. (1984). Memory strategy monitoring in adults and children. *Journal of Verbal Learning and Verbal Behavior*, 23, 270–288.

Primary Power Pack [Computer software]. (1998). Pinehurst, NC: Centron Software. http://www.centronsoftware.com/

Print Shop 22 Deluxe [Computer software]. (2006). San Francisco: Riverdeep/Broderbund. http://www.broderbund.com/jump.jsp?itemType=PRODUCT&itemID=1645

Project Gutenberg. (2007). Retrieved March 8, 2007, from http://www.gutenberg.org/wiki/Main_Page

Public Broadcasting Service. (1995–2006). PBS *teachersource*. Retrieved November 30, 2006, from http://www.pbs.org/teachersource/

Public Broadcasting Service. (1995–2007). PBS *kids*. Retrieved April 16, 2007, from http://pbskids.org/

Public Broadcasting Service. (n.d.). *Nature for teachers*. Retrieved November 25, 2006, from http://www.pbs.org/wnet/nature/teach.html

Pujol, M. (1995/1996). ESL interactions around the computer. CAELL *Journal*, 6(4), 2–12.

Purcell, R. (1996, March 12). The case for research. *Bloomington Herald-Times*, p. A6.

Quia. (1998–2007). *Quia Web*. Retrieved April 16, 2007, from http://www.quia.com/web

QuickTime (Version 7.1.3) [Computer software]. (2006). Cupertino, CA: Apple Computer. http://www.apple.com/quicktime/

Raimes, A. (1983). *Techniques in teaching writing*. Oxford: Oxford University Press.

Raimes, A. (1991). Emerging traditions in the teaching of writing. TESOL *Quarterly*, 25, 407–430.

Rainie, L., & Hitlin, P. (2005). *The Internet at school*. Washington, DC: Pew Internet and American Life Project. Retrieved November 27, 2006, from http://www.pewinternet.org/pdfs/PIP_Internet_and_schools_05.pdf

Raskin, J. (1995). Escape From Planet Arizona [Computer software]. Cambridge, MA: EF Multimedia. [No longer available.]

Rationale (Version 1.1.0) [Computer software]. (2006). Carlton, Victoria, Australia: Austhink. http://www.austhink.com/rationale/

Reading Horizons (Version 4.0) [Computer software]. (2006). North Salt Lake, UT: HEC Reading Horizons. http://readinghorizons.com/solutions/software/rh/features.aspx

Reading is fundamental. (2006). Retrieved December 8, 2006, from http://www.rif.org/

The Reading Matrix. (2000–2005). *Script-O!* Retrieved December 13, 2006, from http://www.readingmatrix.com/quizmaker/index.php

Reeder, K., Macfadyen, L. P., Roche, J., & Chase, M., (2004). Negotiating cultures in cyberspace: Participation patterns and problematics. *Language Learning & Technology*, 8(2), 88–105. Retrieved April 18, 2007, from http://llt.msu.edu/vol8num2/reeder/default.html

Refresh Mobile. (n.d.). *Mobizines*. Retrieved December 30, 2006, from http://www.mobizines.com/what/index.html

Refsnes Data. (1999–2006a). HTML *tutorial*. Retrieved December 10, 2006, from http://www.w3schools.com/html/default.asp

Refsnes Data. (1999–2006b). W3*schools*. Retrieved November 30, 2006, from http://www.w3schools.com/

Regensburg experience. (n.d.). Retrieved December 31, 2006, from http://www.rex-regensburg.de/

Regents of the University of California. (2002–2006). *webcast.berkeley*. Retrieved November 27, 2006, from http://webcast.berkeley.edu/index.html

Reid, J. (Ed.). (1998). *Understanding learning styles in the second language classroom*. Upper Saddle River, NJ: Prentice Hall Regents.

Renniger, A., & Shumar, W. (Eds.). (2002). *Building virtual communities: Learning and change in cyberspace*. Cambridge: Cambridge University Press.

The Report Writer (Version 4.2.4) [Computer software]. (2003). Sai Kung, Hong Kong: Clarity Language Consultants. http://www.clarity.com.hk/program/reportwriter.htm

Research. (2006). Retrieved November 24, 2006, from http://en.wikipedia.org/wiki/Research

Rhodes, B. (2006). *Chalk 'n talk: The old fashioned way to teach*. Retrieved December 16, 2006, from http://international.ouc.bc.ca/chalkntalk/

Rice, P. L. (1987). *Stress and health: Principles and practice for coping and wellness*. Monterey, CA: Brooks/Cole.

Rice, R. E. (1987). Computer-mediated communication and organizational innovations. *Journal of Communication*, 37, 85–108.

Rice, R. E. (1993). Media appropriateness: Using social presence theory to compare traditional and new organizational media. *Human Communication Research*, 19, 451–484.

Richards, C. (2005). The design of effective ICT-supported learning activities: Exemplary models, changing requirements, and new possibilities. *Language Learning & Technology*, 9(1), 60–79. Retrieved April 16, 2007, from http://llt.msu.edu/vol9num1/richards/default.html

Richards, J. C., & Rodgers, T. S. (1986). *Approaches and methods in language teaching: A description and analysis*. Cambridge: Cambridge University Press.

Rigg, P. (1991). Whole language in TESOL. TESOL *Quarterly*, 25, 521–542.

Riley, F. (2006). *Postgraduate courses*. Retrieved December 14, 2006, from http://www.eurocall-languages.org/resources/courses.html

Rilling, S. (2006). An ESL OWL takes flight: Social and curricular issues in an online writing lab. In E. Hanson-Smith & S. Rilling (Eds.), *Learning languages through technology* (pp. 125–136). Alexandria, VA: TESOL.

Rising Concepts. (2007). *Frappr!* Retrieved March 7, 2007, from http://www.frappr.com/

Rivers, W. (1973, June). *Testing and student learning*. Paper presented at the First International Conference of the Association of Teachers of English to Speakers of Other Languages, Dublin, Ireland. (ERIC Document Reproduction Service No. ED086003)

Rivers, W. (2001). Autonomy at all costs: An ethnography of metacognitive self-assessment and self-management among experienced language learners. *Modern Language Journal*, 85, 279–290.

Robb, T. N. (2006). Issue: CALL and the nonautonomous learner: Build it, but will they come? In E. Hanson-Smith & S. Rilling (Eds.), *Learning languages through technology* (pp. 69–76). Alexandria, VA: TESOL.

Robb, T. (n.d.-a) *Tom's page*. Kyoto Sangyo University. Retrieved November 29, 2006, from http://www.kyoto-su.ac.jp/~trobb/

Robb, T. (n.d.-b). *Welcome to the Student List Project.* Retrieved November 28, 2006, from http://sl-lists.net/

Robb, T., & Holliday, L. (2005, December). *The effects of the medium on the quality of message exchange.* Paper presented at the International Conference of the Pacific Association for Computer Assisted Language Learning, Kunming, China.

Robb, T., & Holliday, L. (2006). SL-*lists: International EFL/ESL email student discussion lists.* Retrieved December 7, 2006, from http://www.kyoto-su.ac.jp/~trobb/slinfo.html

Robinson, G. (1991). Effective feedback strategies in CALL: Learning theory and empirical research. In P. Dunkel (Ed.), *Computer-assisted language learning and testing: Research issues and practice* (pp. 155–168). New York: Newbury House.

Robinson, K. (n.d.). *Webgapper.* Retrieved December 6, 2006, from http://newtongue .org/webgapper/

Robinson, P. (1995). Attention, memory and the "noticing hypothesis." *Language Learning, 45,* 283–331.

Robinson, P. (2003). Attention and memory in SLA. In C. Doughty & M. H. Long (Eds.), *Handbook of second language acquisition* (pp. 631–678). Oxford: Blackwell.

RocketReader (Version 8.0) [Computer software]. (2006). New York: RocketReader. http://www.rocketreader.com/

Rodgers, T. S. (2001). *Language teaching methodology.* Washington, DC: Center for Applied Linguistics. Retrieved November 24, 2006, from http://www.cal.org/resources/digest/ rodgers.html

Rollins, D. (2001). *Rubrics.* Retrieved December 10, 2006, from http://www.techtrekers .com/rubrics.html

Root, T. (2000–2003). *Mightycoach.com.* Retrieved December 5, 2006, from http://www .mightycoach.com/

Rorschach, E., & MacGowan-Gilhooly, A. (1993). *Fluency first in ESL.* Retrieved December 9, 2006, from http://eric.ed.gov/ERICDocs/data/ericdocs2/content_ storage_01/0000000b/80/11/18/b5.pdf (ERIC Document Reproduction Service No. ED423662)

Rosetta Stone [Computer software]. (n.d.). Harrisonburg, VA: Fairfield Language Technologies. http://www.rosettastone.com/en/

Rost, M. (1990). *Listening in language learning.* New York: Longman.

Rost, M., & Fuchs, M. (2004). *Longman English interactive 3* [CD-ROM]. New York: Pearson Education.

Rotta, L. M., & Huser, C. A. (1995). *Techniques for assessing process writing.* (ERIC Document Reproduction Service No. ED393893)

Rotter, J. B. (1982). *The development and application of social learning theory.* New York: Praeger.

Rubin, J. (1975). What the "good language learner" can teach us. TESOL *Quarterly, 9,* 41–51.

Rutherford, W., & Sharwood Smith, M. (1985). Consciousness-raising and universal grammar. *Applied Linguistics, 6,* 274–282.

Ryan, R. M., & Deci, E. L. (2000). Self-determination theory and the facilitation of intrinsic motivation, social development, and well-being. *American Psychologist, 55,* 68–78.

Sacks, H., & Schegloff, E. A. (1979). Two preferences in the organization of reference to persons in conversation and their interaction. In G. Psathas (Ed.), *Everyday language: Studies in ethnomethodology* (pp. 15–21). New York: Irvington.

Salaberry, M. R. (2001). The use of technology for second language learning and teaching: A retrospective. *Modern Language Journal*, 85, 39–56.

Salmon, G. (2000). *E-moderating: The key to teaching and learning online.* London: Kogan Page.

Salomon, G. (1979). *Interaction of media, cognition and learning.* Hillsdale, NJ: Lawrence Erlbaum.

Salomon, G. (1990). Cognitive effects with and of technology. *Communications Research*, 17, 26–44.

Samford University. (2006). *PBL process.* Retrieved November 25, 2006, from http://www .samford.edu/ctls/pbl_process.html

San Jose Mercury News. (2006). *The Mercury News.* Retrieved November 30, 2006, from http://www.mercurynews.com/mld/mercurynews/

San Mateo County Office of Education. (1997–2001). *Multimedia project scoring rubric: Scoring guidelines.* Retrieved December 6, 2006, from http://pblmm.k12.ca.us/PBL Guide/MMrubric.htm

San Mateo County Office of Education. (1997–2002). *The PBL web ring.* Retrieved December 6, 2006, from http://pblmm.k12.ca.us/webringinfo.htm

Saskatoon Public School Division. (2004). *What is k-w-l? Know–want to know–learned.* Retrieved December 13, 2006, from http://olc.spsd.sk.ca/DE/PD/instr/strats/kwl/ index.html

Savery, J., & Duffy, T. (1995). Problem based learning: An instructional model and its constructivist framework. *Educational Technology*, 35(5), 31–38.

Savignon, S. (1991). Communicative language teaching: State of the art. TESOL *Quarterly*, 25, 261–277.

Schallert, D. L., Reed, J. H., & Turner, J. E. (2004). The interplay of aspirations, enjoyment, and work habits in academic endeavors: Why is it so hard to keep long-term commitments? *Teachers College Record*, 106, 1715–1728.

Schegloff, E. A., Jefferson, G., & Sacks, H. (1977). The preference for self-correction in the organization of repair in conversation. *Language*, 53, 361–382.

Schiefele, U. (1991). Interest, learning, and motivation. *Educational Psychologist*, 26, 299–323.

Schiffrin, D. (1994). *Approaches to discourse.* Oxford: Blackwell.

Schmidt, R. (1990). The role of consciousness in second language learning. *Applied Linguistics*, 11, 129–158.

Schmidt, R. (Ed.). (1995). *Attention and awareness in foreign language learning.* Honolulu: University of Hawai'i Press.

Schmidt, R. (2001). Attention. In P. Robinson (Ed.), *Cognition and second language instruction* (pp. 3–32). Cambridge: Cambridge University Press.

Schmidt, R., & Frota, S. N. (1986). Developing basic conversational ability in a second language: A case study of an adult learner of Portuguese. In R. Day (Ed.), *Talking to learn: Conversation in second language acquisition* (pp. 237–326). Rowley, MA: Newbury House.

Schofield, J. W. (1995). *Computers and classroom culture.* Cambridge: Cambridge University Press.

Scholl, W. (1996). Effective teamwork—a theoretical model and a test in the field. In E. Witte & J. H. Davis (Eds.), *Understanding group behavior: Vol. 2. Small group processes and interpersonal relations* (pp. 127–146). Mahwah, NJ: Lawrence Erlbaum.

Schön, D. A. (1983). *The reflective practitioner: How professionals think in action.* New York: Basic Books.

Schramm, A., & Mabbott, A. (2006). Implementing an online ESL teacher education program. In E. Hanson-Smith & S. Rilling (Eds.), *Learning languages through technology* (pp. 245–256). Alexandria, VA: TESOL.

Schraw, G., Flowerday, T., & Lehman, S. (2001). Increasing situational interest in the classroom. *Educational Psychology Review, 13,* 211–224.

Schwartz, B. (1993). On explicit and negative data effecting and affecting competence and linguistic behaviour. *Studies in Second Language Acquisition, 15,* 147–163.

Schwartz, B. (2004). *The paradox of choice.* New York: HarperCollins.

Schwartz, D. L. (1998). Doing with understanding: Lessons from research on problem and project-based learning. *Journal of the Learning Sciences, 7*(3/4), 271–311.

Schwartz, J. (1980). The negotiation for meaning: Repair in conversations between second language learners of English. In D. Larsen-Freeman (Ed.), *Discourse analysis in second language research* (pp. 138–153). Rowley, MA: Newbury House.

Schwartz, J. (2003, January 2). Professors vie with Web for class's attention. *The New York Times.* Retrieved March 5, 2007, from http://www.chesslaw.com/profsvcomputers.htm

Schwienhorst, K. (2002). Why virtual, why environments? *Simulation and Gaming, 33,* 196–209.

Schwienhorst, K. (2003a). Learner autonomy and tandem learning: Putting principles into practice in synchronous and asynchronous telecommunications environments. *Computer Assisted Language Learning, 16,* 427–443.

Schwienhorst, K. (2003b). Neither here nor there? Learner autonomy and intercultural factors in CALL environments. In D. Palfreyman & R. C. Smith (Eds.), *Learner autonomy across cultures: Language education perspectives* (pp. 164–180). New York: Palgrave Macmillan.

Science Court (Version 2.0) [Computer software]. (2006). Watertown, MA: Tom Snyder Productions. http://www.tomsnyder.com/products/product.asp?SKU=SCISCI&Subject=Science

Scrimshaw, P. (2004, June). *Enabling teachers to make successful use of* ICT. Coventry, England: British Educational Communications and Technology Agency. Retrieved November 27, 2006, from http://www.becta.org.uk/page_documents/research/enablers.pdf

Scriven, M. (2005). *The logic and methodology of checklists.* Western Michigan University. Retrieved December 13, 2006, from http://www.wmich.edu/evalctr/checklists/papers/logic&methodology_oct05.pdf

Scriven, M., & Paul, R. (2004). *Defining critical thinking.* Retrieved December 15, 2006, from http://www.criticalthinking.org/aboutCT/definingCT.shtml

Sendai museums. (n.d.). Retrieved December 10, 2006, from http://sendai-city-tourism-tohoku-university.blip.tv/file/55530

Sevier, M. (2006). Problems of time and exposure in vocabulary acquisition: An electronic solution. In E. Hanson-Smith & S. Rilling (Eds.), *Learning languages through technology* (pp. 25–40). Alexandria, VA: TESOL.

Shapiro, N., Adelson-Goldstein, J., Hanson-Smith, E., & Fella, E. (1999). The Oxford Picture Dictionary Interactive [Computer software]. New York: Oxford University Press. http://www.oup.com/elt/catalogue/isbn/9295?cc=gb

Sharwood Smith, M. (1981). Consciousness raising and the second language learner. *Applied Linguistics, 2,* 159–168.

Sharwood Smith, M. (1993). Input enhancement in instructed SLA. *Studies in Second Language Acquisition, 15,* 165–179.

Sheerin, S. (1997). An exploration of the relationship between self-access and independent learning. In P. Benson & P. Voller (Eds.), *Autonomy and independence in language
learning* (pp. 54–65). Harlow, England: Longman.

Sheperd, C. (n.d.). *Blended learning in the mixer.* Retrieved December 29, 2006, from
http://www.aboveandbeyond.ltd.uk/features/blended_learning.htm

Shiveley, J., & VanFossen, P. (2001). *Using primary sources to teach critical thinking skills in
government, economics, and contemporary world issues.* Westport, CT: Greenwood Press.

Shneiderman, B. (2002a). *Designing the user interface: Strategies for effective human-computer
interaction* (3rd ed.). Boston: Addison-Wesley.

Shneiderman, B. (2002b). *Leonardo's laptop: Human needs and the new computing technologies.*
Cambridge, MA: MIT Press.

Short, J. A., Williams, E., & Christie, B. (1976). *The social psychology of telecommunications.*
New York: John Wiley.

Sid Meier's Civilization II [Computer software]. (1997). Hunt Valley, MD: MicroProse
Software.

Siemens, G. (2004a). *Connectivism: A learning theory for the digital age.* Retrieved December
10, 2006, from http://www.elearnspace.org/Articles/connectivism.htm

Siemens, G. (2004b). *Eportfolios.* Retrieved December 13, 2006, from http://www.elearn
space.org/Articles/eportfolios.htm

SimCity (Classic version) [Computer software]. (1998). San Mateo, CA: Maxis/Elec-
tronic Arts.

SimCity (Version 4) [Computer software]. (2003). Redwood City, CA: Electronic Arts.
http://simcity.ea.com/

SimCopter [Computer software]. (1996). San Mateo, CA: Maxis/Electronic Arts.

SimTown [Computer software]. (1995). Walnut Creek, CA: Maxis/Electronic Arts.

Sinclair, B., McGrath, I., & Lamb, T. (Eds.). (2000). *Learner autonomy, teacher autonomy:
Future directions.* Harlow, England: Longman.

Singingfish. (1999–2006). Retrieved December 31, 2006, from http://search.singingfish
.com/sfw/home.jsp

Sivert, S., & Egbert, J. (1999). Building a computer-enhanced language classroom. In
J. Egbert & E. Hanson-Smith (Eds.), *CALL environments: Research, practice, and critical
issues* (pp. 41–49). Alexandria, VA: TESOL.

Skehan, P. (1998). *A cognitive approach to language learning.* Cambridge: Cambridge University Press.

Skyhook Wireless. (2006). *Loki.* Retrieved December 30, 2006, from http://loki.com/

Skype (Version 3.0) [Computer software]. (2006). Luxemburg: Skype. http://www.skype
.com/

Slowinski, J. (2000, September/October). The gap between preparation and reality
in training teachers to use technology. *The Technology Source.* Retrieved December
7, 2006, from http://technologysource.org/article/gap_between_preparation_and_
reality_in_training_teachers_to_use_technology/

Smerdon, B., Cronen, S., Lanahan, L., Anderson, J., Iannotti, N., & Angeles, J. (2000).
Teachers' tools for the 21st century: A report on teachers' use of technology. Washington, DC:
National Center for Education Statistics.

Smith, K. (2000). Negotiation assessment with secondary-school pupils. In M. Breen &
A. Littlejohn (Eds.), *Classroom decision-making: Negotiation and process syllabuses in practice*
(pp. 55–62). Cambridge: Cambridge University Press.

Smith, M. (2000). Factors influencing successful student uptake of socio-collaborative CALL. *Computer Assisted Language Learning*, 13, 397–415.

Smith, R. L., Skarbek, D., & Hurst, J. (2005). *The passion of teaching: Dispositions in the school*. Lanham, MD: Rowman & Littlefield.

Smith, W. F. (1989). *Modern technology in foreign language education: Applications and projects*. Chicago: National Textbook Company.

Snow, C. (1972). Mother's speech to children learning language. *Child Development*, 43, 549–565.

Sokolik, M. (2006). Issue: Mismatch or missed opportunity? Addressing student expectations about technology. In E. Hanson-Smith & S. Rilling (Eds.), *Learning languages through technology* (pp. 137–149). Alexandria, VA: TESOL.

Solomon, G. (2003, January). Project-based learning: A primer. *Technology & Learning*, 23(6). Retrieved November 28, 2006, from http://www.techlearning.com/db_area/archives/TL/2003/01/project.html

Sona-Speech II (Version 2.7.0) [Computer software]. (n.d.). Lincoln Park, NJ: KayPEN-TAX. http://www.kayelemetrics.com/Product%20Info/3650/3650.htm

Sony Electronics. (2006). *Sony reader*. Retrieved December 31, 2006, from http://www.sony.com/reader/

Soos, R. (2001, August 1). Multimedia projects: An effective use of technology as a tool in elementary education. *Educators eZine*. Retrieved December 5, 2006, from http://www.techlearning.com/db_area/archives/WCE/archives/soos.htm

Sorsa, D. (2003). *English insight by Don Sorsa*. http://condor.depaul.edu/~dsorsa/insight/

Sotillo, S. M. (2000). Discourse functions and syntactic complexity in synchronous and asynchronous communication. *Language Learning & Technology*, 4(1), 82–119.

Southwest Educational Development Laboratory. (1999). *Learning as a personal event: A brief introduction to constructivism*. Retrieved December 10, 2006, from http://www.sedl.org/pubs/tec26/intro2c.html

Spears, M., Lea, M., & Lee, S. (1990). De-individuation and group polarization in computer-mediated communication. *British Journal of Social Psychology*, 29(4), 121–134.

Special English: Learn American English and much more. (n.d.). Retrieved December 2, 2006, from http://www.voanews.com/specialenglish/index.cfm

Splish Splash Math [Computer software]. (2001). Elgin, IL: Sunburst Technology. http://store.sunburst.com/ProductInfo.aspx?itemid=176629

Spolsky, B. (1989). *Conditions for second language learning: Introduction to a general theory*. Oxford: Oxford University Press.

Springfield Public School District 186. (n.d.). *iMovie examples*. Retrieved December 5, 2006, from http://www.springfield.k12.il.us/movie/

Spurl ehf. (2004–2006). *Spurl.net*. Retrieved December 29, 2006, from http://www.spurl.net/

SRI International. (1995–2004). *Tapped in*. Retrieved November 26, 2006, from http://tappedin.org/tappedin/

St. Louis, R., & Pereira, S. (2003). Student involvement in an EST reading course for remedial students: A case study. *The Reading Matrix*, 3(2). Retrieved December 13, 2006, from http://www.readingmatrix.com/articles/st_louis_pereira/article.pdf

Stahl, G. (2000). A model of collaborative knowledge-building. In B. Fishman &

S. O'Connor-Divelbiss (Eds.), *Fourth International Conference of the Learning Sciences* (pp. 70–77). Mahwah, NJ: Lawrence Erlbaum.

Stanford University. (n.d.). *Stanford on iTunes U.* Retrieved November 27, 2006, from http://itunes.stanford.edu/

Stanley, G. (2006). Podcasting: Audio on the Internet comes of age. TESL-EJ, 9(4). Retrieved December 7, 2006, from http://tesl-ej.org/ej36/int.pdf

Star Trek: The Next Generation: Interactive Technical Manual [Computer software]. (1995). New York: Simon & Schuster.

Starfall Website. (2003). *Starfall.* Retrieved November 20, 2006, from http://www.starfall.com/

Stephens, M. (1998). *The rise of the image, the fall of the word.* New York: Oxford University Press.

Stepp-Greany, J. (2002). Student perceptions on language learning in a technological environment: Implications for the new millennium. *Language Learning & Technology,* 6(1), 165–180. Retrieved June 10, 2007, from http://llt.msu.edu/vol6num1/steppgreany/

Sternberg, R. J., & Williams, W. M. (1996). *Developing creativity in students.* Alexandria, VA: Association for Supervision and Curriculum Development.

Stevens, V. (2000). Designing a CALL facility from bottom to top at the Military Language Institute in Abu Dhabi. In E. Hanson-Smith (Ed.), *Technology-enhanced learning environments* (pp. 21–33). Alexandria, VA: TESOL.

Stevens, V. (2001). EVOnline 2002—*Webheads community event.* Retrieved November 28, 2006, from http://groups.yahoo.com/group/evonline2002_webheads/

Stevens, V. (2003). *Language learning techniques implemented through word processing.* Retrieved December 6, 2006, from http://www.geocities.com/Athens/Olympus/4631/wordproc.htm

Stevens, V. (2005). *Vance's e-zguide "10+ steps to creating simple HTML files."* Retrieved December 11, 2006, from http://www.homestead.com/prosites-vstevens/files/pi/very_basics/starthere.htm

Stevens, V. (2006). Issue: Tools for online teacher communities of practice. In E. Hanson-Smith & S. Rilling (Eds.), *Learning languages through technology* (pp. 257–269). Alexandria, VA: TESOL.

Stevens, V. (2007). *Webheads in Action: Communities of practice online.* Retrieved April 25, 2007, from http://www.prof2000.pt/users/vstevens/papers/evonline2002/webheads_evo.htm

Stevick, E. (1976). *Memory, meaning and method: Some psychological perspectives on language learning.* Rowley, MA: Newbury House.

Stites, R. (1998). *Evaluation of project based learning: What does research say about outcomes from project-based learning?* Retrieved November 25, 2006, from http://pblmm.k12.ca.us/PBLGuide/pblresch.htm

Stockwell, G., & Levy, M. (2001). Sustainability of e-mail interactions between native speakers and nonnative speakers. *Computer Assisted Language Learning,* 14, 419–442.

Storybook Weaver Deluxe [Computer software]. (2004). San Francisco: Riverdeep. http://www.riverdeep.net/portal/page?_pageid=353,157846,353_157847&_dad=portal&_schema=PORTAL

Strauss, H. (2003, October). Wireless classrooms: Evolution or extinction? *Campus Technology.* Retrieved November 27, 2006, from http://www.campus-technology.com/article.asp?id=8287

StreamSage. (2004). *Synchronization.* Retrieved December 30, 2006, from http://www
.streamsage.com/products_services/synch.htm

Strong, B., & Kidney, D. (2004). Collaboratively evaluating and deploying smart technology in classrooms. *Educause Quarterly, 27*(4), 64–67. Retrieved March 5, 2007, from
http://www.educause.edu/ir/library/pdf/eqm0448.pdf

Strudler, N., McKinney, M., & Jones, W. (1999). First-year teachers' use of technology:
Preparation, expectations and realities. *Journal of Technology and Teacher Education,
7*(2), 115–129.

Student-teacher writing pages. (n.d.). Retrieved November 29, 2006, from http://www
.schackne.com/Writing.htm#Link1

Stufflebeam, D. L. (2000). *Guidelines for developing evaluation checklists: The checklists development checklist* (CDC). Western Michigan University. Retrieved December 13, 2006,
from http://www.wmich.edu/evalctr/checklists/guidelines.htm

Sullivan, P. (2000). Practicing safe visual rhetoric on the World Wide Web. *Computers
and Composition, 18,* 103–121.

Suparp, S., Todd, R. W., & Darasawang, P. (2006). Supporting language learning from
a computer game. *CALL-EJ Online, 7*(2). Retrieved April 16, 2007, from http://www
.tell.is.ritsumei.ac.jp/callejonline/journal/7-2/darasawang.html

SuperMemo 2004 [Computer software]. (2004). Poznan, Poland: SuperMemo World.
http://www.supermemo.com/english/smintro.htm

Surowiecki, J. (2004). *The wisdom of crowds: Why the many are smarter than the few and how
collective wisdom shapes business, economies, societies, and nations.* New York: Doubleday.

SurveyMonkey.com. (1999–2006). *SurveyMonkey.* http://www.surveymonkey.com/

Susser, B. (2006). CALL and content-area teaching. In E. Hanson-Smith & S. Rilling
(Eds.), *Learning languages through technology* (pp. 97–107). Alexandria, VA: TESOL.

Swain, M. (1985). Communicative competence: Some roles of comprehensible input and
comprehensible output in its development. In S. M. Gass & C. G. Madden (Eds.),
Input in second language acquisition (pp. 235–253). Cambridge, MA: Newbury House.

Swain, M., & Lapkin, S. (1998). Interaction and second language learning: Two
adolescent French immersion students working together. *Modern Language Journal,
83,* 320–337.

Syque. (2002–2007). *Socratic questions.* Retrieved March 10, 2007, from http://changing
minds.org/techniques/questioning/socratic_questions.htm

Tacey, W. S. (1975). *Business and professional speaking* (2nd ed.). Dubuque, IA: W. C.
Brown.

Tactical Iraqi (Version 3.1) [Computer software]. (2006). Los Angeles: Tactical Language
Training. http://www.tacticallanguage.com/tacticaliraqi/

Tait, A. (2000). Planning student support for open and distance learning. *Open Learning, 15,* 287–299.

Taking TCO to the classroom. (n.d.). Retrieved December 7, 2006, from http://www.class
roomtco.org/

TALLENT Project. (2000). TALLENT: *Teaching and learning languages enhanced by new technologies.* University of Jyväskylä. Retrieved December 14, 2006, from http://www.solki
.jyu.fi/tallent/english.htm

Tam, M. (2000). Constructivism, instructional design, and technology: Implications for
transforming distance learning. *Educational Technology & Society, 3*(2). Retrieved January
25, 2007, from http://ifets.ieee.org/periodical/vol_2_2000/tam.html

Tancock, S. M. (n.d.) *On-line stories*. Ball State University. Retrieved December 8, 2006, from http://web.bsu.edu/00smtancock/EDRDG430/430stories.html

Tangient. (2006). *Wikispaces: Wikis for everyone*. Retrieved December 5, 2006, from http://www.wikispaces.com/

Tardy, C. M., & Snyder, B. (2004). "That's why I do it": Flow and EFL teachers' practices. *ELT Journal, 58*, 118–128.

Tarone, E. (1977). Conscious communication strategies in interlanguage: A progress report. In H. D. Brown, C. Yorio, & R. Crymes (Eds.), *On TESOL '77* (pp. 194–203). Washington, DC: TESOL.

Tavares, R., & Cavalcanti, I. (1996). Developing cultural awareness in EFL classrooms. *Forum, 34*(3), 18–23. Retrieved December 21, 2006, from http://exchanges.state.gov/forum/vols/vol34/no3/p18.htm

Taylor, A., Lazarus, E., & Cole, R. (2005). Putting languages on the (drop down) menu: Innovative writing frames in modern foreign language teaching. *Educational Review, 57*, 435–455.

Taylor, C. (2005, October 18). New member [Msg 2565]. Message posted to http://groups.yahoo.com/group/Real_English_Online

Taylor, C., & Weser, A. (2005). *kobe Bahía Blanca*. Retrieved December 10, 2006, from http://kobebahia.blogspot.com/2005_05_01_kobebahia_archive.html

Taylor, M. (1990). Simulations and adventure games in CALL. *Simulation & Gaming, 21*, 461–466.

Taylor, P. G. (2006). Critical thinking in and through interactive computer hypertext and art education. *Innovate, 2*(3). Available from http://innovateonline.info/index.php?view=article&id=41

TCET. (2001). *Technology lesson plans*. Retrieved November 30, 2006, from http://www.tcet.unt.edu/START/instruct/lp_tech.htm

teAchnology: Rubrics. (n.d.). Retrieved December 13, 2006, from http://www.teach-nology.com/web_tools/rubrics/

Techdictionary.com. (2006). Retrieved November 28, 2006, from http://www.techdictionary.com/domainlist.html

Technology lesson plans for ESL teachers. (n.d.). Retrieved November 30, 2006, from http://www.eslflow.com/technologylessonplans.html

Terrell, T. D. (1977). A natural approach to second language acquisition and learning. *Modern Language Journal, 61*, 325–37.

TESL-EJ. (1994–2007). Retrieved March 8, 2007, from http://tesl-ej.org/

TESL-L: *Teachers of English to speakers of other languages electronic list*. (n.d.). Hunter College, City University of New York. Retrieved March 8, 2007, from http://www.hunter.cuny.edu/~tesl-l/

TESOL. (1996–2004). TESOL *career center*. Retrieved December 14, 2006, from http://careers.tesol.org/

TESOL. (1996–2006a). *Essential Teacher*. Retrieved November 30, 2006, from http://www.tesol.org/et/

TESOL. (1996–2006b). *Principles and practices of online teaching certificate program*. Retrieved December 14, 2006, from http://www.tesol.org/s_tesol/sec_document.asp?CID=244&DID=488

TESOL. (1996–2006c). TESOL: *Teachers of English to speakers of other languages*. Retrieved December 14, 2006, from http://www.tesol.org/

TESOL. (2006). *PreK–12 English language proficiency standards in the core content areas*. Alexandria, VA: Author.

TESOL CALL-IS: *Make the connections*. (n.d.). Retrieved December 15, 2006, from http://www.call-is.org/moodle/

Textamerica. (n.d.). Retrieved December 31, 2006, from http://textamerica.com/

Thakerar, J. N., Giles, H., & Cheshire, J. (1982). Psychological and linguistic parameters of speech accommodation theory. In C. Fraser & K. R. Scherer (Eds.), *Advances in the social psychology of language* (pp. 205–255). Cambridge: Cambridge University Press.

Thein, M. (1994). A non-native English speaking teacher's response to a learner-centered program. *System, 22*, 463–471.

Theme tourism. (n.d.). Retrieved November 29, 2006, from http://themetourism.blogspot.com/

Thinkin' Things Collection 1 [Computer software]. (1995). San Francisco: Riverdeep.

Thomas, E. (2006). Listserv (Version 15.0) [Computer software]. Landover, MD: L-Soft. http://www.lsoft.com/products/listserv.asp

Thomas, J. W. (2000). *A review of research on project-based learning*. San Rafael, CA: Autodesk Foundation. Retrieved December 10, 2006, from http://www.bobpearlman.org/BestPractices/PBL_Research.pdf

Thomas, W. R. (1999). *Educational technology: Are school administrators ready for it?* Atlanta, GA: Southern Regional Education Board. Retrieved December 7, 2006, from http://www.sreb.org/programs/Edtech/pubs/ReadyForIt/Readyforit.asp

Thompson, G. L. (2004). *Through ebony eyes: What teachers need to know but are afraid to ask about African-American students*. San Francisco: Jossey-Bass.

Thorpe, M. (2003). Collaborative on-line learning: Transforming learner support and course design. In A. Tait & R. Mills (Eds.), *Rethinking learner support in distance education: Change and continuity in an international context* (pp. 198–211). New York: Routledge/Taylor & Francis.

TileToy: About us. (n.d.). Retrieved January 26, 2007, from http://www.tiletoy.org/

TileToy press material. (2005). Retrieved March 10, 2007, from http://www.tiletoy.org/

Time and Date AS/Thorsen, S. (1995–2006). *Time and date.com*. Retrieved December 29, 2006, from http://www.timeanddate.com/

TimeLiner (Version 5.0) [Computer software]. (2001). Watertown, MA: Tom Snyder Productions. http://www.tomsnyder.com/products/product.asp?SKU=TIMV50

Tobin, J. (1995). The irony of self-expression. *American Journal of Education, 103*, 233–258.

Torrance, E. P. (1972). Can we teach children to think creatively? *Journal of Creative Behaviour, 6*(2), 114–143.

Torrance, E. P. (Ed.). (2000). *On the edge and keeping on the edge: The University of Georgia annual lectures on creativity*. Westport, CT: Ablex.

Torrance, E. P., & Safter, H. T. (1990). *The incubation model of teaching: Getting beyond the Aha!* Buffalo, NY: Bearly.

Tosh, D., & Werdmuller, B. (2004). *Creation of a learning landscape: Weblogging and social networking in the context of e-portfolios*. Retrieved January 26, 2007, from http://elgg.net/bwerdmuller/files/61/179/Learning_landscape.pdf

TourMaker [Computer software]. (n.d.). Kirkland, WA: Tramline.

Towndrow, P. A. (2005). Teachers as digital task designers: An agenda for research and professional development. *Journal of Curriculum Studies, 37*, 507–524.

Toy, C. (n.d.). *Middle school diaries: The great Maine laptop experiment.* Retrieved November 27, 2006, from http://www.middleweb.com/mw/msdiaries/02-03wklydiaries/CT08.html

Toyoda, E., & Harrison, R. (2002). Categorization of text chat communication between learners and native speakers of Japanese. *Language Learning & Technology, 6*(1), 82–99. Retrieved December 11, 2006, from http://llt.msu.edu/vol6num1/toyoda/

TRACI Talk: The Mystery [Computer software]. (1997). Cupertino, CA: Courseware Publishing International.

Trahey, M., & White, L. (1993). Positive evidence and preemption in the second language classroom. *Studies in Second Language Acquisition, 15,* 181–204.

Treffinger, D. J., Young, G. C., Selby, E. C., & Shepardson, C. A. (2002). *Assessing creativity: A technical guide* (Report No. 02170). Storrs: University of Connecticut, National Research Center on the Gifted and Talented.

Trekmail. (2002–2006). Retrieved December 31, 2006, from http://w2.trekmail.com/

Tribble, C., & Jones, G. (1990). *Concordances in the classroom.* London: Longman.

Trumbull, M. (2005, October 11). The Internet enters a bold second act. *The Christian Science Monitor.* Retrieved November 27, 2006, from http://www.csmonitor.com/2005/1011/p01s03-ussc.html

Trustees of Dartmouth College. (2004). *Collaborative facilities.* Retrieved November 26, 2006, from http://www.dartmouth.edu/~collab/

Tsutsui, M. (2004). Multimedia as a means to enhance feedback. *Computer Assisted Language Learning, 17,* 377–402.

Turkish Ministry of National Education: General Directorate of Educational Technologies. (2004). MONE *Internet access projects.* Retrieved December 7, 2006, from http://egitek.meb.gov.tr/Egitek/EgitekIng/Projects/EgitekIng.htm

TurnHere. (n.d.). Retrieved December 10, 2006, from http://www.turnhere.com/

Tuttle, H. G. (1996). Rubrics: Keys to improving multimedia presentations. *Multimedia Schools, 3,* 30–33.

TVEyes. (1999–2006). Retrieved December 31, 2006, from http://www.tveyes.com/

TVEyes. (2006). *Podscope.* Retrieved December 31, 2006, from http://www.podscope.com/

The U-M software archives. (2000). University of Michigan. Retrieved November 30, 2006, from http://www.umich.edu/~archive/

U.S. Department of Education & SRI International. (1995). *Effects of technology on classrooms and students.* Retrieved November 29, 2006, from http://www.ed.gov/pubs/EdReform Studies/EdTech/effectsstudents.html

U.S. Department of Education, National Center for Education Statistics. (2004). *Internet access in U.S. public schools and classrooms: 1994–2003.* Retrieved November 27, 2006, from http://nces.ed.gov/surveys/frss/publications/2005015/

Uhlirov, L. (1994). Talk at a PC. In S. Cmejrkov, F. Dane, & E. Havlov (Eds.), *Writing vs. speaking: Language, text, discourse, communication* (pp. 275–282). Tübingen, Germany: Gunter Narr.

Ulitsky, H. (2000). Language learner strategies with technology. *Journal of Educational Computing Research, 22,* 285–322.

Ulrich, J. (n.d.). *We real cool by Gwendolyn Brooks.* Retrieved December 29, 2006, from http://www.favoritepoem.org/thevideos/ulrich.html

Ultimate Writing and Creativity Center [Computer software]. (n.d.). San Francisco: The Learning Company/Riverdeep. http://www.riverdeep.net/portal/page?_pageid=353,155572,353_155573&_dad=portal&_schema=PORTAL

University of Chicago. (n.d.). *Poem present: Readings and lectures.* Retrieved December 1, 2006, from http://poempresent.uchicago.edu/

University of Delaware. (1999). *Problem-based learning.* Retrieved December 6, 2006, from http://www.udel.edu/pbl/

University of Essex. (1999–2001). *Electronic generic auction marketplace (e-*GAME). Retrieved November 25, 2006, from http://csres43.essex.ac.uk:8080/egame/index.jsp

University of Houston System. (2005). *Educational uses of digital storytelling.* Retrieved December 11, 2006, from http://www.coe.uh.edu/digital-storytelling/

University of Illinois at Urbana-Champaign, Intensive English Institute. (n.d.). *Grammar safari.* Retrieved December 9, 2006, from http://www.iei.uiuc.edu/student_grammar safari.html

University of Iowa. (n.d.). *Phonetics: The sounds of American English.* Retrieved December 19, 2006, from http://www.uiowa.edu/~acadtech/phonetics/english/frameset.html

University of Southern California, Center for Scholarly Technology. (2006). *What is a wiki?* Retrieved March 9, 2007, from http://www.educause.edu/ir/library/pdf/ELI0626.pdf

University of Texas at Austin. (2006). *World lecture hall.* Retrieved November 30, 2006, from http://web.austin.utexas.edu/wlh/index.cfm

Ur, P. (2002). The English teacher as professional. In J. Richards & W. Renandya (Eds.), *Methodology in language teaching: An anthology of current practice* (pp. 388–392). Cambridge: Cambridge University Press.

Usborne's Animated First Thousand Words [Computer software]. (2004). Watertown, MA: Tom Snyder Productions. http://www.tomsnyder.com/products/product.asp ?SKU=USBFIR

Ushioda, E. (2000). Tandem language learning via e-mail: From motivation to autonomy. *ReCALL, 12,* 121–128.

van Borssum, A. (2005, April). *Scaffolding elementary ESL social studies with realia.* Paper presented at the 39th Annual TESOL Convention and Exhibit, San Antonio, TX.

Van Dijk, J. A. (2005). *The deepening divide: Inequality in the information society.* Thousand Oaks, CA: Sage.

van Gelder, T., & Bulka, A. (2001). Reason!Able [Computer software]. http://www .goreason.com/

van Lier, L. (1996). *Interaction in the language curriculum: Awareness, autonomy and authenticity.* New York: Longman.

Vandergrift, L. (1999). Facilitating second language listening comprehension: Acquiring successful strategies. *ELT Journal, 53,* 168–176.

Veenhof, B., Clermont, Y., & Sciadas, G. (2005). Skills and information and communications technologies. In Statistics Canada & Organization for Economic and Cooperative Development, *Learning a living: First results of the Adult Literacy and Life Skills Survey* (pp. 179–201). Ottawa, Ontario, Canada: Organization for Economic and Co-operative Development. Retrieved January 24, 2007, from http://www.statcan .ca/english/freepub/89-603-XIE/2005001/pdf/89-603-XWE-part1.pdf

Verizon New Media Services. (1996–2006). *Superthinkers.* Retrieved November 25, 2006, from http://www.superpages.com/enlightenme/superthinkers/pages/

Via Voice (Version 10) [Computer software]. (2003). White Plains, NY: IBM. http://www-306.ibm.com/software/voice/viavoice/

Villegas, A. M., & Lucas, T. (2002). *Educating culturally responsive teachers: A coherent approach.* Albany: State University of New York Press.

Vimeo. (2006). Retrieved December 10, 2006, from http://www.vimeo.com/

VIRLAN: *Foreign language virtual environment for primary school children.* (n.d.). Retrieved December 23, 2006, from http://www.educational-concepts.de/pprojects/virlan.html

VITO ActiveTrace (Version 1.21) [Computer software]. (2006). Novosibirsk, Russia: VITO Technology. http://www.activetrace.com/

Vivox. (2006). Retrieved December 31, 2006, from http://www.vivox.com/

VOA: *Voice of America.* (n.d.). Retrieved November 30, 2006, from http://www.voanews.com/

Volle, L. M. (2005). Analyzing oral skills in voice e-mail and online interviews. *Language Learning & Technology, 9*(3), 146–163.

Von der Emde, S., Schneider, J., & Kotter, M. (2001). Technically speaking: Transforming language learning through virtual learning environments (MOOs). *Modern Language Journal, 85,* 210–225.

Voronov, M., & Singer, J. (2002). The myth of individualism-collectivism: A critical review. *The Journal of Social Psychology, 142,* 461–480.

Voyager Info-Systems. (1998–2004). *VoyCabulary.* Retrieved December 6, 2006, from http://www.voycabulary.com/

Vygotsky, L. (1962). *Thought and language* (E. Hanfmann & G. Backer, Trans.). Cambridge, MA: MIT Press. (Original work published 1934)

Vygotsky, L. S. (1978). *Mind in society: The development of higher psychological processes* (M. Cole, V. John-Steiner, S. Scribner, & E. Louberman, Eds. & Trans.). Cambridge, MA: Harvard University Press.

Vygotsky, L. (1986). *Thought and language* (A. Kozulin, Ed. & Trans.). Cambridge, MA: MIT Press. (Original work published 1934)

Vygotsky, L. (1987). *Thinking and speech* (N. Minick, Trans.). New York: Plenum.

Wajnryb, R. (1990). *Grammar dictation.* Oxford: Oxford University Press.

Walker, J. (n.d.) *Your sky.* Retrieved November 25, 2006, from http://www.fourmilab.ch/yoursky/

Walker, R. A., & Lambert, P. E. (1995). *Designing electronic learning environments to support communities of learners:* A tertiary application. Retrieved December 22, 2006, from http://www.aare.edu.au/95pap/walkr95220.txt

Walther, J. (1996). Computer mediated communication: Impersonal, interpersonal, and hyperpersonal interaction. *Communication Research, 23*(1), 3–43.

Walther, J., & Boyd, S. (2002). Attraction to computer-mediated social support. In C. A. Lin & D. Atkin (Eds.), *Communication technology and society: Audience adoption and uses* (pp. 153–188). Cresskill, NJ: Hampton Press.

Ware, P. (2005). "Missed" communication in online communication: Tensions in a German-American telecollaboration. *Language Learning & Technology, 9*(2), 64–89. Retrieved December 20, 2006, from http://llt.msu.edu/vol9num2/ware/

Ware, P., & Kramsch, C. (2005). Toward an intercultural stance: Teaching German and English through telecollaboration. *Modern Language Journal, 89,* 190–205.

Warlick, D. (2006, October). A day in the life of Web 2.0. *Technology & Learning, 27*(3). Retrieved November 29, 2006, from http://www.techlearning.com/showArticle.jhtml?articleID=193200296

Warschauer, M. (1995). *E-mail for English teaching: Bringing the Internet and computer learning networks into the language classroom.* Alexandria, VA: TESOL.

Warschauer, M. (1996a). Comparing face-to-face and electronic discussion in the second language classroom. *CALICO Journal, 13*(2), 7–26.

Warschauer, M. (1996b). Computer-assisted language learning: An introduction. In S. Fotos (Ed.), *Multimedia language teaching* (pp. 3–20). Tokyo: Logos International.

Warschauer, M. (1997). Computer-mediated collaborative learning: Theory and practice. *Modern Language Journal*, 81, 470–481.

Warschauer, M. (1999). *Electronic literacies: Language, culture, and power in online education.* Mahwah, NJ: Lawrence Erlbaum.

Warschauer, M. (2002). Reconceptualizing the digital divide. *First Monday*, 7(7). Retrieved December 6, 2006, from http://www.firstmonday.org/issues/issue7_7/warschauer/index.html

Warschauer, M. (2003). *Technology and social inclusion: Rethinking the digital divide.* Cambridge, MA: MIT Press.

Warschauer, M. (2005). Networking the Nile: Technology and professional development in Egypt. In J. Inman & B. Hewett (Eds.), *Technology and English studies: Innovative professional paths* (pp. 163–174). Mahwah, NJ: Lawrence Erlbaum. Retrieved December 21, 2006, from http://www.gse.uci.edu/faculty/markw/nile.pdf

Warschauer, M. (2006). *Laptops and literacy: Learning in the wireless classroom.* New York: Teachers College Press.

Warschauer, M., & Donaghy, K. (1997). Leokï: A powerful voice of Hawaiian language revitalization. *Computer Assisted Language Learning*, 10, 349–362.

Warschauer, M., & Healey, D. (1998). Computers and language learning: An overview. *Language Teaching*, 31, 57–71. Retrieved December 7, 2006, from http://www.gse.uci.edu/faculty/markw/overview.html

Warschauer, M., & Ware, P. (2006). Automated writing evaluation: Defining the classroom research agenda. *Language Teaching Research*, 10, 157–180.

Weasenforth, D., Biesenbach-Lucas, S., & Meloni, C. (2002). Realizing constructivist objectives through collaborative technologies: Threaded discussions. *Language Learning & Technology*, 6(3), 58–86. Retrieved December 21, 2006, from http://llt.msu.edu/vol6num3/weasenforth/default.html

Weaver, C. (1990). *Understanding whole language: From principles to practice.* Portsmouth, NH: Heinemann.

Webb, N. (1982). Student interaction and learning in small groups. *Review of Educational Research*, 52, 421–445.

Webb, N. (1985). Verbal interaction and learning in peer-directed groups. *Theory Into Practice*, 24, 32–39.

WebCT Campus Edition (Version 4.1) [Computer software]. (2004). Lynnfield, MA: WebCT. http://www.webct.com/

WebFrance International. (n.d.) *Volterre-Fr: English and French language resources.* Retrieved November 29, 2006, from http://www.wfi.fr/volterre/home.html

Weil, M. M., & Rosen, L. D. (1997). *Technostress: Coping with technology @work @home @ play.* New York: Wiley.

Weiss, R., Adelson-Goldstein, J., & Shapiro, N. (1999). *Classic classroom activities: The Oxford picture dictionary program.* New York: Oxford University Press.

Welcome to the famous personages project! (n.d.). Kyoto Sangyo University. Retrieved November 28, 2006, from http://moodle.kyoto-su.ac.jp/wiki/index.php/Main_Page

Welcome to the Kyoto restaurant pages! (n.d.). Kyoto-Sangyo University. Retrieved December 10, 2006, from http://www.kyoto-su.ac.jp/information/restaurant/mainleft.html

Wenger, E. (1998a). Communities of practice: Learning as a social system. *Systems Thinker,*

9(5). Retrieved December 22, 2006, from http://www.co-i-l.com/coil/knowledge-garden/cop/lss.shtml

Wenger, E. (1998b). *Communities of practice: Learning, meaning, and identity.* New York: Cambridge University Press.

Wenger, E. (n.d.). *Learning for a small planet.* Retrieved February 8, 2007, from http://www.ewenger.com/research/index.htm

Western Michigan University, English Education Program. (2003). *Teaching English through technology.* Retrieved November 30, 2006, from http://www.wmich.edu/teachenglish/index.htm

WGBH Educational Foundation. (1996–2006). *Nova.* Retrieved December 6, 2006, from http://www.pbs.org/wgbh/nova/

WGBH Educational Foundation. (2000a). *Bicycle-wheel gyroscope.* Retrieved December 19, 2006, from http://www.pbs.org/wgbh/nova/lostsub/media/bicycle_vid.html

WGBH Educational Foundation. (2000b). *Build a rice paddy.* Retrieved December 19, 2006, from http://www.pbs.org/wgbh/nova/satoyama/hillside2.html

WGBH Educational Foundation. (2000c). *Destroy the castle.* Retrieved December 19, 2006, from http://www.pbs.org/wgbh/nova/lostempires/trebuchet/destroywave.html

WGBH Educational Foundation. (2006). *Getting results: A professional development course for community college educators.* Retrieved November 30, 2006, from http://www.league.org/gettingresults/web/

WGBH Educational Foundation. (2007). *Interactives archive.* Retrieved April 24, 2007, from http://www.pbs.org/wgbh/nova/hotscience/

Wheatley, G. H. (1991). Constructivist perspectives on science and mathematics learning. *Science Education, 75*(1), 9–21.

Wheeler, S., Waite, S. J., & Bromfield, C. (2002). Promoting creative thinking through the use of ICT. *Journal of Computer Assisted Learning, 18,* 367–378.

Where in the World Is Carmen Sandiego? [Computer software] (2002). San Francisco: The Learning Company/Riverdeep. http://www.learningcompany.com/jump.jsp?itemID=146&itemType=PRODUCT&path=1%2C2%2C22%2C90&iProductID=146

Widdowson, H. (1979). *Explorations in applied linguistics.* Oxford: Oxford University Press.

Widdowson, H. G. (1990). *Aspects of language teaching.* Oxford: Oxford University Press.

Wikipedia. (n.d.). Retrieved November 28, 2006, from http://www.wikipedia.org/

Wilkinson, R. J. D., & Foster, S. F. (1997, August). *Assessing task motivation in an LSP programme.* Paper presented at the 11th Symposium on LSP, Copenhagen, Denmark.

Williams, M., & Burden, R. L. (1997). *Psychology for language teachers: A social constructivist approach.* Cambridge: Cambridge University Press.

Willinsky, J. (1998). *Learning to divide the world: Education at empire's end.* Minneapolis: University of Minnesota Press.

Windows Movie Maker (Version 2.6) [Computer software]. (2007). Redmond, WA: Microsoft. http://www.microsoft.com/moviemaker/

Winet, D. (n.d.). *StudyCom English for Internet.* Retrieved November 29, 2006, from http://www.study.com/index.html

Winograd, T., & Flores, F. (1988). *Understanding computers and cognition: A new foundation for design.* Reading, MA: Addison-Wesley.

Witte, E., & Davis, J. (1996). *Understanding group behavior: Small group processes and interpersonal relations* (Vol. 2). Mahwah, NJ: Lawrence Erlbaum.

Wolfe, E. W., & Manalo, J. R. (2004). Composition medium comparability in a direct writing assessment of non-native English speakers. *Language Learning & Technology*, 8(1), 53–65. Retrieved June 10, 2007, from http://llt.msu.edu/vol8num1/wolfe/

Woodward, H. (1994). *Negotiated evaluation: Involving children and parents in the process*. Portsmouth, NH: Heinemann.

World Summit on the Information Society. (2005). *What's the state of ICT access around the world?* Retrieved December 6, 2006, from http://www.itu.int/wsis/tunis/newsroom/stats/

Worldbridges. (n.d.). Retrieved December 10, 2006, from http://www.worldbridges.net/

WorldForge. (1998–2005). Retrieved December 23, 2006, from http://worldforge.org/doc/about

WOW. (2004). *Water on the Web*. Retrieved November 25, 2006, from http://wateronthe web.org/

Wrege, A., & Hickman, T. (2004). *Around the house: A Website for language learning*. Retrieved December 23, 2006, from http://homepage.mac.com/alexander.wrege/qtvr/QTVR/english_home.html

The Writing Lab, The OWL at Purdue, & Purdue University. (1995–2006). *The OWL at Purdue*. Retrieved December 8, 2006, from http://owl.english.purdue.edu/owl/

www.eye.fi. (2006). *Eye-fi*. Retrieved December 30, 2006, from http://www.eye.fi/index .htm

Xiph.org. (1994–2005). *Ogg vorbis*. Retrieved December 30, 2006, from http://vorbis .com/

Yahoo! (2007a). Retrieved April 19, 2007, from http://www.yahoo.com/

Yahoo! (2007b). *Flickr*. Retrieved April 25, 2007, from http://www.flickr.com/

Yahoo! (2007c). *K–12 > Individual school newspapers*. Retrieved April 25, 2007, from http://dir .yahoo.com/Education/K_12/Newspapers/Individual_School_Papers/

Yahoo! (2007d). *Yahoo! Answers*. Retrieved April 25, 2007, from http://answers.yahoo .com/

Yahoo! (2007e). *Yahoo! Groups*. Retrieved April 19, 2007, from http://groups.yahoo .com/

Yahoo! (2007f). *Yahoo! Mail*. Retrieved April 19, 2007, from http://mail.yahoo.com/

Yeaman, A. R. J. (1993). Whose technology is it, anyway? *Education Digest*, 58(5), 19–23.

Yeh, A. (2004). *Let's get physical!* Retrieved December 29, 2006, from http://dcyeh .com/sy0304/2ndsem/groupa_projects/tpr/

Yeh, A. (2004–2006). *Research writing SY2006*. Retrieved December 29, 2006, from http:// researchwriting.blogspot.com/

Yeh, A. (2005a). *Optimum blend: Designing blended learning activities to facilitate effective teaching and learning approaches*. Presentation at the 2005 TESOL CALL Interest Section Electronic Village Online. Retrieved December 29, 2006, from http://dcyeh.com/ baw205/

Yeh, A. (2005b). Poetry from the heart. *English Today*, 21(1), 45–51.

Yeh, A. (2005c, December 8). *To ditch or not to ditch credit cards*. Retrieved December 24, 2006, from http://aidenyeh.podomatic.com/entry/2005-12-08T20_27_30-08_00

Yeh, A. (2005–2006b). *Language and culture*. Retrieved December 29, 2006, from http:// yehlanguageandculture.blogspot.com/2006_01_01_yehlanguageandculture_archive .html

Yeh, A. (2006). *English advertising class: Wenzao Ursuline College of Languages, English Department*. Retrieved December 5, 2006, from http://english-ad.blogspot.com/

Yeh, A. (n.d.). *Aiden Yeh's speech class podcast.* Retrieved August 22, 2006, from http://aiden yeh.podomatic.com/

Yildirim, S., Kocak, S., & Kirazci, S. (2001). Computers are ready but how about teachers: An assessment of Turkish basic education teachers' inservice training needs. In *Proceedings of Society for Information Technology and Teacher Education International Conference 2001* (pp. 1031–1035). Norfolk, VA: Association for the Advancement of Computing in Education.

Yngve, V. H. (1996). *From grammar to science: New foundations for general linguistics.* Amsterdam: John Benjamins.

Yoffe, L. (1997). An overview of ACTFL proficiency interviews: A test of speaking ability. *Shiken: JALT Testing & Evaluation SIG Newsletter,* 1(2), 3–9. Retrieved December 11, 2006, from http://www.jalt.org/test/yof_1.htm

Young, J. R. (2003, November 14). Student "engagement" in learning varies significantly by major, survey finds. *Chronicle of Higher Education.* Available from http://chronicle.com/weekly/v50/i12/12a03701.htm

Young Caucasus Women Headquarter. (n.d.). Retrieved December 3, 2006, from http://young caucasus.neweurasia.net/?page_id=3

Yousendit. (2007). Retrieved April 18, 2007, from http://www.yousendit.com/

YouTube. (2006). Retrieved December 5, 2006, from http://www.youtube.com/

Z Corporation. (n.d.). Z*Printer 310 Plus.* Retrieved November 21, 2006, from http://www .zcorp.com/products/printersdetail.asp?ID=1

Zamel, V. (1987). Recent research on writing pedagogy. *TESOL Quarterly, 21,* 697–715.

Zeinstejer, R., & Al-Othman, B. (2005). *Freedom and future dreams in different cultures.* Retrieved December 22, 2006, from http://alothman-b.tripod.com/skypeproject_ portal.htm

Zellermayer, M., Salomon, G., Globerson, T., & Givon, H. (1991). Enhancing writing-related metacognitions through a computerized writing partner. *American Educational Research Journal, 28,* 372–392.

Zhang, W., & Storck, J. (2001). Peripheral members in online communities. *AMCIS,* 8(1), 29–38.

Zimmer, S., Kratz, L., Gérard, P., & Roelants, A. (n.d.). *jamendo.* Retrieved November 30, 2006, from http://www.jamendo.com/

Appendix A: Professional Associations and Professional Development Resources

Professional Associations

Asia-Pacific Association for Computer-Assisted Language Learning (APACALL)	http://www.apacall.org/
Association for the Advancement of Computing in Education (AACE)	http://www.aace.org/
Association for Educational Communications and Technology (AECT)	http://www.aect.org/
Computer-Assisted Language Instruction Consortium (CALICO)	http://www.calico.org/
Computer-Using Educators (CUE)	http://www.cue.org/
European Association for Computer-Assisted Language Learning (EUROCALL)	http://www.eurocall-languages.org/
International Association for Language Learning Technology (IALLT)	http://www.iallt.org/
International Association of Teachers of English as a Foreign Language (IATEFL)	http://www.iatefl.org/
International Society for Technology in Education (ISTE)	http://www.iste.org/
Japan Association for Language Teaching (JALT)	http://jalt.org/
JALT CALL	http://jaltcall.org/
Pacific Association for Computer Assisted Language Learning (PacCALL)	http://www.paccall.org/main/index .php
Teachers of English to Speakers of Other Languages (TESOL)	http://www.tesol.org/

Special Interest Groups, Other Professional Communities, and E-Lists

Australia Flexible Learning	http://www.flexiblelearning.net.au/flx/go
CALL-IS Electronic Village Online (January-February annually)	http://www.call-is.org/moodle/
CATESOL Technology-Enhanced Language Learning Interest Group	http://www.jazvo.com/tellig/ http://tech.groups.yahoo.com/group/tell-ig/
Computer Learning Foundation	http://www.computerlearning.org/
EDC Center for Children & Technology	http://cct.edc.org/
EduNation	http://www.theconsultants-e.com/edunation/edunation.asp
EVOnline 2002—Webheads Community Event	http://groups.yahoo.com/group/evonline2002_webheads/
ESL/EFL Student Video Production	http://groups.yahoo.com/group/EVOvideo07/
Hot Potatoes Users	http://tech.groups.yahoo.com/group/hotpotatoesusers/
IATEFL Learning Technologies Special Interest Group	http://www.iateflcompsig.org.uk/
JALT CALL	http://jaltcall.org/
Learning With Computers	http://groups.yahoo.com/group/learningwithcomputers/
The LINGUIST List	http://linguist.emich.edu/
Moodle for Language Teachers	http://moodle.org/course/view.php?id=31
Multimedia Educational Resource for Learning and Online Teaching (MERLOT)	http://www.merlot.org/merlot/index.htm
Real English Online	http://groups.yahoo.com/group/Real_English_Online/
Tapped In	http://tappedin.org/tappedin/
TESOL CALL Interest Section	http://www.call-is.org/moodle/
TESOL Video and Digital Media Interest Section	http://lists.tesol.org/read/?forum=vdmis-l (members only)
Webheads in Action: Communities of Practice Online	http://www.geocities.com/vance_stevens//papers/evonline2002/webheads.htm

Journals

CALICO *Journal*	https://www.calico.org/p-5-CALICO%20 Journal.html
CALL EJ *Online*	http://www.tell.is.ritsumei.ac.jp/callejonline/ index.php
Computer Assisted Language Learning	http://www.tandf.co.uk/journals/titles/ 09588221.asp
Essential Teacher	http://www.tesol.org/et/
Internet TESL Journal	http://iteslj.org/
Language Learning & Technology	http://llt.msu.edu/
The Reading Matrix	http://www.readingmatrix.com/journal.html
ReCALL	http://journals.cambridge.org/action/ displayJournal?jid=REC
System	http://www.elsevier.com/wps/find/ journaldescription.cws_home/335/ description#description
Teacher Librarian: The Journal for School Library Professionals	http://www.teacherlibrarian.com/
Technology & Learning	http://www.techlearning.com/
TESL-EJ	http://tesl-ej.org/

Lesson Plans and Information Sources

Alado: Webheads	http://www.alado.net/webheads/
Apple Learning Interchange	http://edcommunity.apple.com/ali/index.php
Blue Web'n	http://www.kn.pacbell.com/wired/bluewebn/
Breaking News English: Technology Lesson Plans	http://www.breakingnewsenglish.com/ technology.html
CALL @ Chorus	http://www-writing.berkeley.edu/chorus/index .html
Collaborative Facilities	http://www.dartmouth.edu/~collab/
College and University Home Pages—Alphabetical Listing	http://www.mit.edu:8001/people/cdemello/ univ.html
Download.com	http://www.download.com/
EduBlog Insights	http://anne.teachesme.com/
Educational Resources Information Clearinghouse (ERIC)	http://www.eric.ed.gov/
Educational Uses of Digital Storytelling	http://www.coe.uh.edu/digital-storytelling/
eThemes	http://www.emints.org/ethemes/index.shtml
everythingESL.net Lesson Plans	http://www.everythingesl.net/lessons/

Guide to Teaching Reading at the Primary School Level	http://unesdoc.unesco.org/images/0014/ 001411/141171e.pdf
Google Scholar	http://scholar.google.com/
Learning Point Associates Publications: Technology in Education	http://www2.learningpt.org/catalog/category .asp?SessionID=317656867&ID=9
Let's Get Physical!	http://dcyeh.com/sy0304/2ndsem/ groupa_projects/tpr/
Linguistic Funland	http://www.linguistic-funland.com/
LiteracyCenter.net	http://www.literacycenter.net/
The Open University LearningSpace	http://www.openlearn.open.ac.uk/
OPPortunities for Teachers and Learners of English for Speakers of Other Languages	http://www.uoregon.edu/~leslieob/
The PBL Web Ring	http://pblmm.k12.ca.us/webringinfo.htm
Problem-Based Learning Network @ IMSA	http://www2.imsa.edu/programs/pbln/
Selected Resources for Language Professionals	http://www.usq.edu.au/users/sonjb/resources .html
Software Selection, Evaluation, and Use	http://oregonstate.edu/Dept/eli/vstevens/day1 .htm
teAchnology	http://teachnology.com/
The Technology Applications Center for Educator Development Technology Lesson Plans	http://www.tcet.unt.edu/START/instruct/lp_ tech.htm
Technology/Gadget/Device/Object Lesson Ideas/Plans for ESL Teachers	http://www.eslflow.com/technology lessonplans.html
TESOL CALL Interest Section Software List	http://oregonstate.edu/Dept/eli/softlist/
Tom's Page	http://www.kyoto-su.ac.jp/~trobb/
The U-M Software Archives	http://www.umich.edu/~archive/
University of Delaware Problem-Based Learning	http://www.udel.edu/pbl/
Virtual=Real	http://ehansonsmith.blogspot.com/
Volterre-Fr: English and French Language Resources	http://www.wfi.fr/volterre/home.html
The Weblog Project	http://www.theweblogproject.com/
World CALL Directory	http://www.call4all.us/home/_all.php?fi=c
Worldbridges	http://www.worldbridges.net/
ZDNet Downloads	http://downloads.zdnet.com/

Self-Access Professional Development and Online Courses

Annenberg Media	http://learner.org/
Atomic Learning	http://www.atomiclearning.com/
Collaborate 1: With One Person or Classroom	http://www.siec.k12.in.us/~west/edu/wwwdo/index.html
Education World: Techtorials Archive	http://www.education-world.com/a_tech/archives/techtorials.shtml
Electronic Village Online	http://www.call-is.org/moodle/
Getting Results: A Professional Development Course for Community College Educators	http://www.league.org/gettingresults/web/
Harnessing the Power of the Web	http://www.gsn.org/web/index.html
iEARN: MovingVoices	http://www.iearn.org/projects/movingvoices.html http://movingvoices.iearn.org/
Information and Communications Technology for Language Teachers (ICT4LT)	http://www.ict4lt.org/en/index.htm
Internet4Classrooms On-line Practice Modules	http://www.internet4classrooms.com/on-line.htm
Knowplace Openweekends	http://knowplace.ca/moodle/course/category.php?id=7
Learning Together Apart	http://www.ilearnitonline.com/lta/moodle/
Learning With Computers	http://groups.yahoo.com/group/learningwithcomputers/
MightyCoach.com	http://www.mightycoach.com/
NCRTEC Learning With Technology Profile Tool	http://www.ncrtec.org/capacity/profile/profwww.htm
Principles and Practice of Online Teaching Certificate Program	http://www.tesol.org/s_tesol/sec_document.asp?CID=244&DID=488
TALLENT: Teaching and Learning Languages Enhanced by New Technologies	http://www.solki.jyu.fi/tallent/index.htm
Teachers' TV	http://www.teachers.tv/video/
Teaching English Through Technology	http://www.wmich.edu/teachenglish/sitemap.htm
Vance's e-Zguide "10+ Steps to Creating Simple HTML Files"	http://www.homestead.com/prosites-vstevens/files/pi/very_basics/starthere.htm
W3Schools	http://www.w3schools.com/

Appendix B: Electronic Forums, Exchanges, and Collaborations for Teachers and Students

Electronic Discussion Lists for Teachers

TESL-L Lists

To join any of these mail forums, first visit **http://hunter.cuny.edu/~tesl-l/** and follow the directions given there. To subscribe to any of the special interest branches of TESL-L, listed below, you must first become a member of TESL-L:

- TESLCA-L: Computer technology and TESL
- TESLMW-L: Material writers
- TESP-L: English for specific purposes

TESOL Member Lists

Members of TESOL have access to a free e-mail list from their main interest section (IS) and caucus, and can join any of the other IS and caucus e-mail lists for a small fee. Lists include several of interest to technology-using teachers, such as those offered by the Computer-Assisted Language Learning IS and the Video and Digital Media IS. To join TESOL and find out more about its programs, go to **http://www.tesol.org/**.

Many TESOL affiliates also have e-mail lists. Check your local affiliate's Web site for more information.

Electronic Discussion Lists for Students

SL Project

Teachers must register with the Student List (SL) Project before their students can sign on to the discussion boards. Organized by Tom Robb and based in a Moodle (**http://sl-lists.net/**), the SL Project for secondary, university, and adult students has the following forums:

- Introductions—All students in registered classes should visit this forum first

For university and adult learners:

- General Chat—This forum is for any topic not covered in the other forums
- Business English
- Culture & Society
- Current Events Around the World
- Global Warming
- Learning English
- Movies
- Music
- Sports

For secondary school learners:

- Teen Talk

Special projects for class collaborations are also possible. To have your class (or individual students) join the SL-Lists, write to Tom Robb at **trobb@cc.kyoto-su.ac .jp** with the subject heading *Student List Project Enrollment Key*. State whether you are a student or a teacher, and give your location and educational institution. Further explanation of the history and purpose of the SL-Lists can be found at *Tom's Page*: **http://www.kyoto-su.ac.jp/~trobb/#sl**.

Gaggle.Net Gaggle Blogs

Gaggle Blogs allow students and educators to interface with the rest of the world in a safe environment, and may be used for regular student online discussions. Gaggle Blogs are filtered for inappropriate words, phrases, and images; URLs are scanned and checked for pornographic content. If rules are violated, the offending blog entry is blocked and sent to the author's administrator e-mail address pending approval. Students can get Gaggle accounts only through their school. A sign-up form for teachers or lab coordinators is linked from **http://www.gaggle.net/**.

MOOs, MUDS, Chats, Blogs, Podcasts, and Other Online Public Community Spaces

Blaxxun	http://www.blaxxun.com/
Buzznet	http://www.buzznet.com/
Click.TV	http://www.click.tv/
Dave's ESL Cafe's Student Discussion Forums	http://www.eslcafe.com/forums/student/
del.icio.us	http://del.icio.us/
The Diary Project	http://www.diaryproject.com/about/

EduNation	http://www.theconsultants-e.com/edunation/edunation.asp
Epsilen Environment	http://www.epsilen.com/Epsilen/Public/Home.aspx
Facebook	http://www.facebook.com/
Flickr	http://www.flickr.com/
Flock	http://flock.com/
Frappr!	http://www.frappr.com/
Friendster	http://www.friendster.com/
Gaggle.Net	http://www.gaggle.net/
Gather	http://www.gather.com/
Google Groups	http://groups.google.com/
MSN Groups	http://groups.msn.com/
MundoHispano: The Spanish Language Learning MOO	http://www.umsl.edu/~moosproj/mundo.html
MySpace	http://www.myspace.com/
orkut	http://www.orkut.com/
Ourmedia	http://www.ourmedia.org/
Paltalk Messenger	http://www.paltalk.com/en/messaging.shtml
Participatory Culture Foundation	http://participatoryculture.org/
PBwiki	http://pbwiki.com/
podOmatic	http://www.podomatic.com/
Radio Handi	http://www.radiohandi.com/
schMOOze University	http://schmooze.hunter.cuny.edu/
Second Life	http://secondlife.com/
Skype	http://www.skype.com/
StudyCom English for Internet	http://study.com/
Textamerica	http://textamerica.com/
Vimeo	http://www.vimeo.com/
VIRLAN: Foreign Language Virtual Environment for Primary School Children	http://www.educational-concepts.de/pprojects/virlan.html
Vivox	http://www.vivox.com/
Wikispaces	http://www.wikispaces.com/
Yahoo! Groups	http://groups.yahoo.com/
Yahoo! Messenger	http://messenger.yahoo.com/
YouTube	http://www.youtube.com/

Guides to Finding Forums, Blogs, Chat Exchanges, and Other Projects

CataList, the Official Catalog of LISTSERV Lists	http://www.lsoft.com/catalist.html
Dekita.org: EFL/ESL Exchange	http://dekita.org/exchange/
ESL: Student Projects	http://iteslj.org/links/ESL/Student_Projects/
The Global Schoolhouse: Internet Projects Registry	http://www.globalschoolnet.org/GSH/pr/index.cfm
Harnessing the Web: Locating Projects and Partners	http://www.gsn.org/web/pbl/find/locate.htm
Intercultural E-mail Classroom Connections (IECC): Related Resources	http://www.iecc.org/Resources.cfm
Linguistic Funland TESL Pen Pal Center	http://www.tesol.net/penpals/
Rachel's Super MOO List: Educational MOOs	http://moolist.yeehaw.net/edu.html
Student-Teacher Writing Pages	http://www.schackne.com/Writing.htm#Link1

Exchange Projects and Collaborations for Students and Classrooms

absolutely intercultural! Blog and Podcast	http://www.absolutely-intercultural.com/
De Orilla a Orilla	http://www.orillas.org/welcomee.html
Dekita.org EFL/ESL Exchange	http://dekita.org/exchange/
Email Projects Home Page	http://www.otan.dni.us/webfarm/emailproject/email.htm
ePALS Classroom Exchange	http://www.epals.com/
ESL: Student Projects	http://iteslj.org/links/ESL/Student_Projects/
ESL Slideshow Exchange Project	http://www.deepmoat.com/moodle/
eTwinning	http://www.etwinning.net/ww/en/pub/etwinning/index2006.htm
Friends and Flags	http://www.friendsandflags.org/
The Global Schoolhouse	http://www.globalschoolnet.org/GSH/index.html
The GLOBE Program	http://www.globe.gov/globe_flash.html
Harnessing the Web	http://www.gsn.org/web/index.html
International Education and Resource Network (iEARN)	http://www.iearn.org/

Intercultural E-mail Classroom Connections	http://www.iecc.org/
Nicenet	http://www.nicenet.org/
Student List Project (SL-Lists)	http://sl-lists.net/
TESL-L	http://www.hunter.cuny.edu/~tesl-l/

Examples of Collaborative Projects

English Class' Podcast	http://dreamteam.podomatic.com/entry/2006-02-04T01_08_39-08_00
kobe Bahía Blanca	http://kobebahia.blogspot.com/2005_05_01_kobebahia_archive.html
Paris-Normandy 2005	http://mgsonline.blogs.com/paris2005/
The Skype Worldbridges Project for EFL in Different Cultures: Argentina and Kuwait Online Presentation at WiAOC	http://worldbridges.com/webheads/audio/ritabuthstudents2005-08-22.mp3
The Spirit of Christmas	http://64.71.48.37/teresadeca/school/spiritofxmas.htm
A Web-Based Students' Collaborative Project	http://alothman-b.tripod.com/162s4_groupboards04.htm

Appendix C: Resources by Subject Area for Sustained Content Learning and Teaching

Note that many of the Web sites in this appendix, though free, require registration by the user.

General Resources Covering Multiple Subject Areas

A number of universities and colleges place all of their educational programming (formerly often on closed television cable) on Internet media. For example, Seattle Community Colleges Educational Television (**http://www.scctv.net/**) offers advanced placement courses for high school students; an online quarterly magazine written by college students; and courses in ESOL, culinary arts, technical writing, and so on. In addition, a number of local newspapers (e.g., San Jose's *Mercury News* [**http://www.mercurynews .com/mld/mercurynews/**]) are online and offer good general content resources for many subjects.

BBC Schools	http://www.bbc.co.uk/schools/
Biography	http://www.biography.com/
blinkx	http://www.blinkx.com/
CBBC	http://www.bbc.co.uk/cbbc/
CNN.com	http://www.cnn.com/
digg	http://www.digg.com/
Discovery.com	http://www.discovery.com/
DiscoverySchool.com	http://school.discovery.com/
Earthcomber Spot Guides	http://www.earthcomber.com/comber/catalog/view.do
Google Earth	http://earth.google.com/
Great Sites for Educators—Links Archive	http://www.idecorp.com/bookmark.htm
Individual School Newspapers	http://dir.yahoo.com/education/k_12/newspapers/individual_school_papers/
The Intersect Digital Library	http://intersect.uoregon.edu/
MIT OpenCourseWare	http://ocw.mit.edu/index.html
MIT World: Video Index	http://mitworld.mit.edu/video_index.php
National Museum of Australia Canberra	http://www.nma.gov.au/index.html

National Public Radio (NPR)	http://www.npr.org/
PBS Kids	http://pbskids.org/
PBS TeacherSource	http://www.pbs.org/teachersource/
Public Broadcasting Service (PBS)	http://www.pbs.org/
SimCity	http://simcity.ea.com/
The Sims	http://thesims.ea.com/
Smithsonian Education	http://www.smithsonianeducation.org/
Video Nation	http://www.bbc.co.uk/videonation/
Voice of America (VOA)	http://www.voiceamerica.com/
World Lecture Hall	http://web.austin.utexas.edu/wlh/index.cfm

Fine Arts

Almost all major museums have created online, interactive treasure houses for teachers and students. Because of the visual and pedagogical support they offer, these sites can become valuable language learning resources, not just for art but for history and culture. (Web sites for drawing and painting are also good resources for inspiring creativity in other areas.)

A Lifetime of Color	http://www.sanford-artedventures.com/
The Louvre	http://www.louvre.fr/llv/musee/alaune.jsp
Metropolitan Museum of Art: Explore & Learn	http://www.metmuseum.org/explore/index.asp
National Gallery of Victoria	http://www.ngv.vic.gov.au/

History and Culture

Most major national museums have Web sites offering lesson plans and other resources that are useful to historical and cultural studies and language learning.

Biography	http://www.biography.com/
British Museum	http://www.thebritishmuseum.ac.uk/
Freeciv	http://www.freeciv.org/index.php/Freeciv
History.com	http://www.history.com/
The Oregon Trail	http://www.learningcompany.com/jump.jsp ?itemID=147&mainPID=147&itemType= PRODUCT&RS=1&keyword=oregon+trail
Regensburg Experience	http://www.rex-regensburg.de/
Sid Meier's Civilization II	http://www.mobygames.com/game/ sid-meiers-civilization-ii

Smithsonian Education   http://www.smithsonianeducation.org/
Windsor Castle Virtual Tour   http://www.bbc.co.uk/history/british/launch_
    vt_windsor_castle.shtml

Literature, Music, and Movies

Poems, stories, and songs can offer students an understanding of their adopted country or one where they will study, as well as provide a means to self-exploration and personal growth—which are often very important for immigrant students. Reading an extended work of literature or studying a body of essays, poems, or songs can form an excellent basis for sustained content language teaching in all types of language programs, even if the curricular focus is not a particular subject area. The Web itself forms a huge body of reading material, but many sites offer lengthy texts or other media that may be read online or downloaded.

Authors' Web sites, such as Judy Blume's Home Base   http://www.judyblume.com/menu-main.html

The Ballad Tree: Song Collections & Indexes   http://www.balladtree.com/links/songs.htm

The British Council Arts: encompassculture   http://www.encompassculture.com/

Favorite Poem Project   http://www.favoritepoem.org/

jamendo   http://www.jamendo.com/

LitLinks   http://www.bedfordstmartins.com/litlinks/home.htm

Little Explorers English Picture Dictionary   http://www.enchantedlearning.com/Dictionary.html

Living Books Library (e.g., *Arthur's Teacher Trouble*, *Just Grandma and Me*)   http://www.riverdeep.net/portal/page?_pageid=353,143803,353_143804&_dad=portal&_schema=PORTAL

On-Line Stories   http://web.bsu.edu/00smtancock/EDRDG430/430stories.html

Poem Present: Readings and Lectures   http://poempresent.uchicago.edu/

Poemar   http://www.poemar.com/

Project Gutenberg Online Book Catalog   http://www.gutenberg.org/catalog/

Math and Science

Downloadable or online software can provide fascinating entry points into the world of content. A Web search by subject area will lead to hundreds of hours of activities in almost any field.

Bicycle-Wheel Gyroscope	http://www.pbs.org/wgbh/nova/lostsub/media/bicycle_vid.html
Build a Rice Paddy	http://www.pbs.org/wgbh/nova/satoyama/hillside2.html
Chemistry Software and Science Teaching Resources	http://www.chemistryteaching.com/
Destroy the Castle	http://www.pbs.org/wgbh/nova/lostempires/trebuchet/destroywave.html
Dig and Deduce	http://www.pbs.org/wgbh/nova/neanderthals/dig.html
DiscoverySchool.com	http://school.discovery.com/
Engineer a Crop: Transgenic Manipulation	http://www.pbs.org/wgbh/harvest/engineer/transgen.html
The GLOBE Program	http://www.globe.gov/globe_flash.html
Google Maps	http://maps.google.com/
Illuminating Photosynthesis	http://www.pbs.org/wgbh/nova/methuselah/photosynthesis.html
Imagination Express (e.g., Destination: Ocean, Destination: Rain Forest)	http://www.riverdeep.net/portal/page?_pageid=353,184442,353_184443&_dad=portal&_schema=PORTAL
Math Magician	http://www.oswego.org/ocsd-web/games/mathmagician/mathsmulti.html
Inside the Jet Stream	http://www.pbs.org/wgbh/nova/vanished/jetstream.html
The NASA SciFiles	http://whyfiles.larc.nasa.gov/
National Aeronautics and Space Administration (NASA)	http://www.nasa.gov/home/
National Geographic	http://www.nationalgeographic.com/index.html
Nature for Teachers	http://www.pbs.org/wnet/nature/teach1.html
NOVA	http://www.pbs.org/wgbh/nova/
NOVA Interactives Archive	http://www.pbs.org/wgbh/nova/hotscience/
NOVA Teachers	http://www.pbs.org/wgbh/nova/teachers/
PBS TeacherSource	http://www.pbs.org/teachersource/
Science Friday Kid's Connection	http://www.sciencefriday.com/kids/
Star Trek: The Next Generation: Interactive Technical Manual	Simon & Schuster

TeachEngineering Resources for
  K–12
http://www.teachengineering.com/

Virtual San Francisco Tower
http://www.natca.net/assets/multimedia/
  gatetogate/sfotower.mov

Water on the Web
http://waterontheweb.org/

Your Sky
http://www.fourmilab.ch/yoursky/

Vocational Education, Business, English for Tourism, and Other ESP

Come Visit Wisconsin!
http://people.uwec.edu/HAYDENDA/pbl/
  wisconsinpbl.htm

English on the Job
http://www.languagesolutionsllc.com/

Internet-Based Projects for
  Business English
http://aei.uoregon.edu/esp/

Outreach and Technical Assistance
  Network (OTAN)
http://www.otan.us/

Resource Generator
http://www.resourcegenerator.gov.au/Login.asp

TurnHere
http://www.turnhere.com/

Dictionaries and Encyclopedias

Freedictionary.com
http://www.freedictionary.com/

Little Explorers English Picture
  Dictionary
http://www.enchantedlearning.com/Dictionary
  .html

MSN Encarta
http://encarta.msn.com/

Oxford Picture Dictionary
  Interactive
http://www.oup.com/elt/catalogue/
  isbn/9295?cc=gb

Wikipedia
http://www.wikipedia.org/

Appendix D: Content-Free Online Tools, Software, and Tutorials

Web Sites and Online Tools

Acrobat Connect Professional   http://www.adobe.com/products/
                                acrobatconnectpro/
Active Worlds   http://www.activeworlds.com/
AirPlay   http://www.airplay.com/Home.tap
A.L.I.C.E. Artificial Intelligence   http://www.alicebot.org/
    Foundation
Audacity   http://audacity.sourceforge.net/
Babel Fish Translation   http://babelfish.altavista.com/
Backflip   http://www.backflip.com/
Blackboard Academic Suite   http://www.blackboard.com/products/
                                Academic_Suite/
BlogCheese   http://www.blogcheese.com/
Blogger   http://www.blogger.com/
Bubbleshare   http://www.bubbleshare.com/
Chalk & Wire   http://www.chalkandwire.com/
Charles Kelly's Online Quiz   http://a4esl.org/c/qw.html
    Generator
College LiveText   http://college.livetext.com/college/index.html
The Compleat Lexical Tutor   http://www.lextutor.ca/
Curriculum Bytes: Assessment   http://www.plrd.ab.ca/sites/bytes/web/
    Tools   resources/links.htm#assessment
del.icio.us   http://del.icio.us/
e-Game   http://csres43.essex.ac.uk:8080/egame/index
                                .jsp
Earthcomber   http://www.earthcomber.com/splash/index
                                .html
Everypoint   http://www.everypoint.com/
Filamentality   http://www.kn.pacbell.com/wired/fil/index.html
Filamentality: Activity Formats http://www.kn.pacbell.com/wired/fil/formats
                                .html

FolioLive	http://www.foliolive.com/
Gaggle	http://www.gaggle.net/index.html
Gliffy	http://gliffy.com/
Gmail	http://mail.google.com/
Google	http://www.google.com/
Google Docs & Spreadsheets	http://docs.google.com/
Google Image Search	http://images.google.com/
Google Scholar	http://scholar.google.com/
Great Sites for Educators—Links Archive	http://www.idecorp.com/bookmark.htm
Groupboard	http://www.groupboard.com/
hellodeo	http://www.hellodeo.com/hello/
Internet Archive	http://www.archive.org/index.php
Introduction to Scoring Rubrics	http://intranet.cps.k12.il.us/assessments/ ideas_and_rubrics/intro_scoring/intro_ scoring.html
KartOO	http://www.kartoo.com/
KEEP Toolkit	http://www.cfkeep.org/static/index.html
Learning Styles Inventory	http://www.learning-styles-online.com/ inventory/
Loki	http://loki.com/
MagazineFactory	http://www2.edu.fi/magazinefactory/
Makers Pages	http://web.archive.org/web/20041010183546/ makers.cet.middlebury.edu/makers/index .htm
MMORPG.COM	http://www.mmorpg.com/
Mobiedge Radio	http://mobiedge.ca/index_files/page0002.htm
Mobizines Reader	http://www.mobizines.com/
Mobot	http://www.mobot.com/
Moodle	http://moodle.org/
MSN Groups	http://groups.msn.com/
MSN Hotmail	http://www.hotmail.com/
MySpace	http://www.myspace.com/
NCRTEC Lesson Planner	http://www.ncrtec.org/tl/lp/
Odeo	http://odeo.com/
OneLook Dictionary Search	http://www.onelook.com/
The OWL at Purdue	http://owl.english.purdue.edu/owl/
PBL Checklists	http://pblchecklist.4teachers.org/checklist .shtml
The PBL Web Ring	http://pblmm.k12.ca.us/webringinfo.htm

PBwiki	http://pbwiki.com/
Play Free Online Games	http://play-free-online-games.com/
Podcasting Rubric	http://www.beaut.org.au/podcastrubric.pdf
podOmatic	http://www.podomatic.com/
Podscope	http://www.podscope.com/
Project Based Learning: Checklists to Support Project Based Learning and Evaluation	http://pblchecklist.4teachers.org/
QuestGarden	http://questgarden.com/
Quia Web	http://www.quia.com/web/
QuickTopic Document Review	http://www.quicktopic.com/documentcollaboration/
Radio Handi	http://www.radiohandi.com/
RubiStar	http://rubistar.4teachers.org/index.php
Rubrics	http://www.techtrekers.com/rubrics.html
Script-O!	http://www.readingmatrix.com/quizmaker/index.php
Singingfish	http://search.singingfish.com/sfw/about.html
Skype	http://www.skype.com/
Socratic Questions	http://www.changingminds.org/techniques/questioning/socratic_questions.htm
Spurl.net	http://www.spurl.net/
StreamSage Synchronization	http://www.streamsage.com/products_services/synch.htm
SuperThinkers	http://www.superpages.com/enlightenme/superthinkers/pages/
SurveyMonkey	http://www.surveymonkey.com/
Tapped In	http://tappedin.org/tappedin/
TaskStream	https://www.taskstream.com/pub/
teAchnology: Rubrics by Category	http://www.teach-nology.com/web_tools/rubrics/
TechDictionary	http://www.techdictionary.com/
ThinkQuest	http://www.thinkquest.org/
ThinkQuest Library	http://www.thinkquest.org/library/index.html
Time and Date.com	http://www.timeanddate.com/
Trekmail	http://w2.trekmail.com/
TVEyes	http://www.tveyes.com/
VoyCabulary	http://www.voycabulary.com/
Web Inquiry Projects	http://edweb.sdsu.edu/wip/
WebCT/Blackboard	http://www.webct.com/
WebGapper	http://www.newtongue.com/webgapper/

Wikipedia	http://www.wikipedia.org/
Wikispaces	http://www.wikispaces.com/
WildVoice	http://www.wildvoice.com/
WorldForge	http://worldforge.org/
Writeboard	http://www.writeboard.com/
Yahoo! Groups	http://groups.yahoo.com/
Yahoo! Mail	http://mail.yahoo.com/
Your Sky	http://www.fourmilab.ch/yoursky/
YouSendIt	http://www.yousendit.com/
YouTube	http://www.youtube.com/
Zoho Writer	http://www.zohowriter.com/jsp/home.jsp

Desktop Tools, Software, and Products

ACE: A Collaborative Editor	http://ace.iserver.ch/
AppleWorks	http://www.apple.com/appleworks/
Audacity	http://audacity.sourceforge.net/
Audio Spotlight	http://www.holosonics.com/index.html
CamStudio	http://www.camstudio.org/
Diva	http://www.diva-project.org/
Eye-Fi	http://www.eye.fi/
FLY Pentop Computer	http://www.leapfrog.com/Primary/GradeSchool/FLY.jsp?bmUID=1167537883286
Heliodisplay	http://www.io2technology.com/technology/overview.htm
Hollywood	http://www.tomsnyder.com/products/product.asp?SKU=HOLHOL
Hollywood High	http://www.tomsnyder.com/products/product.asp?SKU=HOLHIG
HoloTouch	http://www.holotouch.com/
Hot Potatoes	http://hotpot.uvic.ca/
HyperStudio	http://www.hyperstudio.com/
iMovie HD	http://www.apple.com/ilife/imovie/
Inspiration	http://www.inspiration.com/productinfo/inspiration/index.cfm
Keynote	http://www.apple.com/iwork/keynote/
Kid Pix Deluxe for Schools	http://rivapprod2.riverdeep.net/portal/page?_pageid=353,143072,353_143073&_dad=portal&_schema=PORTAL

Microsoft Paint	http://www.microsoft.com/resources / documentation/windows/xp/all/proddocs/ en-us/mspaint_overview.mspx?mfr=true
Microsoft PowerPoint	http://office.microsoft.com/powerpoint/
Microsoft Reader	http://www.microsoft.com/reader/
Microsoft Word	http://office.microsoft.com/word/
myvu	http://www.myvu.com/
Neverwinter Nights	http://nwn.bioware.com/
Nextcode	http://www.nextcodecorp.com/
Nvu	http://www.nvu.com/index.php
Ogg Vorbis	http://vorbis.com/
OpenOffice.org Suite	http://www.openoffice.org/
Photo Story	http://www.microsoft.com/photostory/
Portfolio Products	http://www.aurbach.com/
Print Shop 22 Deluxe	http://www.broderbund.com/jump.jsp ?itemType=PRODUCT&itemID=1645
PTViewer	http://webuser.fh-furtwangen.de/~dersch/PTVJ/ doc.html
Rationale (formerly Reason!Able)	http://www.austhink.com/rationale/
The Report Writer	http://www.clarity.com.hk/program/ reportwriter.htm
Sing That iTune!	http://www.apple.com/downloads/dashboard/ music/singthatitune.html
Sony Reader	http://www.sony.com/reader/
SuperMemo	http://www.supermemo.com/
TourMaker	http://www.field-trips.org/tm/index.htm
VITO Active Trace	http://www.activetrace.com/
Windows Movie Maker	http://www.microsoft.com/moviemaker/
ZPrinter 310 Plus	http://www.zcorp.com/products/printersdetail .asp?ID=1

Tutorials and Exemplary Projects

Come Visit Wisconsin!	http://people.uwec.edu/HAYDENDA/pbl/ wisconsinpbl.htm
Designing an Autobiographical Webpage Using FrontPage 2003	http://viking.coe.uh.edu/~smarsh/fp2003/
How to Set Up a Student Centered Classroom Blog	http://mhetherington.net/blogs/?p=8
How to Videoblog With Blogger	http://www.infodesign.no/artikler/Videoblog_ with_Blogger_211004.html

HTML Tutorial	http://www.w3schools.com/html/default.asp
iMovie Examples	http://www.springfield.k12.il.us/movie/
Internet Assignment: Publishing Webpages	http://www.mythfolklore.net/3043mythfolklore/ weeks/week02/internet.htm
MightyCoach.com	http://www.mightycoach.com/
Multimedia Project Scoring Rubric: Scoring Guidelines	http://pblmm.k12.ca.us/PBLGuide/MMrubric .htm
Problem-Based Learning Network @ IMSA	http://www2.imsa.edu/programs/pbln/
Problem-Solving Introduction	http://literacy.kent.edu/salt_fork/prob_solv/ intro.html
Project-Based Learning Research	http://www.edutopia.org/php/article.php ?id=Art_887&key=037
Tom's Page	http://www.kyoto-su.ac.jp/~trobb/
University of Delaware Problem-Based Learning	http://www.udel.edu/pbl/
Virtual Field Trips at Tramline	http://www.field-trips.org/vft/index.htm
W3Schools	http://www.w3schools.com/
Web Inquiry Project	http://edweb.sdsu.edu/wip/
The WebQuest Page	http://webquest.sdsu.edu/
What Is an ePortfolio?	http://www.danwilton.com/eportfolios/ whatitis.php

Appendix E: Resources for Studying Language Skills, Vocabulary, Grammar, 21st-Century Thinking Skills, and Culture

Web Sites

Around the House: A Website for Language Learning	http://homepage.mac.com/alexander.wrege/qtvr/QTVR/english_home.html
Blue Web'n	http://www.kn.pacbell.com/wired/bluewebn/
Chalk n' Talk	http://international.ouc.bc.ca/chalkntalk/
CNN: Education With Student News	http://www.cnn.com/EDUCATION/
The Compleat Lexical Tutor	http://www.lextutor.ca/
Dave's ESL Cafe	http://www.eslcafe.com/
Educational Testing Service (ETS)	http://www.ets.org/
ELLIS Academic	http://www.pearsondigital.com/ellis/academic.cfm
English Insight by Don Sorsa	http://condor.depaul.edu/~dsorsa/insight/
English Online: EFL/ESL Resources	http://cla.univ-fcomte.fr/english/index_s.htm
English Trailers	http://www.english-trailers.com/index.php
ESLoop	http://www.linguistic-funland.com/esloop/esloop.html
ESLvideo.com	http://eslvideo.com/
Flash Hangman Games for ESL Students	http://www.manythings.org/hmf/
Grammar Safari	http://www.iei.uiuc.edu/student_grammarsafari.html
IATEFL Poland Computer Special Interest Group Internet Lesson Plans (*Teaching English With Technology*)	http://www.iatefl.org.pl/call/j_lesson10.htm
Interesting Things for ESL Students	http://www.manythings.org/
Language and Culture	http://yehlanguageandculture.blogspot.com/
Language Learning Techniques Implemented Through Word Processing	http://www.geocities.com/Athens/Olympus/4631/wordproc.htm

Learning Resources	http://literacyworks.org/learningresources/
Makers Pages	http://web.archive.org/web/20041010183546/makers.cet.middlebury.edu/makers/index.htm
My Language Exchange	http://www.mylanguageexchange.com/
National Public Radio (NPR)	http://www.npr.org/
PEAK English	http://www.peakenglish.com/
Phonetics: The Sounds of American English	http://www.uiowa.edu/~acadtech/phonetics/english/frameset.html
Phrasal Verb Video Dictionary	http://web.li.gatech.edu/~rdrury/600/oral/video/dictionary.html
Randall's ESL Cyber Listening Lab	http://www.esl-lab.com/
Reading Is Fundamental	http://www.rif.org/
Real English	http://www.real-english.com/
Research Writing SY2006	http://researchwriting.blogspot.com/
Skillswise	http://www.bbc.co.uk/skillswise/
StudyCom English for Internet	http://www.study.com/index.html
ThinkQuest	http://www.thinkquest.org/
TOEFL Practice Online	http://toeflpractice.ets.org/
VOANews: Special English—Learning American English and Much More	http://www.voanews.com/specialenglish/index.cfm
Volterre-Fr: English and French Language Resources	http://www.wfi.fr/volterre/home.html

Software

The Authoring Suite	http://www.wida.co.uk/noframes/auth.htm
BetterAccent Tutor	http://betteraccent.com/
Choices, Choices	http://www.tomsnyder.com/products/product.asp?SKU=CHOCHO
ClueFinders 4th Grade Adventures	http://www.learningcompany.com/jump.jsp?itemID=191&mainPID=191&itemType=PRODUCT&RS=1&keyword=cluefinder
The Critical Thinking Company: Software Bundles	http://www.criticalthinking.com/all-abilities/product_bundles.html
Decisions, Decisions: Prejudice	http://www.tomsnyder.com/products/product.asp?SKU=DECDEC
English Discoveries	http://www.edusoft.co.il/en/products/apeed.asp

EnglishNow! for Spanish Speakers	http://store.digitalriver.com/servlet/Controller Servlet?Action=DisplayPage&Locale=en_US&SiteID=transpar&id=ProductDetailsPage&productID=42017500
English on the Job	http://www.languagesolutionsllc.com/
eyeQ	http://www.infmind.com/
First English	http://www.dyned.com/products/fe/
GO Solve Word Problems	http://www.tomsnyder.com/products/product.asp?SKU=GOSGOS
Kurzweil 3000	http://www.kurzweiledu.com/kurz3000.aspx
Learn to Speak English	http://www.amazon.com/The-Learning-Company-381415-English/dp/B00005TQ17
Live Action English Interactive	http://www.speakware.com/
Live Action Spanish Interactive	http://www.speakware.com/
Mind Benders: Deductive Thinking Skills	http://www.brightminds.us/series/013/index_h.html
Mystery at Motel Zero	http://homepages.utoledo.edu/dcolema/motelzero/
New Dynamic English	http://www.dyned.com/products/nde/
Odyssey ELL	http://www.compasslearning.com/solutions/elementary/ell/index.aspx
The Oxford Picture Dictionary Interactive	http://www.oup.com/elt/catalogue/isbn/9295?cc=gb
PLATO Learning	http://www.plato.com/index.asp
RAM: Reading Acceleration Machine	http://www.slu.edu/colleges/AS/languages/classical/ram/ram.html
Reading Horizons	http://www.dyned.com/products/nde/
Rocket Reader	http://www.rocketreader.com/
Rosetta Stone	http://www.rosettastone.com/en/
Sona-Speech II	http://www.kayelemetrics.com/Product%20Info/3650/3650.htm
Starfall	http://www.starfall.com/
Tactical Iraqi	http://www.tacticallanguage.com/tacticaliraqi/
Ultimate Writing Creativity Center	http://www.riverdeep.net/portal/page?_pageid=353,155572,353_155573&_dad=portal&_schema=PORTAL
Web English Teacher	http://www.webenglishteacher.com/
Where in the World Is Carmen Sandiego?	http://www.learningcompany.com/jump.jsp?itemID=146&itemType=PRODUCT&path=1%2C2%2C22%2C90&iProductID=146

Exemplary Web-Based Language- and Culture-Learning Projects

Aiden Yeh's Speech Class Podcast	http://aidenyeh.podomatic.com/
CAE B's Podcast	http://caeb2006.podomatic.com/
Culture Quest	http://coe.west.asu.edu/students/stennille/st3/webquest.html
English Advertising Class	http://english-ad.blogspot.com/
ESL: Student Projects	http://iteslj.org/links/ESL/Student_Projects/
iEARN: MovingVoices	http://www.iearn.org/projects/movingvoices.html http://movingvoices.iearn.org/
International Home Remedies	http://www.otan.dni.us/webfarm/emailproject/rem.htm
Language and Culture	http://yehlanguageandculture.blogspot.com/
Learning Resources	http://literacyworks.org/learningresources/
LQuest: LanguageQuests	http://www.ecml.at/mtp2/LQuest/
Mexican Immigration to the USA	http://www.youtube.com/watch?v=5hjmuFrT0HU
Schoolmaster's Blog: Second Show—Students' Radio Play	http://blog.klemm-site.de/wordpress/?p=13
Sendai Museums	http://sendai-city-tourism-tohoku-university.blip.tv/file/55530
Student-Teacher Writing Pages	http://www.schackne.com/Writing.htm#Link1
Theme Tourism	http://themetourism.blogspot.com/
ThinkQuest	http://www.thinkquest.org/
TOPICS: An Online Magazine for Learners of English	http://www.topics-mag.com/index.html
The WebQuest Page	http://webquest.sdsu.edu/webquest.html
Welcome to the Famous Personages Project!	http://moodle.kyoto-su.ac.jp/wiki/index.php/Main_Page
Welcome to the Kyoto Restaurant Pages!	http://www.kyoto-su.ac.jp/information/restaurant/mainleft.html
Young Caucasus Women Headquarter	http://youngcaucasus.neweurasia.net/?page_id=3

Contributors

Selin Alperer-Tatlı teaches in the Modern Languages Department of Middle East Technical University in Ankara, Turkey, and is interested in applications of flow theory in the classroom.

Jim Buell is an academic professional on a research project involving computer scientists and honeybee researchers. He is working on a doctorate at the University of Illinois at Urbana-Champaign, in the United States.

Chin-chi Chao has a doctorate in language education and is an assistant professor at National Chengchi University, in Taipei, Taiwan. Her research interests include CALL and CALL teacher professional development under sociocultural and dialogical perspectives.

Carol A. Chapelle is professor of TESL/applied linguistics at Iowa State University in the United States, where she teaches courses in second language acquisition, language assessment, CALL, ESL, and linguistics. She is the author of books on technology for language learning, was editor of TESOL *Quarterly* from 1999 to 2004, and is president of the American Association for Applied Linguistics.

Douglas W. Coleman is a professor in the Department of English at the University of Toledo in the United States. A past chair of the TESOL CALL Interest Section and a current member of the editorial board of the journal *Simulation & Gaming*, he has been active in CALL and simulation gaming since the mid-1980s.

Joy Egbert is an award-winning teacher, researcher, software developer, and materials designer. An associate professor of ESL and technology at Washington State University, Pullman, in the United States, her research and teaching interests include learning environments and CALL. She has published and presented widely on both of these topics.

Birgitte Gade Brander has a doctorate in multicultural education and cultural studies and is an adjunct at Suhr's University College in Denmark. She teaches education, health communication, consumer and environmental education, and transcultural studies. Her research interests include democratic citizenship, multicultural conditions in schools, multicultural children's books, intercultural and health communication, and environmental and consumer education.

Susan Gaer is an associate professor of ESL at Santa Ana College School of Continuing Education in the United States. She has a master's degree in TESOL from San Francisco State University and a master's degree in educational technology from Pepperdine University. She has been integrating technology into her ESL classes since 1996. She was chair of the TESOL CALL Interest Section in 2004–2005 and is currently a technology consultant for CATESOL.

Dafne González is a full professor at Universidad Simon Bolivar in Caracas, Venezuela, where she teaches blended English for specific purposes courses and technology-related classes to graduate students and is the coordinator of the Graduate Programs in Education. She holds a master's degree in applied linguistics and a doctorate in education. She is currently the coordinator of the TESOL Electronic Village Online.

Elizabeth Hanson-Smith, professor emeritus at California State University, Sacramento, in the United States, formerly directed its graduate TESOL Program. She was lead designer for The Oxford Picture Dictionary Interactive and pedagogical consultant for Live Action English Interactive, and she distributes her Web-based tutorials, Constructing the Paragraph, free online. She is the author of many articles and books on CALL pedagogy and currently consults and teaches online.

Deborah Healey is the director of the English Language Institute at Oregon State University, in the United States, where she has been combining ESL and computers since 1984. Currently a coeditor of *The* ORTESOL *Journal*, she has written and presented extensively on CALL and administrative uses of computers. Her doctorate is in computers in education.

Torey Hickman is currently a doctoral student and teaching assistant in the Department of Curriculum and Instruction: Educational Technology at the University of Toledo in the United States. He has a master's degree in English (ESL) from the University of Toledo. His current interests are the use of multimedia in second language instruction and instructional design.

Lloyd Holliday is a lecturer in applied linguistics at the School of Educational Studies at La Trobe University in Melbourne, Australia. He has researched CALL since 1987 and was a founding member of the SL-Lists. He also has a special interest in second language acquisition and ethnic minority language maintenance.

Philip Hubbard is a senior lecturer in linguistics at Stanford University, in the United States, and director of the English for Foreign Students Program at the Stanford Language Center. He has worked in CALL since 1982 as a software developer, methodologist, researcher, and teacher educator and has published widely across those areas. He is associate editor of the CALL *Journal* and serves on the editorial boards of the CALICO *Journal* and *Language Learning & Technology*.

Leslie Huff is currently a doctoral student in the Department of Teaching and Learning at Washington State University in the United States. Her focus of study is language and literacy. She has spent 4 years teaching English to all ages of Japanese students in northern Japan.

Keun Huh teaches elementary and graduate students in South Korea. She developed ESL teacher education courses and worked for the distance learning program at Washington State University. Her research interests include classroom research, creativity development in language classrooms, and CALL.

Bill Johnston is an associate professor of second language studies and comparative literature at Indiana University, in the United States, and director of the university's Polish Studies Center. His research interests include second language pedagogy, language teacher education and teacher identity, classroom discourse analysis, and moral dimensions of teaching. He is the author of *Values in English Language Teaching* and numerous other scholarly publications.

Datta Kaur Khalsa is a core faculty member for the graduate program in online teaching and learning at California State University, East Bay, in the United States. She is also a researcher for Developmental Associates, Inc., in Arlington, Virginia, with a research focus on ESL, social computing, online communities, and virtual teamwork as well as policy, training, and organizational structure related to the application of cross-cultural communication in multidisciplinary K–12 curricula.

Joy Kreeft Peyton is vice president of the Center for Applied Linguistics in Washington, DC, and director of the Center for Adult English Language Acquisition, in the United States. She works with teachers, particularly those in deaf education, to use computer-mediated interaction for English language acquisition. She has published extensively on network-based classrooms and computer-based collaborations.

Hsin-min Liu is a doctoral student in applied linguistics at the University of California at Los Angeles in the United States. She holds a master's degree in TESL/applied linguistics from Iowa State University. Her research interests include language testing and authenticity-related issues in language instruction and assessment.

Diane Maloney-Krichmar is a higher education administrator, managing innovative programs that serve the needs of nontraditional adult students. Her research focuses on the use of the Internet and communication/information technology to support educational and health communities. Her publications include work on online communities and a multilevel analysis of sociability, usability, and community dynamics.

Levi McNeil is a doctoral student at Washington State University in the United States. He has worked in South Korea, teaching EFL to university undergraduates. His research interests include language teaching methods, CALL, and language teacher education.

Carla Meskill is an associate professor in the Department of Educational Theory and Practice at the University at Albany, State University of New York, in the United States. Her research interests are the design and research of technologies as they support language education, topics on which she has published widely.

Gina Mikel Petrie is an assistant professor at Eastern Washington University in the United States. Her research interests involve issues of visuality, media, and CALL.

Karen Price has served on more than a dozen advisory boards for entities including Apple, Microsoft, Tandberg, and Annenberg. Affiliated 23 years with Harvard University, as associate director of the Programs of ESL and then as a lecturer at the Graduate School of Education, she now consults full-time in English language and technology at Anne Dow Associates.

Bill Snyder is a professor in the Hanyang-Oregon TESOL Program in Seoul, South Korea, and is interested in flow and task engagement in language teaching and learning.

Rubena St. Louis has a master's degree in applied linguistics from Simón Bolívar University in Caracas, Venezuela, where she teaches in the graduate program and teaches English for specific purposes at the undergraduate level. She is interested in cognition and learning and works in the areas of materials development and evaluation, language teaching methodologies, and autonomous learning.

Alexander Wrege has a master's degree in ESL and is a doctoral student in philosophy of education (with a minor in linguistics). He works as a part-time instructor at the American Language Institute at the University of Toledo in the United States. His interests include human linguistics and the study of political debate through a linguistic and rhetorical filter.

Aiden Yeh, a doctoral candidate at the University of Birmingham in England, holds a master's in English language teaching management. A Webhead, a member of the TESOL CALL Interest Section Electronic Village Online Coordinating Team, and e-list assistant manager of TESOL's Nonnative English Speakers in TESOL Caucus, she lectures in the Department of English at Wen Zao Ursuline College of Foreign Languages in Taiwan.

Senem Yildiz is an assistant professor in the Foreign Language Education Department at Bogazici University in Turkey, where she teaches both undergraduate and graduate courses on materials design and development, program evaluation, and research and study skills. She received her doctorate from Indiana University in the United States. Her research interests include CALL, distance learning, materials design, and evaluation in English for general and specific purposes.

Index

Sexual imagery, 141
Shared repertoire, 379
Sharing, 268, 369–370t
Showcasing, culturally responsive
    teaching and, 369–370t
Side sequences, 164
SILL. *See* Strategy Inventory for
    Language Learning
SimCity, 176–177, 201, 394
SimCopter, 394–395, 395f
The Sims Online, 400
The Sims2, 400
Simulation centers, 157
Simulations
    assessment and, 249–251, 251f
    collaborative learning and, 200–202
    conversation and, 191
    reading and, 176–177, 177f
    software and, 36, 185
    virtual learning environments and,
        391
Situated activities, 302–303
Situated learning, 284–285
Situated nature of texts, 62
Size, class, 419
Skepticism, critical thinking and, 310
Skills
    accessibility and, 25
    acquisition of. *See* Knowledge
        acquisition
    blended learning and, 421. *See also*
        Blended learning
    conditions of flow and, 352–353
    critical thinking and, 311
    direct instruction and, 33–34
    engagement and, 361
    language acquisition and, 2f
    professional development and,
        282t, 283t
    reading, 177–178
    21st-century skills and, 103
Skype, 171, 204
SLA. *See* Secondary language
    acquisition
Small-group discussion, virtual
    learning environments and, 53t
Social blogging, 203

Social cognitive theory. *See* Social
    learning theory
Social constructivist approach to
    education. *See* Constructivist
    approach to education
Social cues, interactive technology
    and, 25–26
Social experience, as condition for
    optimal learning environment,
    91
Social identity, audience and, 62
Social issues, competencies for, 279
Social learning theory, 20, 134
Social needs, 22. *See also* Collaborative
    learning
Social negotiation, blended learning
    and, 410
Social presence, 25
Social problems, 309
Social settings, 377
Social software, educational
    technology and, 1
Socioaffective strategies, 297,
    298–299t
Sociocultural perspective, 327, 377,
    385–387
Socioeconomic considerations,
    345–346. *See* Limited-technology
    contexts
Sociolinguistic approach to language
    teaching, 19–20, 62
Socratic questioning, 104, 307, 317
Software, *See also specific software names*
    assessment and, 238, 239–240,
        262–263, 265–266
    collaborative learning tools and,
        141
    conditional access and, 24–25
    creativity and, 215–217
    critical thinking and, 312–313
    editing, 185
    knowledge acquisition and, 173
    limited access to. *See* Limited-
        technology contexts
    making informed choices for, 155
    one-computer classrooms and,
        50–51
    Oxford Picture Dictionary and, 45

V

Also Available from TESOL

Perspectives on Community College ESL Series
Craig Machado, Series Editor
Volume 1: Pedagogy, Programs, Curricula, and Assessment
Marilynn Spaventa, Editor
Volume 2: Students, Mission, and Advocacy
Amy Blumenthal, Editor

PreK–12 English Language Proficiency Standards
Teachers of English to Speakers of Other Languages, Inc.

Planning and Teaching Creatively within a
Required Curriculum for School-Age Learners
Penny McKay, Editor

Planning and Teaching Creatively within a Required Curriculum for Adult Learners
Anne Burns and Helen de Silva Joyce, Editors

Professional Development of International Teaching Assistants
Dorit Kaufman and Barbara Brownworth, Editors

Teaching English as a Foreign Language in Primary School
Mary Lou McCloskey, Janet Orr, and Marlene Dolitsky, Editors

For more information, contact
Teachers of English to Speakers of Other Languages, Inc.
700 South Washington Street, Suite 200
Alexandria, Virginia 22314 USA
Toll Free: 888-547-3369   Fax on Demand: 800-329-4469
Publications Order Line: 888-891-0041
or 301-638-4427 or 4428
9 am to 5 pm, EST

ORDER ONLINE at www.tesol.org/

TESOL